Alexander Gauri

Office Development Handbook

Second Edition

ULI Development Handbook Series

Urban Land Institute

About ULI–the Urban Land Institute

ULI–the Urban Land Institute is a nonprofit education and research institute that is supported and directed by its members. Its mission is to provide responsible leadership in the use of land in order to enhance the total environment.

ULI sponsors educational programs and forums to encourage an open international exchange of ideas and sharing of experience; initiates research that anticipates emerging land use trends and issues and proposes creative solutions based on this research; provides advisory services; and publishes a wide variety of materials to disseminate information on land use and development.

Established in 1936, the Institute today has more than 13,000 members and associates from approximately 60 countries representing the entire spectrum of the land use and development disciplines. They include developers, builders, property owners, investors, architects, public officials, planners, real estate brokers, appraisers, attorneys, engineers, financiers, academics, students, and librarians. ULI members contribute to higher standards of land use by sharing their knowledge and experience. The Institute has long been recognized as one of America's most respected and widely quoted sources of objective information on urban planning, growth, and development.

Richard M. Rosan
President

For more information about ULI and the resources that it offers related to office development and a variety of other real estate and urban development issues, visit ULI's Web site at www.uli.org.

Project Staff

Rachelle L. Levitt
Senior Vice President, Policy and Practice

Gayle Berens
Vice President, Real Estate Development Practice

Dean Schwanke
General Editor of ULI Development Handbook Series

Jo Allen Gause
Project Director

Nancy H. Stewart
Managing Editor

Libby Howland
Manuscript Editor

**Helene Redmond/
HYR Graphics**
Book Design/Layout

Janice Olson
Book Layout, Chapters 5, 6, and 8

Kim Rusch
Artist

Maria-Rose Cain
Joanne Nanez
Word Processing

Meg Batdorff
Cover Design

Diann Stanley-Austin
Production Manager

Recommended bibliographic listing:

Gause, Jo Allen, et al. *Office Development Handbook,* Second Edition. Washington, D.C.: ULI–the Urban Land Institute, 1998.

ULI Catalog Number: OD2
International Standard Book Number: 0-87420-822-X
Library of Congress Catalog Card Number: 98-85108

**Books in ULI Development Handbook Series
(formerly Community Builders Handbook Series)**
Business and Industrial Park Development Handbook, 1988
Downtown Development Handbook, Second Edition, 1992
Mixed-Use Development Handbook, 1987
Office Development Handbook, Second Edition, 1998
Residential Development Handbook, Second Edition, 1990
Resort Development Handbook, 1997
Shopping Center Development Handbook, Second Edition, 1985

Authors

Principal Author and Project Director

Jo Allen Gause
ULI–the Urban Land Institute
Washington, D.C.

Primary Contributing Authors

Mark J. Eppli
The George Washington University
Washington, D.C.

Michael E. Hickok
Hickok Warner Fox Architects
Washington, D.C.

Wade Ragas
University of New Orleans
New Orleans, Louisiana

Contributing Authors

E. James Burck
The Martin Group
San Francisco, California

Jerry L. Doctrow
Legg Mason Real Estate Services Inc.
Greenbelt, Maryland

Libby Howland
Writer/Editor
Takoma Park, Maryland

Terry J. Lassar
Communications Consultant
Portland, Oregon

Gerard L. Lederer
Building Owners and Managers Association (BOMA)
    International
Washington, D.C.

Paul O'Mara
CMA Management Consultants
Vienna, Virginia

M. Atef Sharkawy
Texas A&M University
College Station, Texas

Steven W. Spillman
Pacifica Companies
Mission Viejo, California

Stephen Spinazzola
RTKL Associates Inc.
Baltimore, Maryland

John A. Walker
Legg Mason Real Estate Services Inc.
Greenbelt, Maryland

ULI Advisory Committee

Kenneth W. Hubbard
Executive Vice President
Hines Partnership
New York, New York

William H. Kinn Jr.
Managing Director
Landauer Associates Inc.
New York, New York

Wayne Ratkovich
President
The Ratkovich Company
Los Angeles, California

Robert N. Ruth
Principal
Tooley & Company
Los Angeles, California

Sam L. Van Landingham
President
Van Landingham Real Estate Advisors Inc.
Columbus, Ohio

Reviewers

Richard J. Bartel
Executive Vice President
Prentiss Properties
Dallas, Texas

M. Jay Brodie
President
City of Baltimore Development Corporation
Baltimore, Maryland

David J. Brotman
Vice Chairman
RTKL Associates Inc.
Los Angeles, California

David M. Childs
Partner
Skidmore, Owings & Merrill
New York, New York

Victor D'Ortona
Director of Development
SSR Realty Advisors
White Plains, New York

Robert Gardner
Senior Vice President
Robert Charles Lesser & Company
Los Angeles, California

Nicholas E. Jahnke
Senior Real Estate Officer
Northwestern Mutual Life Insurance Company
Washington, D.C.

Douglas A. Knaus
President, Central Southeast Division
Insignia Commercial Group Inc.
Houston, Texas

Kevin McCall
President
Paradigm Properties LLC
Boston, Massachusetts

Ehud G. Mouchly
Managing Director
Price Waterhouse LLP
Los Angeles, California

Stephen C. Rozga
Managing Director
H.G. Smithy Company
Fairfax, Virginia

Kristina O. Santry
Vice President
LaSalle Partners
Washington, D.C.

Thomas Storrs
Director of Architecture
Cooper Carry & Associates
Alexandria, Virginia

Joseph S. Summers III
Vice President
Prentiss Properties
Dallas, Texas

William L. Tooley
Chairman
Tooley & Company
Los Angeles, California

Acknowledgments

The Urban Land Foundation (ULF), as part of its commitment to support ULI's core research program, is providing major funding for the new and revised editions of the ULI Development Handbook Series being published during the last half of this decade. The *Office Development Handbook* was funded in part by grants from ULF, for which the Urban Land Institute is very grateful.

Like all ULI development handbooks, this one is the product of the collective efforts of many organizations and individuals. Although it is impossible to mention everyone who participated in the three-year process of producing this book, a number of contributors deserve special acknowledgment.

First, special recognition and thanks are extended to the individuals who drafted major portions of various chapters. Wade Ragas, professor of finance at the University of New Orleans, contributed substantially to the sections on market and financial feasibility analysis in Chapter 2. Mark J. Eppli, assistant professor of real estate and finance at George Washington University, deserves most of the credit for writing Chapter 3 on financing and he developed the case study that is woven into the chapter to illustrate the material. Michael E. Hickok, a principal of Hickok Warner Fox Architects, drafted much of Chapter 4 on project planning and design.

Many other individuals contributed material to these and other chapters. John A. Walker and Jerry L. Doctrow, both with Legg Mason Real Estate Services, helped to develop the scope of Chapter 2 and contributed material on project feasibility for it. Steven W. Spillman, president of Pacifica Companies, helped shape Chapter 3 and provided material on sources of financing for office development. James Burck of the Martin Group wrote the section on ownership structures in Chapter 3. Stephen Spinazzola, vice president of engineering at RTKL Associates (Baltimore), contributed material for the section on building systems in Chapter 4. Paul O'Mara with CMA Management Consultants wrote the initial drafts for Chapters 5 and 6. Gerard Lederer, vice president of government and industry affairs for BOMA International, contributed the discussion in Chapter 8 on the future impacts of major legislative and regulatory changes.

M. Atef Sharkawy of the College of Architecture at Texas A&M University wrote the Chapter 7 case study on Republic Plaza. Terry Lassar, a communications consultant in Portland, Oregon, wrote the case studies on Norm Thompson Headquarters and Crescent 8. Libby Howland, a writer/editor in Takoma Park, Maryland, wrote the case studies on 101 Hudson and the MesseTurm building. David Parham, director of professional development at ULI, wrote the Comerica

Tower case study and Mary Schwartz, a senior associate at ULI, wrote the case study on the Kensington Business Centre.

The material for "High-Rise Office Design and Construction Know-How," a feature box that appears in Chapter 1, was provided by May Tsui of Turner Steiner International. David Mulvihill, senior associate at ULI, wrote two feature boxes—"Rockefeller Center" in Chapter 3 and "1900 K Street" in Chapter 4—and he helped with the research for several topics covered in the handbook.

The handbook also incorporates materials from ULI's *Real Estate Development: Principles and Process, Urban Land* magazine, and other sources—which are cited in the text.

Thanks go to the many organizations and individuals that contributed data, photographs, and other materials. SSR Realty Advisors provided data that were used to develop the case study that weaves through Chapter 2 to illustrate the material on feasibility analysis. Several of the figures in Chapter 3 showing capital market trends were provided by LaSalle Advisors Investment Research. CB Commercial/Torto Wheaton provided data on office market trends. Walker Parking Consultants/Engineers contributed material for the discussion on parking in Chapter 4. Mark Rodman Smith, president of Pario Research, provided material that was incorporated in the discussion of green office buildings in Chapter 8. The sample loan documents included in the appendices were provided by H.G. Smithy Company.

Many architecture and design firms provided many of the photographs. These include Kallmann McKinnell & Wood Architects; RTKL Associates; Hellmuth Obata + Kassabaum; Cesar Pelli & Associates; Pei Cobb Freed & Partners; EDAW; Skidmore Owings & Merrill; Thompson, Ventulett, Stainback & Associates; Arrowstreet; Kohn Pedersen Fox; Kaplan McLaughlin Diaz; and Ove Arup & Partners California Ltd.

A number of ULI staff members and consultants were instrumental in the book's publication. Rachelle Levitt, Dean Schwanke, Lloyd Bookout, and Gayle Berens provided much-appreciated support and direction throughout the writing and production process. Thanks also to Joan Campbell, Adrienne Schmitz, Jennifer LeFurgy, Simone Rones, and Tina Rosan for their help in research and the assembly of photographs. Nancy Stewart oversaw the editing and production process. Libby Howland edited the manuscript, making many valuable suggestions along the way. Helene Redmond expertly laid out the pages—incorporating hundreds of photos, figures, and feature boxes—with the assistance of Janice Olson. Kim Rusch produced several of the graphics for the book. Maria-Rose Cain and Joanne Nanez provided word processing support. Meg Batdorff created the cover. Diann Stanley-Austin managed the printing and binding process with outside contractors.

Finally, thanks go to the members of the ULI Advisory Committee and manuscript reviewers who are listed on page iv. These office development practitioners helped determine the scope of the *Office Development Handbook* and offered insightful comments and practical suggestions throughout its development.

Jo Allen Gause
Principal Author and Project Director
Office Development Handbook

Contents

Foreword

This handbook is the second in the completely redesigned ULI Development Handbook Series, a set of volumes on real estate development that traces its roots back to 1947 when ULI published the first edition of the *Community Builders Handbook*. This initial ULI handbook was revised and updated several times over the next 25 years, at which point, in 1975, ULI initiated the Community Builders Handbook Series with the publication of the *Industrial Development Handbook*. A number of titles were published in this series over a period of years, covering industrial, residential, shopping center, office, mixed-use, downtown, and recreational development. The publication of the *Resort Development Handbook* in 1997 marked the complete redesign of the handbook series and its renaming as the ULI Development Handbook Series.

This second edition of ULI's *Office Development Handbook* is a complete update of the 1981 original edition. Office development is a complex activity that has undergone dramatic changes since the first edition was published. Within these one and a half decades, the office market has experienced the biggest boom and one of the biggest busts in its history. The market has also been through tremendous changes in terms of tenant requirements, building technology, office workplace technology, architectural design, property location and setting, and property ownership and management. To be successful, an office development project must be grounded in an understanding of the complexities and nuances of these changes.

The objective of this handbook, as with all of the handbooks in the series, is to provide a broad overview of the land use and real estate sector under discussion as well as a guide to the development process. As such, this book presents a comprehensive and lengthy discourse on office development, covering such topics as types of office properties, office markets, market analysis, feasibility analysis, project financing and capital markets, site planning, building design, marketing, leasing, operations and management, and trends.

Among the strengths of the book is its reliance on a variety of examples and real-world situations. The case study chapter fully documents 14 office projects, including profiles of downtown and suburban buildings, new construction and renovation and conversion projects, and buildings in the United States, Europe, and Asia.

Numerous other examples are provided in the text or as feature boxes.

Meeting the challenge of office development requires expertise in market analysis, finance, design, construction, property and asset management, and a host of other disciplines. Risks often run high, and fortunes have been won and lost. Office development done effectively should produce a pleasant and productive workplace that is also an attractive asset within its neighborhood and community. Creating such a property requires hard work and imagination. Succeeding can provide both financial and professional rewards. It is hoped that this book will help the reader better understand the office development business and achieve such rewards.

Dean Schwanke
General Editor
ULI Development Handbook Series
April 1998

Office Development Handbook

1. Introduction and Background

Among the various segments of the real estate development industry, office development is arguably the most complex and competitive, and it is also one of the most potentially rewarding. In the United States, the construction of office space has always been a cyclical industry, one whose fluctuations are closely tied to national economic cycles. Despite these fluctuations, the office market has proven itself over time to be remarkably resilient and efficient in meeting the needs of American business.

Office buildings and the business that takes place in them are of vital significance to the U.S. economy. Survey data from the U.S. Energy Information Administration indicate that in 1995 there were about 712,000 commercial office buildings in the United States containing an estimated 10.5 billion square feet of space valued at $642 billion. According to the Bureau of Economic Analysis, this value represents 9.5 percent of gross domestic product. Roughly 20 percent of all nongovernmental office buildings are owner-occupied. The balance is owned by real estate services companies and leased to tenants.

The inventory of U.S. office buildings is diverse, running the full gamut of building size, class, and location. While the average U.S. office building is 14,700 square feet, approximately two-thirds of all office buildings are relatively small—10,000 square feet or less. Small office buildings

A curved glass and aluminum wall forms the entrance to 1250 Boulevard René Lévesque, a 47-story office building in downtown Montreal.

contain about 2 billion square feet of space, or about 19 percent of total office space. Interestingly, large buildings of more than 100,000 square feet make up less than 3 percent of the total number of office buildings, but they contain nearly 39 percent of the commercial office space. They average 254,000 square feet (see Figure 1-1).[1]

According to ULI's *America's Real Estate*, the 25 largest U.S. metropolitan areas contain about 2.1 billion square feet of commercial office space, about one-half of which is found in the central business districts (CBDs) of these cities. Class A buildings, which are the highest-quality buildings in a market, contain almost two-thirds of the total office space in these cities. More than half of the Class A inventory is found in buildings located in the CBDs.[2]

Approximately one in five employed Americans, or about 27 million people, work in office buildings. Office tenants are found in all sectors of the economy, but the largest concentration of office users is found in the services and information sectors, in industries that are considered by many to be the linchpins of the postindustrial economy. Just as most office buildings are relatively small, so are most office tenants. According to Cognetics Inc., an economics research firm, the majority of office tenants employ fewer than 19 people, and only 2.4 percent employ more than 100 people. This implies that while large tenants represent an important segment of the office market, the bread-and-butter demand for office space comes from smaller tenants.[3]

figure 1–1
Commercial Office Space by Building Size, 1995

Building Size	Office Buildings		Office Space (Square Feet)		
(Square Feet)	Number	Percent	Total	Percent	Average Size
5,000 or Under	412,000	58%	1,093,000,000	10%	2,650
5,001–10,000	131,000	18	915,000,000	9	6,980
10,001–25,000	94,000	13	1,580,000,000	15	16,810
25,001–50,000	35,000	5	1,293,000,000	12	36,940
50,001–100,000	22,000	3	1,542,000,000	15	70,090
Over 100,000	16,000	2	4,064,000,000	39	254,000
Total	**712,000**	**100%**	**10,486,000,000**	**100%**	**14,730**

Source: U.S. Energy Information Administration.

This diverse office market provides the setting for this book's overview of the processes and strategies necessary for successful office development. ULI's *Office Development Handbook* looks at office buildings as development ventures and as investments. In the end, however, the success of office developments and the success of office investments depend on the same formula—deliver the right type of office space to the right tenants and keep them happy once they sign on. This book deals with the development of new office buildings, the repositioning of existing office buildings, and the conversion of nonoffice buildings to office uses.

The *Office Development Handbook* is intended as a general introduction to the process of office development and a general reference for many of the people involved in some way with office development, including developers, investors, office tenants, consultants, financial institutions, public officials, and many others.

Chapter 1 explains different categories of office space, provides a brief history of office development in the United States, and describes the key members of an office devel-

opment project and their contributions. Chapter 2 examines the process of determining the feasibility of an office project. Chapter 3 reviews the ways an office development can be financed, the various sources of financing, and the motivations and requirements of lenders and investors. Chapter 4 covers planning and design issues for various types of office developments. Chapter 5 considers the marketing and leasing of office space. Chapter 6 moves on to operations and management. Chapter 7 presents detailed profiles of 14 office projects of various types. And Chapter 8 considers the key issues and trends that are likely to affect office development in the near future.

Categories of Office Space

A developer analyzing the feasibility of a new office building, an investor considering the acquisition or disposition of an existing building, or an office tenant thinking of relocating to a different building—all must evaluate the

Allstate Insurance Company's regional office in Tampa, Florida, is located in a suburban office park. The two 75,000-square-foot buildings are linked by a garden and dining patio.

building relative to other office space that exists in the marketplace. Therefore, it is necessary to differentiate office space based on various building features and characteristics. Office space can be categorized along several dimensions including:

- class;
- location;
- size and flexibility;
- use and ownership; and
- building features and amenities.

Class

Perhaps the most basic feature of office space is its quality or class. The relative quality of a building is weighed by taking a number of characteristics into account, including its age, location, building materials, building systems, amenities, lease rates and terms, occupancy, management, and tenant profile. Office space is generally divided into three classes:

- Class A—Investment-grade buildings, generally the most desirable in their markets, offering an excellent location and first-rate design, building systems, amenities, and management. Class A buildings command the market's highest rents and attract creditworthy tenants. While some older buildings can be renovated and repositioned as Class A properties, Class A space usually is limited to primarily new, highly competitive buildings. In some markets, Class A+ space is a distinct class, consisting generally of one-of-a-kind trophy or signature buildings that feature outstanding

Canterra Tower in Calgary, Alberta, typifies many office towers that were built during the 1980s real estate boom.

Oxford Development Group Inc.

Rather than first having the architect design the building and then telling the civil engineer to put it on the site and then telling the landscape architect to fix it— "and, by the way, we're out of money"—the developer of Maryville Centre, one of the largest business parks in the St. Louis area, began by talking with the site planner and the landscape architect first.

The use of this approach, rather than the level-it-out-and-start-over strategy that was common in St. Louis at the time, enabled Baur Properties to achieve a development that was nearly 50 percent green space. Moreover, the development process was more cost-effective as well as more efficient for the end users.

The result of the process is a 100-acre business park with 850,000 square feet of office space in five buildings and a 300-room hotel. Baur installed stone retaining walls to preserve groves of old pine trees, dedicated large expanses of natural woods as forested patio areas, and put in several miles of walking trails. Other project amenities include a fiberoptic communications system, structured parking, and nearby day care.

The parking structures, which offer tunnel access to the buildings, were terraced into the site to save many trees and plants. While this preservationist approach was important to the developer, it also helped to diffuse initial opposition from the nearby residents. "At the time, all you could imagine was 1.5 million square feet and all those cars in your backyard," says one of those early opponents, "but I'm continually amazed at how nice it is."

While Maryville Centre's neighbors have benefited from the development, the biggest winners are the tenant companies and their employees. The contiguous campuses of Maryville University and St. Luke's Hospital provide educational, recreational, fitness, and healthcare benefits. Maryville Centre employees can take advantage of continuing education classes, training facilities, and internships as well as meeting, sport, wellness, and medical facilities.

Eventually, the business park will have an additional 1 million square feet, for a total 1.85 million square feet in 12 buildings—a task, according to Edward T. "Tee" Baur, chairman of the development company, that will take another ten to 15 years. It also will maintain more than 40 percent green space, walking trails, and wildlife habitat.

Source: Adapted from Birch M. Mullins, "Putting the Land First at Maryville Centre," *Urban Land*, April 1997, pp. 25, 27–28. ∎

Baur Properties

Baur Properties

Maryville Centre, located in suburban St. Louis's I-64 growth corridor, is a 100-acre campus of nearly 900,000 square feet of office space. Landscaping and site planning preserved natural contours, woodlands, and lakes.

Seeking a building that would reflect its identity as a dynamic high-tech company, Silicon Graphics built this landmark 110,000-square-foot building in a suburban corporate campus in Mountain View, California.

Courtesy of Silicon Graphics Inc.

architecture, building materials, location, and management.

- Class B—Buildings with good locations, management, and construction, and little functional obsolescence or deterioration. Class B space is found generally in well-located buildings of an earlier generation that have been maintained to a high standard.
- Class C—Buildings that are substantially older than Class A and Class B buildings and that have not been modernized. Class C buildings are often functionally obsolete and often contain asbestos or other environmental hazards. While data for Class A and Class B office space are available in most markets, Class C space is seldom tracked with any accuracy. Definitions of Class C space, even within a single market, are not standard. Their low values make many Class C office buildings potential candidates for demolition or conversion to other uses.

Location

Within a metropolitan area, various criteria are used to categorize the locational attributes of office buildings, depending on regional development patterns. Downtown is usually a readily identifiable central business district (CBD) that is located at or near the historical core of the central city. CBDs are generally characterized by high-density office buildings that, on average, command the highest rents in the metropolitan area. Major service firms—lawyers, accountants, consultants—and government tenants often prefer downtown locations.

Suburban locations are more difficult to delineate, and they appeal to a more diverse group of office users. Many of the mature suburban communities that ring large urban cores in U.S. metropolitan areas have their own highly concentrated "downtown" office areas that can rival the nearby CBD in terms of rent levels and types of tenants.

Some suburban office nodes are less suburban downtowns than they are major activity or employment centers.

Office clusters are often located near major freeways or beltways, attracting companies and service organizations that do not need to be in the CBD and are seeking high-quality office space at lower rents than in downtown. Examples include the Galleria area in Houston, Tysons Corner in suburban Washington, D.C., and Perimeter Center in Atlanta. Office nodes near major universities or medical centers commonly attract primarily high-tech companies. Examples of such locations include Research Triangle in Raleigh, North Carolina, and Stanford Research Park in Palo Alto, California.

Suburban locations can be characterized also by office corridors—a linear pattern of office nodes that becomes established as employment centers are developed in leapfrog fashion along a major road. Frequently, suburban areas also contain neighborhood office buildings located outside the major nodes, buildings that generally serve the needs of local residents by providing space for professional and other services firms. In exurban locations on the outer fringes of suburban areas, office development is typically in low- to mid-rise buildings that offer abundant parking, access to major roadways, and relatively inexpensive rents.

Office buildings often are located within business/industrial parks. These buildings tend to be small to medium-sized, ranging from one to three stories. Many offer bulk space that attracts companies with large space needs. Many others offer R&D space, including space that can be used for laboratory work.

Size and Flexibility

It can be useful to classify office buildings also by size and by the flexibility they offer tenants. Office buildings are generally put into three size categories: high-rise (16 stories and up), mid-rise (four to 15 stories), and low-rise (one to three stories).

Floorplate size is an important criterion for tenants needing large contiguous blocks of space. In most market areas, large blocks of Class A office space are usually

Many businesses today require large open areas for shared workspace. Furness House, a 1917 historic landmark in Baltimore, was renovated to accommodate such needs.

concentrated in only a few buildings, while blocks of space between 1,000 and 15,000 square feet are quite generally available.

Floor-space flexibility is becoming increasingly important as more office tenants opt for open floor layouts with fewer private offices and more shared workspaces and common areas. Users wanting such layouts, particularly those requiring sizable blocks of space, can be accommodated best in buildings with large efficient floorplates.

Tenants not taking large blocks of space also can be concerned with space efficiency. Most tenants seek space that will give them the ability to reconfigure their office layouts as needed—with as few as possible structural columns, awkward angles, and awkward window placements that might limit this flexibility.

Office floorplates generally range from 18,000 square feet on the small side up to 30,000 square feet or more on the large side. On average, the floorplates of multistory office buildings range from 20,000 to 25,000 square feet. From the developer's perspective, smaller floorplates are generally considered inefficient, because core functions—stairs, mechanical rooms, elevator shafts, and lavatories—will leave an unacceptably small percentage of space per floor as rentable square footage. And, as noted, smaller floorplates tend to be less efficient from a space planning perspective. On the other hand, larger floorplates at a certain point may entail certain structural or design measures—such as an additional stairway

or even an additional bank of elevators—that can prohibitively increase the building's construction cost.

In the final analysis, the optimal floorplate size is determined by balancing a number of factors, including tenant preferences, construction cost, zoning requirements, and expected rental rates.

Use and Ownership

Office buildings can be classified in terms of their users and their owners. Buildings can be either single-tenant (occupied primarily by one tenant) or multitenant structures. A single-tenant building may be owned by the tenant, in which case it is often referred to as an owner/user building, or it may be leased from a landlord. A building designed and constructed for a particular tenant that will occupy all or a majority of the space is called a build-to-suit development. A multitenant building designed for unknown tenants is a speculative development. Also, office space can be included in a mixed-use development that incorporates one or more additional uses, such as retail, residential, hotel, or recreation. Figure 1-2 shows the changing proportions of build-to-suit and speculative office development from 1980 to 1996.

Building Features and Amenities

In many instances, it is important to differentiate office space on the basis of certain building features and characteristics. If, for example, the targeted tenants for a prospective office building are small, cost-conscious high-tech firms, the developer may wish to show how its building stacks up against other buildings in the market area in terms of lease rates and length, electrical power and telecommunications infrastructure, and other features that are determined to be of particular importance to the target market. Other important building characteristics include the availability and cost of parking, and the type and quality of building systems and amenities.

Parking is a major consideration for most office tenants. Its availability and cost can make a significant difference in the lease rates and absorption potential of new or renovated buildings. In a competitive market, the issue of paid parking can become one of the main issues in lease negotiations. A prudent developer or investor will sort competitive buildings by the availability and cost of parking and examine how lease and absorption rates vary by key parking criteria, such as the number of spaces and whether parking is paid or free.

Different office users have different needs, preferences, and priorities concerning the amenities they look for and the requirements they have for power, communications capacity, and HVAC (heating, ventilation, and air conditioning). Office buildings can be looked at in terms of the amenities they offer and the type and quality of their building systems: from retail outlets, health clubs, and restaurants to executive suite services, security arrangement, the telecommunications infrastructure, electrical capacity, HVAC, and energy management systems. Taking inventory of the amenities and types of building systems

that are popular in the market can help a developer or investor understand which building attributes are important to a market segment and identify competitive office space.

Historical Perspective

As a distinct land use, office development has a relatively short history. The offices that existed in the United States during the 18th century housed activity that was secondary to the economy's main activities: producing goods and providing services. The prosperity and expansion of businesses that were spawned by the industrial revolution created a greater need for office space and the advent of modern communications and transportation systems brought forth the age of the modern office building, beginning in the late 19th and early 20th centuries.

The Birth of the Skyscraper

By the latter half of the 19th century, a massive wave of industrialization was sweeping the United States, much of it concentrated in cities. Across the country, central business districts became the focal point for emerging businesses and activities in the public realm: banks, insurance companies, corporate headquarters, newspaper publishers, government offices, professional offices, retail establishments, hotels, cultural institutions, and much more. White-collar workers—a new breed—began to live

figure 1–2
U.S. Office Construction Activity, 1980–1996

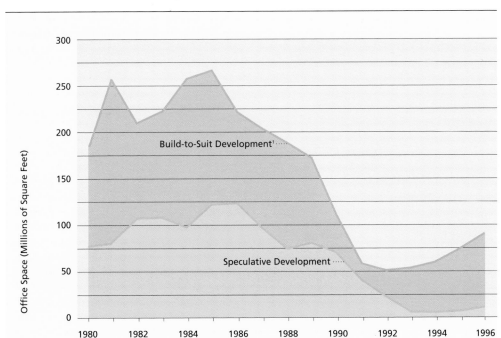

¹Build-to-suit includes bank buildings, light R&D buildings containing primarily office space, corporate build-to-suit buildings, and buildings in which space is leased to government users and the speculative component is not significant.

Sources: LaSalle Advisors Investment Research; CB Commercial/Torto Wheaton Research; and F.W. Dodge.

on the fringes of the crowded and increasingly expensive downtowns, and ride to their jobs on railroads and streetcars.

No symbol of the new prosperous and corporate CBD was more potent than the skyscraper. By the 1880s, the invention of a safe electric elevator had made it possible for buildings to rise above the five to six stories that occupants were willing to climb on a daily basis. Indoor plumbing, electric lighting, and other inventions made interiors livable and functional, while the introduction of steel-frame construction enabled builders to transcend the physical limitations of masonry construction. For masonry buildings, the taller they were, the thicker their load-bearing walls had to be. The new steel skeletons fitted out with light masonry curtain walls and plate-glass windows could soar to hundreds of feet. A half century later, skyscrapers would top 1,000 feet.

Peter and Shepherd Brooks were important early developers of commercial office buildings. In 1873, the Brooks brothers, who hailed from Boston, acquired the seven-story Portland Block, Chicago's first office building equipped with a passenger elevator. The brothers went on to develop many of the structures that became famous as examples of work by the Chicago School, a group of pioneer architects in skyscraper design and the design of modern commercial buildings in the late 19th century. The Brooks brothers hired Owen Aldis, an attorney, to manage the Portland Block and act as their real estate agent in Chicago. By the turn of the century,

Aldis was managing 20 percent of the office space in downtown Chicago. Commercial real estate investment and management was an emerging field, and Aldis and his nephew Graham Aldis were at its forefront. In the words of the late real estate educator James A. Graaskamp: "Aldis was to office buildings what Marshall Field was to retailing."

In 1881, the Brooks brothers and Aldis teamed up with Chicago architects Daniel Burnham and John Wellborn Root to design and construct the city's first ten-story office building, the Montauk Block. This engineering masterpiece was the first steel-frame building in Chicago, although its outside walls were load-bearing. The building boasted two elevators, a unique floating foundation, central heating, full plumbing, and dozens of features to simplify maintenance and prevent fire—and the top floors of the tallest building in town commanded the city's highest rents.

The Brookses and Aldis team developed numerous office buildings in Chicago during the 1880s and 1890s, including the 16-story Monadnock Block, the Pontiac Building, the Marquette Building, and the Rookery, which was restored and renovated as Class A office space in 1992. (See the Rookery case study in Chapter 7.)

All the buildings designed by the Brookses were fully rented when they opened. Among the development guidelines that those developers devised for their office projects were the following: "height sufficient to warrant the use of elevators, as much light as possible, easy mainte-

Intricately carved stone surrounds the entrance to the Rookery, a Chicago building that was designed by renowned architects Daniel Burnham and John Wellborn Root in 1886 and modernized by Frank Lloyd Wright in 1905. The Rookery was extensively restored in 1992.

nance, a high percentage of rentable space, and ornament sufficient to avoid absolute plainness."[4]

In correspondence with the Brookses, Aldis stated his fundamentals of office building design and operation, most of which are still valid:[5]

- Providing ample light and air is a wise investment.
- Second-class space costs as much to build and operate as first-class space. Therefore, build no second-class space.
- The entrance spaces must make a lasting impression. The entrance, first-story lobby, elevator cabs, elevator service, public corridors, and restrooms must be very well designed.
- Generally, office space should be about 24 feet from good light.
- Operating expenses must be constantly borne in mind. The use of proper materials and details will simplify the work.
- The location and future changes in the location of corridor doors, partitions, lights, plumbing, and telephones should be carefully considered.
- Typical layouts should be arranged for intensive use. A large number of small tenants is more desirable than a few large tenants because a higher rate per square foot can be added for small tenants, small tenants do not move in a body and leave the building with a large vacant space when hard times hit, and small tenants do not swamp your elevators by coming and going by the clock.
- Upkeep of an office building is most important. Janitor service must be of high quality, elevator operators of good personality, and management progressive.

With the advent of structural steel, the giant leap into the sky could be realized. In 1883, William LeBaron Jenney, a Chicago engineer and architect, designed the Home Insurance Building, the first true skyscraper and an early product of the Chicago School. The 14-story building was the first to use curtain walls attached to the structural frame. However, Jenney's building resembled its load-bearing masonry wall predecessors more than it resembled the glass-box architecture that would evolve in response to this structural breakthrough.

In New York, where the architecture was more traditional, the first truly tall buildings of the 20th century were born. The Woolworth Building, constructed in 1913, was the first office building to break the 50-story barrier. After a relatively dry spell in building in the years around World War I, the construction of downtown office space burgeoned in the 1920s, in structures of all shapes, sizes, and heights. By the late 1920s, new high-rise building technology, gains in economic productivity, and freely flowing financing from institutional lenders and equity syndicators were fueling a tremendous boom in the construction of speculative high-rise office buildings. The 70-story art deco Chrysler Building, built in 1929, and the 102-story Empire State Building, built in 1930, epitomized this era of giant skyscrapers. The Empire State Building

Built in 1974, the 110-story Sears Tower in Chicago has had a long reign as the world's tallest office building.

was a purely speculative venture. (See "The Story of the Empire State Building" on the following page.)

The Post–World War II Office Boom

The office development boom of the 1920s came to an abrupt end with the depression of the 1930s, which bankrupted many tenants and building owners. A few major office structures were started during the 1930s, most notably Rockefeller Center in New York, which was a forerunner of today's large-scale, urban mixed-use developments and continues to be among the best known of such projects.

For the duration of World War II, most private construction was put on hold, except for development directly related to the war effort. By the end of the war, occupancy in office buildings reached close to 100 percent. Some 20 years of minimal building activity had produced an accumulated backlog of demand for office space, which sparked a nationwide office building boom

The site of the Empire State Building was attractive to its investors because a very large parcel of land, 197 feet by 425 feet, was available. The old Waldorf-Astoria Hotel, which sat on that parcel, was slated to be demolished when the new hotel on Park Avenue was completed. After developer Floyd Brown, who had bought the site in 1928, defaulted on his mortgage payments, the property was sold to the Empire State Company, and the hotel was demolished just few weeks before the stock market crashed in October 1929.

Despite the crash, the Empire State Company, partially owned by the DuPont family and headed by former New York Governor Al Smith, decided to move forward with the project in the face of what it incorrectly perceived

Since it was completed in 1931, the Empire State Building has symbolized New York. Its facade is composed of limestone, granite, aluminum, and nickel. Its art deco design was the height of fashion then and remains stylish today.

to be a brief economic downturn. The company invested a total of $45 million to acquire the site, demolish the hotel, and design and construct the world's tallest building, all in less than 18 months! The actual construction, managed by the general contracting firm of Starrett Brothers and Eken, took less than a year. At the peak of activity, 3,500 construction workers were adding one story a day. By the official opening on May 1, 1931, the building stood 1,250 feet tall, with 85 floors of offices and the equivalent of another 17 floors devoted to the magnificent mooring mast and observation decks.

When completed, the Empire State Building's skeleton consumed 57,000 tons of steel. The finished building contained 51 miles of pipe, 17 million feet of telephone cables, and seven miles of elevator shaft.

One reason for the speed of construction was that in those days commercial leases in New York expired on April 30, and if the Empire State Building were not ready for occupancy on May 1, the company would have to wait an entire year to attract tenants—a costly delay. The rationale for building it so tall was that the syndicate had paid record high prices for a location at 34th Street and Fifth Avenue that was less than ideal for a quality office skyscraper. The principal office districts were at 23rd Street near Madison Square, 42nd Street near Grand Central Station, and downtown around Wall Street. The Empire State Building stood alone in the middle of a low-rise section of hotels, department stores, shops, and loft buildings, relatively far from the Grand Central and Pennsylvania Railroad Stations and several blocks from the nearest subway lines. The extreme height and distinctiveness of the building were designed to serve as an advertising beacon to attract office tenants.

Similarly, key architectural features were intended to maximize the net revenue that could be generated by the rentable space. For example, the building is less bulky than was permitted under the zoning laws. By designing almost the entire building as a setback tower over a wide, five-story base, the developer could increase the rents per square foot because the offices were quieter and had more natural light. By building shallow floors with window access for every office, the developer offered prospective tenants panoramic and unobstructed views and thus eliminated the disadvantage of the location relative to the other tall buildings. In this design, constructing less space per floor made each square foot more valuable. Similarly, rather than building a simple flat rectangular structure that would have produced four corner offices on each floor, the developer recessed the Empire State Building's north and south tower faces so that the extra angles of the structure would yield eight to 12 corner offices per floor, adding significantly to the potential rent.

The physical achievement of the Empire State Building obscures the fact that, like today's projects, it too had to meet legal and financial requirements for feasibility. John Jacob Raskob, one of five partners in the development, asked his architect, William Lamb: "Bill, how high can you make it so it won't fall down?" The real question was, how high and still profitable? The answer depended on a stipulation in New York's 1916 zoning ordinance that above the 30th floor, a building could occupy no more per floor than one-fourth of the total area of its lot. With two acres of ground, the Empire State tower could cover half an acre. Lamb determined that 36 million cubic feet would be a profitable size and then began playing with alternatives. The 16th iteration (Plan K) was it: an 86-story tower. His client Raskob declared: "It needs a hat," and in a creative burst suggested a mooring mast for a dirigible. The 200-foot mast, intended to be an international arrival point for lighter-than-air craft, extended the building's total height to 1,250 feet. Because of high winds, the mast never worked as intended, but it was eventually used for observation. (In fact, during the Great Depression, income from the observation platform offset large office vacancies and kept the Empire State Building in business.)

Unfortunately, all of the developer's sophisticated planning and marketing strategies designed to cope with the basic circumstances of no preleased tenants, a poor location, and a terrible office market during the Great Depression were in the short run to little avail. The building stood mostly vacant throughout the 1930s and was widely nicknamed "The Empty State Building." With the return of full employment and prosperity in the 1940s, however, the building filled up and has proven successful. Rather than being a symbol of a corporate, governmental, educational, medical, or cultural institution, the Empire State Building stands after nearly 70 years as a symbol of commercial real estate development.

Source: Adapted from Marc A. Weiss, "The Story of the Empire State Building," in *Real Estate Development: Principles and Process*, 2nd ed., by Mike E. Miles, Richard L. Haney Jr., and Gayle Berens (Washington, D.C.: ULI–the Urban Land Institute, 1996), pp. 138–139.

that continued to be fueled over the next four decades by unbridled economic growth.

Most of the office construction in the 1950s and 1960s was undertaken by local developers who viewed themselves as investment builders. They constructed buildings with the intention of holding them for an indefinite period. Often, they assembled sites over extended periods of time and warehoused them until the right time to build.

The financing of projects was usually simple in concept. Office developers secured a long-term mortgage commitment (takeout commitment), often from an insurance company. This served as security for a construction loan from a commercial bank. After constructing the building and satisfying any leasing requirements, the developer transferred the loan to the long-term lender. The development entity itself or a few passive partners usually provided the needed equity.

The Suburbanization of Office Development

Beginning in the 1950s, office development began diversifying into suburban areas. The interstate highway system, which started construction in 1956, was a great spur to this shift. Downtown corporate interests lobbied heavily for the federal interstate program to bring highways into the heart of their cities. New expressways radiating in all directions from the central core were expected to bring workers, shoppers, tourists, and middle-class residents to downtowns, and also to reduce traffic congestion on city streets and improve speed and accessibility. Ironically, the downtown expressways turned out to be two-way streets. They allowed businesses and residents to leave the city as well. Together with the beltways and highways that surrounded and bypassed the CBD, the radials opened up new frontiers for development.

Office buildings began to spring up in outlying suburban areas, at first individually, but, by the mid-1960s, also in office parks that grew up near interstate highways. Over the last 25 years, office development has continued to expand outward along the residential growth corridors radiating from cities and towns and into new edge cities. Throughout the country, suburban office districts that rival their region's CBD have taken shape, among them Tysons Corner in the Washington, D.C., area, Irvine/Newport Beach in southern California, and the Galleria area of Houston.

Suburban locations historically have offered many advantages for office development, including lower land and construction costs, liberal zoning ordinances and development incentives, opportunities for ample parking, large sites that can be landscaped and developed with open space, and nearby housing that translates into shorter commutes for employees. Since at least the mid-1980s, however, it has become apparent that suburban business nodes are plagued with the same kind of traffic congestion that originally drove employers from locations in central cities.

Although the demand for office space continues to be strongest in suburban locations, suburban traffic problems and other ills associated with growth are re-

Demand for office space continues to be strongest in suburban locales like this office park in St. Louis.

generating interest in central city locations. In some markets, office developers and investors are finding attractive opportunities for renovation, reuse, and new construction in CBDs and other inner-city locations.

The Tumultuous 1980s and 1990s

From 1979 through approximately 1989, the U.S. office development industry experienced the greatest boom in its history. Developers built an extraordinary amount of new office space. Industry sources estimate that as much as half of the office space ever built in the United States was constructed in the 1980s.[6] But as the decade drew to a close, the industry plummeted into a deep depression and it hit bottom, by most accounts, in 1992. Since then, office development has emerged slowly from the depths, showing the first real signs of solid recovery in 1995.

Office construction cycles usually track national economic cycles, because the factors that drive the demand and supply for office space and those that drive the general economy are closely related. The demand for office space is influenced by a number of factors, among which are the following:[7]

- growth in the overall size of the labor force;
- shifts within the labor force toward or away from office-intensive occupations;
- technological changes that influence the amount of space required per office worker; and

- cyclical movements in overall economic prosperity that influence the rate of growth of space demand from office tenants.

The supply of office space can be influenced by another set of factors, among which are:[8]

- current and expected levels of rents and vacancy in the existing office space inventory;
- the availability and terms of financing for new office space;
- the willingness of city governments to provide financial incentives and the infrastructure needed for major office developments;
- tax law changes that stimulate or suppress office development; and
- current and expected costs of land acquisition and construction on sites suitable for office development.

Said differently, downturns in office markets may be caused by general economic recessions, changes in the capital markets that restrict the supply or drive up the cost of money, and overbuilding that leads to too many buildings competing for too few tenants and buyers. Upturns may be caused by a significant increase in demand as a result of growth in office employment, changes in the capital markets that lead to a plentiful supply of relatively low-cost financing, and speculative responses to rapid increases in rents, prices, returns, and perceived values. These factors and others combined to create the steep cyclical fluctuations experienced by the office development market over the past two decades.

A commercial real estate boom in the late 1960s and early 1970s was fueled by strong economic growth, military spending, and modest inflation. The boom ushered in a bust that lasted from 1973 to 1975 and was induced by the shock of quadrupled oil prices, double-digit inflation, and a severe economic recession. Office development began to thrive once again in the late 1970s, as office employment rose in response to the entry of a large portion of the baby boom generation into the labor market and the increased participation of women in the labor force, and, most importantly, as demand skyrocketed for the services of office-based professionals, notably in the legal, health, business, finance, insurance, and real estate sectors.

During the latter part of the 1970s, annual growth in office jobs averaged more than 5 percent, easily absorbing the supply of new office space. During the 1980s, absorption increased sharply as employment growth remained strong. Except for a recession-related hiatus in 1982, annual growth in office employment continued to exceed 4 percent until 1988, when corporate downsizing, mergers, and consolidations became commonplace and the growth in office jobs noticeably diminished. (See Figure 1-3.)

Despite the healthy increase in office employment during the 1980s, the supply of new office space grew far beyond what the demand could absorb. As early as

figure 1–4

Office Space Production versus Absorption in 31 Major U.S. Markets, 1975–1996

Millions of Square Feet

	Average Annual Completions	Average Annual Absorption
1975–1979	34.5	43.0
1980–1984	96.7	63.1
1985–1989	101.3	75.1
1990–1994	27.9	34.5
1995–1996	6.6	37.0

Source: CB Commercial/Torto Wheaton Research.

1982, a sizable gap between supply and demand had emerged. In fact, in major markets, office space additions exceeded absorption every year from 1980 to 1992.[9] (See Figure 1-4.)

As supply and demand grew more out of balance, office vacancy rates soared to record levels and stayed there. CB Commercial/Torto Wheaton Research's vacancy rate measure for office space in more than 30 major metropolitan areas rose above 16 percent in 1985, and did not fall below 16 percent until 1994. (See Figure 1-5.) Despite rapidly falling office rents and prices, many investors

figure 1–3

U.S. Employment Growth, 1976–1996

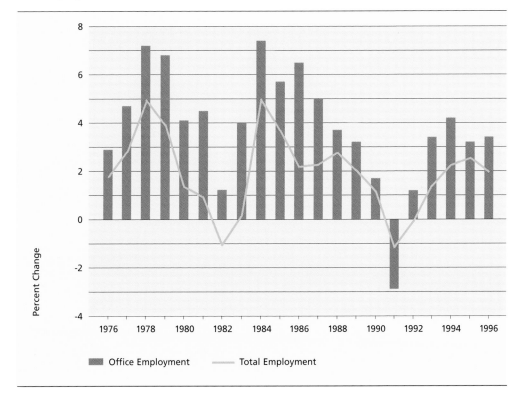

Source: CB Commercial/Torto Wheaton Research.

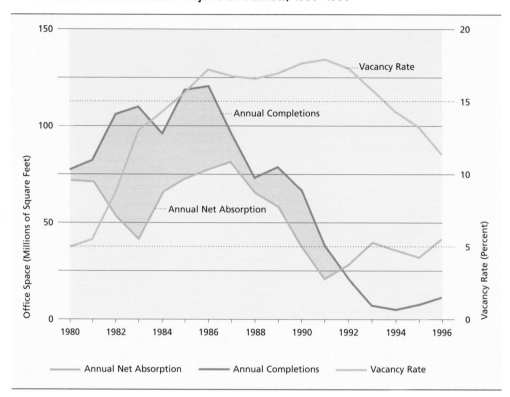

figure 1–5
Office Market Conditions in 31 Major U.S. Markets, 1980–1996

Source: CB Commercial/Torto Wheaton Research.

and developers were undeterred from launching more new construction. Bank lending for office construction actually accelerated after 1987, in spite of the mounting evidence of overbuilding.

The surplus of office space depressed effective rents. After 1987, rent increases vanished from nearly all markets. In many markets, property owners were forced to provide substantial rent concessions. Even fully occupied buildings often generated negative cash flows because their rent levels were so low.

When these negative cash flows began exhausting the accumulated reserves of developers, many defaulted on their loans. By 1990, widespread defaults had seriously hurt hundreds of savings and loan institutions (S&Ls) and banks, especially in the Southwest and New England. In 1990, the investment community finally acknowledged that there was a huge oversupply of office space and that it was driving property values downward by at least 20 percent—and by more than 50 percent in some markets. Money abruptly stopped flowing into real estate.

Why did so much overbuilding occur despite rising vacancy rates and slowing demand? It is generally agreed that a driving force for the superboom was the flood of capital into commercial real estate markets from several sources:

- S&Ls that were swamped with money after having been deregulated in 1983 and newly permitted to invest in commercial properties;

- commercial banks that also were swamped with deposits but were unable to lend to several classes of former borrowers;
- real estate syndicates that received huge tax shelter benefits in the Economic Recovery Tax Act of 1981;
- foreign investors freed by deregulation in their own nations to place more money abroad; and
- U.S. pension funds experiencing record increases in contributions and seeing investment in real estate equities and mortgages as a good way to diversify their holdings of stocks and bonds.

These sources stampeded into commercial real estate, stimulating developers to keep on building offices after 1987, even though vacancy rates had already reached unprecedented levels.[10]

Another key factor that was also to blame in the overbuilding frenzy was poor analysis. Many participants were extremely lax in their analyses of the cost of new projects and their future revenue. In some cases, there was no analysis at all. A developer with one or more recent successes got money for another project on a handshake. Such poor analysis undoubtedly accounts for much of the failure on the part of developers, lenders, and investors to perceive that the demand for office space was growing at a much slower rate after 1986, even though employment was continuing to grow at a healthy pace.

In 1992, the U.S. office market bottomed out. That is, absorption and occupancies reached their lowest level.

Since then, conditions in the office market have gradually improved. Demand for office space has grown modestly but steadily, in large part because the number of small and medium-sized firms is growing and large firms are beginning to absorb space more vigorously as their downsizing plays out, their balance sheets strengthen, and a strong economy encourages expansion plans.

According to economist Anthony Downs of the Brookings Institution, office development cycles are consistent in the sequence of their phases, always proceeding as follows: 1) boom, 2) overbuilding, and 3) gradual absorption. However, says Downs, "the cycles do not have a rigidly fixed duration or amplitude; in fact, both dimensions vary tremendously. That variation is also closely linked to the diversity in length and severity of cyclical movements in general economic activity. Thus, because the general economic expansion of the 1980s had an unprecedented length, so did the boom phase of the office space development cycle. Unfortunately, that length contributed to the creation of a massive oversupply of office space in most U.S. markets for the first half of the 1990s. Even so, by closely observing the many factors influencing office space activity levels, participants in the office market will be able to anticipate when an overbuilt phase will end, to be inevitably replaced by a gradual absorption phase, and ultimately by another boom phase."[11]

Only time will tell if the lessons taught by the last boom and bust will bring more discipline to the marketplace as the 1990s draw to a close with markets heating up.

The Development Team

An office project, whether it is the construction of a new building or the major renovation of an existing one, depends on a complex and multidisciplinary development process. The process is not a linear set of operations. Rather, it is an iterative process involving many interrelated activities and areas of expertise. The larger the project and the more public participation and government involvement, the more complicated is the task of building. In such a complex endeavor, each step has to be weighed and incorporated into the framework of the entire process.

Developers cannot possibly know everything themselves. They need a team of experts. The makeup of the team and the scope of each expert's participation depend on the nature of the particular project, the characteristics of the site, and the local political climate.

It is important to assemble key members of the development team during the feasibility-testing phase. Much of the conceptualization that will be carried into project design is generated during the initial evaluation of the project's feasibility. The added cost of bringing specialists—market analysts, soil engineers, traffic consultants, environmental advisers, and others—on board early represents a protective investment or insurance for developers. Without the advice of such specialists, developers might well purchase sites or buildings with physical, market, or regulatory constraints that will prove fatal

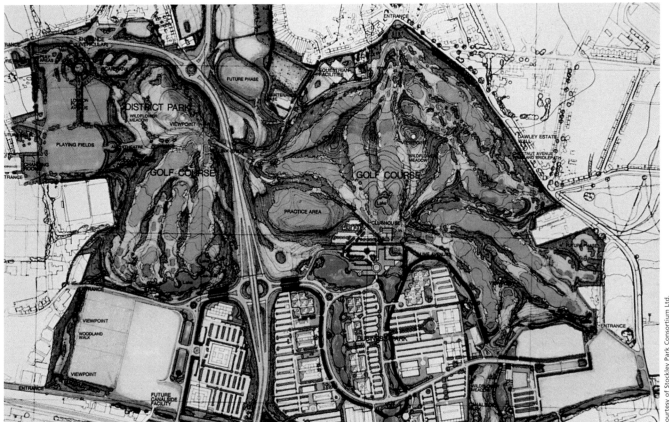

Land plan for Stockley Park, a 350-acre business center—and ULI Award for Excellence winner—located 2.5 miles from London's Heathrow International Airport.

High-rise office development came to a virtual standstill in the United States in the early 1990s, just as a high-rise office building boom took hold in many high-growth countries in Asia and elsewhere. As of early 1998, the three tallest buildings in the world are in Asia, either recently completed or under construction: the T&C Tower in Kaohsiung, Taiwan, an 86-story mixed-use tower; Petronas Towers in Kuala Lumpur, an 88-story mixed-use complex; and the Jin Mao Building in Shanghai, which, when completed in 1998, will be one of the most technologically advanced office buildings in the world. (See the Jin Mao Building case study in Chapter 7.)

The design and construction of such monumental buildings require expertise and systems/materials that may not be available or familiar locally. Thus, American and European high-rise architects, engineers, and construction experts have found themselves in demand around the world.

The worldwide rush to build sophisticated high-rise structures has spread the application of state-of-the-art building technologies and spawned new building technologies. However, problems have also occurred in trying to implement unfamiliar technologies without adequate coordination and supervision of the many and far-flung design and construction participants. For example, if the local construction professionals on a 60-story office building in an Asian city are unfamiliar with the curtain wall technology involved but are responsible for implementing an elaborate curtain wall design by U.S. architectural and engineering consultants—if they must interpret the design specifications and standards, find a manufacturer, and install and maintain the curtain wall—the results are sure to be disastrous.

In such cases, building construction consulting services can help bridge the gap between building owners, local real estate contractors, and American or European design and engineering service providers. Turner Steiner International, the international arm of Turner Construction Corporation, one of the largest general building contractors in the United States, has provided building construction consulting services for over 25 years and is currently active in Asia, the Middle East, Europe, and South America. A building's sponsor generally hires Turner Steiner to coordinate and manage all phases of the development process, much like a fee developer in the United States. May Tsui, the company's business development manager, says that successfully managing a foreign development project requires not only technical and managerial expertise, but also familiarity with the local market

Among the tallest buildings in the world, the twin 88-story towers of Petronas Towers in Kuala Lumpur enclose 4.5 million square feet of space.

The construction of high-rise buildings in Asia has produced advances in the field of building engineering. The composite structural-steel and concrete Grand 50 Tower in Kaohsiung, Taiwan, is built to withstand typhoons and earthquakes, both of which are commonplace in the region.

and the ability to understand cultural differences and overcome knowledge gaps.

As project manager, Turner Steiner wants to be involved from the earliest stages of concept development when basic decisions that ultimately shape the project are made. During the design phase, Turner identifies the components of the construction process and the skills that will be needed, establishes time schedules, and manages the selection of the construction team. It continues to manage day-to-day construction activities through project completion. The company also provides training for local contractors and workers, covering a range of activities from budget control and scheduling to the installation and maintenance of specific building components and materials.

In many parts of the world, the enforcement of contracts depends more on personal relationships than on a judicial system as in the United States. To compensate for limited legal recourse, Turner normally provides its project management services under a no-risk contract. The company never acts as a general contractor and rarely takes an ownership position in international development projects.

■

The two towers of Nadya Park in Nagoya, Japan, are connected by a 165-foot-tall atrium. One tower houses a design center and the other contains multitenant office space, retail stores, and restaurants.

to office development. More positively, the expense of front-end consultants is often repaid in the form of a significantly shorter project design phase.

In general, the developer's role in an office project is to orchestrate the development process and bring the project to completion. The developer's role in the project may continue after it is completed, depending largely on ownership. A fee developer, for example, typically is hired by an owner or investor to see a project through from start to completion, and is paid a fee plus a bonus if certain conditions, such as timely delivery, are met. A fee developer may also be hired by the owner to manage the property when it is ready for tenants.

In contrast, a developer that owns the office project (a developer/owner) continues its commitment until the project is sold, which may be as soon as it is completed or many years later, depending on the developer's objectives. Regardless of the developer's role after the building is up and running, it is the developer's responsibility to function as the team leader throughout the development process.

In most development companies, an individual in the company is designated as the project manager and assigned the responsibility for day-to-day decision making. Throughout the development process, however, owners and investors retain ultimate responsibility for determining how to proceed. Their decisions should be based on the realities of the marketplace and qualified input from all members of the development team.

Most developers, even large diversified development companies, do not retain a staff with all the technical talents needed by the development team. Instead, they hire consultants. One advantage of relying on consultants is that the developer has to pay for expertise only when it is needed. Individual consultants and multifaceted consulting firms can provide consulting services pertaining to every issue associated with office development.

In evaluating prospective consultants, developers should inspect other projects in which they have participated and ask other developers about their qualifications and experience. Developers must also make certain that the most competent members of the consultant's staff are assigned to their projects. Before retaining a consulting firm, developers should meet with key members of the firm's staff to gauge their individual qualifications for the project.

Developers should avoid the pitfall of assembling a team of consultants with experience only in designing and constructing the type of office project planned. The development team also should include individuals with extensive local experience, individuals with knowledge of the market area and local regulatory processes and a demonstrated ability to anticipate public sector concerns and market issues. An appropriate mix of national and local talent is generally most likely to get the job done right.

Effective management of the development team is fundamental to project success. Because the team is made up of a group of players whose tasks are interrelated, tardiness or shoddy work from a single firm can set off

A good architect considers many factors in designing an office building. The design must meet the needs of the building's target market as well as give the project a competitive edge. This building is in Stockley Park business park, near London.

a chain reaction and cause costly delays. Part of the developer's role as team manager is to ensure good communication among the various members of the team. Team meetings to review progress and coordinate work are essential. Such meetings can optimize the efficiency of the undertaking and keep the overall effort on the right track.

It can be useful to think of the office development team as consisting of two broad groups of specialists: the design/construction group and the real estate services group. Members of both groups interact as the need to do so arises.

The design/construction group includes an array of consultants and contractors that perform tasks ranging from site analysis and planning to building design and construction management. The work that they perform and manage represents the bulk of the project's total cost. Effectively managing design and construction services is critical to the success of the development project. The design/construction group can include:

- architects,
- landscape architects,
- land planners,
- engineers, and
- construction contractors.

Various real estate services are also critical in the office development process. They are provided by a variety of consultants, some of which participate in the development process from start to finish and some of which typically perform specific, short-term tasks. The real estate services group can include:

- market consultants,
- appraisers,
- attorneys,
- leasing agents,
- marketing and public relations consultants,

- property managers,
- title companies, and
- surety companies.

Any development team must be structured to meet the needs of the particular project, but most office projects will require the inclusion of each of the following types of experts on the team at some point in time.

Architects

Architects are usually involved in office projects from their earliest planning stages to completion. Typically, an architectural firm can provide the following basic services: predesign drawings (schematics) and final design, design development, preparation of construction contract documents, assistance in the construction bidding or negotiation process, administration of the agreements between the developer and general contractor, and overall project management.[12]

The search for an architect must be thorough. Only firms and individuals with relevant experience should be considered. For example, if the project involves renovation and adaptive use, the architect and other key members of the design and construction team should have renovation experience. The architect should be familiar also with the particular market in which the project will be built. A good architect understands that what works in New York may not work in Dallas. The architect should be licensed in the state in which the project will be built. Local planning and building departments will usually not approve projects unless the architect is state-approved.

Developers should look at buildings (not just plans) by the prospective architects, talk to their clients, and generally ask around. They should interview prospective architects thoroughly to ascertain their level of understanding of the different services they will be expected to provide.

Architects can be compensated by several methods, including payment for time spent and materials used (time and materials agreements) and fixed-price contracts. Fixed-price contracts specify the fee that the architect will receive for completing services listed in the performance contract. The performance of any duties not listed in the contract will require additional compensation. Another approach is to calculate architectural fees as a fixed percentage of a project's hard costs. According to many architects, a percentage fee fairly compensates the architect for extra work, because the higher cost of an elaborate, complex project guarantees higher fees. For developers, the disadvantage of this method is that it provides the architect little incentive to economize.

Landscape Architects

Landscape architects do not just plant trees and flowers. They work with the site's topography, soils, and vegetation to create a distinctive setting that will provide the office project with a sense of place. A project's landscape architect works with the architect to create an exterior environment that enhances the building's design, devises a planting and landscape plan, and incorporates nonbuilding components like plants and trees, benches and other furniture, artworks, and signs into the project. Beyond creating a setting, landscape architects also can help the developer save operating costs by, for example, selecting plants that provide energy-conserving shade. And they can help solve drainage and certain other site problems.

Landscape architects develop preliminary plans and manage the completion of those plans. They obtain bids, produce working drawings and final specifications, draw up schedules, and inspect the site to verify that the contractor implements the plan correctly. Hiring the landscape architect is often the architect's responsibility, but the developer should inspect the recommended landscape architect's work and be comfortable with its design philosophy.

Landscape architects generally work on a lump-sum basis to complete working drawings and specifications

Courtesy of M. David Paul & Associates

McLarand, Vasquez & Partners Inc.

Dixi Carrillo—EDAW

Dixi Carrillo—EDAW

A good landscape architect can create a sense of place for an office project.

Property owners and managers are well aware of the business value of attractive landscapes. However, high-priced landscapes that have been professionally (and expensively) maintained often fail within two or three years after installation, with the remedial cost equaling or exceeding the cost of the original installation.

Since the landscape installation portion of a project is usually included under the general contract for new construction, the general contractor typically has ultimate responsibility for its viability—but only for the duration of the warranty, which is usually one year. However, improper plant installation can remain undetected until after the one-year warranty period has elapsed, leaving the property owner financially responsible for replacing failed plant materials.

How can property owners and managers avoid landscape failures? To help answer that question, a study was conducted at the University of Washington. The study focused on the process of landscape development in commercial and public projects. Its case studies sought to determine flaws in the development process that allowed failures to take place, and to measure the financial impacts of failures.

Low-maintenance naturalized areas were used to update the landscaping at IBM Rock Spring, an office park in Bethesda, Maryland.

One typical case study example is a suburban office park complex where 78 trees were planted in a trough system in a highly visible parking plaza—at an initial cost of $188,000. The plant failure rate was 85 percent. Remedial costs are estimated to be $250,000, or 133 percent of the original landscape cost.

Among the reasons for the project's poor plant performance were the following:

- Plant installation was not supervised.
- Trees were installed from 0.5 to 11.0 inches too deeply in the soil.
- The landscape installation contractor substituted local fill soil for the superior soil that had been specified, a partial reason for its exceptionally low bid on the work.
- The troughs were littered with construction debris, which prevented healthy root growth.
- Events forced a shortening of the time period allocated for installation, which occurred at a time of heavy rains. As the supersaturated soil dried after installation it solidified into a compact masslike concrete.

The study concluded that current construction management practices are a major cause of landscape failure. The overwhelming majority of the projects evaluated experienced high failure rates, which ranged from 10 percent to 90 percent. In all of the projects with high failure rates, there had been essentially no supervision of installation. The property owners and developers had incorrectly assumed that the landscape architects would provide site supervision. However, installation supervision is not typically within the landscape architect's normal scope of work—and the landscape architect is not necessarily trained in proper horticultural techniques.

One important step that a property owner or manager can take to ensure the success of a landscaping project is to retain professional and knowledgeable representation to oversee the entire landscaping process from planning to final installation and development of a long-term maintenance program. Professional oversight of the process increases accountability, which, in turn, promotes the success of landscaping projects.

Another step that can help is to be able and willing to delay the project's opening date if needed. Because landscape installation is the last step of a sequential construction process, building delays can force landscape installation into a time slot that is too short for quality control and that may be a time of unfavorable weather conditions.

Source: Adapted from Joellen Hawn, "How Does Your Garden Grow? Tips on Landscape Maintenance," *Skylines*, June 1996, pp. 28–29.

The land planners for Mitchell Plaza in Skokie, Illinois, were able to preserve and enhance the natural character of the wooded site, even though its size is only 3.4 acres.

and on an hourly basis to supervise the completion of the plans.

Land Planners

Also known as site planners, land planners are usually engaged for office developments involving large sites and multiple structures. Like architects, they are involved in office projects from the earliest planning stages. Their task is to produce an efficient land use plan with good internal circulation, good connections to adjacent uses, well-placed uses and amenities, and adequate open space.

The land planner should work up several schemes based on the development program and design concept, and discuss the pros and cons of each with the developer. The land planner needs input from the developer's marketing, engineering, economic, and political staff or consultants, in order to produce a plan that is marketable, efficient, and feasible—financially and politically. Reputation and relevant projects are the best indicators of a land planner's ability.

Engineers

Architects rely on the technical expertise of a variety of engineers to ensure that the design can accommodate the required physical systems. Structural, mechanical, and electrical engineers are always required, and office projects often require civil engineers, surveyors, and consultants specializing in lighting, parking, traffic, elevators, acoustics, curtain walls, graphics design, environmental remediation, and seismic design.

For the developer, the most prudent strategy is to allow the architect, as head of the design team, to contract directly with the project engineers (and other design consultants) and schedule and coordinate all the design work. Large architectural firms often have in-house engineers. Other firms hire engineers as needed. Architects must work very closely with engineers, and the success of the design phase depends on a good working relationship between them.

The architect usually hires the engineers as subcontractors and is responsible for managing them. Often they are included in the architect's budget. During the initial design phase, the architect works with the engineers to accommodate the project's building systems.

Structural engineers design the building's foundation and basic structural system, largely based on the architect's design and the site's existing soil conditions. They produce drawings for the construction contractor that explain the structural system in detail, especially connections and the sizing of the structural members. Mechanical engineers design plumbing, HVAC, and life-safety systems. Electrical engineers design the lighting, power, and communications systems. Each of these building systems is critically important to the success of the project. The engineers for each must seek to achieve the optimum design that balances cost, tenant requirements, efficiency, and flexibility.

Engineers should be licensed by the state and should be members of a professional engineering society—for example, the National Society of Professional Engineers (NSPE), the American Society of Mechanical Engineers (ASME), or the American Society of Heating, Refrigeration, and Air Conditioning Engineers (ASHRAE).

Construction Contractors

Some development companies have their own construction departments or subsidiaries, while others contract out for construction services.

Construction Manager (CM). Many developers of large-scale office buildings bring a construction manager on board early in the development process to perform a variety of services, both before and during construction. During the design phase, CMs advise the developer and the design team on cost-effective ways to execute the various elements of the design.

The developer's contract with the CM may be for preconstruction consulting only, or it might extend into the construction period. The fee for services during construction might be established in the initial agreement between the developer and the CM. Alternatively, the construction manager may enter into a new construction contract with the developer at the end of the design phase. This typically might obligate the CM to complete the project by a certain date and for a guaranteed maximum price. Under such an agreement, the CM retains all the subcontractors and assumes the risk associated with cost overruns and delays.

General Contractor (GC). Instead of hiring a CM to provide consulting and construction services throughout the development process, developers can hire a general contractor to construct the building. The GC is typically selected through a competitive bidding process, and executes a contract with the developer to construct the project in accordance with the completed construction contracts for a fixed price within a set time frame. General contractors hire subcontractors to perform the various construction tasks: excavation, concrete pouring and finishing, frame construction, systems installations, and so on. Typically, the subcontractors execute contracts with the GC, which pays them as their work is completed.

To find a good contractor, a developer should ask a number of contracting firms to submit proposals or general statements of qualifications that include descriptions of past projects, client and lender references, résumés outlining the qualifications of their key employees, and, possibly, verification that the company is bondable (see the discussion of surety companies later in this chapter). The developer can select a company for direct negotiation on the basis of the responses.

In open bidding, developers send out a notice requesting bids and statements of qualifications. However, most contractors are reluctant to spend time bidding on a project—at least two to four weeks are needed—unless they think that they have a good chance of being selected. As a result, developers using an open bidding process may not attract an adequate number of responses from which to choose.

An effective way to obtain bids from targeted contractors is a two-step process involving a general request for qualifications, which are reviewed, followed by a request for bids from the best three, four, or five contractors that responded to the RFQ. Should a preference for one contractor emerge early in the process, the developer should move right to direct negotiations with that firm. A developer should not feel obligated to conduct protracted bidding if it has already found the right contractor for the job.

The lowest bid is not always the optimal bid. The best contractor for the job may offer other important qualifications: the most relevant experience, unqualified reliability, a strong balance sheet, or the ability to complete construction in the shortest time. The lower carrying costs implied in a shorter construction period can compensate for a higher construction bid.

The contractor's major responsibility is to construct the project. This includes hiring construction workers and selecting subcontractors. The contractor is legally responsible for building a safe structure and must hire the best-qualified parties. Another task for which the contractor is responsible is to set up a schedule for disbursements from the construction lender.

During construction, changes to the original plans may be made for a variety of reasons: perceived market preferences, errors in the plans and specifications, delays, unanticipated conditions, the unavailability of specified materials, the availability of cost-saving alternatives, and a host of other reasons. All change orders are subject to the architect's verification and approval. And, if the developer does not monitor change orders carefully, costs can escalate dramatically. To avoid disputes over change orders, the construction contract should clearly and explicitly define the scope of the work that is included in the contract fee.

Developers can provide the contractor with an incentive to minimize construction costs by sharing with the GC any difference between the actual cost of construction and the contract fee. The developer must make sure, however, that the contractor does not sacrifice quality to receive the bonus.

Developers can negotiate other types of incentives and penalties as well. A bonus for early completion pays the contractor a defined amount for completing the work on or before a specific date. Some contracts pay a bonus based on the number of days ahead of schedule that the work is completed. By the same token, some contracts include a liquidated damages clause or a penalty clause to cover late completion. Not surprisingly, contractors often dislike these clauses, arguing that they destroy teamwork.

Market Consultants

Market consultants have many names, among which are feasibility consultant, market analyst, development consultant, or real estate counselor. Office developers retain market consultants to provide professional assessments of the feasibility of proposed developments. The go/no go decision made by developers is based largely on a market study, which typically is prepared by a market consultant with input from other key team members. Market studies delineate the demand for the proposed project, the current and projected competition, the potential tenants or users, the lease-up or sale time frame, rents or sales prices, and the revenue assumptions for the economic analysis.

Market consultants often participate in the dynamic decision-making process that characterizes nearly all office development projects. During all phases—from site selection to design, financing, and construction—market analysts can help define the needs and preference of the target tenants and position the building in the marketplace.

Some developers perform their own market and financial analyses of a prospective project, then hire a market consultant to be devil's advocate and prepare an independent assessment. An independent assessment from a well-regarded market consultant adds considerable credibility to a project in the eyes of lenders and investors.

Determining the market potential of a downtown site can be difficult, but the rewards are often worth the effort. Completed in 1985, Equitable Tower was the first new building in New York's Times Square area in a number of years, and it helped promote a neighborhood renaissance. Equitable Tower's occupancy rate has always been a strong 90 to 100 percent.

Courtesy of Equitable Real Estate

A comprehensive market study provides evidence on the marketability of the proposed development and suggests how best to position and market it. The market study should profile the tenants or buyers to be targeted and provide insights on the office space needs and amenity preferences of the target market.

Choosing the market consultant is likely to be one of the most important decisions made in the predevelopment period. Although the developer may ask other developers for recommendations, it should also ask lenders— whose decision to provide financing depends on the market data that prove the project's feasibility— which consultants they respect. A developer should choose a market consultant that is familiar with both the local market and the type of office development under consideration.

Aside from being technically proficient, good consultants are able to understand subtle nuances of the market that are not readily apparent to the average observer.

Good market consultants can identify competition that has not yet been built, and thoughtfully analyze political situations.

Before choosing, developers should look over several of the consultant's market studies, making sure that they are comfortable with the assumptions and techniques the consultant uses to appraise a market.

Market consultants might work on an hourly basis in preparing a preliminary analysis or a quick inventory of the market. For larger, more complex assignments, they generally require a fixed-price contract.

Appraisers

Appraisals estimating the value of property before and after development are a critical element in the decision to go forward or not to go forward with a project. Appraisals often are necessary when developers transfer ownership, seek financing, or resolve tax matters. Developers often hire appraisers for market and feasibility studies. Apprais-

Democracy Plaza in Bethesda, Maryland, is a mixed-use complex containing two office buildings, a hotel, and structured parking. A courtyard provides seating and outdoor dining space, and pathways provide pleasant areas for walking and jogging.

ers can also provide real estate counseling over a broad range of services, from investment analysis to courtroom testimony.

The developer must use extreme care in selecting an appraiser. Part of the blame for the S&L debacle of the 1980s rests on the often inflated property valuations performed by appraisers. Federal law has since mandated state licensing or certification of appraisers.

Various designations by the Appraisal Institute certify appraisers for different kinds of appraisal work. Among the designations for appraisers of office properties are the following: Member, Appraisal Institute (MAI)experienced in the valuation and evaluation of all types of property, and permitted to advise clients on real estate investment decisions; Senior Real Property Appraiser (SRPA)experienced in the valuation of all types of property; and Senior Real Estate Analyst (SREA)experienced in real estate valuation and analysis, and permitted to advise clients on investment decisions.

Attorneys

Legal specialists are needed to work on many facets of office development. Structuring taxes, forming partnerships or syndications, contracting with consultants, preparing lease agreements, completing property transactions, and negotiating the public approval process all require attorneys. And no single attorney can be familiar with all these issues.

The developer should choose a law firm that includes attorneys with specific experience in the development issues likely to arise on the project. Developers of similar office projects often can recommend good attorneys. Negotiating the public approval process requires specific skills. Consulting attorneys who have worked in the community is generally a good idea. An attorney with a proven record in cases involving a particular public body might be the proper choice to represent the developer at public hearings. On the other hand, the attorney's ability to work behind the scenes with the local planning staff

and politicians may be more important than his or her effectiveness at public hearings.

Many developers request that a partner of the law firm work on their cases, or they hire a well-established attorney, preferring to pay a little more for presumably the best person for the job. For technical work on syndications, contracts, and similar matters, it may be more cost-effective to work with highly recommended junior associates with three or four years of experience. Attorneys generally bill clients on an hourly basis. The developer should obtain an estimate of the total cost for a given job before authorizing it.

Leasing Agents

The leasing function is one of the most complex financial operations in the development process. Leasing agents must balance the needs of many different users against the owner's needs. Clearly, leasing requires more than quoting the number of square feet available and the price per square foot. Leasing involves negotiating the lease and all of its terms, including the price per square foot, the responsibility for various operating and tenant improvement costs, and any concessions or discounts (such as a period of free rent or cash for improvements furnished by the tenant) that will be given as a signing incentive. Leasing also requires identifying any special tenant needs, such as extra electrical or HVAC capacity.

A developer must decide early in the development process if leasing is to be carried out by in-house staff or outside consultants. The decision is usually based on the project's type and size and on the size and staffing of the development company.

The use of in-house agents is often more appropriate for large projects and large development firms that can carry the cost of permanent employees. The benefit of using an in-house agent is that he or she starts participating during initial planning and becomes very familiar with the project. An in-house agent can provide valuable input on the project's design and marketing.

Smaller development firms are likely to find it more cost-effective to retain outside brokers. Finding the right broker can make or break a project. If brokers are not active in the market and do not aggressively engage prospective tenants, developers can lose valuable time.

The developer should interview representatives from a number of firms in order to select a firm that has experience with the type of office project being developed. During interviews, the developer should present the office project carefully. If the broker does not respond positively to the project, another broker should be found. A broker currently representing competitive developments should not be hired because of potential conflicts of interest. The developer should look for a broker who has faith in the project and who can commit the energy necessary to ensure its success.

The broker is responsible for attracting prospective tenants (or buyers) and persuading them to lease (or buy) the project. An active broker will be well informed about the market, able to identify and recruit interested parties, and prepared to give input to the development team during the early planning stages regarding the type of amenities that are currently favored in the market and other information that can help position the project to attract the target market. A local broker often knows when the leases of local firms will expire. Brokers from large brokerage houses may have information about regional or national tenants.

The working relationship between a developer and broker is defined in a contract known as a listing agreement. Real estate brokers work almost exclusively on commission. The developer should negotiate a commissions schedule—for example, higher commissions in the early months—that will provide an incentive to lease (or sell) the building as quickly as possible.

Marketing and Public Relations Consultants

Even the best office development can founder if potential tenants do not hear its story and cannot differentiate it from competitive projects in the marketplace. Accordingly, marketing and public relations should begin long before ground is broken and continue through the operations phase. Office buildings frequently cannot be started until a significant percentage of the space is preleased. An appropriate marketing strategy can help a broker make that happen.

Public relations firms not only produce news releases, press kits, newsletters, and mailings that convey information about the project, but also promote media coverage and stage events that expose the project in a positive light to the appropriate audiences. Different projects require different approaches. It is the agency's responsibility to determine which tools will be most appropriate and effective; and to provide creative ideas for marketing the project.

Advertising agencies create and place advertisements strategically to promote the project and maximize its exposure. A public relations firm can handle advertising, and an advertising agency can handle public relations.

Selecting a public relations or advertising agency involves attending presentations at which the agencies under consideration offer examples of their work, samples relevant to the proposed project, and promotional ideas for the project. The developer should choose a firm that specializes in the type of office project being developed.

For large projects, many developers find it useful to establish a long-term relationship with a public relations firm by keeping it on retainer and relying on it to provide marketing and public relations services through all phases of the project.

Property Managers

Office property management is much more than caretaking buildings. It includes maximizing the value of the office project and extending its productive life. The ongoing success of an office development depends largely on how well it is managed. Therefore, developers often involve a professional property manager in the early planning and design phases of a project to make sure that operational concerns are addressed in the design.

Once the tenants move in, the property manager manages the building's day-to-day operations, within the framework of an annual budget and a comprehensive physical plan that specifies regular inspections and scheduled maintenance and replacement of equipment.

Managers also represent the developer in the landlord-tenant relationship. They should stay in constant communication with the tenants and quickly resolve any problems that might arise. A developer that receives complaints directly from the tenants should replace the property manager. Property managers often are responsible for filling vacancies as they arise, acting either as the leasing agent or working cooperatively with outside brokers.

Whether to provide management services in-house or to contract with a property management company is a decision that depends on such factors as the size and location of the project, the availability of trained in-house personnel, and whether the developer wishes to maintain a day-to-day role in the project. Many office development companies have property management departments or subsidiaries.

A property management firm should be selected on its track record—how it manages similar office buildings —and the type of compensation it requires. Compensation is typically a percentage of effective gross rental revenue, but it also can be a fixed amount. Leasing commissions often are paid in addition to compensation under the management agreement.

The Building Owners and Managers Association (BOMA) International and the Institute of Real Estate Management (IREM) are good sources for potential property managers. IREM awards the designation Certified Property Manager (CPM) to individuals with the appropriate qualifications and it awards the designation Accredited Management Organization (AMO) to qualifying firms. The AMO designation must be renewed, based on performance, every three years.

Sony Music Entertainment signed a ten-year lease for this complex in Santa Monica, California. The developer renovated it to suit the tenant's needs and to enhance the surrounding neighborhood.

Lowe Development Corporation

Title Companies

Title companies determine the validity of a property's title and guarantee the purchaser and lender that the property is free and clear of unknown mortgages, tax liabilities, easements, and other liens or claims that may cloud the title. They will defend any claims against properties that they insure. What is covered in a title policy varies, and the developer must read the policy carefully before signing it. Most policies follow a standard format, but many real estate investors fail to understand what protection their title policies provide, a misunderstanding that can lead to problems.

When selecting a title company, a developer should make sure that the company has the financial strength to back any potential claims and should research its record of service to ascertain how long it takes to obtain a clean title. Most title representatives work for a commission, and they are very accommodating because they want repeat business.

Title companies provide a number of other services. They can provide—typically free of charge—profiles of properties in which clients are interested. The details include lot size, ownership, property taxes, liens, easements, improvements, grant and trust deeds, notes, and the most recent sales price—and the profiles are accompanied by plat maps and information on comparable sales.

Title companies will prepare a preliminary title report for a fee. This is a reading of the existing title and it specifies current liens against the property. The preliminary title report highlights any potential problems that the developer may need to clear from a property before taking title, but it is not an insurance policy.

Surety Companies

A consultant's or contractor's failure to perform an agreed task may have serious economic and legal consequences. For instance, a contractor's failure to meet obligations could result in a lien on the developer's property. Private development projects do not have to be bonded, but, in most cases, some form of bond is recommended.

Developers may require that contractors be bondable, meaning that they qualify for surety coverage. GCs deal directly with surety companies to obtain performance and payment bonds. If bonds will be required, developers are required to inform all potential contractors before bids are submitted. Contractors consequently adjust their bids to pass on the cost of the bonds to the developer. Bondable contractors generally establish a relationship with one surety company and fix an upper limit of bonding credit, which restricts the amount of bondable work that the contractor can perform.

A surety bond is a three-party contract. The surety company (surety) joins with a principal (usually the contractor) and guarantees the specific performance of an act to the beneficiary (usually the developer).

Surety companies issue three main types of bonds:

- Performance bonds guarantee the developer that if the contractor fails to complete the agreed contract, the surety will see that the work is finished.
- Payment bonds guarantee that the surety will meet obligations if the contractor defaults on payments to laborers, subcontractors, or suppliers. This protects the property against liens that might be imposed in response to nonpayment.
- Completion bonds (often called developer off-site bonds or subdivision bonds) guarantee local municipalities that specified off-site improvements will be completed. Many states require local municipalities to secure such bonds as assurance that the developer will complete the improvements.

Payment bonds and performance bonds usually are issued concurrently, with both bonds often appearing on the same form.

Developers sometimes require bid bonds. A bid bond guarantees the developer that the winning contractors will honor their accepted bids. If, for example, a winning contractor finds out that its bid was significantly lower than the others submitted, it may withdraw the offer. In that case, the surety pays damages to the developer, in theory to compensate for time and money lost. In most states, surety companies must charge uniform rates, and file their rates and underwriting standards with the state insurance department or its equivalent.

Developers differ on the need to secure the various forms of surety bonds. Performance bonds and payment bonds cost roughly 1 percent of the construction cost.

Notes

1. ULI–the Urban Land Institute, *America's Real Estate* (Washington, D.C.: ULI–the Urban Land Institute, 1997).
2. Ibid., p. 43.
3. David Birch, Anne Haggerty, and William Parsons, *America's Office Economy, 1996–2006* (Cambridge, Massachusetts: Cognetics Inc., 1996), p. 11.
4. Kenneth Turney Gibbs, *Business Architectural Imagery in America, 1870–1930* (Ann Arbor: UMI Research Press, 1984), p. 54.
5. James A. Graaskamp, *Graaskamp on Real Estate*, ed. Stephen P. Jarchow (Washington, D.C.: ULI–the Urban Land Institute, 1991), p. 271.
6. David Birch et al., *America's Future Office Space Needs* (Washington, D.C.: NAIOP–National Association of Industrial and Office Parks, 1990), p. 5.
7. Anthony Downs, "Cycles in Office Space Markets," in *The Office Building: From Concept to Investment Reality*, ed. John Robert White (Washington, D.C.: Counselors of Real Estate; Appraisal Institute; and Society of Industrial and Office Realtors Education Fund, 1993), p. 155.
8. Ibid., p. 160.
9. James L. Freund, *History of the Eighties, Lessons for the Future: Commercial Real Estate and the Banking Crisis in the 1980s* (Washington, D.C.: Federal Deposit Insurance Corporation, Division of Research and Statistics, 16 December 1996), pp. 14–15.
10. Anthony Downs, *Banks and Real Estate: How to Resolve the Dilemma* (Washington, D.C.: ULI–the Urban Land Institute; and National Realty Committee, 1991), pp. 8–9.
11. Downs, "Cycles in Office Space Markets," pp. 166, 168.
12. American Institute of Architects, *You and Your Architect* (Washington, D.C.: American Institute of Architects, 1995), pp. 32–38.

2. Project Feasibility

Project feasibility analysis is the process by which developers and investors assess the economic viability of a prospective office development before they commit to the undertaking. Feasibility analysis is not a substitute for the developer's vision, experience, and good common sense. But it is a counterbalance to the storied optimism of developers, a reality test. In feasibility analysis, key assumptions and the developer's vision are examined and continually refined before each major commitment in a project.

The largest boom-and-bust cycle ever experienced in the history of the U.S. office market (see Chapter 1) is still fresh in the memories of most real estate practitioners. When, in the mid- and late 1980s, the future demand for new office space appeared to be enormous, office construction boomed and the competition among lenders and investors to get a piece of the action was intense. Project feasibility frequently took a back seat in decisions to build.

Tax benefits deriving from the use of accelerated depreciation for office buildings and the ability to shelter passive income losses removed investor concerns about real cash flows. Office developers and lending institutions typically did not require an in-depth feasibility analysis and, when they did, they all too often accepted superficial analyses without question. Feasibility studies performed during this period too often relied on short-term trends to project the future demand for and pricing

of office space. They failed to consider the slowdown in demand that was becoming apparent and the large supply of office space that was in the development pipeline. A result of these flawed feasibility studies was massive overbuilding in nearly every market in the country.

The consequences were serious: huge commercial real estate losses and the takeover of failed thrift institutions and their holdings by the federal government. And the analytical deficiencies themselves raised serious questions about the ability of commercial real estate developer/owners and lenders to assess project feasibility. Concerns were also raised about the credibility of real estate professionals who prepared the forecasts of financial performance and many of the property appraisals that accompanied the feasibility analyses of that time.

Since the real estate crash of the early 1990s, the development environment has become far more conservative. Decisions to build, renovate, and finance office buildings are based on an objective assessment of the relevant local market and an assessment of the risk that the proposed project will not achieve its projected cash flow. Before moving forward with new office projects, lenders and investors now require comprehensive feasibility studies that clearly identify the risk potential. Moreover, developers are expected to back up their financial projections with equity.

This chapter describes the process of assessing the feasibility of an office development, the techniques and studies used to evaluate project feasibility, and the pitfalls —approaches and assumptions that may bias or even

figure 2-1
Fairway Center

Project Summary

Fairway Center is a hypothetical suburban office building, which is used throughout this chapter to illustrate various components of a feasibility analysis. Brief descriptions of its main elements follow.

Location

Fairway Center is located 25 miles west of downtown Chicago in what is known as the East/West Corridor. The East/West Corridor is the largest of the five office submarkets in suburban Chicago. It contains about 14 percent of the region's total office inventory and nearly one-third of the region's suburban office inventory. The property is five minutes west of the interchange of I-88 and I-355. Interstate access and visibility are excellent. Development entitlements were established under a planned unit development (PUD) category.

Land and Building

Site Size	4.2 acres (182,500 square feet)
Land Cost	$2,000,000
	$10.95 per square foot of land area
	$13.50 per square foot of net rentable area (NRA)
Building	Class A, six stories plus basement garage and penthouse
	Steel-frame construction, concrete floors on metal deck, granite and glass curtain wall
	148,063 square feet of net rentable area (NRA)
	165,263 square feet of gross building area (GBA)
	Building efficiency ratio of 89.6%
Parking	3 spaces per 1,000 square feet of NRA
	25 basement garage spaces
	425 surface spaces

Development Costs

Building Construction	$11,394,000
	$76.95 per square foot of NRA
	$68.95 per square foot of GBA
Tenant Improvements	$4,540,000
	$30.66 per square foot of NRA
Land Cost	$2,000,000
Soft Costs, Interest, and Fees	$4,050,000
Total Development Cost	**$21,984,000**
	$148.49 per square foot of NRA

Timing

Construction Period	12 months
Absorption Period	18 months to stabilized occupancy

Occupancy

Year 1	60%
Year 2	96%
Stabilized Occupancy	96%, reached at end of year 2

Expected Rents (average rent per square foot of NRA)

Year 1	$16.00
At Stabilized Occupancy	$16.66
Long-Term Rent Growth	4% per year

Expected Operating Costs
(average operating costs per square foot of NRA)

Year 1	$8.00
At Stabilized Occupancy	$8.40
Operating Costs Growth	4% per year

Financing

First Mortgage	$16,500,000 (30-year loan, 9.5% interest, 33% preleasing requirement)
Equity contribution	$5,484,000 (25% of total project cost)

Financial and Performance Indicators

Required Before-Tax Rate of Return	15%
Required Cash-On-Cash Rate of Return	12%
Overall Market Cap Rate	9.5%
Terminal Cap Rate	9.5%
Lender's Minimum Debt Coverage Ratio	1.3 x
Maximum Break-Even Occupancy	85%

The development of Harborside Financial Center, which is located in a former warehouse district that had fallen into disrepair, was spurred by its proximity to Manhattan and public transportation. A tax incentive package improved the project's financial viability and its leasing is aided by a sales tax exemption available to tenants because of the building's location in Jersey City's urban enterprise zone.

invalidate an analysis. Various feasibility concepts are explained in part by way of example, using a hypothetical development called Fairway Center: a 148,000-square-foot, Class A speculative office project located in suburban Chicago. Fairway Center is introduced in Figure 2-1.

The Role of Feasibility Analysis

The process of analyzing the feasibility of a prospective office development has two principal components—market analysis and financial feasibility analysis. While many people use the term "feasibility analysis" to refer to both market analysis and financial feasibility, the two analyses are separate and distinct. Office developers and investors use both market analysis and financial feasibility analysis to identify and evaluate opportunities for constructing new office buildings and for repositioning existing buildings to attract different segments of the market.

Together, these analyses are referred to as "project feasibility analysis." Project feasibility analysis serves as a pragmatic tool for internal decision making through all phases of the development process. Developers use it also to secure debt financing and attract equity investors.

Market analysis and financial feasibility analysis are treated separately in this chapter. Chapters on financing, planning and design, leasing, and management follow. This is a logical order, but it is important to keep in mind that development and investment decisions are made in a dynamic environment. Changing market conditions, design choices, leasing considerations, and financing terms interact to affect the feasibility of an office project.

The market analysis is not simply a report that is generated at some critical juncture in the development process. To be used effectively in planning an office development project, the market analysis needs to be reexamined continually and updated throughout the planning and construction phases. Its performance projections—rent levels, timing of absorption, and occupancy—change as planning and design decisions are made, new information is gathered, and changes occur in the market, such as the possibility of a new competitor. A large tenant might move into the market. Its removal of a significant amount of space from the market would require upward adjustments in the market study's projected absorption, occupancy, and rent levels. Or a major tenant in the market might downsize or vacate. The addition of available space could necessitate downward adjustments in the rent, absorption, and occupancy projections.

The financial analysis integrates all the expectations that affect the proposed project's revenues and costs—leasing projections and forecasts of construction, financing, and operating costs—and tests whether, in combination, they can achieve the financial objectives of the developer, investors, and lenders. Financial analysis is an iterative process. Throughout the development period, the feasibility analysis is continually updated to take into account changes in market conditions and any new in-

At Pearl Street East Business Park in Boulder, Colorado, first-floor flex space combines with office on the upper levels to meet high-tech market demand.

formation that comes to light. The feasibility analysis is used also an internal decision-making tool to evaluate different alternatives and possible changes in design, phasing, financing, or marketing.

The Test of Feasibility

A prospective office development meets the test of feasibility if it is capable of achieving the objectives of the project's owners, lenders, and investors. A project that is financially feasible for one of the various participants in the office marketplace might not be for another with different investment objectives. For example, an organization seeking space for its own use might find that a new office building meets the test of feasibility if the debt service and operating costs total less than what the organization is currently paying in rent. A developer that expects to build and quickly sell an office building will view feasibility from a shorter-term perspective than a developer that plans to build, own, and operate a building and benefit from its long-term appreciation in value. Certain investors in rehabilitation or adaptive use projects may be more interested in the project's ability to qualify for federal rehabilitation tax credits than in its long-term value.

From a build-to-use organization's perspective, a project feasibility analysis should address a number of issues, including the functions of an owned building, the asset's liquidity, long-term asset value, and potential productivity and cost savings compared with other alternatives. Custom layouts and other special design features can improve the productivity of the organization's employees. However, if custom features detract from the building's reuse potential for other occupants or entail higher-than-usual operating and maintenance costs, they also can reduce the building's liquidity and long-term appreciation. The process of determining project feasibility involves weighing many such tradeoffs.

Project feasibility from a developer's perspective may depend on whether the developer is a fee developer building for a client or an owner/developer building

for its own account. Fee developers may be less concerned with the long-term viability of a project and more concerned with the workability of the project's time frame and cost budget. Owner/developers that intend to hold onto the building are more concerned with the project's long-term asset value. Developers that intend to sell immediately are particularly concerned with meeting the quality and occupancy standards of prospective buyers.

For lenders and investors, downside risk is an important calculation in the test of feasibility. Financial institutions begin by evaluating the risk of default. They analyze the performance expectations for a project and then define worst-case scenarios to determine the level of exposure on a loan. Investors in a project also define worst-case scenarios and typically base their disposition or exit strategies on them.

Regardless of who initiates an office project, meeting the test of feasibility requires, at a minimum, the satisfaction of three basic criteria:

- The building will meet all local zoning and building code requirements.
- The building will be designed to meet the needs of the target market.
- The building will generate a net cash flow that satisfies the lending requirements of potential sources of construction loans and long-term loans and provides a reasonable return for equity investors.

Common Mistakes

It is often said that the difference between a real estate veteran and a novice is one downturn. There is a lot of truth to this maxim. Veteran real estate professionals understand from having experienced a recession that the market always turns. They base development strategies on the market's cyclical nature. Novices lacking the sobering lesson of a recession tend to believe that a period of rising demand and rents can continue indefinitely (or at least until the proposed project is complete), and they often overlook information that contradicts this rosy view until it is too late. Conversely, novices working in recessionary markets often wait too long for confirmation that the market has turned, and thus miss key opportunities.

In assessing a project's feasibility, both overconfidence and undue pessimism are to be avoided. The following list of shorthand rules for project feasibility analysis is derived generally from the problems that flawed many feasibility studies conducted in the 1980s and caused them to miss the mark. An appreciation of the pitfalls of feasibility analysis as represented by the items in this list should help both novices and veterans avoid basic analytical mistakes:

- Short-term employment trends do not last. Office developers should study both short-term and long-term employment trends. It is important to understand basic employment factors in order to anticipate what could cause short-term employment patterns to change.
- Most markets cannot absorb a rush of office building. If everyone builds an office building, occupancy and rents will suffer. Office developers should monitor the competition and avoid markets where a stampede of new product is underway or proposed.
- Submarkets within a region differ widely. Office development proposals need to be tailored to their specific market areas. By asking and listening, developers can ascertain important details. What types of tenant are moving into what types of office space? What space is available for sublease? What size firms are moving or growing? What types of amenities and building services are important to which tenants?
- Rising rental rates and appreciation in property values are not inalienable rights. Developers should test their project's sensitivity to varying inflation assumptions, particularly in long-term cash flow projections. One good test of a project's financial feasibility is to run a pro forma analysis with inflation set at zero.
- Better mousetraps are few and far between. Assuming that a proposed project will outperform the market is rarely justified, and developers should be very leery of making such an assumption.
- The times they are a-changin'. Technology, lifestyles, and workstyles are all undergoing considerable change. The impact of change increasingly must be considered in office feasibility analysis.

Market Analysis

An office development generally proceeds on the basis of a succession of market analyses. The various types of studies that are commonly undertaken are summarized in Figure 2-2. Each of these studies is undertaken to answer different questions, and not every project requires all these studies. However, the progression of market analyses—from macroeconomic analysis to local market analysis to site selection and site analysis and project marketability studies—represents a general guide

by which developers can formulate and refine an office development concept.

Office market analyses can range from geographically broad to locally focused. The most general market analyses compare two or more cities or metropolitan areas. Companies looking for multiple office development or acquisition opportunities and firms wanting to relocate sometimes undertake such evaluations. Broad macroeconomic market analyses compare economic and demographic trends in the metropolitan areas, office market trends, and such other characteristics as the availability and cost of labor, housing costs, local taxes, the development climate, and quality-of-life factors.

More detailed macroeconomic analyses of local markets evaluate and compare office submarkets within single metropolitan regions. These analyses examine regional economic trends and various indicators of the strengths and weaknesses of the office submarkets, in order to identify submarkets that merit further analysis.

Outstanding amenities are part of the allure of Atlanta Financial Center, a three-building office complex of 1 million gross square feet. The 18,000-square-foot Buckhead Athletic Club is open to tenants only. Membership at the Buckhead Club, a private dining facility, is open to tenants and community residents.

figure 2-2
Components of Project Feasibility Analysis

Component	Questions to Be Answered	Objective	Estimation of Value	Sources of Value Estimates	Estimates of Absorption
Macroeconomic Analysis (Market analysis covering multiple metropolitan areas and cities)	• What are the current and expected market conditions in the areas being evaluated? • How will market conditions affect office supply and demand? • What are the rates of return on office properties in these areas?	To identify metropolitan areas or cities with favorable office indicators, for further analysis	Maybe, if sophisticated office models are used	Sales prices; present value of future rents	Not generally
Local Market Analysis (Market analysis covering a single metropolitan area, city, or submarket)	• What is the overall office demand/supply situation in the area? • What is the office demand/supply situation in the area's submarkets?	To identify submarkets with favorable office indicators, for further analysis	No	Not applicable	Yes
Site Selection Study (Market analysis)	• What sites are available within the market study area? • What are the advantages/disadvantages of each site?	To select a site among those identified as favoring office development	No	Not applicable	Yes
Site-Specific Market Study (Market analysis for a site that has been chosen)	• Is the site's market area favorable for office development? • How does the site compare with other sites in the same submarket? • How does the site compare with other sites in nearby submarkets?	To verify that the indicators are favorable for office development at the selected site	Not generally	Not usually applicable	Yes
Marketability Study	• What prices, sizes, functions, and features are required to capture a market share at the site(s) under consideration?	To determine the achievable rents and occupancy as well as marketable design and amenity features for an office project at the site(s) under consideration	No	Not applicable	Maybe
Financial Feasibility Analysis[1]	• Are the expected revenues sufficient to cover the operating expenses and debt service on the property? • What financial return can the developer expect for its willingness to assume the risk of development?	To determine if the investor can earn the required rate of return, given achievable market rents, cost of capital, debt service requirements, and operating expenses	Yes	Market prices; present worth of future cash flows	No

[1]Financial feasibility can be broken down into the types of documents generated (key elements), which are discussed later in the financial feasibility section of this chapter.

Estimates of Market Capture	Estimates of Project's Timing	Description of Conditions for Success	Possible Predecessor Studies	Possible Successor Studies	Possible Simultaneous Studies
No	No	No	None	Local market analysis or site selection study	None
Maybe	Maybe	No	Macroeconomic analysis; or can be first analysis in series	Site selection study	Site selection study or site-specific market study
Maybe	Maybe	No	Macroeconomic analysis; and/or local market analysis; usually not the first in the series	Marketability study	Local market analysis
Maybe	Maybe	No	None	Marketability study	Local market analysis
Yes	Yes	Yes	Local market analysis and site selection study (or site-specific market study)	Financial feasibility analysis	Local market analysis and site selection study (or site-specific market study)
No	Maybe	Yes	Local market analysis, site selection study (or site-specific market study), and marketability study	Ongoing financial feasibility analysis; changing market conditions and other assumptions are continually updated in electronic spreadsheet(s)	Investment analyses

Waterford at Blue Lagoon takes advantage of an exceptional site—138 acres with five lakes located adjacent to Miami International Airport. Because of its airport proximity, the development has attracted a majority of its tenants from the international business community.

Neither the broad nor the local macroeconomic market study is concerned with specific sites. Instead, the purpose of these analyses is to identify the most favorable region(s) or regional submarket(s) for office development.

A thorough macroeconomic market analysis helps a developer or investor establish a preliminary concept of an office project it wishes to carry out and identify a market area in which to do it. The next step is a site selection study. The chief criteria for selecting a suitable site or existing building relate to market potential, location, access, infrastructure, physical and environmental constraints, the regulatory climate, and price.

After a site is selected, the developer undertakes a detailed market study to refine projections of market conditions (including competition) for an office development at the specific site. If the site proves favorable, the developer then undertakes a marketability study, which yields specific performance projections—including rents, absorption pace, and occupancy rates—for the development under consideration

Macroeconomic Market Analysis

Developers and investors conduct a macroeconomic market analysis to identify potential development or investment opportunities. This analysis assesses the locational, economic, and market conditions of one or more large market areas and generally focuses on the following elements:

- The underlying economy of the market area and its prospects for growth. What major industries make up the region's economic base? Is the regional economy growing? A stable or dynamic economy provides a generally favorable environment for office investment. An economy showing signs of decline is less inherently promising. Developers must give it considerably

more scrutiny before determining that it may offer a good investment opportunity.
- The growth potential of the office-using sectors of the economy. What kinds of businesses have relocated into the area in recent years? Which local industries are major office-using employers? What trends within these industries may affect how much and what type of office space they will require in the future?
- Supply and demand factors in the regional office market. What are the historical trends, by class of building, in net absorption, occupancy and vacancy rates, and rental rates? How much vacant office space is currently on the market and how much space is planned or under construction?

Turning to the Fairway Center example, we find that an analysis of the Chicago market area (Figure 2-3) is the developer's first step in investigating the feasibility of building Fairway Center. Figure 2-3, which shows demographic, economic, and office market data for the Chicago metropolitan area (MSA), exemplifies the types of data that typically are collected in an office market study's first cut. The actual analysis would involve more comprehensive data—more years of data on each series and more disaggregation of the data series. Vacancy rates, typical rents, and office construction and inventory would be further detailed by submarkets. Office-employment data would be collected in more categories than the FIRE (finance, insurance, and real estate) and business services industrial classifications. The data categories in Figure 2-3 provide a reliable initial indication of the strength or weakness of the overall market. If these broad indicators are not favorable, it is likely that the development team for Fairway Center would search for a non-Chicago market, rather than fine-tune this analysis.

However, the general trends in the Chicago market as described in Figure 2-3 justify continuing to explore the

figure 2-3
Fairway Center: Chicago Office Market Analysis[1]

	1985	1990	1991	1992	1993	1994	1995	1996
Population	7,272,000	7,261,000	7,369,700	7,400,000	7,447,300	7,472,700	7,487,100	7,620,000
Households	2,553,300	2,619,800	2,683,960	N/A	2,725,000	2,748,000	2,780,000	2,795,000
Median Household Income	$28,528	$36,327	$37,447	N/A	N/A	$45,950	N/A	$48,225
Office Employment[2]								
FIRE	236,842	284,386	294,000	281,669	284,156	291,732	299,219	301,461
Business Services	N/A	213,935	N/A	N/A	222,498	240,062	283,186	291,303
New Office Jobs[3]	N/A	N/A	N/A	N/A	N/A	25,140	50,611	10,359
Office Inventory (square feet)	119,500,000	156,400,000	158,800,000	163,000,000	163,000,000	163,000,000	163,000,000	163,221,000
Annual Construction (square feet)	15,600,000	8,800,000	2,400,000	4,200,000	0.0000	0.0000	0.0000	221,000
Downtown	7,100,000	6,800,000	1,800,000	3,800,000	0.0000	0.0000	0.0000	0.0000
Suburbs	8,500,000	2,000,000	600,000	400,000	0.0000	0.0000	0.0000	221,000
Annual Absorption (square feet)	5,900,000	3,900,000	(450,000)	(40,000)	825,000	3,707,000	2,700,000	1,000,000
Vacancy Rate	14.0%	17.3%	18.9%	20.7%	20.1%	17.6%	15.7%	14.7%
Downtown Class A Space	11.0%	16.2%	17.8%	21.0%	20.7%	18.1%	17.5%	17.0%
Suburbs	18.0%	19.4%	21.0%	19.9%	18.9%	16.0%	11.9%	10.5%
Typical Lease Rate (per square foot per year)								
Downtown Class A Space	$20.00	$28.00	$26.00	$24.00	$22.00	$22.00	$22.00	$23.00
Suburban High-Rise Space	$15.00	$21.50	$21.00	$20.00	$20.00	$20.00	$22.00	$25.00
Office Parks	N/A	$14.00	$14.00	$15.00	$15.00	N/A	$15.00	$15.00
Typical Price for Land (per square foot)								
Downtown Site	$350–700	$900–1,600	$900–1,500	$1,000–1,200	N/A	N/A	N/A	$900–1,600
Suburban High-Rise Site	N/A	$15–25	$15–25	$15–25	N/A	N/A	N/A	$15–25
Office Parks	N/A	$5–10	$5–10	$5–10	$5–10	$5–10	$5–10	$5–10

[1]Dollar figures not adjusted for inflation.

[2]Two industry classifications—FIRE (finance, insurance, and real estate) and business services—have a very high proportion of office workers (in many cases, over 90 percent). The office shares of many other industry classifications can be deduced with difficulty, but the effort should be made. In any case, employment in the FIRE and business services sectors constitutes a reliable low estimate of office employment.

[3]New office jobs is the annual gain (loss) in employment in the FIRE and business services sectors.

Sources: Illinois Department of Employment Security; Koll; Draper & Kramer; and *ULI Market Profiles*.

feasibility of undertaking the Fairway Center project. Office employment is a good indicator of the strength of the office market. The number of new office jobs can be translated roughly into office space requirements by applying industry standards for office space per employee. In the Chicago MSA, office-employment growth (as measured by the number of new jobs created in FIRE and business services, two industry classifications known to have high shares of office workers) was a strong 5 percent in 1994 and 9.5 percent in 1995 before slowing in 1996 to just under 2 percent. Between 1990 and 1996, office employment grew at a compound annual rate of 3 percent, showing steady increases since 1992.

Net office absorption, the change in the amount of occupied office space, is another key indicator of conditions in the office market. The Fairway Center analysis shows positive absorption in Chicago in each year since 1993, but absorption was less strong than job growth would lead one to expect. According to U.S. office industry standards, office space allocation per employee is in the range of 200 to 250 square feet. In Chicago in the early 1990s, the number of square feet absorbed per new office employee was far below this standard: 147 square feet of space absorbed per new office employee in 1994; 53.4 square feet absorbed per new employee in 1995; and 96.5 square feet per employee in 1996.

The Dial Corporation headquarters in Scottsdale, Arizona, is a 130,000-square-foot build-to-suit development.

Koyama Photographic

Unusual data indicators, like Chicago's low office absorption rates per employee, should be investigated. The analyst needs to determine how the data were collected and what is included in the various data series. This determination may reveal that subleased space and build-to-suit space were excluded from the absorption data that were reported. In a market with considerable subleasing and build-to-suit activity, such exclusions would cause estimates of absorption per new employee to be artificially low. In a market in which employers have accommodated new employees in excess space that they already owned or leased, the reported absorption and employment growth data would misrepresent absorption per new employee in the same way.

In many markets, the competition between the downtown and suburbs for new office employment is fierce. The prudent developer or analyst examines conditions in downtown and in suburban office markets separately. Some key supply and demand measures provided in Figure 2-3—vacancy rates, rents, construction activity, and land prices—show more momentum for development in Chicago's suburbs than in downtown. During the mid- and late 1980s and early 1990s, the downtown had a consistently lower vacancy rate. In 1992, however, the suburbs began having lower vacancy rates and by 1996 the suburban office vacancy rate was substantially lower than downtown's. Similarly, the Fairway Center analysis shows relatively flat office rents in downtown and respectably growing office rents in the suburbs. On the supply side, the analysis shows a resumption in the suburbs of office construction, which had been nonexistent for years. And finally, land for suburban projects—office parks or high rises—is less expensive than for downtown buildings.

The analysis of these broad market trends lead the developers of Fairway Center to the conclusion that conditions are favorable for office development, particularly in Chicago's suburbs. This type of trends analysis

is only a preliminary step in the market analysis, but it provides a foundation for more focused analyses of the local market and submarkets. In this case, the developers of Fairway Center have learned that the suburbs of Chicago offer opportunities for office development. Their next step will be to narrow their focus down to a specific suburb in which to locate the proposed office project.

Local Market Analysis

A local market analysis explores the dynamics of a single MSA. Typically, its purpose is to identify which submarkets, if any, indicate strong potential for office development. It includes a description of the economic base of the metropolitan area, a review of development trends, and, usually, a detailed assessment of the strengths and weaknesses of office submarkets—covering net absorption, occupancy, and rental rates by class of building, as well as demand by tenant size.

Within a metropolitan area, conditions can vary widely from submarket to submarket. The Washington MSA in the early to mid-1990s provides one example. During that time, office construction and net absorption in the northern Virginia suburbs of Washington, D.C., dwarfed activity in the Maryland suburbs. The northern Virginia market was fueled by the expansion of the communications and electronics industries that have located in this submarket. The Maryland suburbs, with high concentrations of federal facilities and life-sciences companies, experienced less growth.

Analysts generally identify a region's office submarkets less broadly than "the northern Virginia suburbs" or the "Maryland suburbs." Many large metropolitan areas have upward of 30 major office submarkets. The Washington metropolitan area, for example, according to a breakdown by Grubb & Ellis, comprises 33 major office submarkets (see Figure 2-4).

Reston Town Center evokes an urban main street in a suburban locale. Reston, Virginia, is one of the earliest master-planned new towns in the United States, and it set the standard for those that followed. It was conceived in 1962 with several goals, including that of providing "the opportunity to live and work in the same community." The Town Center is among the final phases of Reston's development.

The next step for the development team for Fairway Center is to evaluate the development potential of four suburban office submarkets—the northwest suburbs, the north suburbs, the O'Hare area, and the East/West Corridor. (See Figure 2-5.) These four submarkets contain almost all of suburban Chicago's investment-grade office buildings.

This analysis leads the development team to conclude that the East/West Corridor is the most auspicious location for an office project. Paralleling the I-88 east/west toll road, this area has grown rapidly since 1970, when it contained only 1 million square feet of office space. By 1980, the office space inventory stood at 6.8 million square feet and, by 1995, at approximately 26 million square feet.

The development team's analysis of the East/West Corridor area (Figure 2.6) reveals market fundamentals indicating that this rapid growth has not saturated the market, and that even more office inventory is needed to meet burgeoning demand. The corridor's location, transportation infrastructure, economy, labor market, and capital market all seem to combine to create ready opportunities for commercial development. All four corners of

figure 2-4

Office Submarkets in Metropolitan Washington, D.C., 1996

| | Rentable Square Feet | Vacant or Available Space[1] | | Net Square Feet Absorbed | Average Asking Lease Rate[2] |
		Square Feet	Percent		
District of Columbia					
Central Business District	36,288,706	4,257,113	11.7%	(51,534)	$30.00
East End	28,374,173	2,908,562	10.3	(312,275)	30.47
Georgetown	2,827,068	348,772	12.3	(26,021)	23.73
Southwest	9,782,529	496,208	5.1	144,796	33.19
Union Station	6,933,500	1,099,955	15.9	151,664	30.38
Uptown	8,047,702	790,446	9.8	(135,643)	25.40
West End	4,309,191	349,377	8.1	6,925	30.89
Total District of Columbia	**96,562,869**	**10,250,433**	**10.6%**	**(222,088)**	**$30.11**
Northern Virginia					
Alexandria	8,019,275	657,569	8.2%	(58,743)	$21.68
Arlington County					
Crystal City/Pentagon City	11,354,537	32,415	0.3	54,435	26.36
Rosslyn/Ballston Corridor	15,126,018	913,530	6.0	29,205	24.90
Columbia Pike/Arlington Boulevard	1,092,684	48,445	4.4	(6,238)	16.50
Total Arlington County	**27,573,239**	**994,390**	**3.6%**	**77,402**	**$24.91**
Fairfax County					
I–395 Corridor	7,831,708	611,642	7.8	109,491	18.81
I–95 Corridor	1,847,295	172,782	9.4	67,250	20.05
Merrifield	4,820,804	180,047	3.7	11,016	22.41
Tysons Corner	20,994,480	1,233,957	5.9	1,603,292	22.05
Fairfax Center	10,500,189	729,737	6.9	802,992	20.03
Herndon	3,654,508	331,268	9.1	(23,028)	19.86
Reston	9,421,246	444,031	4.7	509,338	20.61
Route 8/Chantilly	3,346,287	490,672	14.7	244,671	21.95
Total Fairfax County	**62,416,517**	**4,194,136**	**6.7%**	**3,325,022**	**$20.92**
Loudoun County	2,494,843	207,977	8.3%	586,230	$18.66
Total Northern Virginia	**100,503,874**	**6,054,072**	**6.0%**	**3,929,911**	**$22.51**

the Chicago MSA are accessible from the corridor. The addition in 1989 of a highway link between the inner and outer loops (I-294 and I-355) enhanced the appeal of the East/West Corridor. Direct rail connections make the commute from downtown or O'Hare Airport to any point along this corridor only 30 minutes or less. Many Fortune 500 companies have a major presence in the East/West Corridor, partly due to its excellent transportation access.

A key step in performing a local market analysis is to define the market area. Failure to define the market area for a proposed office project can result in the collection of a perhaps overwhelming amount of irrelevant data. A good definition, on the other hand, can limit the data compilation effort to areas in which the developer is interested or which are competitive with a site to which the developer is committed.

Developers or investors generally use one of two methods—location or competition—to define the market area for a particular office project. From a locational perspective, an area around the site is defined as the area in which the building will compete for tenants. This geographic area generally encompasses the submarket in

	Rentable Square Feet	Vacant or Available Space[1]		Net Square Feet Absorbed	Average Asking Lease Rate[2]
		Square Feet	Percent		
Suburban Maryland					
Montgomery County					
Bethesda	7,387,483	712,762	9.6%	111,263	$23.41
North Bethesda	9,047,425	756,141	8.4	484,954	19.54
Twinbrook/Rockville	5,802,352	437,683	7.5	(170,858)	20.90
North Rockville/Shady Grove	7,301,602	534,447	7.3	201,091	18.67
Gaithersburg/Germantown	5,008,577	550,544	11.0	251,074	17.50
Silver Spring/Burtonsville	9,954,945	2,053,666	20.6	(292,895)	17.35
Total Montgomery County	44,502,384	5,045,243	11.3%	584,539	$19.24
Prince George's County					
Laurel/Muirkirk	1,575,491	251,357	16.0	91,288	15.13
Beltsville/Calverton	1,391,828	277,982	20.0	31,580	19.00
Greenbelt/New Carrollton	2,740,078	366,539	13.4	(33,428)	19.27
Bowie/Upper Marlboro	297,160	13,685	4.7	6,519	13.42
College Park/Hyattsville	2,545,625	635,320	25.0	131,125	16.61
Southern Prince George's County	2,424,029	345,795	14.3	57,596	17.92
Landover/Lanham/Largo	3,723,637	674,922	18.1	246,902	15.65
Total Prince George's County	14,697,848	2,565,780	17.5%	531,582	$18.45
Total Suburban Maryland	59,200,232	7,611,023	12.9%	1,116,121	$19.07
Total Metropolitan Washington, D.C.	256,266,975	23,915,528	9.3%	4,823,944	$23.90

[1]Including sublet space.

[2]Rates are quoted on an annual, full-service (gross) basis for Class A and Class B buildings.

Source: Grubb & Ellis.

Repositioning office properties to maximize their value through skillful, limited improvements to public spaces and building systems has become a significant trend in recent years. While repositioning is not a new practice, this kind of activity has increased since the early 1990s, when owners and investors shifted their focus to the management of existing properties in response to oversupplied markets. The following observations pertain to decisions on when and how to reposition a property.

Why?

Many older Class A buildings face big challenges in today's marketplace. They are in competition with newer buildings that have suffered little or no wear and tear, are equipped with state-of-the-art technology, offer flexible space for tenants, and are fully accessible to the handicapped.

William Krouch, vice president of LaSalle Partners, Boston, comments: "Often, you have to make cosmetic changes just to stay in the game." One Winthrop Square, a historic landmark building in the heart of Boston's financial district, is one example. LaSalle Partners wanted to give the lobby—last updated in the 1970s—the atmosphere of a comfortable, elegant, small Boston club, to make it more harmonious with the building's architecture. Outdated signage, stucco on walls and ceilings, and iron grillwork were removed. Mahogany paneling was added to match a traditional fireplace, low ceilings were raised, and new lighting was installed. A new security desk, with a built-in directory and security cameras, contributes to the building's changed image as a safe, comfortable place in which to do business.

A redesigned lobby with mahogany paneling gives Boston's One Winthrop Square a look of being a secure and comfortable place in which to conduct business.

When?

When does it make sense to reposition an older property? The basic economic criterion is simple: if the net present value of the expected future net income after the improvements are made exceeds the costs of the improvements plus the net present value of the property in its current state, investing in the improvements makes sense. Applying this criterion is, however, difficult, since it involves comparing the economics of operating the building in the future under different scenarios, from no improvements to simple cosmetic improvements to complete renovation.

Certain market situations tend to favor investment in improvements to existing buildings. The most common of these is when the demand for higher-quality space is growing but the capacity to add new space is limited. When a large inventory of older buildings is also available, this market situation is likely to spark a great deal of renovation activity.

Another common market situation favoring investment in existing buildings is when the demand for higher-quality space is expanding and a substantial number of older buildings are well located to serve this demand but have very limited marketability in their current condition.

Many older, marginally low-quality buildings are well located and structurally sound, and offer floorplates and other design features sought by prime tenants. Their current lack of competitiveness imposes severe penalties in rent and occupancy. Many owners of such buildings will find it attractive to undertake the improvements that will enable them to compete at higher rent levels and to achieve higher occupancy levels.

Among older buildings, the ideal prospects for repositioning have minimal or nonexistent mortgages or can be purchased cheaply. A property with a low acquisition price can be improved yet still offer lower rents than newer buildings with heavy debt burdens. Rents that are often 10 percent below asking rents at new buildings with similar amenities will do much to win over Class A tenants.

Since the early 1970s, 990 Washington Street in Dedham, Massachusetts, has been a landmark office building along Route 128. Purchased by G.E. Real Estate in 1989, the property was having problems replacing tenants lost through normal attrition. A complete overhaul was needed to reposition it in greater Boston's highly competitive, increasingly sophisticated marketplace.

The renovation involved upgrading and refinishing all public spaces. A cafeteria between two lobbies was relocated to a more suitable space, and the lobbies were reconnected with a public passage. New air-conditioned

The upgrading of public spaces at 990 Washington Street in Dedham, Massachusetts, resulted in increased tenant retention rates and new leases.

Richard Mandelkorn Photography

elevator lobbies in the parking garage solved an HVAC problem caused by unconditioned garage air coming in through elevator cabs. The new arrival sequence, lobbies, and internal circulation spaces, as well as a refurbished tenant amenities package, breathed new life into this tired building.

John Cullnane, senior vice president of Peter Elliot & Company and the property's building manager, describes the results: "Dedham Executive Center has achieved significant retention rates with existing tenants, while new leases have brought its 180,000 square feet of space to 95 percent occupancy and rising."

How?

With the increased activity in repositioning, the age-old real estate goal of using each investment dollar wisely becomes even more critical. This is not the time to make cosmetic changes that are ego-driven rather than market-driven, or to replace systems that are functioning adequately. A property must be assessed objectively before its position in the marketplace can be understood.

First, look at the building and identify its faults. Ask existing tenants and local brokers for their impressions: "What is the building's image in the marketplace?" "What are your overall impressions of the building?" "What are its strengths and weaknesses?" Their answers can be very helpful.

Next, prepare a comparative building analysis. Look at four or five buildings that are competing for your tenants. Rate each of them on key factors such as location, access, floorplate flexibility, image, amenities, and so forth.

Finally, conduct an ADA study to get an overall picture of the facility's compliance. The results will serve as the basis for a risk/benefit analysis, providing a menu of items to be prioritized. Simply conducting the survey generally is seen as one step toward compliance.

"A critical factor in building repositioning is communication with existing tenants," attests Krouch. In his experience, good communication through correspondence is essential, and a clear, extensive signage program during renovations represents money wisely spent. "We look at each renovation as an opportunity to enhance relationships with existing tenants. When you bring tenants into the process, they can see how the improved image relates to them. It's a win-win situation," says Krouch. Good communication helps tenants to plan for a seamless transition, and a professional signage program during construction eases the way as it sends a message to tenants that a high-quality product will result.

Cost control for renovation work is also essential. Given the challenges of renovating older buildings and given the potential for hidden conditions, Krouch considers a 5 percent budget contingency the mark of a well-managed repositioning project. Stick to real estate basics, avoid spending too much, and remember that even small design changes can significantly improve a building's image. High-quality design, good taste, and durability are all key to attracting and keeping tenants.

Successfully repositioning a commercial property involves objectively assessing the property, getting a clear picture of the building's problems and advantages, and incorporating high-quality design to solve problems and make the most of advantages. These processes are all central to achieving the ultimate goals of a repositioning: 100 percent tenant occupancy and greater retention.

Source: Adapted, with additions, from Helen G. Novak and Mark E. Glasser, "Repositioning Corporate Office Buildings," *Urban Land*, October 1993, pp. 12–14.

figure 2–5

Fairway Center: Chicago Office Submarkets Analysis

	Total Inventory[1] (Square Feet)	Share of Total Market
Suburban Submarkets		
Northwest Suburbs	16,020,000	8%
North Suburbs	17,700,000	9
O'Hare Area	14,630,000	8
East/West Corridor	26,600,000	14
West and South Cook County[2]	7,550,000	4
Total Suburban Submarkets	82,570,000	43%
Downtown Chicago	109,500,000	57%
Total Chicago Market	**192,070,000**	**100%**

[1]Inventory of multistory single-use office buildings, all classes.

[2]Small submarket containing little investment-grade office product.

which the proposed project is located and adjacent submarkets. From a competitive building perspective, specific buildings that will compete directly with the proposed project are defined as the market area. A competition-defined market area is usually somewhat broader geographically. The Fairway Center developers used a locational perspective in defining their market area, and thus identified, classified, and evaluated all competing buildings in the East/West Corridor submarket.

The exact extent of the market area for any particular office project depends on many factors, including the following:

- the location of competitive buildings;
- street and road patterns in the area surrounding the building;
- commute times from residential areas;
- proximity to mass transit;
- physical barriers to access;
- land use patterns; and
- psychological or perceptual barriers to access, like unappealing or purportedly unsafe areas that must be traversed to get to the building.

Urban locations and suburban locations tend to have quite dissimilar market areas. For example, the market area for a downtown office building may encompass only a few blocks surrounding the building, while the market area for a suburban office project may encompass several submarkets surrounding a central city. Developers must gauge the scale and characteristics of a proposed project before they can define the appropriate market area.

An office building located at a mass transit station, for example, might be competing with buildings located at other stations more than it is competing with nearby buildings that are beyond walking distance from the station. A definition of its market area would have to take that possibility into account.

A proposed office building's competition typically defines its market area more than the current location of potential tenants defines it. Therefore, defining a market area for an office building differs greatly from defining a market area—the extent of the area from which a facility will draw customers—for a retail facility. However, for certain office developments that function like retail projects, for example a medical office building, customer location is of paramount importance.

figure 2–6

Fairway Center: East/West Corridor Area Analysis

	1980	1995	Percent Change
Office Space (square feet)	6,803,636	25,782,739	279%
Office Vacancy Rate	19.26%	10.61%	(45)%
Net Office Rents[1] (per square foot)			
Class A Space	$11.00	$17.50	59%
Class B Space	$9.00	$12.50	39%
Area Boundaries	York to Highland	Wolf. to Route 59	–
Hotel Rooms	2,272	7,950	250%[3]
Population[2]	658,835	844,000[3]	28%

[1]Average net lease rates.

[2]DuPage County.

[3]Projected.

Tower City Center, a 17-acre mixed-use complex in Cleveland, was developed to revitalize the downtown waterfront and bring viable business and retail back to a deteriorating CBD. The development vision was that the provision of high-quality mass transportation and retail amenities would encourage individuals and businesses to come back to downtown Cleveland. Tower City Center exemplifies the importance of such amenities to office development.

During its heyday, the Terminal Tower complex, which dates from the late 1920s, was a regional and local passenger transportation hub and it offered direct pedestrian connections to adjacent department stores, hotels, and office buildings. By the early 1980s, the office and shopping complex was still intact but shabby, a symbol of the general decline of downtown Cleveland. Forest City Enterprises purchased the complex in 1982 and completed its redevelopment in 1991.

The redeveloped Tower City Center contains more than 1 million square feet of office space in both new and renovated buildings, a 208-room luxury hotel, 360,000 square feet of redeveloped and expanded retail space, an 11-screen cineplex, and 3,150 parking spaces. The center is connected to a renovated transit station, as well as to two adjoining office buildings, a department store, a hotel, and the Gateway area's new 42,000-seat baseball stadium and 21,000-seat basketball arena. Tower City Center's easy accessibility and synergistic mix of uses have succeeded in bringing office tenants back to downtown. The project has catalyzed the revitalization of the CBD.

The renovation of the public transit facilities was a public/private effort. Forest City Enterprises, in partnership with the city and the Greater Cleveland Transit Authority, assembled financing from various public and private sources. State and local rehabilitation tax credits and local real estate tax abatements were also important to the project's financial viability. ■

The renovation of Cleveland's 1928 Terminal Tower complex brought together office, retail, hotel, and mass transit land uses. Tower City Center has become the nucleus of Cleveland's successful downtown revitalization.

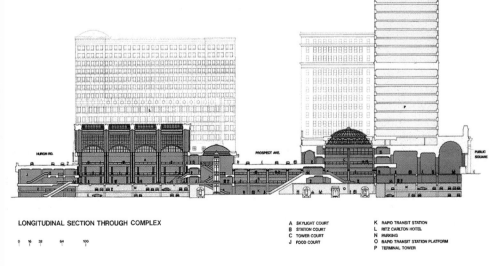

LONGITUDINAL SECTION THROUGH COMPLEX

0   16   32   64   100

A	SKYLIGHT COURT	K	RAPID TRANSIT STATION
B	STATION COURT	L	RITZ CARLTON HOTEL
C	TOWER COURT	N	PARKING
J	FOOD COURT	O	RAPID TRANSIT STATION PLATFORM
		P	TERMINAL TOWER

Tower City Development Inc.

figure 2–7

Factors in Site Selection

Zoning
- Legal use of the site
- Restrictions on density and layout
- Contiguous land uses
- Likelihood of obtaining variances

Physical Features
- Size
- Soils
- Topography
- Hydrology (floodplains, subsurface water)

Utilities
- Sewage
- Water
- Telecommunications (fiberoptic lines, computer lines, cable television, telephone lines)
- Gas
- Oil
- Electricity

Transportation
- Transportation linkages and access
- Traffic patterns and level
- Availability of public transportation
- Access to airport, mass transit

Parking
- Spaces required by zoning and market
- Surface parking vs. parking deck or garage

Location
- Proximity to other office/employment centers
- Proximity to amenities (hotels, restaurants, recreation)
- Proximity to customers/users
- Market perception of location

Environmental Impact
- Adverse impacts on air, water, and noise levels
- Amount and type of waste that the project will generate
- City or county compliance with federal/ state standards for air and water quality
- Other areas of concern, including historic districts, parks, open space, trees, wildlife habitats, wetlands
- Existing environmental hazards

Government Services
- Police and fire service (levels and cost)
- Garbage collection
- Schools, health facilities, and other government services
- Impact fees, property taxes, and permit fees

Local Attitudes
- Defensive (How powerful are antidevelopment forces?)
- Neutral (What social costs does the project impose? What are the benefits to the locality? Is the project in the public interest?)
- Offensive (What are local attitudes toward growth and how can they be used to help shape and refine the project to be built?)

Land
- Cost of land and development costs
- Lease vs. purchase
- Offsite costs (if any)
- View or scenic amenity

Demand
- Population growth (trends and projection)
- Income distribution and probable change
- Employment growth (trends and projection)

Supply
- Existing and planned supply
- Competitive environment
- Amenities offered by competitors

Source: Adapted from G. Vincent Barrett and John P. Blair, *How to Conduct and Analyze Real Estate Market and Feasibility Studies* (New York: Van Nostrand Reinhold, 1988).

Site Selection

Based on the findings of a thorough market analysis, the developer or investor finds a market area that presents the opportunity to develop a particular office product for a particular market segment and then locates a suitable site. This describes how the development process should proceed in theory. However, the development process does not always begin at the beginning. Sometimes it begins with the site.

Perhaps the owner of an underperforming office building envisions rehabilitating it to generate higher rents. (See "Commonwealth Tower" feature box on page 180.) That one owns a site is generally the least justifiable reason for developing it, but the owner of a developable site may be interested in its potential for office space. When a potential site—land or an upgradable building—already has been identified, the developer begins with a site-specific market analysis to determine whether the local market demand and supply dynamics will support the proposed project. This analysis focuses on defining the market area in which the property will compete and on analyzing market demand and supply, as described later in this chapter.

But when the development process does not begin with the site, the developer's local market analysis to identify submarkets with development potential is followed by a review of available sites in the area to identify an attractive development site. The search for a site should not be limited to developable vacant land. The redevelopment or rehabilitation of existing buildings that can be acquired at prices below replacement cost may be a feasible alternative to new construction.

Site selection is a crucial step in the project feasibility analysis. The project's location directly affects the rent and occupancy levels it can achieve. Even office buildings located relatively near each other experience significant location-based differences in rent and occupancy levels. A building within walking distance of a mass transit station, for example, may be able to obtain substantially higher rents than buildings only two or three blocks farther away. Land prices can reflect these large differences in the locational value of sites. Developers choosing sites based on price alone can find themselves unable to compete in the market, even at lower rents. Tower City Center in Cleveland exemplifies the importance of locational amenities to office development (see feature box on page 47).

All of a site's qualities will affect the office building's potential for attracting tenants. Developers should compare the locational, access, and physical attributes of alternative sites to identify potential opportunities and obstacles to development. This comparison should include a review of the rent and occupancy characteristics of the buildings located around each site. It should also note any differences in zoning or allowable development potential.

Jim Goodell, president of Goodell Associates of Pasadena, California, makes the following recommendations regarding site selection:

- Office buildings should be located in areas with a sense of place. The synergy of a mixed-use environment—office uses alongside support uses such as restaurants, shopping areas, and club facilities—generates higher rents and better leasing.
- Suburban buildings should be located close to freeways or roads that feed into the regional traffic system. Good access to adjacent roads is critical. Parcels located on prime highways may have great visibility, but they may not be accessible from those highways. Access for parcels located on major highways or frontage roads may be limited to side streets or even rear streets. The location, number, and arrangement of curb cuts into the parking lot can affect significantly the ease of access to a suburban office building.
- In urban locations, buildings with convenient access to public mass transportation systems command higher rents. Infill sites in established office locations often offer the advantage of established amenities, available utilities and other infrastructure, and office zoning.
- Public approvals for office projects often hinge on traffic loading during peak hours. Busy streets with high traffic counts may be popular with retail developers, but office developers consider them to be a negative factor.
- A site's topography plays an important role in project feasibility. For example, hilly sites may require extensive grading, which will increase construction costs, but they may also provide excellent opportunities for tuck-under parking, which requires less excavation on a hilly site.

In selecting a site for an office project, a myriad of factors must be considered and some complicated issues investigated. A long list of site selection factors is provided in Figure 2-7. Two key site selection issues—the regulatory climate and environmental issues—are discussed in the following sections.

Regulatory Climate. The regulatory climate at the project's location will have a major impact on the viability

Site Selection Databases

Lack of time, money, and experience in the site selection process is causing increasing numbers of companies to begin their searches for a new facility or site by tapping the resources available in existing site selection databases. Communities like these databases too, because they offer some assurance that they will not be overlooked in a search for which they are qualified.

Site selection databases are of particular interest to small- to mid-sized companies—especially manufacturing firms that are managing their own site selection processes and commercial realtors retained to conduct regional or nationwide searches. Most of these companies select sites through a process of elimination. Before tapping a database, they generally develop a set of criteria to use in evaluating potential locations.

The most useful databases provide information that enables companies to put together a short list of prospective communities or sites—quickly, confidentially, and at little or no cost. Such databases can offer everything from local utility rates to information on tax abatement programs. Some provide the information on a confidential basis, ensuring companies that competitors and others will not learn of their plans until they are ready to reveal them.

The contents and accuracy of databases vary. The best are updated for every site search. They include information covering:

- physical characteristics (facility sites, utilities, transportation, labor supply, and other variables of importance to businesses);
- startup and operating costs (facility costs, labor rates, utilities fees, and workers' compensation rates); and
- economic development incentives (tax abatements, free or low-cost land, enterprise zones, worker training programs, and others).

The newest databases are being offered as part of the member-services packages of organizations such as the National Association of Manufacturers, the Society of Industrial and Office Realtors, and other groups whose members typically are in the market for new locations. In most cases, communities pay a nominal fee to be included in these databases, which companies can use at little or no cost.

Source: Craig Throckmorton, "Site Selection Databases," *Urban Land*, May 1994, p. 43.

■

of the development. Zoning, environmental regulations and concerns, and the cost and availability of infrastructure all raise issues that impinge on the feasibility and market potential of the project. Beginning in the earliest planning stages, developers should work closely with public officials to resolve such issues pertaining to the proposed development.

The public sector's role—as a regulator of private development and as a provider of services needed for development—is constantly evolving. In recent years, in a move inspired by fiscal limitations and changing attitudes toward development, governments have shifted the burden of funding public infrastructure improvements that are necessitated by new development to the private sector.

Traditionally, the regulatory concerns of office developers were limited to local zoning and building codes. These codes contained the floor/area ratios (FARs), height limitations, building setbacks, and parking requirements that were the primary determinants of how much space they could build on a site.

In the 1980s, however, a plethora of new regulations aimed at commercial real estate development came into effect. Some of these were motivated by the local community's need to control the negative impacts of office development, such as traffic. Others were motivated by the community's need to bring in more revenue. These dual motivations make the public regulation of office development somewhat ambivalent.

On the one hand, localities welcome office development: it is clean, it generates jobs, and it pays taxes. On the other hand, many localities ascribe their growth pains to commercial real estate development, and in the face of shrinking tax revenue from other sources they have turned to commercial development as a primary source of funds for public infrastructure projects and even social programs, such as low-income housing. As a result, office development is subject to many new types of requirements—known variously as impact fees, systems development charges, exactions, extractions, and proffers—that projects contribute to the provision of related public facilities and programs. Required contributions may include the dedication of land, the construction of public facilities, or the payment of fees to be used for the construction of public facilities. In many jurisdictions, the imposition of such required contributions has pushed up the cost of development dramatically.

Some jurisdictions use their development fee structures to guide the location of new development. Projects proposed for geographic areas in which the jurisdiction wants to encourage investment, which generally are areas that the jurisdiction has targeted for infrastructure improvements, pay relatively low or even no development fees, while stiff fees are imposed on projects proposed for outside the development envelope.

The developer's market analysis must include a careful review of local regulations—master plans, comprehensive plans, zoning ordinances, building codes, and subdivision processes. The analysis should determine how the contemplated office development fits into these plans

125 High Street: Searching for the Ideal Office Site

When New England Telephone, a major Boston employer, was searching for a new headquarters location, it asked Spaulding & Slye, a real estate services firm, to identify potential sites near its current quarters. Right next door was a block that—with some creative development—looked like it just might fit the bill.

The land was not immediately available. The Travelers Insurance Company, which was in the early stages of planning its own redevelopment of the site, owned most of the block and, to complicate the assemblage, the city owned one small piece. On the edge of Boston's expanding financial district, the site was underused, occupied by a 16-story, blue-and-white tile building (an architectural anomaly built in the late 1950s, a time when Bostonians welcomed any development); a 30-year-old central firehouse; three dilapidated 19th-century brick warehouses; and three parking lots.

Ultimately, a joint venture partnership was formed, made up of Travelers Realty Investment Company, New England Telephone, and Spaulding & Slye as development partner. The development concept that emerged was to secure city approval for a 1.5 million-square-foot project by offering unique benefits to the community.

Indeed, 125 High Street offers an unusual assortment and degree of community benefits and involves consid-

125 High Street at a Glance

Development Information	
Site Area	2.5 acres
Gross Building Area	1,963,000 square feet
Gross Leasable Area	1,481,600 square feet
Development Cost	$450,000,000
Office Space	
30-Story Tower	950,000 square feet
21-Story Tower	450,000 square feet
Total Office Space	1,400,000 square feet
Retail Space	19,000 square feet
Parking	850 spaces
Public Facilities	
Fire Station	25,000 square feet
Ambulance Facility	2,600 square feet
Total Public Facilities	27,600 square feet
Atrium	6,000 square feet

erable public participation, even for a city accustomed to public/private partnerships. In return for the developers' underwriting the $5.2 million price tag for a new fire station, the Boston Redevelopment Authority (the city's regulatory agency) deducted that amount from the price of the one-half-acre parcel of city-owned land on which the original firehouse sat. This agreement paved the way for the project's relatively swift, two-year journey through the city's approvals maze.

Designed by Boston-based Jung/Brannen Associates, 125 High Street comprises two granite-clad office towers—a 30-story, 950,000-square-foot building, and a 21-story, 450,000-square-foot structure—that rise above an articulated four- and five-story base. In the middle is a ten-story, skylit atrium that is accessible to the public. New England Telephone rents 15 floors, comprising 520,000 square feet, or 35 percent of the 125 High Street project. The three 19th-century buildings have been meticulously restored and integrated into the new development, adding another 37,000 square feet of office space and paying homage to the area's history.

Parking and delivery services are accommodated underground in a five-level parking garage and in designated off-street areas, enhancing the project's accessible, pedestrian-friendly image. New sidewalk lighting and landscaping further strengthen this image.

The project's two new public facilities—the city of Boston's flagship 25,000-square-foot fire station and its separate 2,600-square-foot ambulance facility—are located at the rear of the complex and face the Central Artery, Boston's main north/south highway. The developer provided both facilities at virtually no cost to the taxpayer.

Construction was complicated by the state's Central Artery/Third Harbor Tunnel project. Underpinning the High Street building and coordinating its structure with the transportation project required moving the eastern footings twice during construction.

The development team faced other challenges as well. Based on extensive wind, shadow, and traffic impact analyses, the project was designed to minimize any adverse effects on its environment. The new firehouse had to be built before the old firehouse was taken out of operation and demolished to make way for the second office tower.

The challenges were met: 125 High Street fills out its block urbanistically with the proud assurance of a project built to last, designed to fit into its historic context, and poised for the approaching 21st century.

Source: Adapted from Diana Miller, "125 High Street," *Urban Land*, October 1993, pp. 38–41. ∎

New England Telephone, in partnership with the city of Boston and Travelers Insurance, reworked a historic building to suit its needs as well as the community's.

and regulations and it should assess the regulatory costs, risks, and timing associated with the proposed project. The regulatory sections of a good market analysis go well beyond the specific ordinances that affect office development in the proposed location, to consider also how public and community attitudes toward commercial development may be used to shape the project. The payoffs of paying attention to community needs and incorporating community uses are well illustrated by 125 High Street, a 1.5 million-square-foot office development in Boston (see feature box on page 50).

Local (and national) building codes are in a constant state of flux, continually revised and updated in response to concerns about and litigation involving building safety and public health and new information on the effects of fire, climate, storms, and earthquakes. In many jurisdictions, stringent new fire, seismic, and energy codes have added to the cost of developing or rehabilitating an office building. The market analysis must consider

Avis Farms Research and Business Park in Ann Arbor, Michigan, respects the land's natural features. A water course and a wetlands area have been preserved. Roads are sited to provide water views and preserve stands of mature trees.

the impact of building code changes on the existing and competitive supply of space in the market area, as well as on the cost of the proposed project. Regulatory requirements that affect site planning and building design are discussed in detail in Chapter 4.

Environmental Issues. Federal and state environmental protection laws and environmental safety laws are widespread and evolving, and they exert considerable influence on office development. The regulatory details of many of these laws have been highly contentious, engendering much conflict over their goals, approaches, and implementation costs—direct and indirect.

Almost all building redevelopment projects involving structures built before the mid-1970s require some degree of environmental remediation (the removal or management of contaminants). The most frequently encountered contaminants in older buildings are asbestos in tiles and pipe coatings, lead-based paint, and polychlorinated biphenyls (PCBs). Office projects on previously used sites often must factor toxic waste cleanups into their costs.

Among laws requiring the protection of environmental resources, those protecting wetlands often exert considerable influence on the location (and design) of office buildings. According to various federal and state laws, office development (which is a non-water-dependent land use, unlike a marina) cannot occur on wetlands unless the developers can demonstrate that there exists no practicable non-wetlands site for the project. Furthermore, the U.S. Army Corps of Engineers, which is responsible for issuing wetlands development permits, and state regulators generally require developers to minimize a development's adverse effects on wetlands and to compensate for any loss of wetlands by restoring or creating wetlands, on site or off site, in a process referred to as wetlands mitigation.

A determination of the probable costs of assessing a site's (or building's) environmental condition and environmental resources; of remediating environmental problems; and of protecting site and community environmental resources or mitigating damage to them is a major element of the site selection process. Developers often bring in environmental consultants at the site selection stage to assess the potential environmental impact of the proposed project on the surrounding community, as well as to determine if the site contains hazardous materials. The "Due Diligence" feature box on the facing page describes the availability of environmental databases that can simplify the identification of sites containing hazardous materials.

A formal environmental study is not typically part of an office market analysis, but lenders often require one. However, if the proposed development will potentially have an adverse environmental effect on the surrounding community, a formal environmental analysis by an environmental consultant is required. Among the community effects of a project that may be considered in an environmental analysis are air pollution, noise levels, shading, and traffic.

Most knowledgeable developers and lenders routinely perform a site contamination due-diligence test before closing on a real estate deal. Such a test, known as a Phase 1 audit, typically involves a review of government records for signs of likely chemical contamination (such as the presence of leaking underground gasoline storage tanks), a site visit, and interviews with current owners and operators. A quicker, less rigorous process for gathering information, called a transactions screen, often is conducted for smaller properties where contamination is unlikely. The transactions screen consists primarily of a review of government records.

The review of government records for either a Phase 1 audit or a transactions screen has been made simple, quick, and relatively inexpensive by the advent of sophisticated environmental databases that can provide the exact location and profile of all known U.S. sites contaminated with hazardous wastes; facilities that generate, store, treat, or dispose of hazardous wastes; underground storage tanks (leaking or not); and garbage dumps. Online access to these databases allows users to screen one or a portfolio of properties from the convenience of their desks.

Operated by private companies, the databases contain information compiled primarily from state and federal government sources, particularly the U.S. Environmental Protection Agency. In addition, the Sanborn Map Company in Pelham, New York, has, since the 1870s, produced maps that are used by insurance companies to locate properties that store or produce hazardous (flammable) materials. Sanborn maps show previous uses of the property, including the location of fuel or chemical storage tanks and where potentially toxic substances were stored.

Given only an address, the firms that operate environmental conditions databases can provide an environmental risk report that identifies potential environmental threats located on the property and in the general vicinity. They typically provide a report listing all potential problem areas and a map showing the locations of contaminated sites, underground storage tanks, and so forth within a one-mile radius of the property. The maps are designed to meet the American Society for Testing and

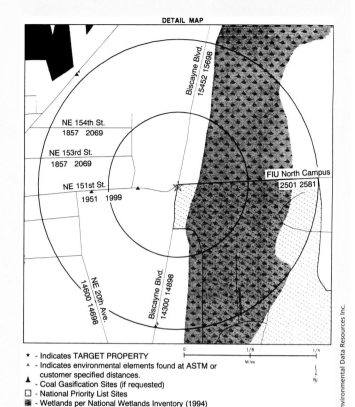

DETAIL MAP

* - Indicates TARGET PROPERTY
▲ - Indicates environmental elements found at ASTM or customer specified distances.
▲ - Coal Gasification Sites (if requested)
☐ - National Priority List Sites
▓ - Wetlands per National Wetlands Inventory (1994)

Environmental Data Resources Inc.

Sophisticated environmental databases can provide maps showing the location of wetlands, contaminated sites, and other factors on and around any specified property.

Materials (ASTM) standard for the records search of a Phase 1 audit and the transaction screen.

Three large players in this very competitive market are Environmental Data Resources (EDR), Environmental Risk Information & Imaging Services (ERIIS), and VISTA Information Solutions. The kinds of services offered by these companies and others like them include the delivery of maps and reports in only two to three days, online access to lists of suspect sites located near a client's target site, maps plotting the location of earthquake faults, and environmental profiles of individual companies or facilities.

Source: Adapted from David Salvesen, "Due Diligence Screens Made Easy," *Urban Land*, June 1994, pp. 8–9. ∎

Federal, state, and local laws dictate the scope of the required analysis. The least stringent type of analysis is an environmental impact statement (EIS). Established by the National Environmental Policy Act of 1969, an EIS is basically a checklist on which the potential impacts of a project are identified. If a project is expected to cause substantial damage to the environment, a full environmental impact report (EIR) may be required under local or state law. In some communities that are particularly

sensitive to environmental concerns, an EIR may be required as a normal course of action.

Demand Analysis

Good estimates of the demand for office space—total demand and demand for space with different characteristics—are an obviously essential element of the market analysis. As will be discussed, estimating future demand is an uncertain, often subjective exercise and, as has been

The U.S. General Services Administration's Public Buildings Service directs the federal government's multibillion dollar building program. GSA is the government's largest civilian landlord. It provides 40 percent of all federal office space in government-owned buildings and space leased from the private sector. More than 1 million employees in more than 100 federal agencies occupy this space. GSA oversees more than 255 million square feet of office space. It leases, constructs, renovates, and manages office space in more than 8,000 buildings—1,900 owned and 6,400 leased.

The agency develops and maintains other facilities, such as courthouses, border stations, laboratories, and data processing centers. GSA also provides security services, childcare facilities, telecommuting centers, and real property disposition services.

In fiscal year 1997, GSA paid private lessors $2.5 billion for 166 million square feet of space. GSA's portfolio is currently split 49/51 between leased and owned space. In the next three to four years, this ratio is expected to shift to about 45/55 as downsizing and efforts to reduce space costs lead to the consolidation of federal operations into government-owned properties.

Even though the government is reducing its leased space, it continues to generate a lot of activity, contract with the private sector for services, and reach out to its neighbors. Over 90 percent of GSA's real estate business is done through contracts with private companies. GSA offers federal agencies an opportunity to negotiate their own leases with private sector landlords through a program it calls "Can't Beat GSA Leasing." GSA strives to improve its customer services through contracts with private sector firms to provide analyses of market conditions, financial analyses, and integrated occupancy services. Up to $3 million a year is spent on integrated occupancy services contracts. GSA operates a Good Neighbor program through which it reaches out to the communities in which it has facilities and participates in business improvement districts.

GSA plans to offer other new opportunities for the private sector. The agency will sign leases for office space in buildings that will be constructed, owned, and operated by private sector entities. The agency is also planning considerable renovation work on government-owned buildings to modernize them to accommodate their users' changed needs. Planned government consolidations will create some interesting redevelopment opportunies for

The twin 18-story office towers of the Oakland Federal Building in Oakland, California, contain 1,075,000 gross square feet of space. GSA acquired the building, which was developed under a 30-year lease-purchase program, after completion of the core and shell.

private sector participants, especially where historic assets are involved.

In 1997, GSA issued a request to developers for use and qualifications for the General Post Office building in Washington, D.C. This represented GSA's first effort to enter into a ground lease for the adaptive use and preservation of a historic landmark. GSA is working with developers, financiers, historic preservationists, and the community to identify viable uses and a private developer for the property. The project is a model that GSA intends to replicate throughout the country.

Continued federal needs mean continued involvement by private sector developers to meet federal space needs. In markets in which private sector rental rates provide better economic alternatives than federal ownership, GSA will continue to rely on private sector services. And with limited federal budgets, it is often preferable from the taxpayer's point of view for the federal government to take advantage of leasing opportunities in privately owned buildings.

Source: Hillary Levitt, Director, Civic Design and Planning, GSA Public Buildings Services. ■

A 300-seat auditorium is made available after hours for public meetings.

A skylit lobby rotunda connects the two towers.

The Oakland Federal Building's entrance.

First Union Management Inc.

Valley North Tech Center in Thornton, Colorado, makes use of workstations in an open floor plan that requires less space per worker than individual offices.

pointed out, analysts and developers should always keep in mind that short-term demand trends live up to their billing as short term. Developers with the ability to decipher long-term trends are better able to put together office developments that stand the test of time and retain their value.

New demand for office space comes primarily from new office-using jobs. Thus, the future demand for office space in a market area is directly related to the growth in office-using jobs. Unfortunately, employment data are not reported in most markets in a way that allows analysts to identify which or how many jobs are located in office environments, particularly at the submarket level. Nor are the data reported in a way that allows analysts to translate employment growth into a number of square feet of demand for office space. Still, analysts can glean important information from standard employment data series about the makeup and strength of the local economic base, as well as a broad understanding of the market dynamics of office space demand.

A second approach to calculating the demand for office space is based on net absorption trends. Net absorption, which is the change in the amount of occupied office space over a period of time, is a direct expression of demand. Both office employment and net absorption are imperfect proxies for office space demand, and developers should not rely on either approach alone in market analyses. When used together, however, the two approaches can provide a reasonable picture of office space demand trends.

Market analysts often multiply the expected growth in office jobs by the estimated average square footage allocated per office employee to calculate the future demand for office space in the market area. The first step in this analytical approach is to look at local employment patterns by industry or types of job. The U.S. Bureau of Labor Statistics (BLS) is a widely used source of data for this purpose. BLS provides employment data for counties or metropolitan areas broken out by job

categories based on Standard Industrial Classification (SIC) codes.

All SIC-code job categories include some office-using jobs. Some, like FIRE (finance, insurance, and real estate) jobs, are strongly office based. But the BLS data do not distinguish between office jobs and nonoffice jobs. Some analysts use employment in one or two SIC codes, like FIRE and business services, as a proxy for office employment (see the Chicago market analysis for Fairway Center, Figure 2-3). But this practice can produce widely inaccurate—very high or very low—estimates of office demand. Analysts may do better by inferring from their own knowledge of the local economy the ratio of office/nonoffice jobs for each locally important job category. Analysts can gain an understanding of the makeup of a local economy by talking to major employers and other professionals who are knowledgeable about the local labor market.

Many state and local planning agencies estimate future employment levels. These estimates can be useful input in a demand analysis. The BLS data on employment growth by SIC codes do not include projections, but the U.S. Department of Commerce, Bureau of Economic Analysis (BEA) provides employment projections for metropolitan areas. The BEA forecasts form the basis of most state and local employment projections. A number of commercial forecasting firms offer employment projections as well.

It is not unusual for employment forecasts for the same market from different sources to be significantly different. Analysts must take care to evaluate the reasonableness of the key assumptions of all the employment projections that they choose to use.

The second step in the employment-forecast method of estimating the future demand for office space is to estimate the average amount of office space per employee. Analysts should be cautious (conservative) in their assumptions in this regard. Ten years ago according to the industry rule of thumb, the average space allocation per office employee was 250 square feet, which including a proportionate share of the lobby, corridor, and restroom space in office buildings. Today, less space per employee is the norm, with many new suburban office buildings providing 200 feet or less per employee.

For many corporate office users, the amount of space allocated per employee is on a downward path. Many companies have cut back on space in order to reduce their occupancy costs. An increasing number of companies are adopting open office space plans with fewer private offices. And technological innovations have eliminated the need for some office jobs altogether, while they have eliminated the need for permanent, dedicated office space for certain other jobs.

For a developer planning an office building, the forecast of total regional demand for office space is less important than is the office demand that is projected for the market area in which the project will compete. Developers and investors must clearly identify the relevant market area for a prospective office project and construct as com-

The completion in late 1996 of a $10 million redesign of Pacific Corporate Towers in El Segundo, California, has revitalized the property. The 1.6 million-square-foot, three-building office complex originally opened in 1984. The window of opportunity for redesign opened in fall 1994, when the project's largest tenant announced that it was leaving due to overall defense industry downsizing. The team formed to determine the next steps for Pacific Corporate Towers initially included GE Capital Investment Advisors and CB Commercial Real Estate Group. In the early stages of drafting a new plan, they recognized that dependence on traditional aerospace and defense tenants was not a viable option and that the project had to appeal to a new tenant population if it was to remain successful.

CB Commercial conducted surveys and other research to identify how, when, and where the asset could best be improved. These included an extensive tenant survey involving more than 500 people at Pacific Corporate Towers. The real estate advisory firm also surveyed successful properties in other markets and conducted an informal market survey among the project's target audiences, including brokers, tenants, and media. The redevelopment team used this information to determine the project's position within the marketplace and to develop a master plan.

This master plan, which was drafted by the Los Angeles–based architectural firm of Johnson Fain and Pereira Associates, identified the priorities for redesign. The firm assessed the challenges facing the property, and with a sensitivity to the bottom line, responded with a series of solutions.

The market dynamics of southern California meant that much more than just a fresh coat of paint, new lobby furniture, and a different parking entrance sign was needed. The redevelopment needed to appeal to companies moving to the coast from downtown and other West-side submarkets and also to take advantage of expected improvement in the southern California economy.

The architect designed a more human-scale and welcoming Pacific Corporate Towers. Comprehensive interior and exterior enhancements created a more functionally balanced property. The center tower lobby was opened up into a central gathering place. Tenants and visitors now can see what is happening in the majority of the project's common areas at the base of the three towers. The project's concierge and main security post are located there. A new restaurant is located off the lobby, and a new courtyard and atrium are just outside. A sports center is planned.

Leasing success has paralleled the project's redesign. The ten-month renovation was completed in time to take ad-

vantage of improvement in the local business climate, and a host of new companies has joined the growing tenant base. As final touches to the project were being completed, leasing agents concluded transactions totaling more than 465,000 square feet of space, valued at more than $50 million. "We anticipate leasing activity will continue at a high level in 1997 and are expecting to announce additional new leases in the coming months," says Grafton Tanquary, a leasing agent with CB Commercial at Pacific Corporate Towers.

Source: Adapted from Dennis Kaiser, "A New Image for Pacific Corporate Towers," *Urban Land*, May 1997, pp. 16–18. ∎

A complete redesign stimulated leasing at Pacific Corporate Towers. Courtyard and lobby areas serve as gathering places for the three-tower complex. Neon edges enhance the night skyline.

plete a picture as possible of employment trends, space requirements, and other demand factors for that market. At Pacific Corporate Towers, a 1.6 million-square-foot office complex in El Segundo, California, for example, a $10 million renovation was based on the development's need to appeal to a new tenant population, which the development team carefully profiled before embarking on the redesign (see feature box on page 57).

The analysis of net absorption trends in the market area can supplement and provide a cross-check for the broad-brush office-employment approach to calculating demand for office space. The absorption analysis should look at trends for different types of office space. Analysts must distinguish between net absorption and leasing activity. Net absorption is the change in occupied office space over a specified time period. Leasing activity is the amount of space that becomes leased or committed in a specified time period. Leasing activity does not account for space that has also been vacated during the period.

But net absorption does. A tenant moves out of 50,000 square feet of space in building X and moves into the same amount of space in nearby building Y: 50,000 square feet of space has been leased, but net absorption is zero.

Because both measures—net absorption and leasing activity—shed light on aspects of office space utilization, they are both relevant in a demand analysis. Most analysts argue that net absorption indicates the real strength or weakness of a market, while leasing activity indicates movement within a market area. By comparing trends in net absorption and leasing activity, analysts can reasonably describe the underlying strength and stability of an office market. For example, a market in which the rate of net absorption and the rate of leasing activity move in tandem over time is more stable than a market in which net absorption and leasing activity (or gross absorption) exhibit widely varying rates.

The market is said to be churning if it has a high rate of leasing activity and a low rate of net absorption. In a

A 200,000-square-foot build-to-suit office facility for Pacific Bell in Anaheim, California.

In October 1995, with more than 20 million square feet of vacant office space to fill in lower Manhattan, New York State Governor George Pataki signed a bill designed to jump-start economic development in the once thriving financial and insurance district. The incentive package offers new commercial tenants a 50 percent real estate tax abatement for the first three years of occupancy and a 30 percent reduction in electricity costs from Consolidated Edison over two years.

The first project to take advantage of the bill, even before it was sent to the legislature, is Manhattan's "hottest-wired" office tower, the New York Information Technology Center (IT Center) at 55 Broad Street. Originally home to the now defunct Drexel Burnham Lambert investment house, the outdated, 28-year-old, 400,000-square-foot, 31-story office tower has been renovated at a cost of $15 million by Rudin Management Company. Confident that lower Manhattan will emerge as a center for multimedia, Rudin targeted the information and telecommunications market for its renovated building. So many companies have already expressed an interest that Rudin is planning to double the center's space.

The facility is one of the few buildings in the world to offer tenants hookups—wired into the building's infrastructure —for high-speed voice, video, and data transmission; a local area network connecting tenants throughout the building; connections to local and long-distance telephone service; satellite communications for videoconferencing and the transmission of visual materials such as X-rays; and high-speed Internet access. The lobby features a ten-foot by 12-foot video wall consisting of 16 SONY multiscan videoprojector cubes. The wall is fed by live video feeds, Internet, Beta tape, laser disk, and CRV disk. It is also connected to a SONY Play Station.

Offices feature high ceilings, conduit paths for cabling, 24-hour air conditioning, 24-hour engineering staff, and round-the-clock security seven days a week. Rents on the first 11 floors start at $15 a square foot. Rudin is planning to put another $10 million into the upper floors, where rents will be somewhat higher. The company hopes to attract video and music production companies as well

The New York Information Technology Center attracts tenants with its high-tech communications systems.

as movie studios, Internet-access providers, and software developers, no matter how small in size.

The IT Center offers flexible space-configuration options such as prebuilt floors for small tenants, serviced business suites, a small-business center, and unfinished tenant floors, all with full expansion capabilities.

Rudin acknowledges that the real payoff will come if the project succeeds in attracting other companies to the area, followed by retailers, restaurants, and shoppers.

Source: Adapted from William Rudin and John Gilbert, "Silicon Alley," *Urban Land*, May 1996, pp. 48–49. ∎

market characterized by churning, tenants are leaving space in one building and taking space in another, both within the market area. While the market may seem to be growing, the amount of occupied space increases little. Churning often occurs in overbuilt markets with falling rents, markets in which the availability of higher-quality space for lower rents and moving incentives offered by building owners lure tenants away from their current locations.

To be most useful, absorption trends data must be collected and analyzed in appropriate detail. Analysts should obtain absorption data for various types of office space in the market, such as by class of building, and by types of tenant. What types of tenants are absorbing how much and what types of space?

There exist various sources of information on absorption and leasing activity. In most metropolitan areas, large office-leasing companies make available—some-

Majestic Realty Company

A state-of-the-art telecommunications infrastructure has helped Crossroads Business Park—a GTE SmartPark in Industry, California—attract and retain tenants.

Business telecommunications systems can cost thousands of dollars upfront and take months to order and install. Tenants of Crossroads Business Park in Industry, California, however, can complete hookups into state-of-the-art fiberoptic telecommunications infrastructure at little upfront cost, often within days or hours. A partnership between Majestic Realty Company and GTE allows tenants of the 110-acre business park to take advantage of the latest in fiberoptic technology easily and quickly.

In the early 1980s, Majestic's senior executives recognized that telecommunications would be pivotal to the success of businesses of all types and sizes. The company envisioned creating a Class A business park that would attract information-intensive businesses requiring advanced telecommunications services. The partnership between GTE, the country's largest local telephone-service provider, and Majestic began in the mid-1980s when Edward Roski, president and CEO of Majestic, expressed interest in GTE's SmartPark® concept.

GTE, with 53 SmartParks in the United States, developed the concept in response to increasing demand for business telecommunications services. In SmartParks, fiberoptic and digital equipment provide tenants with integrated voice, video, and data services—services that are in particular demand from high-tech, medical, and financial industries. Since teaming with GTE, Majestic has been able to offer its tenants office space that is configured in advance with a telecommunications network capable of transmitting rapidly vast quantities of voice communications, video images, and data.

Crossroads Business Park currently totals 500,000 square feet in six buildings, with the capacity to develop 1 million additional square feet. The park is located at the intersection of two major southern California freeways (I-60 and SH-605). Some tenants, including Friendly Hills Medical Group (which operates an 87,000-square-foot data and administration center that occupies one of the park's buildings), have leased space at Crossroads specifically because of its technology infrastructure. Friendly Hills needed asynchronous transfer mode (ATM) services to analyze medical images taken at geographically remote offices. Installing such services in a traditional office building can take weeks, because they require an extensive fiberoptic network and a series of switches and links. Because Crossroads Business Park had a fiberoptic network in place, Friendly Hills had access to ATM within 48 hours of its move-in.

Edison Source, a consultant on energy-efficiency (and a subsidiary of Edison International) chose Crossroads because it may need its technology at a later date. Edison currently does not use the SmartPark technology to its fullest, but the company was reassured by the availability of so many options and the ability of the park's infrastructure to accommodate quickly any changes and upgrades Edison might make. Rick Phelps, vice president of sales and marketing for Edison Source, told the *San Gabriel Valley Tribune*: "We're always looking ahead, and we felt that fiber optics was something that we wanted to have at our fingertips if we decide to take advantage of that technology." According to Tim Cullen, leasing director for Crossroads: "Forward-thinking companies understand that they either need this infrastructure today or will require it in the future."

The SmartPark infrastructure offers tenants connection to a fully redundant SONET ring, a fiberoptic system that sends voice, video, and data signals in opposite directions on two loops. If one loop is interrupted, service instantly continues on the other. Such disaster recovery is important to companies, such as financial institutions, that cannot afford any communications outage. At Crossroads, an on-site, underground digital communications center allows GTE technicians to identify any service disruption and quickly switch transmission paths. Two Crossroads tenants—City National Bank and Square D Company—are connected to the SONET ring through T-1 lines (digital transmission links with a capacity of 1.544 megabits per second). The installation of T-1 lines, like ATM services, can ordinarily take weeks and cost thousands of dollars.

Other tenants, including Majestic Realty Company, use simpler methods of data transmission. To access the Internet faster than it could with an analog modem, Majestic uses ISDN (integrated services digital network), a two-channel digital link that integrates voice and data signals and has a capacity of 64 kilobits per second. General Medical Corporation, a pharmaceutical wholesaler, uses the fiberoptic ring to receive orders by computer 24 hours a day, seven days a week. Crossroads Business Park's infrastructure is designed to accommodate the individual needs of a diverse group of tenants, and the fiberoptic network is designed to grow as tenants expand or require it for different tasks.

Its development as a GTE SmartPark has enhanced leasing at Crossroads Business Park, which absorbed more than 100,000 square feet in 1996. Potential tenants visiting the park are put in contact with a GTE SmartPark consultant, who explains the technology and describes how it can be applied to improve the prospective tenant's business.

Source: Adapted from Jodi Lewis, "Ready Access to Technology: Crossroads Business Park," *Urban Land*, February 1997, pp. 12–13. ∎

times for a fee—periodic office market reports covering the region as well as individual submarkets. These reports typically include a list of office buildings on the market; descriptions of recent, large transactions; and data on trends in lease rates, net absorption, and vacancy rates. Other local sources of information on office space demand include economic development agencies, planning agencies, chambers of commerce, the local chapters of industry associations, universities, and other organizations.

A straight-line projection of either office employment or net absorption is a notoriously unreliable method of estimating office demand. A straight-line projection uses recent trends as the basis for estimating future trends, and thus ignores the all but certain appearance of the next stage in the economic cycle. Nor can an analysis relying on recent historical trends take sufficient account of the predictable industrial and local employment changes that are likely to occur for any number of reasons.

The straight-line projections of office space demand performed by developers and investment institutions in the 1980s contributed to the steep crash of commercial real estate in the early 1990s. Market studies should look beyond actual absorption and employment trends, and consider when national and local business cycles are likely to move into new phases and what impact this will have on the demand for office space in the market area.

The sources of demand for a proposed project generally can be segmented into two major categories: principal users and second-tier users.

Principal users (a building's premium tenants) are generally relatively large and rapidly growing firms. Potential premium tenants may be essentially landlocked in their current locations, unable to expand into contiguous space because tenants that cannot be relocated occupy adjacent floors. If contiguous building floors are essential to their operations, moving becomes their only option. Developers must ascertain the presence of large, high-growth firms in their market area, and their space needs. Other potential premium tenants may be firms preferring a particular location, such as law firms, which often are drawn to buildings with good courthouse access.

Complementary users (a building's second-tier tenants) generally are smaller tenants—such as public relations companies, printers, or graphic arts consultants—that are drawn to a location near their major clients or providing access to many potential clients.

The demand analysis must go beyond general projections of future demand to identify and assess the specific sources of demand for the proposed office building. This should include the identification of potential tenants and potential market niches needing space—by their specific space requirements and typical size requirements. This look at the project-specific demand picture entails the following steps:

- interviews of brokers and other real estate professionals, business organization specialists, and major employers for their perceptions of the need for additional

The conversion of the Blue Hen retail mall to the Blue Hen corporate center was driven by market conditions in Dover, Delaware: too much retail space and an insufficiency of Class A office space. A regional mall built in the 1980s approximately three miles north of Blue Hen had drawn most of Dover's primary retail trade, including Blue Hen's two major anchor tenants. Meanwhile, AEtna Health Plans began looking in 1994 for office space in the Dover area.

To meet its rapidly growing operations, AEtna needed to occupy new space within six months. Blue Realty Corporation, owner/developer of Blue Hen Mall, proposed a nontraditional solution to AEtna's space needs: convert one of two structurally sound but vacant anchor department stores at the underutilized mall. AEtna's evaluation of the proposal determined that the conversion would provide excellent space at a better price-to-value ratio than build-to-suit space and other alternatives. Consequently, AEtna leased 68,000 square feet of a 90,000-square-foot, one-story building, with an exclusive option to lease the remaining space for expansion.

This solution met AEtna's goals. The building's renovation took only four months and it cost substantially less than space in a new office building. AEtna obtained significantly better office space than other options would have provided at a lower rental rate—and, as a bonus, built-in expansion space.

AEtna's move attracted other office tenants to the mall, now known as Blue Hen Corporate Center. The second vacant department store, an 80,000-square-foot building, was leased to NationsBank and converted to corporate office space. On the retail side, service retailers like fast-food outlets and card shops have evinced much more interest in a Blue Hen location since the influx of approximately 1,500 new office employees.

Underused retail facilities, when viewed with a creative eye, can provide excellent, low-cost office space. Given the vast amount of excess mall space around the United States, Blue Hen could become widely imitated. Blue Realty owns approximately 30 acres of undeveloped land around the corporate center to which the developer hopes to attract other major insurance or financial services companies interested in relocating to the Dover market. (The state and county have helped by creating tax relief and training incentives for relocating companies.) Blue Realty's ultimate goal for this site is a corporate campus with a strong retail component.

Note: Articles on the development of Blue Hen Corporate Center include Scott H. Gamber and Joseph N. Brancuto, "The Metamorphosis of Blue Hen Mall," *Urban Land,* September 1995, pp. 66–67; and "Blue Hen Corporate Center," *Architectural Record,* October 1995, pp. 106–107.

Blue Hen Corporate Center's conversion of a 90,000-square-foot department store to corporate offices for AEtna Health Plan saved the health insurance company time and money. The converted space gives AEtna employees a bright, spacious working environment as well as convenient access to retail shops.

facilities in the market and the features that would be desirable in a new building;

- a determination of leasing trends in competitive properties—including vacancy rates, lease rates, and tenant types—to understand current demand;
- a determination of the services and amenities sought by potential tenants or potential types of tenants;
- an assessment of absorption trends to differentiate between new demand and mere churning.

Supply Analysis

Measuring the competitive supply of office space within a market area is a less subjective exercise than measuring demand. A supply analysis has essentially three components: existing space, likely future additions, and vacancy rates.

The first step is to profile existing and proposed office space in the market area. As was discussed in Chapter 1, the most basic feature of office space is its quality or class as measured by various characteristics including location, design, and amenities. Market studies should include an inventory of office space by class. It can be useful to categorize office space in the market by other property characteristics as well, such as size, style, location, lease rates and terms, ownership, tenancy (whether owner- or renter-occupied, whether in single-user or multiuser buildings), type and quality of building systems, and amenities included. A profile of buildings based on property characteristics not only delineates the competitive supply situation, but also provides important information about the local demand for office space and tenant preferences.

Brokers and other local sources such as municipal building departments and permit offices can typically provide data on the supply of office space. Relevant data are increasingly being made available on the Internet (see "Making the Internet/Real Estate Connection" on page 76), but there is no substitute for direct personal contact with knowledgeable market participants.

Users of published data should take care to understand how the data were collected and what was included in the surveys. Some reports cover only buildings larger than 25,000 to 50,000 square feet. Others may include only Class A buildings, or may not distinguish among classes of buildings. Many office space surveys cover only multitenant buildings, and do not include owner-occupied buildings or sublet space.

The market analysis of competitive office supply must include planned projects that may come on line and compete with the project under consideration. Data on planned space are more difficult to obtain and are likely to be less reliable than are surveys of existing buildings within the market area. Some local economic development agencies and planning offices compile lists of proposed projects and track their progress through the approval and development processes. Officials in these agencies are likely to know about projects not yet under construction and to be able to provide details on their size, location, and amenities. Market analysts can confirm and expand upon information from public agencies by questioning the executives of local construction companies about building plans. Some national construction information services can provide information on planned office projects.

Ascertaining the amount of space available for subleasing in a market area is an important element of the supply analysis. Such space is commonly referred to as "sublet" space. In the overbuilt markets of the early 1990s, it was common for tenants to vacate space before the end of the lease period in order to secure less expensive or more desirable space. In many cases, large amounts of sublet space should have indicated to analysts that markets were not as strong as overall leasing data indicated.

Sublet space, even if it remains vacant, is not technically vacant. It is under a lease and the tenant is still paying rent. It is, nevertheless, empty space that is available to be leased. Tenants that vacate before the end of their lease term generally attempt to sublease the vacated space. Often, space available for sublease is offered at a discount and thus is less expensive than other vacant space. The availability of large blocks of sublet space can impinge significantly on the viability of existing and proposed office projects in the market area. It is important, therefore, to include an estimate of sublet space in the analysis of the competition that a prospective project will face.

Vacancy rate trends are another key item in the supply analysis. It is important to analyze movements in the market's overall vacancy as well as vacancy differentials within the overall market that indicate where and in what kinds of space vacancy rates are high or low, rising or falling. Are large blocks of space available for lease? Or, is the supply of vacant space made up mostly of numerous, small chunks of space? How is vacant space distributed among classes of buildings? Are vacancies spread throughout the market area? Or, are they concentrated in certain areas?

The analysis of vacancy trends also provides input for determining a potential project's stabilized occupancy, which is the typical annual occupancy rate for the project after its startup period (and a key variable in assessing a project's feasibility). In the early and mid-1980s, office market analyses on proposed projects routinely projected stabilized occupancies ranging from 93 percent to 95 percent. But, as construction soared later in the decade and demand began to decline, the actual stabilized occupancies achieved by these new office buildings were well below their pro forma projections.

The Integration of Demand and Supply Analyses

At this point—after office-employment trends have been analyzed, existing and potential office space inventoried, and absorption and vacancy trends scrutinized—the analyst can paint a reasonably clear picture of existing office tenants in the market area, their growth prospects, and their office space preferences. The developer now can identify specific segments of office space demand that are currently underserved or are likely to be so in the near future.

When officials at Allstate Life Insurance Company started looking around Chicago a couple of years ago for a building in which to consolidate the firm's regional customer-service unit, they could not find one they liked among the dozens they visited. Allstate wanted a single facility that would house 700 employees, a cafeteria, and an exercise facility, as well as contain space to accommodate future growth. Complicating the search was the requirement that the building be located in the Chicago suburbs near where the bulk of Allstate's workers lived. After months of fruitless searching, the company decided that the only way it could obtain a building that would meet its needs would be to hire a developer to design and build one.

Enter Opus North Corporation, the Chicago-based regional affiliate of Opus U.S. Corporation, a development firm based in Minneapolis. Working closely with Allstate's architect and real estate staff, Opus developed a customized complex in suburban Vernon Hills that meets the company's exact requirements and also provides a flexible floor plan and separate elevator banks so Allstate can lease out space it does not require immediately.

Many firms in the 1990s have adopted the Allstate solution. Build-to-suits were virtually the only type of office development that took place during the first six or seven years of the decade, when activity in most office markets was limited to the slow absorption of excess space. Only in the second half of the decade did rents stabilize and then began to inch upward enough to justify speculative development in some markets.

As the economy continued to improve, growing companies often had a difficult time finding appropriate contiguous space. In some cases, only by building could

The regional corporate headquarters for the computer software tax division of Intuit Inc. in San Diego was designed to meet complex tenant requirements, and the project was built at a highly competitive price.

relocating companies fit under one roof. Furthermore, many companies liked the idea of tailoring a building to fit their needs, instead of being forced to adapt to an existing building's layout and technology.

Build-to-suit projects compared with speculative high rises are sometimes seen as a less glamorous segment of the office development industry. But creating a successful design/build division has its rewards, including solid investment returns and a chance for the developer to diversify its sources of revenue. Builders fortunate enough to develop a strong relationship with national clients also can look forward to repeat business.

A development company's first build-to-suit project "might not seem very profitable because of the learning curve and all the time the staff must put into the project," says Jeffrey L. Swope, managing partner of Champion Partners, a Dallas-based company that has built more than 11 million square feet of office space over the past few years. However, by landing a contract with a big national client and cultivating that relationship, a developer "can wind up with a lot of steady work all over the region or maybe even the whole country," notes Swope, whose repeat clients range from electronics giant Panasonic Corporation to food conglomerate Nestlé S.A.

The design/build segment is one of the few areas in which smaller development firms can compete with big ones on a level playing field. Building speculative office space typically requires a large amount of capital and a substantial credit line, whereas developers of any size are able to arrange financing for a build-to-suit, because the facility has been preleased or presold.

Like all real estate development, build-to-suit projects carry some risks. Even projects that already have been approved by the client and financed by a lender can fall through for a variety of reasons. Many developers will not even pursue government build-to-suit contracts. Merely responding to an agency's request for proposals (RFP) or request for qualifications (RFQ) can involve hundreds of staff hours and several public hearings. The winning bidder can look forward to even more red tape, and the project can be killed at any time by the agency's unexpected budget problems, fickle politicians, or vociferous opponents. Yet, the handful of developers that have mastered the process tend to say that government build-to-suit projects have become a lucrative segment of their businesses.

Many private sector clients tend to stretch the term "build-to-suit" as far as it will go. Wholesale changes can be ordered if the plan that the client approved when it first awarded the contract a few months earlier no longer suits its needs or architectural taste. Even if the devel-

This build-to-suit headquarters building for ConferTech International is located in suburban Denver.

oper can adopt all those changes, a new series of alterations might be ordered again later.

The special needs of different companies constitute a reason why the office build-to-suit market is getting stronger. A generic office building can accommodate the requirements of a typical law firm or accounting practice, but other types of companies need more specialized facilities.

For example, a project that Atlanta-based Carter & Associates is developing in Jacksonville, Florida, for health insurance giant Blue Cross/Blue Shield incorporates not only an extensive fiberoptic network, but also some innovative security components.

A growing number of developers, seeking an edge in the build-to-suit market, are becoming vertically integrated by adding (or beefing up) design, contracting, and brokerage capacity. Some, such as the Stiles Corporation in Fort Lauderdale, Florida, also are making more use of synthetic leases in their build-to-suit operations. In a synthetic lease, the terms of the acquisition and construction financing are essentially based on the credit of the tenant—which means that the interest rate will probably be lower than the rate on a typical real estate loan. As a bonus, the tenant in a synthetic lease can keep both the asset (the building) and the liability (its lease obligation) off of its balance sheet and is not required to charge depreciation expenses for the facility against its annual financial statement.

Source: Adapted from David Myers, "Office Build-to-Suit," *Urban Land*, May 1997, pp. 31–32, 50–51.

■

A comparison of the current rate of net absorption of office space with the existing (and planned) supply of space gives a fairly clear picture of the overall balance between demand and supply in the market. For example, if annual net absorption in the area has been averaging 50,000 square feet and 50,000 to 75,000 square feet of space is available, demand and supply are in balance. If, however, 100,000 square feet of space is available, the market has a two-year supply of office space; and if the market contains 500,000 square feet of available space, it has a ten-year supply.

This simple comparison of current demand and supply represents an expedient way of gauging the market's short-term supply/demand balance, but such a snapshot should never be relied on to predict future trends. To be of any real value, the market analysis must look for factors that could affect absorption of office space in the future and interpret current market conditions accordingly.

The demand analysis has identified office-using industries in the market area and generated historical trends data for them. The market analysis now must search out relevant clues by which it can extrapolate the future. Which local industries are poised to grow? To contract? What new office-using employers might locate in the area? Is the local government taking steps to attract certain types of employers? Are policy changes or program initiatives being considered at the federal or state level that will help or hinder the growth of office employment in the market area?

There are no easy and fast rules for understanding the market at this level. Analysts usually piece together the information they have obtained in scores of interviews with local and regional government officials, civic leaders, employers and trade association representatives, and real estate professionals—to arrive at their reasoned insights on the future of the area's office market. In the end, a site-specific market analysis is only as good as its interpretation of the facts it so painstakingly gathers.

The main tasks in the integration of the demand analysis and the supply analysis are to determine how successfully the proposed office project will compete in the market area and, specifically, to estimate what share of the competitive market it can be expected to capture. The marketability analysis and the market-share analysis are covered in the following sections.

Marketablity Analysis. Several of the preliminary steps involved in the determination of a proposed office building's market competitiveness have been described earlier in this chapter. A market analysis is conducted to identify a site (or to assess the development potential of a specific site) and a target market. As part of the market study, the specific market area in which the project will compete for tenants should be defined precisely and a detailed inventory of the market area's existing and proposed office buildings should be compiled. The inventory can be used to identify competitive projects.

The developers of Fairway Center, for example, identified nine competitive Class A projects from the market study's classified inventory of existing and new office projects in the East/West Corridor office market. Figure 2-8 lists these competitive properties by name. The developers collected data on rents and operating expenses in these competing buildings, and these data will form the basis of the marketability study in which rent levels and operating expenses for Fairway Center will be decided.

Developers need to compare their prospective office project with the buildings with which it will compete. The proposed building's advantages and disadvantages relative to the features offered by competitive buildings are evaluated in order to arrive at an achievable rent. The assessment of how the proposed building stacks up to the competition is really a matter of judgment by the development team, but the team's opinion should be based on the findings of the market analysis.

Based on the competitive advantages/disadvantages of the proposed property, developers can arrive at an adjustment factor—negative or positive—that weighs the position of the proposed property relative to each competitive building. For each competitive building, the adjustment factor is applied to the rent charged, in order to determine an indicated rent for the proposed project. The typical (or, in some cases, average) indicated rent of all of the competitive properties is then assumed to be the rent that the proposed project can expect to achieve, the rent that competitive analysis indicates is achievable.

The rent adjustment process is illustrated for Fairway Center in Figure 2-8. Fairway Center's competitive position is adjusted vis-à-vis each of the nine competitive buildings, according to the development team's assessment of its relative locational, quality, and amenity value:

- Compared with Esplanade Center, Fairway Center is determined to be at a slight disadvantage with regard to location (–5 percent), quality (–5 percent), and amenities (–5 percent), for a total adjustment factor of –15 percent. Therefore, whereas the rent at Esplanade is $19.00 per square foot, Fairway Center can expect to achieve only $16.15 (or 85 percent of $19.00).

- Compared with both Lincoln Center and Oakbrook Terrace, Fairway Center is seen to be similarly disadvantaged. Fairway Center's indicated rent, therefore, vis-à-vis these properties that both command $19.50 per square foot, is $16.58 (or 85 percent of $19.50).

- Compared with Arboretum I and Arboretum II, on the other hand, Fairway Center is seen to have a slight advantage in quality, making its adjustment factor +5 percent. This advantage translates to an achievable rent of $16.80 per square foot for Fairway Center (105 percent of the $16.00 rent commanded by both Arboretum buildings).

- Continuing this adjustment process for the remaining competitive properties, the development team adjusts the $17.00 rent at Westbrook IV and Mid America downward by 10 percent to $15.30 for Fairway Center; the $17.50 rent at Oakbrook Regency downward by 10 percent to $15.75 for Fairway Center; and the

figure 2–8

Fairway Center: Analysis of Competitive Rents and Operating Expenses

Competitive Buildings	Net Rent/Term	Itemized Adjustments[1]	Adjustment (Percent)	Total Indicated Net Rent[2]	Operating Expenses
Esplanade	$19.00/5 years	Location: –5%	–15%	$16.15	$7.45
		Quality: –5%			
		Amenities: –5%			
Arboretum I	$16.00/8 years	Quality: +5%	+5	16.80	6.70
Arboretum II	$16.00/5 years	Quality: +5%	+5	16.80	6.91
Westbrook IV	$17.00/10 years	Location: –5%	–10	15.30	6.30
		Amenities: –5%			
Mid America	$17.00/5 years	Location: –5%	–10	15.30	7.88
		Amenities: –5%			
Oakbrook Regency	$17.50/6 years	Location: –5%	–10	15.75	7.90
		Amenities: –5%			
Lincoln Center	$19.50/3.5 years	Location: –5%	–15	16.58	7.10
		Quality: –5%			
		Amenities: –5%			
Central Park of Lisle	$16.50/5 years	Amenities: –5%	–5	15.68	7.81
Oakbrook Terrace	$19.50/5 years	Location: –5%	–15	16.58	8.50
		Quality: –5%			
		Amenities: –5%			
Typical[3]	–	–	–	$16.00	$7.40

[1] Rent adjustments are subjective, based on the development team's judgment of how the subject office project compares with the competitive project in terms of location, quality, and amenities. A negative adjustment indicates that the subject property is at a competitive disadvantage and the analyst must adjust the rent of the competitive project downward to arrive at an achievable rent for the subject property's space. A positive adjustment indicates a competitive advantage and thus an upward adjustment to the rent of the competitive project to arrive at the rent for the subject property.

[2] The indicated rent for the subject property is the rent of the competitive project adjusted for differences in location, quality, and amenities between the two properties. That is, an analysis of the competitor "indicates" that this is an achievable rent.

[3] The typical indicated rent (or operating expenses) can be an average or another value that falls within the range of indicated rents (operating expenses). The range of indicated rents in this analysis is $15.30 to $16.80 per square foot. The developer of Fairway Center chose $16.00 as the project's indicated rent in the first year of operation, because Fairway Center seemed most similar to Arboretum I and II, which were signing leases at $16.00 per square foot. In the case of operating expenses, the developer of Fairway Center chose an average of the operating expenses indicated by an analysis of the competition.

$16.50 rent at Central Park of Lisle downward by 5 percent to $15.68 for Fairway Center.

The average indicated rent from this analysis is $16.10. Feeling that the most comparable properties are Arboretum I and II, which are signing leases for $16.00, the developers base all financial projections on the following rent scenario for Fairway Center: $16.00 per square foot in the first year of operation, $16.66 in the second year of operation (year in which stabilized occupancy is reached), and long-term growth of 4 percent per year. Because so much subjective judgment is involved in estimating future rents, developers should strive to be safe by erring on the side of conservative estimates.

After determining rents, the next step for Fairway Center's developers is to estimate operating expenses. Their method is to determine the average square-foot operating cost for the nine competitive properties ($7.40 per

square foot) and assume operating expenses will grow by 4 percent per year. Thus, by the time Fairway Center becomes operational (in two years), its operating cost will be $8.00 per square foot. In the second year, this will rise to $8.40, and, thereafter, operating costs will increase 4 percent per year. Predictions of operating costs, like predictions of rents, are full of uncertainties. To be safe, developers should err on the side of overestimating the growth in operating expenses.

In Fairway Center's market area, most of the operating costs of office buildings are being recovered by owners as pass-through expenses to the tenants. In its first year of operation, Fairway Center can expect to collect up to $23.40 per square foot in total rent payments: $16.00 per square foot in base rent plus expense recovery of $7.00 to $7.40 per square foot.

Market-Share Analysis. The next analytical task in the market analysis for a proposed development is to determine the project's capture rate. Regardless of the methodology used, the market analysis must include a realistic estimate of the project's capture rate, along with an explanation of the assumptions used in determining it.

The market analysis has already projected how much office space can be supported in the market area overall. Now the developer must estimate the amount of the market that the prospective office project is likely to capture. Expressed as a percentage, this figure is known as the project's market share. The market-share analysis involves comparing the subject project with competitive projects in terms of location, price, amenities, unique features, and strength of management.

A proxy for a building's capture rate is the share of competitive supply that it represents. The analysis in Figure 2-9 indicates that Fairway Center represents 17.4 percent of the competitive supply of office space. If this share were equivalent to the building's capture rate, Fairway Center could be expected to absorb 95,700 square feet (17.4 percent of the estimated total market absorption of 550,000 square feet over the next several years).

This share-of-current-supply method is a good first cut at estimating a building's capture rate. A building may absorb more or less than its share, depending on its competitiveness. Perhaps a location and amenities that make the building superior to the competition or lower rents that make it more competitive will enable the proposed project to capture extra market share. Analysts need to refine the capture rate estimate to reflect such possibilities. Figure 2-10 shows such a refinement of the projected capture rate for Fairway Center. The building contains only 17.4 percent of the competitive supply in the East/West Corridor market, but the development team thinks that it can achieve a 20.5 percent market share, based on superior location and lower rents. Thus, instead of 95,700 square feet of absorption during pre-

leasing and the first year of operation, Fairway Center can be expected to absorb 113,000 square feet.

Another approach to fine-tuning the estimate of the capture rate for a proposed office project is to analyze how well the building meets the locational, amenity, size, and other preferences of potential tenants. At this point, it is very important that the developer has identified target tenants and has determined their space needs and preferences. If the project, as proposed, does not conform to the building characteristics sought by its target market, it should be redesigned to maximize its potential market share.

It goes without saying that all office tenants are not alike and that all office buildings are not created equal. The details of the demand for space in a market dominated by computer companies are likely to be much different than those in a market with a high number of accounting firms or law firms.

Substantial preleasing is the most reliable test of market demand. Fairway Center's absorption forecast of 113,000 square feet in year 1 was encouraged by its success in preleasing 50,000 square feet to a large corporation before construction began. (Lender concerns had resulted in the imposition of a requirement that one-third of the building's space be preleased prior to the start of construction.)

Once an office project's capture rate has been estimated, the developer should estimate how long the absorption period will take. The basis for this estimate is demand projections and the lease-up experience of similar projects. Rental rates and terms should be estimated. The basis for these estimates is the rents achieved by the most comparable projects in the market area, adjusted for the proposed project's particular competitive position (as was shown for Fairway Center in Figure 2-8). Finally, stabilized occupancy, which is the typical annual

figure 2–9

Fairway Center: First Estimate of Capture Rate and Absorption

Competitive Buildings	Building's Vacant Net Rentable Area (Square Feet)	Building's Share of Competitive Supply	Total Expected Market Absorption[1] (Square Feet)	Building's Share of Expected Market Absorption[2]	Building's Total Absorption in Year 1 (Square Feet)	Building's Absorption in Year 2[3] (Square Feet)
Esplanade	310,000	36.5%	550,000	36.5%	200,750	109,250
Arboretum Lakes	136,000	16.0	550,000	16.0	88,000	48,000
Fairway Center	148,063	17.4	550,000	17.4	95,700	52,363
All Other Competitive Buildings in Submarket	255,937	30.1	550,000	30.1	165,550	90,387
All Competitive Buildings in Submarket	850,000	100.0	550,000	100.0	550,000	300,000

[1]Developer's estimate of absorption in the competitive market over the next few years.

[2]Absorption share assumed to be equal to building's share of competitive supply.

[3]Assumes a roughly uniform rate of first-year absorption for all buildings. In this example, all buildings are assumed to absorb approximately 55 percent of their total expected absorption in the first year.

figure 2-10

Fairway Center: Refinement of Capture Rate to Account for Competitive Advantages/Disadvantages

Competitive Buildings	Building's Vacant Net Rentable Area (Square Feet)	Building's Share of Competitive Supply	Total Expected Market Absorption[1] (Square Feet)	Building's Share of Expected Absorption[2]	Building's Total Absorption in Year 1 (Square Feet)	Building's Absorption in Year 2[3] (Square Feet)
Esplanade	310,000	36.5%	550,000	30.0%	165,000	145,000
Arboretum Lakes	136,000	16.0	550,000	16.0	88,000	48,000
Fairway Center	148,063	17.4	550,000	20.5	113,000	35,063
All Other Competitive Buildings in Submarket	255,937	30.1	550,000	33.5	184,000	71,937
All Competitive Buildings in Submarket	850,000	100.0	550,000	100.0	550,000	300,000

[1]Developer's estimate of absorption in the competitive market over the next few years.

[2]The developer's estimate of absorption share is based on its assessment of how much market share above or below the building's current share of competitive supply that individual buildings can be expected to capture, due to advantages or disadvantages in location and amenities. For example, Fairway Center is competitive in quality with Esplanade, and its rent is $3.00 per square foot less. Therefore, Fairway Center should draw some of Esplanade's market share

[3]Assumes a wide variation in the rate of first-year absorption among the buildings.

occupancy rate for the project after its startup period, should be projected, based upon local market conditions and the experience of similar buildings in the area. These various elements of the project—lease-up period, rental rates, and stabilized occupancy—together with operating expenses constitute the basic ingredients for the cash flow analysis that must be performed as part of the financial feasibility analysis (which is discussed later in this chapter).

To sum up: A typical office market study analyzes the physical and locational characteristics of a site or market, current and future demand for space, and current and future supply of competitive space. Based on these analyses, the developer can estimate the potential capture rate or market share of a particular building on a particular site. It then uses the market-share conclusions to estimate the project's future absorption, pricing, and occupancy. These performance indicators are essential ingredients in the financial feasibility analysis, which determines the economic viability of the proposed development project.

The hypothetical Fairway Center (see Figure 2-1) was conceived following an analysis of office market conditions that indicated the need for Class A office space in Chicago's East/West Corridor market area. Figures 2-3 through 2-10 (not including Figure 2-4 and Figure 2-7) describe the key steps in the market analysis for this development. Fairway Center's program will continue to be refined through the financial feasibility analysis, which is the subject of the following section.

Financial Feasibility Analysis

After the market analysis, the second major component of a project analysis is the financial feasibility analysis.

The proposed project's revenue stream is determined based on the absorption, rent, and occupancy projections from the market analysis. The gross revenue stream (the square-foot rent multiplied by the occupied square feet) together with the development team's estimate of development costs and long-term operating and financing costs is used to project the cash flows that the project will generate over time. A multiperiod cash flow analysis is the major tool for determining a project's feasibility and for convincing lenders and investors to support the project.

Developers use the pro forma cash flows to calculate financial performance measures, such as the cash-on-cash return, the debt coverage ratio (DCR), and the internal rate of return (IRR). Real estate appraisers also use cash flow analyses to estimate the fair market value of proposed projects. How the income and net cash flow projections are used to secure financing for projects is discussed in the next chapter on financing.

The financial feasibility analysis enables developers to determine if a proposed project will generate enough cash flow to pay the debt service on its construction and permanent loans and provide an adequate return on the equity capital invested in the project. Equity investors and lenders that focus on a project's economic potential typically require a financial feasibility analysis.

Evaluating the financial feasibility of the project (or its ability to meet other development objectives) is an ongoing, iterative process that takes place throughout the development process. The process begins, generally, with back-of-the-envelope preliminary calculations that help the developer formulate an idea of what the project will look like, before any formal analyses are undertaken or financial commitments are made.

A series of alternative financial scenarios to test different assumptions usually follows. As the specifics of the proposed project's cost and revenue projections are refined, ongoing feasibility analyses provide an ever clearer picture of the project's financial viability and eventual return on investment. The project's viability is continually tested through financial analyses, which are modified until the associated revenues and costs fit a financial model that meets the developer's objective.

The Elements of Financial Feasibility Analysis

A fully documented financial feasibility analysis for a proposed office building will contain the following key elements: a project summary, a development cost report, a construction cost report, a report on monthly cash flow during the development period, and a report on cash flow during the operations period. These reports will help define the project.

Fairway Center's project summary is provided as Figure 2-1. A project summary should summarize the project's physical characteristics and the assumptions that are to be used in financial analyses of the project's development and operations. Among the items that should be included in the physical description are site and building size, the number of parking spaces, and net rentable square footage. Among the cost and revenue items that should be included are development costs, operating costs, borrowing costs, and assumptions concerning rental rates, occupancy rates, and the length of the lease-up period. It is useful to include financial and performance indicators, such as required rates of return, cap rates, minimum expected debt coverage ratio, and a break-even occupancy level. The project summary usually provides a statement of operational results for the first years of earnings, indicating the differences in the building's performance during lease-up and at stabilized occupancy.

Fairway Center's development costs are shown in Figure 2-11. A development cost report should include all costs related to the development or rehabilitation of the proposed office building, among which are direct construction costs, various soft costs (including money spent on marketing, insurance, permits, taxes, legal services, and overhead), financing costs, and land cost.

Not all feasibility analyses include a separate construction cost report, but it is an essential tool for estimating the adequacy of interim financing and working capital requirements. A construction cost report should provide monthly breakdowns of the cost of various categories of construction work, along with a monthly schedule of how much of each category of work should be completed by that month. The construction categories for which separate budgets and schedules are usually provided include site improvements (grading, utility extensions), off–site improvements (roads, utility extensions), foundation, framework, facade, building systems, and interior finishes for common areas and tenant buildout.

Nor do all feasibility analyses include a report on monthly cash flow during the development period, but this also is an essential tool for estimating the adequacy

of interim financing and working capital requirements. This report should include expected monthly income and disbursements, loan draws and financing charges, and end-of-month balances.

Fairway Center's cash flow from normalized operations is shown in Figure 2-12. Such a forecast of income and expenses at stabilized occupancy enables developers to assess the potential value of the project.

Cash Flow Analysis

At this point, developers can begin to calculate the cash flow that the proposed project will generate. The cash flow analysis builds on assumptions developed in the market analysis about the project's future revenue—achievable rents, the lease-up rate, and the occupancy rate. It also requires estimates of various costs—development cost, operating expenses, taxes, and financing cost. (Development and operating costs are discussed in more detail in Chapter 4.)

Not all office space is alike. Some is arranged in large open areas, often for computer stations. Other space is divided into private offices.

figure 2–11

Fairway Center: Development Cost Estimate[1]

	Total	Per Square Foot of NRA[2]
Hard Costs		
Core/Shell	$9,500,000	$64.16
Site Work, Parking	800,000	5.40
General Conditions	500,000	3.38
Contractor Fee	344,000	2.32
Contingency	250,000	1.69
Total Hard Costs	**$11,394,000**	**$76.95**
Tenant Improvements	**$4,540,000**	**$30.66**
Soft Costs		
Architect/Engineers	$350,000	$2.36
Legal	150,000	1.01
Accounting	75,000	0.51
Advertising/Promotions	250,000	1.69
Municipal Fees	435,000	2.94
Insurance	50,000	0.34
Consultants	280,000	1.89
Administration	250,000	1.69
Contingency	200,000	1.35
Commissions	930,000	6.28
Operating Startup[3]	150,000	1.01
Total Soft Costs	**$3,120,000**	**$21.07**
Interim Interest and Fees	**$930,000**	**$6.28**
Land Acquisition	**$2,000,000**	**$13.51**
Total Development Cost	**$21,984,000**	**$148.47**

[1]Assuming construction started in 1996.

[2]Net rentable area. Note: Fairway Center's NRA is 148,063 square feet and its gross building area (GBA) is 165,263 square feet. This makes for a building efficiency ratio of 89.6 percent. Typically, building efficiency ratios for low-rise suburban offices are often as low as 80 percent, so Fairway Center is an unusually efficient building.

[3]Before building opens.

figure 2–12

Fairway Center: Before-Tax Cash Flow from Normalized Operations[1]

	Total	Per Square Foot of NRA[2]
Income		
Base Rent[3]	$2,466,000	$16.66
Miscellaneous Income[4]	30,000	0.20
Recoveries[5]	1,226,000	8.28
Potential Gross Income	**$3,722,000**	**$25.14**
Vacancy and Credit Loss @ 4%	148,880	1.01
Effective Gross Income	**$3,573,120**	**$24.13**
Operating Expenses		
Utilities	$169,000	$1.14
Repairs and Maintenance	223,000	1.51
Insurance	24,000	0.16
Management Fee	89,000	0.60
Administration	83,000	0.56
Real Estate Taxes	406,000	2.74
Janitorial and Cleaning	143,000	0.97
Security	56,000	0.38
Landscaping	51,000	0.34
Total Operating Expenses	**$1,244,000**	**$8.40**
Net Operating Income	**$2,329,120**	**$15.73**
Annual Debt Service[6]	**$1,664,900**	**$11.25**
Before-Tax Cash Flow	**$664,220**	**$4.48**

[1]Stabilized occupancy at end of year 2.

[2]Net rentable area.

[3]Square foot rent ($16.66) multiplied by NRA (148,063 square feet).

[4]Parking, storage, and miscellaneous.

[5]Common area charges.

[6]Project is assumed to be financed with a $16.5 million first mortgage (9.5%, 30 years) and an equity investment of $5,484,000.

The bottom line of the cash flow forecast (net cash flow) measures the project's potential profitability. Financing sources weigh the project's rate of return (and risks) against the returns (and risks) offered in other investment choices, such as stocks and bonds or other real estate investments, in deciding whether to invest in the project.

A typical cash flow forecast shows cash flow over the expected holding period and includes estimates of the project's gross and net operating revenues, operating expenses, and net cash flow before and after debt service. It is essentially a (projected) profit and loss state-

ment by which developers can determine if the project will meet their financial goals.

Most forecasts of cash flow for an office project take the net revenues analysis a step further, to include a discounted cash flow (DCF) analysis. The aim of a DCF analysis at this point is to forecast the proposed project's financial return and its investment value. Figure 2-13 provides a discounted cash flow analysis covering Fairway Center's first five years of operation. This example does not include a detailed breakout of operating expenses or an income tax analysis.

Before-tax cash flow can be diminished by income tax liabilities, and tax consequences are usually of considerable importance to developers and other equity investors in office projects. The tax implications of investments in

office projects and their after-tax cash flows depend on a host of factors, including the form of ownership, the involvement of the developer/investor in the day-to-day operations of the property, and depreciation methods—all of which are too varied to detail here. Most DCF software packages provide a variety of income tax scenarios from which analysts can choose. Developers and investors should retain legal counsel to advise in all tax matters.

In the Fairway Center example (Figure 2-13), average occupancy in year 1 is estimated at 60 percent and the project's 96 percent stabilized occupancy is expected to be reached at the end of year 2. (One-third of the building's rentable space, or 50,000 square feet, is preleased.) A more complete cash flow analysis would consider the exact timing of tenant move-ins through years 1 and 2. The analysis shows a year-1 operating loss of $74,560. This loss could be much larger if the lease-up period is longer than predicted. In that case, marketing and operating costs still accrue and revenue is delayed.

After year 1, Fairway Center generates positive cash flows—according to the rent, vacancy, operating cost, and debt service assumptions—and meets the project's required minimum 12 percent cash-on-cash rate of return. In year 5, the base rent is assumed to rise by more than the assumed long-term 4 percent per year growth in rents, as the building's rent contracts are renewed within a mature, competitive market.

Fairway Center's investors require a minimum annual before-tax return of 15 percent. Thus, the cash flow analysis uses a 15 percent discount rate to convert annual before-tax cash flow to a present value. While positive cash flow contributes to the overall profitability of a project, office investors generally expect to recover their initial capital investment from a sale or refinancing that captures the project's appreciation in property value. For Fairway Center, the building's expected sale price in year 5 is calculated at $28.4 million.

The standard ratio indicating property value is derived by dividing net operating income by the overall capitalization rate. Fairway Center's sale price—$28.4 million—is derived by dividing its year-5 NOI of $2.7 million by 9.5 percent, a terminal cap rate based on the assumption that the cost of capital in the marketplace will be the same in year 5 as it was when the original investment was made. Sellers often use the (usually higher) NOI in the year following the sale to calculate the value of the property. However, a more conservative approach is used for Fairway Center.

Subtracting selling costs and the payment of the loan balance from the sale price leaves $11.3 million in before-tax net sale proceeds. The present worth of the before-tax net sale proceeds at a 15 percent discount is $5.6 million. The net sale proceeds are not all profit for the investor. To calculate after-tax profit on the sale of Fairway Center, one must deduct from the before-tax sale proceeds of $11.3 million the original equity investment ($5.5 million), loan principal repayments, and any income tax owed.

The sum of the present value of the annual before-tax cash flows (discounted at the owner's required minimum before-tax annual rate of return) and the net proceeds from the sale totals $7.55 million. Since this amount exceeds the original equity investment of $5.48 million, Fairway Center as proposed can be said to be a financially feasible investment.

As noted, Fairway Center's investors require at least a 15 percent return before income tax. The DCF analysis shows that the project is expected to generate a before-tax internal rate of return (IRR) of 21.5 percent over the five-year holding period, which clearly exceeds the required financial performance.[1]

Further proof of Fairway Center's financial soundness is provided by its year-5 before-tax investment value of $24.1 million. (The investment value is the present value of the equity invested at the investor's required rate of return of 15 percent plus the initial mortgage amount—$7.6 million plus $16.5 million. Thus, the investment value exceeds the original cost of developing the property: $21.98 million.

figure 2–13

Fairway Center: Discounted Cash Flow Analysis

	Year 1	Year 2	Year 3	Year 4	Year 5
Expected Occupancy	76%	96%	96%	96%	96%
Income					
Base Rent[1]	$1,808,000	$2,466,000	$2,579,000	$2,693,000	$2,890,000
Miscellaneous Income	15,000	30,000	35,000	40,000	40,000
Recoveries	431,000	1,226,000	1,442,000	1,470,000	1,543,000
Potential Gross Income	2,254,000	3,722,000	4,056,000	4,203,000	4,473,000
Vacancy Allocation	90,160	148,880	162,240	168,120	178,920
Effective Gross Income	$2,163,840	$3,573,120	$3,893,760	$4,034,880	$4,294,080
Operating Expenses	$573,500	$1,244,000	$1,480,000	$1,539,200	$1,600,770
Net Operating Income	$1,590,340	$2,329,120	$2,413,760	$2,495,680	$2,693,310
Annual Debt Service	$1,664,900	$1,664,900	$1,664,900	$1,664,900	$1,664,900
Before-Tax Cash Flow	($74,560)	$664,220	$748,860	$830,780	$1,028,410
Cash-on-Cash Rate of Return	(1.4%)	$12.1%	13.7%	15.1%	18.8%
Present Value of Cash Flow					
(at 15% discount rate)	($64,835)	$502,776	$492,388	$475,002	$511,303
Proceeds from Sale in Year 5[2]	N/A	N/A	N/A	N/A	$28,350,632
Selling Cost (4%)	N/A	N/A	N/A	N/A	$1,134,025
Loan Balance	N/A	N/A	N/A	N/A	$15,879,760
Before-Tax Sale Proceeds	N/A	N/A	N/A	N/A	$11,336,846

Present Value of Before-Tax Sale Proceeds (at 15% discount rate): $5,636,431

Before-Tax Investment Value, January of Year 1: $24,053,064

Before-Tax Internal Rate of Return, January of Year 1: 21.5%

Present Value of Equity Invested, January of Year 1: $7,553,064

[1]Assumes that the average rent per square foot of net rentable area is $16.66 in year 2 (year of stabilization).

[2]Based on year-5 NOI and 9.5 percent terminal cap rate.

Key Financial Ratios

Participants in an office development project use various financial ratios to gauge risk and establish financial feasibility, according to their particular requirements. Developers, lenders, or investors require certain minimum or maximum returns, break-even occupancies, or debt coverage ratios, for example. The values used to calculate such ratios are established in the financial feasibility analysis. The comparison of certain of a project's key financial ratios with the standard requirements of lenders and investors can give its developer an initial understanding of its financial feasibility as proposed.

Analysts for the Fairway Center project calculated four financial ratios to help them establish the development's financial feasibility. The values used in the equations can be found in the analysis of the before-tax cash flow from normalized operations (Figure 2-12).

Debt Coverage Ratio. Lenders generally require a minimum debt coverage ratio, calculated as follows:

$$DCR = \frac{\text{Net Operating Income}}{\text{Annual Debt Service}} \quad \frac{\$2,329,120}{\$1,664,900} = 1.40$$

At Fairway Center, annual operating income covers debt service 1.4 times. Its lender's minimum DCR requirement is 1.3 times. (See "Lender Economic Feasibility Analysis" in Chapter 3 for more on the DCR.)

Cash-on-Cash Return. Investors generally require a minimum cash-on-cash (or equity) rate of return, calculated as follows:

$$\text{Equity Return} = \frac{\text{Before-Tax Cash Flow}}{\text{Equity Invested}} \quad \frac{\$664,220}{\$5,484,000} = 12.1\%$$

At Fairway Center, the forecast cash-on-cash return is barely above 12 percent, which is the minimum rate of return required by the project's investors.

Break-Even Occupancy. Lenders and investors generally require that office buildings at a certain minimum level of occupancy break even in terms of income versus expenses. Break-even occupancy is calculated as follows:

$$\text{BEO} = \frac{\text{Operating Expenses} + \text{Debt Service}}{\text{Potential Gross Income}}$$

$$\text{BEO} = \frac{\$1,244,000 + 1,664,900}{\$3,722,000} = 78.2\%$$

At Fairway Center, the project breaks even when it attains 78.2 percent occupancy. The maximum break-even occupancy allowed by Fairway Center's lenders and investors is 85 percent.

Expected Property Value. Direct market capitalization is the simplest but least accurate means of estimating the likely market value of the property. Overall market capitalization rates for any class of property and location can be secured from knowledgeable local commercial appraisers. Overall capitalization is an estimate of the property value based on the present worth of its current, stabilized net operating income, calculated as follows:

$$\text{Property Value} = \frac{\text{Net Operating Income}}{\text{Overall Capitalization Rate}}$$

$$\text{Property Value} = \frac{\$2,329,120}{0.095} = \$24,500,000$$

Fairway Center's expected $24.5 million market value exceeds its $22 million development cost, and the project therefore meets another measure of financial feasibility.

All these financial ratios meet or exceed the feasibility criteria established by lenders and investors, and Fairway Center's developer can proceed with the project. This is not to say that conditions affecting financial feasibility will not change as the development process continues. Office developers conduct their business in a dynamic environment. They must constantly monitor the impact of changing conditions on financial feasibility. The following section on sensitivity analysis shows how feasibility analysis can move beyond static accounting to become a dynamic planning tool.

Sensitivity Analysis

The importance of monitoring the impact of changing market conditions on project feasibility cannot be overstated. The impact of changes in certain features or assumptions—like development costs, rental rates, or the pace of absorption—can be evaluated by a method called sensitivity analysis.

Sensitivity analysis lets developers evaluate the financial implications of design and construction decisions that will have an impact on operating expenditures or operating revenues. For example, will spending more on initial HVAC systems to lower utility bills later improve the project's feasibility? Will providing certain amenities raise rents or absorption enough to improve feasibility? Developers can use sensitivity analysis also to examine the project's upside and downside potential, which is accomplished by performing analyses using optimistic assumptions first and then pessimistic assumptions for such key variables as rent escalations and vacancies.

What if Fairway Center could achieve a rent of only $15.60 per square foot in year 2, the project's year of normalized operations, instead of the $16.66 indicated by the market analysis? As shown in Figure 2-14, the year-1 NOI and before-tax cash flow both would fall by $218,636; and the year-5 NOI and before-tax cash flow both would fall by $283,593. The sensitivity analysis shows that $15.60 per square foot is about the minimum rent that fairway Center could achieve and still be financially feasible.

The lower income and cash flow that result from an assumed lower rent affect all the key financial ratios that were used to determine Fairway Center's financial feasibility, as shown in Figure 2-15. Under the new rent schedule, Fairway Center just barely meets the debt coverage ratio of 1.3 required by the lender, but it is still comfortably below the 85 percent maximum break-even occupancy required by lenders and investors and the expected property value still exceeds the total project cost, although just barely so.

In contrast, the lower rent structure clearly reduces Fairway Center's cash-on-cash equity rate of return. The cash-on-cash return has fallen to 8.1 percent, which is well below the 12 percent return that the project's investors were seeking. If these investors can settle for the lower return, the project can still go ahead. However, they may be tempted to look elsewhere for higher-yielding investment opportunities.

Sensitivity analysis models have a host of other applications. Developers may wish to determine what rents a potential office project would need to charge to justify its construction in the first place. (Such an analysis sets out to determine financially feasible rents given certain development cost assumptions, rather than setting out to determine the financial feasibility of market-indicated rents.) Developers seeking this information could assume a basic building, apply local construction and development cost data to determine how much it would cost to build, calculate debt service and investment return requirements—and work backward from there to determine the minimum rents that would be needed to meet debt service and provide the desired return on investment.

Developers can carry out sensitivity analyses to test the inclusion of special features in proposed projects—to determine their potential impact on costs, minimum rents, and potential return on investment. Structured parking would be one such feature. A sensitivity analysis

figure 2–14

Fairway Center: Sensitivity of NOI and Cash Flow to Lower Rent and Lower Occupancy[1]

	Year 1	Year 2	Year 3	Year 4	Year 5
Expected Occupancy	60%	96%	96%	96%	96%
Income					
Base Rent[1]	$1,332,570	$2,217,384	$2,319,384	$2,421,437	$2,598,202
Miscellaneous Income	15,000	30,000	35,000	40,000	40,000
Recoveries	418,070	1,159,862	1,400,000	1,436,624	1,490,000
Potential Gross Income	1,765,640	3,407,246	3,754,384	3,898,061	4,128,202
Vacancy Allocation	70,626	136,290	150,175	155,922	165,128
Effective Gross Income	$1,695,014	$3,270,956	$3,604,209	$3,742,139	$3,963,074
Operating Expenses[2]	$534,502	$1,159,772	$1,438,953	$1,491,724	$1,553,357
Net Operating Income	$1,160,512	$2,111,184	$2,165,256	$2,250,415	$2,409,717
Annual Debt Service	$1,664,900	$1,664,900	$1,664,900	$1,664,900	$1,664,900
Before-Tax Cash Flow	($504,388)	$446,284	$500,356	$585,515	$744,817
Compared with results when average rent is $16.66 per square foot (from Figure 2–13)					
Net Operating Income	$1,590,340	$2,329,120	$2,413,760	$2,495,680	$2,693,310
Annual Debt Service	$1,664,900	$1,664,900	$1,664,900	$1,664,900	$1,664,900
Before-Tax Cash Flow	($74,560)	$664,220	$748,860	$830,780	$1,028,410

[1]The average rent per square foot of net rentable area is assumed to be $15.00 in year 2 (year of stabilization), or 10 percent lower than the $16.66 average rent that the market analysis indicated.

[2]Operating expenses are assumed to be 6.8 percent lower in year 1 and year 2 and lower by varying percentages in year 3 to year 5, reflecting the lower management cost and property taxes that accompany lower rents.

for a suburban project might find that the added cost of a parking structure cannot be passed through directly to the tenants and that its inclusion in the project substantially lowers its potential return. For an urban project, rents may be high enough to subsidize a parking structure.

Not long ago, discounted cash flow analyses involved long and tedious calculations and adjustments. Therefore, potentially useful sensitivity analyses were often left undone. Today, personal computers and their spreadsheet models allow developers and investors to almost instantly ascertain the effects that even small changes in assumptions will have on a project's cost, cash flow, and investment value. Spreadsheet models allow developers to perform in a very short time detailed sensitivity analyses on their projects.

Revisiting the Market Analysis

A project's financial feasibility analysis rests heavily on the findings and conclusions of the market analysis, which, in turn, often relies on information from many secondary sources. Before recommending moving forward with a project that appears to be financially feasible, analysts should revisit the underlying data. They should

test the basic numbers again, looking particularly for internal data inconsistencies and possibly questionable or unrealistic assumptions and conclusions. The usual suspects are local market data, construction budget and schedule estimates, rent and absorption estimates, and operating cost estimates. In revisiting the market analysis, analysts should ask the following questions:

- Does the total inventory of competing space in the market area appear to be completely and accurately described?
- Has the analysis missed any construction that is underway or proposed?
- Are the vacancy rate and vacant inventory estimates consistent in their coverage from year to year?
- Has subleased and owner-occupied space been properly accounted for?
- Are the estimates of net absorption in the market area for the recent past plausible? Are the forecasts of net absorption realistic?
- Are the estimates of the project's construction costs and tenant buildout costs realistic? Is the timing realistic?

Real estate professionals use the Internet for four major purposes: communication; real estate research; advertising, merchandising, and promotion; and real estate transactions.

Communication is probably the most ubiquitous use on the Internet, and electronic mail (e-mail)—called the most important two-way communications medium since the telephone—is the most popular of the Internet tools. Properly used, e-mail can give most real estate professionals more flexibility, whether in sending messages to individuals and groups, sending text files, or distributing electronic newsletters, flyers, and magazines.

Research is the second most popular use of the Internet for real estate business purposes. Internet research involves retrieving information provided by various groups and individuals. Search engines (programs that allow users to search the Net by keywords) like Lycos (www.lycos.com), Yahoo! (www.yahoo.com), Excite (www.excite.com), and InfoSeek (www.infoseek.com) can target many large databases of information quickly. (It's best to use several search engines in conducting research since not all information is linked to every search engine.)

Real estate organizations such as ULI (www.uli.org), the National Association of Real Estate Investment Trusts (www.realpage.com/nareit), and many others have created Web sites on the Internet. Many of these organizations post information and publications on their sites, some of it available to the general public and some of it to their members only.

While many private architecture, planning, appraisal, and real estate consulting firms advertise their services on the Internet, some of these firms also provide samples of their research, including market assessments and real estate trends findings. Some such firms provide free information, while others limit access to paid subscribers or employees.

Government agencies—the U.S. Bureau of the Census (www.census.gov) and the U.S. Bureau of Economic Analysis (www.bea.doc.gov) among them—have set up shop on the Internet and offer a wide range of government-sponsored research information, such as census data, SEC filings, and legislative news.

Private real estate companies offer real estate databases that assemble various categories of real estate information and provide links to related information accessible on the Internet. Among these private databases are the Retail Tenants Database (www.retailtenants.com), COMPS—Commercial Real Estate Transaction Informa-

tion (206.65.86.163), and the International Real Estate Directory (www.ired.com).

Some real estate magazines such as *Plants Sites & Parks* (www.bizsites.com) and *Office Buildings* (www.yrinc.com) are on the Internet, as are various city business journals (www.amcity.com) and national newspapers such as the *Wall Street Journal* (www.wsj.com).

Another feature becoming more popular on the Internet is the posting of electronic marketing brochures, property listings, or real estate portfolio information. Researchers can access the homepage of any company with a Web site at any time, download the information desired, and ask for clarification on any item via e-mail. The PikeNet Directory of Commercial Real Estate (www.pikenet.com) lists many firms with a Web presence. As reported by Peter Pike, in their search for office space in the Tampa Bay area, Atlanta Testing and Engineering representatives explored the Colliers Arnold Web site and contacted the firm via e-mail for more information; eventually, Colliers Arnold arranged a lease for 3,000 square feet for Atlanta Testing.

The use of the Internet for actual real estate transactions has been only a fledgling option for real estate professionals, although it seems to offer great promise.

The Internet contains a staggering amount of information, and, except for the sheer entertainment value of it all, much of it is of no use to those in real estate. It takes patience to wade through the ever-growing mountain of material on the Internet, and everyone's interest in, and experience on, the Internet will be unique. But, there is a world of opportunity out there in cyberspace. Making it work for market research is a skill that requires some self-training, networking, and practice.

Source: Adapted from W. Paul O'Mara, "Making the Internet/Real Estate Connection," *Urban Land*, February 1997, pp. 16–20.

figure 2-15

Fairway Center: Sensitivity of Key Financial Ratios to Lower Rent[1]

	$15.60 Rent Assumption	$16.66 Rent Assumption	Industry Standard
Debt Coverage Ratio[2]	1.27 x	1.4 x	1.3 x
	$2,111,184	$2,329,000	
	$1,664,900	$1,664,900	
Cash-on-Cash Return[3]	8.1%	12.1%	12.0%
	$446,284	$664,220	
	$5,484,000	$5,484,000	
Break-Even Occupancy[4]	82.9%	78.2%	85.0%
	$2,824,672	$2,908,900	
	$3,407,246	$3,722,000	
Typical Property Value[5]	$22,222,900	$24,517,000	$22,000,000 (project cost)
	$2,111,184	$2,329,120	
	0.095	0.095	

[1]The average rent per square foot of net rentable area is assumed to be $15.00 in year 2 (year of stabilization). The effect of this lower rent assumption on NOI and before-tax cash flow is shown in Figure 2-14.

[2]At the lower rent, the DCR is minimally acceptable.

[3]At the lower rent, the project's cash flow yields less than the required return in year 2. It would, however, yield a 12 percent return by year 5.

[4]At the lower rent, the project is still below the maximum break-even occupancy allowed by lenders and investors.

[5]At the lower rent, the expected property value barely exceeds the project's development cost.

- Can the project's estimated effective rents and lease terms be achieved? How much lower or higher could the revenues be?
- Are the estimates of absorption for the project reasonable? How much higher or lower could net absorption reasonably be?
- Are the estimates of preleasing realistic and based on likely tenant needs?
- Are the estimates of operating costs reasonable? Could some costs be significantly higher than expected?
- Are the projected tenant buildout allowances reasonable?

The answers to such questions often will produce a range of possible outcomes above or below the assumptions used in the initial financial feasibility analysis. Groups of new assumptions can be made internally consistent. For example, if absorption could be slower, rent assumptions may have to be lowered.

Sets of changed assumptions can be entered in a computer's DCF analysis spreadsheet in a matter of minutes. Recalculation of the entire cash flow analysis is virtually instantaneous. Analysts should seek to identify a variety of absorption, rent, operating cost, and construction cost scenarios. Their goal is to develop a project with little default risk that also offers substantial profits over a wide range of reasonable market conditions. The accomplish-

ment of this goal requires realistic, conservative assumptions about the future.

Note

1. Readers wishing a detailed discussion of the derivation of IRR (internal rate of return) are referred to Mike E. Miles, Richard L. Haney Jr., and Gayle Berens, *Real Estate Development: Principles and Process*, 2nd ed. (Washington, D.C.: ULI–the Urban Land Institute, 1996).

3. Financing

Office development, like real estate development in general, is a capital-intensive business. Significant capital is needed to develop almost any office project—whether it is a 5,000-square-foot garden style office building or a multimillion-square-foot skyscraper. Funds from outside parties are necessary—unless the developer happens to be a corporation that can generate the necessary funds internally or is connected somehow with an insurance company, pension fund, real estate investment trust, or other well-capitalized organization in the development business. The funds to develop office buildings come in two primary forms: debt and equity.

Debt and equity funds for real estate are raised in a variety of capital markets, where conditions are always in flux and competition is often intense. Historically, the capital market for the development of office buildings has depended on local financial institutions and investors. A typical scenario for a thinly capitalized developer with an office project was, first, to solicit wealthy individuals in the community to invest in its ownership (equity investment) and, after a sufficiently large portion (say 20 to 25 percent) of the total cost was accumulated, to approach a local bank for a construction loan. At the same time, the developer would secure long-term, usually fixed-rate financing (known as permanent financing) from an in-

surance company, which would be funded after the building was completed and fully leased.

While the incentives for investors in the real estate development process have remained basically the same, the real estate capital market now comprises a greater variety of funding sources, many of which involve securitization. The securitization of real estate debt and equity provides greater liquidity—an enhanced flow of funds—for real estate investment.

The most common form of securitized commercial real estate debt is commercial mortgage–backed securities (CMBSs), which are put together by banks, mortgage companies, insurance companies, and investment banks. The sale of bonds backed by collateral interests in real estate has increased the flow of funds into real estate debt.

Securitization in the form of real estate investment trusts (REITs) has broadened the sources of debt and equity capital for office projects. REITs can best be described as publicly traded real estate interests or properties.

This chapter begins by looking at the capital market for office development and investment. Within this market, the sources of debt and equity capital are ever changing. The chapter turns next to a discussion of the forms of ownership for office development ventures. This section is intended to help developers and investors understand the legal and tax implications of different ownership structures.

Sections follow on the basic requirements and expectations of lenders and investors in office projects: why

The 32-story headquarters building for the Sinar Group is located in downtown Jakarta.

lenders lend and why investors invest. Then, the focus turns to the primary sources of financing at different stages of development—predevelopment and land acquisition, construction, and operations. Finally, the elements of loan submissions—the financing package—are discussed.

The Capital Markets for Office Development

While the benefits of investing in office development have changed little over the last decade, the sources of debt and equity funds have been undergoing dramatic change. The role of local banks as the primary source of construction loans has been largely taken over by well-capitalized banks with a regional, national or international base. The local partnerships that were once a significant source of equity investment for office developments are now overshadowed by REITs, pension funds, and property trust companies operating nationally and globally.

The shift from private to public sources of capital for real estate development began in the early 1990s, when lending from banks, savings and loan institutions, and other traditional sources of capital was severely curtailed and developers started going to the public markets to raise capital. (See Figure 3-1.) While public markets have supplied real estate debt and equity for many years, their

role since 1992 has expanded quickly in the wake of the real estate recession and capital shortage of the late 1980s. In the 1980s, private sources of debt and equity provided most of the capital that went into real estate. By 1996, public equity and debt markets accounted for more than 40 percent of the year's total net flow of capital into real estate.

The emergence of the commercial mortgage–backed securities market has defined a totally new dimension in the financing of commercial real estate. A mortgage-backed security has as its collateral a pool of commercial mortgages—from a single mortgage to several hundred. Bonds backed by these mortgages have varying risk and maturity profiles based on the characteristics of the underlying property and the priority of the mortgage proceeds in the event of default.

The Resolution Trust Corporation (RTC) was a catalyst for the creation of the CMBS market. The agency found itself owning large portfolios of real estate following the widespread S&L failures in the late 1980s. At first, it tried to sell whole-loan portfolios. But the market for whole loans was limited because of the (temporary) withdrawal from the market of traditional investors in commercial mortgages—banks and life insurance companies. When the RTC was forced to turn to the public capital market, it found that the disposition proceeds it could realize from the sale of interests in CMBSs exceeded what it could realize from sales to private purchasers of whole loans or whole-loan portfolios. Thus, the foundation was

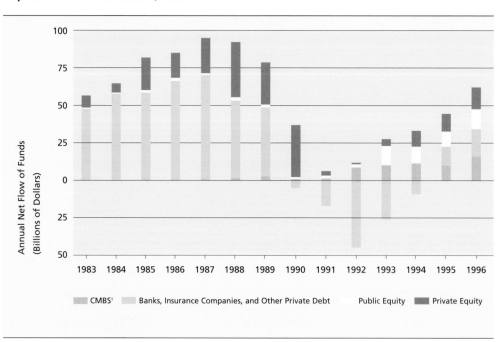

figure 3-1
Capital Flows to Real Estate, 1983–1996

[1]Commercial mortgage–backed securities.

Sources: Federal Reserve; Roulac Group; National Association of Real Estate Investment Trusts; and LaSalle Advisors Investment Research.

figure 3-2
Securitized Commercial Mortgages, 1990–1996

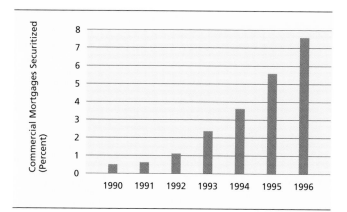

Sources: J.P. Morgan; CS First Boston; Federal Reserve; and LaSalle Advisors Investment Research.

laid for a public market in commercial mortgage–backed securities.

The CMBS market has continued to gain share in overall holdings of real estate debt—from less than 0.5 percent of the value of outstanding commercial real estate mortgages in 1989 to roughly 8 percent (or $81 billion) in 1996. (See Figure 3-2.) CMBSs appeal to institutional investors as an alternative to other fixed-income investments, such as corporate bonds and U.S. Treasury bonds.

This shift of real estate debt holdings into public capital markets has been paralleled by a similar and dramatic shift in the basic sources of equity funds since the late 1980s. The amount of real estate equity raised from REITs, the principal public source of equity funds, grew from less than $1 billion in 1980 to more than $80 billion by year-end 1996. (See Figure 3-3.) Institutional investors such as life insurance companies, mutual funds, and public pension funds that are attracted to the strong performance, liquidity, and diversification benefits of holding commercial real estate in the REIT form are helping to drive the growth of public real estate equity.

Ownership Structures for Office Development Ventures

Real estate ventures can be owned by an individual—a person or a firm—or a group. The ability to bring a real estate venture to profitable reality in harmony with the business and investment goals of its entrepreneurs and investors depends in good part on choosing the right ownership structure. Each form of ownership carries its own legal and tax consequences. Which form of ownership is most appropriate for a particular venture depends on several factors, such as the objectives of the developer or investor, the market conditions, the type of office development contemplated, and the availability of capital.

figure 3-3
Market Capitalization of U.S. Real Estate Investment Trusts, 1980–1996

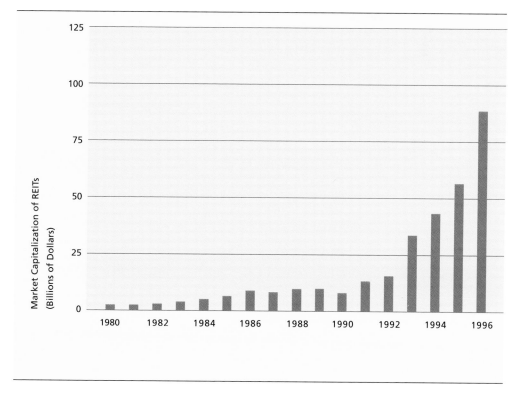

Sources: National Association of Real Estate Investment Trusts; and LaSalle Advisors Investment Research.

figure 3-4

Comparison of Private and Public Real Estate Investments

Private U.S. Property Market (Direct Investment)	Public U.S. Property Market (Securities)
• Avoids stock market risk and thus provides diversification benefit to mixed-asset portfolios (because property investment performance is negatively correlated with stock and bond performance).	• Provides less protection against stock market risk.
• Requires a large number of properties—approximately 50—to provide diversity to property-only portfolios and thus avoid property-specific risk.	• Provides an efficient way to achieve diversification of property portfolios.
• Enjoys less volatile returns at the portfolio level.	• Outperforms direct investing (over the last two decades); performs with more volatility at the company level (because the franchise values of REITs can go up or down).
• Provides a broader range of investment opportunities across the risk/return spectrum.	• Provides access to property types not easily purchased in the private market (such as regional malls or manufactured home communities).
• Informed by a significantly increasing base of information on the property level. However, real-time transaction data are still scarce.	• Faces scarcity of data on the property level. However, the public market is based more on real-time pricing information.
• Experiencing improved liquidity of investments, based on the establishment and expansion of capital markets for private real estate. However, the value-added from private investment is not easily capitalized and traded.	• Allows greater ease in capitalizing and trading on the franchise value of public companies.
• Can align the interests of owners and managers through the structure of the investment.	• Generally closely aligns the interests of investors and management (because of the substantial management ownership of most REITs).
• Provides greater investor control over all decisions, from property management to the timing of sales.	• Property decisions governed by REIT boards of directors.

Source: Adapted from LaSalle Advisors Investment Research.

Figure 3-5 summarizes key features of the major forms of ownership.

Office developers commonly raise capital for a specific project by joint venturing with an institution, such as a pension fund or a life insurance company. Such a joint venture is not a form of ownership per se, and it may take any form the participants desire. These joint ventures are usually organized as limited partnerships in which the institutional investor provides most, if not all, of the capital while the developer contributes development and management expertise. The parties then share in the project's operating cash flow and appreciation in value. In recent years, some institutional partners have been reluctant to share the ownership benefits with the developer, preferring instead to hire the developer for a fee and retain 100 percent ownership of the completed development.

A brief discussion of each of the major forms of real estate ownership follows.

Individual Direct Ownership

Direct ownership of real estate by an individual person or firm is certainly the simplest form of ownership. There are no partners or associates to deal with, no organiza-

tional requirements beyond one's own to satisfy. But this simplicity also entails some disadvantages. Without the protection of a separate tax entity, the direct owner of a property is liable for all the debts and liabilities associated with the property. In addition, a direct owner can encounter difficulties in obtaining debt financing for the project. Direct ownership can also complicate the planning for the succession of the property to another owner(s).

Direct ownership generally is only appropriate for small-scale office developments. For most office developments, the large capital requirements and the need for risk sharing make direct ownership unworkable.

Partnership

In legal terms, a partnership is an unincorporated association of two or more persons or entities. People often refer to a partnership as a joint venture or syndication. During the last 20 years, the partnership has been the real estate industry's preferred organizational form. It gained notoriety as the vehicle that was used to finance the commercial office building boom that essentially was ended by the Tax Reform Act of 1986. That act introduced limitations on the use of passive losses in tax calculations, to curb what was viewed as abusive sheltering of non–real estate income with paper losses from the depreciation of real estate.

A partnership is a reporting vehicle. It is not a taxable entity. It reports items of gross income and deductions from income, and the partners include their share of these items on their individual income tax returns. Among ownership entities, only partnerships have the flexibility to make special allocations of income, gain, loss, deductions, or tax credits to their partners. Partnerships have no limits on the number of partners they can include or on the tax status or nationality of their partners. A foreign individual, corporation, or trust may be a partner in a U.S. partnership.

General Partnership. In a general partnership, all the partners share the risks, rewards, and management of the venture. Any and all partners are liable (jointly and severally liable) for all the debts and obligations of the business. For this reason, wealthy individuals and money partners do not typically enter into general partnerships for real estate ventures, preferring the protection of limited liability provided by limited partnerships or limited liability companies.

Limited Partnership. In a limited partnership, the general partner (or partners) is liable for the partnership's debts and other obligations, while the limited partner (or partners) bears no liability for such debt beyond its contributed capital. Participation by limited partners in the day-to-day management of the partnership is not allowed and if it occurs the limited partners risk loss of their limited liability status.

Limited partnerships are historically the most widely used form of ownership for office properties. The attraction lies in their ability to allocate income (without double taxation) or losses to the limited partners without conferring liability on those partners. Not only does a limited partnership avoid double taxation, but also the income received by partners retains its nature as ordinary

With a gross portfolio in excess of $7 billion, Hines Interests LP in Houston is one of the largest U.S.-based real estate development and management companies still operating as a private entity. Penzoil Place in Houston is part of the firm's portfolio of properties around the world.

Hines Interests LP

figure 3-5

Features of Major Forms of Real Estate Ownership

Ownership Form	Ease of Formation	Minimum/Maximum Number of Owners	Ability to Raise Funds	Management
Individual Direct Ownership	Simple and inexpensive	1/1	Very limited	Flexible and independent
General Partnership	Simple and inexpensive	2/unlimited	Limited	Designated partners
Limited Partnership	Moderately difficult and expensive	2/unlimited	Limited	General partner or agent
Limited Liability Company	Moderately difficult and expensive	2/unlimited	Limited	Member or agent
C Corporation	Complex and expensive	1/unlimited	Good if public company	Continuous and centralized
S Corporation	Complex and expensive	1/75	Limited	Determined by relative share of ownership
Real Estate Investment Trust	Complex and expensive	100/unlimited	Good if public company	Centralized, by advisory group

Source: Adapted from James H. Boykin and Richard L. Haney Jr., *Financing Real Estate*, 2nd ed. (Englewood Cliffs, New Jersey: Prentice-Hall, 1993), p. 288.

or capital gains income. For office developments, the most common type of limited partnership involves a corporate entity established by the developer, which acts as the general partner and manager, and investors—frequently many in number—who are limited partners.

Limited Liability Company

Limited liability companies (LLCs)—a relative newcomer to the scene—combine the advantage of a single pass-through tax, limited liability for investors (members), and no restriction on investor participation in the management of the enterprise. Virtually every state has adopted legislation that allows business organizations to be formed as LLCs.

In general, the members and managers of an LLC are not personally liable for its debts and obligations, regardless of the degree to which they participate in its management. A member's liability is limited to the amount of its capital contribution. Accordingly, creditors may not recover any part of a claim from a member's personal assets if the LLC's assets are insufficient to satisfy it.

The advantages of LLCs—flexibility in allocation of income and loss, flow-through tax benefits, limited liability, and owner participation in management—should make this form of ownership increasingly attractive for office development and investment.

C Corporation

A corporation is an organization separate and apart from its owners. It is a legal entity created under authority of the state. Its scope of activity is limited by an approved charter. Corporations pay income tax on their earnings. Generally, they are solely responsible for their debts. They operate under the authority of a board of directors elected by the shareholders and they continue in existence unaffected by any transfer of ownership or by the death, retirement, or bankruptcy of their shareholders. C corporations can have any number of shareholders—including only one—of any type or nationality.

For office development projects, the corporate form of ownership presents some tax disadvantages. The corporate tax bracket may be higher than the tax brackets of the shareholders. And, corporate earnings that are distributed to the shareholders in the form of dividends are doubled taxed—once as corporate earnings and again as shareholder income. This tax characteristic makes the transfer of an office project's cash flow to investors problematic.

In addition, if a venture under a corporate form incurs losses in its early years, its owners receive no immediate tax benefit (unless the corporation elects to be taxed as an S corporation as explained in the next section). Such losses can only offset corporate earnings in the future. Unlike some other forms of ownership, C cor-

Personal Liability of Owners	Income Tax Treatment	Transferability of Ownership	Operating Agreement
Unlimited	Pass-through; single tax	Simple and inexpensive	N/A
Joint and several liability	Pass-through; single tax	Poor	Written or oral agreement
None for limited partners; joint and several for general partners	Pass-through; single tax	Fair to poor	Partnership agreement
No liability for LLC's debts	Pass-through; single tax	Fair to poor	Operating agreement
No liability for corporation's debts	Double tax	Superior	Corporate bylaws
No liability for corporation's debts	Pass-through; single tax	Impeded by ceiling on number of shareholders	Corporate bylaws
No liability for corporation's debts	Modified pass-through	Superior	Corporate bylaws or trust agreement

porations do not allow losses to be used to offset other current income of the stockholders.

The ability of many corporations to elect to be S corporations or REITs, both of which are described in the following sections, makes the establishment of a C corporation to hold or operate real estate a poor second choice.

S Corporation

In some situations, corporations can elect to be taxed as small business corporations (called "S" corporations after the relevant subchapter in the tax code). Like partnerships, S corporations are pass-through entities, meaning that income (or loss) can be passed through to the investors without being taxed at the entity level. Thus, S corporations do not have to pay a tax at the entity level on income that is distributed to shareholders.

The growing acceptance of LLCs has come at the expense of S corporations, which are used much less frequently than they once were. An electing S corporation must meet a number of varied restrictions and eligibility requirements in order to retain its qualified S status. These include the following: no more than 75 shareholders; no corporate shareholders; no foreign shareholders; no special allocations of income, loss, and cash distributions; and only one class of stock.

Developers and investors considering an undertaking's ownership structure must keep in mind that an S corporation, despite its pass-through tax benefits, is in fact a corporation and is treated as a corporation for purposes relating to organization, reorganization, and liquidation. Although similar to an LLC in that no equity holder is personally liable for the debts of the entity, an S corporation is not a partnership. In considering an S corporation election, investors should not rely on its partnership style tax benefits to shareholders as the sole criterion.

Real Estate Investment Trust

Real estate investment trusts (REITs) are a mutual fund form of ownership that was invented to encourage widespread investing in real estate. If they meet certain technical requirements, they can elect to pass realized gains through to shareholders and take tax deductions for the distributions, thus avoiding a double tax. Otherwise, they are taxable as corporations.

These capital pools provide small investors with an opportunity to invest in managed real estate, to spread risk through diversified holdings, and to acquire interests in properties that would ordinarily be beyond their means. Additionally, REIT shares can be easily sold or transferred. A disadvantage is that tax losses are trapped inside REITs, not permitted to be passed directly to investors as they are by partnerships, LLCs, and S corporations.

A REIT must meet numerous and complicated qualifying standards. On the investor side, a REIT must have

A limited partnership owns the three-building headquarters complex of Sony Music Entertainment in Santa Monica, California. Sony Music occupies the complex under a ten-year lease that is fully guaranteed by its parent, Sony U.S.A., with options to extend for several five-year terms. The average effective rents over the lease term provide the project's owner with a 10.5 percent development capitalization rate.

at least 100 shareholders and it cannot be closely held. Generally, this second requirement means that the five largest individual shareholders cannot own more than 50 percent of the value of the REIT's outstanding stock during the last half of any taxable year.

On the investment side, in order to insure that a REIT is primarily involved in real estate, it must satisfy certain income and assets tests or forfeit its REIT status. At least 75 percent of a REIT's assets must be in the form of real estate assets, cash, and government securities. Finally, at least 95 percent of a REIT's taxable income excluding any net capital gains must be distributed annually as ordinary dividends. The REIT entity incurs an income tax only to the extent it has not distributed to its shareholders 100 percent of its taxable income including any capital gains. REIT qualifying rules are complex and unforgiving, and the administrative costs can rival those associated with large, public companies.

The heating up of the real estate market in recent years has prompted some REITs to use a partnership structure—an umbrella partnership REIT (UPREIT)— to acquire properties. In an UPREIT, the REIT forms an operating partnership in which it retains the sole general partner interest and through which it owns all of its real property interests.

Taubman Centers was the first publicly traded REIT to adopt the UPREIT structure. It raised $295 million in an initial public offering (IPO) in November 1992. A typical UPREIT formation involves a contribution of property to the operating partnership in exchange for limited partnership units in the operating partnership. The units are convertible into REIT shares. The REIT raises cash through an IPO and contributes the money raised to the operating partnership. For the initial property partners, who often are limited partners holding syndicated partnership interests that were acquired in the 1980s, UPREITs offer the advantage of being able to defer the gain they otherwise would have had to recognize had they sold the property or partnership interests directly to the REIT.

Other variations of this theme are also coming into play. DownREITs are the latest refinement in the REIT market for acquiring new properties. A downREIT is any REIT acquisition of property through a subsidiary partnership, and it can provide greater flexibility than an UPREIT in structuring an acquisition when certain business and tax objectives must be met.

Institutions have stepped up their involvement in REITs, which should help to stabilize and increase the size of the REIT marketplace. The availability of capital is one of the determinants of a project's ownership structure. To determine capital availability, developers and owners must understand how lenders and investors will evaluate the economic feasibility of a proposed office development. Knowing what the providers of debt and equity funds require in a project enables a developer to target the most likely sources of financing and to make the best case for the project. Lender and investor requirements are the subject of the following sections.

Parkway Properties started as a REIT in the 1970s under another name. After a long and arduous reincarnation, the REIT has developed a strong portfolio of more than 20 office buildings, including the Woodbranch Building in Houston.

Why Lenders Lend

Because of the large amount of capital necessary to build, buy, or operate an office project, obtaining debt financing often is the developer's most difficult hurdle. Lenders know the key role played by debt financing and frequently tout what they call the golden rule of real estate lending: He who has the gold makes the rules. And since lenders have the gold, they make the rules.

Loan Underwriting Process
A lender's analysis of a loan application for an office development (or its loan underwriting procedure) typically comprises seven steps. The terminology and sequence of the steps may vary from lender to lender, depending on the institution's priority of concerns. As will be discussed later, developers include market and financial analyses in their loan applications. But lenders need to verify the developer's assumptions and independently assess the project's viability. With relatively minor variations, the loan underwriting process for most lenders includes the following steps:

- market analysis;
- location analysis;
- analysis of the site and the proposed improvements;
- analysis of the loan's collateral;
- evaluation of the developer's construction team and property management plan;
- assessment of economic feasibility; and
- evaluation of placement options for the loan.

Much of the data necessary to complete the loan underwriting process flows from the lender's analysis of the property's market. To determine whether the market is strong enough to generate occupancy and rental rates that will justify the proposed development, the lender must obtain satisfactory answers to three questions about demand, supply, and timing. What is

Given the current attractiveness of REITs on Wall Street, it is no wonder that many real estate companies with portfolios of properties earnestly wish to go public. But just as a college student cannot go to graduate school before completing a bachelor's degree, there are many prerequisites to going public, points out Mike Krupa, a vice president and real estate investment banker with Salomon Brothers. Krupa subscribes to seven golden rules for taking a private real estate company public through a successful initial public offering (IPO):

- You generally need a focus by property type—or possibly a geographic focus. Investors want the expertise of management with a proven ability to add shareholder value through acquiring or developing a specific class of property. In addition, many buyers of REIT stocks retain a strong conviction that successful management needs a regional specialty—due to the adage that all real estate is local. As REITs expand, however, investors are becoming more forgiving on the need for a geographic focus.
- You need a critical mass. With some exceptions, an equity offering of at least $100 million to $250 million is necessary to launch a successful public offering, underwriters insist. Otherwise, you will not offer investors the liquidity and float that they covet. And you will not get the research support from sell-side analysts to keep your name in front of investors. As a result, your stock price could suffer. Institutional investors—which are playing an increasingly important role in REIT markets—are especially insistent on REITs with a large market capitalization
- You should have conservative debt to total market capitalization—preferably at a ratio lower than 20 percent. When your debt level is low, investors perceive that you will be able to grow quickly without coming back to the equity markets.
- You need solid management with a track record for creating value. To be sure, the question of what constitutes "solid management" is a judgment call. But certainly Wall Street wants to know that for a period of perhaps five years or longer, you have proven your ability to undertake sound development, make savvy acquisitions, and employ aggressive leasing practices that keep your buildings full and rents high.
- You need a strategic plan accentuating future growth. Even during the original road show—which introduces your management team to prospective investors in many cities —you will be called upon to produce a good story as to why your company will grow and thrive. Expect to be peppered with tough questions about your strengths and weaknesses as a firm.
- You need significant investment by your management. In most cases, a company's executives should go public owning a big stake in the company—so investors know that you have a major interest in the REIT's future.

Ideally, the chief executive should have retained a majority of his or her net worth in the real estate company.
- You need minimal conflicts of interest among your officers. Investment bankers love to talk about an alignment of interests between management and shareholders. That occurs when the primary focus of your management team is on the core business of the REIT— and the REIT is self-run and self-advised. You may have to discontinue any partnerships or outside affiliations that seem to drain attention away from the REIT.

If you decide to jump the hurdle to public ownership, what is the first step? "You need advisers—legal and accounting advisers, as well as Wall Street underwriters," says Richard Schoninger, who heads real estate investment banking for Prudential Securities. There is no harm— or expense—in going straight to Wall Street underwriters for a preliminary glimpse at how an IPO would fly for your company. And good investment bankers will put out the welcome mat, especially for a large real estate firm with an impressive cadre of executives. "People should absolutely come in and chat," says Raymond Mikulich, managing director for real estate investment banking at Lehman Brothers.

What makes a good IPO candidate? "The management of a company provides the edge," states Schoninger. Since we are now at a relatively mature stage in the cycle for new REITs, Wall Street is more demanding in its search for "the deepest and most well-rounded operating companies" that have proven themselves over a lengthy period, he says. Underwriters caution against extremely large executive compensation packages—salary or stock bonuses —during the period when you are attempting to go public. The appearance of greed is unappealing to investors who want to see officers focused on the company's success, not their own personal gain. (And remember, your pay package and perquisites will be disclosed in public documents.)

By the same token, Schoninger stresses that an initial REIT offering should not be structured to appear as a vehicle for the company's management team to bail out. Indeed, Schoninger says underwriters usually discourage officers from selling any of their own stock in a REIT initial public offering because of the "remaining paranoia" of investors who recall the last wave of unsuccessful REIT offerings, most of which tanked in the 1970s. Given their insecurity about what happened in the last REIT cycle, investors want to see strong signs that management is committed to the company's future interests.

Good timing is crucial to a successful public offering and much of it is luck. One force that often is beyond your control when you go public is whether or not investors are in the mood for your type of company. Although underwriters never slam the door on any particular type of REIT or geographic area, their preferences vary across time, notes David Jarvis, one of two managing directors overseeing PaineWebber's real estate investment banking group.

What if you do not want to go public or cannot convince the underwriters of the merits of your deal? Then you have three choices, as outlined by Mikulich. You can sell your portfolio to another REIT or private investor. You can merge with a REIT, retaining an executive role in the larger company. Or you can sit tight—amassing properties and expertise that either make you a more competitive private player with a good niche or allow you to go public one day in the future.

Granted, the cost of capital should remain lower for public REITs than for private players, as Mikulich predicts. But there is no guarantee that REITs will remain the darlings of Wall Street, as they have been of late. And it is unlikely that public real estate companies will ever control a majority of the real estate assets in the United States, except perhaps in a field such as regional malls, where the barriers to entry are high, he says, adding that "there will always be room for quality private companies to make money in the real estate business."

One company delighted with the public arena is Parkway Properties. Started as a REIT in the 1970s under a different identity—and with the intention of investing in mortgages—Parkway hit bottom the same decade. In recent years, it has been going through a long and arduous reincarnation by buying up and liquidating the assets of failed REITs.

Parkway has used the proceeds to build a healthy core portfolio of more than 20 office buildings, notes Steven Rogers, president of the company, which is based in Jackson, Mississippi. It has also converted to an equity REIT, moved onto the New York Stock Exchange, and garnered a research following from analysts at both national and regional investment houses.

"You do not have to be a big company to enjoy the benefits of the public equity markets," Rogers says, pointing out that Parkway now has but $210 million in market capitalization (although it is growing swiftly and completed a $51 million secondary stock offering in January 1997). Small cap REITs (REITs with small market capitalization) like Parkway have their role, says Rogers, especially for individual investors and institutions that favor emerging growth companies. Still, getting investors to pay attention to the REIT has required constant contact with the investment community.

Rogers advises real estate companies that are contemplating a public offering not to be daunted by all the paperwork involved in the deal or its aftermath. "The public disclosure seems to be overwhelming. But you get a lot of help from your accounting firm, law firm, and other professionals," he says. Nor should a small- to medium-sized company fear approaching underwriters about a REIT offering simply because of its size. "There are a lot of investment bankers out there willing to underwrite small companies," Rogers says.

But not everyone is enamored of the public markets. "We've decided definitely to stay private and the main reason is flexibility," says Hasty Johnson, chief financial officer of Hines Interests LP in Houston. Hines has launched a large-scale global strategy and does not want to be tethered by Wall Street.

Hines started in 1957. In 1997, with 2,700 employees, offices around the world, and a gross portfolio in excess of $7 billion, the real estate development and management firm is one of the largest U.S.-based companies of its kind still operating as a private entity. Despite ample opportunities to take the public plunge, it refuses.

"REITs are really valued and driven a lot by current earnings, so they have a more difficult time setting up a new line of business. A few years ago, when we decided to develop in Europe, we had a lot of downtime and went several million dollars in the hole. That would have been more difficult if we had been public," says Johnson. Instead of going public, Hines, along with Dean Witter Reynolds and the Trust Company of the West, is financing its international growth spurt with capital raised through a private investment fund that closed with $410 million in the fall of 1996. Who backed the global fund? Big pension funds, international investors, and a few wealthy individuals.

Although private debt capital from insurance companies is far harder to get than it once was, Hines's sterling reputation has allowed it to secure whatever capital it has needed through a half-dozen large insurance companies that are still willing to back private development ventures, says Johnson. "We definitely watch what is going on in the public markets—because it does affect us. But there is a continued appetite for private investment," Johnson adds. A still more important reason he cites for staying private is to preserve the corporate culture that Hines has so carefully nurtured.

Source: Adapted from Ellen James Martin, "The REIT Surge," *Urban Land*, June 1997, pp. 44–47, 70–73.

■

Darling Park, a 1.6 million-square-foot mixed-use development in Sydney, Australia, was a joint venture between Japanese and Australian investors. The development obtained nonrecourse construction financing through Australia New Zealand Bank.

Michael Chittenden Photography

the market's demand for this kind of space over time? How much competition does the building face from current and future office properties? Is the project's timing good?

The answer to the timing question depends on the answers to several other questions. How long will it take for the new space to be absorbed? Are unanticipated construction delays possible or likely? How would the developer pay for any increased costs associated with the delays? Will market conditions change adversely before the project's completion and lease-up?

The second step in the typical loan underwriting process—a location analysis—involves determining the site's accessibility and suitability for target tenants. Is it convenient to the kinds of amenities, services, and resources that these tenants need or prefer? The location analysis also involves issues of developability. Is the proper zoning in place? Will the community and the project's neighbors support the development? Are utilities avail-

able? Finally, the location analysis involves determining if the site is in an area of growth.

Step three of the loan underwriting process is an analysis of the site characteristics and the building improvements. Are there site constraints to development? Does the site contain species habitat that will have to be protected? Will the site require environmental remediation? Does the proposed building suit its location? For instance, a lavish office tower might be deemed out of place in a low-rise suburban market and, for that reason, not economically viable.

Next on the list of lender concerns is what will ultimately secure the loan. For most loans, it is the property that serves as collateral. The value of the property that the borrower pledges as collateral must exceed the amount of the loan. Lenders seek to determine how attractive the property would be to tenants and potential buyers in the marketplace should the borrower default on the loan.

The creditworthiness of tenants that have signed leases —their willingness and their ability to pay the rent—is often a key consideration in assessing collateral. The signature of certain strong (creditworthy) tenants on a preconstruction lease generates rental income and thus can serve as collateral. This applies most often to single-tenant projects.

Most construction loans are recourse, meaning that in the case of default the lender has recourse to other assets of the borrower in addition to the property pledged as collateral. Thus, the lender's analysis of a loan's collateral includes an investigation of claims against the borrower's assets and associated liabilities. In addition, the lender investigates how the borrower's repayment of its existing liabilities might deplete the assets available to satisfy the lender's future claims.

In step five of the underwriting procedure, the lender analyzes the proposed development's construction team and property management plan. The construction team must have a proven record of completing projects on time and in accordance with architectural and engineering specifications, which is known as building to spec. Missing construction deadlines can cause costs to escalate and missing completion dates can give prelease tenants the right to renegotiate their leases. If a project is not built to spec, the structural and mechanical integrity of the building may be compromised, which can lower the collateral value of the property.

While good property management cannot save a poorly conceived and executed office project, poor property management can destroy a good project. Hence, the borrower's proposed property management plan is an important factor in the loan decision. Good property management includes maintaining an efficient and safe building, meeting tenant space needs, and solving problems and repairing deficiencies that arise in a timely manner.

The cost of replacing high-quality tenants typically exceeds the cost of retaining them. Lenders therefore look for evidence of the management team's skills in tenant relations. They also examine executed leases in order to evaluate the manager's ability to structure favorable lease terms. (Favorable lease terms, from a lender's point of view, are ones that best enable the borrower to service its debt.)

In step six, the lender assesses the project's economic feasibility. This analysis uses data, findings, and conclusions from the preceding analyses. Step six is, essentially, an underwriting step that covers everything from the project's concept to its cash flow and its ultimate sale to the next investor. Its tools are the pro forma cash flow statement (see the financial feasibility section in Chapter 2) and various other single-period and multiperiod analyses. Its goal is to determine whether the development will pencil out. The lender's economic feasibility analysis is discussed in detail in the next section.

If the project passes the lender's test of economic feasibility, step seven—the lender's final underwriting task—is a loan placement analysis. This means deciding whether to hold a loan or sell it—or to not make the loan if the lender is unwilling to hold it and no secondary market exists.

Lenders generally have more than one option for loans. The lender's evaluation of placement options may dictate whether the loan will be funded. One option is for the lender to hold the loan in its own investment portfolio. An increasingly viable option is for the lender to place the loan in a securitized pool of loans that are sold on Wall Street (see discussion of commercial mortgage–backed securities earlier in this chapter). Loans can also be sold—in whole or in part—to other banks.

Lender Economic Feasibility Analysis

The lending decision is based in large part on three key calculations derived from the pro forma financial statements, and lenders therefore insist that the pro formas for a proposed project be carefully constructed and complete. These three calculations are the mortgage constant, the debt service coverage ratio, and the loan-to-value ratio.

Mortgage Constant. The mortgage constant (MC) expresses the relationship between annual debt service requirements (including principal and interest) and the amount of the loan. The mortgage constant is based on market interest rates for commercial mortgages plus the installment to amortize the loan over a set period of time. Specifically, it is the percentage of the loan amount represented by the annual debt service:

$$MC = \frac{\text{Annual Debt Service}}{\text{Loan Amount}}$$

The lender often uses the mortgage constant to determine the maximum loan amount (see following section on the debt coverage ratio). The lender also can use it to calculate the annual debt service when the loan amount is known:

$$\text{Annual Debt Service} = MC \times \text{Loan Amount}$$

The lender can also use the mortgage constant to calculate the maximum loan amount for a known amount

A consortium of banks led by Mellon Bank East N.A. provided the construction loan for the Independence Blue Cross headquarters building in downtown Philadelphia.

of annual debt service (based on what can be justified for the specific project):

$$\text{Loan Amount} = \frac{\text{Annual Debt Service}}{MC}$$

A higher interest rate or a shorter loan amortization period will cause the annual debt service for a given loan to rise, and thus raise the mortgage constant. Many developers pursue a strategy of bargaining for the lowest interest rate and the longest amortization term that the lender will accept, knowing that such a strategy will result in the lowest mortgage constant, the smallest debt service payment, and ultimately the largest loan amount.

Debt Coverage Ratio. For most regional and nationwide lenders such as commercial banks, life insurance companies, mortgage companies, pension funds, and commercial secondary mortgage market conduits, the debt coverage ratio (DCR) is the single most important

figure 3-6

4455 Jefferson Avenue: Project Data and Assumptions

4455 Jefferson Avenue is a hypothetical proposed build-to-suit office building. It has a net rentable area of 162,500 square feet. Before construction, a lease agreement was signed with one tenant to occupy the entire building. The lender's market and financial analyses have led to the following assumptions about the project's financial performance.

Income and Expenses

Rent	$21.00 per square foot
Rent Escalations	2% per year
Parking Income	$125,000
Vacancy Loss	7% of potential gross income[1]
Operating Expenses	$735,000
Real Estate Taxes	$398,000
Cash Reserves	2% of potential gross income[1]

Lease

Type	Modified gross lease
Term	15 years

Permanent Loan

Interest Rate	9.5%
Term	10 years
Amortization Period	30 years
Amount	To be determined

[1] Potential gross income equals potential gross rent plus expense pass-throughs plus parking income.

figure 3-7

4455 Jefferson Avenue: Property Income and Expense Statement

Income	
(a) Potential Gross Rent	$3,412,500
(b) Expense Pass-Throughs	0
(c) Parking Income	125,000
(d) Potential Gross Income	$3,537,500
(e) Vacancy Credit/Loss	(247,625)
(f) Effective Gross Income	$3,289,875
Expenses	
(g) Operating Expenses	$735,000
(h) Real Estate Taxes	398,000
(i) Cash Reserves for Replacements	70,750
(j) Total Expenses	$1,203,750
(k) Net Operating Income	$2,086,125

measure for determining the acceptability of an office development loan application. Lenders also use the DCR to determine the maximum loan amount. The formula for computing the DCR is as follows:

$$DCR = \frac{\text{Net Operating Income}}{\text{Annual Debt Service}}$$

An office property with a 1.25 debt coverage ratio produces $1.25 of net operating income for every $1.00 of debt service. The DCR indicates the adequacy of the development's projected cash flow to service the debt. It also indicates the lender's operating risk. The lower the DCR the smaller the cushion of available NOI, and therefore the higher the lender's operating risk.

For office projects, lenders generally require a DCR between 1.15 and 1.40. Lenders on projects deemed riskier than average require a higher DCR and lenders on projects deemed relatively risk free will accept a lower DCR.

Construction lenders use the DCR to evaluate loans, even though no operating income is generated during the construction period. The construction lender must be satisfied that the anticipated cash flow generated by the project will be sufficient to obtain the permanent takeout mortgage from which the construction loan will be repaid. Thus, short-term construction lenders measure the sufficiency of a project's income using the DCR.

The cash flow (or operating income) analysis for an office project is covered in Chapter 2, using the Fairway Center example. In this discussion of lender feasibility analysis, a different hypothetical project is used as an example. The project—4455 Jefferson Avenue—is a proposed build-to-suit office building, which is introduced in Figure 3-6.

In a loan application, the projected net revenue of the building is of critical interest, because it will be the source of the principal and interest payments on the loan. For 4455 Jefferson Avenue, a lease agreement with one tenant to occupy the entire building was executed before the commencement of construction. Preleasing greatly reduces the risk to the lender, since it promises a known stream of income.

Figure 3-7 is the pro forma income and expense statement for 4455 Jefferson Avenue. Potential gross rent is based on a $21 per square foot rental rate. The tenant's lease is a modified gross lease agreement in which no expenses are passed through to the tenant in the first year of the lease agreement, so zero expense pass-throughs are included in the income statement. (Types of leases are covered in Chapter 5.) Parking income is estimated at $125,000. These three income sources add up to a potential gross income of $3,537,500 a year for the project.

A 7 percent vacancy factor reduces income to $3,289,875: the project's effective gross income. Some developers might argue against the inclusion of a vacancy factor on a building leased for 15 years to a single tenant. Since the building occupancy will be either 100 percent or zero, the tenant will either pay rent on the fully occupied building or it will not pay rent. Lenders, however, are likely to include a vacancy factor in the analysis to reflect the likelihood that the building will eventually be multitenant and possibly not 100 percent occupied.

Total expenses for 4455 Jefferson (also shown in Figure 3-7) are made up of operating expenses, property taxes, and cash reserves for replacement. Typical office building operating expenses include payroll, insurance, cleaning services, utilities, maintenance and repair, and management fees. Operating expenses should be carefully projected during the design phase of development. The Building Owner and Managers Association's annual Experience Exchange Report provides useful information on operating expenses and income based on a survey of U.S. office buildings. Experienced property managers and appraisers are another good source of information for making operating expense projections.

Line (i) in 4455 Jefferson's income and expense statement—cash reserves for replacement—is a contingency account that is used to pay for the replacement of major capital items such as HVAC systems, elevators, or roofs. Capital items generally have a multiyear life and cannot be expensed for tax purposes. As a new building, 4455 Jefferson needs to set aside only a relatively small amount of cash for replacements.

The building's total annual expenses are expected to be $1,203,750. This sum subtracted from the effective gross income returns a net operating income (NOI) of $2,086,125. Two categories of expenses—tenant improvements and leasing costs—are not included in the calculation of NOI. There are two reasons for these exclusions. First, these costs generally are not expensed for tax purposes but are depreciated over the life of the lease or the life of the building. Depreciation is not a cash expense, so these costs are excluded from NOI. A second reason for not including these costs is their irregular nature. They vary from year to year, depending on the square footage of expiring leases, and if they were included the NOI would fluctuate wildly from period to period.

Because of an early commitment to specified rent rates, the developer of the Nestlé USA headquarters building in Glendale, California, needed to minimize financing risks. Thus, before beginning construction, it purchased an interest rate hedge that limited the maximum rate of interest that would be payable under the construction loan.

Lincoln Property Company N.C. Inc.

figure 3-8

4455 Jefferson Avenue: Calculation of Maximum Loan Amount

Potential Gross Income	$3,537,500
+ Vacancy Credit/Loss	(247,625)
Effective Gross Income	$3,289,875
– Operating Expenses	735,000
– Real Estate Taxes	398,000
– Cash Reserves for Replacements	70,750
Net Operating Income	$2,086,125
÷ Debt Coverage Ratio	1.20
Cash Available for Debt Service	$1,738,438
÷ Mortgage Constant	10.09%
Maximum Loan Amount	$17,200,000[1]

[1]Rounded from $17,229,316.

figure 3-9

4455 Jefferson Avenue: Maximum Loan Amount Sensitivity Analysis[1]

Mortgage Constant	Debt Coverage Ratio		
	1.15	1.25	1.35
8.0%	$22,675,000	$20,861,000	$19,315,000
10.0%	$18,140,000	$16,689,000	$15,452,000
12.0%	$15,116,000	$13,907,000	$12,877,000

[1]Maximum loan amounts based on a net operating income of $2,086,125.

Now that a defensible net operating income has been established for 4455 Jefferson Avenue, the lender can apply its debt coverage ratio to determine the income that the project will have available for debt service. As has been noted, the lender determines the DCR based on its assessment of its operating risk. A ten-year loan for 4455 Jefferson would carry a relatively low risk. A 15-year lease has been executed with a creditworthy tenant, and annual 2 percent rent escalations are included. The lender determines that this project must maintain only a 1.20 DCR.

The permanent lender can now calculate the maximum loan amount, based on the NOI, the mortgage constant, and the required DCR. Using the NOI calculated in Figure 3-7, the next step is to determine cash available for debt service by dividing NOI by the DCR. With an NOI of $2,086,125 and a DCR of 1.20, 4455 Jefferson Avenue can support an annual debt service of $1,738,438. (See Figure 3-8).

The second step converts the cash available for debt service payment into a maximum loan amount by applying the mortgage constant (obtained from capital market lenders), which, in the case of 4455 Jefferson Avenue, is determined to be 10.09 percent (equivalent to the installment needed to amortize a dollar at a 9.5 percent interest rate for a 30-year term on a monthly basis). The cash available for debt service divided by the mortgage constant yields a maximum loan amount of approximately $17,200,000 for 4455 Jefferson Avenue, as shown in Figure 3-8.

(Note that lenders often originate a loan for a set number of years, ten in the 4455 Jefferson Avenue example, but amortize the loan over a longer term. By partially amortizing loans, lenders reduce the risk that the value of the property will not be sufficient to refinance the loan in ten years.)

The importance of the lender's debt coverage ratio in the determination of the size of loans cannot be overstated. Whether the loan is securitized through a CMBS or held as a whole loan by a commercial bank or insurance company, the debt coverage ratio is the critical ratio that lenders use to assess the viability of a project. Figure 3-9 illustrates how dramatically the amount of the loan can vary with changes in the DCR and the mortgage constant.

Loan-to-Value Ratio. The third key lender ratio is the loan-to-value ratio (LTV). The LTV ratio expresses the relationship between the amount of a mortgage loan and the value of the property securing it:

$$LTV = \frac{\text{Loan Amount}}{\text{Property Value}}$$

The LTV assesses the risk of borrower default based on a drop in the value of the property. The higher the loan-to-value ratio, the lower the total equity invested in the property and thus the greater the lender's risk, because borrowers with little equity in troubled projects are more likely to default on the loans.

For projects that are still in the conceptual stage, most lenders use a loan-to-cost ratio (LTC) in place of the LTV. This is calculated as follows:

$$LTC = \frac{\text{Loan Amount}}{\text{Total Construction Budget}}$$

(In this chapter, the term "loan-to-value ratio" is used broadly to apply also to construction projects that use cost rather than anticipated value to calculate a loan-to-value ratio.)

As a matter of policy, banks and insurance companies often mandate specific loan-to-value ratios for their investments in different types of real estate. Federal and state regulators often specify maximum loan-to-value ratios for the real estate investments of regulated institutions like banks and insurance companies.

Cap Rates and DCF Analysis. The value of an office development stems from its cash flow. Lenders and other analysts use two primary methods to estimate the value of real estate income: a back-of-the-envelope calculation using the cap rate or a discounted cash flow analysis.

The capitalization rate (usually known as the cap rate) is the rate of return used to derive the present capital value of the future income stream. The cap rate is usually derived through the analysis of comparable properties sold in the market. The more formal definition of the cap rate is the property's NOI divided by its sales price (NOI/sales price). The higher the perceived risk in the property's cash flow, the higher the cap rate that investors will apply to the estimates of future NOI.

Generally speaking, cap rates for office developments that are fully leased at market rents range from 7 percent to 13 percent. (See Figure 3-10.) Most newer properties in good locations are selling at cap rates in the 8 percent to 9.5 percent range. A number of real estate brokerage, appraisal, and consulting firms publish quarterly compilations of cap rates by property type and market area, based on recent transactions.

The back-of-the-envelope cap rate estimate of value is quick and easy. The project's value is derived as follows:

$$Value = \frac{NOI}{Capitalization\ Rate}$$

The low-risk profile of 4455 Jefferson Avenue earns the project a low 8.75 percent cap rate. Thus, the building's value according to the cap rate method is $23,841,400 (based on an NOI of $2,086,125).

Cap rate valuation is a good starting point. However, small adjustments in the cap rate can return large changes in the value of the property. Therefore, most lenders estimate value by means of a discounted cash flow (DCF) analysis, which more explicitly addresses the cash flow of a property over the life of the loan.

Lenders find DCF analysis helpful in the underwriting process for two reasons. First, it takes many variables into account. DCF analysis can take into account differ-

ences in the growth rates of income and expense categories—item by item. Also, by using a higher reversion cap rate—the cap rate that is applied at the end of the holding period when the property will be sold to the next investor—a DCF analysis can account for physical obsolescence, that is, for the additional risk that the next investor will assign to the purchase of a ten-year-old building. Additionally, certain costs (such as tenant improvements, capital improvements, and leasing commissions) that are not included in NOI can be accounted for in a DCF analysis. The second reason why lenders find DCF analysis helpful is that they can assess a property's cash flows in each year (or month) during the term of the loan. (DCF analysis is covered in more detail in Chapter 2.)

A DCF analysis by the permanent lender for 4455 Jefferson Avenue is shown in Figure 3-11. Although the term of the loan is ten years, an 11-year cash flow stream is calculated in order to permit a calculation of the value of the property using the NOI in the first year of operations under a new owner, which occurs in year 11. The next investor will be interested in the cash flow that will be available in the first year that it owns and operates the property rather than in the income that was available to the prior owner.

Dividing the year-11 NOI ($2,761,000) by a reversion cap rate of 9.25 percent yields a property value of $29,850,000 at the end of the tenth year. A 12 percent discount rate applied to the annual cash flows and the reversion sales price returns a present value of $22,422,000 for 4455 Jefferson, significantly below the $23,841,400 that was calculated as the project's value using the direct cap rate approach. The DCF approach yields a lower value primarily because the reversion cap rate (9.25 percent) is higher than the current cap rate (8.75 percent) in order

figure 3-10
Average CBD and Suburban Office Capitalization Rates, 1989–1997[1]

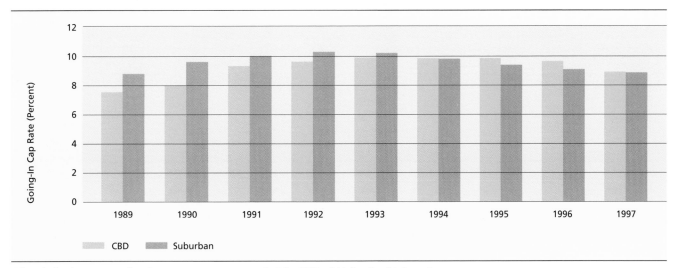

¹All capitalization rates are fourth-quarter averages except that for 1997, which is a the third-quarter average.

Source: Real Estate Research Corporation.

to account for property obsolescence, and also because it subtracts the selling cost from the cash flow.

Now that the lender has an estimated value (or two) for 4455 Jefferson Avenue, it can apply its LTV to determine a maximum loan amount. (See also the discussion on determining the maximum loan amount by means of the debt coverage ratio earlier in this section.) Because the entire building is leased to a single, creditworthy tenant and the lease period (15 years) is longer than the loan term (ten years), the lender is willing to loan up to 80 percent of the value of the building. Rearranging the LTV equation to solve for loan amount produces the following:

Loan Amount = LTV X Property Value
$17,937,600 = .80 X $22,422,000

Based on a DCF analysis of property value and using the LTV approach, the maximum loan for 4455 Jefferson Avenue is $17,937,600. Since this is a proposed development, the lender would also review the loan-to-cost ratio (LTC) to make certain that a minimum amount of equity—an equity cushion—is contributed to the project. In this case, the equity cushion requirement is 20 percent of the property value.

Making Sense of Lender Ratios

The process of underwriting 4455 Jefferson Avenue has been described, but what does it all mean? In short, it means that based on the value of the property the lender is willing to loan a maximum of $17,937,600, and based on the property's cash flow and current interest rates the lender can justify a maximum loan of $17,200,000.

How does the lender reconcile the two values? Recall that the loan-to-value ratio and debt coverage ratio assess two very different risks. The LTV addresses the preservation of the loan principal. It tells the lender how far the value of the property can fall before the principal balance of the loan is at risk. The DCR addresses the sufficiency of the income generated by the project to support the debt service. Because the two ratios assess such different risks, lenders tend to use the lower of the maximum loan amounts in their loan decisions.

figure 3-11
4455 Jefferson Avenue: Permanent Lender's Discounted Cash Flow Analysis

Thousands of Dollars

	Year 1	Year 2	Year 3	Year 4	Year 5	Year 6	Year 7	Year 8	Year 9	Year 10	Year 11
Revenue											
(a) Gross Rent	$3,413	$3.481	$3,550	$3,621	$3,694	$3,768	$3,843	$3,920	$3,998	$4,078	$4,159
(b) Expense Pass-Throughs	0	46	93	143	194	248	304	362	422	486	552
(c) Parking Income	125	129	134	139	143	148	154	159	164	170	176
(d) Potential Gross Income	3,538	3,656	3,777	3,902	4,031	4,164	4,301	4,441	4,586	4,734	4,888
(e) Vacancy Credit/Loss	248	256	264	273	282	291	301	311	321	331	342
(f) Effective Gross Income	$3,290	$3,400	$3,513	$3,629	$3,749	$3,872	$4,000	$4,130	$4,264	$4,403	$4,546
Expenses											
(g) Operating Expenses	$735	$761	$878	$815	$843	$873	$904	$935	$968	$1,002	$1,037
(h) Real Estate Taxes	398	418	439	461	484	508	533	560	588	617	648
(i) Cash Reserves for Replacements	71	73	76	78	81	84	87	90	93	96	100
(j) Total Expenses	$1,204	$1,252	$1,302	$1,354	$1,408	$1,465	$1,524	$1,585	$1,649	$1,716	$1,785
(k) Net Operating Income	$2,086	$2,148	$2,211	$2,275	$2,341	$2,408	$2,476	$2,545	$2,616	$2,688	$2,761
(l) Tenant Improvements	0	0	0	0	0	0	0	0	0	0	0
(m) Leasing Commissions	0	0	0	0	0	0	0	0	0	0	0
Return Analysis											
(n) Property Cash Flow	$2,086	$2,148	$2,211	$2,275	$2,341	$2,408	$2,476	$2,545	$2,616	$2,688	$2,761
(o) Reversion Sales Price	N/A	N/A	N/A	N/A	N/A	N/A	N/A	N/A	N/A	29,850	N/A
(p) Selling Cost	N/A	N/A	N/A	N/A	N/A	N/A	N/A	N/A	N/A	896	N/A
(q) Cash Flow	$2,086	$2,148	$2,211	$2,275	$2,341	$2,408	$2,476	$2,545	$2,616	$31,642	$2,761
(r) Present Value of Cash Flow (at 12% discount rate): $22,422											

Assumptions: Rent growth rate per year: 2.0%. Operating expense growth rate per year: 3.5 %. Vacancy: 7.0%. Real estate tax growth rate per year: 5.0%. Sales commission: 3.0%. Reversion cap rate: 9.25%.

Gramercy Plaza was built for long-term investment, so the key measure of financial success was the project's ability to meet IRR (internal rate of return) targets. Equity invested amounted to 20 percent of development costs, and the goal was to achieve an 11 percent return on equity at full lease-up and a 16 percent IRR.

Mckay Photographics

For 4455 Jefferson Avenue, this is $17,200,000 as derived from the debt coverage ratio. The lender would welcome a loan request by a developer of less than $17,200,000, and it would probably reject a request for an amount in excess of $17,200,000.

Equity Investor Requirements

Except in projects that are perceived as highly risky, such as some adaptive use developments, the lender is likely to supply a majority of the funding for office projects. However, most developers will find that raising equity investment capital is one of the more challenging components of project financing.

Equity investors hold a residual position in a real estate venture, like the owners of common stock in a corporation. The interests of the equity investors are subordinate to the claims that lenders have on the venture's assets. The outstanding debt on the project will always be paid in full before the equity investors receive any return on their investment. Thus, the equity investment in a real estate project is much riskier than the debt investment.

When the property performs poorly, equity investors are in the riskiest position. But when it performs well, they reap most if not all of the upside potential. Equity investors receive benefits in the form of cash flow generated by the project, property value appreciation, and tax advantages. The importance of these benefits varies from project to project, depending on the characteristics of the investor and the type of office development.

It used to be common for office developers to supply the equity investment for their projects, often in the form of land. Today, few developers have sufficient equity capital for a development project and most must solicit equity investors.

Permanent lenders base their feasibility analysis of office projects on a cash flow analysis of the project begin-

ning in the first year of operation. In contrast, equity investors in an office development must assess the return on investment from the time the land is purchased and including the construction period. The following sections consider three office development scenarios—a turnkey development, a build-to-own development, and a joint venture build-to-own development—from the perspective of the equity investor.

Turnkey Development

A project that is planned to be sold to another investor as soon as it is completed and leased is called a turnkey development. The equity investment in turnkey projects can be supplied by the developer or investors or both. Figure 3-12 provides an equity investment analysis of 4455 Jefferson Avenue as a turnkey development that is sold upon its completion.

The turnkey equity investment analysis shows the quarterly cash flows through the two-year construction period. The developer or investors could have supplied the $4.5 million equity investment (land). Had the developer provided the equity, it would receive a return on this investment (assuming the project is successful) as well as fee income from developing the project.

For the sake of simplicity, Figure 3-12 shows consistent quarterly draws of $1,847,000 on the construction loan. In reality, construction draws are based on the actual cost of the construction completed during each quarter, less a retainer. The retainer is an amount of the cost that the lender does not distribute until construction is complete, to ensure that the developer completes the project according to specifications. The retainer is typically expressed as a percent of the construction completed during the quarter, say 10 percent. Construction draws are usually on a biweekly or monthly schedule.

It is important to keep the lender's position in mind when analyzing the return on the (subordinate) equity investment. Interest on the construction loan is usually accrued during the construction period, meaning that

figure 3-12
4455 Jefferson Avenue: Equity Investor Analysis for Turnkey Development
Thousands of Dollars

	Qtr 0	Qtr 1	Qtr 2	Qtr 3	Qtr 4	Qtr 5	Qtr 6	Qtr 7	Qtr 8
(a) Equity Investment (Land)	$4,500	N/A	N/A	N/A	N/A	N/A	N/A	N/A	N/A
(b) Construction Costs	0	$1,847	$1,847	$1,847	$1,847	$1,847	$1,847	$1,847	$1,847
(c) Cumulative Construction Costs	0	1,847	3,694	5,541	7,388	9,235	11,082	12,929	14,776
(d) Accrued Construction Interest	0	0	46	93	142	192	243	295	348
(e) Cumulative Accrued Construction Interest	0	0	46	139	281	473	716	1,011	1,359
(f) Construction Loan Balance (rows c + e)	0	1,847	3,740	5,680	7,669	9,707	11,797	13,939	16,133
(g) Net Sales Price	N/A	N/A	N/A	N/A	N/A	N/A	N/A	N/A	22,427
(h) Construction Loan Amount	N/A	N/A	N/A	N/A	N/A	N/A	N/A	N/A	16,133
(i) Investor's Cash Flow	(4,500)	0	0	0	0	0	0	0	6,294
(j) Investor's Internal Rate of Return:[1] 17.13%									

[1]Stated on an annual basis and calculated on a quarterly basis.

the lender receives no interest payments until the property is operational. Lines (d) and (e) in Figure 3-12 show accrued interest, which must be included in the balance of the loan (line (f)). For 4455 Jefferson Avenue, the construction loan interest rate is a variable rate that is 1.5 percentage points over the prime rate, which was 8.5 percent when the loan was made. At the end of the construction period, the cumulative accrued interest totals $1,359,000. Clearly, any construction delays can be expensive in terms of additional interest costs.

After eight quarters, 4455 Jefferson Avenue is completed and leased by the single tenant, at which point the construction loan funds all the construction costs and accrued interest. The loan balance of $16,133,000 shown in line (f) represents 78 percent of the total project cost, which includes the $4.5 million for land acquisition (a loan-to-cost ratio of 78 percent). And it represents 72 percent of the anticipated net sales price (line (g)) that was calculated by the permanent lender (for a loan-to-value-ratio of 72 percent).

The investor's cash flow during the construction period is shown in line (i) of Figure 3-12. The investor's only cash outflow was for the land purchase, which occurred in time zero prior to construction. During the construction period, the developer receives loan disbursements that cover construction costs. The return to equity in this development comes when the project is complete. For the first seven quarters the investor receives no return; in the eighth quarter it receives $6,294,000, which is the amount from the sale proceeds that remains after the construction lender is paid in full. The investor's return has two components: the original investment ($4,500,000) and profit ($1,794,000). The investor's profit here represents an internal rate of return (IRR) of 17.13 percent, which is the discount rate that must be paid for $4,500,000 to become $6,294,000 in two years (stated on an annual basis and calculated on a quarterly basis).

Build-to-Own Development
Many developers build office buildings with the expectation of holding the property as an income-producing investment. The investment analysis for a build-to-own development is more complex than for a turnkey project. It requires combining the cash flows from the construction period and the holding period. The build-to-own analysis for 4455 Jefferson Avenue (Figure 3-13) combines information from the turnkey analysis (Figure 3-12) and the permanent lender's discounted cash flow analysis (Figure 3-11).

During the construction of 4455 Jefferson Avenue, the only cash outflow occurs in year zero when the equity investor purchases the land for $4,500,000. At the end of construction in year 2, the construction loan totals $16,133,000, as described in the preceding section. However, the permanent lender that will take out the construction loan determines that a mortgage of $17,200,000 is justified (see preceding section "Making Sense of Lender Ratios").

The $1,067,000 difference between the construction loan and the permanent loan reduces the amount of the equity investment in the project. This amount is entered as a year-2 cash inflow on line (r) in the return analysis section of the investor cash flow analysis.

The year-3 through year-13 cash flow shown in the equity investor's cash flow analysis in Figure 3-13 is equivalent to the cash flow for year 1 through year 11 in the permanent lender's DCF analysis (Figure 3-11), except that the equity investor's analysis includes annual debt service of $1,736,000 (line (n)), which reduces the property cash flow (line (o)).

Similarly, the sale assumptions in both analyses are the same, except that in the investor's analysis the outstanding loan balance of $15,515,000 must be repaid. (The loan on 4455 Jefferson Avenue was for ten years, with a 30-year amortization schedule.) After ten years, the outstanding permanent loan balance is reduced by $1,685,000. Subtracting the cost of selling the building

figure 3-13
4455 Jefferson Avenue: Equity Investor Cash Flow Analysis for Build-to-Own Development

Thousands of Dollars

	Year 0	Year 1	Year 2	Year 3	Year 4	Year 5	Year 6	Year 7	Year 8	Year 9	Year 10	Year 11	Year 12	Year 13
Revenue														
(a) Gross Rent	0	0	0	$3,413	$3,481	$3,550	$3,621	$3,694	$3,768	$3,843	$3,920	$3,998	$4,078	$4,159
(b) Expense Pass-Throughs	0	0	0	0	46	93	143	194	248	304	362	422	486	552
(c) Parking Income	0	0	0	125	129	134	139	143	148	154	159	164	170	176
(d) Potential Gross Income	0	0	0	3,538	3,656	3,777	3,902	4,031	4,164	4,301	4,441	4,586	4,734	4,888
(e) Vacancy Credit/Loss	0	0	0	248	256	264	273	282	291	301	311	321	331	342
(f) Effective Gross Income	0	0	0	$3,290	$3,400	$3,513	$3,629	$3,749	$3,872	$4,000	$4,130	$4,264	$4,403	$4,546
Expenses														
(g) Operating Expenses	0	0	0	$735	$761	$878	$815	$843	$873	$904	$935	$968	$1,002	$1,037
(h) Real Estate Taxes	0	0	0	398	418	439	461	484	508	533	560	588	617	648
(i) Cash Reserves for Replacements	0	0	0	71	73	76	78	81	84	87	90	93	96	100
(j) Total Expenses	0	0	0	$1,204	$1,252	$1,302	$1,354	$1,408	$1,465	$1,524	$1,585	$1,649	$1,716	$1,785
(k) Net Operating Income	0	0	0	$2,086	$2,148	$2,211	$2,275	$2,341	$2,408	$2,476	$2,545	$2,616	$2,688	$2,761
(l) Tenant Improvements	0	0	0	0	0	0	0	0	0	0	0	0	0	N/A
(m) Leasing Commissions	0	0	0	0	0	0	0	0	0	0	0	0	0	N/A
(n) Debt Service	0	0	0	$1,736	$1,736	$1,736	$1,736	$1,736	$1,736	$1,736	$1,736	$1,736	$1,736	N/A
Return Analysis														
(o) Property Cash Flow	0	0	0	$350	$412	$475	$540	$605	$672	$740	$809	$880	$952	N/A
(p) Cash Flow Return[1]	N/A	N/A	N/A	10.2%	12.0%	13.9%	15.7%	17.6%	19.6%	21.6%	23.6%	25.6%	27.7%	N/A
(q) Equity Investment	$4,500	0	0	0	0	0	0	0	0	0	0	0	0	N/A
(r) Proceeds from Takeout Loan	N/A	N/A	$1,067	N/A	N/A	N/A	N/A	N/A	N/A	N/A	N/A	N/A	N/A	N/A
(s) Reversion Sales Price	N/A	N/A	N/A	N/A	N/A	N/A	N/A	N/A	N/A	N/A	N/A	N/A	$29,850	N/A
(t) Selling Cost	N/A	N/A	N/A	N/A	N/A	N/A	N/A	N/A	N/A	N/A	N/A	N/A	$896	N/A
(u) Outstanding Loan Balance	N/A	N/A	N/A	N/A	N/A	N/A	N/A	N/A	N/A	N/A	N/A	N/A	$15,515	N/A
(v) Residual Sale Proceeds	N/A	N/A	N/A	N/A	N/A	N/A	N/A	N/A	N/A	N/A	N/A	N/A	$13,439	N/A
(w) Equity Investor Cash Flow	(4,500)	0	$1,067	$350	$412	$475	$540	$605	$672	$740	$809	$880	$14,391	N/A
(x) Internal Rate of Return: 17.70%														

[1]Cash flow return based on property cash flow (o) divided by the equity investment (q) less the proceeds from the takeout loan (r).

and the outstanding loan balance from the reversion sale price of $29,850,000 leaves the equity investor with $13,439,000 in cash. The equity investor's before-tax cash flow shown on line (w) represents an IRR of 17.7 percent over the 12-year holding period. The investor must determine if this return is sufficient to compensate for the risk involved in undertaking this development.

Joint Venture Build-to-Own Development

Joint ventures are a common method of raising capital for office developments. Usually structured as a limited partnership, a joint venture often pairs a developer (the "knowledge" partner) and a financial institution (the "money" partner). The developer contributes experience, reputation, and possibly equity capital. The money partner brings capital to the table.

The terms and conditions of a joint venture are completely negotiable. At the insistence of the money partner, they often include financial incentives for the knowledge partner to bring the project in on time and on budget. To compensate for bearing most or all of the financial risk in the project, the money partner(s) usually requires a preferred return. That means that the money partner will receive its share of the cash flow before the knowledge partner receives its share. The joint venture cash flow analysis shown in Figure 3-14 shows the equity investor's return on its $4.5 million land investment for 4455 Jefferson Avenue, as well as the developer's return from the satisfaction of various performance incentives.

Three financial incentives appear in the developer return portion of the analysis (lines (o) through (t)): a

figure 3-14
4455 Jefferson Avenue: Equity Investor Cash Flow Analysis for Joint Venture Build-to-Own Development
Thousands of Dollars

	Year 0	Year 1	Year 2	Year 3	Year 4	Year 5	Year 6	Year 7	Year 8	Year 9	Year 10	Year 11	Year 12
Joint Venture Return													
(a) Property Cash Flow	0	0	0	$350	$412	$475	$540	$605	$672	$740	$809	$880	$952
(b) Net Proceeds from Takeout Loan	N/A	N/A	$1,067	N/A	N/A	N/A	N/A	N/A	N/A	N/A	N/A	N/A	N/A
(c) Reversion Sales Price	N/A	N/A	N/A	N/A	N/A	N/A	N/A	N/A	N/A	N/A	N/A	N/A	$29,850
(d) Selling Cost	N/A	N/A	N/A	N/A	N/A	N/A	N/A	N/A	N/A	N/A	N/A	N/A	$896
(e) Outstanding Loan Balance	N/A	N/A	N/A	N/A	N/A	N/A	N/A	N/A	N/A	N/A	N/A	N/A	$15,515
(f) Residual Sale Proceeds for Equity Investor	N/A	N/A	N/A	N/A	N/A	N/A	N/A	N/A	N/A	N/A	N/A	N/A	$13,439
(g) Equity Investment	$4,500	0	0	0	0	0	0	0	0	0	0	0	0
Equity Investor Return													
(h) Proceeds from Takeout Loan Split (50/50)	N/A	N/A	$533	N/A	N/A	N/A	N/A	N/A	N/A	N/A	N/A	N/A	N/A
(i) Cash Flow Split (90/10)	0	0	0	$316	$371	$428	$486	$540	$540	$540	$540	$540	$540
(j) Participation Cash Flow Split (50/50)	0	0	0	0	0	0	0	$6	$39	$73	$108	$143	$179
(k) Return of Investment	0	0	0	0	0	0	0	0	0	0	0	0	$4,500
(l) Sale Proceeds Split (75/25)	0	0	0	0	0	0	0	0	0	0	0	0	$6,704
(m) Equity Investor Cash Flow	($4,500)	0	$533	$316	$371	$428	$486	$546	$579	$613	$648	$683	$11,923
(n) Investor Internal Rate of Return: 14.57%													
Developer Return													
(o) Proceeds from Takeout Loan Split (50/50)	N/A	N/A	$533	N/A	N/A	N/A	N/A	N/A	N/A	N/A	N/A	N/A	N/A
(p) Cash Flow Split (90/10)	0	0	0	$35	$41	$48	$54	$54	$54	$54	$54	$54	$54
(q) Participation Cash Flow Split (50/50)	0	0	0	0	0	0	0	$6	$39	$73	$108	$143	$179
(r) Sale Proceeds Split (75/25)	0	0	0	0	0	0	0	0	0	0	0	0	$2,234
(s) Developer Cash Flow	0	0	$533	$35	$41	$48	$54	$60	$93	$127	$162	$197	$2,467
(t) Present Value of Developer Cash Flow (at 20% discount rate): $840													

completion incentive for the completion of the project on time and on budget; a property management incentive for the efficient operation of the property; and a sale incentive for enhancing the value (sales price) of the property.

The completion incentive is a 50/50 split of the net proceeds from the takeout loan (line (o)). The partnership's split of these proceeds encourages the developer to complete the project on time, because if it is delivered late construction interest will continue to accrue (see Figure 3-12) and reduce the net proceeds from the takeout loan. Similarly, if the property is delivered over budget, the added construction costs will reduce the net proceeds from the takeout.

The property management incentive is a participation agreement that encourages the developer to maximize operational returns. The partners have agreed to split the property cash flow as follows: the annual cash flow will be split 90/10 between the equity investor and the developer until the money partner has received a cash flow return equal to 12 percent of its $4.5 million invest-

ment (or $540,000), and cash flow above the point where it returns $540,000 to the investor will be split 50/50. As can be seen on lines (p) and (q), in the early years of operation the developer receives a relatively small cash flow return. However, by year 7 the developer begins benefiting from a larger share of the cash flows. The money partner should be pleased with this arrangement: it receives a 12 percent cash flow return plus half of all net operating income above $540,000. The knowledge partner is clearly motivated to exceed the 12 percent cash flow performance level in order to participate more fully in the property cash flow.

The sale incentive (line (r)) is structured to encourage the developer to design and build the property well and maintain it in a manner that preserves its physical facilities, so that its value increases over the 12-year holding period. After the $4.5 million equity investment has been returned to the money partner and the selling cost has been deducted and the outstanding loan balance paid off, the partners split the proceeds from the sale of the building 75/25. The developer's 25 percent share gives it much to gain from a significant increase in the building's value.

For the money partner in a joint venture project, the primary measure of investment performance is the internal rate of return (IRR). In the case of 4455 Jefferson Avenue, the investor IRR is 14.57 percent.

The developer invested no money on which a rate of return can be calculated, but the present value of its cash flow return can be stated. Applying a 20 percent discount rate to the developer's cash flows (line (s)) throughout the holding period returns a present value of $840,000. This suggests that if the developer were to sell its interest in the development, it would be worth $840,000. In joint venture projects, the developer is likely to be paid also for construction and development services (costs plus a small profit margin). However, the developer's big payoff comes if the office building is a financial success.

Predevelopment Financing

Office development typically involves a series of financing arrangements—predevelopment financing, short-term construction financing, interim financing, and permanent financing—depending on the project's stage in the development process. As a project progresses through the development process, its investment risk generally diminishes. Therefore, the interest rates and rates of return required by lenders and equity investors decrease the further along a development is. Predevelopment debt and equity carry the most risk and the highest expected returns. Financing the purchase of well-designed and -located office buildings with credit tenants carries very low risk and correspondingly low investment yields. For the developer, the critical point is the necessity of assessing the risk/return orientation of various sources of debt and equity when deciding where to go for financing at each stage.

Much of this chapter on financing has been concerned with the motivations and investment needs of the financial partners in office developments. On the project level, lenders are primarily concerned about two loan risks: loss of loan principal and default (or nonpayment of interest). Lenders try to mitigate the loss-of-principal risk by establishing a safe loan-to-value ratio and the interest-payment risk by setting a conservative debt coverage ratio. On a broader level, lenders are also concerned with matching the maturity of their loan assets with the maturity of their liabilities (such as bank deposits, life insurance claims, and retirement payments). Equity investors, on the other hand, are motivated by cash flow, value appreciation, and tax shelter benefits.

Debt and equity investors differ in the amount of risk they will accept. Consequently, they require different rates of return. Debt investors generally are more risk averse. They are less willing to invest in risky projects. Lenders are usually willing to provide the majority of financing for completed developments that have creditworthy tenants secured on long-term leases. With the rental income stream in place and backed by creditworthy tenants, such properties have a low-risk profile. Equity investors will invest in riskier projects or in the risky portions of projects, but they require a higher rate of return for these investments.

Generally speaking, office projects in the predevelopment stage are the riskiest investment option for two reasons. First, any positive cash flow generation is one or more years in the future. The value of office develop-

The Prime Group Inc. developed and owns the 50-story RR Donnelley Building in downtown Chicago. Equity funding came from Kemper Securities Inc. and debt funds were provided by a consortium of primarily foreign banks.

The Fairmont Plaza Office Building in San Jose, California, was developed jointly by the city's redevelopment agency, Kimball Small Properties (KSP), and Melvin Simon & Associates (MSA). The building is owned by KSP, MSA, and Hart Advisors (a pension fund). The land, garages, ground-level retail, and interior public spaces are owned by the redevelopment agency.

Courtesy of the San Jose Redevelopment Agency

125 Summer Street in Boston was developed by a joint venture between the landowner and Cornerstone Properties. Cornerstone Properties has since become a REIT.

Pacifica Companies

Apple Computer Inc. is the single tenant as well as 50 percent owner of the Apple Research and Development campus in Cupertino, California. In order to ensure long-term financial viability, the project is designed for multi-tenant use at the expiration of Apple's lease.

ments is in their income streams. The more distant the stream of income, the riskier the investment. Second, the probability that any project in the predevelopment stage will be completed and occupied is small compared with the probability that projects in more advanced stages will be completed. At the predevelopment stage, it is difficult to obtain equity financing and next to impossible to obtain debt financing without more collateral than that provided by the site.

A number of predevelopment tasks pose substantial completion risk. Some of these high-risk tasks that may need doing at this stage—and thus require front-end capital—are the rezoning of property to office use, securing tenants, completing conceptual designs, and conducting engineering and other studies.

Typically, developers cover predevelopment costs with their own equity capital. But high-risk, high-return capital may be available, usually from a joint venture partner. The usual joint venture agreement for office development is a limited partnership involving a money partner as the limited partner and the developer as the general partner. But developers can joint venture with other kinds of equity partners, including, for example, a landowner, a public utility seeking to selling a brownfield site, a high-profile corporation wishing to demonstrate its commitment to the community, or the owner of a hard-to-sell building.

The investors in other development projects in the neighborhood are a good potential source of equity in the early stages of a project. Whereas outside parties may view a particular neighborhood as risky, local residents or investors that have already committed development funds there may view the development site differently. Also, the proposed office development may provide some indirect benefit for adjacent or nearby property owners. By enhancing the image of the neighborhood, the proposed development could enhance the financial position of the neighboring sites. For that reason, these local investors may be willing to invest in the proposed development.

Obtaining control of the development site is a predevelopment task that can take many forms, from purchase to option to lease agreement. The financing of these alternative approaches to site control is discussed in the following sections. Whatever the approach, finding the funds to control the site is normally the developer's biggest financial hurdle in the predevelopment stage.

Land Acquisition

A variety of sources provide land acquisition funds for office development. Commercial banks are a preferred source of land loans, which they will make mostly to borrowers with other collateral or strong credit histories. S&Ls provide loan funds, but they tend to concentrate on improved sites. Some REITs and financial services companies provide land acquisition financing. Mortgage companies and life insurance companies infrequently finance land acquisition, and when they do it is with the hope of becoming the construction lender and permanent lender. These companies sometimes charge penalties ranging from 0.5 percent to 2 percent of the land acquisition and development loan if they are not the subsequent lender.

Banks, S&Ls, and other sources of debt financing for land acquisition and development invariably offer recourse loans, which are loans that make other assets of the borrower available as collateral for the loan. For the developer, this is risky business. By pledging other assets as collateral for a land acquisition or construction loan, the developer, in essence, places debt against the other collateral to raise capital for the development. A developer who personally signs a recourse loan is usually pledging all of his or her personal net worth as collateral for the loan.

The landowner can provide financing for the land. Such financing is typically in the form of a seller-financed loan (known as a purchase money mortgage) providing 70 to 90 percent of the sales price, with the developer contributing the balance in equity capital. The deed to

A prototype for later large-scale urban mixed-use developments, Rockefeller Center has been a landmark property in New York City for more than 60 years. Located in the middle of Manhattan just a few blocks from Central Park, the 12-building art deco complex was built by John D. Rockefeller Jr. in the 1930s in the depths of the Great Depression. The original property comprised 7 million square feet of space. Although it has been a commercial success since it was built, in the mid-1980s this venerable property became an object lesson in the dangers of inflated projections of rental rate growth and other overly optimistic assumptions.

In 1985, the Rockefeller family trusts sought to liquefy their holdings in Rockefeller Center. With the advisement of Goldman Sachs & Company, they transferred ownership to two partnerships owned by Rockefeller Group Inc. (RGI). A public REIT—Rockefeller Center Properties Inc. (RCPI)—was created to fund the mortgage. The mortgage on Rockefeller Center would be the RCPI's principal asset. The mortgage was scheduled to mature

in December 2007, but RCPI would retain the option of converting the mortgage to a 71.5 percent limited partnership interest in December 2000. Investors eagerly purchased shares in the REIT at $20 apiece, and RCPI raised $750 million in stock and $550 million in convertible bonds. The Rockefeller family trusts took about $250 million out of the deal.

Because of the large mortgage created by the REIT financing, it appeared that the property's cash flow would be about $250 million short of covering the mortgage's scheduled interest payments over the next nine years, a shortfall that RGI would have to make up. In light of the fact that about 40 percent of Rockefeller Center's long-term leases would be up for renewal in 1994, the prospectus downplayed this shortfall. At the time of the offering, New York was in the midst of a real estate boom with rents averaging about $45 per square foot. The prospectus projected midtown rents would increase by 6 percent annually, reaching $75 per square foot by 1995 and more than $100 per square foot by 2000. Based on these optimistic rent projections, the prospectus concluded that the value of Rockefeller Center could rise from its 1985 appraised value of $1.6 billion to between $3 billion and $5 billion by 2000.

In 1989, confident of the revenue increases to come and desirous of owning such a high-profile property, Mitsubishi Estate paid $1.4 billion to purchase a 51 percent interest in RGI. While RGI held some other high-profile assets, Rockefeller Center was clearly the plum property to which Mitsubishi aspired.

By 1994, however, it was clear that the rent projections foretold in the REIT prospectus would not be realized. The real estate market crash of the early 1990s drove rents down in the New York market. Rather than rising to $75 per square foot as predicted, rental rates for Class A space in midtown plummeted to about $30 per square foot. Rockefeller Center's appraised value dropped to just over $1 billion. The $250 million shortfall in the property's cash flow available for debt service spiraled to $600 million, and the prospects for stronger rents were not rosy.

Some unfortunate management decisions by RCPI aggravated the problems. In 1987, RCPI had taken out short-term loans—financed by commercial paper and backed by letters of credit—to retire some of the debt issued two years earlier. But when Rockefeller Center's appraised value dropped by several hundred million dollars in 1994, the banks declined to renew or they reduced their letters of credit. Without the letters of credit, RCPI would be unable to turn over the commercial paper by year's end.

Desperate to refinance the commercial paper by the end of the year, RCPI entered into a questionable and expen-

RGI 1997

Overly optimistic rent projections made in the late 1980s led to problems down the road for shareholders of the REIT that owned Manhattan's landmark Rockefeller Center.

The world-famous plaza at Rockefeller Center at Christmas time.

sive deal with Goldman, Sachs in December 1994. Goldman provided RCPI with $225 million, $150 million of which would be senior debt at the London interbank offered rate (LIBOR) plus 4 percentage points. The remaining $75 million was in 14 percent junior bonds due in 2007 and prepayable only with a 5 percent penalty. Goldman also received a seat on RCPI 's board and warrants and stock appreciation rights that were worth almost 20 percent of the REIT. Additionally, a cash sweep provision guaranteed that any cash flow above a certain level would have to be applied to paying down the Goldman debt.

A subsequent attempt by RGI to buy out RCPI failed as Mitsubishi and the various Rockefeller family trusts could not come to terms on the financing. In May 1995, Mitsubishi put Rockefeller Center into bankruptcy and the property defaulted on its loan. RCPI was now in position to take over Rockefeller Center, but faced a cash flow problem.

Goldman proposed several refinancing schemes, each of which would have been expensive for RCPI and given a larger stake to Goldman. By now RCPI was seeking to

reduce its leverage and extricate itself from the December 1994 deal. RCPI attempted several subsequent deals led by investor Sam Zell, none of which was successful. Goldman's position made it too expensive for an outside entity to purchase RCPI. But a chorus of critics led by Zell complained that Goldman's terms were onerous and had placed the investment bank in a position of potential conflict of interest (as both a lender to RCPI and a member of its board).

RCPI eventually agreed to a buyout at $8 a share from a consortium that included Goldman Sachs, David Rockefeller, Jerry Speyer, and the Agnelli and Niarchos families. Rockefeller's interest in returning to the property was in part to ensure that individual properties would not be split off from Rockefeller Center.

Ultimately, the biggest losers were Mitsubishi and the individual shareholders. Enticed by the prospect of huge returns in the midst of a market boom, these investors failed to look at the rent projections realistically. This failure to objectively read the market's future was an expensive lesson for many.

■

the land is transferred to the developer if the developer meets specific conditions and makes the required periodic payments. Seller financing can be an attractive option for the seller, who can report the transaction as an installment sale and thus defer income taxes. Seller financing can also be an attractive alternative for the developer, which needs to raise only 10 to 30 percent of the land value to control the site for development.

In the purchase money mortgage, the seller/lender may agree to a subordination clause that makes the seller a second-lien holder on the property. By enabling a financial institution to take a first-lien position, the seller makes it possible for the developer to obtain construction financing. Almost without exception, construction lenders require that they have the first lien against the property, guaranteeing in most instances that they will receive all property liquidation proceeds until the construction loan is paid off in full. Only after the first lien is paid in full will the second-lien holder receive any proceeds. Subordination makes seller financing much riskier, and, to compensate, sellers usually require a higher price for the land or an interest-rate premium. Construction lenders and permanent lenders include the debt service payments on seller-financed loans in their calculation of the debt coverage ratio. And if seller financing is in place, construction lenders almost always lower the amount of the loan they will make.

Despite the problems it poses for construction lenders, seller financing can be one of the best alternatives for a cash-strapped developer because of the leverage—the use of borrowed funds to finance the development—that it offers. The confidence that land sellers have about the potential of their land is likely to translate into seller financing that provides a higher degree of leverage for the developer than any available alternative for financing land acquisition. A developer with few assets and little capital may find that seller financing is the only way to obtain title to the land. But, as the next two sections illustrate, ownership is not the only way by which the developer can gain control the land. Other strategies for land control include land purchase options and ground leases.

Land Purchase Option

Under a land purchase option, a developer agrees to pay a landowner a relatively small, nonrefundable cash payment to take the land off the market during a specified option period. The cash payment, which often ranges from 1 percent to 10 percent of the land value, can take a variety of forms. It may be a lump sum paid at the time the agreement is signed. It can take the form of debt service payments on the land loan during the option period. Some land purchase options include bonus payments to the landowner if the property is rezoned successfully to accommodate the use(s) the developer proposes.

A land purchase option is a relatively low-risk method of controlling the site before committing significant resources to the project. While the site is under option, the developer can work on other steps in the development process, like further land assembly, government approvals, rezoning, environmental assessment, due diligence, the signing of anchor tenants, and project financing. If the needed zoning, approvals, tenants, and so forth are forthcoming, the developer exercises the option and commences construction. If, on the other hand, conditions do not favor proceeding with the project, the developer walks away from the option, leaving its nonrefundable deposit with the landowner. Some short-term option agreements require a refund of the deposit according to provisions in the agreement.

Option contracts include a sale contract for the land, but the seller retains ownership until the option is exercised. If the option is exercised, the option payment is usually applied to the sales price. The contract spells out the option price and purchase price, the terms and conditions of the option, how the option can be exercised, how it may be extended, the developer's right of access, the landowner's responsibility to cooperate, and much more. Among the variety of land purchase options that a developer might encounter are the following:

- Straight Option—An owner agrees to sell the land to the developer during a specific period for a set price.
- Escalating Option—Additional nonrefundable payments are required over time to keep the option open.
- Purchase Price Variant of an Escalating Option—The purchase price escalates if the land purchase option is extended in time or if the value of the land is increased through zoning changes or municipal variances.
- Rolling Option—Larger land tracts can be purchased in stages.
- Lease and Re-lease Option—The developer leases the land from the seller for a period of time after which the developer can re-lease or purchase the land.
- Declining Balance Option—A smaller portion of the option payment is applied to the purchase price as the option period goes on, creating an incentive for the developer to exercise the option early.

Ground Lease

Ground leases constitute another method of financing the land component of an office project. Instead of purchasing the land, the developer rents it for a long period of time. A ground lease can protect the long-term financial interests of the landowner while it enables the developer to begin the project with minimal capital.

In a typical ground lease the rental payments are based on the value of the land. Improvements usually are not included in a ground lease. (Lease agreements that cover land and improvements, such as some master leases, are not referred to as ground leases.) Lease terms are typically long (from 25 to 99 years), and the agreement usually contains a provision to extend the lease. A ground lease is usually structured as an absolute net lease, meaning that the lessee is responsible for all expenses associated with the property. Land rents usually escalate according to a predetermined schedule, an agreed index such as the CPI, or changes in the property's rental income.

The developer of Resurgens Plaza in Atlanta leased the airspace over a rail station from the regional transit authority. On less than one acre of land, it erected an economically viable, tax generating, architecturally significant structure.

The use of a ground lease offers advantages and disadvantages to the developer. Among the advantages are that no down payment on the land is needed; the developer's leverage is increased; the developer can sublease the land; and the lease payments are deductible for federal income tax purposes.

From the developer's perspective, ground leases have some disadvantages as well. A ground lease can be difficult to negotiate. It is possible for the escalations in ground rent to grow faster than the building's cash flow. The developer does not participate in future land appreciation. And when the lease term ends, the improvements revert to the landowner. (If the improvements are expected to have value at reversion, the ground lease frequently includes a provision that the developer be paid for the value of the improvements.)

From the landowner's perspective, a ground lease also offers advantages and disadvantages. Among the advantages: a possibly significant improvement in the value

of the land over time; a stream of income that entails few management responsibilities; and ownership of the improvements at the end of the lease. Among the disadvantages to the landowner: the possibility of default by the lessee; less control over the land; and forgone development opportunities during the ground lease period.

Once the developer has secured control of the land, obtained any necessary zoning and planning changes, and met preleasing requirements, it is ready to commence construction—if construction financing has been arranged.

Construction Financing

Commercial banks traditionally have been the primary source of financing for office construction. They still are, but alternatives to bank-financed construction loans are available. Developers can obtain construction loans from pension funds, life insurance companies, and other non-bank lenders that are more known for their role as providers of permanent financing. Larger, well-capitalized developers can issue commercial paper (short-term, unsecured promissory notes) to finance construction. A few well-capitalized developers use only equity to fund the construction of their office projects.

In their search for a construction loan, many office developers look first at local and regional banks. For large projects, national banks and consortiums of banks are likely sources. Construction lenders generally require some preconstruction leasing. The preleasing requirement often ranges from 30 percent to 70 percent of the building's space, depending on market conditions and the developer's experience.

While the real estate asset is typically what is offered as collateral for a construction loan, negotiations between the lender and the developer ultimately determine what secures the loan. An office development's collateral value is based on the cash flow that it is expected to generate upon completion. The collateral value of an unbuilt project may be only a fraction of its completed and fully leased value.

Nonrecourse construction loans put the lender in a risky position during construction and lease-up, because in a foreclosure action it has recourse only to the real estate that secures the loan and not to any other assets of the borrower. However, ever since the real estate mar-ket crash of the early 1990s, construction lenders have routinely sought personal liability or recourse for loans. (Permanent lenders as well have sought at least partial liability for takeout loans.)

The following sections describe the major sources of construction financing for office developers: commercial banks, S&Ls, credit companies, corporate debt, and mortgage bankers and brokers.

Commercial Banks

The dominance of commercial banks in nonresidential real estate lending has grown in the last 15 years. At the end of 1996, banks held about $430 billion in commercial real estate mortgages, which was 41 percent of outstanding commercial mortgages in the United States. (See Figure 3-15.) The large size of banks' real estate loan portfolios has been a matter of concern to investors, debt rating agencies, and government regulators since the late 1980s, when widespread problems in commercial real estate lending surfaced. Despite this concern, banks are likely to remain the dominant debt financier for commercial real estate in the near term. Banks are the only institution around with extensive commercial lending experience at the local level and with ties to regional and national mortgage conduits and loan participation networks.

In their effort to match the generally short-term nature of their primary liabilities (checking account and savings deposits), banks traditionally have concentrated on assets

Plaza East in Milwaukee, a joint venture between Urban Investment & Development Company and Mortgage Guarantee Insurance Corporation, was constructed on a line of credit from First National Bank of Chicago.

with a short-term maturity, like construction loans. The interest rate on most short-term bank loans is tied to money-market rates. Developers should assess the prospect for changes in money-market interest rates when they are estimating construction interest costs.

The terms of construction loans range generally from six months to three years. Developers of large or multiphase projects that require longer-term construction loans may obtain them from a consortium of lenders that may be formed to share the risk of a large loan or a loan with a long time horizon.

Reflecting the higher risk of construction loans, the interest rate is usually higher than on permanent loans. Construction loan rates usually range from 0.5 to 2.0 percentage points above the prime rate (the short-term interest rate banks charge their most creditworthy commercial customers), but they may be as high as 6.0 percentage points above the prime rate depending on market conditions and the bank's assessment of the credit risk posed by the project or the developer. Upfront loan fees (expressed as "points," with one point being equivalent to 1 percent of the loan amount) also vary with the market and the perceived risk of the project or the developer. A charge of one to two points is common on most construction loans. An additional point frequently is charged to extend the loan to accommodate construction delays or a difficult lease-up period.

As was discussed earlier in this chapter (and shown in Figure 3-12), rather than requiring periodic interest payments, most construction loan agreements call for interest to accrue through the construction period. When construction is complete and the building is leased up, the developer obtains a permanent loan or sells the project and, at that point, pays off the total loan amount, which includes the accrued interest and the principal balance.

Banks have changed their construction lending practices dramatically over the past decade. They have become much more concerned about loan repayment in the underwriting process. Thus they have increased prelease requirements and required borrowers to invest more equity. Banks have become key participants in the growth of commercial mortgage conduits, entities that specialize in mortgage origination, mortgage pooling, and the issuance of mortgage-backed securities. (See "Commercial Mortgage–Backed Securities" section later in this chapter for more detail on commercial mortgage conduits.) The relatively newfound ability of banks to sell the mortgages that they originate to investors frees them from having to focus on short-term loans to match their assets, and therefore empowers them to provide a wider variety of loans, including interim and permanent loans. Still, banks underwrite loans destined for commercial mortgage conduits in much the same way, if not in exactly the same way, as they underwrite loans that will be held in their own portfolios.

Savings and Loan Associations

The reputation of S&Ls as thrift institutions—places in which thrifty individuals could safeguard their savings—

figure 3-15

Outstanding Commercial Mortgage Debt, 1996

	Amount (Billions of Dollars)	Share (Percent)
Commercial Banks	$430.2	41%
Life Insurance Companies	192.1	18
Savings Associations	135.8	13
Foreign Investors	111.0	11
Nongovernment CMBS[1] Issuers	91.0	9
Federally Related Mortgage Pools	32.4	3
Pension Funds	28.7	3
REITs[2]	16.2	2
Other	11.8	1
Total	**$1,049.2**	**100%**

[1]Commercial mortgage–backed securities.

[2]Real estate investment trusts.

Source: Equitable Real Estate Investment Management.

took a beating in the late 1980s and early 1990s when scores of thrifts failed from the weight of poor lending decisions. Commercial real estate lending was a major culprit.

Savings and loans used to specialize in long-term home mortgages, using their depositors' passbook and other short-term accounts to fund them. In the late 1970s and early 1980s, however, interest rates rose to historically high levels and short-term rates exceeded long-term rates. The profitability of S&Ls began sinking, and the federal government—which insured S&L deposits through the Federal Savings and Loan Insurance Corporation (FSLIC)—responded by allowing S&Ls to broaden their lending activities and removing interest rate ceilings on their deposits.

Emboldened by rising deposits, the removal of investment restrictions, and the safety net of federal insurance, many S&Ls moved into the commercial real estate business and made risky loans on office and other development projects. Arguably, they did not fully understand the risks. The deterioration of the commercial real estate market in the last half of the 1980s sparked that period's thrift crisis.

Because the federal government insured the deposits, U.S. taxpayers bore the brunt of the damage. The FSLIC was dismantled and its regulatory duties handed over to the Resolution Trust Corporation (RTC), a government corporation created by the Financial Institutions Reform, Recovery and Enforcement Act of 1989 (FIRREA). New rules were promulgated for S&Ls. These institutions still can make land, construction and permanent loans for office buildings, but the strict parameters imposed by FIRREA have reduced their participation in the commercial mortgage market. In 1996, S&Ls held $135.8

billion or 13 percent of outstanding commercial mortgages. S&Ls are not expected to become more active as commercial real estate development lenders in the future.[1]

Credit Companies

Some large U.S. corporations use their power in financial markets to establish entities known as credit companies that issue low-cost debt and relend the money to entrepreneurs. Some of these companies, such as GE Capital and General Motors Acceptance Corporation, provide construction and redevelopment financing. Credit companies profit on the spread between the cost of their funds and the interest rate they charge on loans to developers.

Compared with bank and S&L financing, the lending activities of credit companies are less entangled in federal regulatory oversight. The federal government regulates the investments of banks and S&Ls in order to protect the safety of their (federally insured) deposits. Because credit companies' source of funds is not the deposits of individuals, they are not subject to this kind of regulation. Therefore, they often are willing to lend on projects that are too complex, too risky, or otherwise outside the lending parameters of banks and thrifts.

Corporate Debt

In some cases, corporate debt is also available to finance development directly. Large construction and real estate development companies can issue rated corporate debt, which is debt that is secured by the full faith and credit of the company and is not collateralized by a single project. This money can be used to support land acquisition and development. Corporate debt does not necessarily mature when the projects that it supports are complete.

Corporate debt is a potentially longer-term source of funds than construction mortgages. Development companies can finance several projects with one debt issuance, thereby avoiding the points and fees they would have to pay for loans secured on a project-by-project basis. As a share of total debt financing for real estate development, the amount of debt issued by corporations for development purposes is quite small. However, the use of this type of financing is likely to grow.

Mortgage Bankers and Brokers

Mortgage bankers originate real estate loans, which they then sell to institutions or securities dealers. Mortgage bankers have been a major force behind the growth of the commercial mortgage–backed securities (CMBS) market, which is covered in more detail later in this chapter. They have acted as deal makers in this market, both soliciting business from developers and issuing debt. To date, few construction loans have been pooled as CMBSs and sold on Wall Street. Many observers, however, think that once investors become comfortable with securities based on pools of permanent loans, the pooling of construction loans will be the next step in mortgage securitization.

Mortgage brokers do not lend money. They act as intermediary or conduit between the lender and the developer. They solicit business from developers. They often represent a variety of debt sources, to which they can shop a loan proposal to find the best fit. Brokers' fees are negotiable, typically ranging from 0.25 percent to 1.5 percent of the loan amount and decreasing as the amount of the loan increases. Mortgage brokers generally do not service the loan. Their involvement in the lending process usually ends with the loan's closing.

Interim Financing

Interim financing bridges the gap between construction loans and permanent loans—when such a gap exists. Most construction loans are for projects on which the developer has a permanent loan (or takeout loan) commitment. If all construction loans included an unconditional takeout agreement, the need for interim financing would disappear. But sometimes, obtaining a forward permanent loan commitment is not possible or not advisable for the developer or for the lender. Alternatively, it is possible that when the project is complete the permanent lender will not fund the takeout loan commitment because certain conditions have not been met.

Broadly speaking, permanent lenders require that two conditions be met before they will fund the takeout of the construction loan. The building must be built as specified in the architectural and engineering drawings, in order not to compromise its collateral value. And the NOI must be adequate to service the debt, which means that the building must be leased up sufficiently to meet the lender's minimum debt coverage ratio.

Developers may have to arrange interim financing when no takeout exists or when the construction lender needs assurance that the funds to repay the construction loan will be available even if the requirements of the permanent lender are not met. It is the construction lenders that usually provide interim financing when it is needed.

Thus some construction lenders—especially commercial banks—will commit to convert their construction loans, if necessary, to short-term permanent loans called miniperms, with three- to seven-year maturities.

Committing to interim financing can be a risky proposition. To compensate for the risk, the interim lender often exacts a fee at the time the construction loan is closed and also charges a high risk premium if the interim commitment needs to be funded. The interest rate is likely to be less than the rate on the construction loan and more than the rate on permanent loans on other office projects. From the developer's perspective, an interim loan buys time for the project in the marketplace.

Permanent Financing

Long-term loans on real estate are called "permanent" loans. Historically, the primary sources of long-term debt

LCOR Inc. developed and owns One Penn Square West, a 25-story office building in downtown Philadelphia. The Philadelphia National Bank provided the construction loan and Kennedy Associates, a pension adviser, provided permanent financing.

James Oesch Photography

financing for office development have been life insurance companies and pension funds, with commercial banks playing a limited role. When real estate values dropped in the early 1990s, insurance companies withdrew from the permanent loan market leaving developers, property owners, and the Resolution Trust Corporation (RTC) without a reliable source of long-term property financing. This lack of capital pushed up the financial returns on long-term permanent loans, which lured Wall Street investors into the market. Now commercial mortgage–backed securities (CMBSs) are an important source of funds in the permanent financing landscape.

Permanent loans generally are underwritten with a loan-to-value ratio in the range of 70 percent to 85 percent and a debt coverage ratio of 1.15 to 1.40, depending on the riskiness of the property's long-term value and cash flow. The permanent lender's LTV and debt coverage ratios are of critical importance to the construction lender because, if the completed project falls short of leasing

projections or property value estimates, the permanent lender will be unwilling to take out the construction loan.

Developers usually arrange the permanent financing before they seek a construction loan. When a permanent financing commitment is in place, it is much easier to obtain a construction loan. In most instances, the construction loan's principal and accrued interest both are paid from the takeout loan. Thus, a takeout commitment improves the construction lender's risk position. (As has been noted, takeout commitments are conditioned on the adequacy of the construction and the success of the leasing.) The interest rates on construction loans are typically higher than on permanent loans, giving the developer an incentive to replace the construction loan as soon as possible.

By providing long-term capital, the permanent lender assumes some of the project's long-term market risks. Historically, permanent financing was expected to remain in place through more than one market cycle. The typical loan was for a 30-year term on a fixed-rate, fully amortized basis. More recently, most permanent lenders have attempted to reduce the refinancing risk or the risk that the property's value might fall over time by shortening their loan terms to between five and ten years, and by using a 30-year amortization schedule on these shorter-term loans.

Long-term financing is commonly provided in the form of a mortgage or a trust deed, both of which involve the commitment of property as collateral for the repayment of the loan. Mortgages come in many forms, among which are the following:

- Fixed-Rate Mortgage—The interest rate is held constant during the loan term.
- Variable-Rate Mortgage—The interest rate is tied to an index. Also known as an adjustable-rate mortgage, this instrument protects lenders against rising interest rates and inflation.
- Blanket Mortgage—A single mortgage covers multiple properties, and a release provision allows individual properties to be unmortgaged without retiring the whole mortgage.
- Package Mortgage—Personal (non–real estate) items may be included in the loan.
- Open-End Mortgage—The borrower may obtain additional funds at a later date.

The dominant sources of permanent financing are life insurance companies, pension funds, and Wall Street in the form of commercial mortgage–backed securities. Each of these sources along with a variety of other sources is discussed in the following sections.

Life Insurance Companies

Life insurance companies are able to invest a large amount of capital in long-term mortgages because their cash flow is continuous and predictable. They receive a constant flow of funds from premium payments and they can accurately predict their future outlays from actuarial

figure 3-16
Pension Fund Real Estate Assets, 1993–1996

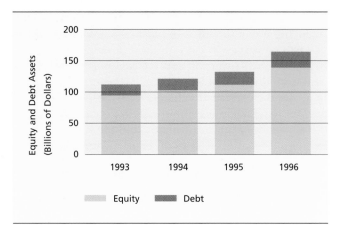

Source: Institutional Real Estate Inc./Roulac Group.

tables. Life insurance companies are a principal source of permanent financing for office development.

Life insurance companies took a hit along with other lenders and investors when the bubble burst from the overbuilding of the 1980s and the value of commercial real estate declined. Since then, new government regulations, new industry standards, and pressure from investors have led life insurance companies to reduce the proportion of their assets held in mortgage loans. Life insurance companies once held one-third of their total assets in mortgages. In 1990, their total commercial mortgage holdings peaked at $255 billion and these have declined since then—to about $192 million in 1996.[2] Despite their recent pullback, life insurance companies remain the second largest institutional provider of commercial mortgages. (Banks are first.) They should continue to be a significant source of permanent loans for office development.

Life insurance companies are also becoming major investors in CMBSs, a growing source of long-term debt financing for office development.

Commercial Mortgage–Backed Securities

Commercial mortgage–backed securities (CMBSs) are bonds collateralized by commercial property loans. As was noted earlier in this chapter, most of the mortgages in CMBS pools are permanent loans, but the use of construction loans as CMBS collateral is expected to grow. CMBSs are a vehicle that channels investor dollars into commercial property loans.

The loans that find their way into CMBS pools are originated by a variety of lenders and debt intermediaries. The recipients of these loans have little if any knowledge of who are the bondholders, the ultimate source of the funding that they receive. Commercial banks, insurance companies, mortgage bankers, and mortgage brokers, among others, are primary originators of such loans. Banks and mortgage bankers are active participants in the securitization process. Life insurance companies are

major investors in CMBSs, which are a much more liquid form of real estate investment than are whole loans.

In securitizing loans, banks and mortgage bankers do not actually supply the funds that flow to the projects for which the loans were originated. They are middlemen, matching sources of long-term debt with users of long-term debt. Private CMBS issuers, or real estate mortgage investment conduits (REMICs), increased their commercial mortgage holdings from $6 billion in 1990 to $91 billion in 1996.[3]

A number of large commercial banks, including Wells Fargo, Chase, Bank One, First Union, and NationsBank, have established their own conduit operations in which some of the loans that they underwrite, originate, and service are pooled and sold in the form of mortgage-backed bonds on Wall Street. Although banks do not hold these loans for investment purposes, they underwrite them using the same ratios that they use for underwriting loans in their own portfolios.

CMBSs are a relatively new source of long-term real estate debt. From all indications, they will continue to grow in volume and in their share of the total market for permanent loan financing.

Pension Funds

After passage of the Employee Retirement Income Security Act of 1974 (ERISA), which required pension funds to diversify their investments (which at that time were mostly stocks and bonds), these funds, often through advisers, began to invest in high-quality real estate assets, including office buildings. Their real estate investments include both debt and equity.

Pension funds provide a significant source of equity for commercial real estate development. (See Figure 3-16.) Like life insurance companies, pension funds have long-term and relatively predictable liabilities that correspond well with real estate assets. Total pension fund assets in 1996 were about $4.6 trillion, with $155 billion—about 3 percent of total assets—invested in real estate.[4]

In the late 1970s and the 1980s, high inflation and the chance to diversify assets made real estate an attractive investment for pension funds. They hired advisers and moved into real estate. Investing continued until the early 1990s, when market values began plummeting and many funds tried unsuccessfully to divest themselves of poorly performing equity real estate. By the end of 1996, however, as shown in Figure 3-16, the market recovery had encouraged the funds to push their equity investment up to around $120 billion. Meanwhile, their mortgage holdings increased to about $35 billion.[5] In addition to direct investment, some funds are now investing in more liquid commercial mortgage–backed securities. Furthermore, recent regulatory changes allow pension funds to invest in REIT stocks.

Pension funds remain an important source of long-term financing for office development. A 1996 survey of pension fund sponsors and their real estate advisers found that most pension funds plan to increase their capital allocations to equity real estate investment over the next five years, by up to 50 percent. Many pension funds will continue to increase the liquidity of their real estate investments by diversifying into securitized mortgage debt.

Other Sources

Among a variety of other sources of long-term office development financing are credit companies, foreign investors, REITs, and municipal bonds.

Credit Companies. Credit companies were described in the "Construction Financing" section earlier in this chapter. Developers often turn to credit companies for permanent financing for unusual or hard-to-underwrite projects. Because they are not subject to the kinds of federal and state regulations that restrict the investment policies of life insurance companies and banks, credit companies can be more flexible about the types of projects to which they lend and the loan structures they establish.

Foreign Investors. U.S. property attracts foreign investment for a number of reasons: the large size of the market, the country's potential for long-term economic growth, U.S. political stability, and the foreign trade deficit. During the 1980s, foreign trading partners with surplus dollars invested heavily in U.S. commercial real estate. In 1988, for example, nearly two-thirds of the Class A office space in downtown Los Angeles was owned by foreigners. Foreign investors owned 20 percent of downtown office space in Chicago; 23 percent in Washington, D.C.; and 21 percent in Manhattan.[6]

Demand for U.S. real estate has varied significantly from year to year. Estimates suggest that foreign investment in U.S. real estate increased in the early 1980s, and moderated and then picked up again from 1983 to 1985. Foreign investment went through a number of cycles from 1985 until the early 1990s, when it declined appreciably, as the value of all U.S. real estate dropped and foreign investors sold off their U.S. holdings. In 1994, foreigners owned 2.5 percent of the value of U.S. real estate.

The Japanese were the most active foreign investors in real estate during the 1980s. In fact, much of the growth in foreign ownership can be traced to the Japanese, whose investment positions in U.S. real estate rose from $744 million in 1984 to a high of $15.2 billion in 1990. Japanese investment activity in the 1980s was encouraged by the huge trade surplus Japan had with the United States, the relatively small size of its own real estate market, and the higher U.S. rates of return. In the 1990s, Japanese holdings of U.S. real estate decreased significantly, to about $8.8 billion in 1996, largely due to low or even negative returns and steep drops in the value of Japanese property investments in the United States.

European investment in U.S. real estate has been more consistent, increasing annually since 1980. Europeans were particularly active from 1980 to 1986 and from 1989 to 1993. Dutch investors, with $5.5 billion in direct investment positions in U.S. real estate in 1996, are the second largest group of foreign owners after Japanese investors.

REITs. Most real estate investment trusts (REITs) provide equity for development projects, but there are a handful of mortgage REITs whose mission is to invest in debt vehicles. REITs are usually publicly traded companies on one of the stock exchanges (NYSE, NASDAQ, AMEX). They are described in detail in the earlier section in this chapter on ownership structures. The lending policies of mortgage REITs vary, and they may provide short-term construction loans as well as long-term mortgages.

Municipal Bonds. Municipalities sometimes issue tax-exempt bonds to help finance the development of commercial real estate projects. Such public assistance is used when portions of a development are public uses or when the municipality wishes to encourage the development of a site, such as an urban brownfields site, or an area, such as a designated urban redevelopment district. This source of financing is limited by strict federal guidelines on how much of a tax-exempt municipal bond issuance can be used for private purposes.

Prairie Stone, an industrial/office park in Hoffman Estates, Illinois, was developed by Homart, the development branch of Sears, Roebuck & Company. Tax increment bonds covered the cost of public improvements and all other funding was provided by Sears, Roebuck.

Courtesy of Homart Development Company

The Corporate Center, a 450,000-square-foot build-to-suit office building in suburban Boston, was a joint venture project between the developer and the anchor tenant. A consortium of U.S. and offshore banks provided the debt financing.

The Financing Package

Office developers seeking financing for a project need to approach lenders or investors with an understanding of the money source's current requirements and policies, strong supporting evidence on the market feasibility of the project, and a well-prepared business plan. They would do well to have anticipated the objections that the lender or investor might raise and to have considered before-hand alternatives that might placate these objections.

In order to secure funds, developers need to compile a professionally organized financing package before they contact investors and lenders. The financing package is typically a developer's first, and possibly only, chance to demonstrate its understanding of the project's investment criteria, relevant development issues, lender requirements, the financing process, and other critical issues.

The developer's financing package plays a significant role in the lender's assessment of the risk posed by both the borrower and the project. A cavalier attitude toward the financing process or an inexperienced reading of the lender's needs will impede the developer's efforts to secure funding. As the saying goes: "There is only one chance to make a good first impression."

An outline of the main elements of a good financing package follows. Most sections of the outline can and should include several subtopics, with care being taken to include all the topics in which the target lender (or equity investor) will be interested. (See Appendix 1 for a table of contents and several sample pages from a preliminary financing package for a permanent loan for an office building.) When preparing the financing package, the developer should always keep in mind the audience, which is the specific lender (or equity investor) to which the project is being pitched. The developer should be prepared to tailor the basic package for delivery to specific lenders or investors. The major elements of a good financing package include:

- table of contents,
- executive summary,
- overview of the proposed development (the offering summary),
- description and location of the project,
- design and construction details,
- schedule of the project,
- project economics,
- market analysis and positioning of the project,
- regulatory approvals and community support,
- the project team,
- sponsorship and financial details (which should be provided under separate cover to assure confidentiality),
- closing observations, and
- exhibits.

Color and graphics—photographs, maps, and graphs—should be combined with narrative to make the points as clearly and strongly and concisely as possible. Developers without experience in putting together financing packages should consider hiring a real estate consultant to help them create an informative and persuasive presentation.

The goal of successful loan submissions is to guide lenders to the conclusion that the loan will be secured by a high-quality asset and that repayment of principal and interest will be assured. It is important to highlight positive aspects of the project, identify risk areas, and clearly state the ways by which risks will be minimized. Developers should be prepared in advance to answer all difficult questions.

The assessment of risk is a paramount factor in the financing of office projects. Investment and loan criteria are established on the basis of the risks involved, with perceptions of risk being different for the developer, the lender, and the investor. Accurate risk assessment is important. Too much optimism can advance a project that should not have been developed. Too much caution can scuttle a project that would have served the market well.

Lenders are often characterized as risk averse. A good tactic for the financing package is to identify various risks and specify ways in which the developer of the proposed project will seek to minimize them. The kinds of risks that could be addressed in this manner can be arranged by category, as follows:

- Borrower Risks—The developer's performance risk is usually measured by such factors as the composition of the development team, the strength of the developer's financial statement (its capacity to cover potential losses), the developer's track record and reputation, and the developer's collateral. Developers with large capital assets and a record of successful undertakings will typically get better loan terms because they pose a smaller performance risk.
- Lender/Investor Risks—The ability of the lender or investor to perform is measured by its financial capability and stability, its approach to business, and its management philosophy.
- Market Risks—The supply and demand climate depends on risk factors like demographic shifts, absorption rate changes, and the development of competitive space.
- Political Risks—Among the risks to a project's successful development that may be called political risks are the developer's ability to navigate through the local approval process, shifts in regulatory or community attitudes, and changes in taxes.
- Design and Construction Risks—Office projects abound with risks related to design and construction, among them the risk that the schedule will be delayed (by weather, strikes, or anything else), that contractors will not be able to obtain bonding or completion insurance, that the budget will be exceeded, and that contracts (especially contracts negotiated to achieve particular objectives like a maximum cost ceiling or a fast-track schedule) will not be met.
- Economic Risks—Interest-rate risk and the risk of recession are the chief economic risks that confront

office developments. Office development typically is highly leveraged, so that rising interest rates can increase development costs to a point where the risk/return tradeoff is unacceptable, but interest-rate risk is an external factor that the developer cannot control.
- Market Preferences—Shifts in consumer preferences, business confidence, location preferences, or design preferences all pose risks to office development.
- Operational Management Risks—Management performance risk can be assessed by reviewing the experience and attitude of the property manager, the management approach, and the operational budgets and schedules. Insurance is a related contract risk.

Once a financing package with top-quality, professional content and appearance has been prepared, the developer can directly contact funding sources. Or it can retain consultants or brokers with real estate investment, development, and finance experience to locate likely lenders or investors.

Developers must allow sufficient time to gather and analyze data, prepare the submission, and complete the loan closing process. A prototypical timetable for the process, beginning after the developer has completed the necessary research and analyses and obtained control of the site, is as follows:

Time required	
Prepare loan submission package	2–4 weeks
Contact lenders and establish preliminary interest	2–4 weeks
Finalize loan terms and begin formal application process	1–2 weeks
Lender due diligence, outside reports, and loan commitment	4–6 weeks
Closing and funding	4–6 weeks

Note that the preparation of the loan submission package and the process of establishing lender interest can take longer than four weeks if the project involves multiple phases, mixed uses, or other complicating factors. Note also that some lenders can close a loan in four weeks, but it can take others up to six months. A sample commitment by a bank for an office construction loan is provided in Appendix 2.

Notes

1. Equitable Real Estate Investment Management, *Real Estate Outlook: 1997* (Atlanta: Equitable Real Estate, 1997), pp. 1–13.
2. Ibid., pp. 1–13.
3. Ibid., pp. 1–13.
4. Institutional Real Estate Inc./Roulac Group, "Roulac Capital Flows Database," *Real Estate Capital Markets Report*, August 1997, p. 10; and Pension Real Estate Association data.
5. Ibid.
6. Mike E. Miles, Richard L. Haney Jr., and Gayle Berens, *Real Estate Development: Principles and Process*, 2nd ed. (Washington, D.C.: ULI–the Urban Land Institute, 1996), p. 33.

4. Project Planning and Design

Wherever a proposed office building is located, whether in a city's core or on a suburb's fringes, its design will be shaped by a unique set of variables. Among the key variables affecting building design are the owner's objectives, local regulatory requirements, the needs of prospective tenants, competition in the local marketplace, site characteristics, the development budget, and available technology.

Outside the parameters set by regulatory requirements, the most important consideration in office building design is the needs and expectations of the future tenants. Targeting and positioning issues—how the building can meet the needs and preferences of specific target tenants —drive all aspects of an office development project from the earliest planning stages and involve the entire development team.

While an office building should be designed to capture a specific segment of the market, the developer must avoid design fads and trends that can render it dated or obsolete before its time. Adaptability must be programmed by design into the building. Today's building may be in use 50 or more years from now. Furthermore, office markets are ever changing. A well-designed building will have the flexibility to meet shifting tenant demands.

The opulent office buildings that many corporations built for their headquarters in the 1980s, for example, do

The 40-story 120 North LaSalle Street building in Chicago meets the significant design challenges posed by a narrow, mid-block site.

not communicate the image of cost consciousness that corporate America wants to project in the late 1990s.

Increasingly, flexibility and value are the drivers of leasing decisions today. In the eyes of many tenants, flexibility means open floor plans that make it easy to arrange and rearrange space as needed, access for the disabled, and the ability to add electrical capacity and supplemental cooling at a reasonable cost. And value means efficient floor plans with high ratios of office space to core space, efficient air-conditioning and heating systems, fast and reliable elevators, a welcoming lobby, responsive building management, and convenient access to amenities—as well as reasonable rents.

Not surprisingly, providing superior flexibility almost always adds to the design and construction costs of an office building, including its structural and mechanical systems. Developers must weigh the tradeoff between market acceptance and cost in the context of the particular market.

The design quality and functionality of a new or renovated office building determine how it will succeed in the competitive market. This chapter addresses a broad range of planning and design issues, from regulatory considerations to site planning, from a building's configuration to its infrastructure, and from a project's skin to its interior layout. It describes the means by which the development of high-quality, thoughtfully designed office buildings can be carried out under the regulatory and market (supply and demand) conditions of today.

Zoning
- What is the current zoning?
- Does the current zoning allow the proposed use?
- Is the proposed use allowed only as a special exception or with other restrictions?
- Is the site located in an overlay zone, such as an urban renewal district or a historic district?
- If so, what are the requirements of that zone?
- Is an environmental impact statement (EIS or EIR) required for approval?
- What is the maximum allowed density (floor/area ratio)?
- What are the building setback requirements (or yard requirements)?
- What are the parking and loading requirements?
- Does the proposed development require any zoning variances or other relief from zoning requirements?
- If so, what is the likelihood of obtaining them?
- How much will it cost to obtain them?

Traffic Analysis
- Will a traffic analysis be required for site plan approval?
- When should the traffic analysis be undertaken?
- Must the development comply with local traffic management plans?
- What off-site transportation improvements will be required?
- How much will they cost?

Site Analysis
- Are any endangered species (animals or plants) on the site?
- Is the soil or water contaminated?
- Who is responsible for the remediation of the contamination?

- How much will remediation cost?
- How long will remediation take?
- Does the site include any floodplain areas?
- Does the site contain any wetlands?
- How will the presence of floodplain areas and wetlands affect site planning?
- Will the floodplain areas or wetlands entail any special site design or construction costs?
- Have soil borings been taken?
- What is the bearing capacity of the soil?
- Will the site accommodate the size of the planned building?
- Will the building be visible from surrounding roadways or adjacent development?

Site and Building Design
- Is the topography of the site appropriate for surface parking?
- Will large amounts of earthwork (cut and fill) be required?
- How will stormwater management be approached?
- Will on-site stormwater detention be necessary?
- Will vegetative clearing be required?
- Will trees be preserved, and in what areas?
- Will the building block sun from adjacent developments?
- Will parking be visible from the main adjacent roadway?

Regulatory Issues

Local regulatory requirements contained in zoning regulations, building codes, and other land use laws establish some basic design parameters of any office building. Maximum floor/area ratios (FARs), height limitations, minimum building setbacks, and requirements that certain elements like parking or open space be provided—all typical provisions in zoning ordinances—obviously affect site planning and the design of office buildings. Some localities have ordinances designed to keep buildings from casting shadows on neighboring property or to keep them from reflecting excessive heat onto other structures. In some localities, design review agencies must approve the materials, style of architecture, location of entries, and various other design aspects of office projects.

Local building codes addressing safety and health concerns also exert a powerful influence on design. Municipalities regularly revise their building codes, spurred, in some cases, by litigation or the threat of litigation concerning safety and public health and, in other cases, by new building methods, technologies, and materials. The regulations that affect building design vary greatly by location. In the early planning stages of the project, office developers must identify all the public requirements that apply to the building and site design.

Zoning and Land Use Controls
The construction or renovation of office buildings is regulated by local zoning and land use ordinances that are established to ensure public health, safety, and welfare, and to exercise control over land uses. Zoning and land use ordinances exercise control over everything from the types of tenants that can occupy a building to the building's distance from the street. Zone by zone, these ordinances designate uses that are permitted by right, uses that require special exceptions, and, frequently, uses that are excluded.

The Merrill Lynch operations campus in Denver is designed to project a unified corporate image but still accommodate stand-alone buildings that can be sold or leased independently.

Zoning regulations often require that public open space be provided. At Union Bank, in Orange, California, public space takes the form of lush gardens with seating that invites passersby in.

Zoning ordinances spell out certain standards to which an office development must conform. These include the amount of building square footage that is permitted on the site, the distance the building must be from the streets it faces, and the minimum (or maximum) number of parking spaces required or allowed. Zoning ordinances also describe the approval process for projects, which can vary depending on whether the proposed project can be developed by right under the existing zoning, or whether it must apply for an exception or waiver to the regulations or obtain a rezoning of the site in order to proceed.

Early in the planning phase of a project, the development team must address several critical zoning and land use particulars that could impinge on the project's viability. Does the zoning ordinance permit a building on the site that is large enough to achieve the rental income on the financial pro forma? What are the parking requirements in the zoning ordinance and can the site accommodate them? Does office development on the site trigger any special

requirements—such as the provision of public spaces or the construction of affordable housing (or contributions to funds that provide parks or affordable housing)?

Developers are advised to consult a zoning attorney who is familiar with the particular jurisdiction and with the office development process, in order to sort through these kinds of questions. Zoning attorneys interpret complex codes and regulations and are able to bring up relevant examples of exceptions and rezonings that have been granted or denied.

Most zoning ordinances empower local planning or zoning commissions to grant exceptions or waivers. Some types of land uses are listed within zoning ordinances as permissible by special exception. The proposed use may be allowed, but only after closer scrutiny by planning officials and usually with certain restrictions. For example, a restaurant may be allowed in a commercial office zone, but only by special exception. Upon review and perhaps a public hearing, the zoning board may grant

Courtesy of Hines Interests LP

The developer of Ravina, a 42-acre office park in Atlanta, made multimillion-dollar contributions to off-site road improvements as a condition of rezoning approval.

the special exception with some restrictions. For example, a restaurant could be restricted to no liquor sales and limited hours of operation.

In many localities, the approval of development plans hinges on exactions (or impact fees or proffers). These generally are requirements that developers provide infrastructure improvements and amenities that benefit the community or mitigate the impact of the development on the surrounding community in exchange for the government's permission to build. Many municipalities offer variances or waivers from zoning ordinances in return for the provision of public facilities and certain amenities. New York City, for example, awards density bonuses (in the form of higher permitted FARs) to developers that provide plazas, galleries, and other special features in their office projects.

Framingham, Massachusetts, a town located about 20 miles from Boston, generally requires that office developments provide 3 percent of the construction cost for off-site improvements. The exaction is in response to the considerable growth—and attendant traffic growth—that the town has experienced over the last 15 years. The Corporate Center, a 450,000-square-foot, build-to-suit office building that was completed in the town in the early 1990s, devoted 5 percent of its construction budget, or more than $2.5 million, to off-site road, intersection, signal, and sidewalk improvements—including the construction of a connector road across the edge of the site to relieve traffic congestion at a nearby intersection.

The exactions required by Framingham for the Corporate Center directly mitigated traffic congestion on and around the site, and thus benefited both the developer and the town. In other jurisdictions, the connection between the exaction and the development project is not so direct. In the District of Columbia, for example, rezonings, height variances, or alley closings for office developments frequently are granted on the condition that the developer will contribute to a fund to develop low-income housing. The rationale is that advantages that are granted to developers should generate equivalent advantages for economically disadvantaged residents of the District. Ultimately, developers must assess the impact of such contributions on the feasibility of their projects.

Transferable development rights (TDRs) are sometimes used for office projects. (See "1900 K Street" feature box on page 122.) TDRs are a special regulatory device that allows the transfer of the development rights that are available on particular designated sites for use on other sites that are usually located in a designated receiving zone. If a property owner wants to preserve, for example, a two-story building on a site zoned for a ten-story building, that owner may sell its right to build the additional square footage to the owner of another parcel of land. The purchase of development rights permits the owner of the transfer site to build a larger project than the zoning allows. Once a site's TDRs are sold, the building density of that site is limited to the square footage allowed under the retained (unsold) zoning rights.

TDRs have not been as widely adopted as their advocates once expected, perhaps due in part to the concern that they sanction the legal overbuilding of receiving sites, which can produce traffic congestion and cast dense shadows on neighboring properties. However, TDRs can help make the renovation of historic landmark buildings economically viable. A historic landmark designation may confer status to a building, but property owners often find that such a designation is detrimental to the value of the property in that it severely complicates and may even prevent major changes to the structure and the facade. If the landmark building has salable development rights, its owner can receive compensation for the building's diminished value.

Office buildings house a high concentration of activity and thus can place significant burdens on public water, sanitary sewer, stormwater sewer, and transportation systems. In areas where growth has been outpacing infrastructure development, many jurisdictions have enacted adequate public facilities (APF) requirements that make new office (and other) development contingent on adequate capacity in the infrastructure systems that will serve it. The reviewing agency, typically, assesses the supply/demand balance for affected public facilities in the area and determines the burden that the proposed office project will place on public infrastructure. Depending on that determination, the developer may be asked to contribute to the upgrading of specific public facilities.

Depending on the size of the project and the current adequacy of public infrastructure, the cost of satisfying

APF requirements can be considerable. The office developer must establish early communications with regulatory officials in order to ascertain the likely extent of any required contributions of public facilities—and the cost.

Building Codes

Building codes mandating certain standards of construction are used throughout the United States to control the quality of all types of construction, including office buildings, in an effort to ensure public health, safety, and welfare. Unlike local zoning ordinances, most building codes are statewide—although interpreted locally—and are based on one of three model national building codes. Some states like New York and California have developed their own building codes. The three model building codes are published by nonprofit organizations of code officials as follows: the Uniform Building Code (International Conference of Building Officials: ICBO), the National Building Code (Building Officials & Code Administrators: BOCA), and the Standard Building Code (Standard Building Code Congress International: SBCCI). These three model code organizations also work together under an umbrella organization, the International Code Council.

The building officials in different jurisdictions can interpret standard building code provisions differently. While one jurisdiction may allow a large floor to be divided into two by a simple two-hour-rated firewall, another may interpret this wall as equivalent to the wall between two separate buildings with zero clearance—a condition that requires a four-hour firewall with no penetrations. Or, to give another example, officials using the same standard building code might treat a multistory atrium in the center of an office building quite differently. One municipality may agree that the space is, in fact, an atrium, which according to the code must contain certain smoke evacuation systems and can have only a certain maximum number of openings to it from the adjacent office space. Another municipality might consider the space to be an open well, a building element that allows the adjacent office space to be designed with more flexibility.

Developers should review a proposed building design with the appropriate building code officials as early as possible, and certainly before the construction documents are complete. For building renovation projects, developers should redouble their efforts to ascertain the design's compliance with the local building code, particularly if the building was constructed before much of the current code was put into effect.

Americans with Disabilities Act

The Americans with Disabilities Act of 1990 (ADA), which went into effect in January of 1992, plays a significant role in the design and operations of office buildings and has a significant impact on cost. Title III of the act mandates that places of public accommodation and commercial facilities provide certain levels of access to persons with disabilities. All buildings constructed after January

Courtesy of Arrowstreet Inc.

The Lotus R&D building in Cambridge, Massachusetts, rises six stories instead of five because the city's approval of an increase in allowable floor area enabled the developer to add an extra story.

The completion of the 1900 K Street building in 1996 generated much excitement. It was the first speculative office building to be constructed in Washington, D.C.'s central business district since the crash of the commercial real estate market in 1990. Just 57 percent of the space was preleased when construction started in early 1995, at a time when demand for contiguous blocks of Class A space was beginning to tighten but the local office market was still far from robust. At completion, the building was 80 percent preleased.

The Kaempfer Company, a local Washington developer, developed and manages 1900 K Street. Dutch pension fund manager PVF Real Estate owns the 346,473-square-foot building, and Aegis Realty Consultants, as asset manager for the owner, provides oversight.

The target market is high-end users, such as prestigious law and accounting firms, that place a premium on superior location and architectural excellence. Designed by Cesar Pelli & Associates, the glass and steel structure offers an excellent location, distinctive architecture, and exceptional amenities that speak to the priorities and requirements of its tenants.

Office space is provided on 13 floors above grade and 1.5 floors below grade, with each floor measuring approximately 26,000 rentable square feet. Underground parking on 2.5 below-grade levels accommodates 220 cars. Windows on all four sides are accentuated by the stainless steel facade and ribbons of Burlington stone. A glass rotunda provides a signature corner entrance, which is topped with a sweeping curved glass corner that continues up to the rooftop terrace. Marble floors and finely detailed wood wall panels enrich the lobby, which is a three-story, light-filled atrium. Seven high-speed passenger elevators serve the office floors and two elevators shuttle between the garage and the lobby. Numerous amenities are included, among which are a full-service concierge, a rooftop terrace, and a 3000-square-foot fitness center for tenants only.

While clearly well appointed, 1900 K Street reflects the more reserved corporate culture that has evolved in the 1990s and shies away from an overt display of wealth of the kind that characterized corporate America and some of its buildings in the 1980s. The design is both elegant and understated, sophisticated but not ostentatious.

As sole financier, PVF Real Estate took a more active role in the development process than does a typical foreign investor. The company was closely involved in many of the details of the project, including the decision to use expensive curved glass to define the building's entrance.

A rounded corner entrance provides an elegant identity for 1900 K Street. This and other design amenities in the 13-story building meet the demands of prestigious tenants.

PVF maintained certain requirements for poststabilization yields and the project's internal rate of return, and Kaempfer recommended a course of action for attaining or exceeding PVF's required returns from among several alternative construction startup dates and lease-up schedules.

The site occupies about one-third of a city block on the southwest corner of K and 19th Streets in the heart of downtown. The developer acquired the six lots that make up the site between 1989 and 1991, just as the commercial real estate market was plunging into recession. Its strategy was to assemble a prime downtown site out of income-producing buildings and hold the properties for future office development.

In 1992, the inventory of new office space in the region peaked and the development team concluded that demand for new high-end office space was about three years out. It was at this point that the team began planning for the construction of a building. After hiring the architect, Kaempfer embarked on a number of preconstruction activities.

One of the more complex aspects of the project was the use of transferable development rights (TDRs) to increase the building's density. The project site falls within the city's TDR receiving zone. Most of the TDRs used were "preferred use" TDRs generated by Kaempfer's commitment to redevelop the Warner Theater (in another part of downtown D.C.) as a viable theater venue. Other TDRs were obtained from three transactions involving historic properties. (In a program to facilitate the renovation of landmark structures, the District of Columbia allows the owners of low-rise historic properties to sell the space above their buildings that would be developable under current zoning regulations. The buyers of this space can use it to increase development densities at other sites.) The four TDR transactions that took place enabled the developer to increase the project's FAR from 6.5 to 10.0, and thereby create a viable development site where others had failed. Requiring numerous approvals including the D.C. Historic Preservation Review Board's, the zoning administrator's, the planning director's, and the mayor's, the TDR transfer took more than 18 months to complete.

The developer undertook a similar administrative odyssey in order to obtain approval for closing an alley. Preparing drawings, drafting legislation, and obtaining approvals from the city council, the public works department, and each of the public utility departments took nearly a year.

By the middle of 1994, the TDR transfer was complete, the alley closed, and asbestos removed from existing buildings. A three-month demolition process began in May 1994, and in September a building permit was finally issued.

Efficient floorplates allowed tenants to lease less space than they had in older buildings, saving them money despite higher square-foot rents.

In early 1993, Kaempfer devised a marketing plan in three phases: preconstruction, construction, and lease-up. The preconstruction goal was to prelease at least 100,000 square feet (30 percent of net rentable area), which was determined to be the minimum amount of committed space needed to begin construction. By the end of the year, the developer had put together a roster of potential tenants and had built two intricate architectural models that could help prospects visualize the finished product.

Within a 15-day period in December 1994, two leases were signed for a total of 195,000 square feet—nearly double the amount of preleased space required to begin construction. Construction began in February 1995 and was substantially complete—including 60 percent of the tenant space—just 17 months later, in June 1996.

The preleasing tenants were relocating from other downtown D.C. buildings, even though their rental rates at 1900 K Street would be slightly higher. To compensate, the building offered several ways to save on overall occupancy costs. Efficiently designed floorplates featuring 30-foot column spacing lent themselves to a wide variety of office configurations within virtually column-free space. Consequently, these tenants were able to make practical use of more of the space they were renting, thus allowing them to rent less space.

A portion of each floor was also designed with extra load-carrying capacity, which allowed tenants to centralize certain weighty office uses—including files and libraries. Without this feature, tenants would be required to spread such office uses across larger areas.

The availability of below-grade office space offered another means for saving on occupancy costs. The lobby atrium directs some natural light to this space, making it suitable for conference rooms, libraries, or administrative functions. By renting below-grade space for such functions, tenants could realize significant rental savings. ∎

Historic buildings can be retro-fitted to provide access to persons with disabilities. At Philadelphia's U.S. Customs House, a renovation included wheelchair ramps.

Courtesy of Ueland Junker McCauley

A wheelchair ramp has been unobtrusively integrated into a hallway off the lobby of the MASCO Building in Boston.

Courtesy of Arrowstreet Inc.

1993 must be fully accessible to the disabled. The law also affects alterations to existing properties begun after January 1992.

ADA distinguishes between places of public accommodation and commercial facilities, and mandates different requirements for the two types of places:

• Places of Public Accommodation—According to the ADA, a privately owned building is a place of public accommodation if it is open to and serves the public. Privately owned places of public accommodation would include hotels, restaurants and bars, movie houses, theaters, retail stores, and service establishments like banks, barber shops, or dry cleaners. They also include recreational and educational facilities and other service facilities such as day-care and senior citizen centers. Private offices typically are not considered places of public accommodation, unless the tenants are medical or other public service providers.

• Commercial Facilities—Commercial facilities are privately owned facilities intended for a nonresidential, commercial use. They include office buildings and warehouses. Some commercial facilities contain areas that are considered places of public accommodation, like multitenant office buildings that contain a restaurant or medical office suites.

Significantly, the ADA is civil rights legislation, administered by the U.S. Department of Justice. It is not a building code. (However, some jurisdictions have incorporated ADA requirements into their building codes.) Enforcement is triggered by the action of an aggrieved party. Persons may file lawsuits concerning newly constructed or altered buildings if they have "reasonable grounds" for believing that discrimination against the disabled exists or is about to occur.

The law requires that new buildings adhere to accessibility guidelines and that architectural barriers in existing buildings be removed at the owner's expense. A provision of the act states that administrators should consider "good faith efforts" and "attempts to comply" in enforcing the law. Priorities in compliance plans include entrances, the routes from sidewalks and parking areas to entrances, restrooms, interior doors, fire exits, and drinking fountains.

For older buildings, the cost of compliance varies considerably from property to property depending on the building's specific conditions and original design. The law has not had a major impact on newer pre-ADA office buildings, most of which were built under state and local building codes that already required accessibility. Compliance with ADA accessibility guidelines has a considerable impact, however, on the cost of renovation of older buildings.

Developers should be familiar with ADA requirements. In renovation projects, the design team should be skilled in integrating accessibility features into existing building designs. Among the sources of publications and other materials that can help developers and architects perform the necessary ADA evaluation are the Building Owners and Managers Association (BOMA), which has published a guide titled *ADA Compliance Guidebook: A Checklist for Your Building*; and the U.S. Architectural and Transportation Barriers Compliance Board (U.S. Access Board), an independent federal agency, which issues a compliance guide called *Americans with Disabilities Act Accessibility Guidelines* (ADAAG).

A federal advisory panel has been working since late 1996 on updating the ADA and clarifying its intent. The formal process for reviewing the panel's proposed changes was expected to begin in January 1998 and could take up to a year to complete. Most of the panel's recommended changes are technical in nature, such as the maximum reach of wheelchair users, which is newly defined as 48 inches (down from 54 inches). The panel has also sought to clarify ambiguous guidelines, such as the one related to the determination of the least possible slope of a ramp, which as it now stands can be variously interpreted.

On the nontechnical side, ADA's intent is sometimes unclear. For example, the courts are currently considering liability issues, on which the intentions of Congress have been interpreted differently by architects and building owners. In 1996, a federal judge in Washington, D.C., decided that the building owner is responsible for ensuring that the building satisfies ADA requirements. In 1997, a federal judge in Florida ruled—in a different case—that ADA compliance is the architect's responsibility.[1]

Transportation Planning

Office development generates traffic that can severely strain transportation systems. Congestion occurs on many of the roads serving office uses, particularly during certain rush hours—in the morning and evening commute periods and at lunchtime. The measurement of potential traffic that will be engendered and its mitigation are important considerations in transportation planning for office projects. Traffic and congestion are not simply issues of infrastructure. They also concern air quality goals. For many office projects, making connections to mass transportation—bus and rail—is another element of transportation planning.

Traffic analysis and traffic control measures are discussed in the following sections.

Traffic Analysis. No other issue generates as much controversy in the approval process for a proposed office development as the project's possible impact on traffic and transportation routes. Most jurisdictions require a professionally prepared traffic study as part of any application for rezoning or for site plan approval, which may be undertaken by the developer's traffic consultant or by the jurisdiction (but generally is paid for by the developer).

The traffic study must address several big questions. How many cars and trucks will enter and leave the site at various times of the day? These data define the project's trip generation. What is the capacity of surrounding roads, highways, and intersections to accommodate existing and new levels of traffic?

As a part of the approval process, office developments such as Chase Plaza at Fountain Square in Atlanta need to undertake traffic studies to assess the impact they will have on surrounding roadways.

Brian Gassel—Thompson, Ventulett, Stainback & Associates

Pearl Street East Business Park in Boulder, Colorado, is served by alternative modes of transportation. One and one-half miles of concrete bike paths connecting with the city's bike path system traverse the 33-acre site and city buses serve the park.

The traffic study helps determine the size and type of any off-site transportation improvements that the developer will be required to make to accommodate the project's traffic impacts. Requirements for off-site transportation improvements can be relatively small items that are clearly related to the office project: the addition of a traffic light at the site's entry, the widening of the frontage road, the addition of acceleration and deceleration lanes to and from the entry, or the addition of turning lanes on the main access road. For large projects, requirements for off-site improvements can be quite extensive. Some developers are required to construct new bridges or interchanges to accommodate the additional traffic generated by their projects.

Off-site road improvements can be an expensive component of an office development. But they do not necessarily represent only an onerous burden on the development. Office projects are more marketable if they are served by an efficient and well-designed road system. If the developer of a new office building or office park makes roadway improvements that facilitate the flow of off-site traffic and prevent congestion near the development, the building's position in the rental market will be correspondingly improved. On the other hand, an office building in a congested area becomes more difficult to lease, and its rental rates can suffer.

Traffic Control Measures. The federal Clean Air Act Amendments of 1990 instituted traffic control measures (TCMs) as a strategy for reducing mobile-source air pollution (emissions from cars, trucks, and buses). Jurisdictions in areas that have not attained a certain level of air quality are required to implement a TCM plan of their own devising (subject to EPA approval). Many individual transportation control measures involve office development and office use.

Among the TCMs that jurisdictions have adopted are expanded public transportation programs, the dedication of highway lanes for the use of high-occupancy vehicles (HOV lanes), ride-sharing programs, and programs to develop pedestrian and bicycle facilities. Funding for many of the capital items in TCM plans—mass transit, HOV lanes, bike trails, and the like—is scarce, and office developers are sometimes required to contribute. Some jurisdictions require employers of a certain size to prepare and implement plans for decreasing peak hour auto trips among their employees. Such plans might include ridesharing incentives and flexible work schedules.

TCM plans may also include trip reduction ordinances that make traffic mitigation a condition of development permits.

Some jurisdictions have reduced their minimum parking ratio (number of parking spaces required per 1,000 square feet of office space) for office buildings in order to discourage some parking—and thus car trips. However, if prospective tenants would prefer more than the minimum number of required parking spaces, developers are free to provide more parking in their projects. On the other hand, some jurisdictions have adopted a maximum parking ratio (number of parking spaces allowed per 1,000 square feet) as a condition of office development permits.

For developers, such a cap on the number of parking spaces may require their involvement in other transportation services to accommodate the transportation needs of tenants and the traffic reduction requirements of the TCM plan. The developer may have to manage a ridesharing program, provide parking incentives for carpools, provide fare incentives for mass transit, and offer shuttle bus service between the project and transit facilities. Such transportation alternatives entail costs that must be included in the project's financial pro forma.

Several solutions for reducing peak hour trips to and from office developments have emerged. The inclusion of retail components in an office project, the provision of housing on the site or adjacent to it, and the provision of pedestrian or shuttle connections to public transportation systems can be effective measures. The developer also can encourage the building's tenants to implement transportation system management (TSM) programs, and offer better lease terms or incentive rewards if they do so.

Site Planning

An office development is more than just the building itself. Visitors and prospective tenants will fail to appreciate the design of any building, no matter how handsome, if they have difficulty locating its parking area or its entrance. The building's environment needs to be well ordered and people friendly, safe and aesthetically pleasing. The progression from the access street to the parking lot or garage must be logical. So must the progression from the parking lot or sidewalk to the building's entrance. Among the key site planning issues for typical office developments are vehicular and pedestrian circulation, the location and orientation of the building, the location of parking, the building's visibility, and landscaping.

A good site plan capitalizes on the site's advantages and overcomes its constraints. For example, a portion of a site that drains poorly and is completely unsuited for the building or parking might be an ideal area for a storm-water detention pond; and the pond could be designed to serve as an attractive water amenity as well. In a good site plan, the various uses and elements that will occupy the site are organized logically and meet the needs of the people who will occupy and visit the office space.

Site planning challenges and opportunities are likely to be different depending on whether the site is in a suburban or urban location. Suburban sites are typically much larger and planning them encounters fewer contextual constraints. They can present numerous land use options. Planning suburban sites involves making choices about building location, the locations of vehicular and pedestrian entrances to the site, the placement of loading and

Do's and Don'ts for Suburban Site Planning

- Don't allow the primary view of the building to be over the parking lot. The siting of the building and the parking should be based in part on a careful analysis of the vantage points from which it will be visible. Topography, traffic patterns, parking requirements, and existing and proposed landscaping are all factors in these siting decisions.
- Do maintain clear separations between service traffic, building-access traffic, and parking-lot traffic. Parking-lot traffic should not travel on lanes that lead to the loading docks. Service traffic should not use the lanes that provide access to drop-off/pickup locations at the building's entrances.
- Do separate pedestrians and vehicles. Driveways and walkways should be arranged to provide pedestrians with passageways through the site that do not cross major traffic access routes. If pedestrian crossings are absolutely necessary, the number should be minimized and they should be clearly marked by special pavements or painted stripes.
- Don't allow the primary building-access road to weave through the parking lot. When the approach to the building goes through the center of a 300-car parking lot, the building can appear to be engulfed in asphalt, leaving a negative impression in the minds of visitors and tenants. A green and landscaped approach to the building along a separate access road can produce a positive impression.
- Do provide as much landscaping as possible. Landscaping is one of the most important and least expensive elements in a site plan, and compared with most other site development expenditures it provides more bang for the buck. But landscaping often is the first item cut during value-engineering.
- Don't crowd the parking against the building. Although suburban office projects must provide

some parking next to buildings to accommodate the disabled, it is generally a mistake to try to put as much parking as possible as close to the building as possible. From the outside, dozens of cars moored against the building present a not particularly appealing sight and obscure whatever landscaping is provided. From the perspective of office workers on the inside, their view of grillwork and headlights is also not appealing.

- Do shield the loading dock from view. Loading docks do not need to be one of a site's focal points. Few tenants or visitors want to observe the delivery of goods. Dense landscaping or the mass of the building itself can be used to hide loading docks from public view.
- Don't locate the loading dock within sight of the front door. This rule sounds simple enough, but loading docks do in fact frequently end up situated near the front door. The reason is that architects generally seek to locate loading docks near the building's elevators, which makes loading and distribution efficient.
- Do use clear and consistent signage. A project's signage should be considered as one single package, from signs indicating parking entrances to those identifying buildings to those providing directions within buildings. Graphically well designed signage elements both enhance the project's overall appearance and assist visitors in finding their ways.

Three four-story buildings sited around a landscaped commons provide more density at Microsoft's Augusta campus in Redmond, Washington, than is usual at the company's other offices. At this campus, the buildings are designed to maximize the amount of private office space and to encourage employee interaction.

service areas, and the configuration of parking. It may also involve extensive landscape design.

Urban site planning, on the other hand, takes more of its direction from the proposed building's context: nearby buildings, pedestrian patterns, traffic patterns, existing utilities and easements, and soil contamination from previous uses.

The following sections discuss some key site planning considerations for office development on both urban and suburban sites. The topics covered are density, vehicular and pedestrian circulation, service and emergency vehicle access, parking, surveys, grading, stormwater management, building siting, and landscaping.

Density

For office land uses, density is measured by a ratio of the building's gross size (in square feet) to the size of its site (also in square feet). This is known as the floor/area ratio (FAR), and it is usually expressed as a decimal and sometimes as a percent. A 54,000-square-foot building on a five-acre site (which equals 217,800 square feet) has an FAR of 0.25 (54,000 ÷ 217,800).

Density, or the amount of built space on a site, is a basic consideration in planning an office development. Most jurisdictions regulate the density of development in office zones by means of maximum permitted FARs, in conjunction with setback and parking requirements and site coverage constraints.

Suburban office developments typically have FARs that range between 0.25 and 0.50. FARs of 0.25 or less usually indicate buildings of one to three stories in height. FARs around 0.50 typically produce two- to five-story buildings. And FARs of 0.75 to 1.00 will likely yield multistoried buildings with structured parking.

The usual FARs for urban office developments range much higher. Urban sites with FARs from 2.0 to 15.0 are not unusual. High-rise office buildings can have FARs of 20.0 or higher, particularly in downtowns dominated by high-rise office buildings. Some municipalities offer de-velopers density bonuses (a higher FAR) on projects that incorporate (or contribute to the funding of) public amenities. Such bonuses are a potentially valuable tradeoff for developers.

The acquisition price of an office site is greatly influenced by its allowable FAR. Generally, the greater the allowed density the higher the land price. Land prices for office sites are sometimes expressed per FAR foot (the total price divided by the allowable square feet of building) rather than per square foot of land.

Land cost is normally a major component of an office project's total budget. The high cost of land encourages developers to build to the maximum allowable density in order to maximize the return on their investment. However, allowable FAR is not the only consideration in determining a project's density. Other considerations that should go into the determination of optimal density include the optimal size of the floorplates (see "Base Building Configuration" section later in this chapter), the amount of open space wanted on the site, the type of parking provided, vehicular and pedestrian circulation patterns, and views.

Furthermore, higher-density development often entails additional costs, which must be weighed against the higher revenue that is achievable with more rentable area. For example, building to the maximum allowable density on a site with an FAR of 1.0 or higher will almost certainly require building structured parking instead of surface parking. However, structured parking adds a considerable amount to the project's construction budget. If the project cannot command rents that are high enough to justify the expense of structured parking, it may be more feasible to build less on the site, provide surface parking, and charge lower rents.

Vehicular and Pedestrian Circulation

Office buildings do not stand alone on a site. They are supported by circulation systems that direct visitors and tenants first to the entrance of the development and then through the site to parking areas and to the building or buildings.

A suburban office development that has (potentially) convenient access to regional roadways can enjoy a great competitive advantage. But that advantage can be more or less negated if the transition from major roads to the site is confusing or inconvenient. The developer of Fairview Park, a master-planned office park in northern Virginia, has used the site's strategic location to good advantage. Located at the intersection of the Capital Beltway and Route 50, Fairview Park is serviced by a dedicated highway interchange that provides immediate access into the development from either direction on the beltway. Guided by well-placed and numerous signs and encountering no traffic signals en route, visitors and tenants find their way from the beltway to Fairview Park with ease.

It can be useful to conduct a traffic access study. Among the factors the developer should consider in assessing the development's access system are the capacity of approach streets and highways to handle traffic generated by the de-

Suburban FARs typically range from 0.25 to 0.50, and yield buildings of fewer than five stories with surface parking.

ITT Building. Courtesy of Valencia Company

Urban FARs yield blocks of high-rise buildings with underground parking.

Chicago Title & Trust. Courtesy of LCOR Inc.

velopment, the location and design of the development's driveways, and the location and design of its facilities for service vehicles. Off-site traffic access improvements may be the financial responsibility of the developer, especially when the sole or principal beneficiary is the office development. As the preceding Fairview Park example shows, developers may find it expedient to construct major off-site improvements, such as a freeway interchange, to solve difficult access problems.

Office-site planners need to design distinct vehicular circulation systems on the site according to the functions they perform. The primary circulation system that moves cars through the site should remain distinct from the circulation routes through parking lots. Cars should never have to back out of parking spaces directly onto primary circulation routes. If possible, the circulation system for service and delivery vehicles should be separated from the primary circulation system for visitors and employees. It should be planned with adequate loading areas

and turning radiuses. If buses—operated by a public transportation authority or by the developer—serve the site, pull-off bus stops should be located along the primary circulation route so that loading and unloading do not block the flow of traffic.

In suburban office park developments with extensive street systems, proper street layout and design is a major consideration in site planning. As a general rule, roads should be located on stable, well-drained soils with adequate bearing capacity. In areas subject to periodic freezing and thawing, good drainage is doubly important because if below-grade moisture freezes and expands it can produce disastrous results. The street layout should respect the natural contours of the site and retain as many existing landscape features as possible. Pavement thickness should be responsive to the bearing capacity of the soil and the ultimate traffic load.

Streets within an office park may be dedicated to the public or retained as private rights-of-way. The choice de-

Clear design cues at One Century Place in Nashville, Tennessee, direct visitors to the building's entrance.

Gary Knight & Associates Inc.

A heavily traveled tree-lined path that recalls the intimate scale of European streets carries pedestrians to 1100 Peachtree Street in Atlanta.

Dixi Carrillo—EDAW

pends primarily on how involved the developer wishes to be in road management and maintenance and on how willing the local government is to accept responsibility for the roads. Developers that primarily sell or lease improved sites for further development often will dedicate the office park's streets. Developers that carry the development process further—construct buildings, lease office space, and continue to own and operate associated service facilities—are more likely to hold the streets as private rights-of-way.

The circulation systems of suburban office parks sometimes neglect the comfort and safety of pedestrians. Parking lots should be broken into human-scale units ("rooms") and be furnished with sidewalks or pathways leading to building entrances. Pedestrians should not have to cross major circulation routes, but in cases where it is necessary, crosswalks should be provided and their locations clearly defined. The crosswalks should be made clearly visible to motorists. In many office parks, pedestrian trails wandering through the site and linked to buildings are a marketable recreational amenity.

If the parking areas are not equipped with sidewalks or pedestrian paths, the drive aisles that access parking spaces should be perpendicular to buildings, so that parkers can walk down them toward the building. If the drive aisles are placed parallel to buildings, parkers have to walk between cars and across drive aisles to reach the building.

Vehicular and pedestrian traffic patterns are also of concern in planning urban sites. For sites with street frontage on two or more sides, where the building's primary entrance will be located is an important decision. Usually, locating this entrance on one of the streets rather than the other(s) will be more advantageous because of traffic considerations, ease of pedestrian access, or the value of the address. Thus, conducting an access study for urban sites can be useful.

Service- and Emergency-Vehicle Access

Deliveries, other than small parcels, should not be made at the visitors entry to an office building. Service and delivery areas should be placed out of view of the tenants, generally in the rear of the building. Loading and service areas should be screened from public view by walls, fences, or landscaping or otherwise removed from view—by putting them below grade or by extending the building's facade to blend an at grade service area into the project's overall design. Also, service and loading areas should be out of the view of neighbors.

Service vehicles should be directed to their destination immediately upon entering the site, and their route should never go through employee or visitors parking areas. Service vehicles require larger turning radiuses than cars. Loading areas should be designed with enough room for service vehicles to maneuver easily and return to the exit route. Some office developments need to accommodate large tractor-trailers, which have special turning requirements.

Local subdivision and zoning codes normally contain specifications for fire- and rescue-vehicle access to the

The Stiles Corporation

Structured parking increases the efficiency of land use. Las Olas Centre in Fort Lauderdale, Florida, sandwiches parking for 600 cars between 40,000 square feet of ground-level retail space and 175,000 square feet of corporate office space. About 20,000 square feet of the two-acre site will be developed as a landscaped plaza with sidewalk cafés.

site and building(s). Fire-engine access to buildings must be unobstructed by objects such as trees, utility appurtenances, or site furnishings. If fire lanes are required around a building, they do not necessarily have to be paved. Sod reinforced by appropriate subbases is an increasingly acceptable alternative material for such fire lanes. Local codes spell out the turning-radius requirements of fire- and rescue-vehicles, and the code specifications are generally strictly enforced.

Parking

Not enough parking and badly located parking are among the most common mistakes made in office development, according to experienced developers, property managers, and brokers. Parking—availability and proximity—is a key factor in an office building's ability to attract and hold tenants. If the representatives of prospective tenants have trouble finding a parking place when they visit a building, the prospects for getting that tenant are low. Parking is a major planning issue in any office development. The parking capacity of suburban buildings typically must exceed that of urban buildings with access to mass transit.

How to determine parking requirements and how to configure parking space are the subjects of the following sections.

Parking Demand Estimates. The minimum number of parking spaces that is specified in most zoning ordinances is often not enough for particular office tenants. The

A well-designed parking structure, landscaped islands, and
pedestrian walkways are all elements of good parking design.
By adding definition to an outdoor public space, a parking
structure can become an inte-
gral part of the overall design
of an office development.

type of tenants that will occupy the building, the building's location, and what the competition is offering all influence how much parking will be required for a particular office development.

Parking demand for office buildings typically has been calculated in terms of the number of parking spaces needed per 1,000 square feet of rentable building space. In theory, an office building in which each employee occupies an average 300 square feet of space would need 3.3 parking spaces per 1,000 square feet of rentable space, assuming that all employees drive. Commuting by other means—carpool, mass transit, foot, bicycle—reduces this parking requirement. Accommodating visitors, on the other hand, raises the parking requirement.

In today's ever changing environment for office development, developers should not rely on old industry standards and rules of thumb to determine the parking needs of their projects. A parking analysis is described in "The Jefferson" feature box on the following page. As this example illustrates, an office building that exceeds industry guidelines for parking and complies with local zoning requirements for parking can still experience a serious parking shortage. Developers must carefully predict employee density among other factors that affect parking demand. A tenant with significant back-office clerical or telemarketing operations, for example, will fit considerably more employees in 10,000 square feet of office space than will a professional services firm. And a law firm or a consulting firm may employ professionals who are frequently on the road, and thus may need less than one parking space per employee.

Parking Configuration. The skillful accommodation and arrangement of parking to provide adequate parking capacity at a supportable cost while avoiding the appearance of a building floating in a sea of asphalt is one of the central goals of site planning. How parking is configured affects other elements of the site design. The more area that is paved for parking, for example, the higher the volume of stormwater runoff; and the more runoff, the greater the need for detention areas; and the more space occupied by stormwater detention facilities, the less open space that is available for landscaping and outdoor amenities.

Planning for parking involves other considerations as well, including security, signage, and accessibility concerns. Adequate parking area lighting is a particular concern for buildings with tenants that operate from 18 to 24 hours daily.

Many factors enter into the decision of whether to provide parking in structures rather than on surface parking lots. Parking garages provide employees and visitors with protection from the elements and, often, parking spaces that are closer to the building. Structured parking is expensive compared with surface parking, but it can give a project a powerful competitive advantage—particularly in areas in which competitive buildings do not all offer it. For office projects in some areas, structured parking might be required to attract the targeted segments of the market.

In general, office buildings with structured parking are perceived as higher-end projects. However, a poorly designed garage—one that is dark or confusing and seems dangerous—is a liability.

As a site's density increases, it becomes necessary to build structures to accommodate the amount of parking needed (and preserve open space). The topography and shape of the site may be determining factors. A relatively flat and rectangular site, for example, can accommodate more surface parking than can a hilly, triangular site of the same size. But even if it is physically possible to squeeze enough surface parking lots out of a site, doing so may be counterproductive if the result is an unappealing sea of parking and little open space.

The site's purchase price is another factor that determines the feasibility of constructing structured parking. From an economic standpoint, structured parking generally begins to make sense as the square-foot cost of land approaches the square-foot cost of constructing structured parking. When cost of the land for surface parking exceeds the cost of constructing a parking structure, it benefits the developer to purchase less land and build structured parking.

Surveys

Site surveys by certified land surveyors are standard planning procedure for both suburban and urban office projects. For sites with a history—where one or more buildings may have once stood—developers should commission both surface and subsurface surveys. The purpose of site surveys is to locate and record various items, including topographical features, spot elevations, utilities that serve or cross the property, any easements that may be in effect, underground storage tanks, the foundations and other remains of previous structures, trees, rights-of-way, and the property lines.

In older sections of cities where 19th- and early 20th-century buildings are common, property lines may be not clearly defined and building foundations may encroach on adjacent properties. Most jurisdictions in which this situation is likely to arise have in place well-established mechanisms for resolving property line disputes. Sometimes longstanding conditions, such as buildings that extend over property lines, that are in noncompliance with current codes are grandfathered, or exempted from the current codes. To formalize the condition, an easement can be drafted between the parties involved.

Soil Borings

Soil borings provide information on the condition and weight bearing capacity of the soil, factors that affect foundation design. Soil conditions can add considerably to construction costs if they necessitate an expensive foundation system. Developers should investigate soil conditions early in the development process, whether the site is urban or suburban.

Soil borings are also undertaken to test for the presence of hazardous materials. Such a test is especially required if known prior uses of the site suggest the likelihood of

The Jefferson: Evaluating a Building's Parking

In 1996, the property manager of the Jefferson, a multi-tenant office building in suburban Chicago, asked Walker Parking Consultants/Engineers to evaluate the building's parking supply. Were its 392 spaces adequate to meet current and future demand? Walker's analysis went as follows.

Existing Parking

The original development plan for the Jefferson building required 3.3 parking spaces per 1,000 square feet of gross leasable area, or a total of 353 parking spaces. The site now provides 392 spaces (3.7 spaces per 1,000 square feet), which exceeds the original requirements by more than 10 percent. Although the current zoning requires 4.0 spaces per 1,000 square feet, the Jefferson was in compliance at the time of construction and is not required to meet the current ordinance.

Parking Use

A survey of parking use on a typical weekday (see table below) clearly shows that the demand for parking exceeds the supply throughout most of the day—even though the 3.7 spaces per 1,000 square feet that the Jefferson provides exceeds national standards and complies with local zoning requirements.

Peak occupancy

8 a.m.	93%
9 a.m.	102[1]
10 a.m.	102[1]
11 a.m.	100
12 noon	98
1 p.m.	98
2 p.m.	100
3 p.m.	100
4 p.m.	96

[1] Includes cars parked illegally in fire lanes or no-parking zones.

Employee Density

Office buildings have traditionally been designed to provide 200 to 300 square feet of space per person. The standard design parameter for employee density is: 200 square feet of building area per person, or five persons per 1,000 square feet. Tenant surveys at the Jefferson show that the building's current employee density averages 170 square feet of space per person, or almost six employees per 1,000 square feet—a higher-than-normal density. Some tenants average only 70 square feet per employee. The largest tenant's density is 129 square feet per person, which is almost eight employees per 1,000 square feet. The original building codes and parking ordinances were not designed to accommodate such high employee densities.

Estimated Parking Demand

A building's parking demand is the sum of employee demand and visitor demand. At the Jefferson, total current demand is 494 spaces (452 employee spaces and 42 visitor spaces), or 4.6 spaces per 1,000 square feet, which is significantly higher than the 3.7 spaces per 1,000 square feet that are now provided. The methods for these determinations of employee demand and visitor demand are explained next.

Two elements of employee parking demand—the driving ratio and a presence factor—were used to calculate current employee demand. The driving ratio is the percentage of employees that drive their own cars, versus carpooling or other commute modes. The presence factor is the percentage of employees that are present at a given time, versus out of the office for business or personal reasons. For the tenant mix at the Jefferson, Walker recommended applying a presence factor of 80 percent. Based on the tenant survey, the driving ratio for the Jefferson is approximately 97 percent, a high but not uncommon rate for suburban office developments. Applying these rates to the Jefferson's 582 employees yielded a current employee parking demand for 452 parking spaces (582 x 0.97 x 0.80).

The tenant survey indicated that approximately 166 visitors arrive by car on a daily basis. Assuming that the average visitor stays two hours, visitor parking spaces will turn over four times per day. With one space serving four daily visitors, visitor parking demand was calculated to be 42 spaces (166 ÷ 4).

Bottom Line

The Jefferson's current parking deficit is 102 spaces (494 spaces needed less the 392 spaces provided). If the tenants' estimates of their employment densities are realistic, the building's future parking deficit will be 316 spaces. Among the available options for resolving the parking shortage are the following: restrict the use of existing parking, encourage the use of alternate modes of transportation, or expand the parking supply. The Jefferson could expand the parking supply by constructing a surface lot, adding a level to the existing parking facility, or a combination of the two.

Source: Marshall J. Kramer, Walker Parking Consultants/Engineers Inc., Elgin, Illinois.

■

soil contamination. A site where a gas station once stood, for example, may still contain the gasoline holding tanks and is also likely to be contaminated with disposed auto fluids and spilled chemicals. The U.S. Environmental Protection Agency has developed guidelines for conducting site surveys and standards for the remediation of contaminated sites.

Earthwork

The earthwork involved in preparing an office site for the construction of building foundations, parking areas, and roads can be extensive. Ideally, the amount of soil cut out of (excavated from) the site will approximate the amount of soil used to fill in the site. A balance of cut and fill avoids expensive hauling costs. It is the job of the civil engineer or the landscape architect to calculate soil requirements.

The need for additional soil from off site depends to some extent on the quality of the site's soils and their suitability for various applications. Highly compacted soil that is primarily clay, for example, can not be used in areas like lawns and gardens that require well-drained soils. Topsoil, on the other hand, is unsuitable as fill material. Topsoil is generally stripped from areas to be excavated, stored on site, and finally spread on top of graded areas that will be landscaped.

Besides being the essential first step in the construction of building foundations, parking areas, and roads, the engineering and grading of earth on an office development site can serve a multitude of other purposes. Grading is used to create the proper siting for buildings and to resculpt undesired landforms or create new ones. It is used to create drainage swales and berms that serve as noise or wind barriers. Grading can gain additional soil depth for planting areas. It is used for aesthetic and informational purposes: to highlight topographic features, add interest to a flat site, capture or hide views, relate the site to surrounding areas, and to control circulation routes.[2] Accessibility standards are a concern in site grading. For example, barrier-free access from designated parking areas to the building must be provided at specified gradients.

Developers should be sensitive to two potentially damaging consequences of grading: erosion and sedimentation. Climate, vegetation, soil characteristics, and slope influence the severity of erosion. Intense and frequent rainfall produces runoff, which is a key cause of erosion. Frozen soil is highly erodible. Wind erosion can be a serious problem in arid and semiarid regions and in areas experiencing drought. Soils of different textures and particle arrangements vary with respect to their moisture-holding capacity. The steeper the slope the higher the velocity of runoff and the longer the slope the greater the collection of runoff.

In general, developers can control erosion and sedimentation during and after construction by following a few principles:

- Use soils that are best suited for the specific situation.

The Prairie Stone industrial/office park uses natural stormwater management techniques to preserve and enhance wetlands. Vegetated swales clean the water and reduce off-site stormwater flows to below predevelopment rates.

- During grading, leave soil bare for the shortest possible time.
- Detain storm runoff on the site so that sediments can settle out.
- Release runoff safely.

Stormwater Management

The impervious surfaces of any office development—roads, sidewalks, surface parking—increase the flow and velocity of stormwater on and from the site and this runoff must be managed. The consequences of unmanaged or mismanaged runoff can include disastrous downstream flooding and a lowered water table.

The aims of stormwater management are to slow stormwater runoff, detain some portion of it on site, clean it according to local requirements, and release it in a controlled and incremental manner into a storm sewer or stream. How complicated the task is for an office project depends on local regulations, the density of the development, and the nature of the site.

Many jurisdictions have adopted a zero runoff requirement, which means that the amount of runoff from a developed site cannot exceed the amount of runoff from the site prior to its development. Such requirements may be imposed because the regional stormwater system is operating near its capacity.

Jurisdictions regulate not only the volume and flow of runoff, but also its quality. As rainwater flows across a developed site, it accumulates chemical substances and particulates—oil and gasoline residues from parking lots, fertilizers and pesticides from planted areas, and soil from undeveloped portions of the site or areas under construction. Many jurisdictions require that stormwater be cleaned before it leaves the site.

The use of stormwater detention ponds is widespread. Detention ponds are designed to allow sediments to settle out before the water is drained from the site. Stormwater management systems are increasingly including aquatic plants that act as a filtering fabric. Judicious

McLarand, Vasquez & Partners Inc.

McLarand, Vasquez & Partners Inc.

planting of vegetation is used to slow runoff and assist rainwater to return to the earth at the site.

Some jurisdictions require developers to implement best management practices (BMPs), which in the case of stormwater management are site engineering practices known to contribute to the improvement of water quality and hydrological systems. Most jurisdictions in the watershed of the Chesapeake Bay, for example, have required developers to adopt BMPs in accordance with the Chesa-

peake Bay Agreement of 1987, a multistate bay and river restoration program.

Stormwater runoff on suburban sites can be detained by a number of methods. The most common method is a dry pond—a low area on the site—to which stormwater runoff is directed by earthen drainage swales or pipes. The pond usually remains dry except after heavy rainfalls. It is equipped with outflow structures that are designed to slowly release stormwater into public storm sewers.

Dry ponds can be aesthetically unappealing. Screening them from view is often not an option, because many municipalities do not permit trees or shrubs to be planted around dry ponds. Such vegetation might conflict with spillways or other drainage structures, and root growth might damage a pond's earthen walls. Steeply sloped sides may have to be lined with riprap (broken stone). If they are more gently sloped they can be planted with grasses and in some cases with smaller decorative plants to add some visual appeal.

Another method by which stormwater can be detained is a wet pond, which is designed to retain a permanent pool of water. A wet pond can effectively control peak stormwater flows and remove pollutants. It also can be designed to be an amenity for an office development. A wet pond is more expensive to build than a dry pond. It requires slightly deeper excavation, and a filtration and circulation system to prevent the water from becoming clouded or stagnant.

A third method of stormwater detention for suburban and urban sites is underground storage. Large concrete pipes located under parking lots are engineered to store a certain, required amount of runoff and to release it into the local stormwater system in a controlled manner. Office developers typically choose this method only if the density of the site is high and the unused portions of the site are too small or otherwise not suited for a dry or wet pond. An alternative to pipe storage is the temporary detention of stormwater on the roofs of buildings and parking garages to reduce peak flows to sewers. But this solution is rarely used, because holding a large volume of water on a building's roof increases the likelihood of leakage.

Building Location

The best placement for an office building on its site and its ideal orientation depend on many considerations having to do with the site's physical features, the internal circulation plan, visibility concerns, and adjacent development—as well as zoning and other land use requirements.

Most developers are concerned, and justifiably so, about the visibility of the proposed office building from surrounding roads and highways. The residents of adjacent neighborhoods also may be concerned about the building's visibility, but for entirely different reasons. While visibility is a key factor in siting, it should not be the only consideration. For example, a location at the rear of the site might provide maximum visibility from an adjacent highway, but it also might require an unacceptably long approach through a large parking lot to reach it. The siting choice should seek a balance between access to the building and off-site visibility.

The topography and geology of the site can be determining factors in the decision on where to locate buildings. An elevated area that could provide good visibility, for example, might be over a subsurface rock formation on which it would be prohibitively costly to build. The presence of distinctive site features that should be pre-

The development of a campus for 3,400 employees and 2,500 automobiles is bound to have an impact on the site's surroundings. The design team for the MCI Network Services Group's 760,000-square-foot corporate campus in Colorado Springs, Colorado, tried to mitigate that impact as much as possible. Surrounding residential areas and existing views were taken into account in siting decisions. Parking lots were terraced and arranged in concentric rings to avoid long views through parking. The low-rise connected buildings were arranged as a U with native landscaping at the center.

served and protected affects the building siting decision, as do on-site and off-site view opportunities.

Unless there is a compelling reason not to, the building siting choice should seek also to respect and fit into the project's surroundings. A new building can continue to uphold existing patterns of development or deliberately break them. Developers must make a conscious decision about their building's role in the development pattern of the surrounding neighborhood.

If, for example, the surrounding buildings are built more or less out to the front property line, they may create a strong and consistent edge along the street. A new office building would reinforce this pattern if it were positioned on the property line. And it would break the pattern if it were set back with an entrance plaza in front. Any decision to break the pattern must be for good reasons.

On many urban sites, office developers have fewer alternatives for siting the building. The building's placement is frequently dictated by the placement of buildings on adjacent lots, the size of the development parcel, and the economic necessity of building out the site to its legal capacity in order to justify the high price of the land—among other factors.

Landscaping

Landscaping has numerous important functions in an office development. A well-designed landscape can effectively project the image the developer wishes the office development to have. Developers use landscape design to convey a powerful statement about the office building to visitors from the moment they enter the site to when they arrive at the building's entrance. A reasonable landscape budget for a suburban office development accounts for between 1 percent and 2.5 percent of total construction cost. This is a relatively small investment for something that can add immediate market appeal to the project and lasts for decades.

Among the many functions of landscaping are the following. It can make diverse buildings appear related. It defines spaces. It provides the material for walls, canopies, and floors. It screens certain uses from view. It makes views. It highlights entrances and other special elements. Trees, shrubs, and ground covers can be used to control soil erosion, lower noise levels, remove pollutants from the air, provide protection from wind and other climatic elements, and alleviate glare.

Irvine Spectrum, one of the largest master-planned business parks in the United States, provides a good example of the use of landscaping (as well as signage and architecture) to create a strong sense of identity for a development. Irvine Spectrum, which is located in Orange Country, California, encompasses 3,600 acres and more than 20 million square feet of business space in diverse settings, including mid-rise office towers, high-tech and biotech complexes, and light industrial buildings.

Consistent landscaping unifies this variety. A typical streetscape in Irvine Spectrum exhibits evenly spaced evergreen trees (palm or canopy style), a single ground cover (turf or ivy), and a formal, clipped-hedge backdrop. Deed restrictions tightly regulate groundskeeping in the business park (as well as building maintenance and improvements to buildings).

Plants and trees are hardly the only materials of landscape design. Landscaping elements include rocks, berms, streams, fountains, sculptures, pavements, retaining walls, trellises, outdoor furniture, and lighting. An office development's landscaping should reinforce the overall site plan, unify the site, and respond to the building's architecture.

The landscaping of the average office building tends to the unimaginative: dull concrete sidewalks, few site furnishings, and unshaded parking lots. This run-of-the-mill building makes no accommodation for informal gatherings, lunchtime picnics, or waiting for taxis. Developers should ask for more from their landscaping. They should use it to create usable places for the people who work in the building: a terrace off the cafeteria or deli, a grove of shade trees with benches and trash receptacles, a sheltered taxi pickup area.

Trees on a site will assist the leasing effort and increase the project's long-term value. Precautions must be taken during construction to avoid destroying mature trees. The soil within a tree's canopy or drip line should be left undisturbed, and developers should require contractors to build fences around any trees that are to be protected. Many trees have survived construction only to die later because their roots were buried too deeply in the final grading. If it becomes necessary to pile two to three feet of fill at the base of trees, a six- to eight-inch layer of gravel or stone should be spread over their roots to promote air circulation or tree wells should be constructed around the tree trunk down to the original level of the ground.

The choice of plant materials should depend largely on the local climate and the building's architecture, which plantings should complement. The building design and landscape design should be combined into a cohesive palette. Some plants are better than are others for particular locations—either because of how well they do in those locations or because of how well they work in those locations. Some trees, for example, grow well in the compacted soils of small parking-lot planters, while others do not. Low, weeping trees do not work well in parking-lot islands where they may scrape cars and annoy pedestrians. When choosing plants, developers need to bear in mind their size at maturity. Plants that grow too tall are not suitable for many landscaped areas, such as around the perimeters of buildings where they might eventually obstruct views. A final important factor in plant selection is the cost of landscape maintenance. Ground cover, for example, may be more expensive to install than grass but it will not require weekly mowing. Developers need to consider the tradeoffs between initial landscaping costs and landscape maintenance costs early in the landscape design process.

Landscape design should begin when the site planning process begins. The inclusion of a landscape architect on the development team is advisable, especially if the development of the site involves the need to preserve existing vegetation, to grade extensively, or to construct stormwater detention ponds.

Base-Building Configuration

Developers must determine several key design parameters at the onset of the planning and design phase, be-

Nestlé USA created public open space to enhance its Glendale, California, headquarters. Fountains, plazas, and gardens combine to form a pleasing environment in the middle of the financial district.

A water element at Nestlé USA's headquarters.

Its wooded site sets the landscape theme for Fairview Park, a mixed-use development just inside the Capital Beltway in suburban Fairfax County, Virginia.

The United Parcel Service headquarters in Atlanta was sited to minimally disturb its natural landscape. Tree coverage was preserved as close as 15 feet from the buildings. The building height was kept to approximately the same height as the existing tree canopy. Over 1.5 miles of new pathways that are open to the public wander through the woods.

A corporate commitment to landscaping was the most important influence on the design concept for United Parcel Service's corporate headquarters complex in Atlanta. The HQ buildings were designed to fit into their heavily wooded site with minimal impact on existing vegetation and topography. Only 12 acres of the site were allowed to be disturbed, six of which account for the building footprints. Trees located as close as 15 feet from the buildings were saved. Where vegetation had to be removed, new plantings were made, using primarily indigenous species in order to maintain a sustainable natural environment. A well was installed to replace city water for the irrigation of planters and lawns. The well is used also to collect stormwater runoff from an adjacent highway, clean it, aerate it, and send it to an on-site wetlands area.

Dominating the site is a broad ravine with a small, meandering creek at its base, along which appear rock outcroppings, waterfalls, and several of the site's largest trees. In fact, the ravine is a created, but very natural looking feature that serves as an element of the stormwater management system.

Twin buildings linked by an atrium each provide 620,000 square feet of office and support facilities space for 1,700 employees. A structured parking garage has 1,800 spaces. The UPS program restricted the average height of the buildings to seven stories. The idea was to create a work environment that is like being in a tree canopy and to prevent the buildings from dominating the site. The five-story atrium connector spans the ravine and houses a 620-seat cafeteria, conference center, executive offices, and a roof garden. Two-story-high loggias provide sheltered passageways between the parking decks and building entrances.

A top priority of the building design was to provide maximum exposure to the outdoors, allowing employees to enjoy the beauty of the wooded site and exposing the interior to natural daylighting. Precast sunscreens, which are attached to the exterior at a 63-degree angle, protect the clear glass windows from solar rays. All the office areas, even those at the center of the large floorplates, receive natural daylight. Except at the corners, most of the perimeter space is in an open office format

fore they can address questions of architectural style or lobby materials. Among these base-building design elements that will guide the whole design process are the following:

- floorplates (size of typical floors);
- structural bays and other design modules (spacing of structural columns, depth from the windows to the core, and distance between window mullions); and

- core (location of elevators, restrooms, stairs, and other building service areas).

The base building's design elements are interrelated and decisions about each element must be made in light of the other elements. The floor plan, for example, must consider the building's core, the exterior design should depend in large part on the floor plan, and the core design should take into account the size of the floors.

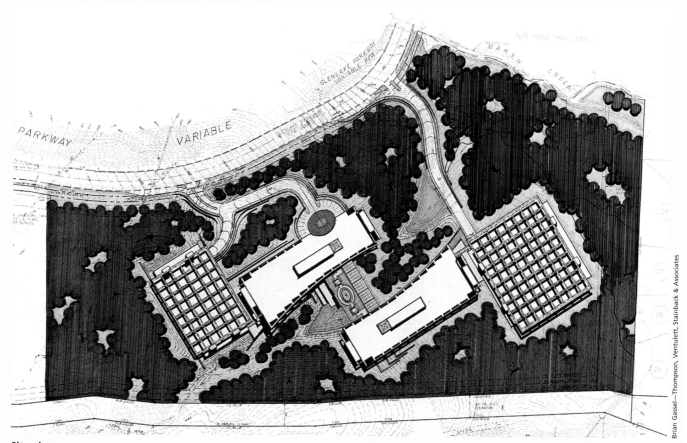

Site plan.

and daylight flows over the cubicle panels. Daylight reaches the enclosed offices, most of which are located in the core, through clerestory glazing that also provides views to the perimeter windows.

The exterior windows are 9.5 feet tall—on floors that have a floor-to-ceiling height of ten feet. The top and bottom sections of the windows are made of green-tinted glass panels. The center section is made of clear glass in order to provide employees with the best possible views to the outside.

The UPS program also called for buildings that are energy-efficient. The interior lighting is energy-efficient and glare-free. On the exterior, lighting is purposefully min-

imized. Lights are mounted low and directed inward, so that safety and security are not compromised and neighbors are not disturbed. Other energy-saving features of the UPS headquarters complex include the cogeneration of heat and power with a gas-fired generator, the use of exhaust air for heat, and digital controls for temperature and lighting.

The UPS headquarters site is open to the public for jogging, walking, and the enjoyment of nature.

■

And what should guide the important base-building design decisions is a design strategy. The goals of the design strategy should be to meet the needs and wants of future tenants and to deliver office space and building services more efficiently and effectively than the competition.

Obviously, then, the developer needs to have a clear picture of who the targeted tenants are and their preferences and expectations for office space. Is the market made up primarily of small tenants in the 2,000- to 5,000-

square-foot range? Does the market comprise primarily back-office operations, which tend to prefer predominantly open office areas? Is the building intended to be a corporate headquarters, which will require large private offices and ample meeting spaces? In each case, the developer will have to make market-specific decisions on the physical design of the office building, while also bearing in mind the construction costs associated with each alternative.

As important as it is to design a building for the targeted tenants, the developer should seek also to ensure the long-term success of the project by considering the needs of future generations of tenants. Even when building for a major tenant, the developer should design the building with enough flexibility to accommodate another major tenant as well as multiple tenants. If an anchor tenant is preleased before the building's design has been completed, the developer will find it necessary to balance

carefully the tenant's preferences against the developer's own need to design a building that will appeal to other tenants in the future.

If, for example, this tenant (with a lease term of ten to 15 years) suggests that its ideal facility will be a single-story building with 50,000 square feet of space, the developer needs to consider this design in light of a realistic exit plan. When the current tenant vacates this unusual building, will the owner be able to attract a buyer or other

The large floorplates at Adobe Systems' 18-story corporate headquarters in San Jose, California, were designed for efficiency and planning flexibility and to facilitate staff communication.

Hellmuth Obata + Kassabaum

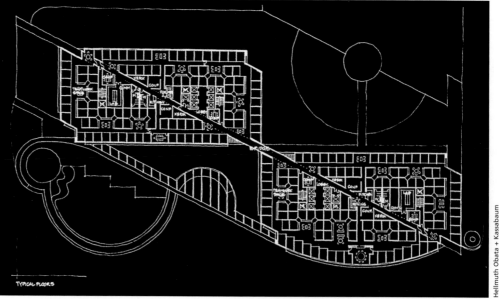

The typical floor is divided diagonally by a "street." Meeting rooms, coffee rooms, and other common areas are located along the Adobe street to provide convenient places for employee interaction.

Hellmuth Obata + Kassabaum

tenants? The developer might propose instead to design a two-story building of the same size, because a 25,000-square-foot floorplate will provide more use options over the life of the structure.

A good market study provides guidance on what design features and amenities will attract particular types of tenant to one office building over another in similar locations. Some seemingly attractive amenities may not necessarily attract tenants, and their inclusion could simply price the building above its market. Certain on-site amenities, such as a day-care facility or a health club, may attract one type of user. For another tenant, the operational efficiency of a state-of-the-art HVAC system or a large column-free floorplate may be of the utmost importance.

If the office building's targeted tenants are operations that are heavy users of communications technology for data collection, manipulation, and transmission, they will need large and open workspaces. Clearly the base building should be designed to accommodate communal work areas. On the other hand, if the targeted tenants are law firms or accounting firms, the design needs to accommodate more private offices. The developer should base these important design decisions on real knowledge of the current marketplace and an educated guesstimate of how current conditions might change.

In thinking about a project's design, the developer should have a clear picture of what competitive buildings are offering. If all the buildings in a market offer basically the same amenities or mechanical systems, therein lies an opportunity to position the building by including some different options and amenities.

While the basic design parameters of an office building must flow from an understanding of the target market, they also must be tempered by the inevitability of change in the marketplace over time. The flexibility to adapt to change is one of the most valuable attributes of a well-designed office building.

Shape (Massing)

The shape of an office building (or its massing) is influenced by a number of factors. These include local zoning regulations, site constraints, the surrounding architectural context, and the known or supposed preferences of the target market. Some jurisdictions require that the upper floors of buildings be stepped back, in order that urban streets lined with large buildings not resemble concrete canyons. Variety in a building's massing, breaking the shape into different forms can avoid the boxy appearance of ordinary office buildings and can decrease the apparent scale of large buildings.

Effective massing can help a building to blend in with the surrounding buildings. An eight-story building squeezed between two six-story buildings in a downtown, for example, could be set back above the sixth story so as to maintain the cornice line of the neighboring buildings.

Designers can use changes in a building's massing to give important visual cues. A change in the massing at the entry, for example, can direct pedestrians to the front door. Smaller massing for top stories of a building along

Stepped upper floors reduce the bulk of this cluster of mid rises at Wilshire Courtyard in Los Angeles. They allow for three levels of rooftop decks as well.

with balconies or roof terraces can indicate the presence of specialty (premium rent) floors.

Rectangular buildings generally yield more efficient use of interior space than do irregularly shaped or curved buildings. In the 1980s, a widespread desire for striking architecture produced a strong movement away from the glass boxes of the 1970s. Office buildings were designed with many angles and corners. However, such buildings now find themselves in the position of being unsuitable for tenants using open floor plans, which do not adapt well to angled spaces.

The site's influence on the shape of a building—which involves considerations of orientation, visibility, topography, and context—varies considerably. In general, urban sites lend themselves to buildings with rectangular shapes, whereas suburban sites can accommodate buildings with more idiosyncratic shapes.

Size

Developers most often determine the size of an office building by weighing several factors and striking a balance among them. Local zoning laws may set a maximum height or a maximum area. How much space the market can absorb is a key consideration. Other important factors include the optimal size of floorplates for the targeted tenants, land costs, construction costs, and site constraints. When land costs are high, as they traditionally have been in central business districts, developers generally want to build as much square footage as permitted by zoning—a strategy that enables them to recover costs within a competitive rental rate structure.

Nevertheless, zoning is seldom the last or only word in the determination of a building's size. The size of the site is a driving factor. Small sites may dictate small building footprints, which may be an argument for tall buildings. However, other site conditions can limit the height of an office building. Constructing a tall building on a site with poor soil conditions, for instance, can be prohibitively expensive.

As a public policy think tank advocating liberal social and conservative economic views, the Cato Institute wanted a building that would embody its dichotomous political philosophy. Furthermore, it would have to address the tight geometry of its downtown Washington, D.C., site. The solution was a building comprising two interpenetrating cubes—an open, light-filled glass cube that contains the lobby and space for receptions and informal activities and a masonry cube that contains the staff offices.

The cost premiums imposed by local building codes on tall buildings sometimes limit their height. These codes often distinguish between mid- and high-rise buildings based on the height that can be reached by fire department equipment. Above that height, building code requirements become stricter and cause construction costs to rise, sometimes prohibitively. Special exit, ventilation, and fire-safety requirements imposed on buildings with heights or floor sizes exceeding certain thresholds can be so costly that they constitute effective limits to size and height.[3]

Ultimately, market demand determines building size. Within the limits prescribed by zoning, the needs and preferences of the target market are balanced against construction costs to calculate the area of the building and the size of its floorplates—and thus its ideal size.

In office buildings constructed today, floorplates generally range from 18,000 square feet to 30,000 square feet or more. A typical multistory office building has a 20,000- to 25,000-square-foot floorplate. A smaller floorplate generally is considered inefficient because a significant portion of the floor space is consumed by the core functions of the building—stairs, elevator shafts, mechanical rooms, electrical closets, and restrooms. This leaves an unacceptably small portion of the floor as rentable square footage. (The ratio of rentable square footage to total square footage is often called the building's efficiency ratio.) Furthermore, from the perspective of space planning for tenants,

small spaces are usually more difficult to use efficiently and flexibly.

Tenants that use open floor plans are a growing share of the office market. They generally prefer large floorplates with few columns. Such spaces can accommodate open office furniture systems and also support teamwork, an organizational strategy that many office-based companies are adopting. Open office formats require less square footage per employee than do more conventional office formats.

Large floorplates may produce more rentable area from the developer's perspective and more flexible space from the tenant's perspective, but they also add to the building's construction costs. Floorplates over 40,000 square feet, for example, may require the addition of a stairway or even require split elevator banks, elements that are very costly.

The determination of optimal floorplate size, then, is a delicate balancing act. The developer must weigh the preferences of targeted and future tenants, construction costs, and zoning regulations against the expected rental rates.

Structural System

An office building's structural system is what supports the building—as opposed to its skin, which protects the interior space from the weather (and is discussed in the "Exterior Materials" section later in this chapter). Among all the components of an office building, the structural system is the least likely to change over time. Exterior skins and mechanical systems may be removed and replaced, but the structure of a building usually remains until the building itself is demolished. In U.S. office buildings, the most commonly used structural systems are steel, reinforced concrete, or a composite system made up of a concrete core with steel framing.

In a steel structural system, a steel skeleton of columns and beams supports the floors, which typically are constructed of concrete poured onto a corrugated steel deck. Steel systems offer several advantages: they are suitable for large buildings and exert a smaller load on the foundations than do concrete structures, they can be erected quickly, they permit long clear floor spans, they can be modified to accommodate changing loading conditions, and they can withstand earthquake loads. Offsetting such advantages is the limited number of steel suppliers, which can cause widely fluctuating prices and long lead times between orders and deliveries to the job site. In addition, compared with concrete, steel usually requires six- to 12-inch-higher floor heights, which can increase dramatically the height and cubic volume of the building and thus the costs of its skin and mechanical systems. For tall steel-frame buildings, wind bracing is also an important design and cost consideration.[4]

The advantages of steel are in many ways the disadvantages of concrete systems. Erecting a reinforced concrete structure takes longer, the foundations must be stronger to carry the greater weight, clear spans are shorter, and making major modifications after completion is more

Although the 30-story Commerce Place towers above its neighbors in Baltimore's generally mid-rise financial district, its use of harmonious colors, materials, and architectural elements results in a pleasing streetscape. The tower's roof echoes that of the historic building in the foreground.

difficult. On the plus side, concrete requires less floor-to-floor height, which reduces skin and mechanical costs. Where building heights are limited, the added floor space that concrete systems allow can be critical. In Washington, D.C., for example, where buildings are limited to a height of approximately 120 feet, concrete construction is the norm. Within the 120-foot envelope, concrete buildings with an average finished ceiling height of 8'6" can achieve two more stories than can steel construction, and thus significantly more leasable space. Also, wind bracing has less cost impact for a concrete structure.[5]

Noting that a variety of structural steel and reinforced concrete systems are available for use in office buildings, architect Henry Brennan of Brennan Beer Gorman in New York suggests basing the selection of the system on the following considerations:[6]

• Flexibility—Is the structure adaptable to changes or modifications required by tenants over the life of the building? Will it accommodate different patterns of loading and walls and openings? Can the floor system easily handle changes in wiring for power and communications?
• Floor Loading—Are floor loading capacities high enough for today's and tomorrow's tenants? Live load on the floor is the weight of occupants, furniture, and equipment. The minimum building code standard for office buildings is 50 pounds per square foot live load plus 20 pounds per square foot partition load. Many tenants today demand heavier loads, either throughout the building or for specific spaces such as storage, files, library, vault, or computers.
• Efficiency—Can the structure support the longer clear spans desired by many tenants in office buildings today?
• Depth of Structure—Will the system support the required depth of structure relative to span, floor-to-floor height, and overall building height?

When Thomson Financial Services, an international high-tech software/publishing company, wanted to consolidate several regional offices into a new corporate headquarters that would make a statement, it reviewed several sites in Boston, Cambridge, and surrounding communities. The firm eventually selected a group of seven brick and timber warehouse buildings in Boston's Fort Point Channel.

The task facing Thomson and the project's designer, ADD Inc, was to create a unified corporate identity in 225,000 square feet of space on 27 floors of seven buildings with dramatically different floor and ceiling heights. Incorporating the buildings' exposed brick, wood beams, and high ceilings into a design that resolved functional and aesthetic issues was a challenging prospect. The design solution had to impart a strong identity throughout the project without disrupting the historical elements of the structures. Most important, it had to unify the diverse floorplates while providing flexibility for expansion and reorganization.

The design team began the process by generating a list of building attributes and concerns and asking questions. Could the exposed timber ceilings remain and still provide even illumination with minimal glare? Could the 11- to 16-foot ceiling heights be maintained without creating uncomfortable proportions in enclosed offices and conference rooms? How could paths between departments be clarified in this maze of buildings?

The designer's response to such concerns evolved into a design menu of architectural components and accent color palettes that was divided into two categories: fore-

Industrial forms and materials combine with warm wood and bright colors to create an inviting interior. The two-story lobby features a dramatic stairway and balcony.

ground and background. Three foreground elements (kitchen/copy/fax areas, storage units, and typical offices) were designed as bold landmarks that could be positioned as needed in vastly different buildings for different work groups. Pavilion structures house kitchen, copy, fax, and recycling functions. Maple-clad towers provide storage for coats or equipment. Offices and conference rooms have sloped maple roofs with skylights and a variety of lighting options. Each department customized its space plan by selecting elements from this menu and accent colors from the project palette. These elements are set against a consistent neutral background of textured paint, carpeting, and office furniture.

These architectural elements link the seven warehouse buildings that have been connected but still maintain their individual entrances and street addresses. The buildings thus serve as neutral enclosures that house distinct working "neighborhoods." This use of pavilions and storage units allows Thomson to grow and change just as an established city grows over time, by connecting landmarks and plazas. And, like the urban landscape it occupies, this workplace can evolve as new people and technologies join Thomson's corporate culture.

Seven warehouse buildings were renovated to become Thompson Financial Services' corporate headquarters. The exterior design uses architectural elements from 19th-century warehouses in a fresh contemporary facade.

Source: Adapted from John H. Uzee, "E Pluribus Unum," *Urban Land*, July 1994, pp. 36–37.

- Stiffness—Is the structure able to withstand lateral forces such as wind and earthquakes? This consideration is especially critical in high-rise buildings.
- Fireproofing—How easily and at what cost can the structure meet fireproof requirements?
- Constructability—How adaptable is the structural system to the standard construction methods in the local market?
- Scheduling—How quickly can the structure be built? The length of time that it takes to erect the structural system can affect move-in dates for tenants and construction costs.
- Cost—What is its relative cost? Alternative systems must be evaluated on the basis of cost. The goal is to select the lowest-cost structure that meets all other project criteria.

Structural Bays and Design Modules

Office buildings are designed using multiple modules of space, which allow for the repetition of structural and skin elements. The basic module is the structural bay, which is defined as the distance between the building's structural columns. The structural bay is generally divided into smaller design modules that provide a grid for co-ordinating interior partitions and window panels for the exterior curtain wall. The sizes of the structural bays and design modules are key elements in both the exterior skin design and in the efficiency and flexibility of the interior spaces. Thus, the determination of structural bay and design module sizes should evolve from the market study's conclusions about the types of space—for example, open office plans or private executive offices—that the targeted segments of the market are demanding.

Closely spaced columns can impose significant limitations on the flexibility of an office building's space. Columns tend to impede the efficient placement of interior partitions and to make the use of modular open office furniture systems less practical.

The structural bays in U.S. office buildings have traditionally measured 25' x 25' or 30' x 30'. Like the size of floorplates, however, the size of structural bays is increasing in response to the growing popularity of open office plans. Bay sizes of 30' x 40' or 30' x 45' are becoming more common. As a rule, bays in multitenant buildings with many small tenants can be smaller.

Large tenants with a preference for open office plans were the target market for 101 Hudson at Colgate Center, a 1.2 million-square-foot Class A office building in Jersey City, New Jersey (see 101 Hudson case study in Chapter 7). The developer designed the building from the inside out to serve the needs of this target market. Large floor areas of as much as 54,000 square feet are the rule. The 13' 10" slab-to-slab heights give most of the building nine-foot ceilings over eight-inch raised floors. Column-free 45-foot clear spans from the core to the outside wall on all sides are the rule—accommodating the wall-to-wall installation of 15-foot square, four-workstation modules. Notched corners bring more light into the interior, an important

consideration for open offices. The deep clear spans were made possible by incorporating a dedicated circulation corridor in the core.

Tenant preferences must be balanced against construction costs. While larger bays provide greater efficiency and flexibility in office layouts, they are almost always more expensive to construct because the longer spans require longer and heavier beams.

The office design generally subdivides the structural bay into modules, providing a grid for the coordination of interior partitions and for the placement of window panels on the exterior. A five-foot design module is a long-used standard. This standard yields interior offices in widths of ten feet (two modules), 15 feet (three modules), or sometimes 20 feet (four modules). With the growing trend toward open space plans in the office workplace, the determination of the size of design modules is just as likely to be guided by the need to accommodate modular furniture systems as by the need to maximize the number of enclosed perimeter offices.

Core Configuration

An office building's core houses many of the building support systems, such as the elevators and elevator lobbies, restrooms, access corridors, mechanical rooms (containing HVAC and other equipment), closets for the distribution of electricity and telephone services, and exit stairs. As a design element, the importance of the core is not as much in its appearance as in its efficiency. Many of the access, circulation, life-safety, and other requirements contained in local building codes have much to do with how an office building's core is designed.

An efficient core is one that takes up as little floor area as possible and is, at the same time, flexible enough to serve the needs of a number of tenants in a variety of sizes. Circulation issues are key considerations in the design of a building's core. The core should be designed to facilitate the flow of people in and out of the building. If access to tenant spaces is poor or if circulation is

At Arrow International corporate headquarters in Reading, Pennsylvania, a tall atrium running the full length of the office accommodates three levels of open work stations suspended by steel columns.

confusing the building can quickly gain a reputation in the marketplace as being unsatisfactory.

The developer must evaluate the efficiency of the building's core configuration during its design phase, when a more efficient plan can still be developed. After the building is constructed it is too late. One measure of the efficiency of the building core is the ratio of rentable space to gross building area. (See "Ways of Measuring Floor Space" section beginning on page 169 for a discussion of the concepts of gross building area and rentable space.) Expressed as a percent, this ratio is called the efficiency factor. In general, an office building with an efficiency factor of less than 85 percent has an inefficient core, while one with a 90 percent efficiency factor —meaning that only 10 percent of each floor is devoted to core functions—has a highly efficient core.

In the design of an office building core, a few elements are more or less fixed. In most cases, the elevators are centrally located and egress stairs are located at the ends of the access corridors and approximately 50 feet from the building's perimeters. (Building codes usually require two egress stairways.) These rules of thumb apply to most speculative office buildings, though they may not be adhered to in the design of highly specialized office buildings for specific tenants.

One of two different basic approaches characterizes the design of most office building cores. One is known as a distributed core and the other as a compact core. (See drawings below.)

In a distributed core, the restrooms, mechanical rooms, and other core elements are located more or less evenly along the length of the access corridor on both sides. Such an arrangement provides flexibility for the placement of numerous tenant entries. Distributed cores are more suitable for buildings that will be occupied by numerous small tenants.

In a compact core, the core elements are tightly packed around the elevator banks. Compact cores are especially useful in buildings that will have one or two tenants per floor, because they will give the tenants more flexibility in the layout of their office spaces.

Exterior Design

Materials, windows, entrances, signage, and lighting: these elements are important aspects of an office building's exterior design and its image. The outside of the building serves a greater purpose than keeping out the rain and wind. The look of the building is a powerful conveyor of a project's image—for better or for worse. The exterior gives passersby and visitors (among whom are prospective tenants and tenants' clients) their first impression of the development, which can be a lasting impression. A number of factors enter into the design of the building's exterior, and one of the most important is the target tenants—their preferences and expectations, and the image that they will want to project to their customers and clients and shareholders.

Of course, tenant preferences change over time. When business was booming in the 1980s, soaring high-rise office buildings were in great demand. Developers hired world-famous architects to design signature edifices. Their buildings were marked by sweeping curves and arches

A distributed core (top drawing) is suitable in general for office buildings with large floorplates and multiple tenants per floor. For buildings with smaller floorplates and one or two tenants per floor, a compact core (bottom drawing) is typically more suitable.

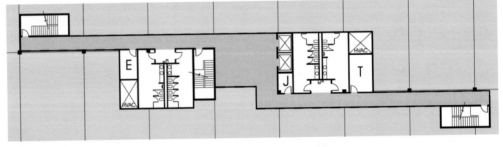

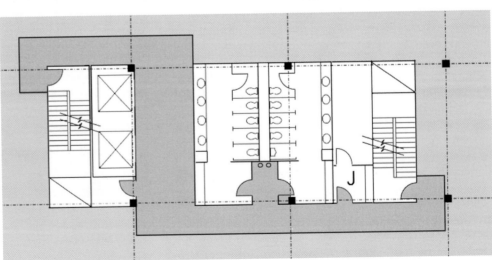

David Whitcomb—RTKL Associates Inc.

and the use of distinctive materials: polished granite, stainless steel, and gold-tinted-glass curtain walls.

However, when office building recommenced in the mid-1990s, after the real estate recession, most new buildings bore little outward resemblance to the trophy buildings of the 1980s. Reflecting office tenants' new-found emphasis on functional, efficient, and flexible space and their distaste for highly visible luxuries, the exteriors of postrecessionary office buildings have become more modest in size, architecture, and choice of materials.

Regardless of current design trends, office developers should aim for an exterior design that conveys enough distinction to add value to a tenant's image and maintain the building's value in the marketplace. At the same time, the developer should avoid design extremes, which all too soon can become dated.

Exterior Materials

An office building's exterior wall, known as its "skin," should be made of materials that are chosen with regard to quality, durability, initial cost, lifetime maintenance expense, and the image they project. Commonly used building-skin materials include brick, aluminum and other metals, glass, masonry, precast concrete, granite, marble, limestone, slate, wood, stucco, and stone. Most office building exteriors combine a number of materials.

Skin materials vary greatly in price, and the same material can differ greatly in price from region to region. Brick and some metal-panel systems are often the least expensive, while precast concrete panels, customized-glass curtain walls, and stone are often the most expensive.

Developers should not select exterior materials based on cost alone. Equally, if not more, important are the building's context and the appearance that is desired for the building. In a suburban setting, brick may be a good choice for a building that is intended to look warm and inviting and is expected to command top-of-the-market

rents. Or, for a building that is intended to appeal to entrepreneurial high-technology firms, the developer might use metal panels and glass curtain walls that give the building the appearance of being on the cutting edge. This deliberate use of typically expensive materials could give the building a significant competitive advantage in certain markets.

In Stamford, Connecticut, 225 High Ridge Road is an example of an office project in which the exterior materials were selected to create a certain look and feel. Gerald D. Hines Interests, the developer of the two-building, low-rise office complex, wanted it to be reminiscent of the large wooded estates that were once prominent in the area. To reflect their classic masonry style, the architect used brick, precast concrete, and clear glass. (See 225 High Ridge Road case study in Chapter 7.)

Maintenance requirements and durability are other key considerations in the selection of exterior materials. In choosing materials, developers should focus on the likelihood of leaks, as leaks are notoriously difficult to locate in facades, and even harder to repair. Also, the skin should be carefully constructed to ensure that it will not look tired and worn in several years.

A properly detailed and well-constructed skin should last the life of the building (or approximately 30 years) without requiring major renovation. But all materials—even masonry, precast concrete, and brick—require periodic maintenance. Exposed to the elements and stressed by movement through settling, joints are a skin's weakest part. Skins that fail usually fail first at the sealant joints around windows or in other places where different materials meet. Curtain wall systems tend to have many joints and therefore often require a high level of maintenance.

Leaks are a risk that the developer should seek to minimize in the exterior design. An office building's skin is more likely than the roof to develop leaks. In the value-engineering process—which is the process by which designers and engineers seek to discover the design and engineering solutions that result in the best possible value within a given construction budget—a watertight skin should be a clear goal.

Entrances

The location of the office building's entrance(s) should be readily apparent to first-time visitors. It is a frustrating experience to approach what one presumes to be the entrance to a building, only to find that the entrance is elsewhere. A variety of design elements can be used to mark the entry. One technique is to mark the entry with a different building material. For example, a building clad in concrete panels could be given a stainless steel entry. A change in the shape of the building can indicate the location of the entrance. For example, the entry area could be recessed or built out from the facade. Or the line of the roof parapet above the entry could be raised or lowered to articulate and draw attention to the point of entry.

If more than one entry is visible from the parking lot, design treatment should be used to indicate the main entry—which usually is the entry that the public uses and that provides the most direct access to the elevator bank. The main entry should be assigned more significance by its materials, massing, or landscaping. It should be located to provide more convenient access for tenants and visitors than secondary entrances.

Developers should give special care to the materials and detailing that surround the building's entry. The

Canopies shelter the entrances and walkways at Apple's research and development facility in Cupertino, California.

entry should be scaled to the comings and goings of people and also should be related to the entirety of the building. Its design should, therefore, echo the exterior design of the building, but its materials and finishes should be of a higher quality and its details more finely rendered. What may be an appropriate detail for the top floor of a six-story precast concrete building might not work as a detail for the entry.

Developers need also keep in mind that the entry design and the lobby design cannot be separated. These two elements should work together to create an entry experience that unites the building's exterior and interior. (See "Lobbies" section beginning on page 171.)

Security is an important consideration in the design of the building's entry. Even if the building has full-time security personnel, an entrance access system—a keypad or magnetic card-key reader—may be required. Such devices should be located in a well-lighted area, clearly visible from outside and inside, and protected from the elements by a canopy or awning.

Exterior Lighting

Exterior lighting should be designed to enhance security within the office site and also to highlight and amplify architectural and landscaping features. Inadequate illumination of entries, parking lots, and other areas on the site not only invites trouble and poses a liability problem, but also hurts the leasing program. Usually security is a major concern of tenants, and unlighted or badly lighted exteriors will give most prospective tenants pause.

Developers should include lighting expertise on the development team. They have turned traditionally to architects and electrical engineers for lighting design services. They are turning more frequently now to lighting consultants for such expertise—particularly when the aesthetics of lighting are a primary concern.

For many years, mercury-vapor, sodium-vapor, quartz, and fluorescent lamps have been used for exterior lighting, because they consume only a fraction of the electri-

A 1940 Greyhound bus terminal was preserved as the main entrance and lobby for a 12-story office and retail building in downtown Washington, D.C. The building's bulk was scaled down to a size below the maximum permitted by zoning so that the terminal would stand out as a distinct element.

city that incandescent lights use. In recent years, the choice of lamps and fixtures has become considerably wider, and many new lighting systems require even less energy and can be designed to achieve distinctive visual effects. Many of the new light bulbs have significantly longer life spans, which reduces operating expense. The placement of lighting, the types of lighting, the levels of illumination, and the types of control systems—manual, timer, or photocell—must all be considered in the project's exterior lighting plan.

Lighting standards for the illumination of parking lots should be placed around the perimeter of the lot or on the centerlines of double rows of car stalls. To protect them from cars, developers should place lighting standards in planter medians and not on the stall lines between cars. Outdoor parking areas should be given an average minimum illumination level of five foot-candles. For structured parking areas, the National Parking Association recommends an average illumination of ten foot-candles.

Windows

The amount of glass used in an office building and the selection and placement of windows are key design considerations. Among the sometimes conflicting factors that have made windows a matter of increasing concern are more stringent energy codes, greater emphasis on reductions in operating costs, and tenant demand for more natural light. Windows can account for up to 25 percent of an office building's heat loss and 30 percent of its cooling load. In the 1970s and 1980s, many office developers selected designs using strip windows—which are continuous horizontal bands of glass that wrap entire floors. Strip windows offer flexibility for the layout of the interior space. However, they can be inefficient in terms of energy use. In recent years, office designers have returned to so-called punched windows—or a facade in which windows alternate with solid panels.

In general, windows should be selected on the basis of the exposure—north, south, east, or west—that they will have. South-facing windows let in solar heat that reduces the building's heating load but increases its cooling load. North-facing windows can lose a significant amount of heat in winter in almost any climate. Large windows on a building's east and west exposures will add to the building's cooling load, unless their heat gain is controlled with careful design. It is easier to decrease window area on east and west exposures than it is to design adequate shading.

Rapid advances in window technology offer many opportunities for improving the energy-efficiency of buildings. In the not-too-distant past, tinted windows or reflective window coatings were commonly used solutions for controlling solar heat gain in the summer. But these tints and coatings can reduce the amount of natural light coming in by as much as 80 percent, and thus require the installation of a higher level of electric lighting. More lighting, in turn, adds to the building's cooling load and a larger cooling load requires larger air-conditioning

Windows are an important and varied architectural element.

The stumbling block for the two principals in midtown Manhattan's Swiss Bank Tower/Saks Fifth Avenue project was the entrance. An innovative design solution helped keep the deal together.

The Swiss Bank Tower/Saks Fifth Avenue complex seems like a textbook example of how to reconcile an array of opposing development forces—retail and office space, new and landmark buildings, and two owners. Saks Fifth Avenue, the venerable New York department store, built in 1924 to resemble a Renaissance palazzo, was joined with a sophisticated new 38-story office tower. In a seamless extension of the department store's selling floors, the tower's nine-story base contains 100,000 square feet of new retailing space.

Completed in 1991, the complex stands on Saks Fifth Avenue land with nine floors occupied by the store and 26 floors occupied by office tenants. Shared facilities include the basement loading docks, mechanical services on the tenth floor, a sky lobby on the 11th floor, a cafeteria on the 12th floor, and an executive club on the 36th floor for the tenants.

The Swiss Bank Tower/Saks Fifth Avenue complex unites a venerable 1924 landmark store with a modern 36-story high rise. The hand-cut limestone tower rises symmetrically behind the store. Its chamfered corners, ribbon windows, and recessed center architecturally respect the store and Rockefeller Center's GE Building.

The bank, based in Basel, Switzerland, and the retailer, then owned by B.A.T. Industries of London, approached the planning table with differing needs for space and image. As each would own and occupy a part of the complex, both parties would have to be satisfied. Otherwise, there would be no deal. The project almost derailed over one question: Who gets the entrance of choice?

Occupying a prime Fifth Avenue block between 50th and 49th streets at Rockefeller Center, Saks wanted to maximize its visibility and display windows along 50th Street. Saks's president, Mel Jacobs, regarded as essential the location of a new store entrance on 50th Street, across from St. Patrick's Cathedral.

Acting as its own developer, Swiss Bank Corporation required a superior location, prestigious address, and a sophisticated image for its new North American headquarters. For the bank, too, a 50th Street entrance became a nonnegotiable demand.

Swiss Bank's U.S. executive vice president Willi Wittner turned to New York City architect Lee Harris Pomeroy. The architect's suggestion that a 50th Street entrance be designed for each party—with an 11th-floor sky lobby for the bank—helped the deal over this hurdle.

Pomeroy's design extended Saks's neoclassical nine-story limestone facade—with its tall windows, fluted columns, and hand-carved stone ornaments—along 50th Street. An embellished bronze canopy (a Saks Fifth Avenue trademark) marked the new entry. By contrast, the bank's 50th Street entry was made elegant and discreet, a three-story portal set back within a flat marble wall. A small but smartly outfitted elevator lobby on the ground floor served as prelude to the 11th-floor sky lobby, a grandly proportioned two-story space with a wall of windows overlooking the spires of St. Patrick's Cathedral.

"With the entrances settled," Pomeroy explains, "the building design became almost a direct blueprint integrating the needs of the office and retail occupants." The common goals of the two owners—column-free floors and in-building loading services—far outweighed their differences.

Combining office and retail floors in a single building required considerable engineering ingenuity. Structural support for a 36-story tower normally would require a continuous vertical transfer of loads to the foundation, but, in this case, the intervening department store had to have maximum column-free space. To resolve this dilemma, the core of the building was moved from the center to the east wall and a structural system was engineered to carry the loads out to the periphery of the base.

Innovative design allowed Saks Fifth Avenue and the Swiss Bank Tower each to have desirable 50th Street entrances.

At the tenth floor, where the base and tower intersect, a massive bridgelike truss supports the transition.

Prompted by the bank's need for instantaneous worldwide communications and electronic funds transfer, state-of-the-art technology was installed, including a fiberoptic communications system, uninterrupted power supplies, and provisions for satellite communications.

Office tenants, primarily financial firms with international operations, have been attracted by the building's advantages: new space in a prime location, sophisticated amenities, open floors, and great views. Two years after completion, the leasable space was completely occupied.

On the urban scale, the Swiss Bank Tower/Saks Fifth Avenue complex works exceptionally well. Its tower complements the neighboring GE Building in Rockefeller Center and the spires of St. Patrick's Cathedral, and its presence can be appreciated by pedestrians. Looking back on the evolution of a multiuse complex that could easily have never gotten off the ground, Pomeroy's favorite compliment is hearing people comment that it seems to have been there forever.

Source: Adapted from Sydney LeBlanc, "Design Helps a (Big) Office/Retail Deal Happen," *Urban Land,* May 1993, pp. 46–47.

■

units. Thus, the net effect of coatings that block both heat and light can be small.

High-efficiency superwindows have come into more common use. Such windows have low-emissivity (low-e) coatings that reflect heat back inside when it is cold outside and back outside when it is hot outside. For insulation, they also enclose an inert gas, such as argon or krypton, between panes. Low-e coatings block infrared waves (heat) while they allow visible light waves to pass through. Superwindows also cut back on the penetration of external noise. These windows entail added costs, but they also can result in considerable savings in the form of downsized HVAC equipment, reduced artificial lighting requirements, and lower operational costs.

Windows were an important part of the design of the Norm Thompson building in Hillsboro, Oregon, a project in which energy-efficiency and employee comfort were important goals. (See Norm Thompson Headquarters case study in Chapter 7.) The building was oriented to the south and its southern exposure was given as much glass area as allowed by the local energy code. Much of the work that would be done in the building involves reviewing art boards and color proofs for retail catalogs, so as much natural lighting as possible was desirable. Instead of tinted class, the designers chose clear, low-e thermal glass that reduces heat loss. They rejected the idea of using skylights because of the significant heat gain involved in skylighting a long building like the Norm Thompson headquarters.

Buildings with window systems that emphasize natural daylighting may have a competitive advantage in some tenant markets. Natural light has been shown by studies to have positive effects on worker productivity. Lockheed Corporation's office building for 2,700 employees in northern California was designed with an emphasis on natural daylighting. Not only were lighting costs reduced by 75 percent and overall energy costs by 50 percent, but also employee absenteeism declined by 15 percent. Many building codes in Europe require that a third or more of an office building's interior light be from natural daylight.

Office building architects and developers have neglected operable windows for many years, but windows that open are making a comeback, especially for office buildings in areas with mild climates such as northern California. For tenants that prefer floor plans with private perimeter offices, operable windows are an increasingly popular amenity. Like natural daylighting, the ability to open windows and let in fresh air—to not feel that one is working all day in a hermetically sealed box—may have a positive effect on employee productivity.

In a building with operable windows, the exterior zone of the HVAC system is somewhat more difficult to balance, but the added operating expense is relatively small. For open office settings and other environments where opening a window would affect several individuals, operable windows may be less desirable and developers should give careful consideration to proposals to include them in the building design.

Because they were absolutely flat, the 1895 Reliance Building's plate-glass windows reflected light evenly and with little distortion. They essentially resembled voids. In 1995, a facade restoration for the 14-story building located in Chicago's Loop was undertaken. The project team sought to create the same effect with insulated glazing. "We needed to get as flat a glass as possible," says T. Gunny Harboe, project architect with McClier, an architecture/engineering and construction firm.

A supplier willing to fabricate nontempered glass was needed. According to Steve Kelley, project manager with Wiss, Janney, Elstner Associates, the facade consultant, tempered or prestressed glass is two to four times stronger than ordinary glass but it is also more prone to warpage since tempering involves heating the glass in a furnace and then rapidly cooling it. Moreover, the rollers that move the glass in the tempering process can make marks on heated glass, and streaks would have been unacceptable in this restoration.

Although the local building code did not require tempered glass, most suppliers felt that sheets of the size needed for the Reliance renovation would be easier and safer to handle in the factory if they were tempered. After an extensive search, the designers finally located a willing fabricator in New York. (The glass is, however, annealed, which involves a process of heating and slower cooling.)

Suppliers also balked at the renovator's request that they match the sight lines of the building's original windows. It was particularly difficult to find manufacturers for the double-hung wood windows, whose meeting rails measured only 1.25 inches high. Manufacturers were concerned that such a thin profile would cause the windows to bow. A willing manufacturer was eventually found, but only because the replacement windows are fixed rather than operable and therefore need only a single wood piece rather than two smaller ones for each meeting rail.

The larger windows also presented problems. Their panes had rested on wood seats that were set into the bottoms of cast-iron frames and held in place by wood stops. The wood had rotted, so that the glass was no longer continuously supported at the base, according to Kelley. Suppliers indicated that framing the replacement glass in the same manner would not meet code requirements. The concern was that the large panels would bow in the wind and pop out of their frames. A framing member with more bite was needed. The solution was to set aluminum frames within the grooves of the original cast-iron mullions so that they were virtually invisible to the eye.

Despite these efforts, the glazing has been met with mixed reviews. The new windows have a slightly distorted reflection largely due to the double glazing, and some critics have complained that they no longer resemble voids. "We got the flattest, clearest glass that we could," Harboe says. "With restoration work, you're sometimes limited by the technologies available."

Source: Adapted from John Gregerson, "Old Reliable," *Building Design & Construction*, March 1997, p. 58.

Jon Miller—Hedrich-Blessing. Courtesy of McClier Corporation

The Reliance Building's replacement windows are set into a restored terra-cotta facade.

The main entry at Nortel's corporate headquarters building in Toronto was designed for high visibility and to give customers and visitors an arrival experience appropriate for a company that creates advanced-technology products. A curved, transparent glass facade invites glimpses into the corporate work environment.

Hellmuth Obata + Kassabaum

Signage

Developers should use signs not only to identify the building and some or all of its tenants and to help employees and visitors find their ways, but also to represent the development. Signs—their design, placement, and content—are an important component of the overall impression of the building that visitors receive.

The best approach is to develop a comprehensive signage program. Design, materials, and color scheme should be well thought out for each type of signage needed:

- project identification at the entry to the site;
- identification of the building;
- directional signs and symbols through the site and in the parking lots and structures;
- the building directory; and
- identification of building services (elevators, restrooms, equipment rooms, and so forth).

To be most effective, all the elements of the signage program should be designed to be compatible in terms of lettering styles, materials, lighting, and color. It can be helpful to carry certain design concepts developed for the signage program, like logos and colors, over into the marketing program—for use in brochures, letterhead, and advertisements. Developers should consult with experienced marketing consultants and graphic designers in developing the signage that, in effect, puts the name of their project in the public eye.

In most municipalities, the types and amount of exterior signage that can be installed at an office development are regulated by ordinance. Sign codes typically control the size of exterior signs and their placement, lettering, and lighting. Developers must comply with guidelines in the Americans with Disabilities Act for the placement and clarity of exterior and interior signs pointing out accessible parking spaces, loading zones, entrances, exits, stairs, and elevators.

Office park developers should determine the location and quantity of entry signage during the site planning phase. Permanent and seasonal landscaping and lighting should be used to enhance entry signage. Care should be taken to locate signs so that they do not interfere with motorists' sight lines.

In some situations, it may be possible and helpful to extend the signage program off site. The example of Fairview Park, a master-planned office park in northern Virginia, has been cited. Located at the intersection of the Capital Beltway and Route 50, Fairview Park is serviced by a dedicated interchange on the beltway. Well-placed and numerous signs along the access road help visitors and tenants find their way from the beltway to Fairview.

The signs that identify an office building and its tenant(s) typically are located close to the building's primary entrance. The design and materials of identity signage should complement the design and materials of the building's exterior. Lighting and landscaping can be used to good effect to heighten the visibility of identity signage.

If permitted by local ordinance and if agreed to during tenant negotiations, a tenant's identification may be mounted on the building. This privilege is usually limited to one tenant that occupies a large percentage of the building. Many tenants negotiate hard for sign privileges. For tenants that will be allowed to mount identity signs on the building, developers should include in the lease a provision that the property owner must have final design approval of their signs. Inappropriate signage can downgrade the image of the development, a result that clearly benefits neither the tenants nor the building owner.

Informational signage should be strategically located and quickly comprehensible. It should clearly identify entrances, parking areas, service and delivery areas, and directions to various destinations within the complex. Informational signage also should be comprehensive and well designed, reinforcing the visual cues that were established in the site plan and facilitating the progress of visitors through the site.

Building Systems

The items that go into an office building's infrastructure —its mechanical systems, electric power and communications capacity, plumbing, elevators and escalators, lighting, and fire protection system—are generally very costly and can become outmoded as new technologies are developed and the needs and preferences of tenants change. Changing organizational structures, operating procedures, and equipment needs on the part of many office-based operations have changed the office workplace so much and at such a rapid pace that the basic infrastructure in many office buildings of the 1970s and 1980s fails to meet the preferences and needs of many firms in the 1990s.

This section discusses the functions of major office building systems and suggests key issues that the developer needs to consider in determining which systems are appropriate for a particular office building.

Heating, Ventilation, and Air Conditioning

Not only is the HVAC system one of the most costly line items in an office building's construction budget (typically 15 percent of the total construction cost), but it is also a major factor in tenant satisfaction. Surveys by the International Facility Managers Association (IFMA) and Carnegie Mellon University's Center for Building Performance and Diagnostics have identified temperature control and air circulation as the number one employee complaint in offices across the United States—accounting for nearly 90 percent of all complaints to building managers. A good HVAC system can do much to enhance the quality of indoor air and the comfort of the work environment. The importance of the HVAC system and its cost make its selection a critically important decision. To make that decision, the developer must consider many factors.

The primary considerations in the selection of an HVAC system include the following:

- the size of the building (floor dimensions, height, and volume);
- the amount of exterior glass;
- the building's orientation and type of skin;
- the cooling load, which is largely a function of the number of occupants, the type and quantity of lighting and other electrical equipment that emits heat, and heat gain through the building's skin;
- the heating load; and
- the number of temperature zones required and other control mechanisms needed.

Ongoing changes in the office workplace are creating a demand for bigger, better, and more flexible HVAC systems. Higher employment densities in many work-

At the 11-building EDS Centre in Plano, Texas, an energy-conserving ice storage system supplements five 1,000-ton chillers.

places, more widespread use of high-tech office equipment that generates heat, and a growing awareness on the part of tenants of the benefits of high-quality indoor air are spurring the development of more efficient HVAC systems and, in particular, better methods of ventilating and cleaning air.

Developers have discovered that tenants increasingly are looking for flexible HVAC systems that can be operated efficiently during hours other than the traditional 9 a.m. to 5 p.m. workday. A multiple-zone HVAC system is a necessity for tenants with employees who work late or on weekends, so that the tenant can avoid having to pay to heat or ventilate an entire floor or larger portion of the building. Such a system divides the building into zones, each controlled by its own thermostat. The more zones in the building, the more precisely can the temperature and humidity be regulated—an advantage, however, that comes at the price of higher installation costs.

In zoning the building, developers should seek to create air-flow zones that are uniform in terms of some basic characteristics—such as orientation to the sun, type of use, and intensity of use. The HVAC requirements for conference rooms, waiting rooms, computer rooms, kitchens, and restrooms are different than they are for general office uses, and these areas should, if possible, be in separate zones that do not include general office uses. The zoning plan should divide large single-use areas into a number of zones as well, in order to provide flexibility for the future reuse of the space. The balance of tenant needs against costs should be the chief criterion in determining the total number of zones in the system and the amount of space included in a single zone. In today's new office buildings, a typical thermostat zone comprises five or six perimeter offices or 1,000 to 2,000 square feet of interior office space. A single zone in an open office plan can be larger than a single zone in a closed-rooms configuration.

The basic goals of a well-designed and functioning HVAC system are to:

- provide comfortable, consistent temperature and humidity levels,
- introduce and circulate adequate amounts of outside air, and
- isolate and remove odors and contaminants from the circulating air.

One person's comfortable temperature may not be another's, and other variables like the uniformity of temperature in the office space and the individual's location near heat-generating equipment, an air vent, or a cold surface, for example, affect comfort levels. The level of humidity affects how hot or how cold is considered comfortable. The American Society of Heating, Refrigerating, and Air-Conditioning Engineers (ASHRAE) Standard 55-1992, Thermal Environmental Conditions for Human Occupancy, describes the temperature and humidity ranges that are comfortable in most office environments for winter and summer conditions.

HVAC systems meet thermal comfort and ventilation needs by supplying a blend of outside and recirculated air that has been filtered, heated or cooled, and, sometimes, humidified or dehumidified. Odors and contaminants are controlled through the use of air-cleaning and -filtration devices and exhaust systems, and by adjusting the quantity of air that is supplied to and removed from each room.[7]

Opinions on how much outside air needs to be brought into the system for proper ventilation have varied substantially over time. ASHRAE Standard 62-1989, Ventilation for Acceptable Indoor Air Quality, is currently under revision to reflect advances in the state of knowledge and practices in indoor-air quality since the standard was published in 1989. Final approval of the new standard may come in 1998. The 1989 standard includes the following features:

- a definition of acceptable air quality;
- minimum standards for flows of outside air to occupied areas;
- the recommendation to control contaminants at their source rather than trying to filter them out of air that is circulated through the system;
- recommendations for the use of heat-recovery ventilation;
- a guideline for allowable carbon dioxide levels; and
- appendices listing suggested possible guidelines for common indoor pollutants.

As with most other office building design issues, the selection of an HVAC system is directly related to the needs of the target tenants. If the building is being developed for a corporate headquarters or a law firm, for example, and most of the space will be made into private offices, the employee comfort and tenant satisfaction gained by establishing an individual thermostatic control zone for each office may be worth the extra installation cost. If, on the other hand, the building is being developed for back-office operations where employees work mostly out of open office cubicles, rents generally will not support such an expensive HVAC system.

Widely Used Systems. The most appropriate HVAC system for an office building is usually the one that provides the best environment for the targeted tenants within an HVAC budget (including operations) that can be justified by the rent that those tenants will pay. Among the variety of HVAC systems available for office buildings, the most widely used center on one of four basic heating/cooling units: central plants, rooftop package units, heat pumps, or individual floor units. Each of these types of HVAC system is discussed in the following paragraphs.

A central plant usually is selected only for large office buildings, typically high rises of 500,000 square feet or more. Such a system consists of a chiller plant and a boiler plant, typically located in the basement or on the roof. Multiple chillers and cooling towers cool water for use in the air-conditioning cycle of the system. Multiple boilers heat water for use in the heating cycle. The boil-

After 60 years of advances in technology, the air-conditioning systems in modern office buildings can provide excellent ventilation and control the temperature and humidity in every part of the space. Are office tenants happy with these systems? By and large, they are not.

One office building manager, whose experience is typical of many others, regularly sends out questionnaires to gauge tenant satisfaction. He says that he can count on a score of six out of seven when it comes to cleaning, lighting, elevators, and access. However, when it comes to air conditioning, he rarely scores above a 4.5. Why is that? His systems are well designed. In fact, most HVAC practitioners would be challenged to improve them.

It is because air conditioning can still get better. The key is individual occupant control of temperature and air motion to create individually ideal conditions.

Independent climate control for private offices has long been an option. But achieving individual control of temperature and air motion for areas with open-top and no-door workstations requires a new approach.

A concept developed by Johnson Controls—the Personal Environmental Module (PEM)—involves an air unit that can be mounted in the knee space under a workstation desk. The unit's fan draws air from two sources—an underfloor supply plenum or the knee space. The mix depends on the temperature that the workstation occupant sets manually, and the occupant also controls the fan speed manually. Air is discharged above the desk in two louvered outlets. The West Bend Insurance Company installed the Johnson system for 390 workers in a new office facility, and experienced a significant rise in productivity.

McGill University sponsored the development of another system, known as Zero Complaint, that uses a vertical air jet to supply air to individuals. Individuals control the volume of air motion on them by directing the swivel on the air jet and raise or lower the temperature with a hand-held remote control.

A Zero Complaint system was installed in May 1994 in the Real Property Department of Public Works Canada in Toronto. McGill University research had found that complaints about the facility's HVAC system averaged about 10 percent (of employees) before May 1994. A survey conducted after four months of individual control found that employee dissatisfaction had dropped to zero percent, and the same results were found in another survey taken a year later.

Much of the reason for increased employee satisfaction from personal control systems comes from the control over air motion that they provide. Equipment manufacturers and building engineers have labored for 60 years to separate all air motion from building occupants. They may actually have gone too far. Given the chance, some 20 percent of an office building's occupants will opt for a level of workspace air motion that is up to four times the 50 feet per minute that is the commercial standard for drafts.

Conventional HVAC systems contain all air motion in a zone that does not extend beyond three feet of the finished ceiling. Air motion around lower workstations is essentially zero. In these systems, air is supplied and returned at the ceiling level, and much of the ventilation component of the system may never reach most building occupants.

Personal control systems are different in that they provide displacement ventilation. Air traverses the workstation from bottom to top, with an air change rate of up to one per minute. The ventilation component of the system is included in the total purging effect, which is why they make the air seem much fresher.

The Johnson PEM is best suited for new buildings with air plenums in raised floors. The Zero Complaint system can be adapted to almost any air-delivery system and is ideal for building renovations.

These approaches represent the third wave in air-conditioning technology. First came comfort cooling (1935–1955), then zone control (1955–1995), and now personal control.

Source: Adapted from Robert T. Tamblyn, "Air Conditioning in the 90s: Giving Control to Individuals," *Skylines*, June 1996, pp. 51–53.

ers and chillers can be powered by electricity, natural gas, or oil, with the choice depending primarily on local energy costs.

Chilled and heated water is piped to air-handling units (AHUs) that are located in mechanical rooms on each floor of the building or in a central penthouse. Each AHU mixes fresh air brought in from the outside with recirculated inside air, and passes the air mixture over heating or cooling coils. The properly heated or cooled (and dehumidified) air is distributed through ducts to the office areas. Variable-air-volume (VAV) terminal units that modulate the volume of airflow to each zone control the temperature in each zone.

A central-plant system offers the building's owner great flexibility, in that the air mixing and distribution system can be modified without affecting the primary chillers and boilers. A central plant is initially more expensive than other alternatives, but it also can be one of the most efficient HVAC systems to operate in terms of energy use. But it is efficient only for a standard pattern of building use. Because the entire central plant system must be activated to heat or cool any space in the building, it can be enormously inefficient and expensive for a multi-tenant building that houses small tenants that need to heat or cool their space during evening or weekend hours. A 10,000-square-foot tenant with 24-hour operations may need to use (and pay for) a system designed to heat and cool an entire high-rise office building. The sophistication of most central-plant systems is another potential disadvantage, insofar as the plant may require an on-site operator, which will add to operating costs.

Some central plants include a system for making ice and storing it in tanks. Using the chillers to make ice at night—when utility companies charge lower off-peak rates —and melting the stored ice during the day to cool the building results in lower energy bills. An ice storage system costs more to install than does a standard central-plant system, and it also can take up more space in the building. However, the rebates that utility companies in some regions of the United States offer for installing equipment that reduces peak hour demand for energy can offset some of added cost, making ice storage a potentially attractive option.

Rooftop package units, a second widely used type of HVAC system, are found most often in small- to medium-sized buildings of less than five stories. The installation cost for a package unit is less than for a central plant, but the operating cost is generally higher. In place of separate chilling and boiling plants, the heating, cooling, and air-handling equipment is all contained in single units (or a single unit) that are mounted on the roof. Using electricity, gas, or oil, the rooftop units mix fresh air with recirculated air, heat or cool the mix, and deliver it to the office areas through ducts. This type of system also uses VAV terminal units for controlling temperature.

A roof-mounted package system eliminates the need for mechanical rooms containing large air-handling units on each floor. This contribution to the building's floor efficiency is somewhat offset by the system's requirement

When Chase Manhattan Bank undertook the comprehensive renovation of its aging 50-story Manhattan office building, One New York Plaza, the installation of energy-efficient building systems was a high priority.

for large vertical shafts to house the ducts that supply conditioned air to the floors and return used air to the rooftop units.

Systems using heat pump technology are a third type of HVAC system. They are less expensive than rooftop units or central plants to install and they work well in buildings with fewer than six stories. Such systems use electricity or gas (and sometimes waste heat) to drive pumps that extract the heat from some heat source— usually air, ground, or water—for use in space heating or cooling. They can thus deliver more heat or cooling out of a given amount of utility-delivered energy than can conventional space-conditioning systems.

Heat pump units can be located on a building's roof or above the ceilings. A water loop heat pump system is common, in which each heat pump is connected to a piped water loop that is also connected to a cooling tower. Air that has been cooled or heated by the heat pumps is delivered through ducts to thermostatic control zones in the building.

A geothermal heat pump system uses the ground as the heat source, usually by means of a piped water loop that passes through underground water wells located around the building. No cooling tower or auxiliary heat source is needed, and this type of system is highly energy-efficient. Geothermal heat pump systems qualify for the energy-conservation rebates that are offered by many utility companies, which can help offset their higher installation cost.

A fourth HVAC system commonly used in office buildings is self-contained air-conditioning systems on each office floor. Floor-by-floor air conditioning is most appropriate for medium- to large-sized office buildings, from four to 30 stories. Water-cooled air-conditioning units are located on each floor, in mechanical rooms that typically are located so that the main air supply ducts can be routed over the restrooms, in order to control noise. Each floor typically houses two units. A cooling tower and pumps are located on the roof, usually adjacent to the elevator machine room, and usually screened. Cooled air is distributed through ductwork on each floor to VAV terminal units for temperature control. The mixing of return air and fresh air on each floor means a substantial reduction in the size of air shafts. Another advantage of this system is that providing off-hour cooling is economical, because only the individual unit and the cooling tower are needed.

Indoor-Air Quality. Indoor-air quality (IAQ) has become a factor of major concern for office building owners, developers, and tenants. The term "sick-building syndrome" came into use in the 1980s, as the workers in one office building after another began complaining of physical discomfort and other health symptoms suffered during the workday. Sick building syndrome describes a situation in which a building's occupants experience health and comfort effects that appear to be linked to time spent in the building, but where no specific illness or cause can be identified. If a diagnosable illness is detected that can be attributed to contaminants found in the building, it is called a "building-related illness." Exposure to toxic materials that may be found in office environments can cause headaches, eye irritation, nose and throat irritation, sinus congestion, fatigue, and insomnia.

IAQ research has revealed the presence of many chemical and bacterial pollutants in office buildings. Among these are bacteria in air-handling systems, ozone emitted from fax machines, chemicals released (off-gassed) from carpets made from petroleum distillates, and hydrocarbons and particulates emitted from printers. One indoor bacterium, Legionella, has caused both legionnaires' disease and Pontiac fever. Operating and maintaining a building in ways that are inconsistent with the design and prescribed operating procedures can create IAQ problems.

Developers should be aware that sick-building complaints are not necessarily related to the quality of the air. Other office environmental factors—such as noise levels, lighting levels and glare, the design of workspaces and equipment, and job-related stress—can contribute to the symptoms that collectively make up sick-building syndrome.

Good indoor-air quality matters. Tenants increasingly consider it as a factor in their evaluations of the health and comfort of the work environment. Excellent IAQ and high ratings on other essential elements of a pleasant indoor environment can give office buildings a significant marketing advantage. In EPA's view, good IAQ is the product of three factors: adequate ventilation rates and air distribution, the control of airborne contaminants, and the maintenance of an acceptable temperature and relative humidity.

Developers should make a healthy indoor environment a key objective of the design process and a key criterion in the selection of materials and building systems. The owners of buildings whose occupants have complained about IAQ need to conduct an investigation of the building to identify the cause and determine the most effective corrective actions.

An EPA publication entitled *Building Air Quality* outlines procedures for investigating the sources of indoor air problems. According to EPA, building owners should focus on four elements in seeking to pinpoint the causes of an IAQ problem or in designing to avoid the development of an IAQ problem:[8]

- Sources—A source of contamination or discomfort may be located in the building, outside the building, or in the building's mechanical systems.
- HVAC—The HVAC system may not effectively remove contaminants from the air or provide temperature and humidity conditions that are comfortable for most occupants (thermal comfort). Inadequate ventilation —caused by insufficient infusions of outdoor air or by ineffective distribution of air within the building—is an important factor in poor IAQ.
- Pathways—There can be a pathway, which is usually the HVAC system, through which a pollutant travels from its source to the air breathed by the building's occupants.
- Building Operations—Building finishes and operational practices frequently are a cause of IAQ problems. Chemicals may be released from building components or furnishings. Cleaning materials emit chemicals, as do stored maintenance supplies. Trash emits odors. Improperly maintained cooling towers and standing water from clogged or poorly designed drains provide favorable environments for the growth of microorganisms.

According to EPA, resolving IAQ problems usually involves a combination of steps addressing the source of pollution, ventilation rates, air cleaning, and education and communication.[9] Each of these steps is discussed in the following paragraphs.

Removing or modifying the sources of pollutants is an effective approach to solving IAQ problems when the

The 16-story National Bank Plaza Building in Phoenix was retrofitted with a fully computerized energy management system (EMS). The system allows the engineering staff to closely monitor and control all heat pump, air-handler, central plant, and lighting functions.

sources are known and if their control is feasible. Routinely maintaining HVAC systems and regularly replacing water-stained ceiling tiles and carpeting are generally effective measures. Venting emissions from sources like copiers and printers and photographic dark rooms to the outdoors and establishing procedures for the storage and use of materials that can pollute—like paints, adhesives, solvents, and pesticides—in well-ventilated areas can help. Allowing time for the off-gassing of building materials in new or remodeled areas before occupancy begins can lessen this source of irritation to building occupants. (Further guidance on this subject is included in ASHRAE Standard 62-1989, Ventilation for Acceptable Indoor Air Quality, and Addendum SSPC 62 to maintain and revise Standard 62.)

Increasing ventilation rates and distributing air more effectively can be cost-effective means of reducing the levels of indoor pollutants. Even when HVAC systems have been designed to meet the ventilation standards in local building codes they may not be operated or maintained in a manner that ensures the achievement of those minimum ventilation rates. As noted in the preceding paragraph, local exhaust ventilation should be considered for removing pollutants that accumulate in specific areas, such as rooms that contain a number of copiers and printers.

Air cleaning can be used to supplement source control and ventilation in efforts to resolve IAQ problems, but the technique has certain limitations. High-performance air filters capture small particles, but they are relatively expensive to install and operate. Mechanical filters do not remove gaseous pollutants. They can be fitted out with adsorbent beds to remove some specific gaseous pollutants, but these beds can be expensive and their effectiveness depends on frequent replacement of the adsorbent material.

Education and communication are important elements in both remedial and preventative IAQ management programs. When a building's tenants, managers, and maintenance personnel are fully aware of the causes and consequences of IAQ problems and keep open their lines of communication, they can work together and thus more effectively to prevent problems from occurring and to solve them when they do.

Energy Management System

The Building Owners and Managers Association (BOMA) International's 1997 Experience Exchange Report for U.S. office buildings, which is an analysis of operating income and expenditures based on a survey of more than 4,000 office buildings, reports that energy costs account for 21 percent of total operating expenses, behind taxes and insurance (accounting for 32 percent) and ahead of repairs and maintenance (16 percent).

Energy costs are of considerable consequence to most companies. In a 1996 survey of facilities managers by the International Facility Management Association (IFMA), nearly 60 percent said that they have raised thermostats during the summer and lowered them in the winter to conserve energy. Meanwhile, companies are investing in energy-efficient machinery and equipment in order to reduce energy costs. More than half of the facility managers surveyed had replaced older equipment with new, energy-efficient models within the preceding two-year period.[10]

Until the late 1970s, the most cost-effective control systems for managing energy use in a building were fairly simple, such as thermostats for temperature control and time clocks that could start and stop equipment. Today, office developers can choose from a wide spectrum of energy management systems, ranging from one in which all building systems, even the most complex, are fully automated to one that provides basic stop and start functions for building equipment. Thanks to rapid technological advancement and the continuing decrease in the cost of microprocessor-based equipment, the majority of new office buildings can afford a modern EMS, and many older buildings can afford an EMS retrofit.

A modern EMS in today's so-called intelligent buildings uses sensors to read temperature, humidity, lighting levels, and other conditions in interior spaces and sends signals back to the system controls, which, in turn, make adjustments. Building systems can be set and controlled remotely through the EMS to operate efficiently and maximize space comfort.

The scope and cost for an office EMS vary widely, depending on the specific needs of the development. The project's design team should tailor the attributes of the

In 1991, the National Bank Plaza in downtown Phoenix began a $3 million renovation. The owners, Grossman Company Properties and Aetna Life Insurance Companies, sought to make the 16-story, 265,000-square-foot building a Class A property that could attract and maintain a tenant base of small professional firms. The project involved upgrading the appearance of the 1980 building and updating its energy systems to make them more efficient and cost-effective. Among the major improvements were the installation of an energy management system, a lighting retrofit, an HVAC retrofit, and the replacement of the cooling towers.

A computerized energy management system (EMS)—the CSI S7000 series—was installed. This allows the engineering staff to closely monitor and control all HVAC and lighting functions, detect malfunctions, and produce monthly energy use reports.

Lighting improvements were undertaken to enhance the aesthetics of the workplace and to save energy costs. Low-voltage recessed halogen lights were installed and, in a second phase, all fluorescent fixtures were upgraded to T8 fluorescent lamps. The annual energy cost savings per T8 lamp is estimated to be more than $17.50. More than 3,000 fixtures were involved, for a total annual savings of more than $52,000 and a payback period of only two years.

On the HVAC front, a high-efficiency heat pump system was installed. The system provides ten thermostatically controlled temperature zones per floor, each approximately 1,500 square feet in size. Designed to compensate for the movement of the sun during the day, the system automatically makes adjustments for outside conditions.

After-hours air conditioning is provided upon request, at an hourly charge. Building engineers can program special orders for air conditioning made ahead of time.

As the renovation progressed, the building's occupancy rose from 40 percent to 95 percent. It was soon evident that the building's aging fluid coolers were undersized for the cooling load imposed during the hot Arizona summers. The replacement of four fluid coolers with two cooling towers and a tube heat exchanger increased cooling capacity from 800 tons to more than 900 tons, and allowed for better temperature control and operational efficiency.

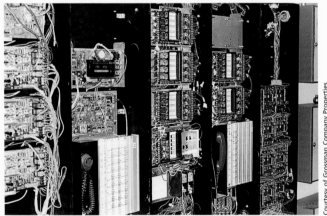

Four coolers (top photo) were replaced by two cooling towers.

An outmoded life-safety system panel (top photo) was replaced.

EMS to the project requirements and budget. In addition, an EMS should be designed with the capability of being expanded in the future.

Electrical System

An office building's base electrical capacity needs to power all the building systems and meet tenant power needs. Office buildings developed as recently as the late 1980s and early 1990s can have base electrical capacity that is vastly insufficient for many of today's high-tech office needs but well within the range of power demanded by many other users of office space. The office developer's selection of appropriate electrical systems should depend on the needs of the targeted tenants, the cost and ease of installation, and operating costs.

In a build-to-suit development, the developer can fairly easily determine the power needs of the user. For a speculative office building, this determination is more difficult. The following discussions of electrical supply, lighting power requirements, and the provision of emergency power focus on some of the key issues that the developer needs to consider when planning the electrical systems for an office development.

Electrical Supply. The local power company brings electrical power to the building's main transformers, which may be owned by the power company or by the property owner and which steps down the incoming power from many thousands of volts to 480 volts. The developer should consider carefully the location of the transformers in relation to the main building's switch gear, because the cost of the installation and cabling may substantially increase as the distance between the switch gear and the transformers increases.

Various mechanical systems within the building require different voltages. The primary HVAC equipment typically requires 480-volt power, fluorescent lighting and some other HVAC equipment typically require 277 volts, some office equipment requires 208 volts, and most general office and computer uses need 110 volts. Transform-

ers are required to step down to each lower voltage. Power is distributed from each type of transformer by circuit breaker panels from which wires are run to individual outlets throughout the building.

Tenants are primarily concerned with the low-voltage end of the spectrum. Their primary concern is the amount of power that is available through the normal 110-volt circuits and wall receptacles for operating computers and other office equipment. In recent years, tenants have generally increased their demand for power from an average of 3.5 watts per square foot to five watts per square foot or more. Many different types of firms, from Andersen Consulting to Hewlett-Packard, typically require seven to ten watts per square foot for their office space. To meet tenant demands as high as this, a building's base electrical capacity must be ten to 13 watts per square foot. (See developer discussions of technologies in office buildings on pages 166 and 167.)

Many R&D facilities and companies involved with computer imaging require 15 watts or more per square foot. Examples of space users with such high energy demands include the state-of-the-art development electronics lab at Tandem Computers' Systems Design Development Building in Cupertino, California, and Sony Pictures Imageworks in Culver City, California.

When tenants tell landlords they need 10 watts per square foot, they may be referring to what electrical engineers call a nondiversified load (or the total sum of power requirements) as opposed to a connected load. In any office, all power-using machinery—equipment, lights, and computers—will not be in use simultaneously. Electrical engineers, through experience and in accordance with municipal electrical codes, apply a diversity factor (or the percent of total power requirements that will actually be needed at any one time) to determine the building's connected load. A tenant's connected load more accurately represents its level-of-service requirements.

The developer's objective should be to supply tenants with all the power they need. However, the developer and

The lead tenant's 25,000-square-foot computer operation was the main reason for installing an instantaneous backup power supply at the Corporate Center office complex in Boston. In the event of a power outage, a bank of batteries stored in the basement immediately provides electricity until a diesel-powered backup electric generator automatically kicks on. A second backup generator powers lights, elevators, and other emergency accessories.

Courtesy of Leggat McCall Properties

electrical engineer should make a considerable effort to determine the tenants' actual requirements. It is also important to estimate accurately the number of watts that must be provided to each floor to operate the building's HVAC systems. Overdesigning the electrical systems in terms of the building's realistic power needs is costly and inefficient. The reduction of electrical power requirements through green design measures and special energy-management measures should be taken into account in determining the building's power requirements.

Interior Lighting. Lighting plays a key role in an office building's design, both as a tool for articulating spaces, highlighting features, and creating atmosphere to influence how tenants and visitors perceive the building and also as an important element of the workplace environment that affects employee productivity.

Lighting accounts for a significant portion of an office building's use of electric power, and installing energy-efficient lighting can save operational expense as well as contribute to an overall reduction in the environmental pollution caused by fossil fuel electricity generation. (See "Patagonia Building" feature box on page 338.) Design innovations in electric lighting (and in daylighting techniques as well) have made it possible to light an office building today using about half the energy that was required ten years ago.

Electronic ballasts and energy-saving fluorescent lamps and reflective fixtures can be used in various combinations to minimize electrical consumption. The quality of light has also been improved. Parabolic fixtures, for example, provide more light for the same amount of energy than do prismatic lenses, with less glare on computer screens. The growing use of energy management systems (see "Energy Management System" section earlier in this chapter) has also contributed to the efficiency of lighting in office buildings. Lighting designers also have made use of the different absorptive and reflective qualities of colors and fabrics to alter the need for lighting in office spaces.

Retrofitting the lighting in older buildings can yield large benefits in energy-efficiency. As the Audubon House case study in Chapter 7 notes, a new lighting system added approximately $92,000 to the cost of the 1992 renovation of the National Audubon Society's century-old headquarters building in New York. This investment in lighting-efficiency was expected to reduce annual electricity expenses by $60,000. Operational savings plus rebates from the local power company, Con Edison, added up to a one-year payback period for the expense of the new lighting system, which included motion sensors for controlling lighting in each room and energy-efficient T8 fluorescent lamps that dim as sunlight is detected.

Integrated ceiling packages are available for office developments, which include direct lighting along with other ceiling elements—sprinklers, sound masking functions, and air outlets. Heat recovery is more efficient when the building's air-handling network is linked to ceiling lighting fixtures, because these fixtures can contribute heat to the system. Integrated systems have the disadvantage of making any necessary moving of lighting fixtures more expensive than it would otherwise be.

Some tenants prefer indirect lighting systems, which are generally not part of the base building design. Indirect lighting, which depends on the reflective capacity of walls, ceilings, and room furnishings, is not an especially energy-efficient method of providing light, but it distributes light more evenly than direct lighting systems and thus produces less glare on computer screens—an important advantage. The ceiling material plays a key role in indirect lighting design. A smooth texture works best, while acoustical tiles, which are designed to absorb sound, often have poor light-reflecting capabilities.

Emergency Power. Modern office buildings typically provide two types of emergency power: 1) electricity required to maintain emergency lighting circuits and elevator access and 2) standby power systems for tenants to keep computer networks and other critical equipment going during power outages. The latter are known as uninterruptible power supply (UPS) systems.

A diesel- or gas-powered generator usually provides emergency power for the base building. The National Electric Code requires that life-safety fixtures and equipment—egress lighting, fire pumps for sprinkler systems, and elevators—be on the emergency circuit. Emergency generators may not be required in low-rise office buildings without sprinkler systems or fire pumps. In these buildings, battery-operated light fixtures provide emergency lighting. Often called battery packs, these fixtures are usually wall-mounted and separate from the building's standard fluorescent ceiling fixtures.

Normally tenants purchase and maintain their own UPS systems. If the landlord provides a UPS system and it fails, the tenant's downtime may be the owner's liability. The building owner should understand any implicit assumption of liability before it agrees to provide a base-building UPS system to tenants.

Uninterrupted power supply is a major concern for tenants that use computer networks extensively. An office building, 101 Hudson, located in the Colgate Center in Jersey City, New Jersey, caters to such tenants. (See 101 Hudson case study in Chapter 7.) The building's electrical system provides seven watts per square foot as the building standard, with riser capacity of up to 11 watts. It offers emergency generators that are similarly high powered and battery farms, which are installed on the building's mechanical floor. Dual feeds deliver electricity to the building, providing redundancy.

Telecommunications

Tenant demand for advanced telecommunications cabling and services—for phone systems, computer networks, data transmission, voice and video conferencing, and other communications technologies—has exploded in recent years. This is clear to anyone who opens a telephone closet or electrical closet in any office building other than one that has been very recently constructed with state-of-the-art telecommunications capabilities. In that closet there will be barely room enough to shine a light through, much less to run more cable through.

Many businesses increasingly rely on communications and data transmission across great distances to conduct their day-to-day operations. Developers need to design their office buildings with the telecommunications infrastructure in place to accommodate such tenants.

Rudin Management has done this. Its New York Information Technology Center (NYITC) in lower Manhattan is a prime example of a building that offers built-in access to advanced telecommunications services. Firms that are heavy users of interactive communications technology but cannot alone support the infrastructure—cabling, satellite dishes, and power—that advanced telecommunications technologies require are its target market. In 1996, the developer gutted the former Drexel Burnham Lambert high-rise building at 55 Broad Street and converted it to multitenant office space. The NYITC offers tenants ready and affordable access to the latest interactive tech-

nology and services, including high-speed-wire access to the Internet, advanced fiberoptic cabling, and two KU-band dishes mounted on the building's roof for satellite transmissions. Rudin plans to make NYITC the hub of a global network of wired buildings, beginning with a second building in London that will be housed in what was once the world's largest cigarette factory.

Traditionally, building owners provide electrical and telephone distribution closets on each floor of the building as a part of the core. The number of closets per floor should be determined by the size of the floorplate. The Electronic Industries Association (EIA) Standard 569 states that a minimum of one telecommunications closet per floor should be provided. Telecommunications closets should be vertically stacked from floor to floor and connected by cable conduits. In its new building at 1200 Avenue of the Americas in New York, the Equitable Life Insurance Society will have two communications providers, Nynex and Teleport, and two communications closets per floor, providing the company with the same kind of redundancy in its communications wiring as it requires in its power supply.[11]

While the landlord traditionally has provided the telecommunications closets and the connecting conduits, tenants typically have been responsible for installing their own wiring and equipment. However, having a state-of-the-art telecommunications system in place has become an advantage in competitive office leasing markets and many tenants may come to expect prewired offices in the foreseeable future. As the following chapter on marketing makes clear, office developments must deliver more than affordable space if they are to succeed. They must provide services and amenities sought by tenants, and telecommunications capacity is one of the most important of these.

Office tenants occupying more that one floor are likely to want to connect computers on different floors into local area networks (LANs). Because of this increased demand for floor-to-floor cabling, developers should con-

Satellite telecommunications center for Dial Tower in Phoenix.

Four Denver-based developers discuss the types of technologies that they are incorporating into their office buildings.

Chetter Latcham
Vice President, Development
Pacifica Holding Company
Englewood, Colorado

Because personal computers have become increasingly more user friendly and more capable of a broad and complex range of functions, they are a virtual necessity for every desk in an office environment.

The proliferation of PCs has led to a significant increase in the demand for electricity by most companies. To meet this demand, Pacifica is delivering two to three times the electrical capacity to new buildings than it did a decade ago. For example, a general office user ten years ago consumed 1.5 to two watts of electricity per square foot. Today, we design the electrical infrastructure in new buildings to accommodate five to seven watts per square foot.

Fiberoptic capability is now mandatory in all our new office buildings. As an owner/developer, Pacifica runs four to eight empty conduits from the street into a building's central phone room to accommodate the multiplicity of phone and fiberoptic cable providers that service our tenants. Telecommunications technology is changing so rapidly that we are providing building access for technology that does not exist yet, but certainly will within the projected useful life of the building.

In today's global economy, business is being conducted 24 hours a day. This has affected what technologies are being put into new office buildings. Technology has allowed companies to link multiple satellite offices worldwide through computer networks, as well as through phone, fax, and data lines. Sophisticated HVAC systems must be in place, at least in certain portions of buildings, to accommodate the 24-hour schedules that this phenomenon necessitates. Today, it is possible to provide a redundant HVAC system that can heat and cool an office in the event of a failure in a portion of a building's mechanical system.

At Pacifica Pointe, our new Class A office building in Greenwood Plaza in Englewood, we have joined with Northern Telecom to provide a videoconference room for tenant use. This technology is still in its infancy, but has experienced exponential growth over the past several years. I believe that the videoconference will become a normal avenue of communications for large companies, which will benefit from a reduction in travel expenses.

The technology sector has been the catalyst for economic recovery in Colorado. It is this same technology that is driving the design of new office buildings.

Richard G. McClintock
President
Westfield Development Company
Denver, Colorado

What building infrastructure to provide is a question every developer asks when faced with hundreds of choices at the beginning of a project. Since technologies are constantly changing, the challenge for the developer is to stay current with advances while remaining flexible enough for growth. The developer needs to figure out how to address the needs of the target market while staying within the budget.

For Westfield Development Company's most recent project, Panorama Corporate Center, a seven-building office park at the intersection of Interstate 25 and Dry Creek Road in south Denver, we targeted high-tech companies, many of which operate on a 24-hour, seven-days-a-week basis. They typically have high population densities and bring along lots of computers, printers, and fax machines. To appeal to these tenants, we focused on their specific technological needs for quick and easy access to communications networks.

The ability of these tenants to communicate long-distance through a variety of means other than the telephone is critical to their operations. Not only does the very nature of their businesses often involve some sort of communications service, but their everyday operations go beyond the traditional office environment. To satisfy their needs, buildings must be equipped with adequate communications lines. Traditional copper-filled telephone lines have limitations on speed and bandwidth. Transmitting video and electronic data requires fiberoptic cables.

At Panorama Corporate Center, we built a communications infrastructure that accommodates this need. We designed an intricate fiberoptic pathway that loops through the entire business park and into and through each building. The companies that supply Panorama Corporate Center tenants with access to their communications lines can use this pathway. Such a preexisting communications infrastructure is less expensive to install than would be retrofitting it onto existing buildings as an afterthought.

The equipment that runs on these massive communications networks needs ample and reliable power. We increased the size of the transformers to provide buildings with 13 watts per square foot for general purpose power. This compares with five watts per square foot for a typical office building. To protect against the potentially devastating financial impact of power outages, we installed automatic turnover switches that, in the event of a power outage, switch the main power feed from one substation to another. One switch backs up an entire building.

John Shaw
Vice President, Real Estate Development
Opus Northwest LLC
Denver, Colorado

Over the past decade, many technological, economic, and social dynamics have contributed to today's changing office environment. Fiberoptic cable, powerful portable computers, cellular telephones, fax machines, and the Internet have modified dramatically the way business is conducted. Enormous quantities of data can be directed to any desired location and users of this information have the flexibility to establish an operational base wherever they choose.

Corporations across the United States have focused their attention on bottom-line performance. For their real estate needs, this means shying away from glamorous high-rise towers in favor of lower-rise office buildings with larger floorplates. These facilities are often suburban and densely occupied.

Some companies, particularly those with large sales staffs, have moved employees out of traditional offices and have implemented alternative officing strategies such as hoteling, sharing space, and telecommuting. For employees still housed in the organization's office space, private offices have been replaced with modular furniture systems.

The continued growth of suburban residential communities and the desire of many employees to work close to home—coupled with the difficulties of commuting long-distance and the scarcity of city parking—continue to make suburban offices appealing.

Opus Office Plaza, a four-story, 143,000-square-foot building in north Inverness Business Park, is a response to these dynamic forces. Each floor plan features 36,000 square feet of open space that was designed to accommodate a variety of office configurations, ranging from an executive suite to high-density modular layouts. Five parking spaces will be allotted per 1,000 square feet of building area.

Electrical service from two separate feeds provides tenants with extremely reliable power at eight watts per square foot. Four fiberoptic cable providers have installed lines to the project, giving our tenants ultimate flexibility in long-distance communications linkage. The heating and air-conditioning system's capacity was designed to accommodate the higher cooling demands caused by the greater power consumption and higher occupant densities of today's offices.

Skip Ahem Jr.
President
Charter Realty Group LLC
Denver, Colorado

A look at the landscape of American business suggests that communications may well be the greatest technological advance of the latter part of this century. With the breakup of AT&T, the proliferation of baby Bells, the aggressive growth of long-distance providers, the advent of fiberoptic connections, and a host of other sophisticated telecommunications technologies, it is difficult for developers to keep up with these changes and with the accompanying growth in the number of companies that offer communications services.

Because I believe that communications access—whether it be voice, data, or visual—is one of the most important services to provide for tenants, I have sought assistance from experts who are current not only on the rapidly changing technology, but also on the changing players in the industry. Such consultants can help the developer sort through and identify the most important aspects of the new telecommunications technologies that tenants will need, and figure out ways to provide telecommunications services efficiently.

Charter issues a questionnaire to prospective tenants to gather information about their communications and technological needs. Once Charter has a picture of a tenant's priorities, it calls in professional consultants who help put together the best mix of transmission, switching, and hardware/software packages. Sometimes the recommended equipment consists of fiberoptic cables augmented by copper-filled wires. At other times, it is necessary to add a wireless component, such as rooftop antennas. The solution, no matter how sophisticated, must be cost-effective and reliable.

Charter believes that the most important means of ensuring the company's future success is to correctly anticipate the technological needs of its tenants and to negotiate ways to provide them with sound solutions. If we do this, our tenants respond by helping us to enhance our basic product: the square footage that we rent.

Source: Adapted from "What Technologies Are You Putting in New Office Buildings?" *Colorado Real Estate Journal*, December 4–17, 1996.

■

Courtesy of Tishman Technologies Corporation

Prefabricated superfloors and superwalls will eventually simplify office cabling. A single cable will replace systems like this central patch frame that interconnects 5,000 separate points.

sider incorporating vertical communications columns—like the building's wet columns that house water supply and drain lines for tenant use—to help organize the web of cables in the building. Equipped with sleeves through the concrete floor slab, communications columns make it possible to run cables to a floor with little disturbance to the tenants above or below that floor. Communications columns should be located near an existing column or adjacent to the building core and at a safe distance from the wet columns. However, vertical cabling has distance limitations, depending on the type of cable used and this approach may not be applicable for high-rise buildings.

Office developers should consider a project's telecommunications services during early site planning. For an office park project with multiple buildings, for example, it is good practice to link the buildings underground with empty PVC pipes that can serve, if required, as communications cable conduits between buildings. Providing these simple links as part of the original site work costs little, whereas retrofitting them can cost a lot more. Any tenant with multiple locations within the office park will benefit from such forethought.

Plumbing

An office building's basic plumbing system is dictated largely by local building codes and the accessibility requirements of the Americans with Disabilities Act. Building codes generally prescribe the number of fixtures in the core restrooms, roof drainage systems, and the size of pipes. The ADA requires that restrooms and drinking fountains be made accessible to the handicapped.

Developers traditionally have controlled the cost of plumbing by stacking the building's restrooms in the building's core and by locating the men's and women's restrooms next to one another. Stacking and proximity are still the most cost-efficient approach to plumbing requirements. However, increasing tenant demand for flexibility in floor plans has made remote restrooms and pantries more common in new office buildings. In buildings with unusually large floorplates (50,000 square feet or more), it may be wise to provide two restroom cores to reduce walking distance for tenants.

Developers can design flexibility into the plumbing system by providing remote sanitary risers, known as wet stacks. The presence of accessible sanitary pipes in remote wet stacks permits tenants to add plumbing fixtures without having to extend pipes from the core, and thus lowers the cost of remote plumbing additions.

Choosing the building's hot-water system is an important design decision. The two most commonly used systems are a central system and a floor-by-floor system. The central system consists of a large water heater located in a mechanical room with a recirculation loop piped into each toilet room in the core. A floor-by-floor system involves individual water heaters on each floor. While a central hot-water system is more expensive to install, it provides more flexibility for the postoccupancy addition of fixtures needing hot water.

Life-Safety System

Most but not all new office buildings are required to install fire-alarm and sprinkler systems. These systems in combination with building code requirements for fireproofing, exit doors and stairways, standpipes, and the like are the elements of an office building's life-safety component. Fire-alarm systems involve a network of ceiling-mounted smoke detectors and alarms that detect fires and notify occupants to evacuate the building. Sprinkler systems extinguish fires. These two elements are discussed in the following sections.

Fire-Alarm System. Most building codes require office buildings to install fire-alarm systems, but the exact design requirements vary from region to region. The most commonly used fire-alarm system is known as an addressable multiplexed system. In this system, each of the devices that constitute the system—smoke detectors, sprinkler flow switches that indicate if a sprinkler head has been activated, and manual pull stations—is given an address that is indicated on the control or annunciator panel when the device is activated. This panel, located near the fire control room or in the lobby of the building, gives firefighters the exact location of the fire.

Sprinkler System. Most but not all new office buildings have sprinkler systems installed. Some smaller low-rise buildings constructed of noncombustible materials (steel or concrete) may not be required by building codes to provide sprinklers. In such instances, however, the developer may choose to add this safety feature to reduce insurance rates, or to meet market requirements.

A sprinkler system is a network of pressurized pipes that are connected to sprinkler heads, which are located in the ceiling and are individually activated by a heat sensor in the head itself. It is predominantly a wet system, meaning that the pipes are filled with water. But in areas like loading docks and parking garages that may experience freezing temperatures, it may be a dry system, meaning that water is not introduced into the piping until a heat sensor or smoke detector is activated. Building codes mandate the frequency and location of the sprinkler heads.

A certain level of water pressure must be maintained for the sprinkler system to work properly. The water main to the building may provide sufficient pressure for sprinkler systems in some low-rise office buildings. But for high rises and for low-rises with inadequate water main pressure, a fire pump will be required to provide added water pressure. Fire pumps cannot be subject to interruptions of electrical service and must, therefore, be wired to an emergency generator.

Elevators

For a multistory building, the elevators are one of the key ways by which the quality of the building is communicated. A building's lobby and then its elevators—their availability and speed and the quality of their interior finish—are the primary elements that shape the initial impressions of tenants and visitors. Elevator waiting time can be a significant factor in tenant retention.

Waiting time for elevators should average no more than 20 to 30 seconds. If the waits are longer, tenants may be disinclined to renew their leases. The determination of how much elevator capacity is needed in an office building is based on the needs of the target market and the building's projected occupancy load. Buildings occupied by large companies that tend to maintain regular work hours will need high-capacity elevator systems

to accommodate peak hour demand. Elevator systems in buildings with predictable rush hours should be able to move as many as 30 percent of the employees in a five-minute period. Buildings occupied by mainly professional organizations that tend to keep irregular hours will experience less peaking of demand. On the other hand, such firms can be less tolerant of time lost waiting for elevators.

The design of elevator cabs is an important consideration. Standard cabs offered by the manufacturers are usually suitable in all but the highest-quality office buildings. Most elevator cabs can be ordered from the manufacturer in a number of different finishes for the metal doors and control panels and for the wall panels (plastic laminate, metal, or wood), and with a choice of lighting schemes.

Designers can use the lobby's materials to good effect inside the elevator cabs. Custom elevator-cab design may involve mirrors, stainless steel, and stone or wood panels. In the selection of materials, the cab's overall weight is of primary importance. Most elevators are rated for a standard weight cab. A cab with a stone floor and walls may exceed the manufacturer's maximum weight standards and require a larger elevator motor. Thus, the developer should make basic decisions on the design of cabs when the elevators are being engineered, rather than after their delivery. An elevator specialist is needed to determine the capacity of the equipment to handle the weight of the proposed cabs, and such a specialist should also be consulted about the overall elevator system—equipment, controls, hoistways, and building code issues.

Interior Design

The interior design of an office building begins with the determination of the building envelope, design modules, bay depths, and floorplate sizes—all of which were discussed earlier in this chapter. These form the basic framework that determines how the various interior elements of the building can be laid out and how well the building will function. Within this framework, the interior design also must accommodate the various building systems—HVAC, power, communications, elevators, plumbing, lighting, and life safety—that were also discussed in this chapter. The overall goals of the interior design should be to meet the needs and preferences of the targeted tenants and to provide flexibility.

The following discussion of interior design begins with an important and often controversial subject: the different ways of measuring space in office buildings. A section on general principles of interior space planning is followed by discussions of specific elements of an office building's interior design—lobbies, corridors, tenant entries, restrooms, and signage. Tenant improvements are covered in the following section.

Ways of Measuring Floor Space

Every office building contains some common area, such as lobbies and cores. How much common area usually

The same materials can be used in the lobby and elevators to intensify the building's image.

In calculating rents, landlords generally factor in a tenant's share of the building's common areas, like this atrium at Becton Dickinson's headquarters in Franklin Lakes, New Jersey.

depends on the kinds of design and building amenities that the target market expects. Developers pass the cost of a building's common area on to the tenants. Landlords typically charge tenants for their usable space plus a prorated share of the common area space. The tenant pays rent at the stated rental rate multiplied by the "rentable square feet." Most tenants are very sensitive to how the landlord calculates their rentable square feet, especially the common area portion.

While rentable area is measured in a variety of ways—and some local markets have their own particular customs in this regard—the measurement standard developed by the Building Owners and Managers Association (BOMA) International has long been the most commonly used method in most U.S. office markets. Through concepts like gross area, rentable area, and usable area, BOMA's standard makes a distinction between the space that a tenant actually occupies on a given floor and its pro-rata share of the common area on that floor.

A building's gross area is the sum of the areas of all its enclosed floors, including basements, mechanical equipment floors, and penthouses. It is measured from the outside finished surface of the permanent outer walls of the building.

Rentable area includes all areas within the building's outside walls, with the exception of the space enclosed by vertical penetrations like elevator shafts, stairways, and equipment shafts. It is measured from the inside finish of the permanent outer walls of the building or from the inside of the glass line if at least 50 percent of the building's exterior is glass. According to local standards, rentable area may include elevator lobbies, restroom areas, janitorial rooms, and equipment rooms. Developers should be careful to use rentable area and not gross construction area in their pro forma projections of rental income.

Usable area for tenants excludes public hallways, elevator lobbies, toilet facilities that open onto public hallways, and other common areas. Usable area is measured from the inside finish of the outer building walls or the glass line to the inside finished surface of the office side of the public corridor. Usable area for full-floor tenants is measured to the building core and includes corridor space. Usable area for tenants occupying less than a full floor is measured from the center of the partitions that separate one tenant's office space from another's.

The ratio of rentable area to usable area (the R/U ratio) is important in determining rents, because landlords generally use it to calculate any tenant's share of the common area rent. For example, in a building with a 1.15 R/U ratio, a tenant that rents 1,000 square feet of usable space will pay rent on 1,150 square feet:

Rentable Area = Usable Area x R/U Ratio
1,150 = 1,000 x 1.15

In the past, the calculation of a tenant's rentable space was usually based on the R/U ratio for its particular floor. In buildings in which certain floors—usually the first floor—contain a lot of square footage devoted to common areas such as lobbies and mail rooms, this method raises problems. A building might have a 1.25 R/U ratio on the first floor and only a 1.10 R/U ratio on the upper floors. Many landlords began using a ratio that was calculated for the entire building.

BOMA came to realize that office projects were increasingly including buildingwide amenities and that the need to capture them in rent calculations was widespread. In 1996, the association issued an updated version of its standard method of floor area measurement. (See feature box on this page.) The revised approach is a buildingwide method that was designed to fairly account for spaces in the building that benefit all tenants—entrance lobbies with concierge desks, conference centers, day-care facilities, exercise facilities, health clubs, building core and services areas, and other common areas.

Lobbies

Creating an image is one important function of a building's lobby, and it serves other important functions as well. For the visitor, the lobby is where his or her most immediate and strongest impression of the office building is formed. The favorable impression that the approach to the building may have made on the visitor will be immediately confirmed or dispelled by the lobby. Image-conscious tenants want a lobby that reflects the image they wish to project, so the lobby plays a key role in positioning the building.

Among its other functions, the lobby is a place of orientation. Lobby design sometimes unfortunately overlooks this role. The design must make the location of key elements—the building directory, the elevators, telephones, and restrooms—clear to visitors. The lobby also is an important element in the building's security. Absent a concierge desk or security station in the lobby, a building

A Bird's-Eye View of the Revised BOMA Floor Measuring Standard

The Building Owners and Managers Association's 1996 revised standard for measuring the floor area in office buildings is full of new definitions for measuring office space. The following is a step-by-step approach that should be followed in applying the standard to an office building. Each italicized term has a new or substantially revised definition in the revised standard. The complete standard contains explanations of each term along with illustrations and guidance for users.

- Determine, for records, the overall *gross building area*.
- Ascertain the *gross measured area* of each floor of the building, applying the concepts of *finished surface* and *dominant portion*.
- Establish the *floor rentable area* for each floor by deducting from each floor's *gross measured area* the area of its *major vertical penetrations*.
- Measure the *usable area* of *office areas*, *store areas*, and *building common areas* on each floor to determine each *floor usable area*.
- Determine the *floor common area* of every floor by subtracting from each *floor rentable area* its *floor usable area*.

- Determine the *basic rentable area* of each floor by applying the *floor R/U ratio* (rentable/usable) to the *floor usable area*. This allocates the *floor common area* to the *floor usable area*.
- Determine the building's *rentable area* by applying the *building R/U ratio* to each *basic rentable area*. This allocates the *building common area* to each *basic rentable area*.

The American National Standard for Measuring Floor Area in Office Buildings, BOMA/ANSI Z65.1-1996, can be ordered by calling 800-426-6292.

Source: Adapted from Brigett Reilly, "Measuring Buildings Better in the '90s and Beyond," *Skylines*, July–August 1996, pp. 16–17.

■

access system that requires a special code or card-key for admittance and a visible security videocamera indicate to would-be criminals that security is taken seriously in the building.

Office building lobbies come in many different sizes and shapes, and lobby design styles come and go. In the 1970s and 1980s, multistory atriums were in vogue. Some lobbies were finished in exotic-wood paneling and featured grand staircases like baronial halls, while others were decked out with skylights that transformed them into greenhouses. Smaller and more intimate lobbies gained popularity in the early 1990s. By the late 1990s, office lobbies were being designed with the highest-quality materials that construction budgets would allow but with less flashy applications than a decade before.

Developers should make lobby design and material selections with one eye on current market trends and the other on the future, in an effort to ensure that the

© Wolfgang Hoyt/Esto

Winter Properties Inc.

Brookfield Management Services Ltd.

Ahmanson Commercial Development Company

A building's lobby projects its image. Clockwise from top left: Seaport Plaza (New York City), the Carriage Works (Atlanta), 120 North LaSalle (Chicago), 320 Bay Street (Toronto).

lobby will not become quickly dated. The overuse of glass block in the 1980s, for instance, gives lobbies executed in that material a dated look today.

Office building lobbies must endure a tremendous amount of traffic. They need to be designed to withstand people's wet umbrellas and snowy boots, delivery hand trucks, and even messengers' bicycles. Clearly, lobbies need to be constructed of durable materials. Designers sometimes do not consider carefully enough the practicality of the materials they select. Thus, long rubber mats covering expensive but slippery stone or terrazzo floors often lead from the front door to the elevators. Or, stainless steel edges must be applied to stone walls to protect their corners. And durability and practicality cannot be the only reasons for selecting materials. Even fine materials of the highest quality can combine to make a cold and inhospitable space in which every footstep echoes and conversation is uncomfortable.

Striking a balance between durability, comfort, and aesthetics is a key objective in lobby design. Tile or stone floors are the easiest to maintain. They can be softened by the use of carpets in some areas, which may require periodic but inexpensive replacement. Wood panels are suitable for walls if they are detailed so that their edges are not exposed to damage. Painted drywall also is an acceptable wall surface, if it is properly protected and maintained.

Furniture in office building lobbies is usually a good idea. Furniture makes the building seem inhabited, provides a sense of human scale, and, even if it is used only by the occasional messenger, makes the lobby feel welcoming. Plants can enhance lobby spaces and soften their echoes. Lighting can be used to create a particular ambiance in lobby areas. A drywall ceiling with coffers or recessed lighting can give a simple lobby more character than can a standard acoustical tile ceiling with fluorescent fixtures.

Corridors

Developers and designers all too often fail to give sufficient consideration to design elements for the office building's core, which is made up of admittedly utilitarian spaces but also is the path to tenants' front doors. Developers of multitenant buildings should orient the elevators and elevator lobbies in a way that can give several tenants lobby presence, which is a highly marketable commodity. Tenants value an entrance directly off an elevator lobby.

On floors with many small tenants, the corridor leading from the elevator lobby to an egress stair typically provides access to the front doors of most tenants. Tenant access corridors should be important public spaces, but all too often they are merely grim, five- to six-feet-wide hallways with poor lighting and inexpensive finishes. By spending some additional money on access corridors—for better lighting, carpeting, moldings, and directional graphics—developers can differentiate a building from those of competitors and attract tenants that are seeking to improve the public image that they project.

Courtesy of Arrowstreet Inc.

At the Somerset Bank headquarters in Somerville, Maine, open workstations define the main circulation path.

The length and location of access corridors vary with the size and shape of the building's footprint. Suburban office buildings can measure 200 feet or longer, and long access corridors may be unavoidable. In such cases, a main goal should be the clarity of the corridor pattern. A long straight access corridor is preferable to a twisting corridor, which can become disorienting.

Access corridors not only lead to tenant entries and exit stairs, but also to toilet rooms, mechanical spaces, and other building service areas. How these areas are distributed can have a great impact on the efficiency of the core and the efficiency of the layout of the tenant spaces. (See "Core Configuration" section on page 147.)

Urban office buildings typically have smaller footprints and more compact cores. For these buildings, the length of the corridor is less of a problem but maintaining the clarity of the corridor pattern still requires good planning and design. The fewer the twists and turns in the corridor, the clearer will be the circulation system. If a loop corridor is required, the number of turns in it should be minimized.

Tenant Entries

The entrances to tenant suites, unlike the lobbies in multi-tenant buildings, project the identity and image of individual tenants. They demand thoughtful design consideration. Developers should take care to differentiate tenant entries from the doors to restrooms or mechanical rooms. Tenant entries might be stained mahogany doors with a glass sidelight. A graphics system might be devised to further differentiate tenant doors.

In urban buildings and in some single-tenant suburban buildings, the core configuration tends to be more centralized around the elevator banks. Since the maximization of usable floor area is generally the goal, tenant entries generally are not located directly off elevator lobbies.

Restrooms

Restroom design matters. The functionality of restroom fixtures is at least as important as their appearance. If a sink counter holds standing water that paints a wet stripe across a hand-washer's new suit, the developer/manager has an unhappy client. The quality of the restrooms conveys strong signals about the quality of the building's management and the property manager's concern for the comfort of tenants and visitors.

Local building codes require a certain number of fixtures per square foot of floor space or per person. Toilets, urinals, and lavatories must be accessible to the disabled.

Practicality guides much of the design of restrooms. Men's and women's toilets are generally installed back to back so that their waste pipes can share a single chase, which saves costs. Lavatories and urinals have smaller waste lines and can be located on walls not containing the chase. The location of restroom doors and sight lines into restrooms are important design concerns. While a person in the hallway may not have a direct view into the restroom, he may have a view into the mirror over the lavatories, which yields the same result.

Restrooms must be finished with materials that are durable enough to withstand frequent cleaning and disinfecting. Ceramic tile is frequently used on restroom floors. Walls are usually covered in tile or vinyl. Marble and granite tiles are widely available and have begun to replace ceramic tile as a common material. Cost-conscious designs may specify tile only for surfaces that are likely to need heavy maintenance, such as the areas behind toilets.

Cleaning and maintenance ease should be considered in the design of restrooms. Wall-mounted toilets allow easier and more thorough cleaning of floors than do floor-mounted toilets. For the same reason, ceiling-mounted toilet partitions are superior to floor-mounted systems.

Ease of maintenance is also an important consideration in the design of countertops. Whether the counter is plastic laminate or polished stone, the sinks should be mounted under rather than through the counter so that the ceramic edges do not overlap it. This makes the cleaning of the countertop easier.

The design and condition of restrooms convey strong signals regarding the quality of the building's management and its concern for the comfort of tenants and visitors.

Interior Signage

The advisability of developing a comprehensive signage program for the entire office development was discussed in the "Exterior Design" section earlier in this chapter. Signage in the office building's interior should be clear, consistent, and distinctive. Consistency and clarity can be achieved by developing a program of signs that specifies colors, fonts, and a size hierarchy.

Such a program might call for the fonts and colors used for the building directory in the lobby and for the identity signs at each tenant's door to be the same, although the shapes and sizes of the signs might differ. Directional signs along hallways and restroom signs might use the same colors and fonts, but perhaps be mounted directly on doors to distinguish them from tenant identity signs mounted on the side of the doorframes.

Interior signage must comply with Americans with Disabilities Act requirements. Braille text must accompany standard text on signs that are intended to guide people through the building and the signage at entrances, restrooms, elevators, and lobbies must be mounted to be visible from a wheelchair. In addition, the international symbol of accessibility should indicate the locations of accessible facilities if not all the building's facilities are universally accessible.

Tenant Improvements

As part of the lease for office space, the landlord usually provides an allowance for tenant improvements (TIs). TIs, which are also called buildouts, fit-ups, fit-outs, or finish-outs, include ceilings, walls, floors, doors, lighting, and electrical and telephone outlets. The size of the TI allowance is determined largely by what the market will bear. In markets where the demand for office space is strong, the allowance might be insufficient to cover the cost of standard tenant improvements. In down markets where tenants are scarce and office space is plentiful, landlords typically offer generous TIs to attract tenants.

Along with the size of the TI allowance, the quantity and quality that the developer sets for TIs are a definite factor in the marketing of the building. The developer must ascertain from brokers and tenants in the market their perceptions of what are appropriate TI standards.

A work letter serves as the formal agreement between the developer and a tenant concerning the amount and quality of improvements that the landlord will provide. It specifies the work that the landlord will do before the lease commencement date, as well as the schedule of costs. The work letter also includes a completion schedule, and since leases typically do not require the tenant to pay rent during the TI phase, developers should try to ensure that the work is done on schedule.

There are three basic types of TI packages: building standard installation, building standard improvements, and fixed construction budget. These alternative approaches are discussed in the following paragraphs.

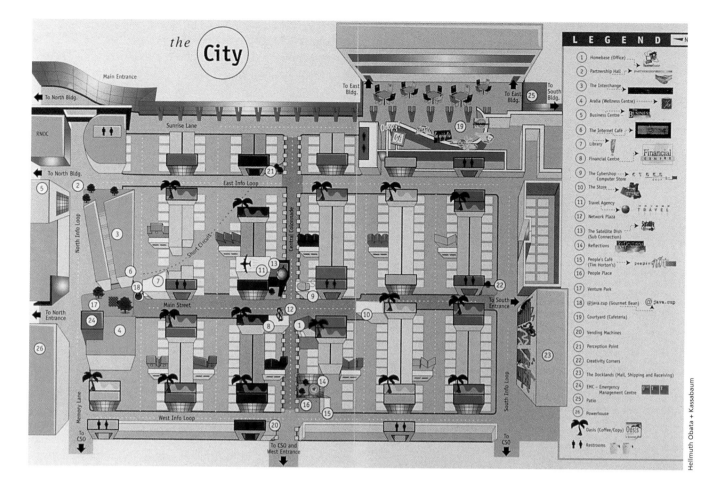

the City

Main Entrance

To North Bldg.

RNOC

To North Bldg.

To East Bldg.

To East Bldg.

To South Bldg.

Sunrise Lane

East Info Loop

North Info Loop

Short Circuit

Central Colonnade

Main Street

To North Entrance

West Info Loop

South Info Loop

To South Entrance

To CSO

To CSO and West Entrance

To CSO

LEGEND

1. Homebase (Office)
2. Partnership Hall
3. The Interchange
4. Aralia (Wellness Centre)
5. Business Centre
6. The Internet Cafe
7. Library
8. Financial Centre
9. The Cybershop Computer Store
10. The Store
11. Travel Agency
12. Network Plaza
13. The Satellite Dish (Sub Connection)
14. Reflections
15. People's Café (Tim Horton's)
16. People Place
17. Venture Park
18. @java.cup (Gourmet Bean)
19. Courtyard (Cafeteria)
20. Vending Machines
21. Perception Point
22. Creativity Corners
23. The Docklands (Mall, Shipping and Receiving)
24. EMC – Emergency Management Centre
25. Patio
26. Powerhouse

Oasis (Coffee/Copy)

Restrooms

At Nortel's world headquarters in Toronto, a former factory has been made into a 1 million-square-foot city. Hallways are marked with street signs and location maps show departments, coffee stations, copier rooms, and other areas of interest within the building.

A building standard installation is based on standards that the developer sets as a minimum level of quality for all tenant work. These standards are stated in a list of items that will be installed in every tenant suite. The list provides details concerning the number of partitions, the types of doors and door hardware, the size and pattern of acoustical ceiling tiles, types of floor coverings, the types and locations of various other elements—lighting fixtures, electrical outlets, switches, individual HVAC

units and HVAC controls, and plumbing connections—as well as paints and other wall coverings, and window coverings.

The developer generally prepares a standard TI work letter that applies to improvements throughout the building. In it, standard installations are usually expressed in terms of quantity per square foot of rentable space: 15 linear feet of drywall partition per square foot of rentable space, for example, or one door and frame with hard-

In the interior design of its Miami headquarters, JPBT wanted to reflect an open-door policy. Designers used layered glass partitions and free-flowing spaces to accomplish this.

ware per 120 square feet. The developer usually bids the standard installation work letter with the base-building construction, in order to include a fixed cost for TIs in the construction budget.

In a building standard installation, if the tenant wants items that exceed the building standard, these will be specified in the landlord's work letter, along with their cost and method of payment.

The second basic type of TI package, building standard improvements, differs little from a building standard installation except that quantities usually are not specified. In essence, this arrangement allows tenants as many building standard doors, frames, hardware, and partitions as they need to build out their space according to their plans.

For the developer, the cost of this type of TI package is more difficult to predict. But some tenants prefer this approach as a way of getting whatever they need as part of their lease. However, buildout items that are above building standard—usually such items as glass partitions for the perimeter of conference rooms, special millwork or cabinetry, special paints or carpets—are not generally included in building standard improvements. The tenant generally must pay for such improvements, unless otherwise determined in the lease negotiations.

The fixed construction budget option, a third basic type of TI package, offers the most straightforward and flexible approach to tenant improvements. In this approach, the developer offers to spend a certain (negotiated) amount of money on TIs. For the tenant, however, fixed-budget TIs may be the most difficult approach. An inexperienced tenant may have little idea of what a negotiated TI budget of $15 per square foot of rentable space will actually buy. The tenant wants to know, for example: Will it allow carpet upgrades or special wall coverings?

On the other hand, fixed construction allowances give tenants flexibility and more choice on how to allocate the buildout budget, especially if the terms of the lease allow unused portions of the budget to be applied toward furnishings or rent abatement. Usually a fixed-budget agreement also allows the tenant to bid the project to general contractors and select the lowest bidder.

How the TI package is structured depends on local market conditions, as well as on the developer's business. If the developer has a construction division, for example, a work letter or building standard package may be a better option than a fixed-budget arrangement under which the tenant can bid the project—because the developer may not be the lowest bidder on the proposed TIs.

Renovations

Office building renovations and projects to adapt buildings to office uses have made their mark on the fabric of many urban communities. Only in recent years has the renovation of older suburban office buildings become a viable alternative to new construction. Suburban buildings built in the mid- to late 1960s are now 30 to 35 years old. Some of these buildings are located in older, close-in suburbs and are now marketable as close-in alternatives to facilities located in outer suburbs and exurban areas.

However, these buildings usually are not up to current market standards. Their mechanical, electrical, and plumbing systems do not meet today's standards and are approaching the end of their useful lives. These buildings were designed without today's concern for energy conservation or operating efficiency. They tend to have many serious problems. For example, 30-year-old uninsulated building facades have begun to leak as the sealants around deteriorating window systems break down.

This section considers the planning and design process for building renovation projects, beginning with the initial determination of building conditions, which has much to do with the decision on whether the project should be undertaken at all. The role of building codes and accessibility standards is discussed, as are the issues involved in replacing or upgrading major components

of older buildings—building systems, the structural system, the facade, and the roof. A discussion of seismic upgrades concludes the renovations section.

Analysis of Existing Conditions

Before making the final decision to renovate an older building, the developer must commit time and money to an evaluation of the structural condition of the building and its major mechanical systems. Only then can the developer begin to know the scope of the renovation process and the cost of complying with local zoning ordinances. Only then can it make detailed cost estimates.

In the predesign phase of a building renovation, the developer and the project's consultants must look for trouble spots. The greatest risk in renovation projects comes from unknown hidden conditions. These might include currently operating mechanical systems that will not last another five years, leaking underground storage tanks long since paved over, or hazardous materials such

Stainless steel and glass bays, hung from the eighth floor of the completely renovated headquarters of the American Chemical Society in Washington, D.C., contrast with the building's weighty precast concrete and add usable space without increasing the floor/area ratio.

Installed in 1959, a 40-foot stainless-steel, acrylic, and Plexiglas mural by Buell Mueller depicting the artist's view of the world of chemistry was carefully preserved in place during the renovation.

as asbestos. The presence of asbestos (and other hazardous materials) can expose a project's owner to long-term liabilities in the form of future health claims that extend well beyond the project's ordinary cash flow projection period.

Building Codes

The identification of all building code violations is the first step in analyzing an existing building. Some existing code violations can be grandfathered into the renovation approvals, unless the building is being renovated for a use other than the one for which it was built. It was once a rule of thumb that only a change in use (from residential to office, for example) would trigger the requirement that the building be brought into full compliance with building codes. Today, however, any major renovation may require improvements in the building's life-safety system.

The acceptability of grandfathered code violations is usually a matter of interpretation by a local code official or fire marshal. Twenty-five years ago, few building codes addressed the issue of smoke evacuation from egress stairwells, but today pressurization is required in all stairwells over seven stories or 75 feet in height as measured to the floor level of the top floor. However, if the renovated building includes sprinklers and a smoke-detector and fire-alarm system that is code compliant, the code official may waive the requirement for stair pressurization. Throughout the United States, code officials are focusing on issues of life safety in office building renovations—in particular, on sprinkler systems and seismic upgrades.

Efforts to encourage the renovation and recycling of buildings in some regions of the United States have resulted in building code amendments that somewhat ease code requirements for qualifying projects.

Accessibility

While the accessibility requirements in the Americans with Disabilities Act are relatively easy to accommodate in new construction, they are often difficult and expensive to incorporate into a renovation. (ADA requirements as they affect office buildings in general are discussed in the "Americans with Disabilities Act" section early in this chapter.) Developers should undertake an ADA compliance study as part of the predesign analysis.

ADA requires that in places of public accommodation existing architectural barriers to accessibility be removed, provided that their removal is readily achievable—a condition that ADA defines as "easily accomplishable and able to be carried out without much difficulty or expense." No standard formula guides this determination. Among the factors that are considered are the cost of the alteration, the financial resources of the site or sites, and the relationship (both geographic and financial) between a parent corporation or entity and the ownership of the particular building.

Judgment of what is readily achievable occurs on a case-by-case basis. Providing a ramp for wheelchair access may be considered readily achievable. Adding an elevator may not be considered readily achievable. In a renovation project, the determination of what is readily achievable depends also on the construction budget.

For historic buildings, ADA includes special provisions that require a lesser level of compliance. If a building is listed or eligible for listing in the National Register of Historic Places or if it is designated as historic under an appropriate state or local law, and if a required accessibility alteration would threaten or destroy the building's historic integrity, the required alteration may be waived.

Building Systems

It is difficult for even an experienced developer to evaluate the condition of the building systems in older buildings. In most cases, the developer should hire a licensed mechanical, electrical, and plumbing (MEP) engineer to thoroughly review the condition, operating costs, and code compliance of the existing systems.

The older the building, the more likely that its systems are inadequate or on their last legs. If the building was built after the mid-1970s, when most jurisdictions implemented energy-conservation standards, the systems may have considerable life left in them. If the building is approaching 30 or more years of age, the remaining useful life of all its systems is quite possibly short.

Structural System

As a rule, a building's steel or concrete structural system tends to outlive its mechanical systems. If there are structural problems, they are often apparent: exposed steel reinforcing bars in spalled concrete columns, cracks in the masonry skin, or cuts in the steel beams made to allow the installation of new ductwork. Such conditions may seem to indicate serious underlying deterioration, but they are not necessarily dangerous or expensive to resolve.

Before undertaking a renovation, the developer must obtain an accurate assessment of the structural integrity of the building and of the actions that will be required to correct any deficiencies. Typically a structural engineer performs this assessment.

The structural assessment should include a calculation of the floor loads—pounds per square foot—for which the building is designed, in order to ascertain if the building meets current codes and determine what types of loads the building can safely bear. Load-bearing capacity affects the kinds of tenant improvements and equipment/furnishings that the building can handle. It is not unusual for buildings—even newer buildings—to be deficient in capacity for areas of highly concentrated loads, such as file rooms.

Another structural consideration for renovations in seismic zones is whether the building will require a seismic upgrade. (See "Seismic Upgrades" section at the end of this chapter.)

Building Facade

The office developer can use three criteria in the evaluation of the skin of the building proposed for renovation: watertightness, energy-efficiency, and aesthetics.

To consolidate its staff in a single headquarters building, Advanced Micro Devices (AMD) purchased a 25-year-old warehouse style building on a 29-acre site in Sunnyvale, California, and gave it a new skin, a new roof with clerestory windows, a two-story atrium, and new mechanical systems.

Hellmuth Obata + Kassabaum

Hellmuth Obata + Kassabaum

A $24.7 million renovation transformed Commonwealth Tower in Arlington, Virginia, from a dated and dark 12-story office building into a bright and modern 15-story tower. The renovated building features light-gray and white precast concrete panels, extensive glazed areas, and a new two-story lobby that reorients the building to a different street. Three new floors provide an additional 66,000 square feet of space.

The 1971 building was vacant when it was taken over by developer London & Leeds in 1987 for the purpose of renovating it inside and out. The developer gutted the building and removed asbestos, leaving only the basic building structure.

One of the developer's primary goals was to increase the leasable space on the site. Several options were explored, including complete demolishment. Analyses by Skidmore, Owings & Merrill (SOM), the project architect, of the structure's joints and foundations and the bearing capacity of the soil verified that the structure could accommodate three additional floors.

After the determination that the building could be enlarged, the next step was to design an exterior that would create a new image for the building. The developer wanted to create a lighter, brighter, and more inviting building that would bear no resemblance to the older one.

The new facade is nearly three-quarters glass—almost the reverse of the original design, which emphasized the opaque portions of the exterior wall. The new exterior also features textured, precast concrete panels that lighten in color from medium gray at the bottom to nearly white at the top of the building.

London & Leeds initially submitted its application for renovating Commonwealth Tower to the Arlington County Board in 1990, but withdrew it following a less than favorable response from the county. The developer resubmitted the application in 1993 following the completion of the county's master redevelopment plan for the area, which included specified goals for the streetscape and surrounding architecture.

The county responded to the application with several requests. The most significant was that the building's entrance be relocated from Nash Street to Wilson Boulevard, which the county's master plan had designated as the area's main street. In spite of the considerable design and construction challenges posed by such a relocation, London & Leeds agreed to modify its plans accordingly.

With the county's approval secured, the building team had only 15 months to complete the renovation in time for the arrival of the first major tenant.

Relocating the entrance proved to be one of most challenging aspects of the project. Because of differing street elevations, the proposed Wilson Boulevard entrance was ten feet lower than the original lobby. Not wanting an entrance that would require steps or ramps, the developer moved the lobby down one level into space that

Skidmore, Owings & Merrill LLP

Michael Dersin Photography. Courtesy of Skidmore, Owings & Merrill LLP

The Commonwealth Tower before renovation (top photo) had a dark, forbidding appearance. After a $24.7 million renovation, it gained three levels and a stylish new facade.

had been occupied by the parking garage. The new lobby had a ceiling height of only nine feet.

Carving an opening in the first-floor slab, which doubled the height of the lobby, solved this problem. The removal of the slab required the installation of additional bracing. How to direct people to the elevators at the back of the new lobby was the next problem that presented itself. A large curved wood wall was installed to direct traffic flow from the revolving door entrance to the elevator bank.

A glass-plank walkway accommodates traffic on the former lobby floor. Light steel tension rods that extend from the slab above support the six-foot-wide, L-shaped walkway. The 1.2-inch-thick plank consists of three pieces of glass, one tempered and two heat strengthened. The designer chose the glass plank because with its lack of bulk it fit better in the limited space between the ground floor and the former lobby floor than would a conventional concrete slab or glass block.

Adding three stories was another challenge. After removal of the roof-mounted mechanical equipment, the concrete columns and roof were prepared for the installation of the new floors. The tops of the columns were cut off 2.5 feet above the existing roof slab, exposing the rebar cages. The original plan was to weld the base plates for the column extensions to the rebar cages, but because of the rebar this solution turned out to be unworkable. Instead, 30-inch anchors were set into the columns.

A ten-by-ten-foot hole was cut into the slabs from the roof down to the ninth floor to permit the erection of a tower crane for installing the steel columns and decking. A tower crane was the only economical way to complete the job, as the use of a truck-mounted crane would have required shoring up the underground parking garage. This would have sharply reduced the number of available parking spaces in the garage, which was required to remain open by an executed rental agreement.

While the three new floors were being constructed, the building's brick facade was dismantled. Because it had been built without the relief angles typically used, the brick was not supported at each floor but from the ground floor up. As a result, the demolition team had to begin at the top of the building and progress downward.

The original floor slabs had followed the chevron outline of the exterior wall. By shaving off the chevron points of the slabs and filling the gaps between chevrons with concrete, the developer gained an additional 2,200 square feet of leasable space on each floor. After analysis of the concrete columns and floor slabs, it was determined that the exterior panels should be secured to the columns

A 1.2-inch-thick glass plank serves as the floor for Commonwealth Tower's relocated lobby, occupying less of the limited space than a conventional concrete slab would have.

rather than the slabs. Support brackets for the panels were attached to each column.

Commonwealth Tower fronts on streets with changes in elevation. The elevation of Wilson Boulevard, for example, decreases by 1.5 stories along the front of the building. Therefore the developer would be unable to obtain accurate measurements—for fabrication purposes—for the precast panels at the ground level until the sidewalks and first-level facade had been demolished. This would have meant an unacceptable two-month gap between demolition and the installation of the panels.

The solution was to begin the use of the precast panels at the second floor. The higher floors could be measured earlier, enabling the precaster to begin panel fabrication earlier. Instead of the precast panels at the first-floor level, masonry covered with handset stone was used. This solution avoided an estimated three-month delay in the project.

The project was completed on time and within budget. A large part of the project's success can be attributed to the developer's having had a clearly stated goal. Rustom A. Cowarsjee, senior vice president for London & Leeds, explains: "Even during the design phase, we were clear on what we wanted to achieve." This focus helped to eliminate wasted efforts by the designers and kept the project moving.

Source: Adapted from Hugh Cook, "Commonwealth Tower," *Building Design & Construction*, October 1996, pp. 40–46.

■

A three-year seismic retrofit of the Pacific Gas & Electric Company (PG&E) headquarters in downtown San Francisco is one of the most comprehensive seismic retrofits of a historic complex in the United States. The project was undertaken to strengthen, restore, and connect the four landmark buildings that housed PG&E's headquarters offices as well as power and telecommunications equipment. The complex had been damaged in the October 1989 Loma Prieta earthquake.

PG&E's board of directors had considered several options for the buildings—including sale, demolition, and expansion. It determined that renovation would result in the least cost to customers and the greatest benefit to shareholders and the city of San Francisco.

William A. Porter

Pacific Gas & Electric interconnected and strengthened two of its buildings without altering their exterior appearance. Both structures are among San Francisco's first steel-frame high rises.

The four 50-foot-wide buildings totaling 533,985 square feet wrap around three sides of a block to create a broad courtyard. They had four separate addresses. The renovation structurally united the two oldest buildings and added connections to consolidate the four buildings into one address—245 Market. The original facades and many historical details were restored.

A shear-wall system replaced the complex's seismic resisting system. A special concrete shear wall forms a U around the center courtyard. It is designed to distribute seismic forces efficiently from the two interconnected buildings to their foundation. Other concrete shear walls were added at the ends of the complex and in the middle.

Construction activities were carefully planned to ensure the uninterrupted operation of the power systems and telecommunications equipment housed in the complex.

The new concrete shear walls needed openings placed so as to direct light and air to the new office space within the old plan and needed also to be compatible with the landmark facades—a design challenge. The new walls use modern materials that relate to the original walls, and the openings are organized to be both structurally sound and aesthetically compatible.

At the same time, the office interiors were modernized to be more functional and flexible. State-of-the-art, energy-efficient lighting and HVAC systems were installed. Approximately 17,000 square feet on the ground floor was converted to retail space. Lease income will help offset the building's operating costs, and retailing will create more activity on the block.

The total cost of the seismic retrofitting of the complex was an estimated $178 million, an amount that was expected to be reduced by at least $20 million through a federal historic building rehabilitation tax credit.

Source: Adapted from Diane Sable, "Past Perfect," *Urban Land*, January 1996, pp. 62–63.

■

Watertightness is a key skin function. Leaks tend to occur where different materials meet—for example, at the intersections of the aluminum window frames and the brick veneer. If the building's ceilings or perimeter walls show evidence of water damage, it is necessary to further investigate the causes, to determine if this is a localized or a buildingwide problem.

Most modern buildings rely heavily on sealants, which are relatively cheap, to prevent water penetration. Metal

or fabric flashing details are more reliable but expensive. In many older buildings, the action of ultraviolet rays has caused sealants to deteriorate, allowing water to penetrate. For a building with chronic leaks, the developer should examine the construction method and apply a new detail or technology.

Energy-efficiency is a second consideration in the analysis of an existing building's skin. Are its windows made of thermal glass? Are the aluminum windowframes ther-

Restored interior spaces include the public lobbies and a variety of distinctive offices. These spaces retain their original ornamental plasters, marble fireplaces, and elegant woodwork.

mally broken? Is the wall insulated? These questions have direct impact not only on the operating expenses of the building, but also on the comfort of its occupants.

Aesthetics is the third major consideration in the evaluation of an existing building's skin. The expensive decision to renovate or replace it because of its appearance should be determined by the competitive market. If the competition consists of buildings of similar age and condition and if the developer's marketing strategy

is to reposition the property at the top of the market, a skin replacement can play an important role. If, however, the developer decides to compete on the basis of lower rents, replacement of the building's skin may not be a priority.

Roof

Nothing in a building, other than the HVAC system, will cause more operational problems than the roof. The roofs of older office buildings typically are built up of alternating layers of asphalt paper and tar. Such roofs are notorious for a lack of quality control during their installation. Many have deteriorated over time and been patched. Leaks in these roofs can be difficult to locate and expensive to repair properly.

If the building's roof needs to be replaced, the developer should evaluate new roof systems carefully. Not only should the roof's expense and performance characteristics be considered, but also its weight. The strength of the structure that will carry the new roof must be determined, especially if the new roof system calls for gravel as its top surface.

Seismic Upgrades

The October 1989 Loma Prieta earthquake that wreaked havoc in the San Francisco Bay Area proved that unreinforced brick and masonry buildings are particularly prone to collapse in seismic events and that concrete-frame buildings are also vulnerable—facts known by structural engineers and required to be addressed by local jurisdictions per California state law. The January 1994 Northridge earthquake in the Los Angeles area pointed out that contemporary wood-frame buildings and steel-frame structures are also vulnerable. After learning of the damage inflicted on steel-frame buildings by the Northridge earthquake, some owners of steel-frame high rises in San Francisco—buildings that had suffered no apparent damage in the Loma Prieta earthquake—had their weld joints inspected and discovered cracks.

In the wake of these devastating earthquakes, engineers have made considerable progress in devising methods for determining the strength requirements of existing buildings and retrofitting them for seismic safety. Yet seismic retrofit is still a complex issue involving difficult choices for building owners. Considerations of safety and cost must be balanced in determining the appropriate level of seismic repair for an office building.

How does a building owner make informed decisions on seismic upgrades? As of 1998, there are no easy answers and no prescriptive standards. While state and local governments often are closely involved as guardians of public safety, the hard decisions rest largely in the hands of individual building owners.

California building codes require the owners of commercial buildings to retrofit them for seismic safety when they make major additions to them or change their structural loads or occupancy. A 1986 state law requires local governments to survey buildings and establish risk-reduction programs in high-risk seismic zones. After

Oakland City Hall—rendered uninhabitable by the Loma Prieta earthquake—has been gracefully restored and retro-fitted with a system of seismic base isolators.

© Victoria Visuals 1996

ten years, the requirements have affected mostly older brick buildings.

The owners of office buildings in California not covered by these codes and requirements are not uniformly required to retrofit their buildings. But if these owners are considering selling the buildings at market value, they generally will conduct a seismic evaluation to determine the appropriate degree of retrofitting and they may invest in a retrofit. Insurance companies and lenders encourage seismic evaluations and retrofitting. The prospect of lower insurance premiums is a strong incentive for building owners to invest in retrofitting, especially if the building is in a high-risk seismic zone.

Water damage from broken fire-sprinkler systems is a common and costly type of damage experienced by office buildings and tenant property in earthquakes. To prevent it, developers must brace sprinkler pipes and design ceiling systems that will not shear off sprinkler heads when the ground shakes.

Tenants may drive the retrofit decision. Many computer and software firms located in Silicon Valley, whether or not they incurred damage in the Loma Prieta earthquake, have determined that they cannot afford to have their operations interrupted by an earthquake. Such businesses have upgraded or plan to upgrade buildings that house critical functions to standards well above normal seismic building codes. Performance-based seismic engineering reduces the chances of interrupted occupancy following future earthquakes.

Seismic upgrades can be highly disruptive for operating buildings. However, by using new materials and methods —and managing the project with meticulous attention— an owner can complete a seismic upgrade without causing undue disturbance, even in tenanted spaces. The 1995 seismic retrofit of the Calais Office Center in Anchorage, Alaska, demonstrates this possibility.

Owned and managed by Wright Runstad & Company, a Seattle-based firm, the Calais Office Center consists of two buildings, one five stories and the other eight. The structures are made of reinforced concrete and the cladding is composed of precast concrete, aluminum, and glass. Each building contains more than 100,000 square feet of office space and each was fully occupied at the time of the seismic upgrade. Neither building was structurally deficient, and both met all relevant standards for existing buildings in Anchorage. Nevertheless, a refinancing deal for the property included a seismic upgrading provision.

Wright Runstad set out to reinforce the interior concrete columns without compromising the property's performance as a workplace or as an investment for the shareholders. Project manager Lindy Gaylord compared the task to "pulling the tablecloth off a dinner table without breaking any dishes or spilling the wine."

The project involved wrapping 164 interior columns (44 percent of all columns) in fiberglass/Kevlar sheets that were saturated with epoxy resins. Called Fibrwrap and first used in 1991, this system greatly increases the shear strength of concrete columns. This method of retrofitting concrete columns in place avoids the extensive disruption that ordinarily occurs with traditional reinforcing techniques using welded and grouted metal.

To minimize disruption, all work was conducted after hours, and work schedules were laid out in 15-minute intervals. The same process was used for each column: protect the tenant space and property; install a prefabricated dust partition around the column; demolish the walls enclosing the column; grind the concrete surface; prepare the wrap material; wrap the column; let the epoxy resins cure for 16 hours; replace the wallboard; and restore the wall finishes. Two test runs—one in an unoccupied space and one in an accommodating tenant's space —were undertaken to perfect the plan and schedule.

Despite the number of steps involved, no tenant workspace was affected for more than two working days and currently affected workspaces were cleaned at the end of the night shift so as to be usable during the day. The ventilation and air-filtration systems were powered up during construction to eliminate dust and odors.

Ironically, just as construction work was beginning in May 1995, an earthquake measuring 5.7 on the Richter scale hit Anchorage. No damage was sustained at Calais, but the quake's timing brought home to its manager and tenants the importance of earthquake readiness and perhaps increased the latter's tolerance of the slight disruptions caused by the seismic upgrade. The project was completed two months later—on schedule and on budget.

Notes

1. Sherie Winston, "New Guidelines Could Clarify ADA," *Engineering News Record*, June 23, 1997, p. 8/2.
2. John Sue, "Landscape Grading Design," in *Handbook of Landscape Architectural Construction*, ed. Jot D. Carpenter (McLean, Virginia: Landscape Architecture Foundation, 1976), p. 35.
3. James Goettsch, "The Characteristics of Today's Office Buildings," in *The Office Building: From Concept to Investment Reality*, ed. John Robert White (Washington, D.C.: Counselors of Real Estate; Appraisal Institute; and Society of Industrial and Office Realtors Education Fund, 1993), p. 25.
4. Ibid., p. 29.
5. Ibid., p. 29.
6. Henry H. Brennan, "Architectural Office Design: From Programming through Construction," in *The Office Building: From Concept to Investment Reality*, ed. John Robert White (Washington, D.C.: Counselors of Real Estate; Appraisal Institute; and Society of Industrial and Office Realtors Education Fund, 1993), pp. 254–255.
7. U.S. Environmental Protection Agency, *Building Air Quality: A Guide for Building Owners and Facility Managers*, DHHS (NIOSH) Publication no. 91-114 (Washington, D.C., U.S. Government Printing Office, December 1991), p. 7.
8. Ibid.
9. Ibid.
10. "Lighting, Heating, Cooling Top FM's List of Energy Guzzlers," *Facilities Design & Management*, June 1997, p. 15/1.
11. John Holusha, "The Name of the Game These Days Is Technology," *New York Times*, August 11, 1996.

5. Marketing and Leasing

Marketing and leasing represent the culmination of the developer's efforts to build, buy, or renovate an office product that fulfills a specific need. To earn a fair return on investment, the developer or owner must fill the building with tenants who will pay a rent that is commensurate with the value of the property. It is the function of marketing to lease or sell office space and produce revenue. Successful leasing brings the owner's or developer's vision and the reality of the marketplace into harmony.

Marketing

Marketing an office project is a process. It involves finding prospective tenants or buyers, as the case may be, convincing them that the space meets their needs better than any other available space, and working with them through the leasing (or buying) negotiation. the project nears completion, but the seeds for a successful marketing effort should have been planted in the initial planning stages and the seedlings thinned and tended in the period before construction started.

The job of finding tenants begins, essentially, by identifying the building's target market, which, as was noted in Chapter 2, is the main goal of the developer's market analysis and feasibility studies during the project's early stages. The marketing function during the feasibility stage goes on to determine the type of office space and the amenities that the target market wants, the rents that target tenants would be willing to pay, and the amount and characteristics of available competitive space. In this way, marketing concerns are incorporated into the developer's design decisions, and, ideally, the office project that is built will meet the target market's specific needs in a cost-effective way. In some cases, the project offers space that has been custom-designed for a specific tenant (or owner).

Another basic element of the marketing program is the effective communication of the building's attributes to prospective tenants (or buyers) at a time when they are in a position to lease or buy. Any notion that office buildings sell themselves was proved false in the overbuilt office market that prevailed throughout the first half of the 1990s. The reality is that in anything other than an overheated market, an office building—no matter how well conceived and executed it is—rarely generates its own market.

Experience shows that a systematic approach to marketing produces superior results. Just as the development of an office building requires a coordinated effort, leasing or selling that building also requires a coordinated multidimensional program. Guided by the market analysis and controlled by a strategic marketing plan and marketing budget, the developer undertakes

Glass and steel contrast with rose-colored masonry at the Cato Institute's building in Washington, D.C.

© Peter Aaron/Esto

Harborside has lured tenants to the New Jersey side of the Hudson and kept them by providing attractive amenities.

The building that is Harborside Financial Center began service as a freight-handling terminal in 1929. The 1.9 million-square-foot building now offers high-tech office space for the back-office operations of financial services, insurance, and shipping companies. The building's Jersey City, New Jersey, site is directly across the Hudson River from New York City and an adjacent commuter transit station (the PATH line's Exchange Place station) links Harborside to the heart of Lower Manhattan, just three minutes away, and to New Jersey's regional transit system. The building's direct accessibility to Manhattan orients it to the downtown New York market more than to the suburban New Jersey market.

The original warehouse had structural advantages that, in the view of Harborside's developer Jones Lang Wootton, made its conversion use as high-tech, back-office space a natural choice. These advantages include the following: a flat-slab design that can carry live loads up to 200 pounds per square inch (and thus accommodate heavy mainframe computers and backup equipment), 13'6" slab-to-slab heights that provide enough vertical space for raised floors (to accommodate underfloor cabling) and complex ceilings (to accommodate mechanical apparatus), and more than adequate rooftop space for equipment such as emergency power generators, satellite dishes, and microwave towers with direct line-of-sight communication to Manhattan.

Given Harborside's functional strengths and market orientation, the developer targeted its marketing at financial services and shipping companies located in Lower Manhattan. In its proactive campaign to lure tenants out of Manhattan, the developer emphasized the building's lower occupancy costs and its functionally superior space for back-office and data operations.

An important feature of the marketing strategy is a package of tax breaks and other economic incentives available to businesses locating in this part of Jersey City. Among these are discounted electricity prices, no corporate income and occupancy taxes, and a 15-year abatement of real estate taxes. In addition, the area's designation as a state urban enterprise zone means that businesses at Harborside are exempt from sales tax on the purchase of business equipment and services.

Tenants relocating out of Manhattan boast employee retention rates of over 95 percent. To duplicate some of the urban amenities that these employees enjoyed in their former workplaces, the developer created a waterfront retail promenade that offers tenants a variety of shopping and dining alternatives, the largest of which is a 600-seat food court. Major tenants include Bankers Trust, Dow Jones/Telerate Systems, Dean Witter, Bank of Tokyo, and the American Institute of Certified Accountants.

Three office towers totaling 4 million square feet are planned for future phases of Harborside, west of the terminal building along a new tree-lined boulevard. All three towers will contain retail space and parking, which will be supplemented by two garages. In addition to the office component, the master plan for the project includes a hotel/conference center, 300 condominium units on two piers jutting into the Hudson River, and a 250-slip marina.

Source: Adapted from "Harborside Financial Center," *Project Reference File*, v. 22, no. 6 (Washington, D.C.: ULI–the Urban Land Institute, April–June 1992).

■

various initiatives to attract and satisfy the needs of prospective tenants. Only within such a framework can the efforts of the sales and leasing professionals produce maximum results. All members of the team must understand how their activities can contribute to the success of the overall marketing program.

The Marketing Strategy

The marketing strategy for an office project is essentially a plan for identifying firms and other organizations within the target market and convincing them to pay rent and occupy the building. The time to begin developing the marketing strategy is during the initial project feasibility phase, after a thorough market analysis has convinced the developer that an office need exists and after the potential target market for the prospective office building has begun to emerge. The marketing strategy lays out how the developer will attract the targeted tenants, who should be on the marketing team, and when the marketing period should start. It should take into account not only the requirements of the unfulfilled tenant market but also the developer/owner's investment strategy. Among the specific elements of a good marketing strategy are the following:

- A description of the project, the target market, and the project's relative position in the marketplace. For example: Who are the prospective tenants? What are their needs? How can the project be differentiated from competitive projects? The marketing plan should include a summary of market conditions in the area—asking rents, concessions, vacancies, lease rates and terms, services and amenities, and historical absorption rates—which, of course, needs to be frequently updated throughout the development process.
- A statement of the project's financial goals. The owners' goals for the project and the investment strategy needed to accomplish these goals should be important determinants of the marketing strategy. The discussion of the investment strategy should cover both the project's financing and the owner's exit strategies.
- Short-term and long-term forecasts of expected financial results. While financial feasibility is a major part of the early planning process and not a result of the marketing strategy, the project's financial objectives will be the basis for the leasing decisions. A project's marketing team must keep in mind that the financial feasibility analysis is updated and revised throughout the development process to reflect new information. Therefore, the marketing strategy must also be revised throughout the development period to reflect changes in the pro forma leasing projections.
- A specific marketing and leasing plan for the project. How will the project be presented to appeal to the target market? By what means will the marketing and sales staff get information to and contact the target market? Under what basic leasing assumptions should the marketing effort operate? As the marketing plan evolves, a list of specific, productive marketing activities should be compiled.
- For an existing building, a statement of work. This should include needed capital improvements, major repairs, and tenant space improvements.

While the major elements of a marketing program for an office building are fairly straightforward, as a practical matter it is more difficult to come up with a hard-and-fast estimate of marketing and leasing expenses than it is to estimate construction costs, for example.

The marketing budget depends on a number of variables, among which are the strength of the market, the number of competing buildings, and the developer's local reputation. A developer's first project in a market area will probably need a larger marketing budget than its fifth building in that market.

To gain market advantage, the developer of Washington Mutual Tower accelerated the building's construction schedule so that it could open a year earlier than any of the competitive projects that were underway in downtown Seattle.

James Frederick Housel

The surest means of leasing an office project is to design it to provide a carefully targeted market with exactly what it needs. Stockley Park is located 2.5 miles from London's Heathrow airport on what was once an unsightly landfill. The business park's efficient and flexible tenant spaces, heavily landscaped setting, and convenient access to recreational amenities and restaurants/shopping have attracted high-tech businesses.

Courtesy of Stockley Park Consortium Ltd.

The marketing period can be shortened if necessary to achieve the marketing objectives. For example, when Wright Runstad & Company was building its 55-story Washington Mutual Tower in Seattle in the late 1980s, three other office buildings were also under construction. The developer realized that the Seattle office market was deteriorating and began an aggressive marketing program to get the building leased quickly. This program involved accelerating the entire development schedule, including the building's construction and marketing. Washington Mutual Tower was thus completed a year earlier than the other three competitive new buildings.

On average, the overall cost for marketing an office project ranges from 3 to 5 percent of the project's anticipated gross revenues. The developer should keep in mind that the marketing budget must be adequate to cover the entire marketing period, not just the flurry of marketing activity that usually accompanies a project's opening.

While it is important to be aggressive in seeking out prospective tenants and marketing to them, a shotgun approach to marketing is costly and inefficient. The marketing strategy should clearly define a target tenant market and develop a specific plan for reaching this particular segment of the market and communicating the merits of the project to it. Spending dollars on marketing a downtown Class A office building to small, cost-conscious firms that do not need to be in the CBD is probably an unproductive use of resources.

Office marketing in general must focus on canvassing the market, developing attractive brochures, advertising, merchandising, and public relations—topics dealt with in the following sections. Working with brokers is covered in the leasing section later in this chapter.

Advertising

Properly conceived and executed, advertising can promote the project's image and attract tenants. Some developers prefer to coordinate the advertising of their projects themselves. Others prefer to hire a professional advertising agency. An advertising agency can prepare a long-range advertising strategy, plan individual ad campaigns, select the best media for presentation, prepare the copy and design layouts, and check the overall performance. The budget for this will depend on the size of the project. Advertising must be conceived and scheduled to work in tandem with merchandising and public relations. However, advertising is a selling tool and therefore the heaviest advertising should be concentrated when and where the lease-up opportunity is the greatest.

All advertising for a project should be unified by theme, logo, and style. A name, logo, and identity design to be used in all printed materials, including ads and letterhead, can be developed as early as when the conceptual plan is completed. The early development of a logo provides a continuity in presentation and image that carries through from the working drawings to the project's entrance treatment and signage, brochures, and advertising.

Advertising for an office building can take many forms. One of these is paid space ads in the media, including media on the Internet. Direct mail can be used to reach specific audiences. Various collateral materials produced by the project—brochures, newsletters, building bulletins, lease proposal forms, Web pages, and audiovisual materials—are or should be considered advertising. Off-site signs and signs advertising a project's availability that are located on the property but visible from a distance are another form of advertising used to market office buildings. Some marketing programs have made use of the Internet by creating a Web homepage for specific buildings or developers.

Space Ads. Although some developers believe that media advertisements are more a public relations tool than a tool for attracting new tenants, advertising in publications can be an effective method of marketing the office building. Advertising the building in local newspapers can help make brokers and prospective tenants in the market area aware of the building and its progress. Advertising the building in national newspapers such as the *Wall Street Journal* and the *New York Times* is costly and generally is not cost-effective for most office projects.

If the professional reading habits of prospective tenants are known, it can be productive to run advertising in trade journals and magazines. Some periodicals target prospective tenants and include guides to available office buildings. These can be effective marketing tools, but the developer must take care with these media, since the dollars spent can easily exceed the results that are achieved. A tombstone advertisement in trade journals to announce a major tenant, for example, may be a way of stimulating momentum in project leasing.

Direct Mail. Direct-mail advertising can be an effective tool for reaching specific audiences. Some developers aim their direct-mail campaigns more at the local brokerage community than at prospective tenants. They use direct mail to supply brokers with promotional brochures and floor plans.

Promotional literature designed for use in a direct-mail campaign should include a low-cost flyer that can be sent out in bulk to potential tenants. For highly targeted mailings, developers can use a more expensive, attractive, and detailed sales brochure. To be successful, any direct-mail campaign must be targeted and repetitive.

Collateral Materials. The wide variety of materials that developers use to communicate information to brokers and potential tenants all should be considered part of the office project's marketing program. These collateral materials should be produced professionally and carefully coordinated with the other elements of the marketing program. Some of the most commonly used types of collateral materials include the following:

- Brochures—Whether the project's brochures are produced in color or black and white, they should not only convey information but also pique the interest of prospective tenants. Brochures should be designed to accommodate the insertion of items such as news clippings, a copy of the work letter, a list of the project's unique features, sample floor plans, the leasing agent's name and telephone number, and a list of specific benefits of the project to tenants.
- Space Availability Bulletin—Usually issued monthly or quarterly, space availability bulletins list vacancies on each floor of the building and include information on asking rental rates, tenant improvements offered, and dates of availability.
- Lease Proposal Forms—The building's lease proposal forms should be formatted so that they can be customized for each prospective tenant. The addition of an attractive, personalized cover can create a favorable first impression.
- Audiovisual Materials—Short slide or video presentations lasting five to ten minutes can be an effective

tool for marketing office real estate. James Bell, senior vice president at TCW Realty Advisors (which has since become Westmark Realty Advisors) in Los Angeles, remarks on the widespread use of such materials: "In recent years, audiovisual presentations have developed into an art form, with sophisticated miniature modeling and extravagant photography and lighting effects often housed in a specially designed leasing center or pavilion. Whether there is a relationship between the amount of money and the leasing effectiveness of the audiovisual presentation is a subject of ongoing debate. However, there is little doubt that some kind of audiovisual presentation is now standard equipment in the marketing of major office buildings."[1]

Signs. Large highway signs are a way of announcing the existence of the building to the public. They usually contain little detail, perhaps only the name of the developer and a telephone number. Bus banners and other forms of transit advertising can be an effective way of getting the project's name before the public, but such advertising can be costly. Local ordinances may dictate the size of signs and where they may be placed.

Visually, the building should promote itself, but placing signs on or near the project to announce space availability is a common practice. An effective sign tells prospects that office space is available and indicates to whom inquiries should be directed. Such signs should be tastefully designed, compatible with the architecture of the building, and located so that they are inconspicuous to the building's tenants and visitors. Signs that must attract the attention of persons in moving vehicles should be perpendicular to the traffic flow and have letters large enough to be quickly read.

The Internet. Marketers of commercial space have been slower than residential marketers to use the Web. Increasingly, however, information on commercial properties is making its way onto the Web. While the num-

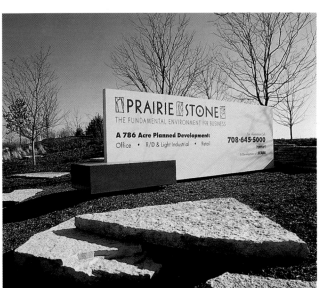

An on-site sign advertises the project.

ber of Web sites devoted to commercial properties is growing, their utility for marketing space has not yet been clearly demonstrated.

Many commercial brokerage houses now maintain their own Web sites that offer searchable property listings, each listing including building specs, floor plans, a description of amenities, and photographs. Other organizations operate sites that provide a clearinghouse for property listings. Real estate service firms have launched Web sites not only to display available properties, but also to maintain a market presence and advertise their services. While property listings on the Internet are becoming more common, many prospective tenants and brokers may not be using them in their search for office space. Web-based property listings can be particularly useful to office users seeking to find space in cities where they are not currently located.

Some individual properties maintain a Web site as part of the overall marketing plan. A case in point is the New York Information Technology Center at 55 Broad Street in New York. This extensively wired multitenant building maintains an elaborate Web site touting its unique features and offering a virtual tour of the property. The site includes a list of the building's current tenants, a calendar of building events, and copies of relevant news stories.

A Web site does the same kind of work as more traditional advertising media. It reaches potential tenants or buyers with information on the project. But so far it is not a transaction tool. As Rod Kimble, president of Rod Kimble & Associates in Tiberon, California, points out: "Even with the use of advanced technology, the leasing and purchasing of real estate remains a very face-to-face process." In time, advances in the design and transmis-

sion of virtual reality could enhance the marketing role of the Web. Some office developers already offer potential tenants multimedia and sometimes interactive "virtual" tours of buildings that are not yet built. As the cost of producing such presentations declines and the technology improves, such techniques are likely to be used on the Web to market office buildings.

Merchandising

Advertising and merchandising for an office project are two sides of the same coin, the purpose of which is to stimulate interest in renting space. They certainly must work together. Whereas advertising is money spent to tell prospective tenants about the advantages of a particular real estate development, merchandising is the use of on-site displays and practices to show these advantages. Merchandising starts with curb appeal, with image. If advertising draws a prospective tenant to a project but the project leaves a negative first impression on the prospect, the advertising money has been spent needlessly.

Creating a favorable impression begins at the development's entrance. A well-designed entrance to an office park or a building is a merchandising essential. The entrance should be modest and designed to blend in with the character of the surrounding community.

The 1993 renovation of the Sears Tower in Chicago, for example, focused on three observations having to do with the building's entrance: the lobby did not conform to the world-class stature of the rest of the building, the elevator system was confusing, and a high volume of tourists created an unreasonable amount of traffic in the office lobby. The John Buck Company upgraded the lobby, brought all the elevators to the same level, and created a separate

55 Broad Street's Web site gives emphasis to the lower Manhattan building's high-tech features.

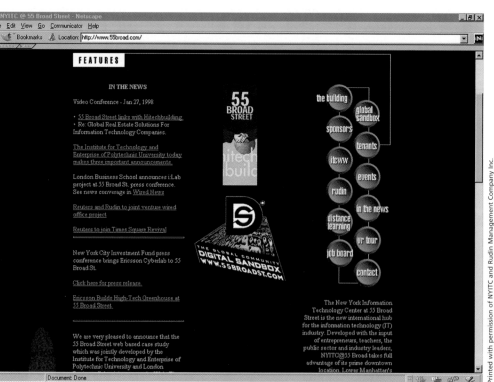

The upgraded office lobby of the Sears Tower in Chicago conveys the appropriate image. In the 1993 renovation, tourists were given their own entrance to the building in order to reduce traffic in the office lobby.

 — caption image credit: Hedrich-Blessing

tourist entrance. The renovation helped the owner reach its occupancy goal a year earlier than expected.

Tools that enable prospective tenants to visualize what finished rentable space might look like are a key part of merchandising. This visualization is difficult, and a model office is often the best technique. Floor-plan displays and handouts also can be useful. In some cases, developers can use CADD technology to depict the space that will be available for prospective tenants and also to allow them to experiment with customizing available space.

While a project is under development, the ideal location for a model office may be in a building overlooking or near the construction site. However, such a site often is not available. In such situations, as soon as the elevators or stairs in a project become usable the developer could set up the model office suite in the first available office space.

A model office suite could include an executive office, a staff office, an open area, and a small conference room, in about 1,000 to 3,000 square feet. The developer should use standard tenant improvements—no extras, no upgrades—in decorating the model office. It is important to show prospects how attractive and comfortable the space can be without added expense.

The condition of the site is important to successful merchandising. Construction traffic must be regulated. Trash must be collected, parking areas policed, and vacant space always kept neat. To project a high-

quality image, developers should spend time and money up front on landscaping, signage, and other visual amenities.

On-site signage is a merchandising element for an office project. It should be simple and used either to inform or direct. The review and approval of the developer should be required before any signage is installed. Having in place a set of uniform sign guidelines is preferable to making decisions on an ad hoc basis. Such guidelines should aim at achieving an orderly and visually pleasant environment while providing enough flexibility to accommodate the many functional requirements of individual signs as well as cost considerations. The developer's signage guidelines should cover all types of signs, from the general to the specific, including exterior signs, parking lot signs, entry signage, directories, elevator signs, directional signs, and the signs identifying individual tenant suites.

The content of signs that are visible from outside the office building typically is restricted to advertising the building's tenants, developer/owner, and property management company. Signs may be mounted on the building. However, a tastefully executed monument sign may more effectively convey the image of the project that the developer seeks to establish.

The developer should be careful about granting a tenant exclusive signage rights. Tenants can use these rights to keep out competitors. James Bell offers the following advice for developers: "Building-top signage rights are frequently used to help capture the major tenant. These rights should not be assignable to subtenants. Lower signage on the building such as 'eyebrow' signage or monument signage is also an effective inducement for many identity-conscious tenants."[2]

Public Relations

Public relations is the creation of a favorable image by means other than advertising. A good public relations effort results in free advertising. The public relations function for an office development can be handled by in-house personnel or farmed out to a public relations firm. Firms providing PR services typically establish their fees in one of three ways: a fixed monthly retainer fee, a fixed retainer with monthly billing for staff time, or a base fee. High-impact marketing may not always be required. In markets with little available space, for example, brokers will be familiar with the few buildings that contain space that could meet their clients' needs. Media relations, promotional materials, and promotional events are the three main avenues of public relations for most office projects.

In marketing an office building, the establishment of good press relations is usually highly useful. Most important is a relationship with the local newspaper(s)—specifically, with real estate, business, and city reporters and editors. Through the course of the development project there will be many appropriate subjects for news releases, among which are the acquisition of the land, the evolving development plans, the signing of tenants, the selection of an architect, various milestones in construction, and innovative program or design elements.

Giveaway promotional items, from paperweights to pens and pencils and coffee cups, can help keep a project in the mind of key audiences, like brokers or reporters. Some office building owners and managers mail items to the brokerage community monthly as part of a campaign to keep up interest and leasing momentum. It may sometimes be advantageous to break through the clutter of competing marketing efforts with a high-impact promotion. For example, the marketing team for One East Wacker in Chicago came up with a Velcro dartboard that depicted the benefits and amenities located within a five- to ten-minute walk from the property.

Staging special events such as press parties and the like is the third main avenue of public relations. Events given prior to the groundbreaking or the grand opening, for example, can result in press coverage and create interest in the project being leased. Events give community leaders and news sources opportunities to preview the project. They can be costly, however, and the developer should monitor their cost-effectiveness. For a standard speculative office building, the advantages of programming special events may be negligible.

Preservation Park: Target Marketing and Leasing

Sixteen 19th-century Victorian residences, 11 of which were relocated to the site, make up the 55,604-square-foot Preservation Park business neighborhood on two blocks adjacent to the Oakland City Center mixed-use redevelopment project in downtown Oakland, California. The historic residences were renovated for use as office and meeting space.

The original project was started in 1982, but the developer bowed out in 1986. Bramalea Inc., the Toronto-based developer of the Oakland City Center project, agreed to take over the development, on the condition that it could change the development concept to target nonprofit, public service organizations. Bramalea stepped up to the plate when it recognized that the unfinished project was a lingering eyesore that would adversely affect the success of the City Center project. The developer

Preservation Park, a two-block business neighborhood, was developed adjacent to the Oakland Federal Building.

Nonprofit, public service organizations lease space in Victorian residences that were moved to Preservation Park from scattered locations and converted to office use.

targeted nonprofit organizations in the belief that they would be willing to occupy unconventional office space within a neighborhood undergoing gentrification. Moreover, the office needs of the growing public service sector were not well served at the time, reinforcing the choice of nonprofit organizations as the target market.

With this new marketing plan and an infusion of additional funding from the city of Oakland as well as the U.S. Department of Housing and Urban Development, Bramalea took over the development, management, and leasing of the project, donating its executive services to the city. The renovation and refurbishment of 11 historic structures and limited on-site improvements were completed by 1991, and 18 months later the project was fully leased.

To develop its marketing strategy, Bramalea first undertook a market survey of nonprofit organizations, pinpointing their space needs and rent levels. The survey, along with a direct-mail campaign, was the principal method of introducing the project to the nonprofit community in the early phases.

Rent-up was successfully achieved over a planned 18-month period, which was long enough to allow Bra-

malea to be selective in the tenants it accepted. The project's cash flow after debt service provides sufficient income to offset ongoing property management and capital improvement costs.

To provide business services for the nonprofit tenants, some space at Preservation Park is reserved for commercial tenants, which currently include a café and a printing/copying shop. A two-tier lease rate system differentiates between the two types of tenants, with lower rates offered to nonprofit tenants and higher rates to commercial tenants.

Preservation Park's conference and banquet facilities generate a valuable revenue stream while they also give the project good market exposure. The conference center, which in 1995 accommodated 691 nonprofit meetings and 112 business meetings, has proven to be a valuable amenity for tenants as well as the surrounding business community. The centerpiece of the conference center is the 3,200-square-foot Nile Hall, which can accommodate meetings for up to 150 people and receptions for up to 200 people.

Source: Adapted from "Preservation Park," *Project Reference File*, v. 26, no. 3 (Washington, D.C.: ULI–the Urban Land Institute, January–March 1996). ∎

PF Bentley

During the real estate glory days of the 1980s, many developers, property managers, and leasing agents used charitable contributions—cash or in-kind donations—to market their office properties. Their reasoning was generally valid: buildings that receive good publicity and make a positive impression on the local community lease up faster. Today, limited marketing budgets require more creativity in the establishment of ties with charitable and community organizations.

A grand lobby is a perfect site for a charity ball or reception.

Facilities can be donated for charitable events at little cost. An office park with a golf course might host a charity event golf tournament. A building with conference facilities could make them available for meetings or lectures. Such events serve as a tenant amenity and generate good publicity for the property.

One of the most common and cost-efficient ways to merge building marketing and charitable involvement is to donate space for special events. Typically, little or no cash changes hands, although the building owner usually provides after-hours heating or air conditioning, security, parking, and janitorial services. Charitable events often attract a community's business and social leaders—who in many cases also are the local corporate decision makers.

Burnett Plaza, a 1 million-square-foot office tower located in downtown Fort Worth, Texas, provides an example. The building donates the use of vacant space on a continuing basis to the local YMCA for the operation of a childcare facility during holidays, teacher in-service days, and school vacations. Tenants can drop off their children at 9 a.m. and pick them up by 6 p.m. During the day, the children are bused to and from a day camp. Burnett Plaza's owners have found that this program helps the building meet two important goals: retention of tenants and support of a local charity.

Sponsorship of a golf or tennis tournament, the proceeds of which are designated for a particular charity or community organization, can be an excellent way to raise a building's profile and benefit tenant relations.

Brown-bag lectures—bring-your-own lunches with a speaker who is usually a tenant or the representative of a local charity—can benefit charities and community groups while marketing a property. Tenants and prospective tenants are invited to attend the lunches, which typically might be on subjects such as estate and tax planning, volunteering, risk management, legal issues, insurance, or financial planning. The speaker usually advertises the event and provides beverages. The property owner merely provides the meeting room. Such events provide opportunities for community building among the property's tenants.

Charitable or community involvement of this sort represents a win-win approach to marketing an office building. Owners get exposure for the building at little or no cost. The events and programs often are an added tenant amenity and they bring recognition to participating tenants. Charities are provided with the opportunities and resources to raise funds and increase community awareness of their causes and activities. Whether or not such efforts translate into greater absorption or higher rents or better renewal rates, they do raise the awareness of the building among the public and its status in the community—which, in the long run, is what marketing is all about.

Source: Adapted from Bob Gibbons, "Building on Charitable Contributions," *Urban Land,* November 1995, pp. 70–72.

More than 100 tenants call the Edgewater Office Park in Edgewater, Massachusetts, home. Located on 135 acres surrounded by 1,200 acres of land designated as an Audubon preserve, the five-building campus provides more than two miles of nature and hiking trails. An important amenity for tenants is its full-service day-care facility.

Courtesy of BOMA

Leasing

The lease is the foundation for the successful financial operation of an office development. It establishes the level of income that the owner/developer can expect to receive from the project. A lease agreement is a negotiated contract between a tenant who will occupy the office space and the owner/operator of the space. Traditionally a broker brings a prospective tenant to the developer and assists in negotiating the lease. However, many developers prefer to negotiate the lease themselves.

The brokerage task of actually finding prospects and bringing them to the table can be performed by outside brokers or in-house staff. The pros and cons of both approaches are discussed in the following sections, as are the common types of leases for office space and certain key elements—term, rates, and tenant improvements—of any lease.

Outside Brokers

The local office brokerage community typically handles 60 to 90 percent of new office space leasing. Outside real estate brokers can be immensely helpful in marketing and leasing office buildings. A real estate brokerage firm is likely to have in-depth knowledge of who are the major competitors and which tenants are looking for space. A brokerage firm frequently maintains large databases that list key items in recently executed leases, including lease rates, terms, concessions, and TI

allowances. Brokers also play an important role in spreading the word about a new development through their contacts with development agencies, local utilities, chambers of commerce, business organizations, and other community groups.

In selecting a leasing agency, the developer should look for firms that have a proven record of success in leasing office buildings of the same type in the market area. It is important also to look at the depth of staff, which is an essential factor in the success of a leasing program. All too frequently, someone with a powerful personality heads the agency but is not sufficiently backed up by a proficient staff. The agency selected should have a staff that can sustain the marketing effort over the life of the project.

In the broker selection, the developer should also consider the firm's or broker's possible conflicts of interest. An agency may be leasing a number of competitive buildings simultaneously, and consequently could not work exclusively on the developer's behalf. It is best to avoid the problems that can come from an overextended broker or potential conflicts of interest. The developer might find it advantageous to select a less well known agency that has no client conflicts and may devote extra effort to the job. However, such an agency may have fewer meaningful tenant contacts than would a more experienced agency.

Commission structures, rates, and payments are always negotiable. Broker compensation depends on a variety of factors, including the condition and competitiveness of the market, market traditions regarding broker compensation, and the type of lease that is negotiated.

A declining commission throughout the lease period is a common method of compensation. A broker might request a 6 percent commission in the first year of a gross lease, 5 percent in the second, 4 percent in the third, 3.5 percent in the fourth and fifth years, and 2.5 percent in the sixth through tenth years. Commission rates for a net lease are typically higher than for a gross lease. It is common to split the commission between the outside broker that makes the lease transaction and a leasing agent. Or the leasing agent might receive an override commission while the outside broker receives the full commission on the lease transaction.

Like the commission rate, the timing of when the commission is paid is negotiable. Frequently, half of the entire commission is paid at the execution of the lease and the other half is paid at the time of occupancy. In cases in which a substantial period of free rent is offered at the beginning of a lease, it is common for developers to pay one-third of the commission at the signing of the lease, one-third at occupancy, and one-third at the commencement of rent.

The developer may enter into a contract with a broker that ensures the broker the exclusive right to negotiate all deals on the building. Alternatively, the developer may opt for an open listing, which allows any broker to act as the primary broker on a deal. Some developers prefer to wait until the midpoint of construction before giving one broker exclusive rights. Variations on the basic exclusive agency contract are almost endless. One common contract provision permits the exclusive agent to list the property with other brokers as an open listing, which allows more widespread marketing of the property.

To avoid misunderstandings and possible litigation, the listing agreement between the developer and broker should include provisions referring to the term of the listing, the developer's approval of rental terms, commissions for lease renewals, and broker obligations, as follows:

- Term—In general, the term of a listing depends on the size of the lease and on what is considered competitive in the marketplace. The developer should not offer a listing term so short that it would be impossible for the broker to be effective. A listing agreement covering an entire office building, for example, would probably not be shorter than six months to one year. On the other hand, a much shorter period might be appropriate for a listing of a 10,000-square-foot space. Regardless of the size of the lease, the developer should seek to include a 30-day cancellation provision that can be exercised in the event of poor performance by the broker.
- Rent—The developer's rent requirements are made known to the leasing agency before it undertakes

the assignment. However, it is advisable to include a clause in the listing agreement that states that the terms of any negotiated lease must be acceptable to the developer.
- Lease Renewals—The agreement between the developer and leasing agent should set out what commissions will be paid for lease renewals. In many cases, tenants renew their leases with no involvement of the broker. Many developers structure their listing agreements to tie commission payments to the direct efforts of the broker. Under such an agreement, the developer would not pay a commission for a lease renewal unless the broker was responsible for convincing the tenant to renew.
- Broker Obligations—In the listing agreement, the leasing agency should undertake to diligently follow the developer's approved marketing plan. A copy of the plan should be attached to the listing agreement.

In-House Leasing Agents

Developers often retain an outside broker during the planning phase of an office project when the marketing strategy is being developed. As a member of the development team, a broker can help determine what types of tenants might be interested in the building and the rental rates they would be willing to pay. When it comes to leasing, however, some developers feel that having an in-house leasing staff offers more advantages than using outside brokers. In-house agents can give a marketing program continuity over time. Also, they typically spend more time at the building than do outside brokers and consequently might better know the property and its attributes. Even when the development firm maintains an in-house leasing staff, continued cooperation with outside brokers is an important element of the marketing program.

An in-house leasing staff involves salary and associated expenses, but it can be less expensive in the long run than commissions to outside brokers. The developer must weigh these advantages against some potential disadvantages, including, most prominently, the possibility that in-house leasing personnel might not understand the market as well as an outside broker and might not have as many helpful contacts.

The decision to rely on in-house leasing personnel depends largely on conditions in the market, the size and in-house expertise of the development company, and the size of the office project. Large office buildings generally have more need for leasing staff over time than do smaller projects and therefore an in-house sales effort might be appropriate for large buildings and for when the landlord owns several buildings in the marketplace. The developer must consider which type of leasing agent is likely to give the project the stronger push. For example, if the current task is to prelease a building that has not yet secured financing, will an outside broker put as much effort into it as will the developer's own staff?

The emergence of new lending sources for office development, such as investment bankers, has spawned a new form of lease, known as a "credit" or "bondable" lease. The mechanics of such a lease assure the lender of lease payments with the same certainty as if the tenant had issued a bond. Financing based on bondable office leases is particularly prevalent in master-lease, single-tenant, and build-to-suit transactions.

Developers also can use bondable leases to attract financing via mortgage-backed securities underwritten by investment bankers. Mortgage-backed securities are rated based on the tenant's underlying senior debt rating, a rating issued by Standard & Poor's and by Moody's. If the tenant's credit rating is more solid than the landlord's, the borrower can achieve a better debt rating based on the tenant's credit rather than on its own credit alone. The new breed of office investors is especially concerned with a stable cash flow and the maintenance of the building's long-term value—which are what the bondable lease guarantees.

Concurrent with the rise of bondable office leases in the 1990s, a variety of strong and increasingly refined tenant protections found their way into leases. High vacancy rates in many office markets gave tenants leverage in lease terms, and they asserted this leverage with vigor. Many of these protections were geared toward avoiding problems with landlords that were cash-strapped, bankrupt, or subject to foreclosure. Despite the recent tightening of office markets, tenants continue to demand favorable terms and conditions in sophisticated leases.

Their increasing clout has made today's office tenants winners. However, developers can also win. Indeed, a lease can be negotiated that achieves the proverbial win-win situation for both the tenant and developer. As a first step in obtaining reasonable protections for occupancy, the tenant should require a definition of the material performance obligations of the landlord related to the tenant's occupancy. (These are the obligations that generally require monetary expenditures, and thus are most subject to neglect when landlords experience financial difficulties.) Wherever possible, the lease should specify minimum guaranteed performance levels for each landlord-provided utility and service.

When negotiating this level of detail, a landlord can protect its cash flow by using performance ranges as opposed to specific values. The lease should ensure that the cost of supplying utilities and services at the requisite levels is recoverable as an operating expense pass-through. As utilities deregulation accelerates, particularly among electric utilities, passing through operating expenses to tenants is growing in importance for landlords.

The parties to the lease must negotiate the allocation of expenses related to obligations to repair the premises and comply with all applicable laws. Both parties must be vigilant in the wake of the Americans with Disabilities Act. Noncompliance can mean steep fines—not to mention the loss of good will—for landlord and tenant.

Once a landlord's obligations are defined, enforcement remains an issue. The most effective way for a tenant to enforce the landlord's obligations is to negotiate self-help remedies that can be invoked when the landlord fails to perform. In negotiating self-help remedies, the parties need to agree on how to treat the sums expended by the tenant.

The tenant also may seek assurance that it will receive applicable lease concessions, such as the agreed tenant improvement allowance. The remedy for unpaid concessions must be negotiated.

The tenant will usually insist that the tenant protections in the lease be ensured in the event of a foreclosure by means of a nondisturbance agreement between it and the lender. The lender, according to such an agreement, recognizes the tenant's rights to self-help, rental abatement, and rental offset remedies if the lender becomes the landlord.

For the tenant, a lease that specifically defines the landlord's obligations concerning the tenant's occupancy and lease concession and that secures the performance of such obligations with self-help and offset rights that are recognized by the lender represents the best and most practical approach to satisfying its major protection objectives. This approach should be acceptable as well to the landlord negotiating a bondable lease if the tenant's ability to interrupt or diminish the cash flow from the building will be subject to notice and cure periods and other express and detailed limitations.

Adapted from Anton N. Natsis, "Structuring the New Bondable Office Lease," *Urban Land*, November 1996, pp. 18–19, 72.

Lobby of First Bank Place, a 1.5 million-square-foot tower in downtown Minneapolis.

Most large office projects use on-site leasing agents to handle walk-in prospects, telephone inquiries, and lease renewals. Often this function is combined with the on-site property management function. When the building has a large amount of vacant space available for lease, such as at the beginning of the marketing period, an on-site agent should be available at all times.

Types of Leases

As negotiated documents, lease agreements come in an unlimited number of forms and contain any number of terms and conditions. As a practical matter, office leases generally fall into one of three categories: gross lease, net lease, and expense stop lease. Retail space in office buildings may be offered under a percentage lease. Each type of lease has advantages and disadvantages for the landlord and the tenant.

Gross Lease. Under a gross lease the tenant pays a fixed amount of rent and the landlord pays all operating expenses. The landlord thus assumes the risk of upticks in operating costs. Long-term gross leases can be particularly risky for the building owner. Over time, increases in operating expenses can erode the net rental stream, particularly if the lease contract does not contain rent escalations that are either predetermined or contingent on some indicator such as the consumer price index.

The gross lease was once the most common form of office leasing, but the net lease generally has replaced it.

Net Lease. In a net lease the tenant pays for certain building expenses—usually operating expenses and real estate taxes—in addition to a base rent. In some instances, property management fees and some building improvements are also the responsibility of the tenant. For the landlord, the advantage of the net lease is that it passes through to the tenants several of the variable expenses, if not all, that are associated with operating an office building—utility and other operating costs, maintenance and repair costs, and property taxes.

Three variations of a net lease exist. Under a single-net lease the tenant pays utilities, real estate taxes, and other special assessments directly associated with the leased space. In a net-net lease the tenant also pays for ordinary repairs and maintenance of the common areas and building systems Under a net-net-net lease (often called a triple-net lease) the tenant pays for all of the above plus some capital improvements. Clearly, the triple-net lease is the most attractive for the landlord, although the market may resist it.

What is included as pass-through expenses in net leases can vary slightly from market to market. Needless to say, the developer should ascertain the local definitions of the various types of net leases so as to avoid confusion in dealings with prospective tenants and brokers.

Expense Stop Lease. Under an expense stop lease the landlord and the tenant share expenses. The landlord pays a stated dollar amount for expenses and the tenant

When completed in mid-1996, Panorama Corporate Center I was the first speculative office building to be constructed in Denver in over a decade. The 100,000-square-foot, three-story project is the first phase of a seven-building, 900,000-square-foot office park located in southeast suburban Denver. Soon after the building was completed, CarrAmerica—an office REIT—purchased the business park and began construction on the second office building, which opened in June 1997.

Panorama Corporate Center's developer, Westfield Development Company, saw an unmet market demand and designed the development to attract technologically intensive back-office space users, such as such as communications and financial services companies that operate telephone and customer-service centers.

According to Richard McClintock, a partner at Westfield Development, the company's development strategy for the business park was to put its money into fiber, not granite. Panorama Corporate Center I was built with few frills—precast concrete instead of granite finishes and surface parking instead of structured parking decks, for example. But it offers the most technologically advanced building systems in the area at rental rates well below those charged at competitive developments. The building features self-healing fiberoptic cable, a fiberoptic loop around and between buildings, power delivery from two substations to protect against outages, high capacity HVAC, and 12 watts of power per square foot instead of the more standard five watts. The floors have few columns, giving tenants large and flexible floorplates.

Panorama Corporate Center I was fully leased prior to completion. Westfield offered flexible lease terms, a policy that CarrAmerica continued. Tenants could chose five- to seven-year lease terms with options to expand (or give back space) every three years. TCG, a technology-driven fiberoptic telecommunications company, says that the building meets all the company's space needs. The developer "made the critical, high-quality infrastructure investments in power, electricity and telecommunications that TCG and other tenants need to maintain an edge in today's competitive market," William Beans Jr., TCG's vice president of customer service, told the *Colorado Real Estate Journal* in 1996.

Panorama Corporate Center targets the market for technologically intensive office space with few design frills.

Courtesy of Westfield Development Company

pays any expenses above that amount. Future-year adjustments can be made in a number of ways.

An approach called a full-stop adjustment is popular with lenders. Allowances are derived—one for real estate taxes and one for operating expenses and insurance. Every year for each allowance category, the difference between the actual cost and the budgeted allowance is debited or credited pro rata to the building's tenants.

Another method is to use a defined base point—usually a base year, which can be the first full calendar year of occupancy—for making future adjustments. This method puts the developer at risk for the base year, and thus provides a strong incentive for the developer to construct a building that operates as efficiently as possible. The full-stop adjustment offers no such incentive.

A third approach to accounting for future expense escalations calls for making annual rent adjustments in accordance with increases in the consumer price index.

Usually 20 to 50 percent of the tenant's annual rent is indexed to the CPI.

Percentage Lease. In its simplest form, a percentage lease is an instrument in which the tenant agrees to pay a rent equal to a stipulated percentage of the gross dollar volume of sales made on the premises. Because total rent charges fluctuate with the volume of business, the landlord receives less rent when times are rough for the tenant and more as the tenant's business prospers. The most common type of percentage lease includes a provision for an agreed minimum rent, which protects the landlord against very low sales performance by the tenant. In a percentage lease developers base the rate and the amount of the minimum rental on several factors, including the ability of the retailer to pay, the kind of business, the volume of business per square foot of leased space, the markup on merchandise, the business value of the location, and the competitive market.

Lease Negotiation

The time to start thinking about lease specifics—type of lease, rates, and other key lease terms—is during the office development's planning phase, when the project is being positioned in the market. Having an idea of what the lease terms will be is essential for determining the financial feasibility of the project. Knowing what type of lease will be used (and therefore how the building's operating expenses will be allocated) is an important factor in the design and installation of building systems and utilities and other building design considerations.

Leasing is a function of general market conditions. Developers are wise to bring in brokers as consultants during the feasibility stage when the marketing strategy is being developed. The leasing strategy must be firmly grounded in the reality of the local market and must also try to anticipate how market conditions might change over the planning period.

Any lease for office space (and retail space in an office building) should include the following information:

- size and location of the space, including the method of measuring the leased space;
- options for expansion, if any;
- duration of the lease, renewal options, and cancellation privileges;
- the rent per square foot and the service it brings;
- interior work to be performed by the developer that is covered by the basic rent;
- operating hours of the building;
- escalation provisions within the term of the lease;
- number and location of parking spaces and the terms of their use (for example, designated or undesignated);
- allowable uses of the leased space (as set forth in local zoning ordinances and the development's rules);

Lee/Timchula Architects

World-class restaurants and shops at Equitable Tower, a 50-story, multitenant office building near Times Square in Manhattan, help give the project the cachet it needs to command top-of-the-market rents. A mid-block arcade facilitates pedestrian access to adjoining buildings.

- date of the tenant's possession; and
- date that the payment of rent commences.

A security deposit may be required to guarantee compliance with the lease conditions as well as to compensate for any damage to the premises beyond normal wear and tear. Most leases also include clauses that allow landlords to adjust rents during the lease term in accordance with changing economic conditions.

Ultimately, the lease terms and conditions are a function of what the market will bear. However, the leases that are executed also must satisfy the requirements of the construction and permanent lenders. Different lenders have different concerns. It is essential for the developer to know lender requirements in order to avoid the possibility of having to renegotiate initial leases in order to finance the building. The developer should work with an experienced attorney before executing any leases. Reliance on standard lease forms is not advisable. Some of the more common concerns about leases among lenders are the following:

- Lenders require that the leases be assignable. Under an assignable lease, the lender can receive rent directly (take assignment of the rents) in the event of default. A major concern of lenders is their ability to get control of a building's cash flow after default and before foreclosure, because the proper maintenance of the building and the continued servicing of its tenants are essential for protecting the interests of lenders.
- Lenders want to be the first party to be awarded condemnation and insurance money in the event of a covered calamity, out of which they will pay the developer. Owners, on the other hand, usually want to receive the insurance money to restore the building, especially if they are obligated to make such restoration under the terms of certain leases.
- Lenders do not like allowing certain pass-through expenses to be offset against lower rent payments, and they dislike pass-through exclusions for increases in management fees and other expenses because all such concessions reduce the ability of owners to cover increased costs.

Almost every clause in an office space lease is subject to some negotiation, but most lease negotiations center on three major items: the term of the lease, the lease rate, and tenant improvements (TIs). These items are discussed in the sections that follow.

Term. Sometimes tenants prefer a long lease commitment and sometimes they prefer to limit their commitment to a short period. The ideal lease period expands and contracts over time in response to changing economic and real estate market conditions. Today, for example, the long-term, fixed-rate office lease is less common than it was a decade ago. Throughout the decade of the 1990s, corporate America has focused on productivity, flexibility, and cost-efficiency. Corpora-

Gradually rising rents in the second half of the 1990s made office construction once again economically feasible in many markets. Monarch Tower, a 25-story office complex in Atlanta, was completed in 1997.

tions' desire to be responsive to their changing needs for office space has translated into a preference for leases with three- to five-year terms. By contrast, in the 1980s when rents were climbing rapidly, office tenants preferred to lock into ten-year leases that could protect them from rent inflation.

While more office tenants today are on shorter-term leases, lease terms of ten to 15 years are still fairly common for lead tenants (the first tenants to lease space in a building), with built-in rent escalations occurring at least every five years and sometimes even annually. Shorter-term leases allow landlords to renegotiate terms to match the rate of inflation, and they give tenants increased flexibility.

Rates. Rental rates vary with the amount of space that the tenant takes and the stage in the project's life that it signs the lease. Lead tenants typically receive lower rental rates and other favorable lease terms. Depending on market conditions, lead tenants are sometimes offered an equity interest in the building.

During the earliest planning stages, the developer must form realistic assumptions about the lease rates that the project can command, and it must update those assumptions throughout the development process. As Richard Kateley, executive vice president and director of research at Heitman Financial in Chicago, puts it: "Unless a building is dramatically superior to the competition's, it is unwarranted to expect that the property will get better than 'market' rents. An analyst must be prepared to spend significant time in the submarket determining exactly what lease terms and conditions prevail and what kinds of deals are being done. Rent is itself a complicated term, and how it is computed locally, and especially how net effective rents are quoted, must be determined. Various concessions (such as abatements, free rent, moving allowances, expensive tenant improvements, and lease buyouts) complicate the task of comparing one lease transaction with another. Effective

In the scramble to maintain occupancy rates, landlords often offer prospective and current tenants a wide variety of perks. Rent holidays, stepped rents, lump-sum payments, and leasehold improvements top the list of popular tenant incentives at the higher end of the cost scale. Understanding the tax angles of various tenant incentives will help landlords develop the most cost-effective inducement packages. Landlords that ignore these tax angles risk incurring hidden costs, as well as unpleasant tax results.

Rent Holidays

A rent holiday, or free rent period, is one of the most popular tenant inducements. While the tenant experiences a cash flow boost, the landlord's cash flow is negatively affected. The landlord (lessor) does, however, receive a tax benefit for granting the rent holiday—a reduction in income during the time rent is not received. Except in certain situations, the lessor recognizes no rental income during the rent holiday.

Another advantage of rent holidays is that the tax benefit is received at the same time. The tax benefits from most other common lease inducements are spread over a much longer period of time.

Stepped Rents

Stepped-rent agreements involve initially discounted rates (generally during the first year of the lease) stepping up to full rates at an agreed point in the lease term. One advantage for the landlord of stepped-rent agreements is that the lease amount is at its peak by the end of the lease term, which means that renewal negotiations start at a high point. For example, if office space is leased for five years at an average of $18 per square foot, but the final year of the lease agreement calls for $20 per square foot, the lessor can start negotiations at $20 per square foot or more.

By receiving reduced rental payments rather than no rent, the lessor avoids the cash flow strain that accompanies rent holidays. The lessor also receives the tax benefit of a reduction of income, except where Internal Revenue Code Section 467 applies. (See below for more on Section 467.) Also, as with rent holidays, the tax benefit is received during the reduced rent period.

Lump-Sum Payments

Lump-sum payments are another common form of tenant inducement. Landlords frequently make a lump-sum payment to cover the tenant's moving expenses, buy out an existing lease, cover furniture and equipment costs, and provide a true cash bonus.

A lump-sum payment made to the tenant must be capitalized by the lessor and amortized over the term of the lease. For example, if a lessor makes a lump-sum cash payment of $50,000 to a tenant for signing a new ten-year lease, the lessor would capitalize the payment and deduct $5,000 during each year of the lease.

When a cash payment is made directly to the tenant, the tenant has received taxable income. If the money is used to pay moving or other deductible expenses, the tenant also has an offsetting deduction. If the allowance that the tenant receives exceeds the amount actually spent, the excess amount is considered income.

A lump-sum payment to buy out an existing lease is not always a practical tenant inducement. Sometimes, it makes more sense for the lessor to sublease the tenant's former space. Subletting, however, can create tax problems for some tenants by resulting in undesirable passive income or a loss. In such cases, one option is to quantify the value of the lease buyout and convert that value into another type of inducement, such as a rent holiday.

Lump-sum payments for furniture and equipment purchased by tenants must be depreciated over the life of the furniture or equipment. In many ways, the tax treatment of lump-sum payments for furniture and equipment is the same as for leasehold improvements. For tax purposes, a rent holiday is generally more advantageous for both the tenant and the lessor than is a lump-sum payment.

Leasehold Improvements

Landlords frequently offer allowances for leasehold improvements as another form of tenant inducement. The tax treatment of leasehold improvements hinges on which party retains ownership of the leasehold improvements. In most cases, the lessor will receive the tax benefits of the cost of leasehold improvements more quickly if it makes a lump-sum payment to the tenant for the improvement costs. If the lessor pays for and retains ownership of the improvements, it receives the tax benefits through depreciation.

When the tenant retains ownership of the improvements, the cash payment from the lessor is recognized as income to the tenant. The tenant depreciates the leasehold improvements over their statutory life, which currently stands at 39 years.

The lessor capitalizes the cash amount paid to the tenant, amortizing it over the life of the lease. The life of the lease may not include any option period, unless the exercise of the option is certain. The option is considered certain if failure to exercise it would result in a substantial penalty or if exercising it would result in a significant economic benefit.

When the lessor retains ownership of leasehold improvements, the tenant is not entitled to depreciation—even if the expenditures pass through the tenant's books. In other words, the inducement has no tax effect on the tenant.

The landlord, on the other hand, capitalizes the amount paid for leasehold improvements and depreciates it over their statutory life (rather than amortizing it over the life of the lease). Changes to the law in the 1996 tax act permit the lessor to take a gain or loss if the improvements are irrevocably disposed of or abandoned at the termination of the lease.

Sidestepping Section 467

Before Section 467 of the Internal Revenue Code came into effect, the postponement of rental income and rent expense through stepped rents and rent holidays offered an ideal opportunity for deferring taxes. In those days it was possible for a cash-basis lessor to defer recognizing income until rent was actually received. An accrual-basis tenant could take a current tax deduction for accrued rent, even though that rent would not be paid until a later year.

Section 467 attempts to smooth out the recognition of rental income that otherwise would have been deferred through rent holidays or stepped rents, thus doing away with the perceived abuse of this opportunity for tax deferments.

Section 467's rent-leveling provisions require rent charged in certain deferred arrangements to be leveled over the length of the agreement. Section 467 applies to lease agreements for tangible property (real or personal) where

- total payments over the lease term (cash plus fair market value) exceed $250,000;
- rent is postponed for more than one year and the lease agreement allocates the rent to a specific calendar year;
- rent increases (or decreases);
- the lease term exceeds 75 percent of the recovery period of the leased property; and
- the principal purpose of the agreement is tax avoidance.

The tax courts determine tax avoidance on a case-by-case basis. They take into consideration the size of the gap between the tax brackets of the lessor and tenant; whether an option exists for the tenant to renew at rents significantly lower than the amounts in the original lease's later years; and whether the lease involves a tax-exempt organization placed between two taxable parties.

Rent holidays or stepped-rent agreements will not be considered to have a tax avoidance purpose where

- rent increases are linked to a price index, such as the consumer price index;
- rents are based on a fixed percentage of the tenant's gross receipts;
- reasonable rent holidays are given at the beginning of the lease term based on the current rental market; and
- rent increases are due to escalations in amounts paid to unrelated third parties, such as insurance, taxes, or maintenance costs.

If a lease agreement does qualify for rent leveling under Section 467, both the lessor and the tenant must allocate an equal amount of rent to each period under the lease. The rent amount is determined by taking the value of all payments that are to be made under the lease terms. This rent accrual is treated like any other debt owed by an accrual-basis taxpayer.

Thus, both lessors and tenants will be subject to the rules governing bad-debt deductions, discharge of indebtedness, and the tax-benefit rule. Interest must be imputed on any of the leveled rent amount that is not paid currently, and the total amount of rent and interest recognized for the entire lease term should equal the total amount of payments under the lease.

When possible, lessors should structure lease agreements to sidestep the provisions of Section 467. Before granting any significant rent holidays or stepped-rent concessions, they should review the tax advantages and disadvantages.

Source: Adapted from Chris Bonfanti, "Reaping the Tax Benefits from Lease Incentives," *Skylines,* October 1996, pp. 30–32.

■

A tenant's two-level reception area in the rehabilitated One Shell Square building in New Orleans.

Hines Interests Limited Partnership

rent [gross rent less concessions], not gross quotations, becomes the comparative measure." [3]

Concessions are incentives that landlords offer to prospective and current tenants to entice them to sign or renew leases. In a soft office market, landlords often have to offer generous lease incentives to retain tenants and fill their buildings. During the commercial real estate recession at the beginning of the 1990s, long periods of free rent became the norm, sometimes

with disastrous results. Lease incentives attracted not only creditworthy office tenants, but also not-so-creditworthy tenants. Since the recovery of office markets in the later 1990s, liberal free rent and other costly lease incentives have become much less common. Even in strong markets, however, landlords often offer some lease inducements to attract or retain highly desirable tenants. "Reaping the Tax Benefits from Lease Incentives" on the preceding page points out ways of structuring tenant incentive packages to yield the best possible tax results for both landlord and tenant.

Tenant Improvements. Every office project has a package of standard tenant improvements (TIs) that the landlord will provide as part of the rental rate. Often, however, tenants will ask for more. Depending on the size of the tenant, the developer may or may not acquiesce to such a request. As discussed in Chapter 4, the work letter establishes how much the tenant and the landlord will pay for TIs, assigns responsibility for arranging for the work, and outlines the criteria for the design and construction of tenant improvements.

There are two basic ways of determining the rate for the standard building items offered to each office unit: a fixed allowance per square foot of leased space or a certain level of improvements per specified area of rentable space—such as one lineal foot of partition per 100 square feet of area, one interior door for each 150 square feet, and one electrical outlet for each 150 square feet. Landlords prefer the latter method, because they can compute the TI costs more accurately. The tenant can change any standard building item, but it pays the difference in cost between the standard item and the substitution.

The fixed allowance may be in the form of cash or a rent credit. It may include a payment for the tenant to do the work normally done by the developer or landlord, if this is the most convenient or easiest way to build out the space. Once the amount has been decided, the tenant should enlist the help of a design professional and prepare a list of all the work that must be carried out by the landlord before tenant improvements can begin. If the space is being conveyed as is, a portion of the TI allowance will go toward work that is typically paid for by the landlord. Among the tenant improvements that are normally the responsibility of the landlord are the following:

- Common Area ADA Compliance—Even with full-floor tenants, landlords should be responsible for insuring that restrooms, elevator call buttons, and door handles meet the requirements of the Americans with Disabilities Act.
- Asbestos—The landlord should be responsible for certifying that the premises are free from asbestos or that any asbestos that was within the structure has been removed or contained.
- Demolition—The two parties must determine which is responsible for any demolition work that is required.
- Windows—The landlord should be responsible for ensuring that all windows and windowframes are working properly.
- HVAC—The landlord should be responsible for ensuring that the heating and cooling units are functioning properly.

The cost of supervising tenant improvements is sometimes passed through to tenants, although tenants often resist paying for it on the ground that such supervision is in the landlord's interest and should be considered a cost of normal building operations.

The landlord may also charge the tenant for the use of elevators and the loading dock during construction, as well as for the cost of providing utilities during this period. Such charges should be limited to the landlord's out-of-pocket costs. The tenant should not be charged if the landlord normally provides the service (freight elevators, for example) during the building's hours of operation.

The tenant is usually required to use the landlord's in-house contractor to perform the improvements or to select a contractor from an approved list. In either case, the tenant should have the right to bid the work to avoid paying an artificially high price that would reduce the value of the TI allowance. Lastly, there should be a clause in the contract to the effect that time is of the essence for both parties in the performance of the TIs.

Notes

1. James Bell, "Space Marketing in Office Buildings by Exclusive Agents or Owners," in *The Office Building: From Concept to Investment Reality*, ed. John Robert White (Washington, D.C.: Counselors of Real Estate; Appraisal Institute; and Society of Industrial and Office Realtors Educational Fund, 1993), p. 336.
2. Ibid., p. 351.
3. Richard Kateley, "Office Marketability Studies," in *The Office Building: From Concept to Investment Reality*, ed. John Robert White (Washington, D.C.: Counselors of Real Estate; Appraisal Institute; and Society of Industrial and Office Realtors Educational Fund, 1993), pp. 196–197.

6. Operations and Management

Office developments involve three interrelated management functions: management of the property to keep it operating efficiently, management of the asset to enhance its value and extend its useful life, and management of the portfolio of assets of which it may be a part. Property management, asset management, and portfolio management can be carried out by the same person or firm, but each function is distinct and involves a different set of responsibilities. (See Figure 6-1.)

Historically, the typical office building was owned by a single investor—often the developer—or a small group of investors, who made the strategic decisions and used in-house resources to manage the day-to-day operations or hired a property management firm. Over the last ten to 15 years, the ownership of office properties increasingly has shifted to entities such as pension funds, insurance companies, and REITs and the role traditionally performed by the single investor has been taken over by professional asset and portfolio managers acting as fiduciaries to the owners and investors.

Figure 6-2 illustrates the relationships among property managers, asset managers, and the portfolio manager for a large portfolio of office buildings. Of course,

every portfolio is different. The roles of the property managers, asset managers, and portfolio manager may expand or contract depending on the composition of the portfolio and the experience and capabilities of the professionals occupying the positions.

In the example shown in Figure 6-2, the property managers are located on site and serve as the direct link to the building's tenants. (Often, several smaller buildings share one property manager.) A property manager's main role is to provide immediate, excellent service to the tenants and to operate the property on a day-to-day basis in a cost-effective manner.

The asset managers in this example focus on several different properties. An asset manager's role is to provide strategic direction to the property managers and, as the owner's representative, to develop long-range strategic plans for the properties, for which the property managers provide input. Asset managers may specialize by property type, geographic location, or both.

The portfolio manager works from an even broader perspective. The role of the portfolio manager is to understand and direct the owner's investment objectives for a portfolio of properties. This requires evaluating the performance of the asset managers, deciding on the capital improvements recommended by the asset managers as necessary to maintain the competitive position of the assets, maximizing risk-adjusted portfolio returns, and directing acquisitions and dispositions.

A 165-foot atrium connects two towers in Nadya Park, a public/private mixed-use development in Nagoya, Japan.

figure 6-1
Property Manager, Asset Manager, and Portfolio Manager Responsibilities

Property Manager	Asset Manager	Portfolio Manager
• Tenant relations and retention	• Development of property strategic plan	• Communication with investors
• Rent collection	• Hold/sell analysis	• Setting of portfolio goals and investment criteria
• Control of operating expenses	• Review of property repositioning opportunities	• Development and implementation of investment strategy
• Financial reporting and recordkeeping	• Justification of major expenditures	• Oversight of acquisitions, dispositions, and reinvestment decisions (oversight of asset management functions)
• Maintenance of property	• Monitoring of property performance	
• Capital expenditure planning	• Management of property manager	
• Crisis management	• Analysis of property performance against competitive properties	• Monitoring of portfolio performance
• Security	• Tenant relations (a shared responsibility with property manager)	• Reporting to investors
• Public relations		• Cash management

Source: *Real Estate Development: Principles and Process* (ULI, 1996).

figure 6-2

Property Manager, Asset Manager, and Portfolio Manager Relationships

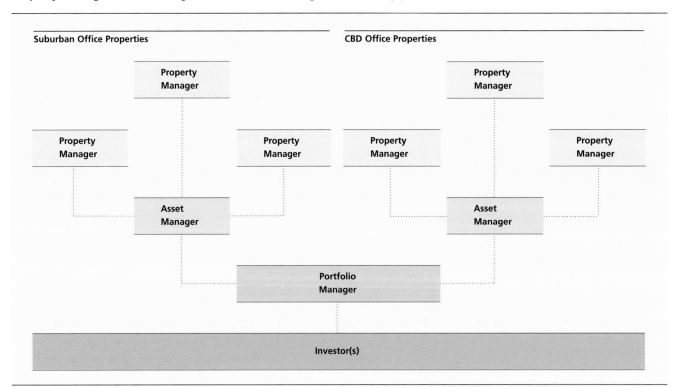

Source: *Real Estate Development: Principles and Process* (ULI, 1996).

This chapter discusses the basic functions of property, asset, and portfolio management. At the end of the day, no property will generate a profit if it is not properly managed. Property management is at heart a service function. All levels of management must focus on providing products and services that meet the needs of current and future tenants. At the same time, all three management functions are involved in adding value to the office investment.

Property Management

The basic functions of the property manager are shown in Figure 6-1. These functions include maintaining good tenant relations, collecting rent, establishing an operating plan, creating a budget, maintaining accounting and operating records, paying bills, supervising or carrying out the leasing function, developing and managing the maintenance schedules, supervising building personnel,

Bishop Ranch 15 is located in the 585-acre Bishop Ranch Business Park in Contra Costa County, California. Software, communications, and multimedia companies have been attracted to the master-planned business community by a high level of services and amenities, which include advanced telecommunications services, free parking, a computerized ridesharing program, and on-site childcare. The business park's owner, Sunset Development Company, does its own leasing, construction, tenant buildout work, and property management.

Courtesy of Sunset Development Company

providing security, addressing issues related to risk management, coordinating insurance requirements, and generally preserving the building's short-term value.

Property management per se begins at the end of the development process, but the broad elements of the property management plan should be set forth in the early conceptual stages of development. Obtaining experienced property management input at this stage of project planning is essential. The management plan should be based on an evaluation of the property's competitive position in the market. It should detail a level of service that will enable the project to compete effectively. If the level of service provided is inconsistent with the competitive objectives, the project is not likely to generate the level of operating income over time that is required to meet the owner's financial objectives. Providing building services of little value to the target tenants can increase expenses without increasing lease rates. To make sure that the building

will be managed to meet the project's objectives, the developer should prepare in the early stages a well-documented management plan that articulates the perceptions of the market analysts.

The management expectations and concerns of prospective tenants should be examined at the project's design stage. This enables the developer to incorporate building features and systems into the design and financial pro forma that are responsive—in terms of initial costs and operating expenses—to the long-term needs of both the prospective tenants and the investors. For instance, if a high level of security is a priority for tenants, the developer may emphasize lighting and visibility of entrances in the building's design and incorporate an electronic security system as well.

Usually there are legal documents—leases and, in office parks, protective covenants—that guarantee the long-term maintenance and appearance of office properties. However, property management must go well

Operations and Management 211

After 150 turnkey tenant buildout projects totaling more than $15 million, W&M Construction Corporation has determined that its clients share some common values. They like to save money. They like to save time. They like to know what they are allowed to do. And they like to know what they should do. The company works for tenants and an owner—often simultaneously—and makes sure that these common values are also common ground.

As an arm of W&M Properties, an agent for properties owned by the Malkin family, W&M Construction operates with the values of the building owner in mind. But as a de facto agent of every tenant that it serves, the firm must undertake buildouts with the tenant's best interest in mind.

In a world in which owner and tenant are often at odds, how can this be done? W&M does it by offering a service called "turnkey space planning" to incoming tenants at Malkin properties and other office properties throughout the United States. The new offices of such tenants range in size from a few hundred square feet to thousands of square feet. Office building owners offer this cost-effective service to lure long-term occupancies. Tenants are eager to work with experienced planners and builders who can navigate local codes, building requirements, and practical workspace issues.

"It's important that the design be in line with the requirements of the building, including the mechanical and architectural building standards," explains Tom Durels, senior vice president of W&M Properties and the construction subsidiary, which is based in Stamford, Connecticut. "These include everything from entry-door heights to ceiling grids, light fixtures to signage to the finishes and hardware used for common area corridors."

How does the process work as a part of leasing office space? W&M typically offers new tenants the services of an architect, free of charge, to help develop a space plan and finish schedule. Based on the plan, the landlord develops a construction budget and adjusts the rental rate to reflect the scope of work. Incoming tenants are offered both rents and space consistent with their needs. The architects and builders that implement this service have to be sensitive to the needs of the tenant and the owner.

Tenants that either cannot or do not want to become involved in the buildout process, because of lack of time or lack of design/build skills, benefit from this service. Most medium-sized and small companies are

Tenant finish work must meet the firm's needs. This teleconferencing center was created for ADP Windward of Atlanta.

Thompson, Ventulett, Stainback & Associates

probably included in this category. But all prospective tenants can benefit in two ways: the process saves the tenant time and it substantially reduces project risk.

"Even with turnkey services, there are important tenant decisions to be made, but there are fewer worries and headaches," says Durels. "And we take the risk. If there is an oversight, we take the risk."

Little wonder that office developers and owners are beginning to offer such services across the United States. Professionals like Durels note that the size of the typical turnkey space planning project is growing, as economic and managerial incentives for turnkey delivery strengthen. "We recently did a full-floor installation at Rockefeller Center," says Durels, "and we were very much in sync with the owner, which has strict rules and needs. And at 1185 Avenue of the Americas, we took care of the 25,000-square-foot headquarters for GGK, the largest privately held U.S. accounting firm."

Working with both owner and tenant requires skills in negotiation and problem solving. "We are constantly fine-tuning, refining, and revising the budgets all along the way," says Durels. "We developed four detailed budgets for the client at Rockefeller Center, so when the project went out to bid, the costs were right in line with the tenant's needs."

Source: Adapted from "Turnkey Space Planning Offers Tenant Advantages," *Buildings,* July 1996, p. 32.

beyond simply maintaining the appearance of the building if the project is to achieve financial success and the landlord's reputation is to remain untarnished. Property managers must provide services that make the work lives of the building's tenants easier. Dissatisfaction with the property's management will almost certainly result in a negative attitude among tenants at lease renewal time, which is the prelude to move-outs. The developer should consider property management to be no less important than project design or project financing.

Renewal of an existing tenant at market rates is much more financially advantageous than signing on a new tenant. Bringing in new tenants generally involves higher-cost TIs, longer downtimes, and higher lease commissions. A high tenant renewal rate (assuming market-rate rents) will improve a project's return for the owner.

Selection of the Property Manager

Many developers prefer to manage their own buildings for two principal reasons. First, property management generates fees that can be another, sometimes more steady source of income for a development company. Second, managing the property allows the developer to maintain close ties with the tenants.

For office building owners that lack the in-house capabilities to manage the property, the services of a well-staffed professional management company are essential. Firms that specialize in property management can offer the advantages of advanced management techniques and systems that individual property owners generally do not possess. Third-party management firms may also attract more experienced people, because they can offer a more varied career path.

With the waxing and waning of development opportunities over the years, many development companies have expanded their business activities beyond building and operating properties for their own account. Many developers now offer complementary real estate services—such as property management—to other investors and owners. Lincoln Property Company, for example, was formed in the 1960s to build and operate residential communities. It later expanded its business to include the development and management of commercial properties. Then, the company's experience with its own properties led to its decision to offer management services for buildings it did not own. Lincoln now offers a variety of real estate services for investors (property management, engineering, accounting, design and construction management, leasing, and financial services) and for corporations (facility management, portfolio management, transactions, and design and construction management). It manages more than 90 million square feet of real estate assets.

Third-party management is governed by a written management agreement that spells out the terms, rights, and responsibilities. The management contract includes the authority to sign leases and other documents, to incur expenses, to advertise, and to make

banking and trust arrangements. It also includes the owner's requirements for recordkeeping, insurance coverage, and indemnification and details of the management fee. The Institute of Real Estate Management (IREM) reports that most management fees are quoted as a percentage of gross income collected over the term of the leases, both new and renewal. Other arrangements may include a base compensation plus fees for special services, such as remodeling, tenant construction, or the sale of a property. Management fees can range from 1 to 5 percent of the gross income.

Unless a building is designed for a single tenant/owner, the developer typically hires the first property manager. (Asset and portfolio managers are usually brought in later by the long-term owner.) The length of the management contract varies, depending on who the owner will be and the nature of the project. The more the property management firm engages in initial marketing and other operations that go beyond the basic functions of property management, the more likely it is that the contract will cover a longer period. A performance contingency is often included in longer-term contracts, allowing the owner to replace the manager should the

---

figure 6-3
Elements of a Standard Management Agreement

Terms, Rights and Responsibilities

Article 1	Properties
Article 2	Commencement date
Article 3	Manager's responsibilities
Article 4	Insurance
Article 5	Financial reporting and recordkeeping
Article 6	Owner's right to audit
Article 7	Bank account
Article 8	Payment of expenses
Article 9	Insufficient gross income
Article 10	Sale of a property
Article 11	Cooperation
Article 12	Compensation
Article 13	Termination
Article 14	Subsidiaries and affiliates
Article 15	Notices
Article 16	Nonassignables, etc.

Schedules

A	Property identification, compensation schedule, and leasing commission
B	Leasing guidelines
C	Monthly report forms
C-1	Chart of accounts
D	Reimbursable employees
E	Subsidiaries and affiliates
F	Insurance certificate

Source: *Real Estate Development: Principles and Process* (ULI, 1996).

property not perform according to budget. Many third-party management agreements are cancelable on 30 days notice, with or without cause. Figure 6-3 depicts the elements of a standard property management contract.

Standard Operating Procedures

The management of an office building or office park revolves around the provision of services. Management services must please the tenants and keep the project in good condition to preserve the value of the investment—at a cost that leaves enough of the rental income to pay a reasonable return on the capital investment.

One of the first tasks for a new building is the preparation (by the property manager) of a customized manual of standard operating procedures that will govern the way the property will be operated. According to Kenneth A. Shearer's guide to office building management, most procedures manuals include an organizational chart showing the property management responsibilities and contain information in the following categories:[1]

- building data;
- general office procedures;
- accounting procedures, guidelines, and requirements (and a chart of accounts);
- payroll;
- reporting;
- taxes;
- purchasing;
- insurance coverage;
- maintenance;
- engineering operations;
- contracted services;
- life safety, emergencies, and security;
- building operations;
- construction;
- tenant relations;
- lease administration policies;
- advertising and promotion;
- special events; and
- personnel policies.

Management Plans, Budgets, and Reports

One of the key functions of the property manager is to develop a three- to five-year operating plan for the building (with guidance from the asset manager) and annual operating budgets to support the plan. Many decisions about an office property should be evaluated over the long term. For example, the annual maintenance expense associated with different options for capital improvements should be analyzed along with the initial costs. The operating plan should be updated at least annually.

The property manager's annual operating budget for the building is normally updated quarterly as the manager tracks the building's actual performance. The property manager needs to provide the owner or asset manager with detailed explanations of any divergences from budget. Presentation of the annual budget to the owner often includes various sensitivity or what-if analyses.

The process of preparing the property's annual budget is time-consuming and complex, especially for a large multitenant building, but it is an extremely important procedure. Each revenue and expense line item from the property's chart of accounts must be carefully considered and detailed to account for all potential revenues and expenses. If revenues are overstated or expenses understated, the result can be financial projections that are overly optimistic.

The importance of realism and accuracy in the pro forma operating budget for a prospective office project cannot be overemphasized. The potential ramifications of overstating or understating net operating income are severe. To avoid the incorporation of errors into the project's operating budget, the developer should involve asset and property managers as early as possible in the development process. As experts in the costs and complications of managing a stabilized office building, asset and property managers are perhaps the development professionals who are most capable of generating realistic operating pro formas.

A credible operating budget requires the development of detailed assumptions describing each line item. The presence of detailed assumptions ensures that everyone involved in assessing the financial feasibility of the project uses internally consistent operating assumptions.

BCE Place in Toronto features 2.6 million square feet of leased office and retail space enhanced by a 2.5-acre public square.

Brookfield Management Services Ltd.

With 1.25 million square feet of space, the Houston Enron Building is one of the city's largest office buildings. The entire third floor was planned to house tenant services, and it includes a credit union, a travel agency, concierge space, training facilities, and a health center.

The income portion of the operating budget for a multitenant office building will include office rents, any retail rents, antenna revenues, parking garage fees, and other miscellaneous income. Operating expenses will include electricity, water and sewer, fuel, payroll, employee benefits, cleaning supplies, repairs, decorating, advertising, management fee, administrative costs, all taxes, insurance, security, window washing, landscape services, trash removal, and possibly snow removal. Cash flow from operations is the balance remaining after all income has been added and all expenses have been deducted.

The property manager usually prepares a monthly or quarterly statement of operations that enables a comparison of the property's actual performance with its projected performance as contained in the budget. Two items make up the operating statement: a rent roll and a disbursement statement. The rent roll lists all tenant data, including income, charges, and lease expirations. The disbursement statement is a detailed record of funds expended. Other documents may be prepared from time to time to supplement the basic operating statement.

The accounting requirements for the operation of an office building vary depending on the complexity of the property and the needs of the owner. Accounting for a single-tenant building will be much more straightforward than for a large multitenant office tower. And the owner of a single building will have different accounting requirements than institutional owners. Whatever the ownership or tenancy of a property, the accounting system must provide timely and accurate information about all facets of operation that affect the asset's value. The Building Owners and Managers Association's chart of accounts (see Figure 6-4) includes line items that cover the operations of most office properties in sufficient detail. Property management software packages typically incorporate BOMA's basic format and can accommodate the addition of new accounts to fit individual situations.

Tenant Retention

Generally, only if the office project succeeds in retaining tenants can it achieve its investment objectives. Replacing tenants is costly, and the money lost through vacancy is never recovered. Karen Krackov, a property manager with Faison & Associates, notes that reasonable costs involved with tenant retention should be regarded as value-adding investments because they help the project avoid the greater expenses related to securing new tenants and meeting their needs.[2]

Retaining every tenant is not always possible. For example, a tenant may need to expand when the building has no space available. But most tenants can be retained if the management understands what they want and provides superior service on a daily basis.

Property managers use a variety of methods to retain tenants. They try to establish a good communications channel with tenants and to ensure that staff follows up on tenant requests. They solicit tenants for suggestions on improving building management. They produce newsletters dealing with subjects like lease rates and management issues. They try to anticipate and be responsive to tenant needs and questions. Leroy Finch, president of Finch and Barry Properties, says: "Giving tenants personal attention gives them a better sense of control over their investment."[3]

Kevin McCall, president of Paradigm Properties LLC, thinks that in today's office market, with its huge base of space competing for tenants, success will come to landlords that differentiate themselves from competitive projects by offering superior tenant services. Leasing decisions today, McCall says, are driven by more than just the space itself. Tenants—especially the smaller 3,000- to 10,000-square-foot tenants that are the heart of many office markets—are looking for value, which means that they are looking at bottom-line costs and at services.

How can a property offer services that are one step ahead of the competition? McCall suggests that first and foremost the property manager should strive to establish relationships with tenants. The manager that understands the nature of a tenant's business and its problems can better orient building and management services to help the tenant achieve its space goals. Managers should think of tenants as both companies and individuals. Companies make the leasing decisions and

---

figure 6-4

Summary of BOMA Chart of Accounts for Office Buildings

Revenue/Income	Miscellaneous Income	Utilities	Leasing Expenses
Office Rent	• Vending machines	• Electricity	• Advertising/promotion
• Base rent	• Telephones	• Gas and fuel	• Commissions
• Pass-throughs	• Signs	• Purchased steam	• Professional fees
• Escalations	• Late charges	• Purchased chilled water	• Tenant alterations
• Lease cancellations		• Water and sewer	• Leasing costs
• Rent abatements	**Operating Expense**	• Tenant reimbursable	• Rent abatements
• Tenant services	**Cleaning**	expenses	• Buyouts
Retail Rent	• Payroll, taxes, fringes	**Roads/Grounds/Security**	**Fixed Expenses**
• Base rent	• Contract services	• Payroll, taxes, fringes	• Real estate taxes
• Percentage rent	• Supplies and materials	• Contract services	• Building insurance
• Pass-throughs	• Trash removal	• Other expenses	• Personal property tax
• Escalations	• Other expenses	**Administrative**	• Other expenses
• Lease cancellations	• Tenant reimbursable	• Payroll, taxes, fringes	
• Association dues	expenses	• Management fees	
• Tenant services	**Repairs and Maintenance**	• Professional fees	**Amortization and Depreciation**
Parking Income	• Payroll, taxes, fringes	• General office expenses	• Amortization of free rent,
• Daily/transient	• Elevators	• Other expenses	buyouts, commissions
• Monthly income	• HVAC	**Parking Operations**	• Depreciation of building,
• Annual income	• Electrical	• Payroll, taxes, fringes	improvements, equipment
• Other services	• Structural/roof	• Cleaning	
Other Space Rent	• Plumbing	• Repairs and maintenance	**Finance Expense**
• Storage space	• Fire and life-safety	• Utilities	• Interest
• Antenna space	• Other expenses	• Roads/grounds/security	• Ground rent
• Express parcel drop-offs	• Tenant reimbursable	• Administrative	• Financing costs
• Shared services	expenses		• Income taxes

Source: Building Owners and Managers Association (BOMA) International.

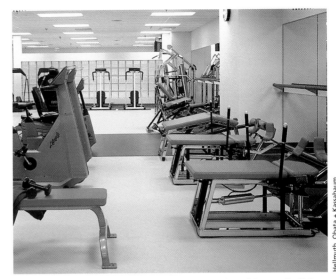

Hellmuth, Obata + Kassabaum

A day-care center and a fitness center are amenities that enhance the quality of the workplace at the National Archives II building in College Park, Maryland.

pay the rent. Providing amenities and services that target the individuals who work in the building makes the tenants' employees happy and therefore helps assure lease renewals. Also, such amenities and services can become a source of additional building income.

Adding special convenience-oriented services and amenities can improve the work lives of the building's individual tenants. Conference rooms made available for rent at below-market rates, childcare centers, health clubs, convenience stores, dry cleaners, and restaurants are examples. Many fairly simple services that do not cost the building much can be effective in terms of tenant satisfaction. A shoeshine service, various automotive services (such as car washing and detailing, or window replacement), video rentals, free newspapers, and ATM machines in the lobby are examples. Concierges are an increasingly desirable amenity in downtown office buildings, where they provide special services such as obtaining theater and sports tickets and making reservations for building tenants and corporate visitors.

Extra building services are a tenant retention tool only so far as the services and amenities offered are important to the building's tenants. An on-site day-care facility, for example, would probably go mostly unused in a building with tenants whose employees spend a great deal of time traveling or working out of the office. On the other hand, for tenants that operate more conventionally, a day-care facility could be a major attraction. The decision on whether to offer a particular service or amenity must be made by weighing the cost of providing the service against its ability to attract and retain tenants.

As landlords have come to realize the importance of effective property management, they have placed greater emphasis on identifying individuals capable of performing the necessary tasks. At the same time, more training opportunities have emerged, including programs offered by several associations. For example, the Institute of Real Estate Management, an affiliate of the National Associa-

tion of Realtors, offers a designation as certified property manager (CPM). The Building Owners and Managers Institute offers a designation as a real property administrator (RPA).

In an effort to encourage professionalism, these organizations offer courses and other materials on topics such as systematic recordkeeping, techniques for anticipating and responding to tenants' needs, negotiating leases, legal responsibilities to tenants, and sales/marketing techniques. A number of real estate services companies have established in-house training organizations—Koll College, Trammell Crow University, and Prentiss Properties University are examples—to supplement the educational opportunities offered by industry associations and to provide company-specific training.

To enhance tenant retention, some leading property management companies have started to use benchmarking systems by which they compare financial and nonfinancial performance measures from their properties with other office properties, using BOMA averages and statistics compiled by benchmarking firms.

Compass Management and Leasing spearheaded the industry's move to comprehensive benchmarking with its Magnet program, which tracks more than 50 performance measures for an office property. The program monitors, for example, the number of tenant calls per month complaining that some part of the space is too cold. This number can be compared with the calls-about-temperature performance of other buildings of a particular size, buildings in a particular area, a company average, or a national average. If a building's performance falls within an average range, no follow-up is needed. If the performance is worse than average, the property manager will investigate and take corrective action. If the performance is better than average, the portfolio manager can investigate the cause and use what was learned to raise the standard of performance on other properties.

Surveys of tenants are another way to measure property management performance. Prentiss Properties and other property management companies use REACT©, a customer survey program administered by CEL & Associates, to measure tenant evaluation of the following characteristics of the property and its management:

- readiness to solve problems;
- responsiveness and follow-through;
- appearance of the property;
- quality of management services;
- quality of leasing services;
- property rating;
- relationship rating; and
- tenant's renewal intention.

Responses are graded on a numerical scale of 1 to 100, with a score of 85 and above considered outstanding. A company's scores can be compared with the scores from other surveys by national property management companies in CEL's database.

Building Operations

The four major operational items that are the daily bread of most office property managers are general property maintenance and janitorial services, elevator service, HVAC services, and security. Most tenants take these items for granted, noticing them only when things go wrong. But if they do go wrong, tenant satisfaction will take a nosedive. And good maintenance is also necessary for preserving the value of the property.

A property manager's responsibility for security includes, but is not limited to, interior security, traffic control, and emergencies such as fires, power failures, and bomb threats. Preventing criminal acts against inhabitants and property in the office building is a major concern. It is not possible to prevent every crime, but certain measures can deter many would-be criminals and thus minimize crime.

It is useful to think of security measures as belonging to one of three categories: site elements such as fences or lighting, human resources such as security guards, and electronic elements such as access control systems and closed-circuit television for remote surveillance.[4] According to security consultant William F. Blake, the risk of crime at office buildings can be significantly contained by management attention to the following five dimensions of security:[5]

- Access Control—Access control starts at the property's boundary and continues inward to the building's various components. While access control is more than a matter of keys and locks, keys and locks are the most often neglected element. Management must institute strict controls on master keys and limit the distribution of keys to justifiable business requirements. Card-key access systems combined with personal identification badge systems can significantly reduce unauthorized access. Control of the storage

of keys and access cards is as important as the control of their issue and use.
- Exterior Lighting—Adequate levels of light are a significant deterrent to violent crime. The type and number of lighting fixtures that are needed depend on the reflective quality of the building, the penetration of light from surrounding areas, and landscaping features. Light-color building exteriors and cement parking lots reflect more light than do dark colors and asphalt parking lots. Property managers should inspect lighting regularly and replace nonworking lights.
- Security Features Maintenance—Neglected grounds and obviously deteriorated fences and lighting suggest, like nothing else can, vulnerability, an easy target. Proper exterior maintenance for security purposes includes tree and shrub control to eliminate hiding places. Property managers should be aware of the operational status of all security devices, which necessitates a regular maintenance schedule and documented inspections.
- Security Force—Property managers should not base their minimum standards and qualifications for security guards solely on state laws or requirements. When using building security services, property managers should develop a detailed contract that outlines personnel qualifications, training standards, and service expectations.
- Warnings—Property managers should keep tenants notified of criminal incidents and advise them about precautions they should take. Crime notices should be short, factual, and to the point—and not inflammatory.

How much time and expense should be devoted to general maintenance depends on several factors, including the size of the building, the building's design efficiency, and the type of building materials used. The property manager should establish itemized cleaning, repair/replacement, and preventative maintenance schedules for common areas (including carpets and painting) and building systems (including HVAC, plumbing, and elevators). Many property management companies use proprietary software that tracks preventative maintenance and schedules tenant service calls.

Property managers generally rely heavily on outside contract services for routine operational chores. It is common to outsource janitorial services, security services, parking garage operations, and sometimes engineering services in order to avoid the administrative burdens of maintaining a large in-house staff.

However, as Michael Steele, president of Equity Office Properties, notes, this practice "has its price." When many or most of the people providing building services are not direct employees of the owner, the ability to build an effective property management team is reduced. "Contract employees are not privy to the marketing goals of the property," says Steele, "nor do they hear firsthand of the image that the owner wishes to project to the tenants.

The finish for the Wichita, Kansas, advertising firm of Sullivan, Higdon & Sink is designed to be casual yet professional and exciting for both clients and employees.

The Harborside Financial Center, located on New Jersey's Hudson River waterfront, offers the latest technology and tight building security to its target market: the back-office operations of financial services, insurance, and shipping companies located in New York City.

Property owners concerned about tenant retention must expand the ownership team [and take] steps beyond traditional property management boundaries into the arena of education, motivation, and communication." [6]

If maintenance work is contracted out, the property manager should make sure that the contract spells out the areas to be cleaned, the frequency of each cleaning, the elements of the basic cleaning function (vacuuming, dusting, mopping floors, waxing floors, emptying wastebaskets, and so forth), and the provision of special services.

Asset Management

The competitive office market of the 1990s and the increasing ownership of office properties by institutions and REITs has created a greater need for strategic planning and management of office properties aimed at achieving the return objectives of their owners over the assets' holding periods. Slower rates of property appreciation over the last decade have forced owners to turn to more aggressive management techniques.

The process of managing properties to their fullest investment potential has become known as "asset management." Some building owners have the necessary resources to carry out asset management, like property management, in-house, while others, such as institutional owners and REITs, tend to hire asset management companies for this purpose. The asset manager acts as the owner's representative and is responsible for managing the long-term financial performance of several properties. To ensure that the return objectives of an owner are achieved, the asset manager develops a long-range strategic plan for the properties, with input from the property managers.

Asset managers often specialize in a certain type of property or in a geographic location, or both. A very

Topnotch cleaning and maintenance are essential for tenant retention.

Dixi Carrillo—EDAW

experienced manager may be responsible for eight to ten properties, depending on the potential leasing opportunity of each. Properties that are largely vacant require more of an asset manager's time than do properties that are fully leased.

For owners, asset management is a means of preserving and adding value to property. Asset management is a relatively new discipline and the role of asset managers is still evolving. From the perspective of a single property, the asset manager is responsible for the overall performance of the property in accordance with the goals of its owner. The asset manager typically develops a comprehensive long-term strategic plan to maximize the value of the property. This plan includes the project's and the market's history, existing and projected competition, possible renovation or other capital improvements, tenant retention strategies, leasing and marketing strategies, and an exit strategy for the project's owner. In addition to monitoring the ongoing performance of properties, the asset manager often manages such activities as the acquisition, sale, or refinancing of properties. The asset manager may also be responsible for securing financing for new development, structuring joint ventures, and performing sale-leaseback analyses.

In addition to overseeing the implementation of the business plan for a newly completed or acquired property, the asset manager makes decisions concerning subsequent remodeling, restructuring, and re-leasing programs on an ongoing basis. As market conditions change, the asset manager repositions the building to accommodate new tenant needs. For a distressed property, the asset manager must determine its strengths and weaknesses and then effect changes that improve the functioning as well as the perception of the building among current and potential tenants. Examples of effective repositioning include the Commonwealth Tower in Arlington, Virginia (see feature box on page 180) and the State Street Bank Building in Boston (see case study in Chapter 7).

Strategic Planning Process

The asset manager's fiduciary role is to manage property assets in a way that will achieve the owner's financial objectives. To do so, the asset manager clearly must first understand what those objectives are. If an owner intends to hold an office building for long-term appreciation, for example, significant capital improvements may be justified to achieve that end. If, on the other hand, the owner wants to get as much income as possible from the building and then sell it at a modest gain, a major capital investment may be uneconomic.

Starting with a clear understanding of the owner's expectations for the property and the owner's expectations of the asset manager's role, the asset manager can develop a multiyear strategic plan for the property. In essence, this is the action plan for achieving the long-range objectives. Among other elements, a property's strategic plan should include the following elements:

- owner's objectives;
- information about the property and an assessment of its problems and opportunities;
- a plan to meet the objectives;
- the expected holding period;
- an exit strategy; and
- an implementation strategy—which includes marketing, leasing, and administrative plans.

Figure 6-5 summarizes the major elements of the property strategic planning process. Once the strategic plan has been agreed upon, the next step is implementation. For the plan to be credible and achievable, resources must be devoted to its implementation that are commensurate with the goals. If, for example, the goal for a new office building is to reach 80 percent

occupancy within a year and it is only 15 percent leased at the end of the development period, implementation will probably require a fully staffed team of aggressive leasing agents armed with a full complement of marketing tools. The implementation of a strategic plan for a property asset includes putting together the staff required to manage the property and carry out the marketing and leasing program.

The strategic planning for an office building does not end with the development of a plan. Rather, it is a dynamic process. Strategic plans should be reviewed at least annually, and more frequently if circumstances dictate. Ideally, the asset and portfolio managers should look at the property with fresh eyes each year and ask themselves: "If we didn't already own this asset, would we acquire it today? If not, why not?" Forcing an office property to be "reacquired" each year can invigorate the planning process and slough off the inertia that is endemic in the property management business.

Capital Expenditures

The capital program for the property—what type of capital expenditures will be made and when—is a key component of the strategic plan. Ideally, a new project

figure 6-5
Property Strategic Planning Process

Define and Analyze Property's Problems and Opportunities
- Physical description
- Operating history
- Market conditions
- Strengths and weaknesses compared with competition

Evaluate and Revise Objectives Based on Current Information
- Local market/competition
- nvestor needs
- Tenant requirements
- Portfolio and other considerations

Consider Alternatives and Generate a Plan to Meet Objectives
- Review major decision points
  - hold or sell?
  - rehabilitate?
  - change the use of the building?
  - change the manager/leasing agent?
- Create a new pro forma for the property based on the plan

Implement the Plan
- Staffing
- Marketing program
- Operating budget
- Capital program

Source: *Real Estate Development: Principles and Process* (ULI, 1996).

The John Hancock Center's $22.5 million redevelopment revitalized the 100-story, 2.8 million-square-foot Chicago landmark. Prior to renovation, the vast majority of retail space was vacant, and office occupancy was at 47 percent. After renovation, the building achieved 98 percent retail and 91 percent office occupancies. The tower was built in 1970 and its renovation was completed in 1995.

will need little additional capital expenditure. In practice, however, even new projects that have been well conceived will require some additional capital investment, either to remedy construction or design deficiencies not covered by warranties, such as inadequate drainage in a parking lot, or to meet expanded tenant requirements.

The upkeep of an office building and its basic components is predictable in the same way that the maintenance requirements for a new car are predictable. Accordingly, the property or asset manager should prepare a ten-year schedule of capital expenditures at the time that a new building is completed or an existing property is acquired.

A repair and maintenance schedule for three major components of an office property—roof, cooling tower, and elevators—is shown in Figure 6-6. Tenant improvements related to the re-lease of space when the initial terms of tenant leases expire should be included in the

capital program. Changes in government regulations or changing market requirements may give rise to capital expenditure requirements. Many building renovations today incorporate features—life-safety improvements, new types of security systems, asbestos removal, energy management programs, and retrofits to provide improved access for the disabled—that were not contemplated in the original development pro formas. The rapidly increasing business use of computers and telecommunications technology often requires owners to modify tenant space—for example, to provide raised floors, fiberoptic cable, or new riser systems for telephone lines.

The asset manager should make sure that recommended capital improvements add more value than they cost. The asset manager walks a fine line between spending too much capital, which can drain a property's cash flow, and spending enough capital to maintain the property at the market standard and extend its useful life. In general, scheduled preventative maintenance projects are usually less costly and less disruptive to tenants over the long run than crisis-driven emergency repairs.

Portfolio Management

With the emergence of securitized commercial mortgages and institutional ownership of real estate portfolios, sophisticated portfolio management has come of age. Institutions, pension funds, and other owners of large real estate portfolios are willing to invest in real estate portfolio management. Portfolio management is the method by which investors determine their investment goals and carry out a plan to meet their objectives.

The portfolio manager is responsible for structuring the portfolio of real estate assets to meet the investor's specific needs. The task of establishing portfolio goals starts from an understanding of the investor's investment goals. The portfolio manager develops and implements a portfolio strategy that will meet these investment goals. Implementation of a portfolio strategy involves analyzing the properties in the portfolio and taking actions—selling, trading, or acquiring properties—to bring the portfolio into harmony with the investment goals.

The portfolio manager is ultimately accountable for the portfolio's performance. Compensation is generally contingent on the successful implementation of the agreed investment strategy. The portfolio manager needs an understanding of major national trends, current market conditions, and market statistics as well as a close knowledge of the owner's objectives in order to devise and implement plans that will enhance the risk-adjusted returns of the portfolio.

Many factors affect the risk and the return of a real estate portfolio. Portfolio managers strive to achieve the perfect match of assets that yields the optimal portfolio, but this goal is never reached. According to LaSalle Advisors, many institutions find that the quantification of risk in a real estate portfolio is an elusive goal. Yet without measures of risk, the assessment of whether an investor is being sufficiently compensated for its holdings is difficult. To evaluate the equity portfolios it manages, LaSalle Advisors performs a risk/return analysis that relies on a series of objective measures of risk. The analysis is based on a multivariate model consisting of three broad categories of risk and ten different risk factors (see Figure 6-7). By applying this risk/return analysis at the portfolio level, a portfolio manager can consider whether the overall trade-off between risk and return fits the objectives of the investor.[7]

Each property in a portfolio of real estate assets should have an exit strategy, which is a plan for how the owner will dispose of the asset. The exit strategy delineates how long the asset will be held, when will it be sold, to whom it will be sold for what purpose, the sales price, and in what condition the property must be to meet this objective.

Like all decisions regarding a portfolio of real estate assets, the plan to acquire, develop, or divest of office buildings is a function of the owner's objectives. Investors looking for opportunities to create shorter-term value might redevelop a property for a new use and sell it upon lease-up. Other investors may be looking to develop a property for their own occupancy. The

figure 6-6

Long-Term Capital Budget Program

For Building's Roof, Cooling Tower, and Elevators

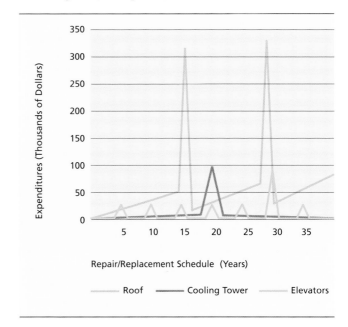

Source: *Real Estate Development: Principles and Process* (ULI, 1996).

figure 6-7

Real Estate Risk Factors

Property-Specific Risks
- Return orientation (income versus growth)
- Tenant risks (credit and rollover)
- Obsolescence/capital improvements

Market Risks
- Supply-side risks
- Demand-side risks
- Capital market factors

Liquidity/Structure (Entity-Specific) Risks
- Leverage
- Ownership structure
- Legal/environmental issues
- Market capitalization (size of entity)

Source: LaSalle Advisors Investment Research.

investor's objectives will dictate the property type, size, location, financing, and timing of acquisitions and dispositions.

Office Property Acquisitions

The portfolio manager devises a set of acquisition guidelines based on the answers to the following kinds of questions. Will the assets be geographically diversified to minimize portfolio risk? Will any market area contain too few properties to permit efficient asset management? Is the investor's interest limited to Class A buildings in central business districts? Or is the investor interested in buildings of lesser quality that offer potentially greater risks and rewards? Will a candidate property's potential vacancy in the near term deter investment? Or will the potential for strong long-term appreciation make suitable the acquisition of a currently weak property?

Office acquisitions for property portfolios should be guided by four major factors:

- the economic environment;
- real estate market conditions;
- characteristics of the property; and
- expected financial return and the investment structure.

Establishing criteria for these four parameters of an office property will give the portfolio manager a means by which to measure the performance of various potential candidates for acquisition.

For an office acquisition, real estate market considerations include the size, composition, and conditions of the office market. The broader economic considerations include the size of the metropolitan area, the stability of its economy, and the expected rate of employment growth. Growth expectations constitute the market risk.

Among the property characteristics that should be considered in any acquisition decision for a real estate portfolio are such tangibles as size, age, location, lease terms, and physical condition of the building. Intangibles such as image and other perceived advantages should also be considered.

Financial return and investment structure considerations include the amount of risk and leverage that is acceptable, the rate of return, and how the investor intends to participate in the acquisition—as a single owner, in a syndication, in a joint venture, in a limited partnership, as a REIT, or in another format. The investor should not acquire a property if it cannot allocate the resources—superior management, construction expertise, leasing talent, capital, or simply patience—that are necessary to add value to the asset.

Office Property Dispositions

The sale of an office building typically occurs at one of three points in its development cycle. It may be sold when stabilized occupancy occurs, and such sales have the potential to yield the highest internal rate of return for the investors. Or, it may be sold after the first full year of occupancy when the first CPI or fixed rent adjustments occur, or after the original leases start to roll over (or after the first rent escalations occur).

In dispositions, the building must be positioned for sale. Richard Peiser, director of the Lusk Center for Real Estate Development at the University of Southern California, notes five actions that can be taken to help position a building for sale:[8]

- a thorough inspection of the mechanical and other systems by a hired building inspection team, including a report that can be shown to prospective buyers;
- summarization of the project's income and expenses and the putting in order of its accounting records;
- cleaning and other measures to ensure a well-landscaped and well-maintained appearance;
- preparation of a summary of all the outstanding leases; and
- creation of a marketing brochure that describes the project's tenants, management, location, and position in the market and highlights its unique and noteworthy qualities.

Some properties will appeal to a broad market while others will appeal to just a narrow market. The portfolio or asset manager may be capable of accomplishing the sale of a building, but often a broker or some other intermediary is engaged for this purpose. An appraisal is conducted to determine the fair market value for a property. Typically, however, two prices are set: the asking price and the minimum selling price. This gives the broker the flexibility of a range of prices.

Office Property Appraisals

Investors may require periodic appraisals of the properties in their portfolios. The portfolio manager may choose to hire a different appraiser for each property or to rotate appraisers after a set period of time. It may be cost-effective for a portfolio to retain an appraiser for an indefinite period in order to avoid having to bid each appraisal.

An appraisal is an opinion of market value based on a factual analysis. A typical appraisal determines the market value of a building as is—or, according to the Code of Federal Regulations on Banks and Banking, "in the condition observed upon inspection and as it physically and legally exists without hypothetical conditions, assumptions, or qualifications as of the date the appraisal is prepared." Such an appraisal results in what is referred to as the "market value as is on appraisal date" (or the "market value as is").

The appraisal or valuation of an office property generally takes one of three common approaches: the income approach, the sales comparison approach, or the cost approach.

The income approach derives the value of a property by using the estimated net income over the life of the

Assuring a well-landscaped and well-maintained appearance is important in positioning a building for sale.

structure, discounted to determine its present value. Among the items that are considered in appraisals following the income approach are historic income and expenses compounded over the projection period, effective market rents, the building's leases (including projected vacancies), initial and terminal capitalization rates, and the internal rate of return. Income appraisals must use supportable cap rates and IRR rates.

The sales comparison approach is also known as the market value approach. This method seeks to derive the value of a property by comparing the recent sales prices of similar properties—known as comparables. It requires examining certain characteristics or circumstances of the sales (timing, motives, and financing) as well as the characteristics of the comparables (rents, location, size, age and condition, quality of construction and finishes, tenant appeal, functional utility, office unit sizes, and highest and best use).

Using the cost approach, the appraiser estimates the replacement cost of the structure, less depreciation, and the land value. This approach has been abused, mostly in the failure to include an appropriate amount of depreciation. Appraisals generally subtract physical depreciation, but it is easy to omit functional depreciation and economic depreciation (which usually is called external obsolescence). Functional depreciation refers to the cost of curing a functional deficiency or to the capitalized rent loss of a functional deficiency. Economic depreciation refers to the loss of value by local economic circumstances. It belongs in any appraisal, especially for buildings in a distressed market.

Notes

1. Kenneth A. Shearer, ed., *The Investors' and Owners' Guide to Office Building Management* (Homewood, Illinois: Irwin Professional Publishing, 1991), pp. 4–5.

2. Karen J. Krackov, "Add Value to Properties to Make Tenants Return," *Washington Business Journal,* July 11, 1997, p. 36.

3. "The New Owner," *Metro Chicago Real Estate,* June 1997, p.1.

4. Robert Kevin Brown and Alvin L. Arnold, *Managing Corporate Real Estate* (New York: John Wiley & Sons, 1993), pp. 434–435.

5. William F. Blake, "Security First," *Journal of Property Management,* July–August 1996, pp. 24–26.

6. Michael A. Steele, "Retaining Tenants into the Next Century," *Skylines,* April 1995, p. 13.

7. *LaSalle Advisors Investment Strategy Annual 1997* (Chicago: LaSalle Advisors, 1997), p.14.

8. Richard B. Peiser with Dean Schwanke, *Professional Real Estate Development: The ULI Guide to the Business* (Chicago: Dearborn Financial Publishing; and ULI–the Urban Land Institute, 1992).

7. Case Studies

Downtown Projects, New Construction

Centex Building, Dallas
A ten-story, 186,000-square-foot speculative office building that provides suburban style amenities.

Comerica Tower, Detroit
A 1 million-square-foot office building developed by a public/private partnership.

Jin Mao Building, Shanghai
An 88-story mixed-use tower featuring state-of-the-art building systems.

MesseTurm, Frankfurt
A 72-story, 680,000-square-foot (NRA) world-class office tower by a U.S. developer abroad.

Republic Plaza, Singapore
A 1.1 million-square-foot tower that features dramatic architecture and advanced building services.

Downtown Projects, Renovation

Audubon House, New York
The environmentally responsible remaking of a century-old, eight-story department store by its owner for its own headquarters plus leasable space.

The Rookery, Chicago
A painstaking restoration of a splendid 109-year-old, 12-story building that retains the building's history and also obtains Class A rents.

State Street Bank Building, Boston
The extensive updating of a 34-story, 1.1 million-square-foot, 1964 office building without an interruption of occupancy.

Suburban Projects, New Construction

101 Hudson, Jersey City
A 1.2 million-square-foot office tower that carefully targets the technology-driven operations and technical support divisions of financial services companies

225 High Ridge Road, Stamford, Connecticut
A 240,000-square-foot, two-building office complex within a parklike setting that focuses on the efficiency and flexibility of the tenant space.

Crescent 8, Greenwood Village, Colorado
An 87,400-square-foot office building that is the first structure in a planned town center for an almost fully developed business park.

Norm Thompson Headquarters, Hillsboro, Oregon
A build-to-suit, leased 54,519-square-foot headquarters facility designed to be environmentally sensitive while adhering to a strict rent budget.

Suburban Projects, Renovation

640 Memorial Drive, Cambridge, Massachusetts
Redevelopment of a 1913 automobile assembly plant as a speculative, multitenant biotechnology laboratory and office facility, featuring developer financing of tenant improvements.

Kensington Business Centre, Tulsa
The conversion of a mixed-use suburban retail mall to a mixed-use office complex, made possible in part by the trend to open offices and modular furniture.

Centex Building
Dallas, Texas

Downtown Dallas was one of the most overbuilt office markets in the United States when Harwood Pacific Corporation undertook the second phase of its International Center complex—a ten-story, 186,000-square-foot speculative office building. At the end of 1996, when the building had been complete for two months (and was fully leased), the central business district had a 37 percent vacancy rate, which represented 11 million square feet of empty office space.

In 1995, before construction had started, Centex Corporation, a Dallas-based financial services and real estate company, looked at the blueprints, signed a 15-year lease for nine of the ten floors, and gave the building its name. Centex made no alterations to the design, either before or during construction. The building stands adjacent to Harwood Pacific's six-story, 100,000-square-foot Rolex Building, which was completed in 1984.

The $40 million project targeted tenants—particularly in service industries—located in downtown Dallas that wanted suburban style amenities. Financing was 100 percent equity from Harwood Pacific's European investors. Square-foot rents are in the mid-$20s. When Centex moved into its new building over the 1996 Thanksgiving weekend, nearby high rises were pulling in rents of only $17 to $21 per square foot. A year later, the recovering downtown market was commanding rents from $19 to $30 a square foot.

The ground floor contains 11,472 square feet of rentable retail space, on which rents average $17 per square foot. A bank occupies a majority of this space, under a five-year lease. A full-service restaurant occupies the remaining retail space.

The development vision for the International Center was a handsomely landscaped mid-rise office campus in a central business district. Taking advantage of a great location, Harwood Pacific patiently set the stage for development success with extensive landscaping, innovative site planning and building design, state-of-the-art building systems, and a plenitude of parking.

Site
Harwood Pacific's International Center is an office campus on a $5 million assemblage of land—more than 80 lots totaling 15 acres—located on the northern edge of the Dallas CBD. This location gives tenants easy access to many downtown amenities, including cultural facilities (the Dallas Symphony Center and Dallas Museum of Art), the West End historic district, and commercial centers (the financial institutions of central Dallas, the World Trade Center, and Infomart). While this CBD-edge location provides access to nearby amenities, it also avoids some of the drawbacks—like traffic congestion—of a more downtown location.

The site is in a city- and state-designated enterprise zone, which provides new commercial developments like the Centex Building with tax abatements that can last up to ten years.

Transportation access is excellent. The site is accessible from four major freeways, near a Dallas Area Rapid Transit (DART) hub, just seven minutes from the Dallas Love Field airport, and only 25 minutes from Dallas/Fort Worth International Airport.

Equally important, the Centex Building enjoys tremendous visibility. The site is basically an island between on-ramps and off-ramps for the North Dallas Tollway, which leads into the CBD and out to much of the metropolitan area's executive housing.

Development Process
When Harwood Pacific Corporation broke ground on the Rolex Building in the early 1980s, its president, Gabriel Barbier-Mueller, envisioned the structure as the first phase in a three-phase project that would create the International Center. The envisioned campus of mid-rise office buildings rising from a European-style garden would transform its surrounding run-down neighborhood into an upscale business district.

Then markets across the country and particularly in overbuilt Dallas were devastated as they were hit by the double whammy of recession and overbuilding. By the early 1990s, many of downtown Dallas's gleaming office towers, many of them only a few years old, were sitting almost empty.

The International Center was put on hold for nearly a decade. But it was far from moribund. The Rolex Building continued to generate stable rents, which kept its European investors happy, and Barbier-Mueller kept busy cultivating (literally) the company's master plan.

The original 15-acre assemblage consisted largely of run-down houses and businesses. In the eyes of the local real estate market, the area had a negative image. To change those unfavorable perceptions and set the stage for the project's development, Harwood Pacific hired the SWA Group, a Dallas-based land planning and landscape architecture firm, to create and implement a landscaping plan.

The company intended to warehouse the property by turning it into a nursery. When construction became

The development of the Centex Building met a market demand for Class A mid-rise space in downtown Dallas in the mid-1990s.

Formal gardens link the three phases of the International Center office campus—the Centex Building, the Rolex Building, and a 220,000-square-foot office building under construction.

feasible once again, the on-site plants would be used for the International Center's landscaping design. The ramshackle buildings on the property were demolished, and the SWA Group planted more than 350 mature oak and sweet gum trees in groves, which have more than doubled in size since the first planting. The landscaper also planted grass and installed seasonal containers, built new sidewalks, and installed attractive streetlights throughout the property. In effect, the landscaping created an urban oasis that unified this once incoherent site. Several people offered to buy the trees, but Harwood Pacific chose to keep them in the park.

"We showed potential tenants, investors, and the real estate community that vacant land waiting for development did not have to be an eyesore, that it could be made into a park in the middle of the city," says Barbier-Mueller.

Harwood Pacific's landscaping program not only transformed people's image of the area. It also eventually facilitated the project's approval. "The city council practically bent over backwards to give us what we needed, including all of our approvals and the tax abatements," says Barbier-Mueller.

When Harwood Pacific decided in 1992 to proceed with the second phase of International Center, the real estate community thought the company was being reckless. At that time, conventional wisdom insisted that speculative office development in downtown Dallas would have to wait a decade or longer, because it would take that long to work off the overhang.

But Harwood Pacific had a plan. "We decided to make a better product," says Barbier-Mueller. "And we could keep our costs down by avoiding some of the inefficiencies and frills of the 1980s."

A standard issue 20-story office tower would have created a more commanding presence in the skyline, but it would not have fit into the plan for a mid-rise office campus and it did not meet market demands of the early 1990s. The typical office tenant in the Dallas CBD needed an average of 150,000 square feet. A tenant of that

size in one of downtown's 20- to 30-story office towers was one of many anonymous tenants, in a high rise that looked like almost every other high rise. By contrast, a tenant of that size in a ten-story mid-rise building was the major tenant and sometimes the only tenant. It would gain both prominence and control over its environment. And it could avoid parking shortages and some of the operating inefficiencies that can be a problem in multitenant high-rise towers.

Centex Corporation leased the new building because of its location in downtown Dallas, its size, and the suburban style amenities that it offered. Also important in its choice was Harwood Pacific's track record for excellent and consistent tenant services. Harwood Pacific manages the buildings it develops.

Design

"I believe that real estate should operate like the computer industry," says Barbier-Mueller. "We must strive to come out with constantly better—and less expensive—products. One way to do that is by rethinking the planning and design process."

Space Flexibility. The first step in the design of the Centex Building was the space planning, and the emphasis of the space planners was on efficiency and flexibility. Maximizing the flexibility of the floor space in order to have a building that could serve the current and future needs of a large variety of tenants meant minimizing the number of columns. This was easier to accomplish in a ten-story building than it would have been for a high rise, with its multiple cores and multiple shafts.

It was decided to create nearly column-free space. This would not only maximize the flexibility of the space, but also would be most suitable for today's flatter corporate hierarchies. Columns hinder attempts to design uniform offices and workspaces, because some modules will always get stuck with a column.

Harwood Pacific aimed to appeal to prospective tenants by demonstrating that a move from more but inefficient space to less but efficient space would save on rent and other overhead costs and make their workspace more productive.

The design architect, DMJM/Keating, created an attractive and cost-effective design that adhered to these requirements for efficient floor planning. Nearly 165,000 square feet of the 185,000 total square feet are net rentable office area and an additional 11,000 square feet are net rentable retail area—for a 95 percent efficiency ratio. The building's rectangular shape helps make it efficient, and its column-free structural design gives it the flexibility to adapt to future workplace and technological changes. Both the owner and the tenant will benefit over the long term in terms of money saved.

And the savings do not end there. The design emphasized long-lasting construction materials and surfaces that require minimal maintenance. There is very little carpet and wood in the building, but there is a lot of stone. Cleaning cannot damage the wall base. Harwood Pacific has budgeted just $6.50 per square foot for annual operating expenses.

Although the building is only ten stories tall, it incorporates many of the fine touches of a high-end downtown high rise, including a large lobby with a double-height ceiling, limestone walls, granite floors, and stainless steel and copper trim finishes.

The development includes a dedicated mailroom facility staffed by USPS personnel and an adjacent health club facility. The tenants get the best of both worlds: the quality of a high rise and the cost savings and distinction of a mid-rise.

Building Systems and Infrastructure. To serve today's technologically driven workplace, the Centex Building was designed with state-of-the-art mechanical, cable, and information systems. The HVAC system, for example, with one air-handling unit per floor and VAV (variable-air-volume) fans, is zoned. Each 1,500 square feet of office space is a temperature zone that can be controlled by touch-tone telephone. Fine-grained temperature control zones mean energy savings for the tenants. The building provides eight watts of electric power per square foot. Tenant security is provided with 24-hour access control monitoring.

The building's energy-saving features cost more money up front, but they mean lower operating costs over the long term, which saves money for the tenants and the owner. For example, the building's energy-efficient lighting fixtures cost $175,000 more than would standard fixtures. But they also consume less energy and cost less to maintain in the long term. Their added cost will be paid back by operational savings in under five years. These systems also provide the building with a good hedge against obsolescence.

Harwood Pacific spent $250,000 on a custom-designed software package for coordinating the building systems, the components of which are from different vendors. The operating control system is designed to enable the building management to operate the building systems and maintain and fine-tune the equipment in the most

Top-quality finishes in the lobby give the Centex Building a high-end downtown feel.

efficient manner, saving on energy consumption, maintenance costs, and repairs over the long term.

Parking. Zoning requires most downtown Dallas office towers to provide one parking space per 1,500 to 2,500 square feet of office space. Most buildings just meet that requirement, which, however, does not necessarily meet today's office needs. Many firms, particularly in the financial services industry, have adopted open office space plans and other alternative office strategies that effectively mean more employees in less space. Thus, many employees in downtown Dallas must resort to off-site parking lots.

Ample parking is an amenity at the Centex Building. A three-story parking garage provides 614 parking spaces, which works out to 3.3 spaces per 1,000 square feet of gross building area. The garage is half underground and half above grade. Additional visitor parking is available on-site.

Landscaping. Extraordinary landscaping is probably the most immediately noticeable feature of the International Center and certainly one of its most popular features with the tenants. The three office buildings (the third is under construction) are built around a 1.5-acre European style lobby-level garden that sits on the roof of the parking garage. Connecting arched bridges with intricate trusses that complement the garden below provide tenant access.

The central garden actually comprises three gardens: the Oak Motte, the Bowling Green, and the Ilex Allee (which contains 12 "secret" gardens). More than 100 trees have been planted in seven-by-seven-foot pits in this garden, including live oak, river birch, magnolia, sweetgum, and hollies. Other elements of the garden's landscaping include evergreen topiary hedges, flowering vines, perennials, aromatic herbs, manicured lawns, gravel pathways, and tree-shaded benches. At the center are an arabesque water garden and a reflecting pool. The garden is illuminated for nighttime enjoyment and special events. The restaurant in the Centex Building will use a portion of

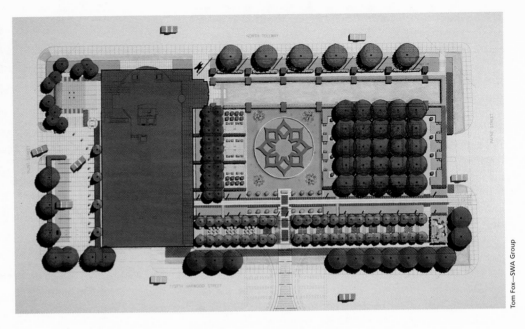

Reminiscent of the formal gardens of Europe, the landscape plan for the 1.5-acre garage rooftop provided an image and a powerful marketing tool for the project in an overbuilt market.

the garden for outdoor dining and even provide music for dancing beneath the stars.

The center's landscaping and its earlier nursery warehouse have proved to be a major marketing coup. The International Center received so much free publicity from the trees and landscaping in the years before Phase 2 construction began that Harwood Pacific did not have to produce leasing or marketing brochures for the Centex Building or its Phase 3 office building. In fact, the developer did not have to advertise the office buildings at all.

"In effect," says Barbier-Mueller, "we spent our marketing budget on landscaping. Because of the landscaping, everybody knew about our buildings and the new neighborhood. And everybody was a winner—our tenants, our neighbors, Dallas, and, of course, Harwood Pacific's bottom line."

The Centex Corporation has followed the developer's lead by using a tour through the gardens as part of its recruitment program.

Experience Gained

The Centex Building was so successful and market demand for this product was so great that in October 1996 construction on Phase 3 started. The new ten-story, 220,000-square-foot building will have its own parking garage with three spaces per 1,000 square feet of building space. It will have 20,000-square-foot floorplates and state-of-the-art mechanical, electrical, cabling, and telecommunications systems. At groundbreaking, the newest building was two-thirds leased by Jones Day Reavis & Pogue for a 15-year term. A sundry shop and deli will occupy part of the ground floor retail space.

Location is always important, but a good location is not always obvious. Although the International Center's location has proved to be a great boon, when Harwood Pacific started the development many people thought that the deteriorating neighborhood was absolutely the wrong location. Barbier-Mueller knew the location would work if the company could transform the neighborhood

to fit the development vision, and it used innovative methods—like creating a 15-acre park—to make the transformation happen.

The International Center may prove the absolute necessity of landscaping for many office projects. For the International Center, landscaping serves not merely as an amenity, but also as an imagemaker, a public gesture of goodwill, and a powerful marketing tool. In the developer's view, landscaping is also a key element in the work process. People thrive when they can see (and visit) trees and flowers and sky. People's productivity and satisfaction fall sharply when all they see is concrete.

Probably the key lesson of this office development is that developers must know their market intimately. They must pay attention to market details and not be limited by the market soothsayers who only glimpse the broad picture. Yes, Dallas was badly overbuilt when Harwood Pacific began construction on the Centex Building. But the building was not adding more of the same product to the market—one more tower in a crowded skyline. The developer found an overlooked (even ignored) market niche, and built what tenants wanted. It created a human-scaled office campus in a downtown that had everything to offer tenants except Class A mid-rise space. Giving the people what they want but do not have will bring success every time.

Project Data: Centex Building

Land Use and Building Information

Site Area	2 acres
Gross Building Area (GBA)	185,589 square feet

Net Rentable Area (NRA)

Office	164,909 square feet
Retail	11,472 square feet
Total	176,381 square feet

Floor/Area Ratio	2.04
Parking (all structured)	614 spaces

Office Tenant Information

Occupied NRA	100%
Average annual rents	$25 per square foot
Average length of lease	15 years

Retail Tenant Information

Occupied NRA	100%
Average annual rent	$17 per square foot
Average length of lease	5 years
Number of tenants	2

Development Cost Information

Total development cost[1]	$40,000,000
Development cost per gross square foot	$216
Development cost per net square foot	$227

Annual Operating Expenses

Estimated expenses	$6 per square foot

Developer/Owner

Harwood Pacific Corporation
2651 North Harwood
4th Floor
Dallas, Texas 75201
214-871-0871

Architects

Gromatsky DuPree and Associates (architect of record)
2626 Cole Avenue
Suite 100
Dallas, Texas 75204
214-871-9078

DMJM/Keating (design architect)
3250 Wilshire Boulevard
Los Angeles, California 90010
213-368-2800

Landscape Architect

The SWA Group
2211 North Lamar
Suite 400
Dallas, Texas 75202
214-954-0016

Land Planner

Brockette/Davis/Drake Inc.
4144 North Central Expressway
Suite 1100
Dallas, Texas 75204
214-824-3647

Development Schedule

1992	Planning started
1992	Site purchased
1992	Leasing started
1995	Construction started
10/1996	Project completed

Note

[1] Includes site acquisition.

Comerica Tower at Detroit Center
Detroit, Michigan

The 44-story, 1 million-square-foot Comerica Tower at Detroit Center rises 620 feet above Detroit and is Michigan's tallest office building. Its gabled roof and Gothic spires make it immediately identifiable on the Detroit skyline. Comerica Tower provides a vital link between Detroit's financial district to the north, the government center to the south, and the Renaissance Center housing the global headquarters of General Motors to the east.

Comerica Tower was conceived in the late 1980s, when Detroit's office market was going through one of the bleakest times in its history. When the big three automobile companies began downsizing at the end of the national recession, the entire region, which was dependent on the automobile industry, suffered a big hit. This plus a rash of relocations to Detroit's northern suburbs left downtown office buildings in desperate competition for the tenants that remained.

As dismal as this office occupancy scenario was, Hines Interests LP still saw an opportunity to build new Class A office space for the significant base of legal and accounting firms, auto companies, and other credit tenants interested in maintaining a city address. Not a single new office building had been developed in the central business district for more than 12 years. Hines was confident that it could turn the tide. In fact, the developer was able to convince a sophisticated group of yield-sensitive investors and risk-averse lenders to commit funds to this project in a city that was considered to be an unsafe and unpromising site for investment.

A public/private partnership between the city and Hines was established to develop the 44-story Comerica Tower and an attached parking facility. The partnership's implementation of an ambitious plan resulted in an office building that was 65 percent preleased when construction started and 100 percent leased six months before the building was completed in December 1991. The blue-ribbon tenant roster boasts some of the country's leading businesses, including accountants Ernst & Young and Arthur Andersen Consulting; the law firm of Dickinson, Wright, Moon, Van Dusen and Freeman; J. W. Thompson Advertising; and NBD Corporation, a major financial company.

The successful Comerica Tower at Detroit Center has catalyzed an emerging renaissance in Detroit and is its symbol. Architectural critics have called the building traditional, conservative, and graceful, and the public and tenants also admire its design. The building's Gothic topping—a somewhat controversial design element—has received generally excellent reviews and it fits well into the city's variegated skyline.

Development Process and Strategy
The city's $29.7 million financial contribution to the project had three components: a $7 million urban development action grant (UDAG) loan; a $16 million contribution to the land purchase through its borrowing capacity under Section 108 of the federal Housing and Community Development Act; and a land grant—the Bates Street right-of-way and parking lot—valued at $6.7 million.

However, funding for most of the $249 million project came from private sources. The Sanwa Bank of Chicago provided a $165 million first mortgage and four limited partners and the general partner (Hines) contributed $54 million in equity.

The public/private partnership called for a jobs program that would ensure the participation of Detroit residents, small businesses, and minority- and women-owned businesses in the construction of the building and the provision of construction materials and design and construction services. Comerica Tower's $105.7 million construction contract was competitively bid to contractors with the following guidelines: residents of Detroit would make up at least 50 percent of total person-hours worked, minority-owned businesses would be awarded at least 10 percent of the subcontracts, and women-owned businesses and small businesses would each be awarded at least 5 percent of the subcontracts. Hines and city officials monitored these goals throughout the project—and they all were achieved.

Comerica Tower commands a strategic location in downtown Detroit on a two-block site at the intersection of Jefferson and Woodward Avenues. When the site was acquired, a 30-year-old, poorly maintained, and obsolete Greyhound bus station, a parking facility, and a motel occupied the eastern portion. The western parcel was empty, the buildings having been demolished several years earlier in an effort to facilitate new development. The street separating the two parcels was little more than a pedestrian walkway between the City-County building and buildings north of the project site.

A variance negotiated with the city for a zero lot line along Woodward Avenue provided several benefits. It enhanced a view corridor to Hart Plaza, the Detroit River, and Windsor, Ontario, across the river. It also enabled the land planners to incorporate large, landscaped pedestrian plazas on the north and south sides of the site and a pedestrian walkway between the tower and the parking garage. These elements provide an inviting gathering place and a welcome amenity, as well as

The 44-story structure's Gothic roofline provides a distinctive profile on the Detroit skyline.

a framework for further urban improvements in the neighborhood.

Achieving a space-efficient design was the primary challenge for Comerica Tower. Its Class A space would have to compete with the many older downtown Class B and Class C buildings available at severely discounted rental rates, as well as with newer suburban space. Since the building could not compete on the basis of rents per square foot, Comerica Tower's success depended on its being able to offer tenants a more competitive total occupancy cost. This meant offering higher-quality amenities, greater space efficiencies, and lower operating costs than other downtown buildings. The tower structure was designed to accommodate 25,000-square-foot floors with column-free 45.5-foot spans. With this highly efficient floorplate configuration, tenants coming into Comerica Tower from lower-rent space needed to lease only 82 to 85 percent of the amount of space they needed in less efficient buildings, and thus could keep their occupancy costs about the same.

Hines determined that Comerica Tower's prospective tenants had two critical needs: convenient and secured parking and a safe and secure building. The first requirement was met with a 2,070-space, seven-story parking garage. The second was met by making security a top priority in all aspects of the building's design. Comerica Tower was designed to feel both accessible and secure at the same time. Instead of one large lobby, Hines created two more intimate yet impressive 30-foot-high lobbies

with multicolored marble walls, one fronting Woodward Avenue and the other facing the garage on Randolph Street. The smaller lobbies are easier to secure. State- of-the-art building access and security surveillance technology systems are important tenant amenities.

While great architecture and public spaces were important priorities for both the developer and the city, Comerica Tower had to be an economically viable project first and foremost. If the building failed to attract a full complement of tenants paying pro forma rents, it would fail to serve as a catalyst for the revitalization of downtown Detroit. In fact, a partially filled financial failure would depress the area even further, an outcome that the city was anxious to avoid.

Comerica Tower has been economically viable since it opened in early 1992. The building was 65 percent pre-leased before groundbreaking and 100 percent leased to seven tenants six months before the completion of construction. In return for long-term commitments to the project, several tenants were permitted to customize their space to include internal staircases, private elevators, and, in one case, a 30-foot-tall glass atrium library on the 40th floor. At opening, more than 80 percent of the parking spaces in the garage were leased under terms that are coterminous with the office leases.

Comerica Tower's leasing strategy includes long lease terms and contractual rental rates (with specific periodic increases) that include a full pass-through of operating expenses.

The architecture refines essential elements of a Gothic cathedral to modern simplicity. These views of the lobby (top photo) and entrance show the high quality of Comerica Tower's design and materials.

Design

In 1992, John Gallagher, *Detroit Free Press* architecture reporter, wrote that Comerica Tower reveals "how constrained architects of even a major project are by economic factors. [It] is good architecture, but it illustrates the old art-versus-economics tug-of-war, and architect [John] Burgee resolved it as well as anyone could."

Burgee knew that the low real estate values in Detroit called for a conservative approach. However, conservative does not have to mean unattractive and uninviting. Burgee and longtime partner and mentor Philip Johnson included in their design graceful arches, a gabled roof, impressive interiors, and a dramatic Gothic spire—all of which helped to create an impressive new Class A address in Detroit.

The building's stonework and Gothic-inspired detail fit the city's strong but conservative image and complement its rich architectural character. But behind the ultra-thin granite facade, which is one inch thick, tenants conduct business in modern state-of-the-art office space.

A glass-covered connector on which the gabled roof design is repeated joins the tower and the parking structure. The parking garage is also carefully designed. Arches and bays with iron grillwork break up its scale and help create a pleasant backdrop for the tower and other neighbors.

Experience Gained

The vindication of Hines' confidence in a location that investors had long ignored shows that a careful identification of unmet market needs can be rewarding. Comerica Tower proves that the prospect of a predictable and distributable cash flow can attract yield-sensitive and risk-averse investors to a city that is not on their target investment lists.

Comerica Tower also demonstrates the feasibility of selective revitalization in overlooked urban locations. Like Comerica Tower, such projects may require a combination of public and private funds in order to assemble an attractive financing package and move forward.

Comerica Tower has stopped the flow of office tenants from downtown Detroit to the suburbs. In 1996, the project generated more than $14 million in real estate tax revenues. Furthermore, the success of Comerica Tower has sparked interest in other urban programs, including infrastructure development, retail development, improvements on Woodward Avenue, and improvements in the Kennedy Square neighborhood.

The development's attention to detail is carried through to the garage, which gains character through the use of arches and iron grillwork.

A three-story library occupies the top of the building.

Site plan.

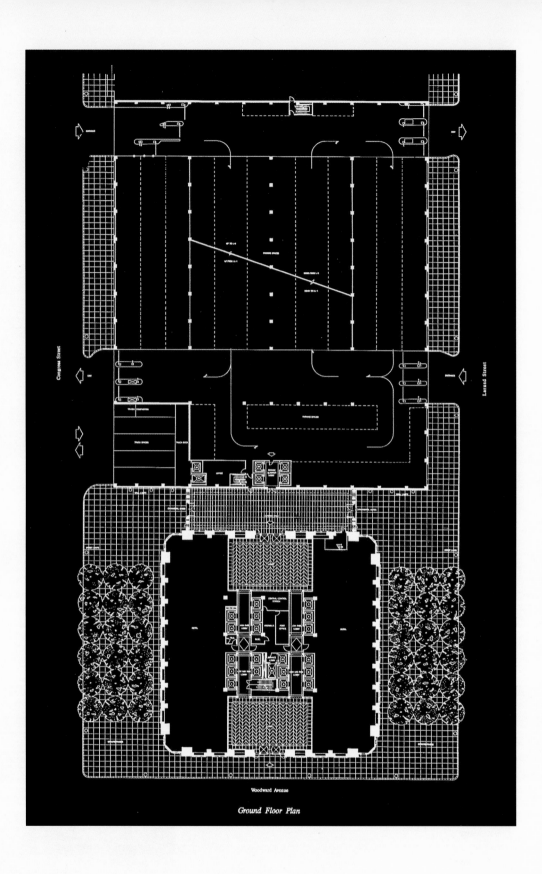

Ground Floor Plan

Project Data: Comerica Tower at Detroit Center

Land Use and Building Information

Site Area
4.6 acres

Gross Building Area (GBA)
Office	1,213,160 square feet
Retail	15,900 square feet
Total	1,229,060 square feet

Net Rentable Area (NRA)
Office	941,454 square feet
Retail	15,900 square feet
Total	957,354 square feet

Building Height
44 stories

Typical Floor Size
25,000 square feet

Parking
Structured	2,068 spaces
Surface	162 spaces
Total	2,230 spaces

Land Use Plan
	Acres	Percent of Site
Buildings	1.2	26%
Parking structures	1.7	37
Paved areas[1]	1.7	37
Total	4.6	100%

Office Tenant Information
Occupied NRA	100%
Average annual rent	$18 per square foot
Average length of lease	15 years
Typical terms of lease	Net of operating expenses; 15-year renewal at market rate; tenant improvements
Typical tenant size	100,000 square feet
Largest tenant	386,149 square feet

Retail Tenant Information
Occupied NRA	100%
Annual rent	$18 per square foot
Terms of lease	15 years; net of operating expenses
Average tenant size	15,900 square feet
Number of tenants	1

Development Cost Information
Site acquisition	$19,231,000
Site improvement and building construction	166,473,000
Soft costs	63,011,000
Total Development Cost	**$248,715,000**
Development Cost per Gross Square Foot	**$202**
Development Cost per Net Square Foot	**$260**

Annual Operating Expenses (1996)
Taxes	$2,432,200
Insurance	115,300
Services[2]	1,878,700
Maintenance	1,119,200
Janitorial	1,725,900
Utilities	1,404,800
Management	703,800
Total	$9,379,900

Financing
Sanwa Bank, Chicago (first mortgage)	$165,000,000
Section 108 grant	16,000,000
UDAG loan	7,000,000
City of Detroit land grant	6,715,000
General partner equity	5,000,000
Limited partner equity	49,000,000
Total	$248,715,000

Developer
Hines Interests Limited Partnership
200 Renaissance Center
Suite 1200
Detroit, Michigan 48243

Owner
One Detroit Center Limited Partnership
500 Woodward Avenue
Suite 2850
Detroit, Michigan 48226

Design Architect
John Burgee Architects, with Philip Johnson

Production Architect
Kendall/Heaton Associates
3050 Post Oak Boulevard
Suite 1000
Houston, Texas 77056

General Contractor
Walbridge Aldinger
613 Abbott Street
Detroit, Michigan 48226

Development Schedule
1988–1989	Site purchased
1987	Planning started
3/1990	Construction started
1989	Leasing started
12/1991	Project completed

Notes
[1] Surface parking and roads.

[2] Includes salaries and building services.

Jin Mao Building
Shanghai, China

In 1995, the China Shanghai Foreign Trade Centre Company, a foreign trade group owned and operated by the Chinese government, started construction on the Jin Mao Building in Shanghai. The 88-story tower—which will be the tallest building in China upon its completion—is located in Shanghai's rapidly developing Pudong district, across the Huangpu River from downtown Shanghai's famed Bund with its early 20th-century row of former foreign banks, clubs, and corporate headquarters.

Scheduled for completion in 1998, the state-of-the-art mixed-use Jin Mao Building has office space on the first 50 floors and a Grand Hyatt hotel on the upper 32 floors. A six-story annex contains additional function areas for the hotel, a conference and exhibition center, an auditorium, and a retail galleria. Three underground levels hold the building's parking garage, emergency power plant, sewage treatment facility, boiler and chiller facilities, and the hotel's back-of-house space.

Development Boom

By the early 20th century, Shanghai was China's largest, most prosperous, and most international city, with many European style buildings and a worldwide reputation for decadence and intrigue. Shanghai's glory days ended when the Communists seized power in China in 1949. The new leaders considered the port city a symbol of foreign capitalism and vice. They cut off its lifeblood—foreign trade —and let the once-vibrant city stagnate for nearly 40 years.

Shanghai's current turnaround started at the beginning of 1990, when Communist party leader Deng Xiaoping ushered in national economic reform with the slogan: "To get rich is glorious." He decreed that Shanghai —still the country's largest metropolis—would be transformed into a symbol of China's economic might and serve as the country's financial, trade, and industrial gateway to the outside world in the 21st century.

The Pudong New Area, which lies just across the Huangpu River from downtown Shanghai, covers 200 square miles. Representing 8 percent of the land area of Shanghai, it was an area of villages and farmland until 1990, when the municipal government announced its creation as a development district. Pudong's nerve center is Lujiazui, an 11-square-mile district. Lujiazui is China's only free trade zone. The Jin Mao Building is located in the heart of Lujiazui.

Between 1992 and 1997, the central government spent nearly $10 billion on the development of (state-owned) buildings and infrastructure in Pudong, and it has committed to invest an additional $36 billion by the turn of the century. But the central government is not the only investor in the area. In the first half of the 1990s, Pudong attracted an additional $34 billion of foreign investment, primarily from Asia, particularly Hong Kong, Japan, and Singapore. The area is abloom with factories, warehouses, high-tech industrial parks, and housing developments for the workers at plants operated by Volkswagen, Xerox, PepsiCo, Mitsubishi, Coca-Cola, and Sony among others.

In 1995, for example, more than 220 high-rise buildings were completed in the city. Between 1995 and 1997, the amount of office space in Shanghai rose by approximately 37.7 million square feet. Nearly 6.5 million square feet of the city's new Class A office space is located in Lujiazui, and by 1999 Lujiazui is expected to contain 13.2 million square feet of Class A office space.

And that is a problem. Shanghai is already severely overbuilt, with the office sector particularly hard hit. In 1996, Lujiazui had a 69 percent office vacancy rate. Some buildings were 90 percent empty. Some projects have been stopped in mid-construction due to funding shortages.

But not all office properties are in the doldrums. Well-designed, well-located, and well-capitalized projects have proved surprisingly scarce, and that has made all the difference to some developers. The demand from western companies for high-quality office space that can support the latest technologies is so great in Shanghai and supply of space of that caliber is so tight that occupancy rates for the finest buildings stand at nearly 100 percent.

Project Background

The developer, which is a consortium of more than a dozen companies, wanted to build a premier project that would serve this demand for high-end commercial space and also symbolize the country's financial strength. In fact, it wanted to build—through the finest design, workmanship, materials, mechanical systems, layout, and location—a world-class international standard office tower as the centerpiece of Lujiazui.

The company chose a 5.68-acre site that was occupied by a village of one- and two-story wood and masonry buildings. On the basis of an international competition, Skidmore, Owings & Merrill (SOM) of Chicago was selected to provide architectural, engineering, and planning services for the Jin Mao Building. SOM engaged a number of consulting firms, including the Shanghai Institute of Architectural Design & Research as local architect and engineer for the preconstruction phase, and the East China Architectural Design & Research Institute as local architect and engineer for the construction phase.

The 88-story Jin Mao Building encompasses 1.1 million square feet of office space, a 1.3 million-square-foot luxury hotel, conference facilities, retail space, and underground parking, including space for 1,000 bicycles.

Skidmore, Owings & Merrill LLP

The Shanghai Jin Mao Contractors, which serves as lead contractor, is a joint venture that includes the Shanghai Construction Group, Ohbayashi Corporation, Campenon Bernard SGE, and Chevalier Development International. The subcontractors are a combination of Chinese and international firms, including Nippon Steel of Japan for structural steel, Mitsubishi of Japan for elevators, Gartner of Germany for the curtain wall, ROM of Germany for the HVAC, and Cegelec of France for the electrical en-

gineering. Zhu Qi Hong, managing director of the China Shanghai Foreign Trade Centre Company serves as project manager.

After residents were relocated and the existing village was demolished, construction of the Jin Mao Building began in August 1995.

Development Strategy

To attract and serve the target market—large multinational corporations interested in opening offices in China —the developer decided to add a retail galleria and a high-end hotel to the office element. The 3.1-million-square-foot building was planned to be a dynamic mix of synergistic uses and a total environment of high-end services.

The first 50 floors of the Jin Mao Building, totaling 1.1 million square feet of net rentable space, are dedicated to office use. Some members of the developer/ owner group will occupy several floors, but the majority of the office space will be leased to outside tenants. The average floorplate is 26,000 square feet.

A 555-room Grand Hyatt hotel occupies floors 53 through 85. The hotel's 1.3 million square feet of building area includes a grand ballroom, an auditorium, and a fitness club. A dramatic atrium rises from the 56th-floor skylobby to five levels above the 88th floor. A private club and restaurant are located on floors 86 and 87, while a spectacular observatory on the 88th floor will be open to the public for a nominal fee. The five levels above the observatory and three underground levels house mechanical equipment, and there is parking for 1,140 vehicles— and 1,000 bicycles—below grade (and for an additional 35 cars around the building).

A six-story, granite and steel podium building on the tower's west side contains the retail space as well as 56,500 square feet of function areas for the hotel and 17,000 square feet of back-of-house space. The 11,000-square-foot conference and exhibition center will house small trade-oriented shows. The 10,000-square-foot auditorium has 400 seats and will be used for film showings and live performances. The podium building's retail galleria contains 85,750 square feet of net rentable area.

The Jin Mao Building's main pedestrian entrance is on the north side of the tower, facing a handsome park. The vehicular drop-off for office visitors is on the east side of the building, and the main entrance and motor court for the hotel is located on the south side. The building's service and parking entrances are on the west side of the building at the base of the retail podium.

The building itself occupies 2.67 acres of the 5.68-acre site. Landscaping takes up 1.19 acres. Roads, surface parking, and other paved areas account for the bulk of the remaining acreage.

The design team was careful to fit the Jin Mao tower into its immediate surroundings. Landscaping at the base of the building creates a public park, with pathways defined by raised beds of trees and flowers. The trees form a shaded canopy and the raised planter edges serve as park benches. Pools that are crossed by bridges at each

A new landscape is taking shape in Shanghai. Since city-wide infrastructure is lacking, high rises like Jin Mao incorporate their own power generation, sewage treatment, water purification, and telecommunications facilities.

building entrance define the periphery of the tower. A large plaza on the north is the front door to a large park that is being developed across the boulevard.

Engineering Challenges and Innovations

The site for the building posed a series of extraordinarily difficult engineering challenges. The region is prone to typhoons and occasional earthquakes. The site is a delta of clay and sand, with no bedrock within 328 feet. And groundwater starts several feet below the surface. The structural engineers had to design a foundation that could support the 88-story tower, provide high load carrying capacity, and limit settlement allowances. It also had to be essentially waterproof.

The building's foundation starts with a grid of 429 hollow steel piles (213 feet long and 3 feet across) driven 262 feet below grade. They are the longest steel-pipe piles ever used for a land-based building. The piles were driven to a layer of stiff sand which provides some bearing capacity, but the foundation depends primarily on pile surface friction to provide support.

A below-grade slurry wall was built around the water-logged site. This was done after the pile driving was complete, because it was feared that the strong vibrations might damage a wall. The slurry wall forms a waterproof container for the building's underground facilities, and a hydrostatic pressure relief system drains any water that may get in.

Finally, construction workers poured a 15-foot-thick concrete mat to complete the building's foundation. This is one of the largest concrete mats ever constructed.

Construction crews worked 24 hours a day to erect the tower. The reinforced concrete core is 33 inches thick at its base and 18 inches thick at the top and spanned by concrete web walls for the first 53 stories. The open core that begins on the 56th floor makes possible one of the tallest atriums in the world.

To design a stable and strong structure that can withstand the site challenges—wind, seismic events, and poor soil—SOM's engineers conducted extensive seismic and other analyses. Wind studies were based on the current built environment and the Pudong district's master plan. (Uncertainty about the chances that two high rises planned near the Jin Mao Building would actually be built added to the analytic challenge.) Of particular concern were the typhoons that sweep up the China coast and the effects on the building of wind gusts.

Jin Mao was designed to survive the most extreme wind and seismic events. How? Eight supercolumns fabricated from structural steel sections encased in reinforced concrete are positioned in pairs and centered on four of the tower's eight sides. Although the floorplates narrow as they taper to the top of the building, the supercolumns remain essentially vertical to maximize the building's structural depth. A deeper section is more resistant to lateral forces.

Three sets of eight outrigger trusses, each two stories high, connect the supercolumns to the concrete core at floors 24 and 26, 51 and 53, and 85 and 87. These monumental steel trusses act like stiffeners between the central core and the outside columns. As the core tries to bend in a typhoon or seismic event, the trusses on four sides restrain it.

The tower includes other steel components designed, like the eight supercolumns used to create column-free office interiors, to assume only gravity loads. Steel floor framing was used to reduce weight and speed construction. The steel trusses support composite metal decks and concrete slabs.

Drift analyses performed by the wind tunnel at the University of Western Ontario demonstrated that the use of reinforced concrete and steel without supplemental dampers would provide enough structural support in strong winds. The perception of building movement by occupants will be minimal and well within internationally accepted limits.

Design

The owners wanted the Jin Mao Building to represent the energy and determination of the people of Shanghai, as well as Shanghai's confidence in its future. The SOM design team conceptualized a structure that is contemporary in its architectural expression and state-of-the-art in its systems—and, at the same time, reminiscent of the first Chinese skyscrapers, which are the ancient pagodas that still form the center of many Chinese towns and villages.

Like the classical pagodas, the Jin Mao Building steps back in a series of setbacks that increase in frequency as the building ascends—in a cadence relating to the number 8 and fractions thereof. This tapered design accommodates larger floorplates for offices on the lower levels and smaller floorplates on the hotel levels. Schematic design for the project began in March 1993.

The number 8—considered by the Chinese to be lucky—is incorporated throughout the building design. The tower rises 88 stories. The floorplate is an octagon. Inside the building, most of the floor-plan elements are eight-sided. On the office levels, eight exterior steel columns are interspersed among eight perimeter super-columns to create an efficient column-free floor span. The project's scheduled completion date of August 8, 1998 even respects the lucky number—the eighth day of the eighth month of the ninety-eighth year.

The exterior of the Jin Mao tower is a state-of-the-art curtain wall of high performance silver-blue reflective glass arranged to emphasize the building's verticality, an expressed aluminum and stainless steel mullion system, and silver ceramic frit patterns. The exterior of the six-story podium building is composed of granite, stainless steel, and anodized silver aluminum. During the day, the tower seems to change form as the sun moves along its metallic and articulated surface. In the evening, the illuminated tower and its crowning spire will form a glowing beacon on the Shanghai skyline.

An unusual feature of the Jin Mao Building is its very high aspect (height/width) ratio, which makes it one of the most slender occupied high-rise structures in the world. Jin Mao's floors are approximately 174 feet across, and the building rises to 1,380 feet. Its aspect ratio is thus 8/1, which may be compared with the 6.6/1 aspect ratio of the Sears Tower in Chicago.

On the office levels, the floor spans are column-free and all of the building services—elevators, washrooms, and mechanical systems—are located in the central core, giving the building flexible and efficient office space. That the office space also provides stunning views of the city is a big bonus.

On the hotel levels, the building's central core opens up into a spectacular 37-story, 498-foot-tall atrium. Glass elevators run up and down the glazed elevator shafts at the atrium's center. Corridors are cantilevered off the core. The typical hotel floorplate is 18,800 square feet.

Two express elevators rise from the concourse retail area, which is one level below grade, to serve a single destination: the 12,375-square-foot glass-walled observation deck on the 88th floor. The observation deck's dark terrazzo floor is inlaid with cast-bronze Chinese characters and medallions that were inspired by the building. The floor offers tenants, guests, and visitors a dramatic 360-degree view of the new Shanghai rising out of a welter of construction cranes.

Combining office, hotel, residential, and retail uses on one site, mixed-use developments often resemble a city within a city. Many projects in Asian cities like Shanghai where infrastructure either is still rudimentary or is being overwhelmed by a construction boom take this familiar development model one step further. They must be essentially self-sufficient in terms of infrastructure—from telephone systems to sewage treatment plants—that is not otherwise reliably provided.

The Jin Mao Building has some of the most complete city-within-a-city infrastructure systems in Asia, including high-voltage electrical transformers and switch gear and a sewage treatment plant—along with the usual building systems for providing heat, cooling, and emergency power.

Jin Mao also incorporates cutting-edge building and mechanical systems. The building makes full use of the newest developments in intelligent building systems to operate and maintain the life-safety, security, and HVAC systems; to conserve energy; to offer technologically advanced communications systems; and otherwise to oper-

Skidmore, Owings & Merrill LLP

A state-of-the-art curtain wall sheathes one of the world's slenderest high rises. In some aspects of its design, Jin Mao is reminiscent of classical Chinese pagodas.

The structure is engineered to create column-free office interiors.

Skidmore, Owings & Merrill LLP

ate and control the building. For example, an intelligent building system can automatically inform building management whenever HVAC components need service or replacement, and thus save the added overhead costs caused by worn-out parts.

At Jin Mao, computers will manage most systems, thereby reducing the building's operational manpower and energy requirements. The computerized system will know when and where any electrical circuits fail and will match and adjust HVAC output to load requirements. Occupancy sensors regulate HVAC and lighting, particularly in the hotel guest rooms. The system accurately tracks tenants' use of building resources—from an office tenant's weekend use of air conditioning to a hotel guest's use of the Internet—and puts it on their bills.

The occupancy sensors and other equipment enhance the building's life-safety and security systems. If a fire breaks out, for example, firefighters will know which spaces are occupied, and which are not.

Jin Mao provides a full range of state-of-the-art tenant services quickly and economically. For example, in Shanghai, companies must sometimes wait six months for telephone service. In the Jin Mao Building, tenants can obtain hookups to telecommunications services—including Internet access, satellite communication services, and teleconferencing capabilities—in a day.

Jin Mao also takes advantage of recent advances in HVAC systems. The building uses a highly energy-efficient VAV (variable-air-volume) system coupled with a constant-volume fresh air system and constant-volume supply to the space to provide a better, fresher air supply than conventional systems. The system recovers heat by exhausting heat from the hotel guest rooms to the guest room ventilation supply.

Intelligent systems and state-of-the-art mechanical systems cost more up front, but they generate tremendous savings in operating costs, efficiency, and manpower over the long term. All these different building system components can be found in buildings in the United States and around the world. Jin Mao, however, is unique in the completeness of its intelligent building system.

Marketing

First Pacific Davies (China), a company that is based in Hong Kong and has offices throughout Asia and Australia, is the marketing and facilities management agent for Jin Mao. It also helped to fine-tune the original design to best serve the market.

First Pacific Davies will market Jin Mao to the 80,000 clients in its database, targeting companies that fit Jin Mao's tenant profile, such as corporations with regional offices in China that need the most modern office space. The firm will team with Stauback in the United States to reach the U.S. and Canadian markets and with Weatherall, Green & Smith of London to reach major European markets.

Experience Gained

SOM took the challenges presented by the Jin Mao Building and turned them into opportunities to test new materials, new technology, and new solutions. Advances in composite structural systems were incorporated into the building to meet the challenges of occasionally severe weather, potential seismic activity, and poor soil conditions. Most very tall high-rise buildings use steel structures alone. Jin Mao's use of reinforced concrete in its core and supercolumns provided greater structural performance at reduced costs. Composite structural systems were developed in the United States, and are becoming increasingly sophisticated in Asia.

SOM designed some cutting-edge mechanical and building systems, which can be effectively adapted for other buildings, even in locations with more extensive public infrastructure services. Of particular benefit to large U.S. building operations, from hotels to office buildings, are intelligent building systems that can track and bill tenants' use of building resources and also provide efficient and cost-effective controls for mechanical operations and maintenance programs.

Jin Mao is a strong reminder of the importance of location, superior building design, and a full menu of building amenities for keeping an office building viable in good times and bad. Unlike the less than first class high rises in Pudong, which are going begging for tenants, Jin Mao has what it takes to remain a premier (and fully leased) building on Shanghai's skyline for decades to come.

Site plan.

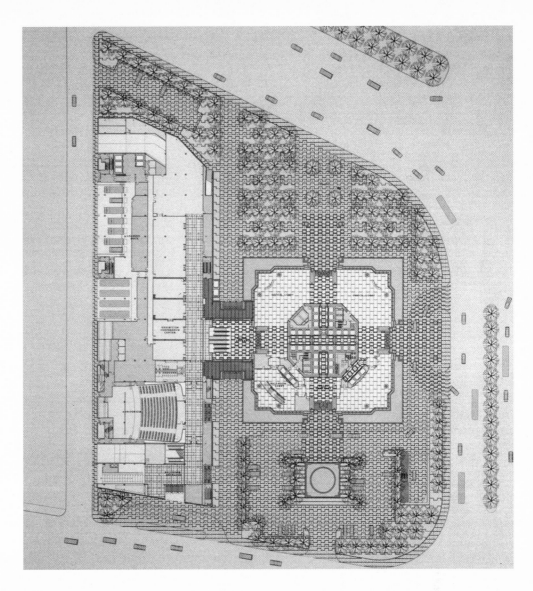

Typical floor plan.

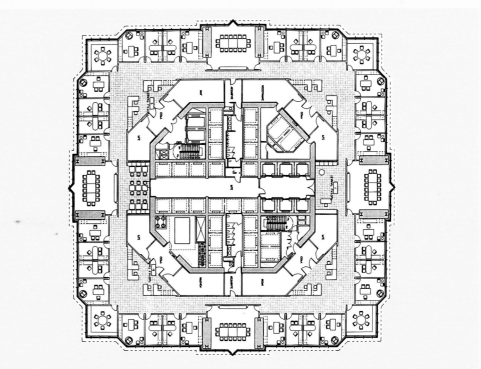

MesseTurm

Frankfurt, Germany

In the view of executives of Tishman Speyer Properties (TSP), the successful development of the MesseTurm, a world-class office tower in Frankfurt, is prima facie evidence of the exportability of professional property development practices. The process of planning, financing, designing, constructing, marketing, and managing this building was basically business as usual for the New York–based developer. Being in Germany did not alter the essentials of the TSP development process, but the peculiarities of the local building process and market called for many cultural adjustments and gave rise to some interesting times. The fact that the project was planned and marketed as an American style building for an international market gave TSP an edge over local developers.

Founded in 1978, Tishman Speyer Properties has developed a portfolio of office buildings, mixed-use centers, and residential properties that is valued at more than $6 billion. A 1988 agreement with the Frankfurt fairground authority, Messe Frankfurt, to build an office tower on the fairgrounds was the firm's first undertaking in Germany.

The project's development was directed as a branch operation from U.S. headquarters. As TSP began to take on other projects in Frankfurt and Berlin, it established a German company, Tishman Speyer Properties Frankfurt LP, chiefly in order to signify a permanent presence in the market and thus attract talented German real estate professionals. Conceptually, the German office, with about 75 employees, duplicates the headquarters operation in terms of specialties: development, design and construction, leasing and marketing, finance and accounting, and property management. TSP calls the integration of these five specialties from the concept stage forward its Pentaplan.

Development Process

The original planning for an office tower on this site preceded TSP's involvement by three years. In 1985, the management of the Messe Frankfurt (Frankfurt fairgrounds) proposed a program that included a 215,000-square-foot exhibition hall and a 900,000-square-foot office building on the eastern third of the fairgrounds. Proceeds from the office development would pay for the construction of the exhibition hall. How well the new buildings would complement the site's landmark Festhalle (festival hall) built in 1909 and its other meeting and exhibition facilities was a primary concern of the Messe management and city officials.

Murphy/Jahn, a Chicago-based German-American architectural partnership, won the Messe's design competition for this project, and a Hamburg-based financial firm was selected to develop it. But the developer bowed out in 1987 when the stock market and office market were both in the doldrums. In early 1988, the Messe approached Citibank and Citibank, in turn, went to Tishman Speyer Properties.

From the start, says Katherine Farley, TSP managing director, "Citibank indicated that it was prepared to provide the financing in some fashion and that TSP should concentrate its attention on making the fundamental deal with the Messe for the ground lease on the property." This required learning the rules of the game for U.S. investors in Germany, especially from a tax standpoint. TSP tax expert Paul Galiano considers tax efficiency, in particular the avoidance of double taxation, to be one of the major challenges for a U.S. developer overseas. Working out the structure of the MesseTurm acquisition and the details of the investment partnership required much consultation with local German law and accounting firms. In Europe, partnerships are an uncommon business arrangement.

Nonetheless, the development deal came together very quickly. In the six months from early 1988, when the idea of TSP involvement was broached, to July 1988, when ground was broken, the lease was negotiated, a partnership structured, and the design of the building modified in some major ways. Construction was similarly fast-tracked.

In March 1988, a ground lease was signed. It was for 99 years with automatic renewal for a second 99-year term. Ground rent for the first 35 years was prepaid. After 35 years, annual ground rents will be set by a formula based on the building's income. The initial ownership partnership involved Tishman Speyer Properties, Citicorp/Citibank, and the Kajima Corporation—each with a one-third interest. Tishman Speyer has stayed on in a management role as well as a partial equity owner, after having sold a portion of its partnership interest to Nomura in 1990.

Essentially, what the partners had bought was a long-term ground lease and the approved development rights for an office tower.

TSP likes to work with overlooked, nonprimary locations that are "possible to cultivate," adding value by turning them into destination locations. The MesseTurm site was on the outskirts of downtown. But architecturally, the building was a standout. At 842 feet, it would be the

Towering over the low-rise exhibition and meeting halls of the Messe Frankfurt (Frankfurt fairgrounds), the slender campanile-like MesseTurm marks the east end of the fairgrounds. Together with the classical 1909 festival hall and a new exhibition hall/entrance pavilion that was also designed by Murphy/Jahn, it defines a piazza.

tallest office building in Europe. The product of an international design competition, the slender and articulated skyscraper would contrast with the boxlike modernist structures dominating Frankfurt's high-rise office scene. When finished, the MesseTurm instantly became a signature building in Frankfurt and, appearing widely on postcards and posters, even a symbol of the city. TSP managing director Geoffrey Wharton notes that the city of Frankfurt and its inhabitants "accepted the building long before the commercial market accepted it." In time, adds Wharton, the MesseTurm in fact became a prestige address and new office development has occurred in its vicinity, making this "a much stronger location than when we built it."

TSP's first exercise was to study the existing design of the building, with Helmut/Jahn continuing its involvement as project architect. Not wanting to lose time taking the building through the approval process, the developer confined its consideration to design elements that could be changed without disturbing the basic approval. "We were very careful to understand which were the types of things that could be changed and which were the things that could not be changed," reports Farley.

Essentially, it was this design modification process that provided the development opportunity. As Farley explains, based on the cost of the original design and local investors' expectations of the market, local investors considered this development very risky. The goals of the design modifications were to make the building more suitable for high-rent international tenants and to make it more efficient. Revisiting the design obviously increased the project's design costs. Some of the design modifications that were made added to the cost of construction, while others lowered the cost or shortened the construction schedule—but overall the new design saved considerable capital costs. "The result," says Farley, "is that the numbers looked better to us than to others. The design changes that we made are what really made this building work."

Design and Construction

Although the redesign could not tamper with the already approved basic shape of the building—its height and massing—TSP was able to make some major modifications to the building's design. Notably, the developer created more rentable space, designed a simpler frame, changed the elevator system, changed the facade, and completely revamped the HVAC system. TSP also worked with the general contractor to accomplish a fast-track construction schedule and to accommodate precompletion occupancy. Dealing with German construction standards and market preferences and subcontractors' own brand of design/build construction practices was a constant and varied challenge.

Rentable Space. The number of stories was increased by compressing several high-ceiling stories at the top of the building to more typical floor-to-ceiling heights. A lot of mechanical equipment was eliminated from mid-rise floors to provide rentable space. After a hard-sell campaign to convince German code officials that interior pressurized stairways were a safe alternative to perimeter stairs, a campaign that involved bringing on board a fire and life-safety consultant, Schirmer Engineering, to argue the case and organize field trips to high-rise buildings in the United States, the building's stairs were relocated from the perimeter—where they took up prime rentable space—to the core.

After the redesign, the building's efficiency—the ratio of rentable space to gross square footage—was still a low 67 percent. The MesseTurm is one-third core because of the market's preference for very narrow lease spans. The typical distance from the windows to the core is just short of 25 feet, compared with typical lease spans of 45 feet in U.S. high rises. In Europe in general, narrow lease spans are a matter of custom and cultural preference. In Germany, they are a matter of labor law as well. By law, workers must be within a certain distance of a window. A basement level restaurant in the MesseTurm had to rent 200 square feet on an above-ground level so that its

Main entrance to the Messe-Turm. Red granite was selected for the facade to match the red sandstone that is used in many of Frankfurt's most architecturally significant buildings.

employees could take periodic breaks in windowed space. Because small floorplates are so inefficient in buildings requiring substantial core services, Europeans generally do not build tall office buildings.

Foundation. Because of Frankfurt's deep compressible-soil strata, many buildings supported by concrete mats have had troublesome problems with differential settlement. TSP brought in a U.S.-based foundation consultant, Mueser Rutledge, to oversee the finalization of the foundation design by the local geotechnical consultant. The 20-foot-thick, 20,000-cubic-yard mat—one of the world's largest—was safeguarded against tilting by the addition of 64 reinforced concrete outrigger piles (four feet in diameter and up to 130 feet long) to act in conjunction with the mat. The foundation system was successfully tested when the construction of a subway project next door caused a long-term sloping water table across the building's footprint.

Frame. A U.S. developer would ordinarily use steel rather than reinforced concrete for framing such a tall office building. However, German builders are used to concrete, and concrete is more economical than steel in Germany and eminently workable for narrow high rises where interior columns are not necessary. Furthermore, the structure was "one of those things that could not be changed" without jeopardizing the approval, and the local building officials would have had to be convinced of the safety of spray-on fireproofing had steel been used.

The frame was, however, simplified in the redesign to permit the continuous foundation-to-top load-bearing core to be slip-formed in seven stages, thereby accelerating the construction schedule. The exterior structure of perimeter columns and spandrel beams was gang-formed inside and out and built ahead of the floors. The original beam-and-slab floor system was redesigned to a flat-plate floor slab (formed with a metal deck) that permitted the exterior structure to be built ahead of the floors. Irwin G. Cantor PC of New York was brought in to facilitate the frame redesign. The new design resulted in cost savings beyond those resulting from the efficient sequencing of construction.

Elevators. The original design included a restaurant/observatory near the top of the building, which necessitated an elevator skylobby that made the vertical transportation system inefficient. The restaurant use was brought down to the tenth floor and the elevators were arranged into more efficient groups. Twenty high-speed elevators arranged in four zones offer direct service to the office floors, two elevators are dedicated for service use and freight, and two elevators are used to take visitors to the tenth floor restaurant. The two underground floors are also served by escalators from the lobby and the plaza.

Facade. The original approvals called for using an experimental, 30-minute fire-rated glass on the building's exterior that would cost about three times as much as normal double-pane glass, and the permitting authorities were fairly insistent that it be used. But the developer was even more adamant against, and, in fact, put a provision in its contract with the Messe Frankfurt that voided the

Courtesy of Tishman Speyer Properties

A curve of glass defines the 60-foot-high lobby, which features polished red granite and stainless steel.

deal in the event that the requirement could not be changed. The developer's life-safety consultant played a key role in persuading the permitting officials that this very expensive glass was superfluous in light of the building's other fire-control systems.

The MesseTurm's facade is a curtain wall of red granite and insulated blue-gray, slightly reflective glass framed in aluminum. The granite of the columns is polished (dark red) and that of the spandrels is flamed (light red). The granite recalls the red sandstone in which several of Frankfurt's architecturally significant buildings are clad, including the cathedral, the city hall, and portions of the Festhalle. The glass is energy conserving.

HVAC, Power, and Lighting. Tito Sarthou, TSP chief engineer, brought in mechanical/electrical consultants Jaros Baum and Bolles to completely redesign the systems to international standards, conserve space, and provide the flexibility, capacity, and control systems that a world-class office building aimed at an international market would have to have.

Germans and many other Europeans tend to object to cold air conditioning, drafts, and fan hums. When it is as hot as 95°F outside, Germans like their indoor air about 10°F lower. Because TSP was building for an international clientele, however, it wanted to be able to provide temperatures as low as Americans tend to like. The solution was twofold: high cooling capacity along with controls allowing room occupants to adjust temperatures and an overdesigned air-handling system with large fans that deliver the air at as low a speed and as noiselessly as possible.

Electrical power and lighting were also designed to international standards, which were higher than German standards. The offices are typically equipped with separate switches for the outside and inside ceiling light fixtures to accommodate German tenants' desire to control operating costs.

Fast-Tracking and Early Occupancy. Tenants began occupying lower-level floors in October 1990, 27 months after groundbreaking and ten months before the building was completed. Turning around a 42-month first-occupancy schedule to a 27-month schedule was largely a matter of convincing the contractor that it could be done. Accommodating occupancy before the upper portion of the building was complete became possible by dint of another "show-and-tell" effort.

In choosing the general contractor, TSP interviewed six contractors that had made bids before its involvement in the project. In its decision to go with Hochtief AG, the developer put great weight on the potential GC's responsiveness to new ideas and different ways of doing things. Hochtief was awarded the foundation and structural work alone, for a lump sum. If Hochtief subsequently could guarantee completion of the building at a mutually agreed target price, it would be retained. If not, TSP was free to hire another builder. While the foundation and early structural work proceeded, the developer and contractor value-engineered and refined the design. The developer eventually negotiated a fixed-price contract with Hochtief.

Charles DeBenedittis, TSP managing director responsible for design and construction, points out that value-engineering is not new to German and other European contractors, but that the usual modus operandi is a fixed-price design/build contract based on preliminary architectural drawings, under which it is in the contractor's interest "to value-engineer the hell out of the job by taking shortcuts and reducing quality." The difference in the construction of the MesseTurm is that the developer stayed involved in the process and retained the right of approval on all design choices.

To achieve its goal of early occupancy, the developer again had to convince doubtful public officials, as well as the contractor, that it could be safe and practical to bring tenants into the lower half of the building while major construction was still taking place on the upper portion. The life-safety consultant explained in great detail how the smoke detectors, sprinklers, stairway pressurization, and smoke purging system could operate under such conditions. Code officials and Hochtief construction managers were brought to New York and shown around a building whose structure was still going up while tenants occupied lower-level floors.

Construction Standards. From exterior window materials to the location of stairways, from window shades to carpet tiles, the developer found it necessary on countless components of the building to persuade the local officials—in a permitting process often led by the fire

A multizone elevator system was one of the major modifications of the building's original design that the developer undertook to save capital costs and appeal to an international market.

department rather than the building department—that its preferences were safe. Generally, what TSP was seeking was an updating of the codes, or the substitution of standards used elsewhere on first-class buildings for German standards that were either outdated or developed for buildings other than high-rise towers. "We spent many months proving to them that new systems were prudent," says Charles Reid, TSP's project manager for the Messe-Turm, "and we got some through and some not." The education process included tours of modern buildings in other European cities. In most cases, says DeBenedittis, "if you go through the procedures and take them through the testing—which can take a lot of time—the Germans are open and willing to make changes to building standards that are often unrealistic for modern office towers."

Determining German market preferences was a matter of much talking to office tenants and brokers, going through buildings, and, notably, working with Helmut Jahn, whose early architecture education was in Germany. Some local market preferences—for example, tiled floor-to-ceiling toilet partitions and marble finishes and polished metal handrails for fire stairs—proved too expensive. The speculative office market seems to have come around to accepting the U.S. style for many of these building elements.

An interesting case of local market adoption of a U.S. practice concerns drywall. In 1988, the Germans were using masonry and plaster or movable partitions to create interior office spaces. TSP arranged for a subcontractor to form a company to install drywall and brought in personnel in to run it. Within six months, says Reid, German builders from all over had begun to adopt this system and now it is widely used for speculative office buildings.

German standards for structural materials and finish materials are high, with fire safety and toxicity usually being the most prominent criteria. High material costs added to high labor costs make for buildings that on a square-foot basis can cost perhaps twice as much as they do in U.S. cities. The MesseTurm's facade, says DeBenedittis, may have cost disproportionately more than it would in New York, "but it never had a single leak in it, which is unheard of in the United States."

The German design/build culture caused some headaches in the developer's dealings with subcontractors, especially in the HVAC trades. Despite contracts that were quite specific, in the American style, as to what would be provided, mechanical contractors not infrequently would redesign on their own without telling TSP construction managers. They would, says Sarthou, take it upon themselves to decide that the chilled water capacity specified was excessive, and cut down on the size of the chillers. Some work had to be redone when such changes were made. In the United States, it is common for the various disciplines—mechanical, structural, and architectural—to work things out on paper via shop drawings. In Germany, it is common for tradespeople to work those things out in the field as they are measuring, cutting, and installing. TSP found the quest for good local engineering people who would adapt to its way of construction management to be very difficult.

Marketing

The strategy for marketing the MesseTurm was to create a project that would appeal to international tenants. But, given that Frankfurt was a new market for TSP and that the MesseTurm was coming in at the top of the Frankfurt market, the developer wanted to build in enough flexibility to attract German operations as well—and foreign operations with local employees. Thus, as noted, the design adhered to international standards while it took into account, as much as possible, the idiosyncrasies of German preferences in office environments. The air conditioning is customizable and unusually quiet and draft-free; the floors are very heavy to minimize noise; and tenants can easily opt to use all or only some ceiling lights as they see fit.

On the other hand, public areas are expensively finished and maintained to suit an image-sensitive clientele, although most German tenants would prefer lower maintenance costs. (Convincing the German companies that are MesseTurm tenants to pay added charges for top-notch maintenance was not an easy sell.) And despite Germans' strong preference for windows that open, the MesseTurm's are fixed. Other features and amenities that were designed to heighten the MesseTurm's international appeal include a high level of security (including card-operated turnstiles at the lobby level, lobby attendants, and a separate access system for deliveries),

concierge services, high-capacity electrical power with flexible distribution systems, and the building's high profile, literally and figuratively.

As it turned out, it was fortunate that the MesseTurm was designed flexibly to suit German tenants as well as the target group of companies. Two German tenants occupy more than 60 percent of the building's rentable area: Deutsche Bundesbank and Credit Suisse (Deutschland) AG. Many tenants—among them, international law firms, financial services firms, and the like—have used the MesseTurm like an incubator, testing the market from small spaces and growing into larger spaces as their businesses grew. Other businesses, naturally, failed to establish themselves in the marketplace and vacated. As of mid-1997, the building was 100 percent leased, with leases that tend to be long term. On balance, says Wharton, who was in charge of international leasing for TSP at the time of the MesseTurm's development, "the market has grown into the building" and the developer's confidence in the site and its willingness to hold out for tenants prepared to pay for world-class quality have been vindicated. The MesseTurm has achieved rents that are well above what the potential investors had been projecting before TSP arrived on the scene.

Experience Gained

Market insiders sometimes believe there is a limit to what can be done in their market, notes Katherine Farley. They are psychologically restrained by the existence of an indicator—perhaps a rent level—that has never been exceeded. Outsiders are not so hobbled. Investors in Frankfurt in the late 1980s did not think rents could go above 48DM because they never had. TSP, looking at the international business market, could take a broader view of Frankfurt's market potential and be confident in its conclusion that higher rents could be sustained. Farley adds that two other factors also helped give TSP an edge over most local investors. First, Europeans (excluding the British) are culturally uneasy with the concept of ground leases as a financing security. They would rather own the land. Second, the scale of the MesseTurm intimidated local investors who are used to buildings of about half its size or less.

Developing outside of one's culture presents a variety of challenges from etiquette to business customs. Compared with how it conducts business in the United States —informally, entrepreneurially—TSP found many cultural differences working in Germany. Relationships are much more formal, business dealings are not on a first-name basis, legal and loan documents are much simpler and shorter, and organizations are clearly structured with titles making plain who does what. In Germany, says Farley, "there's a rule for everything, which makes you nuts." But, she adds, at least the rules are out in the open, which makes working in Germany a lot easier than in some cultures in which even discovering the rules is a challenge.

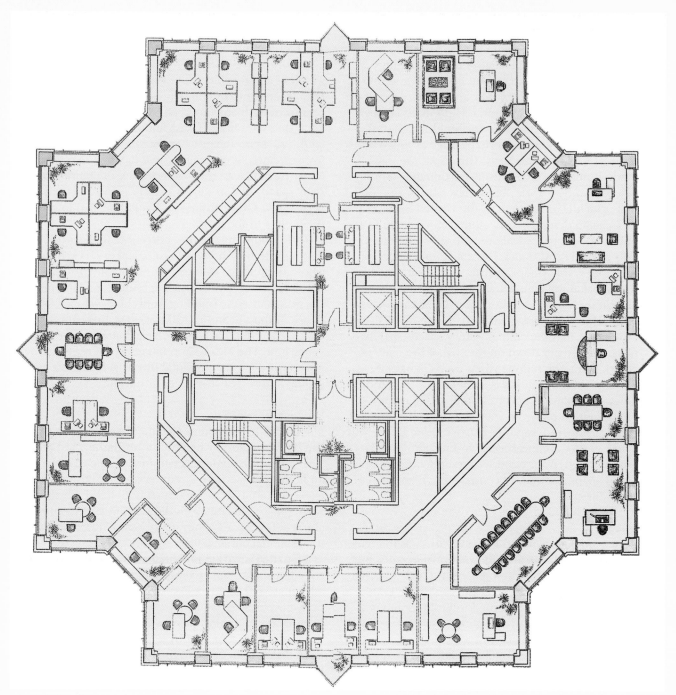

Typical floor plan.

Project Data: MesseTurm

Land Use and Building Information

Net Rentable Area (NRA)

Office	664,000 square feet
Retail	6,600 square feet
Storage	11,300 square feet
Total	681,900 square feet

Typical Floor Size — 12,400 square feet

Building Height — 72 stories

Parking (all structured)[1] — 930 spaces

Office Tenant Information

Occupied NRA — 100%

Largest Tenant Sizes

Credit Suisse (Deutschland) AG	212,000 square feet
Deutsche Bundesbank	203,000 square feet
Goldman Sachs & Company	37,000 square feet
Reuters AG	36,000 square feet

Developer

Tishman Speyer Properties
520 Madison Avenue
New York, New York 10022
212-715-0300

Property Manager

Tishman Speyer Properties of Frankfurt LP
MesseTurm
6000 Frankfurt/Main
Germany
069-9754-10

Architect

Murphy/Jahn Inc., Architects
35 East Wacker Drive
Chicago, Illinois 60601
312-427-7300

General Contractor

Hochtief AG
Bockenheimer Landstrasse 24
6000 Frankfurt/Main
Germany

Development Schedule

1/1988	Planning started
3/1988	Site leased
7/1988	Construction started
10/1990	Occupancy started
9/1991	Project completed

Note

[1] Parking is provided on two floors under the adjacent exhibition hall built by the Messe Frankfurt at the same time as the office building. An underground walkway connects the parking to the building.

Republic Plaza
Singapore

City Developments Ltd. (CDL), Singapore's largest property company, had two important goals in the development of Republic Plaza. One was to deliver top-quality office space to Raffles Place, Singapore's business and financial center. The other was to raise the construction standards for office space in this market. The developer succeeded in producing a visually expressive 66-story "crystal-cut" office building—as high as one can go in Singapore—that stands out on the city's skyline and offers exceptional building amenities. The tower and a ten-story building that shares the same podium together total 1.1 million square feet of space. A 95 percent occupancy rate is proof of its marketability. Beyond the space the project brought into the market, the development of Republic Plaza involved an innovative design and construction process that focused on advanced construction techniques, value-engineering, and the dependability of the building's infrastructure and other operating services. The development has won a number of international awards, both for its commercial real estate aspects and for its architecture and technical advances.

Development Process

Singapore is one of the most successful commercial and financial centers in its region. Its office sector is supported by thousands of local and multinational businesses. Raffles Place, the capital city's center of commerce, is home to numerous multinational companies and more than 200 financial and banking institutions.

The Republic Plaza site, which is a 999-year leasehold, enjoys good accessibility. Major roads flow directly to its entrance. A tunnel was built from the building's basement to a main station in the city's rapid-transit system through which run trains going all over the island.

The Hong Leong Group, CDL's parent company, acquired two of the nine land parcels making up the site in the 1980s. Acquisition of the remainder of the site required immense efforts over a considerable period of time. The CDL Group owns hotels and leisure facilities worldwide in Europe, the United States, Asia, and Australia. Its vision for Republic Plaza was to develop a dynamic landmark that would stand out on the Singapore skyline.

CDL brought together a multidisciplinary, multinational team. At the peak of activity, some 42 experienced project management, design, engineering, and construction professionals fielded 1,100 workers from 12 different countries.

The engineering and construction of the building were meticulously planned and managed, and value-engineering and design revisions were applied throughout the process, resulting in some significant saving. The focus of value-engineering ensured that money was spent on building performance and marketability.

Alternative designs were considered before each major design decision was made. And precise budgetary targets were set for each component. Overall, CDL shaved 15 percent off the building's square-foot construction cost compared with an earlier comparable building by the developer. The eventual design of the structural system, for example, was selected after the consideration of at least six approaches. The design chosen required 8,500 tons of steel, but did not entail any compromise in quality over an alternative that would have required 14,000 tons—almost two-thirds more.

The building was designed to stand on caissons, of which there are 14, each more than 16 feet in diameter. Detailed value-engineering resulted in caissons that are 35 percent more efficient than similar structures used for other tall buildings in the area. Twelve sophisticated remote-control excavators made the work of excavating for the caissons efficient.

Republic Plaza's small site (1.8 acres) and the proximity of underground rail structures made the foundation work particularly complex. Supporting the basement excavation required the design of a special ground-anchor system. Soil movement had to be controlled, which necessitated an instrumentation program. Rail tunnels were monitored to measure any distortion. In restricted areas near the tunnels, the rotary hammer method of installing pile casings was used to minimize vibration. The piles were engineered to ensure that no load transfer would be carried to the subway tunnels.

Precise timing and planning enabled the structural system to be erected in 574 days, which was two months faster than scheduled. The composite structure consists of a central reinforced concrete core to which an exterior steel frame is tied. The core was constructed with two independent, self-climbing jumpforms with hydraulic jets. These forms worked efficiently in a cycle of five days per floor, and the core construction was able to keep approximately three floors ahead of the steel erection at all times.

The steel columns were designed with welded fins for increased shear resistance at the lower level of the building. The crews used lasers to check the alignment of the columns, and results were fed back to the steel suppliers so that they could make adjustments for deviations in the steel fabricated for the next section of construction.

Republic Plaza stands at Singapore's financial hub. It is a state-of-the-art office building designed to resemble a quartz crystal.

The views from Republic Plaza of the city, the harbor, and the sea are an important marketing factor.

The lobby features polished granite and a cascading water fountain.

The design involves profile changes as the building rises, and these required the fabrication of special inclined sections. Specialist steel engineers from Japan worked on site for three months to assure the accuracy of alignment.

A rigorous quality-management system was put in place to control the construction of the curtain wall, which involved more than 10,000 separate panels. Complex sequencing was involved, from design and detailing in the United States to the incorporation of parts and accessories from many Asian countries, to assembly and weather sealing in Singapore. The construction managers used a global computer network to trace the manufacturing and delivery process for each component from when it was ordered until when it was installed. The panels were delivered to the site in floor-by-floor batches.

Limited ceiling space meant that special air-conditioning ducts were required and that the coordination of the mechanical, electrical, and communications systems would have to be carefully managed. A cage to hold all the wiring, pipes, and ducts was designed. These cages were fabricated on the site and installed floor by floor, resulting in faster jointing.

Republic Plaza was financed through shareholder equity and loans from two bank consortiums. The mortgage financing arrangement involved shared equity of 10 percent. The construction cost was approximately $200 million.

Design

Republic Plaza was conceptualized as a development that would be thoroughly compatible with the market and commercial priorities of the 21st century. The design by architect Kisho Kurokawa was inspired by the structure of a quartz crystal. It dramatizes the tower's verticality with profile changes made with crystal-like cuts. The lower portion of the building is octagonal and aligned with the streets. The upper portion is turned 45 degrees, not only to achieve the crystal effect, but also to capture views of

the harbor and the sea. Like a crystal, the tower has a pyramidal top. The building is clad in pink polished granite and features large expanses of tinted glass.

The project design incorporates many intelligent-building features. The typical floorplate ranges from 9,488 to 14,747 square feet and is column-free, providing optimum flexibility for space planning and design. Raised access flooring and trunk-line channels divided into three compartments and installed flush with the floor allow for flexibility in cabling for power and tele-communications within the office spaces. Knockout floor panels are provided to facilitate the construction of internal staircases for multifloor tenants and dedicated data risers are provided so that multifloor tenants can easily connect their computer and telephone networks.

Marketing considerations led the developer to install a highly efficient elevator system that includes 15 double-decker passenger elevators divided into two zones. Waiting times at peak hour are 17 seconds. The building offers

a flexible air-conditioning system that incorporates efficient zone and temperature controls, variable-air-volume air-handling units, a chilled water supply for after-hours office use, and a backup chiller. Parabolic mirror-optic light fittings provide energy-efficient lighting.

Two independent power sources along with four standby and two backup generators provide reliable and secure power. Tenants need not fear any disruption of work from power outages. Security features include closed-circuit TV monitors, door contact alarms, well-located guardstations, and a smart-card system that controls elevator access to the office floors after hours. Among the other intelligent-building features designed into Republic Plaza are a fully automated car-parking system, a fire-safety system with distributed intelligence that screens out false alarms, and a state-of-the-art automated building management system that enhances operational efficiency and tenant safety.

CDL joint ventured with the Club Corporation of America to create the exclusive Tower Club on the top

Different parts of the complex curtain wall were designed and fabricated around the world, and the developer used a global computer network to track the manufacturing and delivery processes for each component.

floors of the building. Membership is by invitation only. At the Tower Club, members enjoy a magnificent view of the city skyline as well as many club amenities, including dining facilities, private dining and function rooms, a boardroom, a health club, and private lockers for cigars.

Marketing and Management

Republic Plaza began preconstruction marketing in 1991 and an aggressive full-scale marketing program in 1993, which included media advertising, printed brochures, TV coverage, press releases, and videos produced for overseas audiences. Every development event such as groundbreaking or the initiation of another phase of the construction was made into a media event. Mock-up models of the lobby and office suites were built to demonstrate the high quality of the finishes. A dramatic view of surrounding buildings was provided in the walk-through models, and was a good selling feature.

Republic Plaza is represented by Jones Lang Wootton and managed by City Project Management Ltd., a subsidiary of CDL. The building was 70 percent preleased before the building was completed. One year after completion, it was 90 percent leased, and it is currently 95 percent leased and experiencing a high rate of lease renewals. Its completion ahead of schedule gave it a market advantage. With its premium location, outstanding views, high-quality design, advanced building infrastructure features, and exclusive amenities such as the Tower Club, Republic Plaza commands one of the highest office rental rates in Raffles Place.

The basic management philosophy is to be customer-oriented and proactive. Meeting the expectations and special needs of tenants is a management goal at every level of service. Management is selective in choosing tenants, in order to maintain the building's image.

Experience Gained

According to the developer of Republic Plaza, the process is where a development succeeds or fails. Teamwork, timing, and tenacity are the main elements of a successful project. Such developer attributes are probably most essential when the project involves an international construction and engineering team that requires skillful coordination. Selection of the contractor is crucial. The more prestigious the development, the more options the developer will have because many contractors want to be associated with an important building.

This project also proved the importance of flexibility and continuous reassessment. The design was complete when it was decided to increase the project's square footage by 100,000 square feet. Accommodating this change was challenging and the solution was innovative—the construction of a second tower over the podium, supported by the installation of more pilings below the building. And the addition improved the profitability of the development.

Finally, if an exclusive club is part of the project, membership can be jumpstarted by creating a well-connected board of governors. The Tower Club formed a 35-member board of governors and the board members introduced their friends to the club and the membership roster grew.

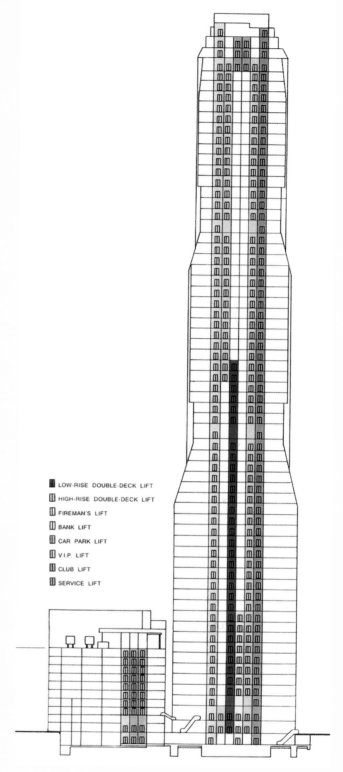

■ LOW-RISE DOUBLE-DECK LIFT
▥ HIGH-RISE DOUBLE-DECK LIFT
▥ FIREMAN'S LIFT
▥ BANK LIFT
▥ CAR PARK LIFT
▥ V.I.P. LIFT
▥ CLUB LIFT
▥ SERVICE LIFT

Tower section looking north. Fifteen double-decker elevators divided into two zones limit peak hour waiting times to 17 seconds.

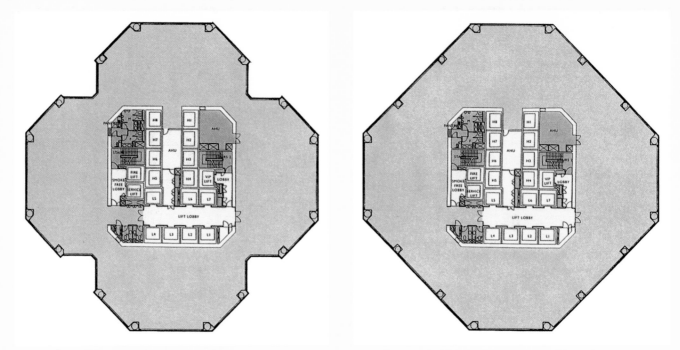

Plans of typical low-rise floors: 14th to 18th on left and 19th to 20th on right.

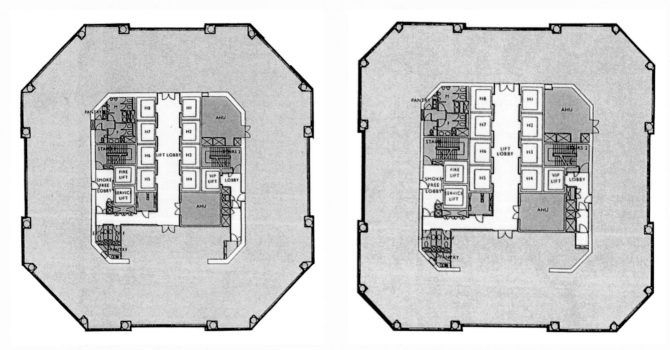

Plans of typical high-rise floors: 37th to 44th on left and 51st to 59th on right.

Project Data: Republic Plaza

Land Use and Building Information

Site Area	1.8 acres

Gross Building Area (GBA)

Office	746,500 square feet
Retail	37,400 square feet
Residential	116,100 square feet
Parking	143,800 square feet
Theater	56,200 square feet
Total	1,100,000 square feet

Net Rentable Area (NRA)	795,000 square feet
Typical Floor Size[1]	9,515–15,027 square feet
Building Height	66 stories
Floor/Area Ratio	14.14
Parking (all structured)	508 spaces

Office Tenant Information

Occupied NRA	95%
Average Annual Rent	$905–$132 per square foot
Average Length of Lease	3–6 years
Typical Terms of Lease	Rent includes service charges
Average Tenant Size	16,600 square feet

Major Tenant Sizes

Bank of Tokyo-Mitsubishi	80,000 square feet
Bank of America	75,000 square feet
ING Barings	55,000 square feet
Rabobank	40,000 square feet

Developer

City Developments Ltd.
36 Robinson Road
#20-01 City House
Singapore 068877, Singapore
65-221-2266

Architects

Kisho Kurokawa Architects and Associates
11th Floor Aoyama Building
1-2-3 Kita Aoyama, Minato-ku
Tokyo 107, Japan
03-3404-3481

RSP Architects Planners & Engineers Ltd.
15 Scotts Road
#07-00 Thong Teck Building
Singapore 228218, Singapore
65-737-7544

Development Schedule

1980s	First land leases
1990	Planning started
12/1991	Construction started
1996	Phase 1 completed
1997	Phase 2 completed

Note

[1] Net rentable area.

Audubon House
New York, New York

The National Audubon Society, one of the nation's leading environmental groups, has renovated a century-old, eight-story building into one of the most energy-efficient, environmentally responsible office buildings ever designed. In undertaking this project, Audubon's goal was to demonstrate that environmentally responsible development could be achieved at market cost using readily accessible, off-the-shelf technology and materials.

Audubon acquired the building, located at 700 Broadway in Lower Manhattan, in 1989 for $10 million. The former department store had been largely vacant for over ten years. By its reuse of an existing structure, the society hoped to realize direct economic, environmental, and social benefits.

Currently, the building's fourth through eighth floors provide office space for Audubon's 170 employees, the second and third floors are leased to other nonprofit organizations, and the ground level is leased for retail use. On the roof level are a newly built conference center and mechanical room.

Development Process and Approvals
Audubon had been paying more than $1 million a year to lease 40,000 square feet in a conventional high-rise office building. Given market conditions in New York in 1987, as well as the nonprofit firm's ability to secure tax-exempt financing, Peter Berle, the society's president, was convinced that building ownership was a cost-effective alternative.

Audubon chose the Croxton Collaborative as the project's architect and interior designer based on the firm's work on the Natural Resources Defense Council's headquarters space in Manhattan, a project that involved the renovation of four floors within a conventional office building in an environmentally sound manner. The architect chose Flack + Kurtz Consulting Engineers, a firm recognized for its expertise in the design of energy- and cost-efficient buildings, to oversee the Audubon project's engineering.

The Audubon House development team relied upon a multidisciplinary design approach in which the architect, engineer, interior designer, and owner collectively participated in the design and development process. Audubon scientists worked closely with the Croxton Collaborative throughout the design and specification process to evaluate the environmental impacts of materials and systems. All major design, engineering, and purchase decisions were tested against three criteria. Is it environmentally sound? Is it cost-effective? Can it be achieved through the use of off-the-shelf products that are readily available to everyone?

In analyzing the building's energy-related systems, the development team carefully projected their payback periods (a payback period being the amount of time it takes to offset any additional cost of a system with operational savings). The conventional development standard that says added costs should be paid back in two to three years was, Audubon perceived, shortsighted and inhibitive to environmentally responsible development. The developer therefore adopted a cumulative five-year maximum payback standard.

During the approval process, the development team encountered an unexpected obstacle: a New York City code that required Audubon to repair and strengthen the vaulting under the sidewalk so that structurally it could support a fully loaded fire truck. This unforeseen expense, together with the need to reinforce the roof's steel frame, added 15 percent to the cost of the project.

Design
The building's design and environmental performance focus on four key areas: energy conservation and efficiency; direct and indirect environmental impacts; resource conservation and recycling; and indoor-air quality.

The development team used the computer modeling software DOE-2, developed by the U.S. Department of Energy, to calculate the interplay between fundamental building components. Designers analyzed the relationships among the thermal shell (roof, perimeter walls, and windows), the HVAC system, and the electrical system, factoring in such influences on energy use as the building site, weather patterns, incoming daylight, and shadows. DOE-2 was able to calculate the relative financial savings associated with individual energy-saving devices as well as overall energy efficiency. A study grant from the local utility company, Con Edison, made the use of DOE-2 financially feasible.

The designers determined that decreasing the need for artificial light would substantially reduce energy consumption. In addition to daylighting techniques, the design incorporates an energy-efficient, state-of-the-art task-ambient lighting system to focus light where it is needed when it is needed. Occupancy and daylight sensors automatically adjust or terminate lighting based on need. The task-ambient design and use of natural lighting not only meet aesthetic standards, but also have been proven to increase worker productivity by reducing eyestrain, headaches, and fatigue.

The design and development of Audubon House successfully confront many of the environmental problems associated with the development of conventional office buildings, including excessive resource consumption, depletion of natural resources, and poor indoor air quality.

The design meets high standards for aesthetic appeal, habitability, building performance, and cost.

© Jeff Goldberg/Esto

© Jeff Goldberg/Esto

The architect also undertook a comprehensive upgrade of the building's thermal shell, which, because of the age of the building, required a complete retrofit of the structure with high-performance insulation. The development team searched widely for an environmentally benign, high-performance insulation, eventually selecting a product called Air-Krete. In addition, energy-efficient windows and skylights incorporating heat-mirror technology were installed. This readily available glass deflects the majority of the sun's radiant heat outward, keeping the interior cool in summer, and deflects convection heat inward, conserving heat in winter, while allowing the greater part of the visible light spectrum to pass through.

Upgrading the building's thermal shell helped the design team downsize the heating and cooling system by approximately 50 percent. All of the building's heating and cooling needs are met by a single source, a gas-fired chiller/heater located on the building's top floor.

The heating and cooling system is directly linked to an air-circulation system that delivers regular mandated infusions of filtered outside air at a rate of at least six changes per hour. The air-circulation system and its high ratio of fresh air were designed to combat indoor-air pollution. The project's cooling and ventilation system does not rely on a central air-distribution unit, but rather on air-handling units in fan rooms on each floor. Filtered air enters the building on the roof and is distributed directly to the fan rooms, where it is mixed with circulated return air. The circulation system's low-velocity airflow keeps moisture from being carried through, and the system's design prevents the accumulation of standing water. These features help prevent the growth of harmful bacteria and fungi.

The project established strict guidelines for the purchase and installation of building materials and products. Builders were required to use recycled building materials wherever possible. In addition, the content of potential building materials and furnishings was scrutinized to minimize chemicals and solvents, such as formaldehyde and benzene, that contribute to indoor-air pollution.

Construction

Not including the unexpected costs for the sidewalk vaulting and rooftop framing, the project's overall cost of $122 per square foot was well within the New York City market rate. The project's development cost excluding site acquisition was $146 per square foot. The Audubon Society's strict adherence to environmentally responsible design parameters and its choice of unconventional building materials made this renovation process quite unusual in several ways.

One departure from usual practices was that materials from the demolition were sorted and recycled. The demolition subcontractors were required to arrange for the recycling of masonry, concrete, metal, and other materials. This recycling of materials was successful, with the exception of glass and oil waste.

In the initial phases of construction, many of the subcontractors wanted to use more familiar, less expensive

Croxton Collaborative's strategic incorporation of custom-designed glass panels, along with skylights and floor-to-ceiling windows, throughout the office interior allows for maximum penetration of natural light.

materials. The design team was able to alleviate tensions caused by the strict material requirements by reiterating the goals of the project and pointing out the competitive advantage subcontractors could gain by acquiring skills with new materials.

Early in the renovation, the architect determined that a subfloor layer would have to be placed over the original floors, which were heavily damaged. Conventional subflooring is commonly made of interior grade plywood, which emits formaldehyde. The architect selected an alternative material, Homasote. Although residential builders had used Homasote for its superior acoustical properties, this was one of the first large-scale commercial applications of the material.

Audubon House was also one of the first commercial buildings to use Air-Krete insulation. New walls were constructed in the exterior cavity and filled with wet, air-blown Air-Krete foam, a material made of magnesium compounds mixed with dolomite that hardens like cement. Rigid fiberglass insulation was used on the roof.

Operational Savings

The energy-saving features installed in Audubon House were designed to reduce operating costs by an estimated $100,000 a year. The building was projected to use 62 percent less energy than a comparable code-compliant building.

The design and installation of the lighting system added approximately $92,000 to the cost of the renova-

Natural lighting helps to reduce energy consumption considerably. The building uses an estimated 62 percent less energy than a conventional building of comparable size.

tion. In return, lighting-efficiency was expected to reduce annual electricity expenses by $60,000. Also, Audubon received $31,000 in rebates from Con Edison for installing the energy-efficient lighting. Audubon estimated that the payback period for the lighting system would be approximately one year.

After a $72,000 conservation rebate from Con Edison, the cost of the gas-fired heater/chiller exceeded that of the most advanced electric cooling system available by $102,000. The compact unit was estimated to save approximately $18,000 in annual utility costs (compared with a conventional electric-powered unit) and to free up rentable space in the building worth roughly $15,000 annually. Audubon estimated that the payback period for the chiller/heater would be three to five years. The overall HVAC system (including variable-speed fans and other features) generates an additional $10,000 in annual savings.

Recycling chutes added about $185,000 to the cost of the renovation. Audubon's aggressive recycling program for the building was planned to reduce dramatically the organization's garbage hauling fees, which amount to $12,000 annually.

Audubon House's healthy work environment—its superior ventilation, air quality, and lighting—was expected to save the National Audubon Society thousands of dollars as a result of increased employee satisfaction, attendance, and productivity. Altogether, Audubon estimated that its decision to buy and renovate the 700 Broadway building would save the organization $1 million a year, compared with remaining at its old address.

Experience Gained

In developing this building, the National Audubon Society proved what it set out to prove: that an office building can be a star performer in environmental terms and economically. It is possible for developers to consider environmentally responsible design parameters—including energy efficiency, the sustainable use of resources, and healthy indoor-air quality—on an equal footing with the traditional criteria of cost, schedule, functionality, and aesthetics. Development practices can respond to many environmental concerns and still produce cost-effective and highly functional buildings.

In the operations phase, the owner/tenant learned that it takes time for a building like this with advanced energy-conservation technology to achieve its maximum projected efficiency. Managers need time to learn how to properly manipulate and monitor this technology in use.

The developer attributes the successful application of innovative technologies in the renovation process to its multidisciplinary design approach, which integrated the expertise of architects, interior designers, engineers, and environmental professionals throughout the development process. When Audubon House was being developed, information on what products and property management strategies are truly environmentally sound was limited. Since that time, in no small measure thanks to this project, the information base has expanded considerably.

Source: *Audubon House: Building the Environmentally Responsible, Energy-Efficient Office* (New York: John Wiley & Sons, 1994).

Project Data: Audubon House

Land Use and Building Information

Gross Building Area (GBA)

Office	90,300 square feet
Retail	20,700 square feet
Total[1]	111,000 square feet

Gross Leasable Area (GLA)

Retail	17,788 square feet

Building Height[2]	9 stories
Typical Floor Size	9,350 square feet

Development Cost Information

Site acquisition	$10,000,000
Renovation costs	14,000,000
Soft costs[3]	2,200,000
Total Development Cost	$26,200,000
Development Cost per Gross Square Foot	$236

Owner/Developer

The National Audubon Society
700 Broadway
New York, New York 10003
212-979-3000

Architect/Interior Designer

The Croxton Collaborative
1122 Madison Avenue
New York, New York 10028
212-794-2285

Development Schedule

12/1989	Site purchased
1/1990	Planning started
4/1991	Construction started
11/1992	Project completed

Notes

[1] Includes 22,700 square feet below grade.

[2] Includes rooftop level.

[3] Includes $1.4 million for architecture/engineering and $215,000 for project management.

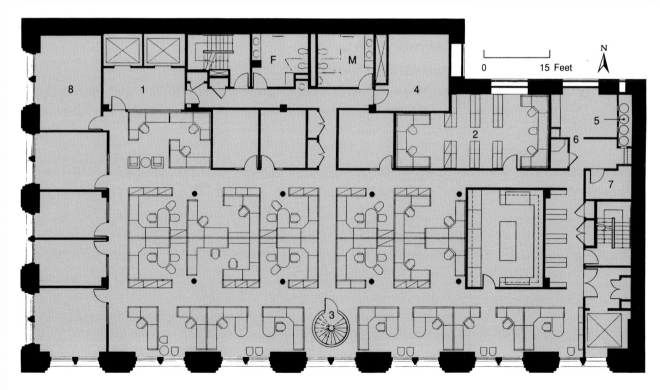

Key to Typical Floor Plan

1	Vestibule	5	Recycling Chutes
2	Library	6	Pantry/Copy Area
3	Convenience Stair	7	Electrical Closet
4	Mechanical Room	8	Conference Room

The Rookery

Chicago, Illinois

Following one of the most extensive restorations of a historic office building ever undertaken, the 109-year-old Rookery Building, located in the heart of Chicago's financial district, has reclaimed its former splendor. With painstaking exactitude, Baldwin Development Company and its restoration architect have brought back elements of the Rookery's three eras—Daniel Burnham and John Wellborn Root's original 1886 design, Frank Lloyd Wright's 1905 modernization of the interior, and a 1931 remodeling by William Drummond—while at the same time renovating the office floors to compete with the most expensive, recently constructed office space inside Chicago's Loop.

Though the Rookery was designated a National Historic Landmark in 1972, it stood blackened and crumbling from decades of neglect and artless makeshift alterations until the late 1980s. L. Thomas Baldwin III, a successful futures trader with no previous real estate experience, bought the building in 1988 and embarked on a three-and-a-half-year, $110 million labor-of-love restoration. Opening in 1992 in an oversupplied market, the Rookery nevertheless met with critical, leasing, and financial success.

Building History and Development Process

When the 12-story Rookery opened in 1886, it was one of the tallest and most expensive office buildings of its day, and also one of the first built on speculation. The Central Safety Deposit Corporation, the original developer and owner of the building, held the land on a 99-year lease from the city of Chicago. Central Safety Deposit owned the property until it reverted to the city in the early 1980s.

Occupying a quarter block on the corner of LaSalle and Adams streets, the Rookery was heralded for its hollowed-square plan, which gave every office direct exposure to natural light and ventilation, as well as for its many technological innovations. These advances included a metal-frame construction, one of the most extensive early uses of electricity, and the provision of hot and cold running water. The contrast between the Rookery's dark reddish-brown brick and granite exterior—often described as Richardsonian or Romanesque, yet in fact its own style—and the dazzling light and ornamentation inside is as striking today as it was 100 years ago.

John Wellborn Root's genius for making graceful use of light and space is evident in the Rookery's two-story light court and the cast-iron glass-enclosed oriel stairs that spiral up the 12-story light well. The light court, with its lacy glass ceiling, mosaic floor, and curvilinear staircases,

received immediate acclaim. In 1905, when Root's heavily ornamented interior surfaces were thought to be dated, Frank Lloyd Wright was hired to modernize the public spaces. Without making any structural changes to the building, Wright reclad much of Root's cast-iron ornamentation with expanses of white Carrara marble, nearly every surface of which was covered with intricate Moorish style incising filled with gold leaf.

In 1931, William Drummond, who once worked for Wright, won a design competition to modernize the building. The Drummond modernization made significant structural alterations to the Rookery. The two-story street entrance lobbies were gutted and rebuilt as single-story spaces, and the original four marble staircases were removed from the entrances. Also, the original hydraulic open-cage elevators were replaced with electric elevators in enclosed shafts and elegant elevator doors were installed that are still in use today. During the next 50 years, numerous small alterations diminished the original design of the building. The most unfortunate of these was the tarring over of the glass ceiling above the light court, apparently to prevent leaks.

When ownership of the Rookery reverted to the city of Chicago in the early 1980s, the city realized that extensive work was required to make the landmark building functional. It decided to sell the property while retaining easements to preserve the architectural integrity of the exterior and key interior spaces. In 1983, Continental Illinois Bank, whose headquarters was located next door, bought the Rookery and announced a five-year restoration plan. The bank had completed a thorough cleaning of the outside of the building when financial misfortune forced it to halt the renovation and put the Rookery back on the market.

In December 1988, L. Thomas Baldwin bought the 293,962-square-foot Rookery from Continental for $28 million cash, formed Baldwin Development Company, and began to assemble a team to renovate the building. It took nearly two years to obtain financing, which came from Europe after 100 top U.S. banks turned down the project. The original construction loan came from ING Bank in the Netherlands. A Dutch real estate fund came in as a joint venture partner, and a major U.S. corporation made an additional equity contribution in return for restoration tax credits plus a share of the residual value. The project qualified for a 20 percent federal tax credit on the total construction cost, amounting to $14.5 million. No other incentives were available for preservation.

Designed by Daniel Burnham and John Wellborn Root in 1886 and later modernized by Frank Lloyd Wright, the Rookery stood vacant and deteriorated in downtown Chicago until the late 1980s. Now restored to its historical grandeur, the Rookery sets the standard for the renovation of landmark office buildings.

Nick Merrick—Hedrich-Blessing/Baldwin Development Company; and McClier Corporation

Design and Renovation

Baldwin was determined to disprove the widely accepted notion that historic buildings are not Class A buildings and that the cost of expensive, high-quality restoration cannot be recovered in rents. Baldwin's strategy was to restore the Rookery's historic architectural features and to incorporate up-to-the-moment heating, air-conditioning, electrical, elevator, security, and telecommunications systems into the upper office floors without losing the feeling of the old building. Essentially, floors three through 12 would be a gut rehab with the exception of the old Burnham and Root library on the 11th floor, which would be fully restored.

The development team did not attempt to restore the Rookery to its original design. Rather, the team restored elements from the building's major design and construction eras in some instances, reconstructed them in others, and added some new features. The focus of the restoration was to return the first two floors—the public spaces—to the Wright period. Thomas "Gunny" Harboe of McClier Corporation, chief restoration architect for the project, used surviving documentation of the building and fragments of original materials as guides in reconstructing the light court and street lobbies. Researchers made use of microscopes and computers to discern and replicate original materials, colors, and patterns. Workers

employed some decidedly low-tech materials techniques as well. For example, they laboriously removed 20 coats of paint from the copper-plated cast-iron oriel stairs by means of low-pressure dry-blasting with crushed walnut shells.

Harboe tracked down dozens of sources for the specialized materials and craftsmanship needed to restore the public spaces. For instance, after sandblasting the iron fretwork in the light court ceiling, workers replaced the tarred and painted-over original glass with 5,000 pieces of clear patterned glass fabricated in Tennessee. A Chicago foundry used cast aluminum to duplicate the patterned cast-iron fronts of the stores that face the light court. Harboe traveled to Italy to select the 25,000 square feet of Carrara marble needed to reconstruct the LaSalle and Adams street lobbies as they were in the Wright era.

As much as 200 ounces of 23-carat gold leaf was used to fill in the arabesque patterns incised into Wright's white marble walls and columns. A particularly tough challenge was replicating the double-ribbed glass globes in the ten Frank Lloyd Wright light fixtures hanging in the light court. A small firm in Pennsylvania finally made them to Harboe's satisfaction. Among the restoration details for the many-splendored light court, the reconstruction of Root's mosaic floor (which had been torn out in the

A 1930 remodeling completely destroyed the two-story space of the LaSalle Street lobby. The lobby's reconstruction had to replicate the Burnham and Root walls and the Wright stairs to reflect the developer's aim of restoring the building to its 1910 look.

Drummond modernization) is the crowning touch. The new floor was crafted locally with Portuguese marble at a cost of $1 million.

An important feature that was added to the building is a glass roof capping the open light well. The simple glass roof protects the ceiling of the light court ten floors below as well as the original walls of the light well, which are white glazed with yellowish terra-cotta banding over the windows.

Tenants and Financial Performance

The Rookery opened in May 1992 with 48 percent of the space leased, at a time when commercial space in downtown Chicago was extremely oversupplied. Brooks Brothers opened a 12,174-square-foot store on the ground floor of the building before renovation was completed. Other early tenants were Brinson Partners, a financial trading firm that occupied the top three floors, and Quantum Financial Services, which leased one floor. As of early 1995, the office space was 86 percent leased and the retail space was 77 percent occupied. The Rookery's average asking lease rates of $26 per square foot for office space and $32 to $54 per square foot for retail space match those of the newest Class A space.

The 24,000-square-foot office floors have varying floor-to-floor heights. Brinson Partners, still the largest tenant,

has expanded into another floor, leasing a total of 92,978 square feet, and has plans to lease half of an additional floor. On average, office tenants lease 15,000 square feet of space. The Rookery has added six new retail tenants on the ground and mezzanine levels since Brooks Brothers moved in: Ameritech Cellular Services, Copies Now, Papyrus, Scudder, Wall Street Deli, and Quick & Reilly.

The success of the Rookery can be measured with several yardsticks. The restoration of this architectural treasure, for example, has received many honors and awards. More important than design awards, however, from a real estate perspective, is the building's success with tenants as demonstrated by the top rental rates it commands and its healthy occupancy level. Finally, in the words of Robert Fraley, chief financial officer for Baldwin Development Company, "the combination of some creative financing, rapid lease-up, and a stroke of luck on interest rates has enabled the Rookery to meet its required debt service."

Experience Gained

The Rookery is an outstanding restoration. The developer's strategy of restoring historic architectural interiors on the ground and mezzanine levels while adding state-of-the-art HVAC, electrical, elevator, security, and telecommunications systems on the office floors succeeded

Workers painstakingly removed 20 coats of paint from the copper-plated cast-iron oriel staircase by dry-blasting with crushed walnut shells.

in retaining the feeling of the old building while providing Class A office space. This project sets the standard for future commercial renovations and proves that the cost of expensive, high-quality restoration can be recovered in Class A rents.

The Rookery project underlines the importance of thorough research to properly determine the real scope of a historical building restoration project. Details are essential. It is important to assemble the complete proj-

ect team early in the game, so that each member has full knowledge of the scope and objectives as the project evolves. And it is also important to be flexible and careful. Exploratory demolition at the Rookery, for example, uncovered salvageable or reproducible original historic elements.

The hollowed-square plan gives inside offices exposure to natural light and ventilation. The new glass roof protects the ceiling of the light court ten floors below.

The two-story light court was restored to its Frank Lloyd Wright period. Storefronts face the lobby on the ground and mezzanine levels. Office floors overlook the light court's sparkling ceiling, which is made up of 5,000 pieces of glass.

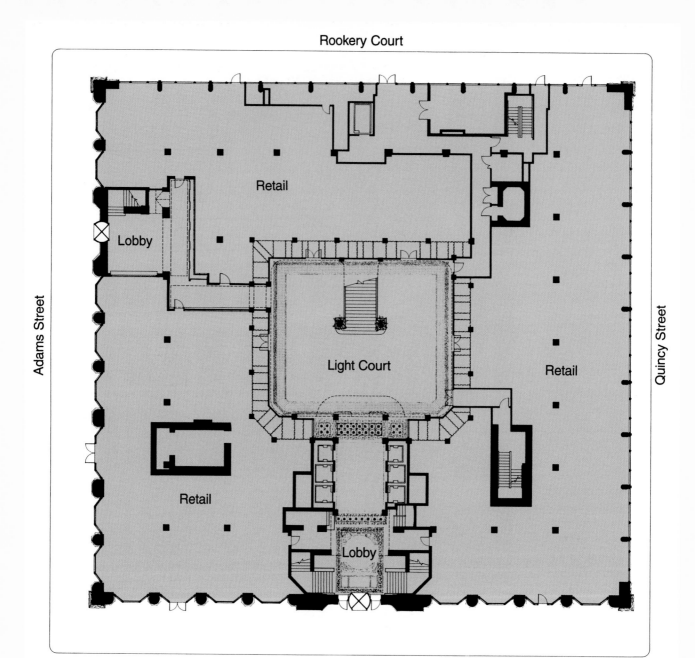

Ground-floor plan.

Project Data: The Rookery

Land Use and Building Information

Site Area	1 acre
Gross Building Area (GBA)	293,962 square feet

Net Rentable Area (NRA)

Office	211,314 square feet
Retail	22,374 square feet
Other	11,234 square feet
Total	244,922 square feet

Typical Floor Size	24,000 square feet
Building Height	12 stories
Floor/Area Ratio	6.75

Office Tenant Information

Occupied NRA	86%
Average annual rent	$26 per square foot
Average length of lease	10 years
Typical tenant size	15,000 square feet
Largest tenant size	92,978 square feet
Number of tenants	12

Retail Tenant Information

Occupied NRA	77%
Annual rents	$32–$54 per square foot
Average length of lease	10 years
Average tenant size	3,685 square feet
Number of tenants	6

Development Cost Information

Site Costs

Site acquisition	$27,120,000
Curbs/sidewalks	77,000
Demolition	1,840,000
Total	$1,917,000

Construction Costs

Base restoration	$20,776,000
Tenant finishes	25,715,000
Permits	227,000
Total	$46,718,000

Soft Costs

Architecture/engineering	$1,384,000
Project management	4,922,000
Leasing/marketing	2,568,000
Legal/accounting	1,153,000
Taxes/insurance	2,531,000
Construction interest and fees	19,678,000
Consultants	1,044,000
Total	$33,280,000

Total Development Cost	$109,035,000
Development Cost per Gross Square Foot	$371
Development Cost per Net Square Foot	$445

Developer

Baldwin Development Company
209 South LaSalle Street
Suite 400
Chicago, Illinois 60604
312-553-6100

Owner

Rookery Partners Limited Partnership
209 South LaSalle Street
Suite 400
Chicago, Illinois 60604
312-553-6100

Restoration Architect

McClier Corporation
401 East Illinois
Suite 625
Chicago, Illinois 60611
312-836-7700

Development Schedule

12/1988	Site purchased
1/1989	Planning started
1/1990	Construction started
1/1991	Leasing started
5/1992	Project completed

State Street Bank Building

Boston, Massachusetts

Today, many owners of high-rise office towers built in the 1960s and 1970s are faced with the decision of whether to invest in extensive renovations in an effort to compete with the newer generation of office buildings, or risk slipping into Class B status. Hexalon Real Estate, owner of the State Street Bank Building at 225 Franklin Street in downtown Boston, took this gamble and proved that older office buildings can have enduring value. Built in 1964, the 34-story building was the first modern skyscraper constructed in Boston's financial district. As one of only two buildings in Boston's skyline with a lighted sign—a result of the city's prohibition of such signs in 1966—State Street Bank has been a familiar landmark for generations.

In 1978, Hexalon Real Estate, a REIT managed by CGR Advisors in Atlanta, bought the office building from C.P.I., the property's previous owner. However, State Street Bank, the building's anchor tenant, retained a purchase option as a condition of the sale and continued to operate in the building. In 1985, with Boston's building boom in full swing, Hexalon bought the bank's option. Despite the building's healthy 95 percent occupancy, the new owner knew the status of the building was deteriorating along with its value. Inherent safety concerns as well as a state law requiring the installation of sprinkler systems in all Boston's commercial buildings by January 1, 1997, prompted Hexalon to address the presence of asbestos in the building. The loss of a 170,000-square-foot law firm and the occupancy of a major tenant at below-market rates further compromised the building's future economic viability. In addition, State Street Bank, which occupied approximately 450,000 square feet, was considering moving to new Class A office space.

In 1987, Hexalon made the decision to reposition the building. The REIT then hired LaSalle Partners to implement the repositioning and manage the property. In early 1989, a three-phase repositioning project was initiated that included improvements to the plaza, lobby, and building systems; an extensive asbestos abatement program; and new tenant finishes (which were made necessary by the abatement program). A significant portion of this internally financed renovation was completed by March 1994. The final phase covering the building's midrise portion (floors 13–22) was delayed until November 1995, when the space was vacated, and was completed in 1997.

In May 1997, Beacon Properties Corporation purchased the State Street Bank Building from Hexalon for $275 million (or $254 per gross square foot), and Beacon Management Company took over as the property manager.

Repositioning Strategy

Hexalon Real Estate and LaSalle Partners began the repositioning by taking a hard look at the State Street Bank Building's strengths and weaknesses. Among the building's strengths they counted its desirable downtown location, many advantageous design features such as efficient floorplates and large window bays, the spectacular views of Boston it offered, its proximity to public transportation (in a downtown where over 75 percent of employees use public transportation), and various amenities —including a spacious plaza and parking. Parking was available both in the building and at the adjacent Post Office Square park and garage complex, of which Hexalon was an equity shareholder. Among the building's most significant weaknesses were the presence of asbestos, antiquated building systems, and some aesthetic drawbacks. The HVAC, fire protection, and elevator systems needed upgrading. The black-slate exterior plaza was nondescript. The wood-paneled lobby was austere, vast, and dark. The tenant-floor finishes were, in most cases, nearly 25 years old.

After comparing the estimated costs of renovation with the expected improvement in lease economics, Hexalon elected to proceed with a major repositioning program in early 1989. At this time, the Boston office market was showing signs of deteriorating. The owner wanted to complete the first phase of the repositioning program before Class A lease rates declined dramatically.

Design

Altering the building's precast concrete exterior to give it a modern look would have entailed enormous costs. It was decided to simply thoroughly clean the exterior and concentrate the renovation dollars where they could make the greatest impact—on the plaza, lobby, and building systems. The idea was to make no apology for the building's 31-year-old exterior and to greet visitors with the impression of a modern, first-class office building from their first step into the lobby.

The 32,000-square-foot plaza that encompasses the building on all sides was completely repaved with two types of granite pavers. Numerous large raised flower beds were added, each one surrounded by fine marble benches. Viewed from street level, the inviting plaza softens and modernizes the exterior and creates a more enticing approach to the building.

© Peter Vanderwarker. Courtesy of Jung/Brannen Associates Inc.

The renovated State Street Bank Building continues to be a landmark on the Boston skyline. Renovation dollars were spent where they would have the most impact—on the outside plaza, the lobby, the building systems, and asbestos abatement.

The lobby has been upgraded to Class A status with polished Italian marble, mahogany panels, and soft recessed lighting.

Mahogany latticework carries the design theme throughout the lobby level.

The fully renovated lobby tastefully incorporates finishes of late 1980s elegance—three varieties of Italian marble, polished bronze, and mahogany paneling and latticework. New mechanical, plumbing, and electrical systems were installed, as well as an emergency electrical system. The elevator system was modernized and the cabs were architecturally renovated.

Construction

The 33 tenant floors above the lobby level of the building are divided into three sections—low-rise (floors 2–12), mid-rise (floors 13–22), and high-rise (floors 23–33)—each served by an independent bank of elevators. Because the building was heavily occupied during the renovation, the construction was scheduled in phases. LaSalle Partners believed it was imperative that the tenants' daily business operations be interrupted as little as possible. From the beginning, LaSalle stayed in constant communication with the tenants, letting them know what to expect during each step of construction, and responding to their concerns.

The first phase of the repositioning program—the renovation of the main lobby, plaza, elevators, and other public areas—was substantially completed by late 1990. To minimize tenant disruption, half of the lobby was completely renovated before work on the second half began. Work in the elevator lobbies was also scheduled in phases to ensure that appropriate access to all floors was maintained. Elevators that served fully occupied floors were refurbished mostly at night and during the weekends. The renovation of the plaza was as carefully scheduled as the interior renovation. The schedule allowed work on only three of eight sections of the plaza at one time, thus maintaining access to two of the four lobby entrances throughout the process.

The first phase of the program also included renovation of the 11 floors in the high-rise section of the building (floors 23–33), which began in March 1990 and was completed in early 1991. The general contractor had the luxury of working primarily in vacated space for this part of the project.

Phase 2 involved the 11 low-rise office floors (floors 2–12) and was the most challenging in terms of scheduling and logistics. State Street Bank had renewed its lease for this space in 1990, so the asbestos abatement, which must be done in a totally contained environment, had to take place in occupied space. Furthermore, the comprehensive nature of the tenant fit-out mandated that the floors be empty for the contractors. To isolate contractor workspace and keep the tenant functioning at the same time, bank operations were relocated two floors at a time to temporary office space located on vacant high-rise floors. The renovation of the low-rise floors and the restacking of State Street Bank was completed in early 1994. The final phase of the repositioning of the building began in November 1995, when the mid-rise space (floors 13–22) was vacated. These floors again opened for occupancy in January 1997.

Marketing

The renovation had a significant impact on tenant retention, specifically that of the anchor tenant, State Street Bank. Hexagon's ability to convince State Street Bank that the renovation would transform the building into a facility that would be functionally and aesthetically competitive with new buildings resulted in the tenant renewing its lease for a 20-year term. Another 225,000 square feet of space in the high-rise section was leased before the renovation of that section was complete and the remaining 250,000-square-foot, mid-rise section was leased to several smaller tenants.

The repositioning of the State Street Bank Building generated an approximate 25 percent improvement in lease economics on the first 700,000 square feet leased after the renovation was started. This represents the approximate difference in rental rates between Class A and Class B buildings in Boston from 1989 to 1992, the period when most of this space was leased. The building's new rental competitiveness confirms that the renovation has secured the State Street Building's position as one of the city's premier Class A office buildings.

Experience Gained

LaSalle emphasizes that tenant relations is a key element in the renovation of an occupied building. Developers should do whatever is reasonably possible to minimize disruption of tenants' daily business activities. Communication with tenants and neighboring buildings is vital. Tenants and neighbors are more tolerant of the unavoidable inconveniences caused by a major renovation if they have been fully informed about the program, the plans, and the end result, and if they have up-to-date information concerning current renovation activities.

Tenant relations are also served by giving the project early credibility. The decision to completely renovate half of the lobby before starting the second half turned out to be a winner. Although this was not the least expensive approach, it had the advantage of enabling existing and prospective tenants to fully appreciate the finished product at an early stage.

The behavior of contractors is a similarly important part of tenant relations. Developers should view the contractors as building employees. LaSalle Partners held contractors to the same high standards regarding tenant service that it holds for its own employees. In the eyes of the tenants, the contractors working in the building during the renovation were direct extensions of the owner and manager. The attitude and demeanor of contractors did much to defuse potential problems with tenants during the renovation of the State Street Bank Building.

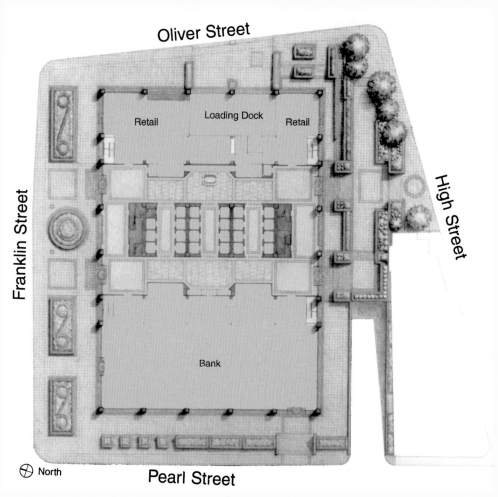

Site plan.

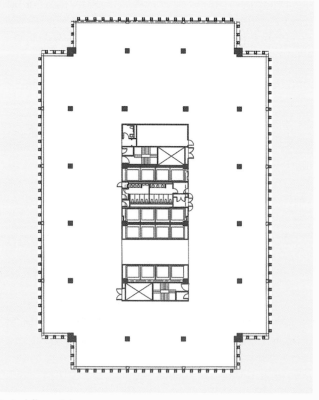

Typical floorplate.

Project Data: State Street Bank Building

Land Use and Building Information

Site Area	1.2 acres
Gross Building Area (GBA)	1,080,821 square feet
Net Rentable Area (NRA)	916,637 square feet

Typical Floor Size

Floors 1–5	50,000 square feet
Floors 6–33	25,000 square feet

Floor/Area Ratio	20.68
Parking (all underground)	200 spaces

Land Use Plan

	Acres	Percent of Site
Buildings	0.8	67%
Landscaped areas	0.4	33
Total	1.2	100%

Office Tenant Information

Occupied NRA[1]	100%
Average Annual Rent[2]	$36 per square foot
Length of Leases[2]	5–10 years
Typical Terms of Lease[2]	10-year term; gross rent; annual escalations for operating expenses and real estate taxes

Tenant Sizes[2]

Largest tenant	450,000 square feet
Next largest tenant	250,000 square feet
Other tenants	14 tenants of various sizes occupy the remaining 216,000 square feet

Development Schedule

1978	Site purchased
1987	Planning started
1989	Construction started
1989	Leasing started
1990	Phase 1 completed
1994	Phase 2 completed
1995	Phase 3 completed
1997	Property sold[3]

Renovation Cost Information

	Phase1	Phase 2	Phase 3	Total
Plaza	$4,328,000	–	–	$4,328,000
Lobby	5,451,000	$494,000		5,945,000
Public areas	1,629,000	779,000	$1,336,000	3,744,000
Arch maintenance	2,085,000	1,003,000	901,000	3,989,000
Restacking	–	1,684,000	–	1,684,000
Life safety	2,260,000	985,000	737,250	3,982,250
HVAC	8,570,000	7,103,000	2,807,000	18,480,000
Elevators	1,731,000	–	465,000	2,196,000
Plumbing	244,000	138,000	–	382,000
Electrical	1,764,000	1,697,000	–	3,461,000
General contractor fees	6,516,000	1,620,000	1,034,000	9,170,000
Asbestos abatement	11,796,000	10,582,000	6,697,000	29,075,000
Consultants	4,907,000	1,523,000	320,000	6,750,000
Administrative	2,157,000	1,036,000	508,000	3,701,000
Bus duct	–	1,310,000	–	1,310,000
Total	$53,438,000	$29,954,000	$14,805,250	$98,197,250

Total Development Cost	$98,197,250
Development Cost per Gross Square Foot	$91
Development Cost per Net Square Foot	$107

Property Manager[3]

LaSalle Partners Management Limited
225 Franklin Street
Boston, Massachusetts 02110
617-451-9700

Owner[3]

Hexalon Real Estate Inc.
950 East Paces Ferry Road
Atlanta, Georgia 30326
404-266-1002

Architect

Jung/Brannen Associates Inc.
177 Milk Street
Boston, Massachusetts 02109
617-482-2299

Notes

[1] As of May 1997.

[2] As of December 1995.

[3] In May 1997, Hexalon sold the property to Beacon Properties Corporation (617-439-3131); it is now managed by Beacon Management Company (617-227-6743).

101 Hudson

Jersey City, New Jersey

101 Hudson is a 1.2 million-square-foot Class A office tower with ground-floor retail. It was built essentially to the specifications of its major tenant. The building is the first project in Colgate Center, a master-planned, mixed-use community on a prime waterfront location that offers spectacular views and is well served by transit. It was designed to meet the special power, HVAC, and space planning needs of its target market—the technology-driven operations and technical support divisions of major financial services firms.

Conceived and built during a difficult time for office development, 101 Hudson carefully targets the technology-driven operations and technical support divisions of financial services companies—users with special space and building infrastructure needs. The developer, LCOR Incorporated, ascertained these needs through its office development experience and six months of discussions with a space search team from Merrill Lynch.

The building rises 42 stories. It is the first development in the 42-acre Colgate Center, a master-planned, mixed-use business district on the Jersey City waterfront where Colgate-Palmolive manufactured consumer products into the 1980s. The 15-year master plan calls for 6 million square feet of office space, along with more than 1,200 residential units, 300,000 square feet of retail space, a hotel, and a marina. When the development of 101 Hudson started, the Jersey City office market had a vacancy rate of 35 percent. Completed in 1992, the building was fully leased about 18 months later at rents that met the pro forma expectations.

Site

The views from Colgate Center are among the most spectacular in the world. The Statue of Liberty and Ellis Island are clearly visible to the south, and it looks as if the World Trade Center would span the Hudson River if it were to topple westward. The public transportation network serving the site is similarly impressive. The World Trade Center is three minutes away by PATH subway.

Before Colgate closed on the site, it secured zoning in accordance with a master plan created by Brennan Beer Gorman/Architects, the firm that also would design 101 Hudson. The company then demolished the existing manufacturing structures in conformity with a state-approved site cleanup plan. The city street grid was extended to the waterfront to link the development to the Paulus Hook neighborhood to the west. Paulus Hook is a recently gentrified residential area that had housed many of the workers at the Colgate plant. The master

plan emphasizes high standards of design, the preservation and reestablishment of view corridors, and open space—particularly along the waterfront.

Colgate-Palmolive had been the city's largest employer. To attract new jobs, the waterfront was designated a state urban enterprise zone (UEZ), and 101 Hudson was able to qualify for a tax abatement that fixes real estate taxes at 2 percent of the construction costs for a 15-year period, providing a significant marketing advantage. Furthermore, tenants in the building can qualify for unemployment tax breaks, hiring tax incentives, and a waiver on sales taxes on the purchase of goods and services used on site.

Development Process

In 1988, LCOR offered a contract on the site (with closing set for the end of 1989) in order to secure a major tenant and financing. The developer began meeting with a project team from Merrill Lynch in early 1989. At the weekly or biweekly meetings, Merrill Lynch explained its requirements, and the developer refined the schematic design to meet them. As the design and basic economics of the project were evolving, Merrill Lynch was evaluating locations throughout the metropolitan region. Finally, the securities firm decided to pursue a New Jersey location, and among the alternatives was 101 Hudson—a building that had been designed to its specifications. In August 1989, Merrill Lynch made a commitment to lease 600,000 square feet—half the building.

LCOR had only five months to close the deal with Colgate. It put together a traditional financing package that included equity from the State Teachers Retirement System of Ohio and debt in the form of a construction miniperm loan from the Bank of Montreal and Tokai Bank. Merrill Lynch required occupancy of its space by January 1992, which meant an aggressive construction schedule. Ground was broken in January 1990. To meet the schedule, Merrill Lynch completed its tenant installation while LCOR completed the core and shell. The building came in on time and on budget.

Design

The 75,000-square-foot site was large enough to allow the architects to give Merrill Lynch the large floors it wanted. The developer carried the base-building specifications it had negotiated with Merrill Lynch through to the upper floors. 101 Hudson was designed from the inside out for users with high-energy and other nonstandard requirements. Slab-to-slab heights are generous—13'10"—giving most of the building nine-foot ceilings over eight-inch

The location of 101 Hudson just across the river from Lower Manhattan offers tenants quick and easy access to many points in the region.

Lenscape Inc.

In keeping with the design guidelines of the Colgate Center master plan and the preferences of its corporate tenants, the building was designed to have a conservative, substantial appearance. It has the distinction of being the tallest building in New Jersey.

raised floors. The live load on clear spans is a high 100 pounds per square foot. Column-free, 45-foot clear spans from the core to the outside wall on all sides are the rule —accommodating the wall-to-wall installation of 15-foot square, four-workstation modules. Notched corners bring more light into the interior, an important consideration for open offices, and provide extra corner sites for closed offices. The deep clear spans were made possible by incorporating a dedicated circulation corridor in the core. Two oversized freight elevators handle the heavy pallets of paper that Merrill Lynch continually moves in.

Uninterrupted power supply is a major concern for high-tech office space users. 101 Hudson's electrical system provides seven watts per square foot as the building standard, with riser capacity of up to 11 watts. Emer-

gency generators are similarly high powered, and battery farms are installed on the mechanical floor (the 15th). Electricity is delivered to the building by dual feeds, providing redundancy. The electric utility, Public Service, supplies the electricity from its most state-of-the-art substation, which also incorporates redundancies.

A sophisticated HVAC system offers building standard cooling designed to handle a cooling load of eight watts per square foot—delivered through tenant-controlled air-handling units on each floor—and supplemental chilled water designed to handle 11 watts per square foot. The building is also equipped with two domestic water feeds and nine fiberoptic feeds from three vendors.

The exterior design uses rich materials and textures for the first 50 feet of the building and then makes a

101 Hudson is the first building in Colgate Center, a 16-parcel master plan for a 24-hour urban district with a waterfront orientation.

Courtesy of LCOR

subtle transition to precast concrete. The award-winning precast spandrels have a distinctive, molded chevron pattern. A grand entrance and lobby announce that this is a Class A building. Parking is located on four levels above the lobby.

Marketing

Except for some of the small tenancies that took space on the multitenant floors, most tenants actually need the advanced power and communications capabilities that the building offers. These include Lehman Brothers, which leased 400,000 square feet; Prebon Yamane, a currency trading company; other trading operations; a compensation consultant; and a communications company that has installed a switching station to service the New York metropolitan area.

Occupancy costs are a major selling point for 101 Hudson. Construction methods, measurement standards, and operating procedures combine to make rents highly competitive. In addition, the Jersey City UEZ offers incentives—sales and real estate tax abatement, lower utility rates, and employment benefits—that make the financial package even more attractive.

Management

101 Hudson provides its tenants gross services while using a net lease concept. To the extent possible, each tenant has separately metered chilled water and electricity. Each tenant has an industrial cleaning contract. A work-order system allocates expenses directly to each tenant for its use of building staff services.

Experience Gained

The building's design has proved to be highly marketable. Tenants seeking technologically advanced infrastructure have found considerable built-in value at affordable prices at 101 Hudson. LCOR has become the development manager for Colgate Center and is contemplating another office building, this one about 430,000 square feet, which

it will design to incorporate the same kind of technology amenities and building infrastructure.

Providing building services à la carte, the developer has learned, goes a long way toward eliminating friction with tenants over service charges.

In the developer's view, spending more money on the exterior would have raised rents, but it would not necessarily have added value. By adding a granite base to a well-designed precast, non–curtain wall tower, the developer was able to construct a building that is both attractive and durable.

This project underlines the value of targeting the specific needs of office users in the design of the building. Everything that was done for Merrill Lynch made it easier to lease the rest of the building to tenants with similar needs. Every element of the design was driven by a specific user need. The design includes no frills or gimmicks for their own sake, and thus has produced a highly functional and efficient building.

Courtesy of LCOR

The granite floor, art deco columns, and light fixtures featured in the building's lobby exemplify the high standards of design at Colgate Center.

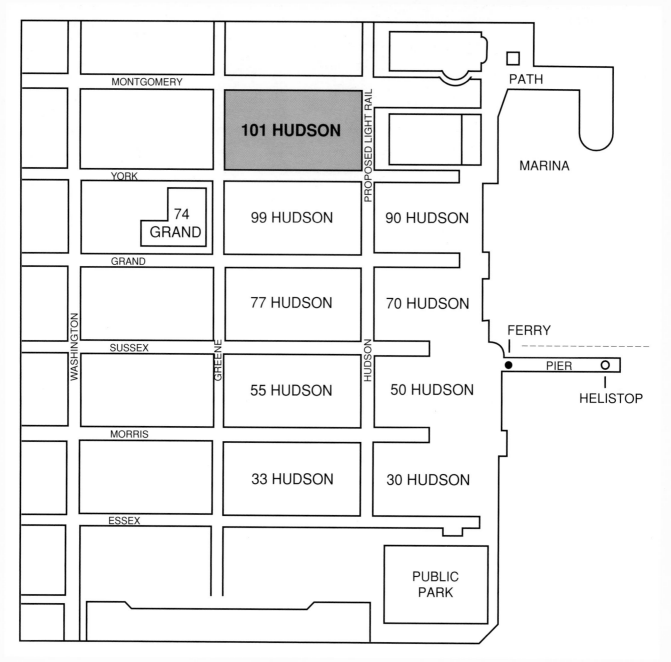

Master plan.

Land Use and Building Information

Site Area — 1.79 acres

Gross Building Area (GBA) — 1,506,000 square feet

Net Rentable Area (NRA)

Office	1,200,000 square feet
Retail	20,000 square feet
Total	1,220,000 square feet

Typical Floor Size

Low-rise floor	54,000 square feet
Mid- and high-rise floor	28,000 to 32,000 square feet

Building Height — 42 stories

Floor/Area Ratio — 19.3

Parking (all structured) — 850 spaces

Office Tenant Information

Occupied NRA — 99%

Average Annual Rent

Full-floor tenants — $28–$32 per square foot

Average Length of Lease — 5–15 years

Typical Terms of Lease — Net lease, with gross services

Tenant Sizes

Merrill Lynch	600,000 square feet
Lehman Brothers	400,000 square feet
Most other tenants	1 full floor (32,000 square feet average); or 2 floors; and some smaller tenants on floors 36 and 37

Retail Tenant Information

Occupied NRA	25%
Number of tenants	2
Average tenant size	2,000 square feet
Average annual rent	$25–$40 per square foot
Average length of lease	5–10 years

Development Schedule

2/1989	Planning started
8/1989	Anchor tenant obtained
12/1989	Site purchased
1/1990	Construction started
2/1992	Initial occupancy

Development Cost Information

Site Costs

Site acquisition	$27,300,000
Site improvements	1,400,000
Total	$28,700,000

Construction Costs

Superstructure	$61,000,000
HVAC	13,500,000
Electrical	8,200,000
Plumbing/sprinklers	4,000,000
Elevators	10,200,000
Fees/general conditions	16,900,000
Finishes	7,200,000
Graphics/specialties	1,200,000
Other	3,700,000
Total	$125,900,000

Tenant Improvements — $23,500,000

Soft Costs

Architecture/engineering	$3,900,000
Project management	1,600,000
Leasing/marketing	10,900,000
Legal/accounting	3,500,000
Taxes/insurance	4,300,000
Title	400,000
Construction interest and fees	28,600,000
Other	1,800,000
Total	$55,000,000

Total Development Cost — $233,100,000

Development Cost per Gross Square Foot — $155

Development Cost per Net Square Foot — $191

Developer

LCOR Incorporated
101 Hudson Street
Jersey City, New Jersey 07302
201-451-3300

Architect

Brennan Beer Gorman/Architects
515 Madison Avenue
New York, New York 10022
212-888-7663

Engineers

Jaros, Baum & Bolles (MEP)
Severud Associates (Structural)
General Contractor
Morse Diesel

225 High Ridge Road
Stamford, Connecticut

The 225 High Ridge Road office complex, a 221,630-square-foot two-building facility, is located one-half mile north of downtown Stamford, Connecticut, in Fairfield County. With more than 40 million square feet of office space, 5,000 hotel rooms, and the corporate headquarters for 25 Fortune 500 firms, Fairfield County has become a nationally recognized office location. Unlike most other suburban locations in the metropolitan New York area, Fairfield County has largely retained its suburban character and natural beauty. The site at 225 High Ridge Road was the last one available for development in the north Stamford area.

Developed by Gerald D. Hines Interests at a total cost of $53 million, the project opened its first building in the spring of 1990, 15 months after the start of construction. The second building was completed three months later. Currently fully occupied at top rental rates, these buildings were 97 percent leased at completion—a striking contrast with the 20 percent vacancy rate for Class A office space that Stamford averaged in the first four years of the 1990s.

Site and Plan
The 225 High Ridge Road complex sits on a 14-acre parcel within a 30-acre master plan developed in conjunction with Waldenbooks, whose recently expanded headquarters building is located just to the south. In December 1986, Waldenbooks had acquired a 23-acre site adjacent to its seven-acre headquarters property to accommodate its expansion requirements. At that time, Hines and Waldenbooks agreed to seek approval for a unified master plan of the 30-acre parcel and stipulated that after approval was obtained Hines would purchase the portion of the property not required for the Waldenbooks expansion.

The New York office of Skidmore, Owings & Merrill prepared the master plan for the coordinated development and also designed the two Hines buildings. Following an extensive review process involving complex environmental remediation, the approvals required to develop the master plan were obtained, and the property was subdivided in late 1988.

The three low-density office buildings and connecting roadways blend into the secluded parklike setting of the 30-acre property. The master plan achieves a consistency in design through common treatment of outdoor lighting, landscaping, and signage. Though compatible in design and similar in scale, the Waldenbooks building and 225 High Ridge Road have distinctive identities. The

mature vegetation in the center of the property and the shared main entry drive from High Ridge Road separate and define the two areas.

A 1.1-mile fitness course with ten exercise stations curves through the woods. This heavily used amenity is open to the public as well as project tenants and has been the staging area for community-sponsored events such as the Stamford Marathon.

The site's frontage along High Ridge Road is opposite an established residential area. To minimize any disruption to the neighborhood, the buildings are set back on the property and entry signage is unobtrusive. The 225 High Ridge Road complex is completely separated from a residential neighborhood at its northern boundary by a massive berm and thick buffer of trees. The eastern section of the site is heavily wooded, contributing to the sense of privacy and place.

Design
An oval set into the wooded landscape forms the basis of the site plan for 225 High Ridge Road. At the center of the site sits an oval-shaped courtyard, which is the focal point of the project and across which the East and West Buildings face each other. A curved arcade connects the two buildings and provides access to some building services, including a cafeteria and a fitness center.

The oval shape of the courtyard is repeated in the landscaping around the buildings and in the arrangement of the parking areas, where 339 parking spaces are distributed evenly around the two buildings to minimize walking distances. To preserve the existing vegetation, designers included an additional 332 parking spaces in an underground garage, for a total ratio of more than three spaces per 1,000 square feet of office space. Traffic circulation within the project is facilitated by a ring road. From the main entry drive, visitors approach the two buildings through the central courtyard, which features a stand of birch trees more than 20 feet in height.

The classical masonry style architecture of the two buildings employs brick, precast concrete, and clear glass. The effect is reminiscent of the large estates that once dotted the area. David Childs, senior architect for the project, says, "The idea was to create a sense of arrival at important buildings, akin to what is found at a college campus."

Unified through siting and symmetry, the buildings achieve individuality through separate entrances marked by central pavilions. Incorporating a distinctive brick pattern, the entrance pavilion for each building terminates

The elegant lines of 225 High Ridge Road are reminiscent of the large estates that once existed in the area. At the center of the wooded site, the East and West Buildings face each other across a central courtyard, which is the focal point of the project. A curved arcade provides a connection between the two structures, and offers protection from the weather and access to services in the complex.

An oval design motif appears in the barrel vault over the central pavilions of the buildings and the curve of the connecting arcade, as well as in the site plan itself, which forms an oval in the wooded landscape.

Each building has a secondary entrance from its surface parking area.

Building interiors feature lobbies with 22-foot ceilings and richly colored slate flooring in a distinctive rosette pattern.

in a barrel vault that is repeated on the outer entrances, providing a strong architectural identity for the project when viewed from either the courtyard or High Ridge Road.

Tenants

The buildings have been designed to achieve a maximum of efficiency and flexibility in tenant office facilities. Large rectangular floorplates offer tenants contiguous expanses of space that can be easily planned to accommodate modern office formats and to allow for expansion, providing an advantage for tenants anticipating continued growth. Ranging in size from 35,000 to 40,000 square feet, the floors have been configured to optimize usable space and to accommodate either open office or partitioned layouts. Oversized windows, more than seven feet tall and six feet wide, offer natural light and views of the outdoors. A central core, two major entrances on the ground floor, and regular column spacing at 30-foot intervals offer flexibility in planning small and medium-sized office units.

Two years into its ten-year lease, Chrysler Capital Corporation, originally the only tenant in the East Building, subleased nearly 60,000 square feet of its 115,000 square feet to Bristol-Myers Squibb Company. The space proved so easy to subdivide that it was accomplished with no disruption in the rental stream.

Learning International, the largest tenant in the West Building, occupies 55,000 square feet. U.S. Trust Company of Connecticut and Centerchem each lease 10,000 square feet of space. Six other tenants range in size from 2,000 to 8,000 square feet.

Experience Gained

In the developer's view, the planning and design for a business location must focus on the occupancy experience. The developer should concentrate on providing services that will make the space work from the tenants' perspective and on making the space efficient and flexible in layout and operation.

The developer thinks that a well-conceived project combines form and function. The design concept for this project had both—form in the plan and architecture aimed at creating a sense of place as well as stately, tradition-inspired buildings, and function in the provision of technologically advanced building systems and a wide array of amenities and services to serve tenants. The combination proved to be a winning one, as evidenced by high occupancies at 225 High Ridge Road.

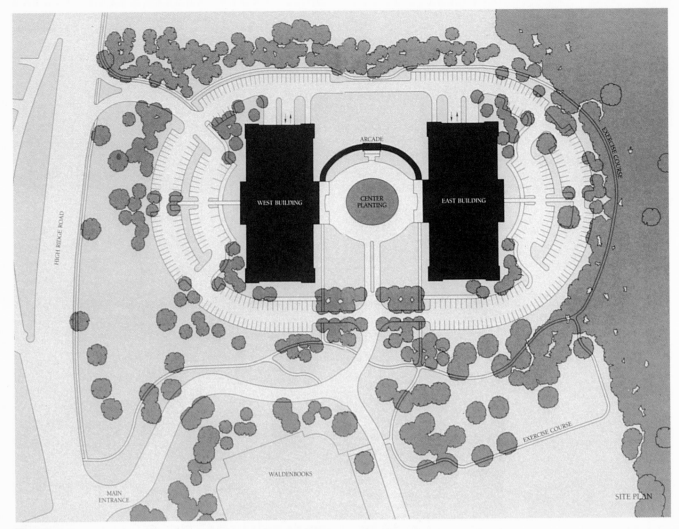

Site plan.

Project Data: 225 High Ridge Road

Land Use and Building Information

Site Area	14.63 acres
Gross Building Area (GBA)	240,000 square feet
Net Rentable Area (NRA)	221,630 square feet
Average Floor Size	35,000 square feet
Floor/Area Ratio	0.38

Parking

Structured	332 spaces
Surface	339 spaces
Total	671 spaces

Land Use Plan

	Acres	Percent of Site
Buildings	1.60	10.9%
Paved areas[1]	2.40	16.4
Landscaped areas	6.01	41.1
Other	4.62	31.6
Total	14.63	100.0%

Office Tenant Information

Occupied NRA	100%
Average annual rent	$17.71 per square foot
Length of leases	3–10 years; typical lease 5 years
Typical terms of lease	Tenant improvements at $10 per square foot
Average tenant size	50,000 square feet
Tenant sizes	1,156–58,249 square feet

Annual Operating Expenses (1993)

Taxes	$572,000
Insurance	32,000
Services[2]	514,000
Maintenance	175,000
Janitorial	226,000
Utilities	617,000
Management	241,000
Total	$2,377,000

Development Schedule

3/1987	Planning started
3/1987	Leasing started
11/1988	Site purchased
1/1989	Construction started
4/1990	Phase 1 completed
7/1990	Project completed

Development Cost Information

Site Costs[3]

Site acquisition	$10,606,629
Excavation	450,000
Grading	312,500
Sewer/water/drainage	375,000
Paving	314,105
Curbs/sidewalks	249,000
Landscaping/irrigation	902,500
Miscellaneous	480,600
Total	$3,083,705

Construction Costs

Superstructure	$11,106,206
HVAC	1,857,720
Electrical	1,333,500
Plumbing/sprinklers	1,523,000
Elevators	463,200
Fees/general conditions	2,030,330
Finishes	1,586,238
Graphics/specialties	55,760
Change orders and tenant work	5,879,620
Total	$25,835,574

Soft Costs

Architecture/engineering	$2,193,000
Project management	3,070,000
Leasing/marketing	6,570,000
Legal/accounting	240,277
Taxes/insurance	415,000
Title	57,094
Construction interest and fees	475,000
Miscellaneous	600,000
Total	$13,620,371

Total Development Cost	**$53,146,279**
Development Cost per Gross Square Foot	$221
Development Cost per Net Square Foot	$240

Developer/Manager

Gerald D. Hines Interests
Houston, Texas

Architect

Skidmore, Owings & Merrill
New York, New York

Notes

[1] Surface parking and roads.

[2] Includes cafeteria, van service, and building management services.

[3] Site improvement costs include on-site and off-site improvements.

Crescent 8

Greenwood Village, Colorado

Crescent 8, which was completed in January 1996, was the first speculative office building developed in the south Denver metropolitan area in more than a decade. The 87,400-square-foot building is the first phase of a six-building complex, Crescent Town Center (the Crescent), that is under development within an 870-acre business park, the Denver Technological Center (DTC or Tech Center). Tech Center, which lies some ten miles southeast of downtown Denver at the junction of two major freeways (I-25 and I-225), is situated in two jurisdictions—the city of Denver and the city of Greenwood Village—and is the gateway to Denver's edge city known as Southeast Corridor.

The business park was started by a developer in 1962 and is now owned by the Peninsular and Oriental Steam Navigation Company (P&O), a British firm with extensive real estate holdings in the United States, most of which are concentrated in Atlanta, Denver, and Houston. With more than 950 companies and 30,000 employees, it is the largest employment center in the Southeast Corridor. Recently, it has drawn an influx of media, communications, energy, technology, financial, and service firms. The more than 10 million square feet of development at DTC includes 7.5 million square feet of office space. Some two-thirds of the business park has been developed.

Crescent Town Center, conceived as an urban nucleus within the suburban office park and designed as its focal point, occupies a 4.2-acre site at DTC's major crossroads—DTC Boulevard and East Belleview Avenue. The collection of six buildings and two parks fronts on an elliptical road. Compared with other development at DTC, Crescent Town Center is more intensely urban and is planned to blend a greater diversity of land uses, including ample public spaces. In the plan for the town center are restaurants, hotels, more office space, perhaps some retail and residential uses in later phases, and a variety of public amenities—including parks, an amphitheater, fountains, and a reflecting pool.

The Crescent's first building, Crescent 8, was fully leased almost immediately after its completion, with CommNet Cellular taking 61,000 square feet (70 percent of NRA). Tech Center's developer and property manager, TCD North, has started construction on two additional office buildings and sold the land for a 128-room hotel that is now under construction. A 6,000-square-foot restaurant, operating under a land lease, opened in November 1996. At buildout, Crescent Town Center will total approximately 650,000 square feet.

Project Feasibility

TCD North made the initial decision to proceed with Crescent 8 partially out of necessity. In 1995, the Texaco Corporation, a major tenant at Tech Center, exercised an option to take over the remaining space in a ten-story building owned by TCD North. TCD North had been leasing space on the tenth floor, which it shared with a law firm, and was hard-pressed to find another 20,000 square feet of prime space within DTC, where vacancy rates for prime space were less than 4 percent. The developer decided that the time was right to go ahead with Phase 1 of Crescent Town Center as a speculative venture.

A strong overall market, however, was actually the driving force behind the decision to develop this spec project. The go-go years of the mid-1980s had produced a glut of spec development that propelled Denver's office vacancy rate to one of the highest in the nation and during the late 1980s, Tech Center's developer had retrenched by mostly ceasing the active development of new projects and focusing on land sales.

However, by 1994, the market had picked up and strengthened significantly. Following a decade of nearly no new spec development in the Denver region, vacancy rates were tightening at around 8 percent and office lease rates were rising fast. Moreover, square-foot lease rates at Tech Center were in the mid-teens. (Rents at Tech Center since 1994 have climbed to the mid-$20s, meaning that office space in the business park is now priced between $5 and $10 per square foot above space in downtown Denver.) "We believed there was a viable market for spec development," notes Peter Culshaw, DTC executive vice president, "and we wanted to be the first out of the box." Crescent 8 was the first of three spec office projects developed by DTC in 1996 and 1997. "Although we're still land developers," says Culshaw, "we are now taking advantage of having capital in the right market circumstance to build vertical product."

Although DTC was prepared to build Crescent 8 as a spec project, CommNet Cellular, a firm that provides rural cellular telephone services in the northern and western states, committed to 61,000 square feet at Crescent 8 shortly after construction started. Holland & Hart, the law firm that had shared space with TCD North in the Texaco building, leased 8,000 square feet. Based on the quick lease-up of Crescent 8, TCD North started development of Oracle Center, a 90,000-square-foot spec building at another DTC location, and Crescent 7, a spec office building that opened in spring 1997.

Crescent 6
Crescent 7
Crescent 8
Ameri Suites
Yia Yia's Euro Bistro
Crescent 5
East Belleview Avenue
Crescent 3
Crescent 4

Crescent Town Center was designed to be a focal point for Tech Center. The intersection of East Belleview Avenue and DTC Boulevard is intended to become the business park's new l00 percent corner.

Development Strategy

Most of the buildings at Tech Center were developed in the early 1980s, and they are characteristically large (300,000 square feet plus) buildings, many of them above15 stories. Many tenants wanted a signature building, designed with elegant, soaring elevations and an expensive granite or limestone skin. This type of building necessitated costly structured parking so that employees would not have to walk too far. The floorplates were generally small, irregular, and inefficient.

By the early 1990s, tenant preferences had shifted dramatically. TCD North's development strategy for Crescent Town Center was formulated around this shift. "I don't think this market is going to see a lot of extravagant architecture over the next cycle," observes Peter Culshaw. "We're targeting a market that is more conservative and corporately acceptable."

In office projects built at DTC in the 1980s, floorplates typically ranged between 17,000 and 20,000 square feet, with some being as small as 14,000 square feet. Today's tenants prefer to be housed on one or two floors. They want larger floorplates that offer a more attractive ratio of useable to built space. Crescent 8 features rectangular floorplates of 24,000 square feet, only four interior columns, and average bay depths of 40 feet. "If we had built a building twice as tall with floorplates half the size, we would not have attracted CommNet Cellular as a tenant," notes Culshaw.

Another theme in the development of Crescent Town Center is to give smaller tenants an identity (their own street address) within the vast business park. Midrise buildings allow smaller tenants to have a larger presence within the building than they would in a high-rise office tower. This was one of the attractions for Moore Realty, which jointly developed Moore Plaza—a 40,000-square-foot building on the Crescent 7 site—with TCD North. Like the other buildings on the Crescent, Moore Plaza features two separate entrances—a symbolic front door that faces visitor parking and opens directly onto the Crescent and an employee entrance that connects conveniently with the parking behind the building. Moore Plaza was completed in spring 1997.

Crescent 8's sizable floorplates reflect a key trend in office use: the accommodation of more employees in smaller workspaces. Whereas office densities used to range from 2.5 to three employees per 1,000 square feet, now companies plan on five to seven employees per 1,000 square feet, says Michael Barber, the architect and land planner of Crescent Town Center. Higher occupancy densities increase parking needs. Parking ratios at Tech Center have risen steadily through the years, from three spaces to more than four spaces per 1,000 square feet. At Crescent 8, there are 330 parking spaces—four per 1,000 square feet. Seventeen of the spaces are located in front of the building for visitors. Sixty-six executive parking spaces are provided—20, as called for in the original plan, are below grade while 46 are in a carport that was added to the project when CommNet requested additional covered parking after construction had started. The remaining tenant spaces are tucked behind the building on a surface parking lot. Parking, except for the executive spaces, is free.

As noted, many of the high-rise towers built in DTC in the 1980s came with expensive parking garages. At Crescent Town Center, only 20 percent of the parking is structured. This change is indicative of an important general reallocation of the office project construction budget that has occurred at DTC over the past decade. Instead of investing in unique architectural designs and costly building skins, Tech Center tenants now would rather spend their money on more practical amenities such as additional power, more cooling capacity, and fiberoptic access.

Three separate power substations serve DTC, making it an ideal location for computer-driven companies that depend on an uninterrupted power supply. DTC has a high concentration of high-tech and telecommunications firms, which increases electrical power demands in the business park. The earlier standard of two to 2.5 watts of power per square foot of space has been increased to four to five watts. Crescent 8 provides four watts per square foot, while Crescent 7 provides five watts.

The project development manager for TCD North, Ron McDaniel, observes that "the issue typically is not so much volume of power, but rather the number of available circuits. So, we provide more circuit breakers in our buildings." McDaniel notes further that even though many employees now use several computers with larger monitors, new equipment is generally more efficient and uses less power than earlier versions. Typically, most computer applications in use in an office setting at any one time are fairly simple and do not require inordinate amounts of electricity.

Crescent Town Center includes amenities—custom light fixtures and railings, wide sidewalks, water features, formal park areas, and park furniture—that people usually associate with urban places.

Crescent 8 was constructed over the confluence of two old streams, one of which was piped under the visitor parking lot. The second stream was exposed, channeled to protect adjacent properties, and integrated into the open-space network.

Contrary to the commonly held view in the industry that significantly more power will be needed in office buildings, the reality is that most tenants use no more than 3.5 watts per square foot, according to McDaniel.

Higher employee densities and the use of an increasing amount of power in office buildings mean higher cooling loads and thus a need for more air conditioning. Crescent 8 offers greater air-conditioning capacity than older DTC buildings.

A key element of TCD North's development strategy at Crescent Town Center was to create a multiuse environment. Because it is primarily an office development, most of Tech Center virtually shuts down after 5 p.m. TCD North aimed to transform the business park's southeast corner into a lively activity center during the day and in the evening. This would be accomplished by offering a diversity of uses at the town center, including hotels and destination restaurants. In November 1996, the first restaurant, Yia Yia's (operated by PB&J, a Kansas City restaurant chain), opened and was instantly popular, requiring lunch reservations a week in advance. Several large apartment complexes located adjacent to the Crescent, provide a ready-made restaurant market. A second restaurant is expected to be built in the near future.

Adding to the mix of uses at the Crescent are public facilities and open-space amenities. A reflecting pond and fountain, parks with sitting areas, a gazebo, and a small grass amphitheater were jointly financed with the Goldsmith Metropolitan District, which manages and maintains these spaces. The district built and maintains 18 visitor parking spaces as well. Additional park elements are planned, including a carillon clock tower and an interactive water feature.

AmeriSuites purchased the Crescent 9 site on which it is constructing a 128-room extended-stay hotel. Unlike the other two full-service hotels at DTC, AmeriSuites has no restaurant. Part of the attraction of the site for the chain was the presence of Yia Yia's across the street. There

is a scarcity of hotels at DTC, and discussions are underway to locate another hotel at the Crescent 6 site. For the Crescent 5 site, TCD North is considering condominiums as one potential use.

Crescent tenants benefit from shared parking opportunities deriving from the multiuse development strategy. The popular Yia Yia's needed extra valet parking spaces during evening hours, and so the restaurant arranged to use space in the lots behind Crescent 8 after 5 p.m.

An additional advantage of the multiuse development strategy, according to Culshaw, is that "it enabled us to take advantage of more than one development segment, thus prolonging our cycle during the uptake." The diversification benefits of multiuse development appealed to DTC's parent company, but P&O was not much interested in mixing different uses within single buildings. P&O's general approach, notes Culshaw, is to finance only projects that can be easily liquidated and that appeal to conservative institutional investors. Culshaw is thinking about the inclusion of some ground-floor specialty retail space at the Crescent 5 and 6 sites, but he anticipates that P&O will be hesitant, unless he can demonstrate that the nonoffice component will not impede the eventual sale of the buildings. Culshaw's separate buildings approach to multiuse makes the future disposition of those buildings easier.

Another advantage of a building-by-building approach to the development of a synergistic multiuse urban center is that the whole project can be developed incrementally. This was an important economic consideration for DTC's owners, who preferred to invest gradually in bite-size pieces rather than to undertake comprehensive infrastructure programs at the start of development. Because DTC may eventually sell some of the Crescent projects, like AmeriSuites, the mechanical systems of the separate buildings are not intertwined and each building is operated independently. However, the tenants benefit from some shared services, such as security and marketing.

The development strategy aims to create an activity center within the business park that will stay lively after the 9-to-5 workday. Backlighting the Crescent buildings at night helps attract evening activity.

Planning and Design

The architectural design standards for the Denver Technological Center are said to be among the toughest in Denver. The quality of development in the business park is controlled by these standards—covering such elements as color palette, building materials, landscaping, lighting, and signage—and an Architectural Control Committee (ACC) that reviews designs. DTC developers credit these tools with the preservation of strong property values in the park.

However, the design review process has failed to address some important urban design issues. Like many business parks planned 25 years ago, DTC is divided into vast superblocks that are irregular in shape and not organized into a conventional grid pattern. The resulting road pattern resembles a curved maze, and visitors have difficulty finding their way around. Within the superblocks, the typical development pattern has been a central office tower surrounded by parking and an outer perimeter of green lawn—meeting DTC's requirement that 30 percent of the site be open space.

This pattern is called the "fried-egg syndrome" by Michael Barber, an architect whose firm has designed a number of DTC projects including the Crescent and who has served for several years on the ACC. Barber places some of the blame on the site-specific design review process, which treats each project as an isolated entity and fails to consider how buildings relate and connect to form a pattern of development and create the public realm.

His firm has authored new design review criteria for multiphase projects at DTC, like the Crescent Town Center. These criteria call for the review of individual projects as part of the relevant general development plans.

The master plan for the Crescent has a design agenda: create a new address; create an actual center for the Denver Technological Center; create a strong visible element as an orienting device; and provide a rich blend of public spaces and pedestrian-oriented amenities. The ultimate goal is to make the intersection of East Belleview Avenue and DTC Boulevard the business park's 100 percent corner. Consolidating the open space at the center of the development and tucking most of the parking behind the buildings would avoid the fried-egg syndrome. After experimenting with a number of different geometric forms, the designers selected an ellipse because it would give each individual pie-slice site favorable depths and good frontal exposure on the street.

The site for Crescent 8 was a veritable obstacle course of easements and water lines. The building was constructed over the confluence of two old streams. One was piped under the visitor parking lot, while the other was exposed, channeled to protect adjacent properties, and integrated into the open-space network.

"The idea of extending public places through a collection of private buildings is not new," says Barber. "What is new is placing a dense ring of urban buildings in a suburban business park." Crescent Town Center has a floor/area ratio of nearly 0.5, which makes it considerably denser than most DTC projects. It also includes high-quality amenities—custom light fixtures and railings, wide sidewalks, water features, formal park areas, and park furniture—that usually are associated with urban developments. Culshaw initially envisioned a central skating rink, but the idea was nixed because of potential complications from underground utility lines. The two restaurants are designed with their backs to the road and facing the park, much like Central Park's Tavern on the Green. Patrons can sit at outdoor tables in warm weather.

The exteriors of each of the six Crescent buildings will be of precast concrete. The molds will be altered subtly to give each building an individual identity. "The idea," notes Barber, "is to create a family of buildings, where each member has a separate, identifiable character." Architectural precast panels offer several economic advantages, particularly in the Denver area, which is home to two of the country's best fabricators of precast concrete. A major cost savings comes from speedy construction.

Experience Gained

In Denver's recovering speculative office market, Crescent 8 was a testing-of-the-waters project. The developer says that the building probably should have been larger, given the market strength indicated by the building's quick lease-up. One of the limitations of a building this small is that it is difficult to justify giving up rentable space for back-of-house uses. For this reason, Crescent 8 has no loading docks, its storage areas are insignificant, the

building engineer is housed elsewhere, and no building-wide shower and locker room facilities are provided. A larger building offers economies of scale that allow more of these amenities to be provided. Crescent 7, for example, with 135,000 square feet of rentable space, has a dedicated engineer's office. McDaniel says that the threshold is around 120,000 square feet. Lacking such amenities, Crescent 8 is only a Class A– building, in contrast to Crescent 7, which is a Class A or Class A+ building.

The plan to create an urban nucleus within a suburban business park turned out to be a definite market draw. Tenants have been attracted also by the opportunity to have their own street address and separate identity. Small tenants in the Crescent's medium-sized buildings have a larger presence than they would have in a high-rise office tower.

Crescent 8's developer emphasizes the importance of commissioning analyses by a third party to test out whether the various building systems are functioning as planned. Had market conditions allowed, more time would have been allocated to the building's commissioning.

"If there was anything we underestimated," says Culshaw, "it was the enormous amount of time we needed to spend on fairly small details." The developer team paid scrupulous attention to planning for the functional needs of the building's tenants—planning efficient floorplates, HVAC, and electrical capacity. TCD North has learned to budget more time into the development schedule to allow for close attention to functional details.

Crescent Town Center features a reflecting pond and fountain, park spaces with seating, and a small grass amphitheater. The fact that Crescent 8 leased up shortly after construction started spurred the development of Crescent 7 (left), which opened in spring 1997.

The exteriors of all the Crescent buildings will be of precast concrete, but each will derive an individual identity from subtle alterations in the molds.

Project Data: Crescent 8

Land Use and Building Information

Site Area	4.2 acres
Gross Building Area (GBA)	87,400 square feet
Net Rentable Area (NRA)	83,400 square feet
Typical Floor Size	24,000 square feet
Floor/Area Ratio	0.48

Parking

Covered or enclosed	66 spaces
Surface	264 spaces
Total	330 spaces

Land Use Plan

	Acres	Percent of Site
Buildings[1]	0.9	21.4%
Paved areas[2]	2.2	52.4
Landscaped areas	1.1	26.2
Total	4.2	100.0%

Office Tenant Information

Occupied NRA	100%
Average annual rent	$22.50 per square foot
Length of leases	5–7 years
Largest tenant size	61,000 square feet

Development Cost Information

Site Costs

Site acquisition	$1,800,000
Site improvements[3]	455,000
Total	$2,255,000

Construction Costs

Shell	$5,000,000
Covered parking	570,000
Tenant finishes[4]	2,165,000
Total	$7,735,000

Soft Costs

Architecture/engineering	$320,000
Permits/testing/taps	125,000
Miscellaneous	70,000
Sales commissions	360,000
Contingencies	210,000
Development fees	210,000
Financing	400,000
Total	$1,695,000

Total Development Cost	**$11,685,000**
Development Cost per Gross Square Foot	**$134**
Development Cost per Net Square Foot	**$140**

Developer

TCD North Inc.
8350 East Crescent Parkway
Suite 100
Englewood, Colorado 80111
303-773-1700

Architect/Master Planner

Michael Barber Architecture
303 Sixteenth Street
Suite 300
Denver, Colorado 80202
303-595-7070

General Contractor

Weitz-Cohen Construction Company
899 Logan
Suite 600
Denver, Colorado 80203
303-860-6600

Development Schedule

2/1995	Planning started
5/1995	Construction started
5/1995	Leasing started
1/1996	Project completed

Notes

[1]Includes parking structure (0.3 acres).

[2]Surface parking and roads.

[3]Includes $55,000 in off-site improvements.

[4]Includes $1,670,000 in base allowance for tenant finish and $495,000 in additions for tenant finish.

Norm Thompson Headquarters
Hillsboro, Oregon

For its new headquarters, Norm Thompson Outfitters, a retailer based in Portland, Oregon, and known for its progressive business practices and unique catalog items, wanted a building that was a physical manifestation of its corporate credo: "Escape from the Ordinary." The 49-year-old company had outgrown its former space and wanted to consolidate operations at one location. Its distribution center was in West Virginia, where it had been relocated in 1994 because the company's primary customer base was on the East Coast. However, all other facilities were in the Portland area.

Norm Thompson's goals for its new headquarters building were resource- and energy-efficiency, a natural setting, a high-quality working environment, and a typical office building price tag. Not wanting to own the building, the firm sought an outside owner to construct a build-to-suit facility that it would lease. It issued a request for proposals (RFP) that specified the building's size, cost, and green development goals.

The Trammell Crow Company was selected. The developer found a site in the rapidly growing suburb of Hillsboro, about ten miles west of downtown Portland. Trammell Crow brought in Washington, D.C.–based Riggs Bank N.A. as trustee for the Multi-Employer Property Trust pension fund to finance the land purchase and building construction.

The 54,519-square-foot, two-story, tilt-up, concrete- and steel-framed building was completed in September 1995. It met the tenant's strict rent budget and environmental goals. The building's primary green elements are its recycled materials, a self-sustaining landscape, and energy-efficient heating, air-conditioning, and lighting systems. Its innovative architecture and energy-saving features have won numerous design awards.

Site
The site was attractive to Norm Thompson for several reasons. Together with the three adjacent acres on which Trammell Crow acquired an option, the 4.95-acre site was large enough to accommodate almost a doubling of the company's size at some future time. Although it is on a ten-year lease, Norm Thompson clearly views its new headquarters as a long-term investment. Some 120 employees work there. Depending on the time of year, another 100 to 400 employees work at the company's incoming-calls center, which is housed in 30,000 square feet in a building one-eighth mile to the west, which the Multi-Employer Property Trust purchased and expanded and leases.

The site's semirural setting and business park amenities appealed to Norm Thompson. The parcel features mature trees and natural wetlands to the east and south. Its configuration made it possible to orient the building to the south and thus maximize natural daylighting. The presence of designated wetlands guaranteed that views of majestic Douglas firs and other luxuriant vegetation would be permanently protected.

Not only was the site aesthetically pleasing, but it was also the least expensive of the four parcels that Norm Thompson was considering. The site is part of the Tanasbourne Commerce and Corporate Center, an 800-acre master-planned development by the Standard Insurance Company, which functions mainly as a land developer, selling off individual parcels. Planned in the early 1980s, Tanasbourne was designed as a mixed-use community of residents, jobs, shopping, and entertainment. In the early 1990s, a sluggish economy was stymieing the development of commercially and industrially zoned land and vacancy rates for flex space hovered around 20 percent. The only land sales of any note happening at Tanasbourne at that time were for apartment projects and retail development.

Thus, when Trammell Crow was negotiating to purchase eight acres in 1994, the land was relatively inexpensive. The large wetlands on the site and a lack of visibility from the freeway also drove down the price. More recently, a general resurgence in high-tech and associated industries has boosted the market for commercial and manufacturing development. Intel Corporation, one of the region's main chip manufacturers, has built a large facility one mile west of Norm Thompson's. The growing tendency of businesses to locate back-office uses outside downtown is also driving this market.

Trammel Crow also saved money on impact fees. Standard Insurance had already paid the traffic impact fees that the county required for development on the site.

Planning and Design
Architecture and Interior Design. The corporate culture at Norm Thompson is casual and nonhierarchical. Suits and ties are a rarity. An open office format would, it was felt, support the egalitarian work ethic as well as foster creative brainstorming and collaborative teamwork. The architects were challenged to come up with a design that would facilitate communication among employees.

The usual perimeter of executive suites was eliminated, which gave space planners more flexibility to arrange floors efficiently and save money. Individual workspaces

The building is stepped back from the south edge to embrace the curved wetlands. The site's configuration made it possible to orient the building to the south, thus maximizing its use of natural daylight.

are smaller than usual, and informal gathering places where staff can exchange ideas are more numerous than usual. Hallways are wider than usual, so that people can stop and talk without blocking traffic. Individual work cubicles are next to common meeting areas with long tables, so that staff members can collaborate on projects without having to walk across the building to a conference room.

Several closed conference rooms are available to staff by reservation. The company's administrative, executive, human resources, and computer services departments are located on the first floor. The creative staff—copywriters, designers, and marketing planners—is on the second floor. Vendor rooms, which are where manufacturers' representatives display their new product lines, are located on the first floor so as not to disrupt the creative work on the second floor.

The interior is designed as an open loft, a concept that forgoes secondary finishes and thus exposes underlying structural elements and mechanical systems. This fits in with the functional, less-is-more overall design approach for the building. "After all," says Norm Thompson CEO John Emrick, "we're in the business of designing and producing products and I like to think that our building functions with the efficiency of a factory, in the best sense of the word."

By eliminating individual offices and minimizing the use of secondary finishes, such as suspended ceilings, the designers limited the number of different materials used in the building, which maximized overall resource-efficiency. At first, some staff members were concerned that the open offices would be distractively noisy, a fear that, apparently, has not been realized.

Emrick notes that although the company went with a basic two-story, tilt-up concrete structure, it did not want a "vanilla building." So the designers, Sienna Architecture Company, subtly tweaked the generic box format to add visual interest. The rectangular building is stepped back from the south edge to embrace the curved wetlands. The bland white surfaces of the tilt-up slabs are punctuated with perforated-steel light shelves, which, besides adding architectural character, also channel daylight into the building. Concrete reveal patterns form shadow lines on the outside walls to help articulate the elevations. Southern facing second-floor balconies and operable windows on the east and west sides add exterior detail—and let fresh air and natural sounds into the interior.

"Because this was a green building," notes lead project architect William Ruecker, "we looked to the natural surroundings for inspiration." A water theme—deriving from an adjacent river and the company's roots as a vendor of hand-tied trout flies made on Norm Thompson's kitchen table—drove the architectural form. The hallways are open, meandering, and curved. Where the hallways converge on the first floor adjacent to the lobby is the "gorge," a canyon with milestone (a mix of cement powder and crushed windshield and bottle glass that resem-

Steel light shelves channel daylight into the building while adding architectural interest to the tilt-up slab building's exterior.

bles stone) floors and milestone walls that tilt and are irregular. On the second floor, a walkway veers out precariously over the atrium lobby, much like a suspension bridge.

Confined to a tight budget, the architects emphasized specific design elements that would give the building character and enhance the work environment, such as the balconies, the light shelves, and the lobby. The atrium lobby plays on the idea of bringing the outdoors indoors. The lush outdoor green scene comes indoors through a picture window on the north side and blends with the lobby's light-colored maple paneling and palette of natural colors, so that inside and outside merge into one verdant landscape.

Materials. One of Norm Thompson's requirements for environmental appropriateness was that the building feature materials that represent the least cost to the environment. This corresponded to the company's recycling program, which specifies recyclable packing materials and, whenever possible, soy inks and recycled paper for printed pieces.

Recycled products were also used throughout the new headquarters building. The lobby floor is made of remilled Apitong wood that was salvaged from the floors of defunct railroad boxcars. Similar to mahogany, this wood from the Philippines is from an endangered tree that is no longer harvested. For the most part, wood was used sparingly throughout the project and the other wood used was harvested only from certified sustainable forests.

The designers opted for a steel structural system instead of wood, because steel is recyclable. Milestone (see above) was used to finish interior walls and floors. Milestone can be refinished much like hardwood floors. The partitions in the restrooms were made from a material that is 90 percent recycled plastic bottles. Recycled paints were used as primer, but not as finish coats because the colors were limited. Thus, surplus paint stocks were used only as primer. Overall, the recycled materials that were used cost the same as comparable nonrecycled materials.

The entire life cycles of potential building materials and furnishings were evaluated. The designers considered the manufacturing processes, the performance of the materials as building products, and what would happen at the end of the product's life. The goal was to protect natural resources and give a second life to existing products. Window frames, for example: Frames high in recycled aluminum content were selected instead of frames high in virgin aluminum content, because aluminum mining causes ecological damage and its manufacture uses high amounts of energy.

Jane Emrick, one of Norm Thompson's owners, notes that when original materials had to be used because appropriate recycled materials were unavailable or were not sufficiently durable, a selection criterion was that the manufacturer made other products of recycled materials. The designers evaluated materials also for potential off-gassing of volatile organic compounds (VOCs), a primary cause of sick-building syndrome. Another resource-conserving element in the development of the building was the establishment by Trammell Crow of procedures to recycle construction materials on site, in order to minimize the amount of refuse sent to the landfill.

Natural Landscaping. Norm Thompson's goal of preserving and creating a natural, resource-conserving outdoor environment as a high-quality office setting was achieved. Portland-based landscape architects Walker & Macy created a sustainable landscape using indigenous trees, shrubs, and wildflowers. Compared to the landscaping that is standard in many suburban office parks, native vegetation requires less water, fewer herbicides and pesticides, and less maintenance. The north portion of the site features shade-tolerant plants including ferns and vine maples, while on the building's south side a meadow of wild flowers slopes down to the wetlands. Once the plants are established, it should not be necessary to water them.

Plants are also used in the site's natural runoff filtration systems. Drainage from the building and parking lot is directed to a bioswale, which is a channel that uses vegetation to slow the flow of water and remove impurities before it drains into the wetlands.

Energy-Efficiency

A southern exposure with tall windows and high ceilings maximizes the building's natural daylighting and energy-efficiency. The building uses as much glass as is allowed by the local energy code. It is clear (untinted to give catalog designers natural light for reviewing art boards and color proofs), low-e (low-emissivity) thermal glass, which reduces heat transmission. The use of skylights was rejected because they would produce significant heat gain in a building this long and not be cost-effective.

The daylighting program revolves around a system of light shelves made of steel. The large rectangular shelves placed seven feet above the floor extend inside and outside the building to reduce glare and channel natural light deep into the building. They work by reflecting light up toward the exposed interior metal roof decking, which like a mirror diffuses light through the building. Seventy-five percent of the building's light fixtures are energy-efficient T8 fluorescent lamps that dim automatically when natural light is available.

Norm Thompson agreed with Trammell Crow to pay the additional capital costs of energy-saving features in the form of higher rents. The catalog company was willing to exceed its rent budget of $0.76 per square foot per month for the sake of lower operating expenses, and its schedule required that this investment in energy-efficiency be recouped through operating savings within eight years.

When the Norm Thompson building was in initial planning, Portland General Electric (PGE) was developing a pilot energy-savings program for commercial buildings called Earth Smart Commercial to complement a similar program it had for residential projects. (See "Earth Smart Commercial at a Glance" below.) The Norm Thompson headquarters was the first green building certified under the new program.

PGE staff members worked with the building's development team on design, equipment selection, payback schedules, and available incentives for investments in energy-saving equipment. G.Z. (Charlie) Brown, professor of architecture at the University of Oregon, ran computer analyses of different variables—for example, sun angle, window size, and paint color—to determine what specific combinations of building elements and energy-efficiency measures (EEMs) would achieve the greatest efficiencies. Brown's modeling showed, for example, that certain daylighting measures and window options would reduce the building's requirements for cooling capacity

---

figure 7-1

Earth Smart Commercial at a Glance

To qualify for Portland General Electric's Earth Smart commercial buildings program, buildings must incorporate certain specified energy-efficiency measures (EEMs) plus other green features, which they may choose from sets of options that PGE lists in four categories, as follows.

Energy-Efficiency	Quality Indoor Environment	Environmental Responsibility	Resource-Efficiency
All buildings require:	Select at least two of the following:	Select at least two of the following:	Select at least one of the following:
• Whole building energy analysis	• Low-toxicity building products (use a minimum of three)	• Indoor-water efficiency	• Recycled-content building products (use a minimum of four)
• Specific requirements for building envelope, HVAC, and lighting systems	• Fresh air ventilation	• Environmentally appropriate landscaping (includes naturescaping and integrated pest management)	• Wood from certified sustainable forests
• Building commissioning	• Natural daylighting	• Construction site recycling	
Earth Smart/Green buildings require:		• Interior recycling storage area	
• Energy-efficiency package that achieves 20 percent minimum savings		• Efficient transportation (includes secure bicycle parking and access to mass transit)	
Earth Smart/Gold buildings require:			
• Integrated design process			
• Energy-efficiency package that achieves 30 percent minimum savings			

Source: Portland General Electric.

figure 7-2

Incremental Cost Analysis of Energy-Efficiency Measures (EEMs) by System

	Incremental Project Cost	Annual Cost Savings	Simple Payback (Years)	Payback after PGE Incentive (Years)
Glazing				
Low-E Glazing	$12,466	$1,961	6.4	4.8
Tinted Low-E Glazing	18,968	1,712	11.1	11.1
Thermal-Break Low-E Glazing*	35,767	3,397	10.5	7.9
External Shading	44,800	2,020	22.2	22.2
Landscaping Shading	2,835	–809	3.5	3.5
Optimized Window Area	28,818	237	1	1
Reflective/Insulation				
Reflective Roof	$9,581	$314	30.5	30.5
Light-Colored Exterior	0	–91	0	0
R-19 vs. R-11 Wall	6,373	269	23.7	23.7
R-30 vs. R-19 Roof	39,484	687	57.5	57.5
Lighting				
T8 Electronic/Compact Fluorescent*	$5,415	$5,503	1.0	–0.2
Occupancy Sensors*	4,292	878	4.9	2.7
Daylighting/Exterior Shading*	107,579	11,191	9.6	7.2
HVAC				
Heat Recovery	$7,500	$170	44.1	44.1
Variable-Speed Drives*	6,300	589	10.7	8.0
Fan-Powered VAC*	5,000	4,958	1.0	0.8
Oversize Ductwork*	5,000	1,413	3.5	2.7
EMCS-OSS and Supply Reset*	27,500	5,414	5.1	3.8
Mass Cooling	38,325	–2,851	[1]	[1]
Norm Thompson Analysis				
Package Selected (*Marked Items)	$196,853	$22,667	8.7	6.2[2]
HVAC-Capacity Savings	–28,000	–	–	–
Total after HVAC Change	$168,853	$22,667	7.4	5.3

[1]System's payback is greater than 99 years.

[2]Additional incentives from the Oregon Department of Energy's Building Energy Tax Credit (BETC) reduced the payback period to 4.1 years.

Source: Portland General Electric.

by nearly 47 tons, which would save about $28,000 in capital outlays.

The Brown and PGE analyses persuaded the developer to invest in certain EEMs. See Figure 7-2 above for a list of the EEMs that Norm Thompson selected (those marked by asterisks). Oversized HVAC ducts are equipped with electronic variable-speed fans that operate only when needed to save energy. Heat generated by occupants and electrical equipment is recovered and used in the heat-ing system, which almost eliminates the need for other heat sources. Heat recovery coils transfer energy between the exhaust and ventilation air streams, reducing the need for primary energy for heating or cooling ventilation air. A computerized comprehensive energy-management system schedules the operating hours of equipment and resets discharge air temperatures and volume to ensure efficient operation. According to company studies, after one year of operation the Norm Thomp-

The lobby features some of the recycled materials that are used throughout the building. Its floor is made of remilled Apitong wood salvaged from the floors of decommissioned railroad boxcars. All other wood used in the building was harvested from certified sustainable forests.

The open loft concept eliminates secondary finishes to expose underlying structural elements and mechanical systems. An advantage of this format is that it uses fewer materials and thus maximizes overall resource-efficiency.

son building had spent only 60 percent of what a more traditional building would have spent on heating, cooling, and lighting—for a 40 percent saving in operational energy expenses.

PGE's Earth Smart program required that Norm Thompson conduct a commissioning analysis of the energy system to ensure that it performed as planned. A consultant, Portland Energy Conservation, was hired for this task and was involved in the design and construction process so that it could determine the intent of the system and assign responsibility for its performance. The consultant continues to review the system's performance and to work with the tenant to ensure its understanding of how to operate it.

Certification under the Smart Earth program qualified Norm Thompson for a 25 percent rebate from PGE on its investment in the energy-efficiency measures. A state tax credit program for energy-conserving expenditures together with the PGE rebate lowered the incremental cost of the energy-saving features by about 55 percent. The incremental cost was about $3.70 per square foot. The credits and rebates and the saving in operational energy expenses that has been realized make the payback time for the EEMs 4.1 years—far exceeding the company's original requirement that they pay for themselves within eight years.

Marketing Green Development

Encouraged by the success of its first green building, the developer is currently pursuing opportunities to devel-

op other green projects in the Portland area. Trammell Crow principal Steve Wells views energy-saving features as a definite draw for build-to-suit projects, particularly in a market like Portland where the environmental ethic is strong.

Green "would be a much harder sell" in a speculative project, says Wells. Tenants are apt to balk if the investment in green features is too steep. However, some resource- and energy-saving features at the Norm Thompson building were not that expensive. The drip-irrigation system, variable-speed drives on the HVAC, oversized ceiling ducts, and occupancy sensors added no more than $15,000 to total costs, he says. But other green features—the integrated daylighting package and the comprehensive energy-management system—were far more costly.

Trammell Crow Company has developed custom-designed buildings for high-tech users. The Norm Thompson building, however, involved a more comprehensive program of specific tenant improvements than the developer is accustomed to providing. The developer was initially uncomfortable with Norm Thompson's request for open ceilings and extra wide corridors, even though some office users have begun to express a preference for loft type spaces.

Nonetheless, should Norm Thompson leave the building, there is some risk that future tenants might want more traditional ceilings. Similarly, the curved shape of the wide corridor on the first floor might not appeal to a future tenant. When the developer agreed to build the corridor to Norm Thompson's specifications, it assumed the risk of potentially having to rebuild it for a future tenant. Likewise, the daylighting system and interior light shelves might be less useful to a future tenant that preferred private offices to an open office plan. On the other hand, future tenants would be attracted by the building's handsome exterior, attractive site, and overall low-cost basis.

Experience Gained

The architect, the developer, and the tenant all learned from their experience in developing a green building. The architect, for example, would set a less aggressive minimum of electrical lighting than the approximately 30 foot-candles selected for this building. The lighting strategy was to keep the level of light used to navigate around the workstations low and provide supplemental task lighting. But Norm Thompson employees were used to much brighter lighting, around 100 foot-candles. Thus, they perceived their new workspace as inordinately dark. In future projects, says William Ruecker, he would probably set a minimum closer to 40 foot-candles and would educate employees on what to expect.

The complicated daylighting system had several unanticipated consequences. Such a system requires that at least 80 percent of interior surfaces be highly reflective, but some of the dark accent colors that were used on the wall segments soaked up too much light. Ruecker cautions against using any dark colors, and says that he would now be more inclined to select white for the wall finishes. Also, a smooth ceiling painted off-white would have produced a higher reflectivity value than the galvanized metal ceiling that was used.

The steel light shelves did not work perfectly. Their perforations—which were intended to give the building's inhabitants glimpses of sky and also to bounce sunlight back into the rooms—were mistakenly made too large by the fabricator. Therefore, light is inadequately filtered and reflected away from the windows, producing some glare. Solid light shelves would have worked better.

The glare problem was made worse because some workstations were placed flush against the window, although the original design had called for four-foot aisles between the windows and workstations. Sun angles create disturbing glare for individuals who work next to the windows.

Ruecker notes that far more sophisticated computer modeling programs for daylighting are now available than when the Norm Thompson building was designed. These programs can more accurately anticipate the consequences of such variables as the size of the perforations.

Steve Wells points out that resource-efficiency and cost saving are often linked. For example, the project's concrete tilt-up construction used a limited number of building materials and it was relatively inexpensive. And the open loft design with its minimal use of secondary layering materials, such as suspended ceilings, minimized cost.

Wells stresses the importance of commissioning for green projects that incorporate complicated energy-saving measures. Trammell Crow contractors carried out some of the commissioning analysis. With hindsight, Wells would not have attempted to do so much of the commissioning in-house. It would have been better to have relied more extensively on the expertise of the commissioning firm, which was far more experienced in this specialized type of analysis.

The limited budget was a major constraint on the project. Some of the decisions would undoubtedly have been easier if the budget had been more flexible. "With a rent limit of $0.76 a square foot, you basically get a standard box in the suburbs," says William Ruecker. "The challenge was to create architecture within these limits."

The strict budget precluded some design elements and the implementation of certain sustainability measures. For example, the Emricks had wanted to restore and enhance the wetlands, which had become monocultural and no longer functioned as a habitat. In situations like this where specific items exceeded the budget, "our approach," says Jane Emrick, "was to do without or do later, rather than compromise on a job half done." The wetlands project was put off until a future date.

Despite the glare and their initial hesitations about the lighting and about working in an open office environment, the employees generally like the new building. They take pride in pointing out the building's use of recycled materials to vendors and other visitors. "Our employees just feel good about the building," says John Emrick.

In green developments, all the systems must be finely integrated and the building process is far more interactive than in a standard project. This interactive process requires extensive collaboration among members of the development team. It involves many meetings and much time.

The Norm Thompson headquarters development succeeded because all the key players—developer, architect, contractors, and tenant—were working as a team toward the same purpose: sustainability and appropriate environmental design. "Without Jane and John Emrick championing these goals from within," says William Ruecker, "the project wouldn't have gone forward. It takes a team and people with vision at the top to make projects like this happen."

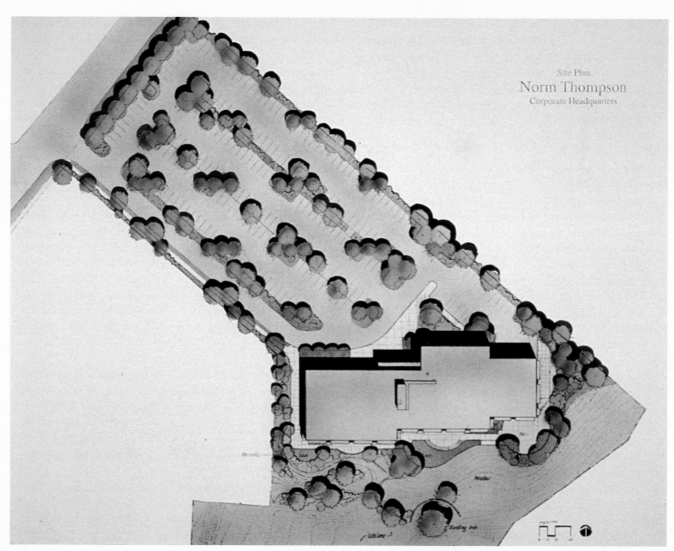

Site plan.

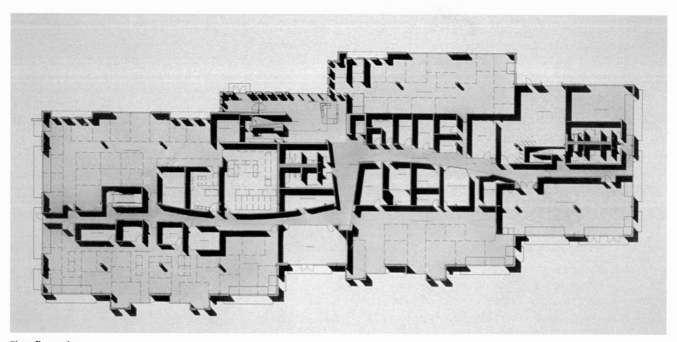

First-floor plan.

Project Data: Norm Thompson Headquarters

Land Use and Building Information

Site area	4.95 acres
Gross building area (GBA)	54,519 square feet
Net rentable area (NRA)[1]	54,519 square feet
Typical floor size	27,260 square feet
Floor/area ratio	0.25
Parking (all surface)	206 spaces

Land Use Plan

	Acres	Percent of Site
Buildings	0.64	12.9%
Paved areas[2]	1.99	40.2%
Landscaped areas	2.32	46.9%
Total	4.95	100.0%

Office Tenant Information

Occupied NRA	100%
Average annual rent	$9.62 per square foot (triple net)
Average length of lease[3]	10 years
Largest tenant size[3]	54,519 square feet

Development Cost Information

Site Costs

Site acquisition	$646,000
Site work and utilities	317,800
Total	$963,800

Construction Costs

Shell	$2,188,400
Interior improvements	1,206,000
Green features[4]	201,700
Utility rebates	(46,900)
Total	$3,549,200

Soft Costs

Architecture/engineering	$172,800
Project management	185,400
Leasing/marketing	233,300
Title	28,900
Taxes/insurance	10,900
Construction interest and fees	157,000
Total	$788,300

Total Development Cost	**$5,301,400**

Development Cost per Gross Square Foot	**$97**

Developer

Trammell Crow Company
8930 S.W. Gemini Drive
Beaverton, Oregon 97008
503-644-9400

Owner

Riggs Bank N.A. as trustee for
The Multi-Employer Property Trust
Washington, D.C.

Tenant

Norm Thompson Outfitters Inc.
3188 N.W. Aloclek Dr.
Hillsboro, Oregon 97124
503-614-4600

Architect

Sienna Architecture Company
Portland, Oregon

Development Schedule

4/1994	Planning started
12/1994	Site purchased
1/1995	Construction started
7/1995	Project completed

Notes

[1] According to BOMA standards, the NRA for a single-tenant building is the same as its GBA. If this were a multitenant building, its NRA would be approximately 52,900 square feet.

[2] Surface parking and roads.

[3] Single tenant.

[4] Incremental cost of energy-saving features, including some that are not counted among PGE's energy-efficiency measures.

640 Memorial Drive
Cambridge, Massachusetts

Originally designed and developed as the Ford Motor Company's first multistory automobile assembly plant, 640 Memorial Drive in Cambridge, Massachusetts, is now home to light industrial, manufacturing, and office tenants. Redeveloped by the Massachusetts Institute of Technology (MIT), the 236,250-square-foot, five-story building was transformed into a speculative, multitenant biotechnology laboratory and office facility.

MIT considered rehabilitating the building for university uses (such as dormitory, administration, or classroom facilities). However, given the property's intrinsic commercial real estate potential, MIT chose to redevelop the historic structure into a commercial asset designed to capture and accommodate the region's expanding high-tech and biotechnology industries.

The redevelopment was spearheaded by the MIT Real Estate Office, a semi-independent division of the university created in 1977 to maximize the institution's return on real estate assets not used for academic purposes. Acting as the owner, developer, and sole financier of the project, MIT plans to use the property's income to assist in the funding of university-related development initiatives.

Site
Constructed in 1913, the building was one of a variety of similar facilities conceived around the prevailing manufacturing technology—the vertical assembly line. Ford moved its plant elsewhere in 1926, because new horizontal manufacturing procedures had rendered its vertical system obsolete.

MIT acquired the property in 1956 and until 1984 leased the facility to Polaroid, which used it to manufacture components for instant cameras. From 1984 to 1987, part of the building was leased to a video display projection company. When the building became vacant in 1987, MIT began to examine alternatives for the structure's redevelopment.

Development Process
In 1988, MIT solicited competitive bids from developers for the redevelopment of 640 Memorial Drive. The only physical requirement attached to the request for proposal (RFP) was that a significant portion of the original building's architecture be retained. More than 40 expressions of interest were received. By 1989, however, the Boston real estate market was in a severe downturn. The unavailability of financing for speculative development made it impossible for MIT to redevelop the property through a venture with an outside interest.

Convinced that the old assembly plant could generate commercial income, MIT's Real Estate Office recommended that the facility be redeveloped by the university into a commercial asset. But not until 1990 did the MIT board give the go-ahead for the university's real estate office to begin investing hard dollars in the project's development.

The decision to redevelop the historic structure as a speculative facility aimed at biotech firms was based on several parameters, including the building's physical attributes, its proximity to biotech and medical research and development activity, and MIT's unique knowledge of the market for biotech real estate.

Financing
At the time of 640's development, the financial resources available to emerging biotechnology companies were limited, except for funding from venture capital firms. MIT recognized that financing deficiencies had created pent-up demand for office and laboratory space near research centers. The university was able to proactively respond to this market demand by financing 640's tenant improvements. In some instances these TIs included substantial lab and manufacturing fit-outs that cost up to $70 per square foot.

MIT financed the buildout for all six of the building's tenants and is amortizing the improvements over the life of the leases. The university also offered what it called "venture leasing" for a targeted biotech tenant with high growth potential. (The tenant now occupies 48,000 square feet of space.) Under this arrangement, as an additional risk premium (over and above the buildout financing), MIT acquired stock warrants in the company much like a venture capital fund would. Should MIT desire, the warrants can be exercised in the future.

Design
Originally designed by John Graham, the old industrial structure has an elaborate exterior that made it particularly amenable to conversion to office use. The building features a brick and terra-cotta facade. The east, south, and west exteriors exhibit decorative features such as a terra-cotta cornice line, arched windows with terra-cotta lintels, and a clock tower. A five-story glass and steel train shed running the entire length of the structure originally dominated the rear of the building.

Conversion of the building began in August 1991 and was completed in March 1994. MIT had decided early in the project to retain and restore the building's highly

Formerly a Ford Motor Company manufacturing facility, 640 Memorial Drive features 40,000-square-foot floorplates and a highly ornate facade that presented a unique opportunity for office conversion.

© Steve Rosenthal

decorative facade and other historic characteristics as faithfully as was economically possible. While qualified to be listed on the National Register of Historic Places, the building was not officially listed as the result of an agreement between MIT and the Cambridge Historic Commission. MIT pledged to cooperate with the commission on an informal basis to address its concerns and desires.

Most of the building's terra-cotta cornice was sound, but the window structures had deteriorated. To keep down costs, fiberglass molding, fabricated to look like the original terra-cotta molding, was used to cover the cornice. In other areas, precast concrete was used to replace numerous odd-shaped terra-cotta pieces. Old small-paned windows were replaced with windows with wider panes that were more appropriate to the building's intended new use.

The multistory glass and steel train shed was transformed into the building's lobby and public entrance. While a major part of the train shed was demolished, the design team preserved the structure's central portion, transforming its five window bays into an atrium. The

Blending both old and new, the building's renovated front reflects its high-tech tenant profile.

Located on the banks of the Charles River, the renovated building offers laboratory, research, and office facilities to Boston's rapidly expanding biotechnology industry.

lobby's new mullions and structural steel were painted white in order to distinguish the new construction from the original structure. The lobby design succeeds in incorporating the building's dominant historic features into a space that overall has a contemporary feel.

The area behind the main building was occupied by surface parking and storage sheds. The structures were demolished to increase the parking area. One of the original side buildings was demolished and replaced with a similar single-story structure that extends the front of 640 and houses a cafeteria and multipurpose rooms.

Accommodating parking required creative design and engineering. The site was too small to provide adequate surface parking. Adding structured parking was too expensive. The solution was to use 80 parking spaces at an MIT-owned lot that is located three blocks away. An on-call taxi service shuttles employees between the building and the off-site lot. Each tenant's parking share is divided between the building's lot and the off-site lot, requiring the tenant to determine how to allocate the spaces to its employees. Parking spaces are generally charged to the tenant at $60 per month for on-site spaces and $40 per month for off-site spaces.

Construction

The building was in excellent condition structurally. The interior support columns required no repair or replacement. The columns were spaced at 23 feet apart, which made the building suitable for office use. However, because the previous use had not required level floors, it was necessary to top the floors with poured concrete to make them even and suitable for office use.

The building's outdated mechanical systems were replaced with two new gas-fired boilers and eight new rooftop HVAC units. In order to market the building as an office and biotech facility, mechanical systems were installed that gave tenants the flexibility to improve the systems as needed. Space on the roof was also provided for tenants to add their own air-handling equipment.

Given the age and previous industrial uses of the building, the need for environmental mitigation was minimal. A limited amount of asbestos and some lead paint were found and removed. Two 20,000-gallon oil tanks located in a storage bunker also were removed.

Marketing and Tenants

Because the facility had fallen into serious disrepair, the development team was forced to rely heavily on architectural renderings and models to attract tenant commitments. Lifeline Systems was the first tenant to sign, committing to 105,000 square feet. But by late 1991, Lifeline had downsized and the firm restructured its lease down to 74,000 square feet. This proved advantageous for leasing up the remainder of the building because it opened up some more flexibility in options for accommodating a variety of smaller tenants. Millennium Pharmaceuticals moved into the building in January 1994, two months before construction was completed. Within three months, the three last tenants had moved in.

The steel and glass former train shed has been redeveloped as a lobby and common area.

Detail of side cornice.

Experience Gained

MIT's education and research focus gives the institute a unique knowledge of emerging trends in the biotech industry. It took advantage of this knowledge and thereby gained a competitive advantage in the marketplace for this kind of commercial real estate. Also, MIT's ability to finance tenant improvements internally was key to its ability to successfully capture the pent-up demand for biotech office and laboratory facilities in the Boston metropolitan area, because start-up biotech companies did not have access to adequate financial resources.

Not only did the developer have a special edge. The building too had a lot going for it. Its historic design and its historic original use worked together to define a strong marketing image for the property.

Site plan.

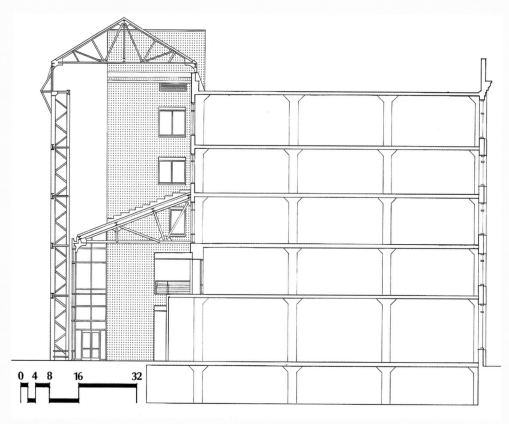

Elevation.

Project Data: 640 Memorial Drive

Land Use and Building Information

Site area	5.3 acres
Gross building area (GBA)	236,250 square feet
Net rentable area (NRA)	187,201 square feet
Typical floor size	37,105 square feet
Floor/area ratio	1.02
Building height	5 stories

Land Use Plan

	Acres	Percent of Site
Buildings	1.0	18.9%
Paved areas[1]	4.0	75.5%
Landscaped areas	0.3	5.6%
Total	5.3	100.0%

Tenant Information[2]

Occupied NRA	100%
Annual Rents	$22–$32 per square foot[3]
Average Length of Lease	5–10 years
Typical Terms of Lease	triple net
Tenant Sizes	6,800–74,000 square feet

Number of Tenants

5,000–10,000 square feet	2
10,000–50,000 square feet	3
More than 50,000 square feet	1
Total	6

Development Cost Information

Site Costs

Site acquisition	$1,600,000
Site work	702,509
Total	$2,302,509

Base Building Cost

Concrete	$801,289
Masonry	1,576,329
Steel	1,123,419
Roof	271,850
Doors/windows	1,406,859
Walls/partitions	900,130
Floors	263,420
Painting	185,388
Elevators	573,633
Plumbing/fire safety	580,288
HVAC	2,707,088
Electrical	813,944
Total	$11,203,637

Tenant Improvements	$5,995,914

Soft Costs

Architecture/engineering	$1,109,027
Project management	126,730
Leasing/marketing	727,857
Legal/accounting	153,449
Taxes/insurance	636,360
Construction fees and interest	970,410
Total	$3,723,833

Total Development Cost	**$23,225,893**
Development Cost per Gross Square Foot	**$98**
Development Cost per Net Square Foot	**$124**

Annual Operating Expenses (1995)

Taxes	$482,994
Insurance	13,104
Services	44,928
Maintenance	119,809
Janitorial	35,568
Utilities	387,506
Management/payroll	149,760
Miscellaneous/cafeteria	44,928
Total	$1,278,597

Developer

Massachusetts Institute of Technology Real Estate Office
238 Main Street, Suite 200
Cambridge, Massachusetts 02143
617-253-1483

Architect

Tsoi/Kobus & Associates
P.O. Box 9114
One Brattle Square
Cambridge, Massachusetts 02238
617-491-3067

Development Schedule

1956	Site purchased
1957	Planning started
1958	Leasing started
1959	Construction started
3/1994	Project completed

Notes

[1]Surface parking and roads.

[2]A majority of the building's tenants occupy a combination of office and laboratory space. Two tenants—totaling 14,500 square feet—occupy only office facilities.

[3]The base rents are $10.00–$13.50 per square foot. The amortization of tenant improvements adds $12.00–$22.00 per square foot.

Kensington Business Centre
Tulsa, Oklahoma

The Kensington Business Centre in suburban Tulsa is an 814,000-square-foot mixed-use office complex created out of a mixed-use retail mall of the same size that was sold to the developer in 1991 for $12 million. The seller was the Resolution Trust Corporation. The upscale Kensington Galleria, which was completed in 1984, had failed to capture its intended affluent market and had lost its sole anchor tenant—Dillard's Department Store—and many of its other retailers. But the Galleria's 183,000-square-foot office tower continued to lease and its 407-room hotel limped along with low occupancies.

The new owner, Ruffin Properties, a property owner/manager based in Wichita, Kansas, with a portfolio of hotels around the United States and 4 million square feet of office and industrial properties in Wichita and Tulsa, saw the handwriting on the wall. The demand in Tulsa was for office space, particularly high-tech office space. The market did not need another mall.

In mid-1993, Ruffin convinced United Video Satellite Group (UVSG), a satellite communications giant with five subsidiaries—Prevue Networks, UVTV, Superstar, SSDS, and Spacecom Systems—to move its headquarters from elsewhere in Tulsa to the proposed Kensington Business Centre, where it would take over the former Galleria mall and a small portion of the former Dillard's. Thus began the lease-driven conversion of the Kensington Galleria to the Kensington Business Centre. The conversion, which was completed in 1994, includes the office reuse of the 270,000 square feet formerly occupied by the Galleria and Dillard's, a reconfiguring and reflagging of the hotel, a change in the anchor tenanting for a 51,000-square-foot linear shopping center annex, and few changes to the office tower.

Plans are underway for a Phase 2 expansion of the mixed-use business center, which is expected to add another 228,000 square feet of office space. Tulsa's office market is currently strong. Some office space is renting for $15 per square foot and 1.26 million square feet of space was absorbed in 1996, a level not seen since the early 1980s. However, speculative development will probably not resume until rents reach $18 to $20 per square foot.

Planning and Design

The Kensington Business Centre is located on a 40-acre site at 71st Street and South Lewis Avenue, less than a 20-minute drive due south from downtown Tulsa and just northwest of the Oral Roberts University campus and the CityPlex Towers. North and west of the site, neighborhood shopping centers, office buildings, and multifamily apartments are the dominant land uses. Farther to the west is the Arkansas River, which, because it bisects the Kensington Galleria's intended market area, deserves part of the blame in the eyes of some analysts for the shopping center's failure. On the south are more office uses and multifamily housing and to the east, high-income, single-family homes. The site is located in the Lewis office submarket, one of the most dynamic office submarkets in suburban Tulsa.

The Kensington Business Centre combines office space and a business hotel in a megastructure built at grade level. The original megastructure was laid out with the office tower at the southeast corner, the L-shaped hotel at the northwest corner, and the department store in the northeast corner, with the Galleria (the retail mall) in the middle connecting the office space and hotel space. The building was (and still is) surrounded on three sides by 2,200 surface parking spaces. The new business center has retained the office tower and hotel uses and turned the former mall and department store into office uses. A linear retail annex anchored by Office Depot is located in another building at the southeast corner of the site.

In the original megastructure, the design sought to capture the synergy of the mix of uses. The office, hotel, and retail uses were fully integrated. Escalators, elevators, and stairs provided easy access between levels. The mall and the department store and the mall and the hotel were connected on two levels, and the mall and the office building were connected on one level. For example, the second level of the mall contained a food court located near the hotel entrance to encourage pedestrian movement between the mall and the hotel.

The design for the conversion to a business center with office space for a few large tenants has restricted the pedestrian movement considerably. While employees at UVSG, which occupies the space that was formerly the mall, still have direct access to the hotel, hotel patrons are restricted from entering UVSG. The hotel is no longer accessible from the office tower through the new UVSG space. Now, office tower employees wishing to enter the hotel must go outside and through the main hotel entrance.

Beginning in December 1993, Ruffin Properties executed the buildout of the former mall for UVSG, according to specifications set forth by UVSG. (Ruffin collaborated with UVSG throughout the design process.) Three of the former mall entrances were retained as office entrances, but their look changed completely. A waterfall

A view from the south of the former Kensington Galleria, now the Kensington Business Centre. Downtown Tulsa, which is almost due north of the Galleria, appears on the horizon.

that had been just inside the mall's main (north) entrance was removed and replaced with a display of colorful banners advertising various UVSG products and divisions. UVSG's reception area was located just inside the southeast entrance, which was formerly the entrance to the atrium of the Galleria. Modular office units now occupy the former food court (up the stairs at the back of the reception area and to the left). Vestiges of the mall structure remain throughout—for example, the connections between the two levels. UVSG replaced the escalators with staircases and landings.

From the staircases, one can view the firm's technicians busy at work. The company's office design puts an emphasis on modular workstations, which vary in design by the work functions they accommodate. UVSG's different subsidiaries use office space differently. Some are able to achieve a high employment density and concentrate their employees in relatively small areas. But some areas of this workplace house space-intensive functions. Among these areas are the satellite transmission rooms, uninterruptible power supply rooms, telephone switching equipment rooms, and computer rooms. The aver-

age space per employee in the UVSG offices is around 200 square feet.

Former boutiques have been transformed into rooms that house state-of-the-art telecommunications facilities, like the multiple monitors and broadcast rooms belonging to the Prevue Channel, part of the Prevue Networks. Another vestige of the former mall is the tall trees and plants on the lower level. These were kept to enhance the open floor plan of the UVSG headquarters.

The two-story department store space also underwent considerable design changes in its adaptation to office space. Two tenants—Tulsa National Bank and MicroAge, a computer services firm—had different requirements.

The bank occupies about half of the ground floor of the former Dillard's. This space had 14-foot ceilings and imported-marble floors, which made it ideal for a classic bank interior. The major changes made in the conversion were some remodeling of the interior and the addition of drive-in facilities.

MicroAge leased the other half of the ground floor and a large share of the upper level. The company's second-floor reception area is the former lingerie department.

An architectural space frame and corporate sign announce the southeast entrance to United Video's headquarters in the Kensington Business Centre.

The openness of the office design is nowhere more apparent than in United Video's atrium

An original escalator from a ground-floor entrance provides the primary access to MicroAge's reception area and second-floor offices.

The 407-room Sheraton hotel was refurbished throughout and converted to a 382-room Marriott Southern Hills, a full-service business hotel containing 43,000 square feet of flexible meeting space in 16 meeting and banquet rooms. The rooms were wired to accommodate voice and data transmissions through modems and to provide access to the Internet—and also cosmetically improved.

The hotel centers on an atrium that provides natural light. A terra-cotta and green color theme is used and the public areas feature oriental rugs, plantings, brass railings, and original art works. The conference rooms and restaurants are expensively finished and furnished. Before the hotel renovations, average occupancy was 48 percent at an average room rate of $69.99. Since the renovation, occupancy is at 65 percent at a room rate of $109.99.

Few changes were made to the exterior of the structure, but the building's appearance was substantially changed. Windows were cut into the glass-reinforced concrete walls of the former mall and department store spaces, to bring natural light into the office environments. (These office areas also gained in brightness when interior walls were eliminated to implement open office plans.) A second exterior change was the addition of a space frame as an architectural design element to emphasize the southeast entrance to UVSG.

Many design changes were involved in the building's transformation to Kensington Business Centre, but the key to the project's economic viability was that the structure did not require much change. If the developer had had to make sweeping changes to the existing structure, the costs of the conversion would likely have outweighed the rents it could achieve. Rents, albeit rising, had not reached a level that would justify new construction. Also important was that much of the necessary infrastructure was in place and suitable for office tenants. Adding expensive new building systems might have cost more than the new use would justify.

The energy management, life-safety, telecommunications, and security systems at Kensington Business Centre incorporate advanced technology in their engineering. The entire complex shares a central heating and cooling plant. An advanced energy management system monitors temperatures within each zone and adjusts operations accordingly. The EMS manages air handling, the functioning of mechanical and electrical units, and routine maintenance. A well-insulated concrete roof enhances the energy-efficiency of the building. A state-of-the-art audible notice and alarm system protects occupants from fire. To attract high-tech tenants, the developer installed a state-of-the-art fiberoptic terminal that all tenants can access—although not all do currently.

Leasing and Marketing

The leasing of Kensington Business Centre drove the deal. Informal discussions between Ruffin and UVSG

In United Video's conversion of the retail space, these stairs replaced an escalator. Employees of Superstar, a video programming subsidiary of United Video, occupy the modular workstations on the lower level.

A corner store space on the second floor was converted to a conference room, complete with Italian-marble tables and state-of-the-art video equipment.

Ex-stores turned broadcast rooms are a common sight at United Video's headquarters.

United Video's main entrance was the north entrance to the mall. Where there had been a waterfall, the company created a display of color televisions (left) showcasing its products and services.

that indicated the willingness of UVSG to move its Tulsa headquarters to the Kensington Business Centre location got the project moving. UVSG's first lease was for approximately 75,000 square feet, which it later expanded to 200,000 square feet. Thus, the office space was significantly preleased prior to conversion, although significant preleasing was not a condition of financing since the project was financed by cash put up by Ruffin Properties. The former Dillard's was also completely leased before the project was completed. New leases currently average around $15 per square foot.

With Kensington Business Centre 100 percent occupied and Kensington Office Tower 98.5 percent occupied, the owner's current marketing activities are directed at maintaining positive tenant relations. Other maintenance marketing focuses on commercial listings in trade publications.

The Tulsa Southern Hills Marriott is a separate operating entity with full-time sales and marketing staff. Its marketing is targeted to the business community and relies on face-to-face meetings with meeting planners in organizations, attendance at trade conferences, and the distribution of kits describing the hotel's meeting and room facilities and related amenities.

Experience Gained

Office use has undergone a paradigm shift, and it is this shift that made Kensington Business Centre's former retail space suitable for conversion to office space at a rea-

sonable cost. KBC succeeded in large part because office employees now share space whereas previously they operated out of private offices, because open office plans and modular furniture have replaced interior walls and traditional office furniture.

This model of retail conversion is replicable. In downtown Tulsa, in fact, the Williams Center Forum, which is another upscale mall that was built in the late 1970s, is being transformed into office space primarily for the Williams Companies. This conversion will yield large floorplates as did the Kensington Business Centre conversion.

Ruffin Properties spent more than a year evaluating alternative retail leasing plans for the mall. But everything kept coming back to the market's strong demand for high-tech office space. Much of the success of this project can be ascribed to good market analysis—and some significant preleasing by credit tenants. Being approached by a good-quality anchor tenant removes a lot of the risk from the project.

Fostering and maintaining a good relationship with tenants is of paramount importance to a successful office project. Ruffin Properties' management staff is located at the Kensington Business Centre in the office tower—always accessible to the tenants and always able to respond quickly to their needs.

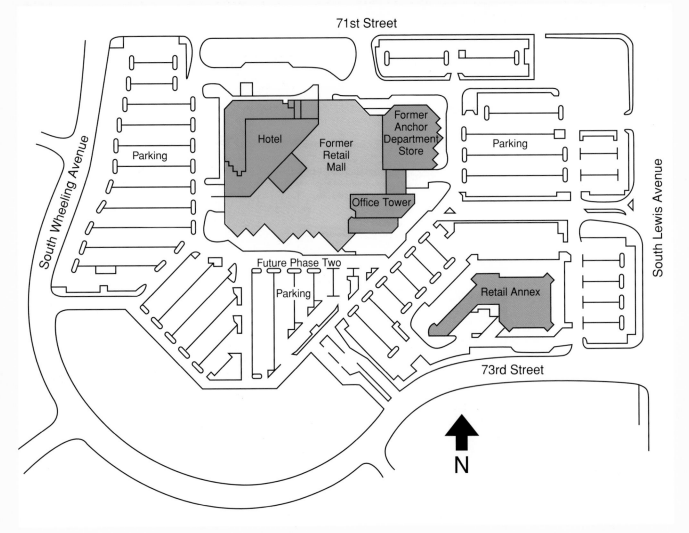

Site plan.

Project Data: Kensington Business Centre

Land Use and Building Information

Site Area	40 acres

Gross Building Area (GBA) Phase 1

Office[1]	453,000 square feet
Retail	51,000 square feet
Hotel	310,000 square feet
Total	814,000 square feet

Net Rentable Office Area (NRA)

Office tower	164,000 square feet
Converted office space	236,000 square feet
Total	400,000 square feet

Floor/Area Ratio	0.47

Parking (all surface)	2,200 spaces

Land Use Plan

	Acres	Percent of Site
Buildings		
Hotel	1.45	3.6%
Office	6.57	16.4
Retail	1.17	2.9
Total	9.19	23.0
Paved Areas[2]	26.56	66.4
Landscaped Areas	4.25	10.6
Total	40.00	100.0%

Tenant Information

	Before Conversion	1997
Occupancy		
Office tower	82%	99%
Converted space[3]	45%	100%
Hotel	48%	65%
Retail annex	91%	95%
Average Rates		
Office	$9.21 per square foot	$10.68 per square foot
Retail	$1.75 per square foot	$9.70 per square foot
Hotel	$69.99 per night	$109.99 per night
Major Tenants		
Office tower	Dyco Petroleum	Callidus Technology
	Unit Corporation	Unit Corporation
Converted space[3]	Dillard's	United Video Satellite Group
	Sipe's Food Stores	Office Depot

Development Cost Information

Site Acquisition Cost	$12,000,000

Converted Space Construction Costs

	United Video	MicroAge	Tulsa National Bank
Superstructure	$760,500	$210,233	
HVAC	385,000	73,825	
Electrical	875,000	273,625	
Plumbing/sprinklers	365,000	59,786	
Elevators		50,000	
Fees/general conditions	1,480,000	21,142	
Finishes	803,600	361,500	
Graphics/specialties	54,718	21,848	
Other	3,000	13,434	
Total	$4,726,818	$1,085,393	$746,137

Converted Space Soft Costs

	United Video	MicroAge	Tulsa National Bank
Architecture/engineering	$115,000	$3,500	
Project management	70,000	54,270	
Leasing/marketing	450,000	100,000	$75,000
Taxes/insurance	100,000	48,000	37,000
Other	3,000	3,111	
Total	$738,000	$208,881	$112,000

Total Converted Space

Development Cost	$5,464,818	$1,294,274	$858,137

Hotel Renovation Costs

Lobby	$158,600
Rooms/kitchen	2,034,000
Public areas	207,900
Meeting rooms	321,600
Infrastructure	140,000
Total	$2,862,100

Total Development Cost	$22,479,329
Development Cost per Gross Square Foot	$28

Developer

Ruffin Companies
Wichita, Kansas

Property Manager

Ruffin Properties
Tulsa, Oklahoma

Space Planners (United Video space)

Page Zebrowski Architects
bellwether design ltd.
Tulsa, Oklahoma

Notes

[1] Includes 183,000 square feet in the office tower and 270,000 square feet of converted retail space.

[2] Surface parking and roads.

[3] The Galleria and department store spaces that were converted to office uses in 1993 and 1994.

8. Trends

Office development has always been a highly cyclical industry characterized by frequent booms and busts. Suggesting what today's developer or investor should do to ensure relevance (and success) in tomorrow's office market is a hazardous undertaking. The playing field for office development is composed of many elements, including the national economy, capital markets, labor force trends, business structures, and technological innovation. Undoubtedly unforeseen changes in these basic forces will influence office markets in unexpected ways. Developers and investors can see ahead only a year or two with any level of confidence.

While office market conditions cannot be predicted with any level of confidence beyond the turn of the century and while a blueprint for the office building of the future cannot be drawn with any certainty, trends already in progress indicate some of the directions that office development is likely to take. This chapter discusses some of these trends, beginning with locational trends. Suburban locations will continue to capture most new office development. At the same time, selected downtowns will see their office markets revive. Also, older office buildings will offer renovation and reuse opportunities.

On the financing front, the most important trend in the 1990s has been the explosive growth of public securities tied to real estate. The big question for the next several years is whether the late 1990s flood of capital into real estate will lead to overbuilding.

Major legislative and regulatory changes will have an impact on some important aspects of office development. ULI asked the Building Owners and Managers Association (BOMA) International, the leading advocacy organization of the commercial real estate industry, to comment on some of these impacts and possible developer responses. This chapter's section on regulatory issues that will affect office developers—telecommunications deregulation, electricity deregulation, the phasing out of CFCs and certain other coolants, the new edition of the guidelines for the Americans with Disabilities Act, and powered platforms for window washing—was provided by BOMA.

Finally, the trend of designing buildings from the inside out for maximum space efficiency, changing office cultures, and operating efficiencies is likely to strengthen. The key design adjectives for the successful office buildings of tomorrow will be flexible, efficient, intelligent, and green. Functional considerations will take precedence over aesthetic considerations, although architectural character remains an important criterion for tenants.

The Wayne Dalton corporate headquarters building in Holmes County, Ohio, was designed from the inside out to suit the company's work processes.

Apple Computer Inc. chose a low-rise campus style environment for its R&D office complex located in Cupertino, California, at the gateway to Silicon Valley.

Hellmuth Obata + Kassabaum

Locational Trends

Office development will continue to occur predominantly in suburban locations, at least into the early 21st century. Over the past 25 years, office-based employment not only grew enormously, but also shifted its center of gravity from the central business districts of America's cities to the suburbs. The real estate boom of the 1980s brought about a rapid decentralization of office activity. In 1970, 80 percent of the office space in the nation's 50 largest metropolitan areas was located in CBDs. By 1994, these CBDs contained only 39 percent of regional office space. Suburbs have accounted for three out of every four square feet of new space occupied since 1970. More recently, the absorption of office space in suburban markets has outpaced that in CBDs by three to four times.[1]

Market conditions in many CBDs are improving (see next trend), but suburban locations offer some strong advantages for office development. Enabled by advances in information and communications technology to operate in whole or in part from suburban locations, many companies are attracted by lower suburban rental rates and closer white-collar labor markets. Lower employment costs in suburban locations may also be an important factor according to research from MIT's Center for Real Estate, which reveals that workers are willing to trade off lower wages for shorter commutes.[2] However, the commuting advantage in many suburban locations is being eroded by suburban traffic problems arising from a failure to make necessary infrastructure improvements.

In some suburban markets, the deepening concentration of technology-based companies will continue to generate new demand for office space. Among these markets are such areas as Silicon Valley, North Carolina's Research Triangle, Boston's Route 128 technology corridor, and the Dulles Airport corridor in northern Virginia.

The next two decades may be much more favorable for downtown office markets than were the previous two. Some central cities are experiencing an office market revival. Downtown office markets around the United States have shown a remarkable recovery from the nearly comatose condition that characterized most of them throughout much of the 1990s. In 1997, the nation's Class A downtown office market, for the first time since the 1980s, was the best-performing property category in CB Commercial's National Real Estate Index. In price and rental gains for Class A properties, downtowns outperformed their suburbs in 1997, although suburban office markets overall experienced higher occupancy rates and absorption.[3]

Rising rents and a shortage of space in some suburban markets have been responsible for some of this revival of activity in downtown office markets. But some office users appear to be looking more closely at downtown locations for other reasons as well, including transit access and urban amenities. Office construction in suburban locations, according to some experts, is proceeding at a pace that will surpass demand by mid-1999, while demand for office space in downtowns is expected to outpace construction at least through the turn of the century.

Certain characteristics will make some downtowns more attractive than others for office development, among them a mix of land uses (residential, retail, commercial, tourist, cultural, entertainment, educational, and governmental), a sense that the streets and sidewalks are safe, the availability of convenient mass transit, and a pedestrian-friendly and lively ambiance. Quality-of-life factors will attract employers seeking to hire young professionals. Downtowns that empty out shortly after 5:00 p.m. will not be seen as prime office locations.

Another factor supporting downtown office markets is the willingness of REITs to invest in them. Among the downtown office markets that have already attracted a concentration of REIT investments are Atlanta, Boston, Chicago, Dallas, Houston, Los Angeles, Newark/Northern New Jersey, Philadelphia, and Washington, D.C.

Metropolitan markets with high office-using employment growth will provide the best opportunities.
Price Waterhouse uses projected office employment to predict the top U.S. metropolitan office markets. Based on rates of growth in office employment, the top markets are Austin, Charlotte (North Carolina), Fort Worth, Las Vegas, Miami, Phoenix, Riverside (California), Salt Lake City, Seattle, and Tucson. Based on the number of new office jobs, the top markets are Atlanta, Boston, Chicago, Dallas, Houston, Los Angeles, Minneapolis, Northern New Jersey, Phoenix, Seattle, and Washington, D.C. All of these markets will be ones to watch in the coming years.

The redevelopment of obsolete buildings is a growing office development and investment niche.
Most urban areas are saddled with a glut of functionally obsolete but otherwise structurally sound, well-located office buildings, industrial properties, and other older structures that can be repositioned to compete successfully with new office space. In those downtowns where the demand for office space is outpacing new construction, renovation activity should experience an upsurge. Grubb & Ellis suggests that conditions in many CBDs are prime for office renovation projects: little or no office construction, rising rents, a large supply of Class B and Class C properties, and municipal governments anxious to keep businesses in the city.[4]

The outfitting of Class B properties with Class A infrastructure is likely to become a growing phenomenon. Such updated buildings can find a market among startup companies—especially those in the high-tech sector—that are unable to afford the higher rents of more traditional office projects. In some cities, including San Francisco and New York, clusters of software and multimedia firms have begun to emerge, mostly occupying Class B and Class C space.

Downtown office rehabilitation projects are being helped along increasingly by incentives, such as property tax abatements, offered by municipal and state governments seeking to promote private investment in obsolete buildings in central cities.

Another public sector incentive that is gathering steam and spurring private development in central cities is the loosening of stringent cleanup requirements for brownfield sites. Such sites can be attractive for office and industrial parks.

Market Discipline and Financing Trends

The continuation of the current expansion will increasingly test the theory that the last great boom (and bust) taught the office market a lesson.
Once again, plenty of money is fueling the acquisition and development of office buildings. The explosive growth of public real estate capital markets in the form

The development of the 390,000-square-foot corporate headquarters of Indiana Farm Bureau Insurance put an abandoned 70-year-old tire and rubber factory to a new use.

Ratio Architects Inc.

of REITs and commercial mortgage–backed securities (CMBSs) has contributed much of this fuel, but pension funds, commercial banks (still the leading source for commercial mortgages), and private investors as well as other sources of real estate funding have also opened the money faucets. At issue over the next several years when capital is likely to be plentiful will be the quality of investment and lending decisions.

There are those who worry that the capital markets—particularly the public markets—will not have enough discipline to control the flow of capital when the currently strong office market softens. Vernon George of Hammer, Siler, George Associates, a market analysis firm in Silver Spring, Maryland, represents this view in the following observation: "Tenant optimism and new space appetite is strong and getting stronger as the economy and capital markets continue to provide real momentum. But the beat-the-other-projects-into-the-market psychology is already becoming a threat to the market's balance in the future."[5]

And there are others who argue that a number of factors—including the restrained growth in new space, a consistent growth in demand, and the increasing influence of the public markets—will limit overbuilding in this cycle to a modest event. In this view, public markets are more likely to make corrections quickly, and thus dampen the amplitude of the cycle's ups and downs. Multifamily apartment REITs provide a recent example of quick public market adjustments. As certain apartment markets, such as Atlanta's, began to soften after a spate of construction activity, the value of stocks in REITs that were heavily invested in these markets also declined. Helping the public markets to react quickly to any softening of the office market will be the ready availability—to stock analysts and other market participants—of relevant information on tenant moves, employment patterns, and absorption trends.[6]

The appetite of REITs for office properties should continue to grow.

The volume of securities issued by both REITs and CMBS conduits set records in 1997. Office buildings accounted for 40 percent of the value of all property assets acquired by REITs in the fourth quarter of 1997, and the strong fundamentals of today's office market should continue to attract the interest of these investors.

The growing number of mutual funds that are targeting REITs is one of the underpinnings of the REIT marketplace. Assets in REIT mutual funds rose from $1.5 billion in 1994 to an estimated $10 billion in late 1997. T. Rowe Price, for example, recently established the T. Rowe Price Real Estate Fund, a no-load fund to invest in REITs and in companies involved in the operation, development, management, and financing of commercial properties.

Stockley Park, a landscaped business park on a former landfill just outside of London, serves as a model for the reclamation and redevelopment of urban brownfield sites.

An obsolete warehouse facility in Sunnyvale, California, was converted to a state-of-the-art headquarters building for Advanced Micro Devices.

Ratio Architects Inc.

The future involvement of REITs in office development (as opposed to acquisition and management) is uncertain.
Investors have been cautious in their initial responses to some recently formed office REITs with substantial development underway.

Sam Zell, the manager of Equity Office Properties and several other REITs, thinks that most REITs cannot effectively incorporate development into their operations. The top priority of REITs needs to be tight management to control costs, he says, but if they are involved in developing properties the talent and attention of the staff will be attracted to the deal-making development jobs rather than the REIT management jobs. In Zell's opinion, demand will be strong for firms that develop properties for sale to REITs.

REITs will dominate certain office markets as they consolidate, acquire properties at a rapid pace, and focus their sights on a limited number of markets.
Spieker Properties, for example, controls more than 80 percent of the Kruse Way office submarket in Portland, according to Grubb & Ellis. Currently, more than half of REIT investment by value is located in only 20 urban areas. REITs with a large presence in local markets will be able to influence rents in those markets.

The concentration of office ownership and management in large REITs is likely to lead to some efficiencies of scale.
Arguing that the real estate industry is generally unsophisticated when it comes to the operation of properties, Sam Zell thinks that well-run REITs can grow their businesses by becoming better operators and integrating the operations of multiple properties. Zell sees opportunities for multiproperty REITs in the bulk purchase of various goods and services, including electricity, as well as in the sale of services associated with office operations to building tenants.

The REIT format may attract more pension fund money into real estate.
Pension funds first started diversifying into real estate in the late 1970s, and many observers predicted that real estate would eventually constitute 10 percent or more of their assets. But it currently makes up only about 3 percent. Probably no class of financial institution has a more ambivalent attitude about real estate based on the experience of the last decade. However, pension funds are increasingly investing in REITs, and some observers think that their allocations to REITs will grow rapidly. Some pension funds are considering converting some or all of their real estate portfolios into REITs.

The CMBS market will capture an increasingly large share of the overall real estate debt market.
Traditional lenders, particularly insurance lenders, have started to substitute debt securities for whole loans and this trend is likely to continue. The size and diversity of CMBS mortgage pools is becoming much larger, which decreases their risk. Most of the current CMBS inventory is in investment-grade properties that pose little credit risk, but certain CMBS loan pools are likely to suffer defaults in the future and cause some bumpiness in the CMBS market.

Insurance companies may become more aggressive players in the large-loan marketplace.
Insurance companies have been retrenching from the equity markets, mostly because of the poor match-up between their short-term liabilities and the long-term investment horizons of real estate ownership. Like pension funds, some insurance companies are considering the rollover of their real estate holdings into REITs. On the other hand, insurance companies have become more active of late in real estate debt markets, competing with CMBS conduits and Wall Street. Their total mortgage holdings declined in 1996 but started to rise modestly during 1997. As noted, some insurance com-

panies have started to invest in the CMBS market in preference to whole loans.

Notable Regulatory Issues[7]

The deregulation of telecommunications will provide office developers with new opportunities and introduce new complexities into the development process.
The federal Telecommunications Act of 1996, various subsequent federal communications on the subject, and various state utility commission decisions have combined with advances in technology to eliminate the former boundaries between local and long-distance telephone companies, cable companies, cellular phone service providers, and Internet access providers. This confronts office developers with some new questions, including who should wire a building and what new revenue opportunities may be available.

Office developers no longer necessarily want the local telephone company to wire their buildings. In fact, in most cases it will be in their best interest to retain ownership over what is referred to as the "last mile" of wire in order to take advantage of the competition among telecommunications providers for access to a building's tenants. Investors with a sophisticated understanding of the increasingly competitive telecommunications industry will insist that a return from the last mile of wire be included in any developer's business plan.

Developers that incorporate the inside wiring—the building's communications network—into their business plans have an additional benefit to sell in predevelopment marketing to investors and tenants. It is like including a parking lot in the business plan as an additional source of operating revenue and a tenant amenity. Tenants and telecommunications providers will pay for use of the building's communications network.

The provision of communications services as a part of office building operations is not a new concept. Shared tenant services (STS systems) were introduced in office buildings a number of years ago. The new twist is that many telecommunications providers can be given simultaneous access to the building's communications wiring, whereas access was restricted formerly to the company providing the STS. The sale of access to a building's wiring network can become a significant source of revenue as local and long-distance phone companies, cable companies, and Internet access providers compete to serve the building's tenants.

Another growing market opportunity is provided by the explosion in wireless technology applications and its demand for rooftop space. A developer would be well advised to market rooftop leases in the building's preconstruction stage. There is a well-financed, growing sector of rooftop users—potential anchor tenants that may not need an inch of space below the building's roofline. The developer should survey them to determine their special needs for rooftop space and support

areas in order to accommodate these needs at the highest possible price in the market. Rooftop prelease commitments can be a financing plus.

The deregulation of electric utilities will also introduce important changes in the way office buildings are developed and operated.
Electricity deregulation has occurred or will soon occur around the country. It holds out the promise of price

The Demand for Office Space

Pessimists about the future of office space demand argue that technology and the more efficient management of space, as well as continued corporate downsizing, will empty vast amounts of office space that will never be reabsorbed.

At first glance, this scenario seems plausible. However, it simply is not supported by the facts. In reality, these factors—more technology in offices, innovations in space management, and corporate downsizing—have accompanied a steady rise in the amount of office space used per worker over the last 15 years. From 1980 to 1995, the average amount of space per office worker rose by 13 feet (or 9 percent)—from an estimated 142 square feet to 155 square feet—for an annual increase of just under one square foot (or roughly 0.6 percent).

Some of the increase in space per worker reflects a response to falling real rents. Demand for office space is elastic in relation to rent. Although not precisely known, this demand elasticity is probably roughly 0.1, meaning that a 10 percent reduction in real rents will cause the demand for space per worker to increase by 1 percent.

The actual increase in space demand from 1980 to 1995 can be adjusted for the impact of decreases in real rents. Demand elasticity suggests that rent decreases were responsible for a 4 to 5 percent increase in the average amount of space per worker, accounting for somewhat more than half of the total 13-square-foot increase. Had rents remained stable, the average space per worker would have reached only about 149 square feet in 1995. Adjusted for rent decreases, the annual increase in the average amount of space per office worker from 1980 to 1995 was roughly 0.4 square foot.

Three key forces are driving the demand for space per worker steadily upward: technology, the changing mix of office workers, and the growing use of movable walls and partitions.

First, the application of advanced technologies to office work has greatly reduced the need for certain types of space, such as typing pools. At the same reductions ranging from 10 percent to 50 percent, which can affect office development in a number of ways.

For example, in a deregulated power market landlords may find that they can best meet tenants' needs and their own needs for lower operating expenses by purchasing power. As large buyers, office building management companies will be able to obtain better prices. Many owners will modify triple-net leases to make themselves the exclusive power purchaser for tenants.

Power deregulation will also have an effect on the economics of incorporating energy-efficient systems into the design of office buildings. As the price of electric power drops, the payback period for the added upfront costs of energy-efficient lighting fixtures and electric HVAC systems will lengthen. Furthermore, competition in the power marketplace will cause many utilities to reduce or eliminate their rebate programs for energy-saving measures in the design and operation of office buildings.[8]

time, it has created new demand for other types of space, such as video conferencing facilities and financial trading floors.

Second, even though modern space management practices allow less space for both professional workers and support workers, more space is required because the ratio of professional to support workers has become much larger—and professional workers use larger amounts of space. Thirty years ago, armies of office clerks—the staple of office operations then—were accommodated in tiny amounts of space per clerk. Modern office operations are characterized by many more managers per worker and seemingly endless numbers of attorneys, accountants, and other professional workers—all typically using more space than clerical workers.

Third, the use of movable walls and partitions—introduced into the office market in the 1980s in projects involving the renovation of older buildings—has enabled space use to increase.

Telecommuting is often mentioned as a factor that will depress future demand for office space. However, according to a study by the U.S. Bureau of Labor Statistics, only 100,000 Americans (out of approximately 20 million who claimed to work at home in 1994) work exclusively from home. The others who work at home reported that they also have offices at their places of employment. Even if the number of employees who telecommute exclusively were to triple over the next decade, the impact on the future demand for office space would be minuscule. If each of these 200,000 new telecommuters vacated 160 square feet of office space, the total amount of demand for space that would be affected is 32 million square feet, which is less than 0.5 percent of the U.S. office stock.

Another commonly used argument by analysts who predict a weakening of demand for office space is that firms are downsizing. However, most of this activity today is better characterized as outsourcing. The same task whether performed by a large firm or by a smaller firm with a core competency in that task requires roughly the same number of workers, so out-

sourcing shuffles but does not reduce employment. In fact, employment in the United States has been growing by some 1.7 million workers per year even as downsizing has spread.

The demand for office space over the next decade depends on changes in three interacting factors: the average amount of space per office worker, the number of office workers, and real rents. If real rents rise by 30 percent over the next decade, the demand for space per office worker will fall by roughly 3 percent. This decrease in demand will be offset by the continued 0.4 square feet per worker per year rent-adjusted growth in space demand, suggesting that average space per worker in 2005 will be 155 square feet, as it was in 1995. In the meantime, projected employment growth will increase total demand for office space by about 1.25 percent annually over the next decade. All told, an additional 800 million square feet up to perhaps 1.5 billion square feet of office space will be absorbed, or as much office space as currently exists in New York City doubled plus in the entire Chicago metropolitan area.

Innovations in technology and space management have not reduced the need for office space. What they have done is change the uses for office space and the types of space that are needed. Office space will continue to change in terms of design and location. Older space will require capital expenditures to remain competitive, but businesses will still need office space. While the ways in which office space is used will change in unforeseen ways, it is safe to say that the increase in the demand for office space over the next decade will be massive.

Source: Adapted from Peter Linneman, "Will We Need More Office Space?" *Urban Land*, May 1997, pp. 11, 69.

The Montreal Protocol, an international treaty, will affect the choices that office building developers make concerning air-conditioning systems and also safety precautions for mechanical rooms.
The Montreal Protocol limits the manufacture of chlorofluorocarbons (CFCs) and other ozone-depleting chemical compounds that are used as coolants. In choosing an air-conditioning system, developers will have to match its useful life to reasonable expectations concerning the supply of refrigerant for the system. Systems that will outlast the availability of their coolant should not be chosen. The U.S. Environmental Protection Agency can provide a list of affected coolants and the sunset dates for their manufacture.

None of the post-CFC refrigerants is as energy-efficient as CFCs, so the cost for operating air conditioning will rise. Furthermore, the post-CFC refrigerants are significantly more flammable and developers must therefore take stricter safety precautions in accordance with local codes. In choosing a cooling system, the developer of an office building should make sure that the mechanical engineer's estimates of the operating cost of alternative systems have taken into account the efficiency of the coolant and that the legal supply of the coolant is sufficiently assured.

A new edition of the ADAAG will liberalize most accessibility requirements of the Americans with Disabilities Act.
The federal government will release a new edition of the Americans with Disabilities Act Accessibility Guidelines (ADAAG) in late 1998. According to BOMA's reading of the draft of these guidelines, most of the accessibility guidelines affecting office buildings will be liberalized, and buildings that comply with current standards and continue to make good faith efforts to comply in the future should be in compliance with the new standards.

One exception to this general liberalization of the rules concerns the height of functional fixtures such as light switches and fire alarms. The new ADAAG is expected to lower the maximum allowable height to 48 inches (from 54 inches). The prudent developer planning a building today should install fixtures at 48 inches to save the cost of a later retrofit.

Another ADA issue concerns whether an owner may look to the building's architect to defend any claims that the building violates the ADA. Federal court rulings to date have clouded the issue, and BOMA International has joined the Justice Department in petitioning the courts to clarify the matter, which they no doubt will. In the interim, the prudent owner will contractually obligate the architect to indemnify the owner against claims relating to ADA violations.

The developers of buildings rising above 130 feet may consider installing roof anchors that can support powered platforms for window washing.
Despite the efforts of some parties to require the use of a powered platform for window washing for building exceeding 130 feet, it is unlikely, in BOMA's view, that the federal government or any state government will actually mandate such a requirement. However, depending on cost considerations, the installation of appropriate roof anchors during the construction of new buildings would allow the use of powered platforms and would also be of use to window washers using controlled-descent equipment.

Design Trends

Scenario modeling will become more important as a technique for designing office buildings.
"What if?" scenarios based on potential changes in tenant preferences will be used to analyze the adequacy of proposed designs for a variety of situations. For example, what if tenants in place need more space or do not need as much space? Will the design of the building and its HVAC and electrical and communications systems easily accommodate different ways of subdividing space? If a major tenant relocates after ten years, is the space flexible enough to accommodate the needs of a different (unknown) tenant(s).

Office tenants will have a wide array of choices in tomorrow's office market. The buildings that succeed in the foreseeable future will be those that are flexible and adaptable to changing work practices and technologies. They will provide floor space and infrastructure (especially power supply, telecommunications wiring and air conditioning) that is arranged to make the reconfiguration of work areas convenient and cost-effective. New office buildings that cannot be adapted to changes in the work place will find themselves waging a losing battle with the increasingly obsolete buildings of the 1960s, 1970s, and 1980s that can offer lower lease rates.

Outside of downtowns and other locations with high land costs, most new office buildings will be low rises or mid rises.
Their advantages compared with high-rise buildings include smaller and less expensive foundations, building systems that are easier to design and operate, and a higher efficiency ratio (the ratio of rentable square footage to total square footage). The taller the building, the greater the need for elaborate life-safety systems and the greater the impact of building systems on construction cost and the building's efficiency ratio.

Business organizations will increasingly adopt open-plan offices.
The message for developers and owners is clear. Office buildings must be flexible. If their interiors cannot be reconfigured, they run the risk of becoming obsolete.

The space allocated to private offices within many office layouts is shrinking. Whereas the basis for the allocation of office space in most business organizations traditionally has been the firm's hierarchy, many organizations are moving toward space configurations based on work performance needs. Whereas office layouts once reflected the organizational chart, more and more they reflect patterns of workplace interaction and job-based requirements for equipment and space.

Many organizations have implemented or experimented with a variety of nontraditional (nonterritorial) office practices like hoteling and telecommuting that, in general, tend to reduce the amount of space set aside for individual employees and increase the amount of shared space. Telecommuting and other nonterritorial workplace strategies have received a lot of press, but the evidence to date does not support the notion that virtual space will replace the need for physical office space. Most jobs require face-to-face interaction, and teamwork and collaboration are at the heart of the creative process.

Workstyles and workplace technologies will continue to change.
Thus, office developers must design interior layouts with built-in flexibility. The universal grid, also called univer-

sal plan, in which all space planning is based on a standard module of, for example, eight-by-eight feet is one approach to built-in flexibility. The universal plan is designed to enable the power and telecommunications infrastructure to be easily upgraded or improved and to allow companies to reconfigure work areas as often as needed. Any module can support a variety of types of workspaces—from individual workstations to collaborative work areas to files and equipment—depending on the organization's preferences, and changing from one type of workspace to another does not involve significant construction costs.

As modular planning evolves, the premium space in offices will be reserved for the shared work areas.
Many organizations in the future will choose to locate private offices near the core of the building so that the employees working in high-density open areas can have direct access to natural light and views.

The open floor plans at Northern Telecom's Brampton Centre outside Toronto typify trends in office space configuration. Space planning today focuses on employee interaction, satisfaction, and productivity. Open-plan offices emphasize the easy rearrangement of workspaces to meet changing needs.

Hellmuth Obata + Kassabaum

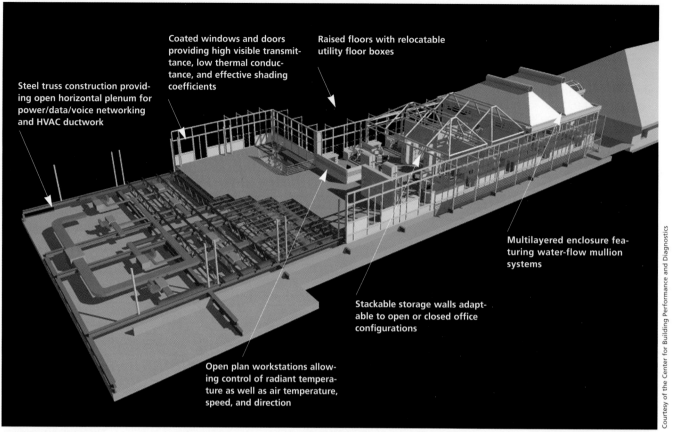

Steel truss construction providing open horizontal plenum for power/data/voice networking and HVAC ductwork

Coated windows and doors providing high visible transmittance, low thermal conductance, and effective shading coefficients

Raised floors with relocatable utility floor boxes

Multilayered enclosure featuring water-flow mullion systems

Stackable storage walls adaptable to open or closed office configurations

Open plan workstations allowing control of radiant temperature as well as air temperature, speed, and direction

Carnegie Mellon University's Center for Building Performance and Diagnostics assesses the impact of new building systems on worker satisfaction and building performance.

More variation in floorplate size is appearing in the market and, whatever their size, floorplates will become narrower and taller ceilings and windows will become more common.

A major reason for these design trends is that they allow more natural light into the building and let it reach more of the interior. In the future, fewer irregularly configured office buildings will be designed because they tend to be less space efficient, often losing 5 to 10 percent of net usable space compared with rectangular buildings, and also because they tend to be less flexible in terms of interior layout options.

Considerations of interior flexibility also underlie the ongoing trend to design rentable space with as few structural columns as possible.

Columns greatly limit options for reconfiguring interior spaces and they interfere with the use of modular furniture for open office plans. New office buildings will be designed with larger structural bays—30' x 30' or larger—than those commonly found in existing office buildings.

System interface has become the new frontier in office building infrastructure.

Most new buildings incorporate systems that are smart, but efforts to coordinate them and to adjust the design of the building so that everything works together for maximum efficiency continue to encounter problems

that tax the ingenuity of designers and engineers. A facility known as the Center for Building Performance and Diagnostics (CBPD) on Carnegie Mellon University's Pittsburgh campus has been developed to study techniques for the effective integration of all the components of office buildings—from their mechanical, electrical, and communications infrastructure to building envelopes and modular office systems furnishings. Developed by the Advanced Building Systems Integration Consortium (ABSIC), an industry-university collaboration, the CBPD is expected to lead to the development of new products and systems for office buildings.

The use of accessible underfloor conduits to deliver telecommunications cabling and electric power to tenants will become standard.

The explosion in the use of computers and other high-tech equipment in the office workplace has rendered many buildings constructed only a decade ago already obsolete in terms of the cabling infrastructure that they can offer tenants. Newer buildings with underfloor grid access systems provide far more workspace flexibility, allowing furniture to be rearranged without the necessity of rewiring for telephones and computer networks. Design innovations have allowed decreases in the depth of access floors, from between six and eight inches to four inches today. The latest super-shallow flooring is even less deep and can be incorporated into buildings without lowering ceiling heights or adding structural bracing.

Demands on HVAC and power systems will continue to grow.

New office buildings must provide substantial—and expandable—HVAC systems. The increased density of people in many workplaces is one major factor and another is the increased use of office equipment that generates heat and off-gases. Furthermore, as noted in the preceding discussion of various regulatory issues, air-conditioning systems are being designed with different refrigerants, and these changes have caused some operational problems. Tenants are demanding more flexibility to manage temperatures and airflow in their spaces and to obtain HVAC on demand during the building's nonoperating hours. Tenants are demanding better ventilation, and, increasingly, natural ventilation.

As more fresh air is introduced into a building's HVAC system, more energy will be required to heat and cool it. Demand for greater operating efficiency is likely to bring about changes in the engineering of mechanical systems. While the efficiency of these systems has already been enhanced by such techniques as economizer cycles and sophisticated energy management systems, building owners and operators may turn to alternative systems—such as ones involving ice storage or geothermal energy—to cut operating costs.

New HVAC and power demands will require further changes in the design of buildings. In order to assure that all office areas—not just those near the building's core—are adequately served, new buildings will have to be designed with sufficient slab-to-slab height to accommodate the distribution of electricity and HVAC output in raised floors or lowered ceilings. New cutting-edge energy-efficient systems will rely more on building design, especially the design of the envelope, to keep heating and cooling loads within certain limits.

One example of many of these design trends in action is the Gap corporate office building in San Francisco that opened in November 1997. The building was designed by Ove Arup San Francisco & Partners with William McDonough Architects and Gensler Associates. Designed to accommodate changes in both technology and work practices, it is also energy-efficient. Its lighting needs are almost entirely satisfied by daylighting. A raised access floor for cable and air distribution reduces the cost and time involved in rearranging workstations and moving partitions. The thermal mass of the structural floor slab is used to cool supply air at night so that the chillers need to run less during the day. Although designed to operate as an air-conditioned structure, the building can also be naturally ventilated.

The competitive office buildings of tomorrow will be big on services and amenities that enhance the comfort, convenience, and security of the occupants.

These buildings will provide an array of services that include central network facilities, teleconferencing

facilities, day-care centers, car washes, video stores, and exercise centers. More companies maintain operations after hours, before hours, and weekends and more employees work flexible hours. To accommodate these operating practices, buildings will have to offer a high level of security.

Finally, and also importantly, the owners and developers of office buildings will respond to tenants' growing demand for better indoor-air quality and lower operating costs by designing green buildings.

Green buildings are designed and built to be energy-efficient, to minimize the use of nonrenewable resources, and to respect the natural environment.

Europe and Asia are at the leading edge of green design. The design goal for the 981-foot-high Commerzbank in Frankfurt, Europe's tallest building, was to fully integrate the architecture with environmental concepts to create an elegant structure that could be built quickly and operated economically. Completed in mid-1997, the 1.2 million-square-foot, 57-story triangular office tower represents a new standard of environmental friendliness in high-rise office buildings.

Operable windows on the exterior and in the atrium can provide natural ventilation for all office spaces, and it is estimated that natural ventilation will be used for space conditioning as much as 60 percent of the time. For more extreme weather conditions, the building's mechanical air-conditioning system will be used. Con-

Europe's tallest building, the 981-foot-high Commerzbank in Frankfurt, Germany, makes use of stacked gardens as natural ventilators.

Ian Lambot/© Ove Arup & Partners

Detailed environmental analysis and planning made a simple tilt-up concrete distribution center and office building into an energy-efficient and comfortable workplace that also is a model for resource conservation and pollutant reduction. Completed in 1997, the 184,000-square-foot Patagonia distribution center and office facility in Reno, Nevada, was designed by the Miller|Hull Partnership of Seattle, Washington. The designers addressed five major areas of environmental impact: global emissions, local interactions, energy conservation, resource use, and the indoor environment.

The list of the building's environmentally sensitive design features is long:

- careful siting along the Truckee River to provide solar exposure and views;
- sensitive natural landscaping, including the restoration of a river ecosystem to the south of the building, the preservation of high-alpine habitat to the west, the maintenance of native high-desert vegetation elsewhere, and xeriscaping around the building;
- the on-site treatment of runoff using bioswales and detention ponds with an oil and water separator;
- extensive daylighting by means of spectrally selective glazing, light shelves, and tracking skylights;
- high-efficiency lighting—T8 fluorescent lamps and metal halide lamps—and sophisticated lighting controls;

The Patagonia distribution and office facility in Reno, Nevada, is a model of energy-efficient building systems and green technology. Energy savings should offset the added costs of installing the green features within three years of operation.

- passive ventilation, including a nighttime flush cycle in the distribution center;
- high-performance insulation and glazing;
- passive heating and natural cooling strategies supplemented by high-efficiency radiant and geothermal HVAC systems;
- water-conserving plumbing fixtures and irrigation systems; and
- a reuse-sensitive design that incorporates elements—such as high floor-to-ceiling heights and simple structural systems—that will facilitate the adaptation and reuse of the building.

A great many of the materials that were selected are also noteworthy for their environmental sensitivity or nontoxicity:

- sustainably harvested wood and reclaimed wood for decking, stair treads, millwork, and window frames;
- concrete with a 20 percent fly ash content for the footings;
- binder-free Miraflex fiberglass insulation and CertainTeed fiberglass batt insulation with a 50 percent recycled content;
- low-VOC interior paint with a 50 percent recycled content and low-VOC exterior paint with a 50 percent to 90 percent recycled content;
- acoustical ceiling tiles with an 85 percent recycled content;
- formaldehyde-free Meadwood straw panels for interior sheathing and formaldehyde-free Medite for custom casework;
- drywall with 10 percent recycled paper facings and 15 percent reclaimed or flue-gas gypsum;
- ceramic tile with a 70 percent recycled glass content and installed with a nontoxic adhesive;
- Forbo natural linoleum flooring; and
- Envirolon carpet made from recycled plastic.

Miller|Hull prepared a report on the process the designers went through for this project. This report lists the green features that were considered for the project and provides a variety of information on each one: its specific environmental benefits, whether it was accepted or rejected, the reasons for rejection (such as cost, timing, and lack of familiarity), and manufacturers. This analysis makes the Patagonia building a strong learning experience. (For information about the report contact the Miller|Hull partnership, 206-682-6837.)

The cost/benefit analysis for the energy-conservation measures—high-performance insulation, radiant heating, displacement ventilation, daylighting, lighting controls, and efficient lighting fixtures—proves that the "use of these systems is clearly economical even

for a building such as this," in the words of Aidan Stretch, architect for Miller|Hull. This analysis comparing the base case (a similar structure built to code) and the Patagonia building follows:

Annual energy use	
Base case	2,023 MWh
Patagonia	812 MWh
Savings	1,211 MWh
	(60%)

Annual operating cost	
Base Case	$161,838
Patagonia	$ 64,837
Savings	$ 97,001
	(60%)

Capital cost of energy-conservation measures	
Base case systems	$162,000
Patagonia	$752,900
Energy-conservation measures	$590,900
Simple payback	6.09 years
Net present value of conservation investment (at 10 percent interest over 20 years)	$146,045
Return on investment	45%

Miller|Hull estimated the reduction in air pollution that the Patagonia building's lower electricity usage would achieve, based on data from the U.S. Environmental Protection Agency's Green Lights program that seeks to reduce the emissions from U.S. power plants by lowering their electricity generation requirements:

Annual emissions reduction	
CO_2	938 tons
SO_2	6,840 kg
NO_x	3,120 kg

Many factors went into the decisions on which green elements to include. According to Stretch, for example, after the high-performance insulation had been added to the building's perimeter walls, the proposed radiant heating system did not meet the Patagonia's payback standard, although it was used in the warehouse in order to increase comfort.

Source: Adapted from *Environmental Building News*, September–October 1996, pp. 8–9.

Motorized louver blinds, chilled ceilings, and a fresh air ventilation system make the Helicon, a London office building, a leader in the field of energy-efficiency.

Peter Mackinven/© Ove Arup & Partners

crete floors for thermal storage and other passive energy-conservation techniques further reduce normal HVAC needs. The bank's column-free floors are built around a central atrium that extends the full height of the building to provide natural light, cross-ventilation, and views. High daylight levels reaching nearly 50 foot-candles at individual workstations minimize the need for artificial lighting.

The Helicon, a glass-clad commercial mixed-use development in London designed by architects Sheppard Robson, is another leading-edge green building. It has 110,000 square feet of office space above two basement and three above-ground retail floors. The building's naturally ventilated triple-glazed exterior includes motorized shading blinds between the outer skin and inner windows. Chilled ceilings reduce cooling costs. The Helicon has proved to be energy-efficient, quiet to operate, and inexpensive to maintain.[9]

Two early U.S. prototypes of green development are the National Audubon Society's headquarters building in Manhattan (see Audubon House case study in Chapter 7) and the Natural Resources Defense Council's (NRDC) offices in Washington, D.C. Both of these projects sought to demonstrate that an environmentally sensitive office building could be developed at market cost using readily available off-the-shelf technology and materials. Both emphasized the use of cost-effective techniques for saving energy in the building's operation and the use of renewable and recycled products with low toxicity as building materials. In both cases, compared with similar standard buildings the energy-conserving features cost more up front but operating costs are considerably less.

Most of the green office buildings that have been built in the United States have been developed by companies for their own occupancy. As occupants, they have been willing to invest in energy-saving building features because the added costs will be offset over time with lower operating costs.

A 48-story office tower being constructed by the Durst Organization Inc. at 4 Times Square in Manhattan is the first large multitenant building in the United States to adopt the latest design standards for energy conservation, indoor-air quality, and recycling systems. It also specifies environmentally friendly building materials. Designed by Fox & Fowle Architects, 4 Times Square is scheduled to open in 1999.

Energy conservation features in the building include the use of natural gas–fired absorption chillers for heating and cooling in lieu of conventional electric systems; an exterior curtain wall that minimizes thermal transmission and allows a minimum of 30 percent humidity to be maintained inside year round; oversized windows that admit natural light but reject ultraviolet rays; exterior wall insulation that is more than twice as thick as standard wall insulation; solar energy generation through photovoltaic cells placed on two sides of the tower; internal chutes to collect materials for recycling; and water conservation fixtures.

To improve indoor-air quality, 4 Times Square's ventilation system will allow 50 percent more fresh air to circulate through the building than the current code requires and the ventilation system will be used to flush air out of specific floors when necessary, such as when offices are being painted. Each floor will have individual air-handling units that can be programmed locally by tenants to control air quality as well as temperature. When the concentration of carbon dioxide in the air rises above a preset point, more fresh air will be circulated.

To extend the same green design principles to tenant improvements, Durst developed a set of buildout guidelines that encourages tenants to conserve energy and choose carpeting and furniture that do not emit toxic vapors. The developer felt that tenants would accept these guidelines if their benefits—lower energy costs and higher employee productivity—were clearly explained. One year after the start of construction (with two years to go), 80 percent of the space had been leased and the buildout guidelines, according to Durst, had been enthusiastically embraced by the tenants.

Douglas Durst, president of the Durst Organization, says that some of the high rise's green features cost more up front but are expected to lower operating costs by approximately 15 percent compared with a similar building constructed without them. Durst expects to see a payback of the added costs within five years of operation.[10]

Notes

1. William C. Wheaton, "Office Growth in the 1990s: Downtowns versus Edge Cities," *Urban Land*, April 1996, p. 67.

2. Ibid.

3. CB Commercial, National Real Estate Index, 3rd quarter 1997.

4. Grubb & Ellis, *1998 Real Estate Forecast* (Northbrook, Illinois: Grubb & Ellis Company, 1997).

5. ULI–the Urban land Institute, *ULI 1998 Real Estate Forecast* (Washington, D.C.: ULI–the Urban Land Institute, forthcoming 1998).

6. ERE Yarmouth and Real Estate Research Corporation, *Emerging Trends in Real Estate 1998* (Chicago: Real Estate Research Corporation, 1997).

7. ULI asked the Building Owners and Managers Association (BOMA) International which regulatory issues would have an impact on office development. This section represents the advocacy organization's response.

8. For more details on utility deregulation issues and response plans for building owners and managers, see Building Owners and Managers Association International, *Power Shopping* (Washington, D.C.: BOMA International, 1996).

9. Helene Murphy and Leslie Morison, "Innovation in Building Design," *Urban Land*, December 1997, p. 41.

10. "In Times Square, It May Pay to Be Green," *Wall Street Journal*, July 16, 1997, p. B10.

Sun and Associates; and Fox & Fowle Architects

The Durst Organization's 4 Times Square in Manhattan is the first large multitenant office building in the United States to be developed as a green building.

Appendices and Index

Appendix 1
Sample Preliminary Package for an Office Building Permanent Loan

TABLE OF CONTENTS

LOAN REQUEST

Amount	$[amount]
Term	Quote requested for a [number]-year term
Amortization	[number] years
Funding	Immediate
Borrower	Borrower entity (legal name, type, state of incorporation/registration); list of individuals and entities with major ownership
Security	First deed of trust on [number] acres of land and a [number]-square-foot (NRA) office building built thereon
Use of Funds	Payoff of existing financing of $[amount] with [name of lender]; coverage of estimated transaction costs of $[amount]; and equity recapture

PROPERTY DESCRIPTION

Site	[number] acres ([number] square feet)
Zoning	[zoning category] (allows for various light manufacturing, office, and retail uses)
Building	Two-story, L-shaped office building; brick on block construction with steel frame; one elevator; two-story lobby area; exercise room with showers for tenant use
Size	[number] square feet of NRA; [number] square feet of GBA
Year Built	1998
Parking	[number] spaces ([number]/1,000 square feet of NRA)
Roof	Built-up membrane with stone ballast on 1.5-inch, 22 gauge metal decking
Fire Protection	Wet sprinkler system (full building coverage)
Tenancy	Currently 92% leased to nine tenants; major tenants include: [tenant name], [number] square feet, 10-year lease; [tenant name], [number] square feet, 7-year lease

LOCATION AND MARKET SUMMARY

Address	2500 Prospect Avenue Shorewood, Arizona 53000
Location	In the Summit Business Center; on Prospect Avenue one-quarter mile north of its intersection with Summit Drive. Summit Drive is a major north/south arterial that accesses the I-495 Shorewood Beltline one mile north of the subject property. The location is about ten miles northwest of the Shorewood CBD. I-495 provides access to the rest of the metropolitan area.
Market	Twenty-five buildings totalling just over 1.5 million square feet have been developed in the Summit Business Center over the past ten years. Only two sites remain undeveloped. This is an attractive office location because it is near the region's residential growth corridors and a wealth of hotel and retail amenities on Summit Avenue. As evidenced by the subject property's rapid lease-up, this submarket is tight. Estimated vacancies are in the 5 percent range. Market rents range from $18.50 to $24.50 per square foot, with tenant improvements averaging $5.00 on rollovers and $15.00 for new tenants.

PRO FORMA

	Per Square Foot	Total
Income		
Rental Income[1]	–	$600,000
Expense Reimbursements	–	30,000
Total Income	–	630,000
Less Vacancy at 5%[2]	–	31,500
Effective Gross Income	–	$598,500
Expenses[3]		
Real Estate Taxes	$1.01	$28,000
Insurance	0.19	5,410
Contract Services	1.00	27,794
Payroll	0.50	13,897
Repairs and Maintenance	0.86	24,000
Utilities[4]	0.65	18,000
Professional Fees	0.18	5,100
General and Administrative	0.50	13,897
Management Fee at 4%	0.86	23,940
Total Expenses	$5.76	$160,038
Net Operating Income	–	$438,462

[1] Based on overall rent roll.

[2] Overall vacancy rate in the submarket is 5 percent.

[3] Based on owner's projections, except for the management fee at 4 percent of effective gross income.

[4] Electricity is separately metered for each tenant, and tenants pay electric costs directly.

RENT ROLL
[month, year]

Suite	Tenant	Square Feet	Total Annual Rent	Annual Square-Foot Rent	Lease Term	Escalations	Comments
[number]	[name]	[number]	$[amount]	$[amount]	[start/end]	[describe]	[options, etc.]
[number]	[name]	[number]	$[amount]	$[amount]	[start/end]	[describe]	[options, etc.]
[number]	[name]	[number]	$[amount]	$[amount]	[start/end]	[describe]	[options, etc.]
[number]	[name]	[number]	$[amount]	$[amount]	[start/end]	[describe]	[options, etc.]
Total		[number]	$[amount]	$[amount]			

Appendix 2
Sample Commitment for an Office Building Construction Loan

Proposed Borrower
c/o Developer
5000 Locust Avenue
Anytown, USA

re: $5,000,000 Construction Loan
[name of property]

Dear Developer:

We are pleased to advise you that [name of bank] hereby offers to provide [borrowing entity] a commercial real estate construction loan on the terms and conditions set forth below:

AMOUNT: $5,000,000 (the "Loan")

BORROWER: [borrowing entity] (the "Borrower")

TERM: The Loan shall begin on the day of closing of the Loan and shall end on the day that is 18 months after the first day of the first month after closing. Interest shall accrue on the outstanding principal balance of the Loan at a rate of prime plus one (1) percent interest only. Provided that no default has occurred, the maturity date may be extended for six (6) months, at the option of the Borrower, upon 30 days written notice to the Bank and the payment of an extension fee of $[amount].

PROCEEDS: The proceeds of the Loan shall be used to pay off the existing land loan and construction escrow. The approximate use of funds is as follows:

Pay off loan	$[amount]
Construction escrow	$[amount]
Closing costs	$[amount]
Interest reserve	$[amount]
Total	$[amount]

SECURITY: The Bank will require a first deed of trust on the land and all related improvements to the Property mentioned above, together with a first lien security interest on all equipment, fixtures, and other personal property of the Borrower located on and necessary to the use and occupancy of the Property, and the Borrower's interest as landlord in all leases and contracts on the improvements and the security deposits and rents payable thereunder.

COMMITMENT FEE: In consideration for the issuance of this commitment, the Borrower shall pay to the Bank a nonrefundable commitment fee equal to [amount]% of the Loan, or $[amount], which shall be deemed fully earned upon acceptance hereof by the Borrower, and is not refundable for any reason. The Borrower has paid $[amount] on account of said fee, and the remaining $[amount] shall be due and payable at settlement. If the Loan shall fail to close for any reason other than default hereunder by the Bank, the commitment fee will be retained by the Bank as liquidated damages, not as a penalty. The Borrower agrees that as liquidated damages the amount of the commitment fee is reasonable.

ACCURACY: This commitment is subject to the accuracy of all of the information contained in your loan package and other supporting information provided to us by you or your representatives. Should any information be determined to be inaccurate, the Bank may withdraw this commitment at its discretion. The Bank will not be obliged to fund the Loan at any time when there has been a materially adverse change in your financial condition or deterioration to the subject property or improvements.

APPRAISAL: At least fourteen (14) days prior to settlement, the Bank shall have obtained an appraisal on the land and proposed improvements based on the final plans and specifications by an appraiser engaged on your behalf by the Bank. All fees incurred in connection with such appraisal shall be paid by the Borrower. The cost of this appraisal is $[amount] and must be submitted with the completed commitment letter.

EQUITY: The maximum Loan will be no more than seventy-five percent (75%) of appraised value or the amount of this commitment. If the appraised value of said Property is not sufficient to meet the 75% loan-to-value requirement, you will have the option to reduce the loan amount to meet the 75% requirement, or to post additional real estate collateral.

COSTS: The Borrower is to bear all costs of settlement including the Bank's counsel, recordation taxes and fees, mortgage title insurance, appraisal, transfer taxes, and the fees of the Bank's construction inspector for the review of the plans and specifications and construction inspections.

TITLE INSURANCE: At least three (3) days prior to settlement, the Borrower is to furnish the Bank a mortgagee's title insurance commitment for the Property from a title company acceptable to the Bank, together with true and complete copies of all documents or instruments enumerated as exceptions to title, in form and substance satisfactory to the Bank in its sole judgment. Within fifteen (15) days of settlement, the borrower is to furnish the Bank a mortgagee title insurance policy satisfactory in form and substance to the Bank and insuring the Bank's deed of trust as a first lien on the Property in the amount of the Loan.

CONSTRUCTION: No work is to commence nor is any material to be stored on the site prior to recordation of the loan documents unless the mortgagor can obtain an acceptable title policy excluding mechanics liens exceptions. Construction must begin no later than thirty (30) days after settlement as may be extended by mutual agreement. A cost analysis, in trade breakdown form, reflecting the various subcontractors and material suppliers shall be furnished by the Borrower and reviewed by the Bank's construction progress inspector prior to the first construction draw request. In the event the Bank's construction progress inspector's review determines, in his sole opinion, that the plans and specifications are inadequate or that construction costs are unreasonable, the Bank may withdraw the commitment.

DISBURSEMENT: The loan proceeds will be disbursed into a construction progress fund administered by the bank as trustee. Interest will not be charged until funds are disbursed from this account.

BUILDING AND LOAN AGREEMENT: Funds shall be advanced under the terms of a building and loan agreement as construction progresses. Requisitions in AIA form will be submitted monthly and approved by the Bank's construction progress inspector. Advances shall be limited to ninety percent (90%) of such requisition until the project is completed. The ten percent (10%) retainage payment is contingent upon receipt of the final release of liens from the general contractor and all subcontractors, final approval by the construction progress inspector, and a use and occupancy permit from the county. All disbursements are subject to a title bring-to-date satisfactory to the Bank.

REQUIREMENTS PRIOR TO THE FIRST CONSTRUCTION DRAW:

1. One set of plans and specifications.
2. Copy of the building permit and evidence that zoning requirements have been complied with.
3. Builder's all-risk insurance policy, including vandalism and malicious mischief, naming [name of entity] as mortgagee and loss payee under the mortgage clause as their interest may appear. Borrower shall provide hazard insurance during the entire term of the Loan in amounts satisfactory to the Bank and name the Bank as mortgagee in such policy. Such policies shall require a 30-day cancellation notice.
4. Certificate of workman's compensation and copies of public liability policy for the borrower and contractor.
5. Location survey.
6. Water and sewer permit (if applicable).
7. Evidence of utility availability.
8. Soil test.
9. Copy of grading permit.

SIGN: At the expense of [name of entity], we reserve the right to erect a temporary sign at the construction site indicating financing is provided by [name of entity].

SURVEY: At least three (3) days prior to the settlement date, the Borrower shall cause to be submitted to the Bank, for approval by the Bank, a location survey of the property prepared by a licensed surveyor approved by the Bank, showing any existing improvements thereon and the locations of easements, encroachment (if any), and all other matters affecting title to the property. Such survey shall be satisfactory to the Bank in its sole discretion, and shall be deemed "current" only if it is dated within thirty (30) days of the settlement date and is otherwise acceptable to the title company for purposes of removing any current survey exception from the title insurance policy required by the terms hereof.

SITE PLAN: At least three (3) days prior to the settlement date, the Borrower shall cause to be submitted to the Bank, for approval by the Bank, a site plan showing the proposed location of the building, any existing improvements thereon, the locations of easements, encroachments (if any), and all other matters affecting title to the property.

ORGANIZATIONAL DOCUMENTS: At least five (5) days prior to settlement, the Borrower shall submit to the Bank a copy of the Borrower's Partnership Agreement, any amendments thereto, and Borrower's Resolution to borrow, which documents shall be satisfactory to the Bank in its sole judgment.

FINANCIAL INFORMATION: The Borrower agrees to furnish to the Bank, on an annual basis, the following financial information:

1. Tax returns on Borrower and key individuals.
2. Current rent rolls.
3. Copies of new leases.

GUARANTORS: The Borrower's payment of the Loan and performance of the obligation contained in the deed of trust and other documents evidencing, securing, and providing for disbursement of the Loan shall be jointly, severally, and unconditionally guaranteed by [name of entity]. The Guarantor(s) will furnish to the Bank at such time or times as specified by the Bank, such financial statements and other information concerning the financial condition of such Guarantor(s) as the Bank may from time to time require.

BROKERAGE: The Bank shall not be required to pay any brokerage fee or commission arising from this commitment and the Borrower agrees to defend, indemnify, and hold the Bank harmless against any and all expenses, liabilities, and losses arising from such claim in connection therewith, including payment of reasonable attorneys' fees.

CONDEMNATION: At the time of settlement of the Loan, no proceeding shall have been threatened or commenced by any authority having the power of eminent domain to condemn any part of the Property that the Bank deems substantial.

NONASSIGNABILITY OF COMMITMENT: This commitment is issued directly to or for the benefit of the Borrower and may not be assigned by or on behalf of the Borrower by operation of law or otherwise, without the express written consent of the Bank, which consent may be withheld by the Bank at its sole discretion.

LEASE(S): The Borrower shall submit to the Bank for its review and approval a copy of all executed lease(s) on the property. Said lease(s) shall be satisfactory in form and content in the sole discretion of the Bank. Said lease(s) shall be subordinate to the deed of trust securing the Loan. On or before the settlement date, and upon each and every request thereafter, the Borrower shall submit to the Bank a rent roll pertaining to the property certified as to its correctness by the Borrower. At settlement, we will require an assignment of rents and leases to be executed. In addition to the assignment of rents and leases [name of bank] will require the following: The building must be preleased up to 50%, or [number of] square feet, prior to settlement/disbursement of funds.

SECONDARY FINANCING: During the term of the Loan, no additional financing or refinancing by any other lender shall be secured by a lien on the Property without the prior written consent of the Bank.

SETTLEMENT COSTS: The Borrower shall pay all taxes and assessments due on the settlement date, and all recording fees and taxes, costs of title examination, title insurance premium, survey and appraisal expenses, attorney's fees, and any and all other expenses incurred by the Bank in connection with the negotiation of, preparation for, closing, and servicing of the Loan. The Borrower shall also pay all expenses incurred if the Loan fails to close through no fault of the Bank.

SETTLEMENT: Settlement is to be conducted by the Bank's counsel unless the Borrower chooses another attorney. If any attorney chosen by the Borrower is used, the Bank's counsel must approve all documents prior to settlement. The Borrower shall pay to the Bank's counsel all fees for services performed either in preparation or review of loan documents or other matters related to this transaction whether or not the loan closes.

SURVIVAL: The terms and conditions of this commitment, where applicable, shall survive the settlement of the Loan and shall continue in full force and effect, unless otherwise modified or amended in writing and signed by the Bank. No agent or broker is authorized to act in this loan transaction on behalf of the Bank. Time shall be of the essence in all matters covered by this commitment.

ADDITIONAL ITEMS: In addition, there will be other supporting documentation relating to this transaction. This documentation will contain the customary covenants and agreements pertaining to construction and permanent financing thereof that are usually required by the bank.

ADDITIONAL COVENANTS: [any additional covenants].

There are no other representations concerning this loan commitment except as set forth in writing. Any change in any terms and conditions of this commitment must be in writing by the Bank. Upon failure to comply with any requirements by the Borrower or if a requirement cannot be met for any reason, this commitment may be withdrawn at the Bank's option.

You may indicate your acceptance of this commitment by signing and returning the original of this letter, the environmental fee, and the appraisal fee for a total of $[amount] by no later than [date]. Settlement must occur on or prior to [date]. This period is extended to allow time to meet the prelease requirement. In the event these deadlines are not met, this commitment is automatically withdrawn.

Sincerely,
[signed]

Index

225 High Ridge Road (Stamford, Connecticut), 149, **288–93**

Tysons Corner (Washington, D.C.), 7, 13

■

Umbrella Partnership REIT (UPREIT), 87

Underfloor conduits, 336–37

Uninterruptible power supply (UPS) systems, 165

Union Bank (Orange, California), *119*

United Parcel Service (Atlanta, Georgia), *140*, **140–41**, *141*

Universal plan, 335

University of Washington: landscaping study by, **22**

Urban enterprise zones, *33*, **188**

Urban Investment & Development Company, *108*

Urban projects: and access, 49; and design issues, 128, *129*, 131, 133, 138, 173; and feasibility, 46, 75; and site selection, 49; trends concerning, 329. *See also* Central business districts; Downtown projects

U.S. Customs House (Philadelphia, Pennsylvania), *124*

Utilities, *48*, 49, 128, 200. *See also* Building systems; *specific system*

■

Vacancy, 14, 15, *15*, 63, 75, 92–93, **199**

Valley North Tech Center (Thornton, Colorado), *56*

Vehicular circulation, 127, **127**, 128, 130–31, *130*. *See also* Traffic

Virginia, northern, 40, **42–43**

VISTA Information Solutions, **53**

■

W&M Properties, **212**

Walker Parking Consultants/Engineers, **134**

Washington, D.C.: base-building configurations in, 145, 147; local market analysis for, 40; submarkets for, *42–43*, **42–43**

Washington Mutual Tower (Seattle, Washington), *189*, 190

Water Garden (Santa Monica, California), *136*

Waterford at Blue Lagoon (Miami, Florida), *38*

Wayne Dalton Corporation (Holmes County, Ohio), *326*

Wells, Steve, 308, 309

Westfield Development Company, **166–67**, **201**

Westmark Realty Advisors, 191

Wharton, Geoffrey, 248

William H. Natcher Building (Bethesda, Maryland), *163*

William McDonough Architects, 337

Wilshire Courtyard (Los Angeles, California), *143*

Windows: and design issues, 140, 147, 148, 151, *151*, 153, **153**, *154*, **154**; and marketing and leasing, 207; trends concerning, 327, 334, 336, 337, 341

Wiss, Janney, Elstner Associates, **154**

Woolworth Building (New York City), 11

Worst-case scenarios, 34

Wright, Frank Lloyd, *10*, 268, *269*, 270, *273*

Wright Runstad & Company, 184–85, 190

■

Zell, Sam, **105**, 331

Zero complaint system, **158**

Zoning: and design issues, 118–21, *119*, *120*, 125, 131, 137, 143, 144, 177; and feasibility, 34; predevelopment checklist for, **118**; as regulatory issue, 50, 52, 118–21; and renovation, 177; and site planning, 131, 137; and site selection, *48*, 49